...elia Lobelia Lobularia Callistephus Nigella Myosotis Convolvulus Delphiniu...
...themum Zinnia Salpiglossis Salvia Eschscholzia Agera... ...Mentzeli...
...sis Coreopsis Doronicum Papaver Verbena Tropaeolu... ...thu...
...alva Stokesia Astilbe Pulmonaria Astrantia Catanan... ...ner
...nia Hemerocallis Trollius Crocus Galanthus Muscari Chionodoxa Tulipa Darwi...
...arcissus Hybrids Narcissus Species Iris Species Iris Bulbs Ipheion Freesi...
...aria Zantedeschia Sedum Thymus Dianthus Zauschneria Aubretia Veronic...
...stium Leontopodium Nierembergi... ...erus Alyssum Corydali...
...odium Geranium Saponaria Silene ... ...n Soldanella Aethionem...
...ntilla Philadelphus Hydrangea Deut... ...othus Ipomoea Mahoni...
...amellia Spiraea Enkianthus Florib... ...oses Hybrid Tea Rose...
...rnum Pieris Chaenomeles Pyracantha Fothergilla Magnolia Laburnum Sorbu...
...melis Acer Climbing French Bean Dwarf French Bean Purple-podded Frenc...
...Beetroot Long Beetroot Sugarloaf Chicory Curly-leaved Endive Land Cres...
...Crisphead Lettuce Loose Leaf Lettuce Corn Salad Nasturtium Radish Winte...
...omato Outdoor Tomato Container Tomato Annual Broccoli Perennial Brocco...
...Autumn Cabbage Savoy and Winter-maturing Cabbage Red Cabbage Earl...
...d Endive Kale Kohlrabi Ruby Chard (Seakale Beet) Swiss Chard (Seakale Bee...
...nter Purslane Globe Artichoke Asparagus Cardoon Trench Celery Self-blanch...
...nd Marrow Spaghetti Marrow Melon Pumpkin Summer Squash Forcing Carro...
...choke Parsnip Long Parsnip First Early Potato Second Early Potato Maincro...
...Leek Maincrop Leek Maincrop Trench Leek Onion Spring-sown Onion Onio...
...a Balm Basil Bay Bergamot Borage Caraway Chamomile Chervil Chives Di...
...age Salad Burnet Sorrel Summer Savory Sweet Cicely Tansy Tarragon Thym...
...awberry Early Strawberry Perpetual Strawberry Summer Strawberry Wineberr...
...te-season Apple Cooking Apple Crab Apple Sweet Cherry Morello Cherry Fi...
...an-trained Peach Peaches under Glass Quince Damson Greengage Cookin...
...Calathea picturata Calathea zebrina Chlorophytum Cissus Codiaeum Coleu...
...Fatsia Ficus benjamina Ficus elastica Ficus pumila Fittonia Gynura Heder...
...Rhoicissus Sansevieria Saxifraga Scindapsus Scirpus Setcreasea Soneril...
...Aphelandra Azalea Begonia semperflorens Begonia tuberhybrida Beleperon...
...Columnea Cyclamen Euphorbia Exacum Fuchsia Hibiscus Hoya Hydrange...
...ningia Spathiphyllum Strelitzia Streptocarpus Adiantum Asplenium Blechnu...
...ystichum Pteris Chamaedorea Chamaerops Chrysalidocarpus Cocos Cyca...
...s Tulipa Vallota Aporacactus flagelliformis Cephalocereus senilis Cereus peru...
...nocereus Ferocactus Gymnocalycium Lobivia Mammilaria Notocactus Opunti...
...Crassula Echeveria Euphorbia Gasteria Kalanchoe Kalanchoe blossfeldian...
...mea Ananas Billbergia Cryptanthus Neoregelia Nidularium Tillandsia Vriesi...
...Dodontoglossum Paphiopedilum Phalaenopsis Pleione formosana Vand...
...rtus Podocarpus Polyscias Punica granatum Sageretia Theezans Cosmo...
...elia Lobularia Callistephus Nigella Myosotis Convolvulus Delphinium Lunari...
...num Zinnia Salpiglossis Salvia Eschscholzia Ageratum Lavatera Mentzeli...
...sis Coreopsis Doronicum Papaver Verbena Tropaeolum Potentilla Polyanthu...
...alva Stokesia Astilbe Pulmonaria Astrantia Catananche Bergenia Brunner...
...nia Hemerocallis Trollius Crocus Galanthus Muscari Chionodoxa Tulipa Darwi...
...arcissus Hybrids Narcissus Species Iris Species Iris Bulbs Ipheion Freesi...
...aria Zantedeschia Sedum Thymus Dianthus Zauschneria Aubretia Veronic...
...stium Leontopodium Nierembergia Santolina Juniperus Alyssum Corydali...
...odium Geranium Saponaria Silene Iberis Sisyrinchium Soldanella Aethionem...
...ntilla Philadelphus Hydrangea Deutzia Magnolia Ceanothus Ipomoea Mahoni...
...amellia Spiraea Enkianthus Floribunda Roses Old Roses Hybrid Tea Rose...
...rnum Pieris Chaenomeles Pyracantha Fothergilla Magnolia Laburnum Sorbu...
...melis Acer Climbing French Bean Dwarf French Bean Purple-podded Frenc...

HAMLYN
ALL COLOUR
PLANT
DIRECTORY

HAMLYN ALL COLOUR PLANT DIRECTORY

HAMLYN

This book brings together material from three gardening titles,
Hamlyn All Colour Flower Gardening, Hamlyn All Colour Kitchen Gardening and Hamlyn All Colour Indoor Gardening,
previously published by Reed Consumer Books Limited.
Additional text by William Davidson, Suzy Powling, Jenny Plucknett and Stella Vayne.

Line drawings by Vicky Emptage, Sandra Pond and Will Giles;
colour illustrations by Jim Robins and Rod Sutterby; symbols by Coryn Dickman.

This edition first published in Great Britain in 1993
by Hamlyn, an imprint of Reed Consumer Books Limited,
Michelin House, 81 Fulham Road, London SW3 6RB
and Auckland, Melbourne, Singapore and Toronto

© 1993 Reed International Books Limited

ISBN 0 600 57939 5

A CIP catalogue record for this book is available at the British Library

Produced by Mandarin Offset
Printed in Hong Kong

The Publishers would like to thank the following organizations and individuals
for their kind permission to reproduce the photographs in this book

A-Z BOTANICAL COLLECTION 171R, 225L, 312L, 313R; K&G BECKETT 117R; BIOPHOTOS/HEATHER ANGEL 362L;
PETER BLACK 351R; BOYS SYNDICATION 255, 260R; PAT BRINDLEY 50L, 68L, 79R, 258, 294R, 299L, 301R, 319L, 333, 341R, 345;
W.H. BROWN/KATH WILLIAMS 358, 360, 361L, 363R, /SU CHIN EE 363L; CAMERA PRESS 246, 311;
BRUCE COLEMAN LTD./ERIC CRICHTON 296L; ERIC CRICHTON 20, 21, 31R, 32L, 35R, 47R, 55R, 65R, 70L, 76, 79L, 81L, 83L, 84R, 92R, 93R,
94L, 95R, 99L, 111L, 145L, 160R, 174R, 262L, 270R, 275, 277L, 280R, 281L, 283, 287L, 291L, 292R,
293L, 297R, 298L, 300, 301L, 307R, 309L, 315R, 318L, 319R, 320R, 321R, 324R, 325L, 326R, 327L, 328L, 329R, 330, 331L, 334R, 335R, 337L, 338R,
339R, 340R, 346, 347, 350, 352, 353, 355; W.F. DAVIDSON 261R; BRIAN FURNER AGENCY 114L, 145R, 210L, 235L;
GARDEN PICTURE LIBRARY/DEREK FELL 28L, 54L, 61, 75R, /DAVID RUSSELL 171L; GOOD HOUSEKEEPING/JAN BALDWIN 256; DEREK
GOULD 27R, 53L, 64R, 83R, 89R, 113R; MELVIN GREY 299R; IRIS HARDWICK LIBRARY 239L; JERRY HARPUR 77; ANTHONY HUXLEY 37R;
GIUSEPPE MAZZA 327L, 336R; TANIA MIDGELY 26R, 30R, 34R, 71R, 81R, 109L, 124L; NHPA/M.SAVONIUS 46R; CHRIS PAGE 304L, 305, 306L,
307L, 308R, 314L; FRANCES PERRY 334L; PHOTOS HORTICULTURAL 93L, 109R, 154, 160L, 170R, 290L, 313L, 317, 341L;
REED INTERNATIONAL BOOKS LTD. 14, 139L, 147R, 148R, 156L, 157L, 161L, 163R, 168R, 176, 180L, 182, 183R, 186L, 188R, 190, 196R, 199R,
201L, 215L, 225R, 226L, 227R, 228, 229, 230R, 236L, 238L, 240, 241, 242L, 244R, 245R, 267L, 286R, 344L; /REX BAMBER 166L,
/THEO BERGSTROM 263R, /MICHAEL BOYS 25R, 31L, 36, 48R, 60, 67R, 68R, 74L, 78, 82R, 85L, 92L, 98R, 100R, 103R, 105L, 108R, 115R, 118,
122L, 123L, 139R, 140R, 148L, 162R, 164L, 165R, 180R, 186R, 197L, 199L, 201R, 206, 207R, 208, 211R, 212R, 213R, 214R, 218L, 230L, 238R, 239R,
265L, /W.F.DAVIDSON 273L, 289L, / MELVIN GREY 203, 302, 356,
/JERRY HARPUR 8, 23R, 24L, 30L, 33R, 35L, 38, 39, 40, 41L, 42, 43R, 44L, 45L, 46R, 49L, 50R, 51, 52L, 53R, 54R, 55L, 56L, 57, 58R, 59R, 63L, 65L,
66R, 69, 71L, 72, 73, 74R, 80L, 84L, 86R, 87R, 88, 89L, 90, 91, 94R, 99R, 100L, 102, 103L, 110L, 112, 113L, 115L, 116, 117L, 121, 124R,
125R, 138L, 149L, 162L, 211L, 226R, 235R, 236R, 244L, 298R, /NEIL HOLMES 33L, 64L, 87L, 98L, 107L, 138R, 140L, 141R, 144L, 147L, 149R, 150R,
151L, 156R, 163L, 164R, 167R, 170L, 174L, 175R, 177, 187L, 189L, 192, 193R, 196L, 197R, 198L, 200R, 215R, 216L, 217R, 219R, 224R,
227L, 237R, 242R, 243L, 245L, 269L, 295R, 323, /ANDREW LAWSON 141L, 167L, 169R, 175L, 187R, /JOHN MOSS 263L, 335L,
/ROGER PHILLIPS 267R, 286L, 288L, 304R, 344R, /PETER RAUTER 266L, 268R, 269R, 270L, 272, 273R, 278L, 280L, 285R, 290R, 292L, /
MARK WILLIAMS 10,11,12,/GEORGE WRIGHT 22, 23L, 24R, 26L, 28R, 29, 32R, 41R, 43L, 44R, 45R, 47L, 48L, 52R, 56R, 59L, 62, 63R, 66L, 67L,
75L, 80R, 86L, 101, 104R, 105R, 106, 108L, 110R, 111R, 120, 122R, 125L, 155L, 168L, 181L, 183L, 191L, 198R, 217L, 243R, 274L, 294L;
HARRY SMITH COLLECTION 25L, 27L, 34L, 49L, 58L, 70R, 82L, 85R, 95L, 96, 97, 104L, 107R, 114R, 123R, 144R, 146, 150L, 155R, 157R, 166R,
188L, 189R, 191R, 193L, 200L, 207L, 209, 210R, 212L, 213L, 214L, 216R, 218R, 219L, 224L, 237L, 260L, 261L, 264L, 265R, 266R,
268L, 271, 274R, 276, 277R, 278R, 279, 281R, 284, 285L, 288R, 289R, 291R, 295L, 296R, 297L, 306R, 308L, 309R, 312R, 315L, 318R, 325R, 326L,
328R, 329L, 331R, 337R, 338L, 339L, 340L, 342, 351L, 354, 359L; SPECTRUM COLOUR LIBRARY 264R; SUE STICKLAND/
HENRY DOUBLEDAY RESEARCH CENTRE 126; PETER STILES 262R, 320L, 324L; SUTTONS SEEDS LTD. 287R, 293R; SYNDICATION
INTERNATIONAL LTD./BERNARD ALFIERI 37L, 336L; THOMPSON & MORGAN 151R, 165L, 181R; WARD LOCK/BOB CHALLINOR
FROM Art of Indoor Bonsai by John Ainsworth 359R, 361R, 362R; ELIZABETH WHITING & ASSOCIATES 250, 310, 314R, 349.

CONTENTS

Introduction 6

IN THE FLOWER GARDEN 8

Annuals 20

Perennials 38

Bulbs 60

Alpines 76

Shrubs 96

Trees 118

IN THE KITCHEN GARDEN 126

Peas and Beans 136

Salad Vegetables 142

Fruiting Vegetables 152

Leaf Vegetables 158

Stalk and Shoot Vegetables 172

Squashes 178

root vegetables and tubers 184

Bulb Vegetables 194

Herbs 202

Soft Fruit 220

Top Fruit 231

PLANTS FOR INDOORS 246

Foliage Plants 258

Flowering Plants 282

Ferns 302

Palms 310

Bulbs 316

Cacti 322

Succulents 332

Bromeliads 342

Orchids 348

Bonsai 356

Glossary 364

Index 366

INTRODUCTION

The choice of plants available to the gardener today can be bewildering in its breadth and variety. The *Hamlyn All Colour Plant Directory* makes life easier by focussing on a great range of popular, easy-to-grow plants, all of which deserve a place in the modern flower or kitchen garden, or inside the house. The book tells you how to look after the plants you have already and what to look out for when touring the garden centre or nursery in search of new ones.

'In the Flower Garden' opens the book, offering over 175 beautiful high-performance flowering plants, some of them old favourites, others less familiar. They have been grouped according to type – annuals, perennials, bulbs, alpines, shrubs and climbers and trees – and organized by colour within each chapter, so whether you are looking for warm reds and pinks or cool blues, you will quickly find the plants that are right for you.

The kitchen garden section includes a good selection of plants which will make feeding the family from the garden a real pleasure. There are plenty of salad vegetables for summer eating, a splendid array of root, bulb and fruiting vegetables to eat cooked or raw, and good choices of soft and top fruits and herbs.

During winter, when little may be happening out-of-doors, houseplants become even more important. The third section of The *Hamlyn All Colour Plant Directory* includes a beautiful array of all types of indoor plants, from ferns to cacti and from palms to spring bulbs. They are divided into 10 main groups, each with its own characteristics: foliage plants, flowering plants, ferns, palms, bulbs, cacti, succulents, bromeliads, orchids and bonsai.

Each of the three sections begins with an invaluable survey of the practical skills and techniques which will help the gardener or houseplant grower create and maintain an excellent selection of plants. Each chapter within each section also starts with valuable practical advice on growing the particular group of plants in it.

A superb colour photograph illustrates each of the more than 450 plants in this book and the text for each includes a concise description of the plant, advice on growing and propagating it successfully and details of other varieties which may be available. Special tips, many of them illustrated with a line drawing, highlight special information about the plants.

Easy-to-use reference symbols, explained in the keys below, are printed under each plant's photograph. They indicate its dimensions, flowering times, degree of hardiness and optimum growing conditions.

To sum up, the detail supplied on each plant in this book makes the *Hamlyn All Colour Plant Directory* an invaluable reference book for all keen gardeners, whatever their level of experience.

KEY TO SYMBOLS

THE FLOWER GARDEN

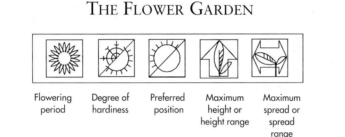

Flowering period — Degree of hardiness — Preferred position — Maximum height or height range — Maximum spread or spread range

THE VEGETABLE AND HERB GARDEN

THE FRUIT GARDEN

INDOOR GARDENING

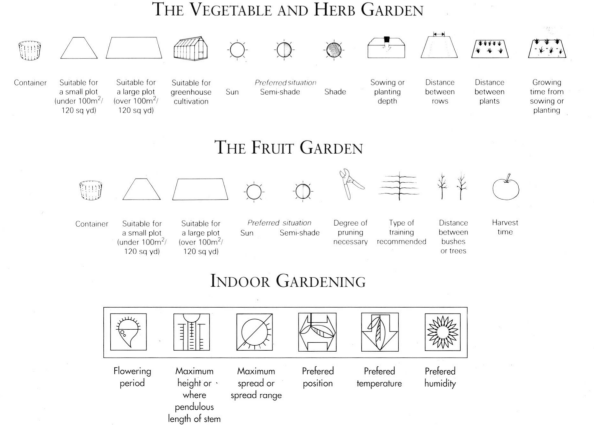

The Vegetable and Herb Garden: Container — Suitable for a small plot (under 100m²/ 120 sq yd) — Suitable for a large plot (over 100m²/ 120 sq yd) — Suitable for greenhouse cultivation — Sun — *Preferred situation* Semi-shade — Shade — Sowing or planting depth — Distance between rows — Distance between plants — Growing time from sowing or planting

The Fruit Garden: Container — Suitable for a small plot (under 100m²/ 120 sq yd) — Suitable for a large plot (over 100m²/ 120 sq yd) — *Preferred situation* Sun — Semi-shade — Degree of pruning necessary — Type of training recommended — Distance between bushes or trees — Harvest time

Indoor Gardening: Flowering period — Maximum height or where pendulous length of stem — Maximum spread or spread range — Prefered position — Prefered temperature — Prefered humidity

IN THE FLOWER GARDEN

Gardening is one of life's most creative activities. Whether a garden extends to several acres or is confined to a few square yards, the gardener brings it to life, deciding what to plant and where, what to move – and sometimes what to discard.

All these decisions are affected by certain factors which must be taken into account in order to achieve success. The most important of these are climate, site and soil. To a large extent you must work with what you are given – human beings have no control over the weather, for example – and it is essential to identify these factors before you can accommodate or improve them.

CLIMATE Climate includes many variables – rainfall, humidity, temperature, wind and intensity of light – which influence the kind of plants that will thrive in the region where you live. The first factor to take into account is whether a particular plant can withstand the lowest temperatures likely to occur. Most of the plants described in this book are hardy in temperate zones, meaning that they need no protection at any point in their life cycle – provided you live in a temperate zone. Some, however, will only thrive against a warm, sunny wall. Half-hardy plants need protection during the winter, such as a cloche or a covering of straw or hessian; tender plants need permanent protection such as that afforded by a greenhouse, but a few can be set outside in the heat of summer.

There are plants with particular likes and dislikes, such as clematis, which likes a cool root run, or camellia, which should not be placed where early morning sun after frost might damage young growth. To help a plant give of its best, it is important to observe these individual requirements. Plant some *Alchemilla mollis* where it will cast shade over the roots of a clematis, and do not site your camellia on a wall which gets the morning sun.

RAINFALL Excessive rainfall causes a problem in gardens where drainage is poor, though this can sometimes be corrected. Even so it may make life difficult for plants like alpines and others that like a sunny, dry bank. Some flowers are badly damaged by rain – white roses, for example – and wind after rain can be devastating. Lack of rain is a more general problem. In areas where rainfall is low, it makes sense to concentrate on plants that can cope with drought *(see page 18)* and to use moisture-retentive mulches of peat, leaf-mould, spent hops, garden compost, well-rotted manure or pulverized bark on plants that need it – particularly shrubs, roses, trees, dahlias and sweet peas.

SUN AND SHADE There are many splendid plants that will only give of their best if they receive a full day's sunshine. However, many more will be sustained by just a few hours every day, and most gardens, however ill-favoured they seem, will enjoy some sunshine for at least part of the day. The blessing is that there are so many desirable plants which prefer shade or semi-shade *(see page 18)*. Take note of the source of the shade and plan accordingly: a large tree will not only cast a correspondingly large shadow, but take all the nutrients from the soil around it, so that no other plants can thrive. A shaded wall will be cool but need not be bare: clematis, jasmine, honeysuckles and some roses will do well in such a situation *(see page 18)*.

WINDS Occasional fierce winds are a hazard most gardeners try to become philosophical about. On sites where strong winds are a more regular feature, it makes sense to erect barriers in the form of quick-growing dense hedges or fences that can be clothed with climbers – both are better than brick walls, which can trap pockets of frost. Flowering shrubs suitable for hedging include deutzia, forsythia, fuchsia, lavender, pyracantha, roses, santolina, lilac and viburnum.

SANDY SOIL

The particles of sandy soil are relatively large so that water drains away quickly, taking valuable nutrients with it. In periods of drought, the soil tends to dry out. The advantage of open-textured soil is a good air supply to plants' roots, encouraging deep development. Sandy soils are light, easy to work and warm up quickly. The best way to improve fertility on such soils is to incorporate quantities of organic manures of any type. Keep well-watered in dry weather.

CLAY SOIL

Generally cold and wet, clay soils do not admit much air to the root systems of plants, inhibiting the development and as a result reducing the amount of top growth. Because they are slow to warm up, clay soils are inhospitable to early-flowering varieties. Clay soils can be improved, and again the means of doing so is plenty of organic matter Clay soils also benefit from so-called 'green manures' (*see page 11*). It is advisable to apply lime to break down the soil's close structure and improve drainage. Apply ground limestone at 100g/m^2 (4oz per sq yd) every other year in the autumn. Clay soils retain their fertilizer content well, and plants rarely suffer from drought. Roses and many perennials like a well-maintained clay soil.

UNDERSTANDING THE SOIL

Plants derive the nourishment they need in order to thrive from the soil. Keeping the soil in good condition is a gardener's most important task. The first step is to identify the type of soil in your garden – bearing in mind that a large plot may contain more than one type. The ideal soil is known as loam: it is dark, has a crumbly texture, drains well but retains enough moisture to supply plants' need for water. It has a high content of decaying organic matter, sustaining plenty of earthworms and beneficial insects and contributing to fertility. Loamy soils warm up relatively quickly, making it easier to succeed with early-flowering varieties. The only requirements for keeping loam in good condition are generous applications of well-rotted compost or other organic matter (*see page 11*). 'Green manures' (quick-growing crops such as mustard or red clover that are dug back into the soil while still young and green) are also effective for improving poor soils and maintaining good loam. Like many other ideals, loam is a rarity. Some soils may approach it, but in practice most approximate to one of the types illustrated on pages 10 and 11.

ACID OR ALKALINE? Soil acidity is determined by the amount of lime in the soil. A very chalky or limy soil is said to be alkaline; one which contains little lime is said to be acid. Acidity is expressed on a measure known as the pH scale. Handy, easy-to-use kits are available to test the soil. Mix a small quantity of soil with the indicator fluid in the kit and compare the colour with those on the chart supplied. A neutral soil (green) will have a pH reading of 7. Any reading higher than this (blue) indicates an increase in alkalinity; a much lower reading (red) indicates high acidity. Loamy soils are generally slightly acid with a pH reading of 6.5. This is the level preferred by most plants (including vegetables). Sandy soils are usually acid, though not excessively so. Clay soils need lime. Chalky soils obviously are not, even if, as is sometimes the case, the top few centimetres are slightly acid: for a long period, enough limestone will be brought to the surface by cultivation to balance this out. Peaty soils are notably acid and require heavy dressings of lime every three years. Lime should be applied to the soil surface, preferably

CHALKY SOIL

Soils on chalk are characteristically pale, light in texture and quick-draining. Chalk, or limestone, is an active chemical which combines with certain elements in the soil and renders them unavailable to plants. Deprived of essential trace elements such as iron, manganese, boron or zinc, some plants suffer from serious deficiency diseases and cannot survive. Plants which hate lime include rhododendrons, azaleas, most heaths and heathers and camellies. Happily, the list of lime-tolerant plants (*see page 18*) includes many beautiful species. Again, improvement is down to plenty of organic matter to prevent the soil becoming impoverished.

PEATY SOILS

Dark brown in colour and low in nutrients, peat contains a plant material which because of poor drainage has not completely decomposed. It is essential to improve drainage, by structural means if necessary (laying drains 12-18in/45-67cm below the surface), by regular cultivation (digging in plenty of organic matter) and by applying limestone except in those areas where you might grow plants such as rhododendrons, azaleas or heathers, which like the acidity of peat.

in the autumn or early spring. Delay the use of any artificial fertilizer for eight weeks thereafter. Little can be done to affect alkalinity, and such soils cannot support acid-loving plants like rhododendrons.

IMPROVING THE SOIL All soils benefit from the incorporation of organic matter, not only to replace nutrients used up by plants and to maintain fertility, but also to improve the soil structure. There are a number of forms of organic matter which can be used for this purpose. The best type of animal manure is wheat-straw based horse manure, but it is too strong to be used fresh. Let it rot down completely first – this will take 3-6 months. Well-rotted manure is usually spread on top of the soil in the autumn and dug in in the winter, and should be incorporated into the planting hole when planting roses and trees.

Compost is formed from rotted vegetable matter such as lawn mowings and kitchen waste – for example, potato peelings and crushed eggshells. A compost heap is an excellent source of bulky organic material. Purpose-built compost bins are useful for small gardens. Start with a 15cm/6in layer of coarse material like straw to allow air to circulate while keeping the temperature up, and add the waste material in batches, an 20cm/8in layer at a time to prevent it compacting down. Water lightly if it looks like drying out. Add small quantities of farmyard manure if available and dust occasionally with ground limestone to speed up decomposition. In summer this process takes about three months, in winter at least twice as long.

Leaf-mould is one of the easiest composts to make. It is a very slow procedure but produces one of the best surface mulches and is a useful ingredient for potting composts. It takes two years for a heap of leaves to rot down to a good crumbly consistency. If you have the space and the leaves – which are, after all, completely free – make a simple frame in a dry shady spot from four posts pushed into the ground with wire netting stretched around them. Peat is useful on very light soils, efficiently retaining water in dry weather, and is an excellent mulch for roses. But peat is a non-renewable natural resource, and some gardeners are reluctant to use it. Other useful organic substances are spent hops, seaweed, wood ash in small quantities and spent mushroom compost.

The handwritten labels on the garden plan read:
- Delphiniums. Up to 5 feet
- Lupins. 3 feet average
- Nigella (love in the mist) - 2 feet
- Dianthus approx 2ft
- Geranium endressii 1 foot
- Lobelia up to 4in
- Lavender
- 1 2 3 4 5 feet

PLANNING YOUR GARDEN

Strategies for garden design differ according to whether you are starting with a virgin plot or working with some established features. There are advantages and shortcomings to both situations.

THE FIRST STEP With a virgin plot, although getting the soil into shape is likely to be a major task, in terms of design you can let your imagination have free rein. In the case of an established garden, you will know what kinds of plants are likely to thrive, and are certain to have inherited at least one feature, perhaps a mature tree or fine hedge, which provides a focal point or good background and gives an air of permanence.

THE PLAN Before drawing up a plan, list all the practical functions your garden must fulfil, such as a play area for children, an area for drying washing or a plot of herbs near the house. You will need somewhere to keep garden tools, and can site a shed for storage where it will be inconspicuous, yet not using up a favourable spot better suited to a deserving shrub. Make a plan on paper by all means, but do not let armchair planning take over from walking around the garden at different times of day, noting how the light falls and how the garden looks from different angles. Remember, too, to take into account what you can see, or would rather not see, in your neighbours' gardens and beyond.

If you do not know where to start, have a look at as many other gardens as you can. Literally hundreds of them, great and small, are open to the public and are unquestionably the best source of ideas.

FORMAL DESIGNS Garden designs are basically formal or informal. A large formal garden is difficult and costly to maintain, but a formal design can succeed very well in small gardens, particularly in town, and need not be demanding once laid out, especially if paving is used rather than lawns and planting is confined to shrubs, low-maintenance perennials and bulbs. Such designs are enhanced by a limited colour palette, giving a sense of peace and order. Silver, green and white is a justifiably popular combination. It associates well with paving and statuary and allows for focus on the shape of individual plants. Concentrating on any single flower colour will have the same effect, though soft blues and yellows tend to be more successful than vivid pinks, reds or orange.

In formal gardens straight lines predominate, balanced with carefully controlled curves, and each element must be in harmony with the rest. Plants with handsome foliage are particularly appropriate here, especially if they can be grouped around a small pool. Some plants with attractive foliage described in this book are the shrubs potentilla, mahonia, santolina, pieris, camellia and species clematis, with enkianthus and fothergilla for autumn colour, and the perennials alchemilla, euphorbia, pulmonaria and bergenia. Dwarf tulips and narcissi are bulbs worth considering.

INFORMAL DESIGNS Restraint and simplicity are essential to garden design, even if the end result is informal and apparently random, as in the ever-popular cottage garden. In such designs the rounded lines of generously planted bushy specimens, twining climbers and arching stems are held in check by straight-line boundaries of paved paths and low hedges. The paths will be of soft-coloured materials like brick or York stone, laid so that thyme, for example, can take hold between the cracks. Hedges might be lavender or santolina. Against a permanent backdrop of shrubs and climbers such as rambling roses, fragrant honeysuckle and scrambling *Clematis montana*, cottage gardens are populated by a wide range of perennials and annuals.

The selection of suitable plants reflects principles relevant to any mixed planting for beds and borders. There must be plants that give height situated at the rear, in this case delphiniums, lupins or lilies perhaps. Colours will be varied, with clumps of the eye-catching poppies and marigolds judiciously set among dense-leaved plants as a green foil.

Getting the palette right – for blues and pinks will inevitably be equally well represented by the likes of love-in-a-mist, forget-me-nots, crane's-bills and cornflowers – takes considerable skill and a certain amount of trial and error. It is comforting to remember that, whatever the effect they are striving for, many gardeners eventually discard up to half their original choice of plants before they feel they have it right. Patience is probably the good gardener's most valuable asset.

A WILD AREA Many people now like to incorporate a 'wild' area in their garden if they have the space. This will not in fact be an area left to nature – that is the opposite of a garden, after all – but one that appears to be so. In the open it might well include bulbs such as *Narcissus cyclamineus* which can be planted in sweeps to fend for themselves. This type of planting is called naturalizing, and typically uses plants like daffodils and crocuses whose foliage is grass-like. Under trees, *Cyclamen neapolitanum*, lily-of-the-valley and snowdrops do well. The area between 'wild' and cultivated garden might well be marked by a strip of long grass, bordering the lawn.

LAWNS Making and caring for lawns is beyond the scope of this book, but in terms of design it is worth pointing out that a swathe of grass – as well kept as you can manage – is the most obvious evergreen element you can include. It is a neutral space against which all other plants are set, restful to the eye and a perfect backdrop to the plants displayed in the border.

GARDEN TASKS

Gardens are places for relaxation and contemplation, it is true; nevertheless there are a number of jobs which need regular attention.

WEEDING Weeds are unsightly and compete with plants for nourishment from the soil. Perennial weeds should be resolutely dug out and burned and will disappear within 2-3 years. Annual weeds should be removed as soon as seen, never let them get to the flowering stage. Use ground cover plants and mulches to smother weeds.

WATERING Seedlings which have just been planted out and container-grown perennials and shrubs should be watered in and kept lightly and frequently watered until established. In summer, an occasional good watering at a cool time of day is ideal. To conserve moisture, apply mulches and protect plants from wind, which dries out the surface

DIGGING If you are starting a garden from scratch in a plot attached to a new house, revitalizing an existing garden or setting out a new border, digging will be essential to clear the ground of rubble and unwanted vegetation, simultaneously aerating the soil.

FEEDING All plants need nitrogen, phosphate and potash plus some trace elements such as iron and zinc to grow. Nitrogen is important for leaf growth, phosphate for root development and potash for flowers. Organic fertilizers contain varying amounts of these substances, which they release gradually into the soil. Chemical fertilizers may contain a balance of all three or one may predominate. Organic gardeners are anti chemical fertilizers because they believe that they make plants prone to pests and diseases without feeding the soil in the long term. On the credit side, chemical fertilizers are easy to use and produce quick results. A compound fertilizer is best, applied as a light top dressing at the rate of 15g/m² (½ oz per sq yd). Spread the fertilizer evenly by hand, three or four times during the season.

PROPAGATION

Raising your own plants is a tremendously satisfying process, and can provide new material for very little expense. Different methods are suitable for different types of plants.

CUTTINGS Cuttings may be taken from various parts of a plant. For the plants in this book stem cuttings are most generally used. They are usually rooted in a growing medium of equal parts (by volume) peat

This well planned planting shows skilful handling of plant colour, height and form. Toning shades of green provide the backdrop to strong punctuations of colour.

SOFT CUTTINGS

These are immature non-flowering shoot tips. Many perennials and sub-shrubs are increased in this way, for example pelargoniums. Make a sharp cut just below a node and remove the bottom pair of leaves before placing the cutting in the rooting medium. Sometimes it is best to take a cutting with a heel, as described below. Soft cuttings take 10-30 days to take root.

SEMI-RIPE CUTTINGS

These are firmer than soft cuttings. They are usually taken in summer and do not need added heat; a cold frame is the best environment. Shrubs and heathers are increased in this way. Take a cutting from a healthy side shoot, if necessary with a heel, a small piece of older wood, attached. Cleanly cut off the soft tip and remove the lowest pair of leaves before inserting in the rooting medium. Keep the frame closed and spray on warm days to keep it moist. The cuttings should be ready for planting out in nursery rows the following spring. Any that have not rooted should be discarded.

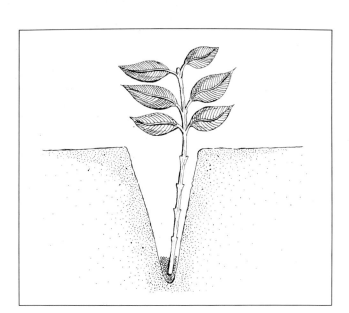

Hardwood Cuttings

These are suitable for trees, shrubs and roses. Take a cutting between 15 and 37cm/6 and 15in long (only 25cm/10in for roses), with a heel if necessary (rose cuttings need a heel). Remove all but the top three pairs of leaves. If there is an unripened shoot at the tip, cut back to a suitable bud. Take out a V-shaped trench 25cm/10in deep in good, weed-free soil and place a shallow layer of sand at the bottom to assist drainage. Insert the cuttings to half to two-thirds their length against the vertical side of the trench and push the soil back from the other side. Plant very firmly. Leave for at least a year, or until the rooted cuttings have increased to a healthy size, before transferring to the permanent positions.

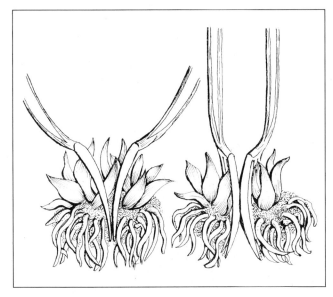

Division

Most perennials are increased by division, and some need dividing from time to time if they become overcrowded. Lift the plant when dormant – between autumn and spring. Separate the sections by hand, trowel or two forks (*above*) in the case of larger plants. Discard the central, woody sections and replant the outer parts. Tough crowns such as lupins should be washed free of soil and the sections cut up with a sharp knife. Make sure each part has roots and buds before replanting.

and sand, though in certain cases other mixtures have been recommended. In order for a cutting to take root it needs light, warmth and moisture. The size of the cuttings and the best time of year to take them are given in the individual entries. Most cuttings of hardy plants taken in summer will root readily in a cold frame without heat. Cuttings taken from growing plants in cold seasons require some heat. An electrically heated propagator is a good way of providing this.

Hardwood cuttings are used for trees, shrubs, old roses, species roses and miniature roses and are taken between autumn and spring when the plant is dormant. Semi-ripe cuttings are used for increasing shrubs and heathers; and soft cuttings are used to propagate many perennials and sub-shrubs, like pelargoniums.

RAISING PLANTS FROM SEED Most plants can be raised from seed, though some take literally years to germinate. In practice you will find it useful to raise most of your annuals in this way. Seeds of hardy annuals may be sown outside in spring in a well-prepared bed. Water the soil the day before. Mark out shallow drills with the side of a hoe, sow the seed thinly along the row and cover lightly with soil. Alternatively, scatter seed on the ground and rake it in. Firm the soil with the flat side of the rake. Water well, with a fine rose the day after sowing and again a week later.

Half-hardy annuals can be raised from seed sown indoors from spring onwards. Fill a seed tray with moist seed compost and press down evenly and firmly. Place the seeds on top, evenly spaced. Cover with 5mm/¼in of sifted compost and water in gently until the compost is thoroughly wet. Cover with a sheet of glass or polythene and place in a heated frame or propagator; or cover with a plastic bag and place in a warm dark place, such as an airing cupboard. Check daily for moisture on the inside of the bag, which should be flicked off. As soon as the seed leaves appear, remove the cover and move to a protected position in the light.

THINNING Thin the seedlings out when they have two or three true leaves (not the tiny seed leaves that appear after germination has taken place). Take care not to disturb the seedlings left behind (a wooden ice lollipop stick makes an efficient 'trowel') Retain only the strongest and discard the weak ones.

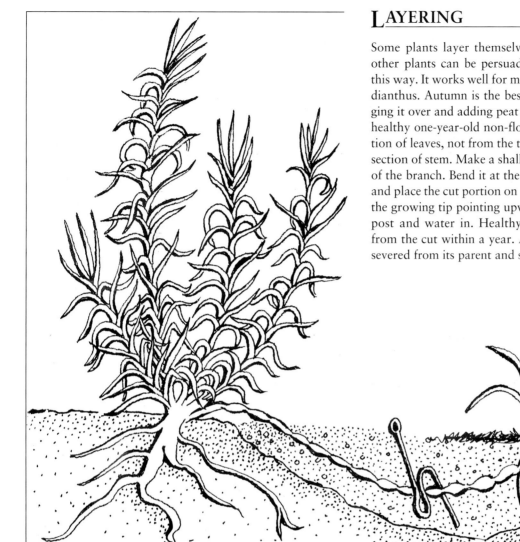

LAYERING

Some plants layer themselves naturally and a number of other plants can be persuaded to reproduce themselves in this way. It works well for many shrubs and is often used for dianthus. Autumn is the best time. Prepare the soil by digging it over and adding peat if it is on the light side. Select a healthy one-year-old non-flowering branch. Remove a portion of leaves, not from the tip itself but the next 30cm/12in section of stem. Make a shallow sloping cut in the underside of the branch. Bend it at the cut, without breaking the stem and place the cut portion on the ground. Peg it in place, with the growing tip pointing upwards. Cover the cut with compost and water in. Healthy roots should have developed from the cut within a year. At this point the branch can be severed from its parent and set in its permanent position.

PRICKING OUT When the true leaves appear the seedlings can be pricked off into trays or 7.5cm/3in pots of potting compost. Prepare planting holes with a pencil, spacing them 4cm/½in apart. Carefully remove a small clump of seedlings with a plastic plant tag or similar tool, holding them by the leaves, never the roots. Separate them gently and lower them one by one into the planting holes. Use a pencil to firm the compost around each one. Water in using a fine rose watering can. Place the tray in a cold frame or on a windowsill away from direct sunlight for two to three days, then move into a sunlit position. The compost should be kept moist. Harden off the seedlings gradually by exposing them to increasing amounts of fresh air during the day. When they are hardened off they may be planted in their permanent positions. Make sure the soil is moist when planting and take care not to damage the root system when transferring the young plants from the trays or pots to the flowerbed.

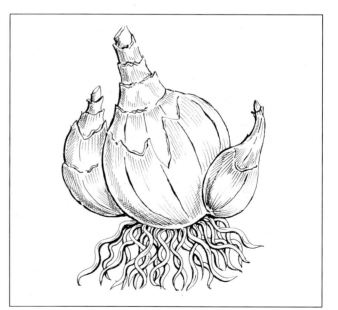

OFFSETS

These are small bulbils or cormlets naturally formed at the side of a parent bulb. They are easy to detach from the parent when lifting for storage and are best planted in a nursery bed for 2 years until they reach flowering size.

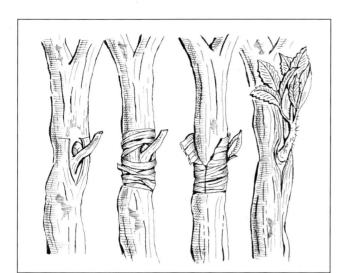

BUDDING

A relatively complex form of propagation used for certain types of roses and some ornamental trees. Basically it involves taking a bud from the plant you wish to increase and inserting it in a T-shaped cut on suitable rootstock. The bud must fit the cut very closely and be tightly bound with raffia. When it has 'taken', the rootstock is cut down to just above the bud. Any shoots appearing from the rootstock itself must be removed, or they will take over the plant.

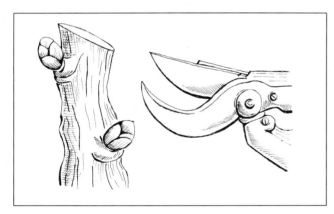

PRUNING

A certain mystique is attached to pruning, but it is based on simple enough principles. Many shrubs must have some branches or shoots periodically removed in order to keep their shape and go on producing good flowers. A tangled mass of stems is not only unsightly but prevents healthy air circulation, encouraging pests and diseases. Use good sharp secateurs to make sure all pruning cuts are clean. Remove branches or stems close to an outward-facing bud with a cut sloping away from it as shown above. Pruning to remove damaged wood can be done at any time. Many gardeners go over shrubs in spring for this purpose to clear up the devastation of winter, simultaneously removing weak branches and shortening by half any that are unsightly. Shrubs that flower on the previous season's wood, such as deutzia, *Spiraea x arguta* and *Mahonia aquifolium* (as ground cover) are pruned immediately after flowering. Cut back hard to a new shoot. Shrubs that flower on new shoots such as deciduous ceanothus, fuchsia, santolina and most spiraeas may be pruned in early spring to encourage healthy, compact plants . Cut the previous year's shoots to 2 or 3 buds from their base.

PLANT FINDER

DROUGHT-RESISTANT PLANTS

ANNUALS Centaurea, Mesembryanthemum, Salvia, Zinnia
PERENNIALS Catananche, Helichrysum, Hemerocallis, Oenothera
ALPINES Aethionema, Iberis, Juniperus, Santolina, Saponaria, Sedum, Thymus
BULBS Crocus chrysanthus, Gladiolus, Iris danfordiae, Narcissus cyclamineus, Scilla peruviana
SHRUBS Cytisus, Hibiscus, Lavandula

PLANTS FOR SHADE

ANNUALS Asperula
PERENNIALS Aquilegia, Bergenia, Convallaria, Fothergilla, Helleborus, Polyanthus, Pulmonaria, Tiarella, Viola
BULBS Cyclamen, Eranthis, Galanthus
SHRUBS Mahonia, Rhododendron
CLIMBERS Clematis, Jasminum, Lonicera, Wistaria, Pyracantha, roses including 'Danse du Feu', 'Caroline Testout', 'Parkdirektor Riggers' and 'Paul's Lemon Pillar'

LIME-TOLERANT PLANTS

ALPINES Erodium, Helianthemum
SHRUBS Deutzia, Forsythia, Fuchsia, Philadelphus, Rosa species, Spiraea, Syringa, Viburnum
CLIMBERS Clematis, Lonicera

A KEY TO THE SYMBOLS USED IN THE INDIVIDUAL FLOWER GARDEN PLANT ENTRIES APPEARS ON PAGE 7

PESTS AND DISEASES

PESTS

PROBLEM	DAMAGE CAUSED	REMEDY
Aphids (greenfly, blackfly)	Sap sucked; honeydew emitted, virus diseases spread	Spray with pirimicarb
Capsid bug	Leaves tattered or with tiny holes	Spray with systemic insecticide
Caterpillar	Leaves, stems, flowers eaten	Spray with permethrin or trichlorphon
Earwig	Flowers, shoot-tips, young leaves eaten	Trap with straw-filled inverted flowerpots on canes among plants; kill with malathion or HCH
Eelworm	Plants weakened, leaves and stems distorted	Destroy infected plants, do not grow again on same site
Froghopper	Sap sucked under cuckoospit	Spray with fenitrothion
Leaf miner	Pale tunnels in leaves	Remove infested leaves; spray with pirimphos-methyl
Lily beetle	Leaves eaten	Spray with pirimphos-methyl
Mealy bug	Sap sucked, virus diseases spread by small insect enclosed in white 'wool'	Spray with malathion
Narcissus fly	No flowers; weak, grassy leaves; maggots in bulbs	Destroy infested (soft) bulbs
Red-spider mite	Sap sucked; foliage desiccated; fine webs spun	Spray with fenitrothion or malathion
Rhododendron bug	Leaves mottled, yellow above and brown below	Spray leaf undersides with pirimphos-methyl
Sawfly	Leaves eaten or rolled under	Spray in late spring with pirimphos-methyl
Scale insects	Sap sucked, virus diseases spread by small, limpet-like insects	Spray with malathion
Slugs and snails	Young plant leaves eaten	Scatter methiocarb thinly among plants
Tarsonemid mite	Stems, flowers distorted and scarred; leaves, stems spoon-like	Dig up and burn affected plants; do not grow again on the site
Thrips	White speckles, then grey patches on leaves, flowers	Spray with fenitrothion
Vine weevil	Lower leaves holed and notched; grubs on roots, plants wilt	Dust lower leaves and soil with HCH
Whitefly	Sap sucked; virus diseases spread	Spray with permethrin

DISEASES

Anthracnose of willow	Small brown canker on stems; die back of stem tips; blotched leaves fall	Spray with thiophanate-methyl
Azalea gall	Hard green reddish or whitish swellings on leaves and buds	Cut out and burn infected stems; spray with copper fungicide
Bacterial canker	Leaves full of holes; stem cankers with oozing gum; general weakening	Cut out infected wood; spray with benomyl
Blackspot	Rose leaves develop black spots, fall early	Rake up and burn all leaves at end of season; spray with bupirimate and triforine
Botrytis (Grey mould)	Parts of plants rot, become covered in grey fur	Remove and burn infected parts; spray with benomyl
Bud blast	Rhododendron buds turn brown, develop black pinhead spore capsules and fail to open	Cut off infected buds; spray with fenitrothion to control leafhoppers that spread the disease
Canker	Rough brown sunken areas on stems	Cut out and burn; spray with thiophanate-methyl
Chlorosis	Leaves yellowed; growth stunted on alkaline soils	Grow plants on acid soils. Water with iron sequestrene; feed well
Clematis wilt	Collapse of mature shoots, usually on young plants	Cut back to ground level; water with benomyl
Coral spot	Raised orange pustules on woody stems	Cut out infected wood and burn; paint wounds with sealant
Die-back	Woody stems die at tips	Cut out infected wood back to healthy tissue
Fireblight	Shoots, flowers look burned, turn brown and wilt	Cut out infected stems back to healthy tissue; paint wounds with sealant
Fusarium wilt	Lower leaves and stem bases turn brown and rot	Destroy infected plants; do not grow species again on the same ground.
Honey fungus	Stems die back (or plants even die) for no visible reason. Fungal 'bootlaces' found in soil; honey-coloured toadstools on site	Dig up and burn infected plants; dig up all tree stumps. Water soil with fungicide
Leaf spot	Dark blotches on leaves	Spray with copper fungicide in spring. Prevent by growing on good soil
Lilac blight	Black spots on leaves; shoots wither	Cut out infected wood; spray with bordeaux mixture
Mildew	White powder or downy deposit on leaves and stems	Cut out badly infected growth; spray with benomyl
Peony wilt	Leaf bases of herbaceous peonies turn brown and rot	Destroy infected buds or plants. Prevent by spraying with dichlofluanid
Petal blight	Petals covered by translucent spots, especially in wet weather	Remove and destroy infected blooms
Root rot	Roots turn brown and rot, killing plant	Destroy infected plants
Rust	Yellow spots on upper leaf surfaces, orange pustules below	Destroy infected plants; spray others with mancozeb. Prevent by growing resistant strains
Scab	Reddish-brown spots on leaves; black spots on corms	Dip corms in calomel dust
Sclerotinia	White fungal growth coats stems, makes plant collapse. Black resting bodies overwinter in soil	Destroy infected plants. Do not grow dahlias on site
Virus diseases	Leaves distorted, marbled, yellowed; plant often stunted	Dig up and burn; control insect disease-carriers

ANNUALS

Annuals are plants that complete their life cycle in one season, while biennials need two seasons, producing leaves in the first year, flowers and seeds in the second.

Sometimes the distinctions between types are affected by climate; for example, in cooler zones the perennial antirrhinum is grown as an annual. Sometimes annuals perpetuate themselves, scattering seed that readily germinates where it falls. Love-in-a-mist *(Nigella damascena)* is an annual that provides you with flowers year after year in this way.

Annuals have a multitude of roles to play in the garden. They are particularly valuable when you are starting from scratch and are confronted with bare patches of earth, with a few young shrubs and perennials as yet too small to have much effect. Seeds of annuals sown in the spring will provide a colourful display for the whole of those first summers while more permanent plants are becoming established. This also gives you an opportunity to play with ideas about colours and

arrangements of colours within particular beds: does a palette of soft blues and pinks look pleasing near the house? Will a dull corner be brought to life with gleaming reds and yellows? Experiments with annuals help you make decisions that have longer-term effects on the overall appearance of your plot.

Even when the basic framework of the garden, provided by trees, shrubs and perennials, is beginning to take shape, most gardeners like to introduce a fresh note of colour into the summer garden by using annuals. The fun lies in ringing the changes and trying out different colour combinations and new varieties of plants each year. Both house and garden benefit from this versatility, as many annuals last well as cut flowers. Serious flower arrangers who need a steady supply of plant material may consider devoting a patch of the vegetable garden to their favourites so that they do not have to deplete the garden's display.

Annuals are relatively time-consuming, calling for regular watering, staking in some cases, weeding and dead-heading. The amount of space you allocate them will therefore depend to some extent on the amount of time you have available to devote to them. Another consideration is cost: if you do not raise your own plants from seed, buying them as bedding plants from a garden centre or nursery can prove expensive.

SITING Choose and site carefully to make the most of your purchases, planting them in tight groups to make an impact rather than setting them too far apart just to fill a space. When designing a bed of annuals, the usual common-sense rules apply about placing tall-growing specimens such as larkspar (*Delphinium ajacis*), cosmos and lavatera at the back, with clumps of medium height in the centre and dwarfs for edging at the front. Low, spreading plants will help to smother weeds, too. Try to strike a balance between different shapes, including some straight-stemmed showy speci-

mens like rudbeckias and some that provide a cloud of delicate colour like gypsophila. Contrast the ragged heads of cornflowers (*Centaurea* species) with daisy-like chrysanthemums and frilly sweet peas.

CONTAINERS Annuals come into their own in the planting up of containers. The bleakest spot can be completely transformed by pots, tubs, window-boxes and hanging baskets spilling over with summer flowers. As well as pelargoniums and impatiens (*see Perennials*), petunias, marigolds, lobelia and lobularia do well in containers. For successful results it is important to remember that all containers dry out quickly and need regular watering. Larger containers with correspondingly greater amounts of compost retain moisture longer. Wind dries out the compost as quickly as the heat of the sun.

HANGING BASKETS Hanging baskets are an ingenious way of displaying summer-flowering plants and have become very popular. Wire baskets permit you to trail flowerstems through the mesh, but are slightly

This beautiful display of Convolvulus tricolor *(left)*, Lychnis coronaria *(front) and* Cosmos *(back) fills the herbaceous border with colour during the summer.*

tricky to plant up. Balance them on a heavy bucket while you work. Line the basket with a small amount of moss which has been soaked in water and wrung out. Cover with a layer of potting compost. Set plants around the edge, carefully pushing the root balls between the wires. Cover with compost and another batch of plants. Continue in this way until the basket is full. Solid plastic containers with a water reservoir incorporated have a flat base which makes planting and maintenance easier.

Annuals grown in containers need a good peat-based compost with a shallow layer of drainage material at the bottom. Soak the compost thoroughly several hours before planting up and do not let it dry out at any time. Within 2-3 weeks the plants will require supplementary feeding, preferably in the form of liquid fertilizer. Dead-head regularly to encourage the flowering.

21

COSMOS

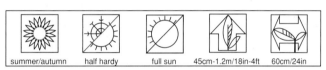

summer/autumn	half hardy	full sun	45cm-1.2m/18in-4ft	60cm/24in

Native to South America, these daisy-like flowers bring vivid colour to borders or containers well into the autumn. Varieties are available in shades of yellow and pink.

PROPAGATION Sow seeds in early spring under protection and with gentle heat. Prick out the seedlings into boxes as soon as they are large enough to handle and harden off before planting out 4-5 weeks after sowing.

GROWING Cosmos like a light soil that is not too rich, and do best in warm, dry weather. The delicate stems need the support of stakes. Dead-head the flowers regularly.

VARIETIES *C. sulphureus*: 'Bright Lights' (*above*) bears small double flowers in yellow, orange and scarlet; 'Sunny Gold' is a dwarf strain with small golden flowers. *C. bipinnatus*: all varieties have fern-like leaves, with flowers of white or deep pink up to 12.5cm/5in across, and reach 1.2m/4ft in height. Choose from 'Candy Stripe', 'Gloria' and 'Sensation Mixed'.

POSSIBLE PROBLEMS Generally trouble-free.

RUDBECKIA

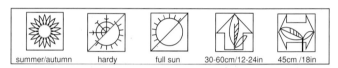

summer/autumn	hardy	full sun	30-60cm/12-24in	45cm /18in

Rudbeckia hirta, the original Black-eyed Susan, is treated as an annual, though strictly it is a perennial like its relatives *R. laciniata* (the coneflower) and *R. nitida*. Its bright yellow or orange flowers with contrasting dark centres are eye-catching candidates for the border and make good cut flowers.

PROPAGATION Sow seed in early spring in trays in a cold frame or greenhouse. Prick out the seedlings when large enough to handle and plant into the flowering site.

GROWING Annual rudbeckias like a dry, free-draining soil, unlike the perennials which prefer heavy, moisture-retentive loam. They tolerate dappled shade but prefer a sunny position. In the open, support the plants with stakes.

VARIETIES 'Marmalade' bears orange flowers up to 7.5 cm/3in across; 'Rustic Dwarfs' (*above*) are of equal size in shades of orange and bronze.

POSSIBLE PROBLEMS Generally trouble-free.

▧ CUT FLOWER TIP

The height and size of these flowers make for a striking flower arrangement, but make sure the vase is tall enough, as the stems are fragile and need support.

▧ PLANTING TIP

These flowers are perfect for planting close to the house, where they will contrast effectively with brick walls or evergreen edging such as privet or box. The bright daisy-like blooms appear in late summer, just when the main display of summer-flowering border shrubs begin to dwindle.

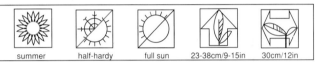

TAGETES

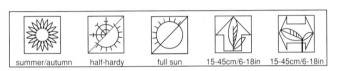

summer/autumn	half-hardy	full sun	15-45cm/6-18in	15-45cm/6-18in

Tagetes patula, the French marigold, is in fact a native of Mexico. Various strains produce flowers of yellow and orange, sometimes blotched with crimson or bronze, some with double flowers. Very long-lived, they add a bright note to the border and make good cut flowers.

PROPAGATION Sow seeds under protection in early spring and prick the seedlings out into boxes when they are large enough to handle. Harden off before planting out in late spring. Pinch out any premature flowerbuds. Seeds may be sown directly into the flowering site in late spring.

GROWING Marigolds are not fussy about soil, but like a sunny, open site. Dead-head regularly to encourage continued flowering. Discard at the end of the season.

VARIETIES Of the many good named varieties, try 'Naughty Marietta', yellow, blotched maroon; 'Monarch Mixed', compact double flowers ranging in colour from yellow to deep mahogany; 'Queen Sophia' syn. 'Scarlet Sophia', double flowers, russet-red laced with gold. *T. patula* is crossed with *T. erecta* to give Afro-French hybrids such as 'Suzie Wong' which are compact and early flowering.

POSSIBLE PROBLEMS Damp conditions cause grey mould.

GAZANIA

summer	half-hardy	full sun	23-38cm/9-15in	30cm/12in

Only in the very mildest areas can gazanias, natives of South Africa, be grown as perennials; elsewhere they are treated as annuals. The brilliant daisy-like flowers of cream, yellow, orange, crimson or mauve will only open in direct sunlight. The narrow leaves are grey on the underside.

PROPAGATION Sow seeds in very early spring in gentle heat. Prick seedlings into pots when they are large enough to handle. Harden off and plant out in early summer when all danger of frost is past. Tip cuttings may be taken in summer and overwintered in the greenhouse before planting out the following year.

GROWING Gazanias must have full sun; they like well-drained soil, and do well in coastal gardens.

VARIETIES Choose from named hybrids such as 'Chansonette' (*above*), lemon, apricot, orange, carmine red; 'Sundance', large blooms, wide range of colours including cream; 'Mini Star', compact strain, yellow, gold, bronze, red.

POSSIBLE PROBLEMS Damp weather may cause grey mould.

■ ORGANIC TIP

Ideal for companion planting near roses, or vegetables such as tomatoes, as they attract hover-flies whose larvae eat aphids by the thousand. The hover-fly has a short feeding tube, and so an open-structured flower like tagetes, whose pollen is easily accessible, is an ideal food source.

■ PROPAGATION TIP

Take cuttings of basal side shoots in mid to late summer. Dip base in hormone rooting compound and plant in sandy soil in pots. Overwinter in greenhouse.

GYPSOPHILA

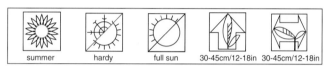

summer · hardy · full sun · 30-45cm/12-18in · 30-45cm/12-18in

Commonly known as baby's breath or chalk plant, *Gypsophila elegans* is covered with masses of tiny white or pink flowers throughout the summer. It makes a cloudy haze in the border and is indispensable in flower arrangements.

PROPAGATION Sow seeds in the flowering site in early spring or late summer. When the seedlings reach 10-15cm/4-6in, provide twiggy sticks or thin brushwood as supports.

GROWING Gypsophilas need very well-drained soil, preferably alkaline; dress acid soils lightly with lime. Cutting down the stems after flowering may induce a second flush of flowers in late autumn.

VARIETIES 'Alba Grandiflora', 'Covent Garden', white flowers; 'Rosea', vivid pink.

POSSIBLE PROBLEMS Generally trouble-free.

NEMESIA

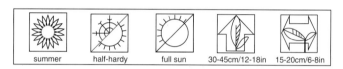

summer · half-hardy · full sun · 30-45cm/12-18in · 15-20cm/6-8in

The velvety flowers of nemesia are like a smaller version of antirrhinums, and come in an equally dazzling range of colours suitable for the summer border. The bushy plants bear their flowers in clusters above pointed, light green leaves.

PROPAGATION Sow seed in early spring under protection and with gentle heat. Prick the seedlings out into boxes when they are large enough to handle. Harden off before setting plants into their flowering positions in late spring.

GROWING Nemesias are cheerful, showy plants, but the blooms fade quickly if in very hot sun. Set in well-drained but moisture-retentive soil and keep well watered, especially in dry spells. Dead-head regularly. Discard plants after flowering.

VARIETIES 'Blue Gem', small, sky-blue flowers; 'Carnival Mixed' (*above*), a compact strain at 23cm/9in high, in red, white, cream, yellow, orange, bronze and blue.

POSSIBLE PROBLEMS Foot rot or root rot infection may cause plants to collapse at ground level.

▦ CUT FLOWER TIP

With its cloudy mass of tiny flowers, this is a must for flower arrangers as a background for more dramatic blooms; it is very effective at softening what might otherwise be a rather stark or formal arrangement. It is best to cut blooms early in the morning or last thing at night, and place in water immediately.

▦ PLANTING TIP

These flowers make ideal pot plants for the conservatory or greenhouse. Do not allow roots to become dry. Pinch out to encourage bushiness.

PETUNIA

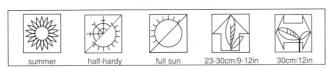

| summer | half-hardy | full sun | 23-30cm/9-12in | 30cm/12in |

Summer bedding would not be the same without the trumpet-shaped flowers of petunia hybrids providing a focus of colour that is vivid without being gaudy. Ideal for window-boxes and tubs, the trailing varieties combine particularly well with lobelia, alyssum, fuchsias and pelargoniums.

PROPAGATION Sow seed in early spring under protection with gentle heat. Prick the seedlings out into boxes when they are large enough to handle and harden off before planting out in late spring.

GROWING Petunias like reasonably fertile, free-draining soil and a warm, sunny position. Give them an occasional high-potash feed. Water regularly, especially if in containers, and remove faded flowerheads regularly. Discard after flowering.

VARIETIES Numerous named hybrids are available. Multifloras bear a profusion of 5cm/2in blooms; Grandifloras carry fewer, but larger, flowers. 'Resisto Mixed' (*above*): multifloras, red, pink, yellow, white, blue; 'Multiflora Double Mixed', large frilled flowers; 'Super Fanfare Mixed', grandifloras, double flowers.

POSSIBLE PROBLEMS Aphids on young shoots.

MOLUCELLA

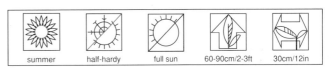

| summer | half-hardy | full sun | 60-90cm/2-3ft | 30cm/12in |

A particular favourite with flower arrangers, *Molucella laevis* or bells-of-Ireland should not be overlooked as a useful addition to the summer border. Its green spires add height and provide the perfect foil for more showy plants. Each tiny white flower is surrounded by a light green, bowl-shaped calyx. No named varieties are available.

PROPAGATION Sow seed under protection in early spring. Harden the seedlings off before planting out in late spring. In favoured locations seed may be sown directly into the flowering site in spring and the seedlings thinned to 23cm/9in apart when they are large enough to handle.

GROWING Ordinary well-drained loam is best. Give molucellas a sheltered site. Pull up and discard plants after flowering.

POSSIBLE PROBLEMS Generally trouble-free.

▦ ORGANIC TIP

Annuals like these are ideal for attracting beneficial insects into the garden, including bees for pollination. (Pollen is transferred from flower to flower by insects in search of nectar. The pollen sticks to the insect, and is then rubbed off on the next flower it visits on it's search for food.

▦ DRIED FLOWER TIP

The intriguing green flowers of this plant are excellent for drying, to provide winter colour in the home. For best results, cut just before the flowers open.

GODETIA

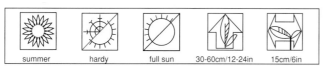

| summer | hardy | full sun | 30-60cm/12-24in | 15cm/6in |

These Californian natives produce brightly coloured flowers for the summer border or for cutting. The plants are compact, with mid-green, pointed leaves, and bear trumpet-shaped blooms of red, cerise, peach or pink, often edged with white. The best-known species, *Godetia amoena whitneyi*, syn. *G. grandiflora*, is often listed under clarkia in gardening catalogues.

PROPAGATION Sow seeds outside in spring if they are to flower the same year. Thin seedlings to 15cm/6in apart. Sow in early autumn for flowering the following year. Protect with cloches in colder areas and do not thin the plants until the spring.

GROWING Godetias do best in light soils. Over-rich soil encourages leaf production at the expense of flowers.

VARIETIES 'Azalea-flowered Mixed' , semi-double flowers with frilled petals; 'Sybil Sherwood', salmon pink; 'Crimson Glow' (*above*), dwarf variety; 'Double White', large white flowers with golden eye.

POSSIBLE PROBLEMS Stem and root rot may cause the plants to collapse.

LOBELIA

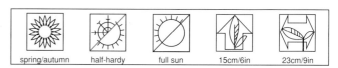

| spring/autumn | half-hardy | full sun | 15cm/6in | 23cm/9in |

Lobelia erinus, a perennial treated as an annual, is an indispensable element in summer bedding schemes, while the trailing varieties are invaluable in window boxes and hanging baskets. Their diminutive size and intense colours – blue, magenta or bright white – make lobelias good companions for petunias, pelargoniums, French marigolds and fuchsias.

PROPAGATION Sow seed in pans under protection and with gentle heat in late winter. Prick out the tiny seedlings in groups of 3 or 4 into trays and grow on until all danger of frost has passed. Plant out in early summer.

GROWING Annual lobelias like light, free-draining soil. If grown in containers, be careful not to let the soil dry out.

VARIETIES 'Cambridge Blue', compact, pale blue flowers, light green foliage; 'Crystal Palace', compact, dark blue flowers, bronze foliage; 'Rosamund', carmine-red, white centre; 'Snowball', white.

POSSIBLE PROBLEMS Damping-off and root rot may cause plants to collapse.

■ SPECIAL CARE TIP

Black root rot occurs when the same type of plants are always grown in the same bed. Avoid this and plant tagetes or calendula nearby to prevent attack by aphids.

■ PLANTING TIP

Plant trailing lobelia in a hanging basket for an eye-catching display. In hot weather syringe with water every evening and soak the basket once a week.

LOBULARIA

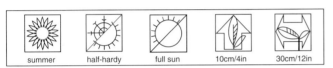

summer	half-hardy	full sun	10cm/4in	30cm/12in

Lobularia maritima is a close relative of alyssum, which it closely resembles, bearing masses of tiny sweetly scented flowers. This dwarf plant is often used in summer bedding schemes, window boxes and hanging baskets, in company with lobelia. It is also suitable for rock gardens and will grow in the crevices of paving or as an edging.

PROPAGATION Sow seeds under glass in early spring. Prick out young plants and harden off before planting out in early summer. If sowing outdoors where the plants are to grow, wait until late spring and thin seedlings to 15cm/6in intervals when they are large enough to handle. Garden plants sometimes self-seed.

GROWING Remove dead flowers regularly with sharp scissors and flowering will continue for 2-4 months.

VARIETIES Choose named varieties such as 'Rosie O'Day' (*above*), rose-pink; 'Little Dorrit', white, also known as 'Little Gem'; 'Lilac Queen' and 'Violet Queen'.

POSSIBLE PROBLEMS Generally trouble-free.

CALLISTEPHUS

summer/autumn	half-hardy	full sun	60-75cm/24-30in	30 cm/12in

The China aster, *Callistephus chinensis*, bears chrysanthemum-like blooms from high summer to the first frosts. They are bushy plants with flowers in all tones of pink, red and purple or white; they may be double, semi-double or single, pompon or feathered. The Duchess strain has thick, incurving petals.

PROPAGATION Sow seed outdoors where plants are to flower in late spring; thin seedlings to 30cm/12in apart when they are large enough to handle.

GROWING Light, free-draining soil is best, but any good garden soil will do. Choose a site protected from wind. Stake the taller varieties before the flowers open. Dead-head regularly for successive flowering. China asters are susceptible to wilt; to prevent the occurrence of this disease, do not grow them on the same plot for 2 consecutive years.

VARIETIES 'Miss Europe', ball type, pink; 'Fire Devil', Duchess strain, wilt-resistant, bright scarlet; the Giants of California strain has large, ruffled flowers; 'Milady', dwarf selection in numerous colours.

POSSIBLE PROBLEMS Wilt causes plants to collapse; cucumber mosaic virus causes yellow mottling of leaves.

▓ PLANTING TIP

This is a very reliable carpeting plant for tubs, dry-stone walls, paving, or rockeries, providing a mass of tiny flowers. To plant in a wall, or in a crack in paving stones, wrap the roots in a piece of old turf well soaked in water and insert in a prepared hole.

▓ PLANTING TIP

The dwarf varieties are excellent for growing in tubs or containers on a patio or balcony, where you can provide a sheltered site protected from the wind. Callistephus will bring a splash of colour to the garden in late summer and early autumn when many other plants look tired. Dead-head regularly.

Nigella

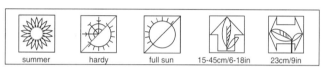

summer	hardy	full sun	15-45cm/6-18in	23cm/9in

Popularly known as love-in-a-mist, *Nigella damascena* is one of the group of plants typical of the English cottage garden. It looks well with lupins and aquilegias against a background of clematis and old roses. The leaves are delicate and fern-like; the flowers, usually blue but sometimes pink, resemble cornflowers.

PROPAGATION Sow seeds in the flowering site at intervals throughout the spring. Protect with cloches in colder areas. Thin out to 20cm/8in apart when the seedlings are large enough to handle. Love-in-a-mist does not transplant well.

GROWING A well-drained soil is best, and a position in full sun essential. Plants often self-seed, giving you new plants in succeeding years (though not necessarily where you would choose to put them).

VARIETIES 'Miss Jekyll', bright blue semi-double flowers; 'Persian Jewels', mixed colours – pink, red, mauve, purple, blue and white.

POSSIBLE PROBLEMS Generally trouble-free.

Myosotis

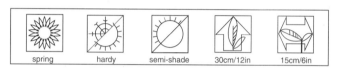

spring	hardy	semi-shade	30cm/12in	15cm/6in

This biennial member of the forget-me-not family bears sprays of tiny, fragrant blue flowers that provide drifts of colour in the border. They can be naturalized in woodland or raised under glass for cut flowers.

PROPAGATION Sow seed outdooors in a seed bed in late spring; thin the seedlings to 15cm/6in when they are large enough to handle. Transfer to the growing site in early autumn for flowering the following spring. Plants grown under glass should be transferred to 7.5cm/ 3in pots of compost. They need no winter heat and should flower up to 6 weeks earlier than those outdoors.

GROWING Forget-me-nots are not fussy plants, but do best in semi-shade in moisture-retentive soil that has been previously enriched with well-rotted compost or leaf mould.

VARIETIES 'Blue Bird', deep blue flowers; hybrids with *M. alpestris* include 'Carmine King', deep pink, 'Marine', clear blue and 'White Ball'.

POSSIBLE PROBLEMS Plants may die in soil that becomes waterlogged in winter.

▦ DRIED FLOWER TIP

The sky-blue, saucer-shaped flowers, surrounded by feathery foliage, are excellent for cutting, but leave some to develop into seed. The striking seed pods, green with maroon stripes, look well in dried flower arrangements. Cut the pods when swollen, tie in loose bundles and hang in warm air to dry.

▦ PLANTING TIP

Good in the herbaceous border, these tiny blue flowers are also useful for planting in bare rose beds to bring colour before the roses begin to bloom.

CONVOLVULUS

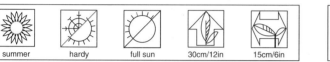

| summer | hardy | full sun | 30cm/12in | 15cm/6in |

Mediterranean in origin, *Convolvulus tricolor* is a garden relative of bindweed, though happily much less rampant. Like its other familiar cousin, ipomoea (morning glory), it bears open, trumpet-shaped blue flowers which appear throughout the summer and (unlike morning glory) stay open all day.

PROPAGATION Sow seed in the open in spring, covering with cloches to protect from cold until the plants are established. Thin seedlings to 12cm/5in when they reach 5cm/2in in height.

GROWING Give *C. tricolor* a sheltered site on ordinary, well-drained soil. Keep the young plants free of weeds. Remove faded flowerheads to ensure a succession of blooms.

VARIETIES 'Blue Flash' (*above*), dwarf variety, bushy plants, deep blue flower with yellow and white eye; 'Crimson Monarch', cherry-red flowers; 'Sky Blue', light blue.

DELPHINIUM

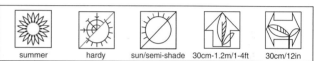

| summer | hardy | sun/semi-shade | 30cm-1.2m/1-4ft | 30cm/12in |

There are two types of annual delphiniums, namely *D. ajacis*, known as rocket larkspur, and *D. consolida*, the common larkspur. Both are typical cottage garden plants, their tall spikes clothed with flowers of blue, white, pink or purple. They bring height and grace to the summer border, and are suitable as cut flowers.

PROPAGATION Sow seed directly in the growing site in successive sowings throughout the spring. Thin the seedlings to about 30cm/12in depending on variety. Alternatively sow seed in the autumn and protect with cloches over winter.

GROWING Delphiniums need well-cultivated, fertile soil and a site sheltered from wind. Provide twiggy sticks for support for taller varieties.

VARIETIES *D. ajacis*, Hyacinth-flowered types: thickly set, double flowers, on blunt stems up to 60cm/24in high; *D. consolida*, Giant imperials: up to 1.2m/4ft, branching out from the base; Stock-flowered types: up to 90cm/3ft, best for cutting.

POSSIBLE PROBLEMS Slugs and snails damage young shoots. Crown, root and stem rot cause plants to collapse. Cucumber mosaic virus shows as mottled leaves.

ORGANIC TIP

Plant in or near the rose bed or vegetable garden to help minimize aphid attacks: the open flowers attract hoverflies whose larvae eat greenfly.

PLANTING TIP

In order to allow sufficient room between plants the rule is usually that the distance between plants should be equal to their height when fully grown.

However, you can vary this rule for very tall plants with small leaves, like delphiniums. Plant them the equivalent of half their finished height apart.

LUNARIA

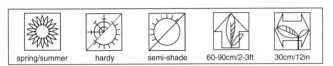

| spring/summer | hardy | semi-shade | 60-90cm/2-3ft | 30cm/12in |

No flower arranger's garden is complete without honesty, grown less for its purple flowers than the silvery round seed pods that follow. The biennial *Lunaria annua (above)* is the best choice as the perennial variety *L. rediviva* self-seeds very easily and may become invasive.

PROPAGATION Sow seeds in an outdoor seedbed from spring to mid-summer. Thin the seedlings to 15cm/6in when they are large enough to handle. Transplant to the growing site in early autumn to flower the following spring.

GROWING Any soil will do. If collecting stems with seed pods for drying, pick in late summer before they are damaged by cold winds.

VARIETIES 'Munstead Purple', tall rose-purple flowers; 'Variegata', crimson flowers, silver-spotted leaves. Mixed varieties are available.

POSSIBLE PROBLEMS Club root causes distortion of roots but does not affect the visible part of the plant. If it occurs, do not use the same site for honesty (or any member of the cabbage family) for three years.

ASPERULA

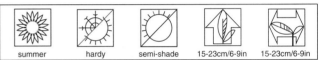

| summer | hardy | semi-shade | 15-23cm/6-9in | 15-23cm/6-9in |

Asperula orientalis is a neat, low-growing plant with attractive star-shaped leaves and clusters of tiny blue flowers that are lightly scented. Good at the front of the border or for cutting, this species may also be grown as a pot plant. No named varieties are available.

PROPAGATION Sow seed outdoors in late spring directly in the flowering site. Thin seedlings in two stages to a final spacing of 10-15cm/4-6in. For pot plants, sow under glass in early autumn, placing 5 seeds to a 12.5cm/5in pot of compost, and overwinter in gentle heat.

GROWING Asperulas do best in moist soil. When the plants are 10cm/4in high, stake them with twiggy branches for support. Discard plants after flowering.

POSSIBLE PROBLEMS Generally trouble-free.

▨ DRIED FLOWER TIP

The white central wall of the seed pod is the part used for dried arrangements: the outside part should be carefully stripped off.

▨ ORGANIC TIP

The common form of asperula – A. odorata – is also known as sweet woodruff and is sometimes grown as a herb. The flowering stems are used medicinally, as they have sedative, diuretic and antispasmodic properties. The dried leaves and stems are used to make a herbal tea.

DIANTHUS

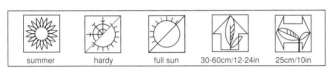

summer	hardy	full sun	30-60cm/12-24in	25cm/10in

Although this member of the dianthus family is a perennial, *D. barbatus*, or sweet william, gives best results when grown as a biennial. The dense flat heads of fragrant flowers range in colour from white through pink to deep cherry red. Some are marked with concentric rings of a contrasting colour. They look best grown in groups in the border, and are very popular as cut flowers.

PROPAGATION Sow seed under glass in early spring at 13°C/55°F. When large enough to handle, prick out seedlings into boxes at 7.5cm/3in apart and grow on at 10°C/50°F. Harden off and plant out in the flowering site in early summer.

GROWING A position in full sun is best, in ordinary, well-drained alkaline soil. Dress acid soils with lime before planting out.

VARIETIES There are no named varieties of sweet william, but hybrids known as 'Sweet Wivelsfield' bearing larger flower-heads have been developed.

POSSIBLE PROBLEMS Carnation ring spot causes deformed plants. Brown spots on leaves are caused by leaf spot.

CENTAUREA

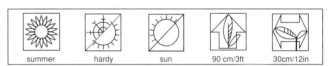

summer	hardy	sun	90 cm/3ft	30cm/12in

Centaurea cyanus, the cornflower, is a sturdy border plant with blooms of pure blue, pink or white that make excellent cut flowers. Its cousin sweet sultan, *C. moschata*, reaches only 60cm/24in and bears fragrant flowers of white, yellow, pink or deep purple.

PROPAGATION Sow seeds in the open where they are to grow in spring, or in the autumn with the protection of cloches over winter for early flowering the following year. Thin the seedlings to 23cm/9in apart.

GROWING Any fertile, well-drained soil is suitable. Choose a site protected from winds and give taller varieties the support of twiggy sticks. Dead-head regularly to encourage prolonged flowering.

VARIETIES *C. cyanus*: 'Dwarf Blue' (*above*); 'Polka Dot' includes a variety of colours; 'Dwarf Rose Gem' is a compact pink-flowered variety good for growing in pots. *C. moschata*: no named varieties, but *C. m. imperialis* is a reliable form with large flowers.

POSSIBLE PROBLEMS Petal blight; rust.

▇ PROPAGATION TIP

These are quite easy to propagate from non-flowering side-shoots in early summer. Strip foliage from the lower section of the cutting, and dip end in hormone rooting powder. Fill a seed box or small pots with sandy soil or potting compost, make a suitable hole with a dibber and firm in each cutting.

▇ ORGANIC TIP

An ideal plant for attracting insects. The flowers provide a good supply of nectar, especially for bees, whose long tongues can easily reach the nectar source.

ANTIRRHINUM

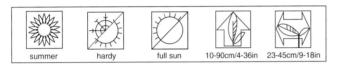

summer	hardy	full sun	10-90cm/4-36in	23-45cm/9-18in

Commonly known as snapdragon, *Antirrhinum majus* is a perennial usually treated as an annual, although in very favoured areas it may survive the winter. Modern varieties are available in all colours except blue, and the profuse tubular flowers look stunning in a summer border. They also make good cut flowers.

PROPAGATION Sow seeds in very early spring indoors with gentle heat. Prick the seedlings out into boxes when they are large enough to handle and harden off before planting out in late spring. Alternatively raise plants during the summer in a cold frame for planting out the following year.

GROWING A well-drained soil, previously enriched with well-rotted compost, is best. Pinch out growing tips to encourage bushy growth, unless single stems are required for cutting. Dead-head regularly.

VARIETIES Always choose rust-resistant varieties from the following divisions. 'Maximum', up to 90cm/3ft, many colours – the Rocket group is a vigorous strain; 'Nanum', up to 45cm/18in – 'Cheerio' is a sturdy hybrid; 'Pumilum', dwarfs at 15cm/6in. 'Tom Thumb Mixed' and 'Pixie' are reliable types which may also be grown in the rock garden.

POSSIBLE PROBLEMS Rust is the major problem. Aphids may damage young shoots.

■ ORGANIC TIP

This popular border plant is also an ideal choice for the organic garden, since the sweet scent of the pouch-shaped flowers will attract bees. Plant in a sunny border to ensure that it continues flowering throughout the summer.

LATHYRUS

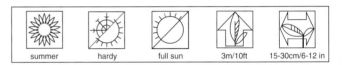

summer	hardy	full sun	3m/10ft	15-30cm/6-12 in

The sweet pea, *Lathyrus odoratus*, climbs by means of leaf tendrils. Its wing-petalled flowers are coloured white, pink, red, lilac or cream, and are sometimes strongly scented. They are extremely popular as cut flowers.

PROPAGATION Sowing can take place either in very early spring in a heated greenhouse or in late spring directly in the flowering site. To speed germination, soak the seeds in water for 12 hours before sowing. Prick out seedlings from early sowings into 7.5cm/3in pots and harden off before planting out in late spring. Plants may also be raised from summer sowings in a cold frame and set out the following year.

GROWING Sweet peas thrive on rich soil. Dig plenty of well-rotted compost or manure into the growing site before planting out. Provide pea sticks or posts and wires for support. Pinch out plants at 15cm/6in high to encourage side shoots. Pick the flowers regularly.

VARIETIES The popular Spencer group includes 'Swan Lake', white; 'Noel Sutton', deep blue; 'Leamington', lavender; 'Princess Elizabeth', coral pink and cream; 'Carlotta', carmine red. 'Knee-Hi', dwarf type, supported with light brushwood makes a bush about 1.2 x 1.2m/4 x 4ft, many colours available.

POSSIBLE PROBLEMS Slugs on leaves; mildew may occur.

■ CUT FLOWERTIP

They are ready for cutting when the bottom bloom on each stem is in full colour. If not cut, remove the flowers as they fade to encourage new growth.

SCHIZANTHUS

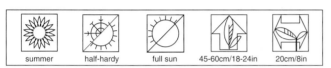

| summer | half-hardy | full sun | 45-60cm/18-24in | 20cm/8in |

Schizanthus are erect plants with delicate light green foliage, bearing a profusion of orchid-like blooms throughout the summer. Flowers may be pink, salmon, red, yellow or white and their fluttering petals have given rise to the popular name butterfly flower. They do well in tubs and as cut flowers.

PROPAGATION Sow seeds under protection at 16-18°C/ 60-65°F in early spring. Prick out the seedlings into 7.5cm/3in pots when they are large enough to handle and harden off before planting out in late spring 10-15cm/4-6in apart. Alternatively sow directly into the flowering site in mid-spring, thinning the seedlings to the recommended planting distances when large enough.

GROWING Soil that has previously been enriched with well-rotted organic matter gives best results. A position in full sun is essential for sturdy plants. Pinch out tips of young plants to encourage bushy growth and stake with split canes if necessary. Discard the plants after flowering.

VARIETIES Choose varieties of the hybrid *S. × wisetonensis* such as 'Butterfly': pink or white, large flowers, or 'Star Parade': compact form, all colours.

POSSIBLE PROBLEMS Aphids may damage growing tips.

CHRYSANTHEMUM

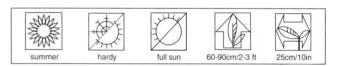

| summer | hardy | full sun | 60-90cm/2-3 ft | 25cm/10in |

Chrysanthemums comprise a huge family of very varied plants. The most popular annual variety, *Chrysanthemum carinatum*, has bright green, coarsely dissected leaves and cheerful daisy-like blooms 5cm/2in or more across. Petals yellow at the base and banded in pink and white, red or purple radiate from a flat, purple, central disc. Double-flowered versions are available. The species *C. coronarium* has a yellow centre and yellow and white flowers. *C maximum (above)* has single white flowers with yellow centres and toothed leaves. Annual chrysanthemums prolong the life of the summer border by flowering well into the autumn.

PROPAGATION Sow seed directly into the flowering site towards the end of spring, and thin the seedlings to 25cm/10in when large enough to handle. In warmer areas, an autumn sowing – protected with cloches over winter – gives large, earlier blooms the following year.

GROWING Chrysanthemums like fertile, well-drained soil and a sunny position. Pinch out the first growing tips to encourage long side stems for cutting. Although the stems are strong, supporting canes may be advisable on windy sites.

VARIETIES 'Monarch Court Jesters', many colours, single flowers; 'Flore-Plenum', yellow/white, compact double flowers

POSSIBLE PROBLEMS Aphids and earwigs can be problems.

ORGANIC TIP

Avoid attack from aphids by planting beside tagetes, papaver or nasturtiums. These attract hoverflies whose larvae eat large quantities of aphids.

ORGANIC TIP

To avoid damage by earwigs, set a traditional trap. Place a flower pot filled with dried grass or straw upside down on a cane near the flower heads.

The earwigs, which are nocturnal creatures, will crawl into the pot to avoid daylight - simply remove the pot once a week and burn the grass or straw.

ZINNIA

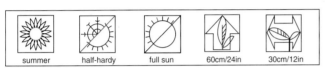

summer	half-hardy	full sun	60cm/24in	30cm/12in

The most popular annual zinnia, *Zinnia elegans*, is native to Mexico; the vivid colours of its luxurious blooms certainly have an exotic air. The species is bright purple, but its varieties include yellow, pink, scarlet, orange, white, lavender and violet; some are double-flowered, others are banded in a contrasting colour.

PROPAGATION Sow seed under protection at 16-18°C/ 60-64°F in early spring. When the seedlings are large enough to handle, prick them out into small peat or fibre pots so that the roots will not be disturbed when transplanting. Harden off before planting out in late spring.

GROWING Zinnias like free-draining, fertile soil and a sunny, sheltered site. Pinch out the growing shoots on young plants to encourage a bushy shape. Remove faded or rain-damaged flowerheads.

VARIETIES Dahlia-flowered strain: 'Giant Double Mixed' (*above*), double flowers, all colours; 'Canary Bird', yellow; 'Envy', lime green. Burpee hybrids, double flowers with wavy petals, are available in all colours. Varieties of the 'Pumila' type are only 15cm/6in high: 'Early Wonder' is a good mixture.

POSSIBLE PROBLEMS Cucumber mosaic virus causes mottled leaves.

SALPIGLOSSIS

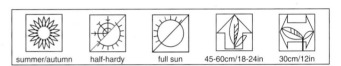

summer/autumn	half-hardy	full sun	45-60cm/18-24in	30cm/12in

Salpiglossis sinuata is such an exotic-looking plant that it is difficult to believe it is so easy to grow – or that it belongs to the same family of plants as the potato. Sometimes called painted tongue, sometimes the velvet trumpet flower, its tall, graceful, slightly sticky stems are clothed with narrow leaves and crowned with blooms all summer long. The colour range includes red, pink, orange, gold, yellow or blue, streaked with a contrasting colour.

PROPAGATION Sow seeds in late spring directly in the flowering site and thin seedlings to 25cm/10in apart when large enough to handle.

GROWING Salpiglossis are unfussy about soil type, as long as it is reasonably fertile. An open, sunny site is best, though in exposed positions stems will need the support of split canes. Remove dead flower spikes regularly.

VARIETIES 'Splash', compact plants, early flowering, many colours.

POSSIBLE PROBLEMS Aphids may infest the stems. Foot or root rot causes plants to collapse.

◼ ORGANIC TIP

Dig compost into the herbaceous border in early spring. After planting, mulch with well-rotted manure or compost to help conserve moisture.

◼ SPECIAL CARE TIP

This exotic plant comes originally from the Andes. It does need a sunny, sheltered position – if conditions are not suitable, you could consider growing this in the conservatory or greenhouse, where it will provide a bright splash of colour, or in a sheltered spot on a patio or balcony.

SALVIA

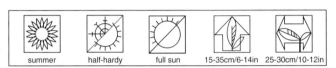

summer	half-hardy	full sun	15-35cm/6-14in	25-30cm/10-12in

The genus *Salvia* includes a number of species, among them the herbs sage and clary. *S. splendens*, a perennial grown as an annual, is an established favourite in summer bedding schemes, especially of the formal type. Its dense spikes of true scarlet flowers last into early autumn. Modern varieties include pink, purple and white-flowering forms.

PROPAGATION Sow seeds in pans in early spring at 18°C/64°F and prick the seedlings out into boxes when they are large enough to handle. Harden off in a cold frame before planting out in late spring.

GROWING Salvias need a warm, open, sunny site on moderately rich, free-draining soil. Do not let them dry out in hot weather. Remove faded flowerheads regularly.

VARIETIES 'Blaze of Fire', 'Tetra Scarlet', both early flowering; 'Tom Thumb', only 20cm/8in high, red or white; 'Dress Parade', all colours.

POSSIBLE PROBLEMS Low temperatures inhibit growth, causing stunted plants and yellowing leaves.

ESCHSCHOLZIA

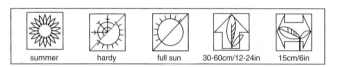

summer	hardy	full sun	30-60cm/12-24in	15cm/6in

Eschscholzia californica, the Californian poppy, is a dazzling candidate for the summer border, especially on dry soils. It blazes with colour – red, orange, yellow or pink – right through to the autumn. The flowers are followed by cylindrical seed pods, 7.5cm/3in long and blue-green in colour.

PROPAGATION Successive sowings ensure a long flowering season. Sow seeds in the flowering site at 2-week intervals throughout the spring, thinning the seedlings to 15cm/6in when they are large enough to handle. Alternatively, sow in early autumn and protect with cloches over winter for flowering the following year.

GROWING For brightly coloured blooms a poor, sandy soil is best. Flowers required for cutting should be picked when in bud. Self-sown seedlings do well in succeeding years.

VARIETIES 'Ballerina', mixed colours, semi-double flowers with fluted petals; 'Mission Bells', mixed colours, only 23cm/9in high; 'Harlequin Hybrids' *(above)*.

POSSIBLE PROBLEMS Generally trouble-free.

■ PLANTING TIP

Practise companion planting to avoid aphids, which spread diseases as they feed on neighbouring plants. Remove any diseased leaves immediately.

■ PLANTING TIP

If space is limited, it is worth remembering that this plant has a tendency to overrun the garden, if it gets the chance. Self-sown seedlings do well, thriving even on poor soils. To avoid self-seeding, dead-head the plants regularly and do not allow the seed pods (which look very attractive) to form.

AGERATUM

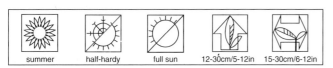

| summer | half-hardy | full sun | 12-30cm/5-12in | 15-30cm/6-12in |

Ageratum houstonianum is a native of Mexico and is sometimes listed as *A. mexicanum*. It produces mounds of small, soft-looking, daisy-like flowers amid heart-shaped leaves. It is an excellent choice for edging or for the front of the border, since the blue, white or pink flowers bloom from early summer through to autumn.

PROPAGATION Sow seeds in gentle heat in early spring and prick the seedlings off into boxes at 5cm/2in apart when they are large enough to handle. Harden off before planting out in early summer.

GROWING A well-drained fertile soil is best. Water the plants well in dry weather and dead-head regularly to ensure a succession of blooms.

VARIETIES Choose F_1 hybrids such as 'Blue Surf', 'Fairy Pink' or 'Summer Snow'.

POSSIBLE PROBLEMS Foot rot and root rot may occur, causing plants to collapse.

LAVATERA

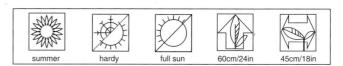

| summer | hardy | full sun | 60cm/24in | 45cm/18in |

Lavatera trimestris is an annual cousin of the perennial mallow, with larger flowers – they may be 10cm/4in across – which are excellent for cutting. Both pink and white forms are available. Lavatera makes a beautiful bushy plant whose long flowering period well justifies a place in the border.

PROPAGATION Sow seed in the flowering site in spring, or in the autumn for flowering the following year. Thin the seedlings to 45cm/18in apart when they are large enough to handle.

GROWING Light, well-drained soil is preferred. An over-rich soil will encourage foliage at the expense of flowers. Stake young plants with twiggy branches when they reach 10cm/4in in height. Discard plants after flowering.

VARIETIES 'Silver Cup' (*above*), bright pink; 'Mont Blanc', white.

POSSIBLE PROBLEMS Leaf spot and rust may occur.

■ PLANTING TIP

Ageratums are among the few annual bedding plants that will tolerate dry soil and light shade. As well as planting in the border, use them to make a colourful carpet of flowers around the base of trees and large shrubs, where other plants will not thrive.

■ SPECIAL CARE TIP

This is a tender flower, so plant in a sunny, sheltered position, especially in cooler regions or exposed gardens. Protect from cold, drying winds.

MENTZELIA

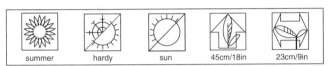

summer	hardy	sun	45cm/18in	23cm/9in

A native of California, *Mentzelia lindleyi* is distinguished by stunning, bright yellow flowers 5cm/2in wide with glossy heart-shaped petals. Numerous fine gold stamens cluster in the centre of each flower. Lightly scented, mentzelias make a vivid splash of colour in the summer border. They are also known as *Bartonia aurea*. No named varieties of the species are available.

PROPAGATION Sow seeds directly in the flowering site in spring and thin the seedlings to 23cm/9in apart when they are large enough to handle.

GROWING Mentzelias do best on well-drained fertile soil into which well-rotted organic matter has previously been incorporated.

POSSIBLE PROBLEMS Generally trouble-free.

MESEMBRYANTHEMUM

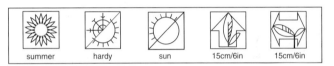

summer	hardy	sun	15cm/6in	15cm/6in

Commonly known as the Livingstone daisy, *Mesembryanth-emum criniflorum* is a succulent, low-growing plant best as informal edging for the summer border or in the rock garden. The small but vivid flowers may be apricot, pink, magenta, orange or white; they only open in full sun. The correct botanical name is now *Dorotheanthus bellidiflorus*. No named varieties of the species are available.

PROPAGATION Sow the seeds under protection and with gentle heat in early spring. Prick the seedlings off into boxes when they are large enough to handle and harden off in a cold frame before planting out in late spring. Seeds may also be sown directly into the flowering site in mid-spring, thinning seedlings to 30cm/12in.

GROWING Any well-drained soil will do, but light sandy soils are preferred.

POSSIBLE PROBLEMS Foot rot may cause plants to collapse at ground level.

ORGANIC TIP

Supply enough nutrients by digging in well-rotted manure or compost in early spring and give the border a dressing of fish, blood and bone meal before planting.

SPECIAL CARE TIP

Although this plant is easy to grow, it is susceptible to foot rot, shown by blackening of the stem base before the plants collapse. Foot rot is often caused by waterlogged ground, so make sure that drainage is adequate. If your soil is unsuitable, grow this plant on a rockery, where drainage will be better.

PERENNIALS

The term perennial is used to describe any long-lived plant that is non-woody (as shrubs and trees are). Herbaceous perennials are those that die down in the autumn and reappear in spring.

This is a large, diverse and useful group of plants. It would be easy to fill your garden with nothing but perennials and still have plants of all shapes, sizes and colours. This was the principle behind the nineteenth-century herbaceous border, which – though stunningly beautiful from late spring to late summer – had the disadvantage of descending into dullness from late autumn to spring. The modern mixed border makes the most of the qualities of perennials while compensating for their shortcomings with shrubs, bulbs, annuals and biennials. Unlike the herbaceous borders of old, which were traditionally rectanguiar but very large – often 3 m/10 ft deep and three times as long – the mixed border can be irregular in shape. Today curved lines are preferred to strict symmetry except in the most formal settings. Borders are smaller and, where space permits, island beds in the middle of lawns are popular. Again, curved lines are preferable; an indented oval is a pleasing shape and one which makes it easy to get close to plants that need attention. In any but the narrowest borders, it is a good idea to set stepping stones into the soil here and there to enable you to approach plants at the back for staking, dead-heading and other routine tasks like cutting down the stems after flowering and division when necessary. Bear in mind the space that most perennials need, and do not try to cramp them in too small an area. If your border is very narrow, dwarf shrubs, bulbs and a climber at the back might be a better combination.

The long life of most perennials is what makes them an attractive proposition to today's busy gardeners. Perennials are a more or less permanent fixture, with the exception of some short-lived species like delphiniums and hollyhocks (*Althaea rosea*), which need replacing after about five years. Because of this longevity perennials should be chosen and sited with almost as much care as you would bestow upon a shrub or tree. This applies particularly to species like peonies and Christmas roses (*Helleborus niger*), which greatly resent disturbance but, if left alone, will bloom through countless seasons. Other species, by contrast, need to be divided regularly not only for propagation purposes but to look their best. Astilbe, coreopsis and viola fall into this category.

CHOOSING PERENNIALS When designing a flowerbed where the principal elements are perennial, it is useful to make a plan on paper (*see page 12*). This will enable you to site plants of different heights and colours in a pleasing relation to each other, bearing in mind flowering time, the ultimate spread of the plants and their particular requirements as to site and soil. Always set perennials the correct distance apart, and if the bare space between them when they are young and small displeases you, fill it up with annuals. Eventually the perennials will fill up the gaps. Indeed, many make excellent ground cover plants, giving a luxurious effect

and smothering weeds. Some perennials which perform this function are bergenia, brunnera, *Euphorbia robbiae*, *Geranium endressii*, pulmonaria and stokesia.

Because flower colour is the single most important factor affecting choice of plants, the entries in this book have been arranged in colour groups as far as possible. Other design considerations to be taken into account are height and quality of foliage. Tall plants which should be situated at the back of the border or towards the centres of an island bed are some campanulas, delphiniums, echinops, hollyhocks, lupins and mallow (*Malva alcea*). A border should be twice as wide as the tallest plant in it. The middle range includes *Alchemilla mollis*, astilbe, catananche, *Monarda didyma*, peonies, poppies and trollius. At the front of the border you might place low-growing plants such as *Bellis perennis*, *Oenethera missouriensis*, dwarf coreopsis, geraniums, potentilla, polyanthus, *Stokesia laevis* and violas. Alchemilla, euphorbia, pulmonaria, bergenia and brunnera are among perennials prized for their foliage.

Sedum spectabile, in the foreground, is a striking border plant with year-round interest derived from its attractive grey-green leaves.

Hardy perennials can be purchased in containers or bare root direct from the nursery or garden centre. The planting procedure is identical whichever way they arrive. Dig a hole with a trowel or spade about one and a half times as large as the root ball. Set the plant in the hole so that its crown (the point at which the annual stems arise) is about 2.5cm/1in below the surrounding soil surface. Fill in around the roots and firm with fists or feet, depending on the size of the plant. To save on expensive garden centre bills, ask your friends and neighbours if you can take cuttings or make divisions from their perennials to establish in your own garden.

The choice of perennials is so wide that they can be used to contribute to any type of garden design – there is undoubtedly a perennial for every situation. It is this versatility that makes them the most valuable group of plants.

ALCHEMILLA

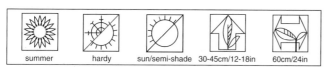

summer	hardy	sun/semi-shade	30-45cm/12-18in	60cm/24in

Commonly known as lady's mantle, *Alchemilla mollis* (*above*) is less valued for its flowers than its handsome leaves, which are light green, palmate and particularly attractive after rain when droplets settle on the leaves. Clusters of tiny, star-shaped lime-green flowers appear in early summer and are very long-lasting. These plants look their best at the front of a border. There are no named varieties of the species. *A. alpina,* at 15cm/6in, is a smaller species suitable for rock gardens.

GROWING Set out plants between autumn and spring when the weather is favourable. Alchemillas like moist, well-drained soil and a position in sun or partial shade. Set twigs around the plants for support and cut the stems right back after flowering.

PROPAGATION Divide established plants in autumn or spring. Plants usually produce numerous self-sown seedlings which do well.

POSSIBLE PROBLEMS Generally trouble-free.

EUPHORBIA

spring/summer	hardy	semi-shade	60cm/24in	90cm/3ft

The euphorbia family comprises a great many plants including annuals and shrubs. Among the evergreen perennials *E. robbiae* (*above*) is particularly attractive, with upright stems, whorls of dark green leaves and loose heads of lime-green flowers and bracts. It makes excellent ground cover under trees. Plants like euphorbias and alchemillas (*see left*) are invaluable elements in a garden design where patches of green are used as a foil for the bright colours of summer flowers. There are no named varieties of this species.

GROWING Set out young plants in spring, in light, well-drained soil. While most evergreen euphorbias tolerate some shade, *E. robbiae* will thrive even in full shade. Exposed windy sites are not suitable. Remove flowerheads when the colour fades. Cut plants back in late summer to keep them bushy.

PROPAGATION Take 7.5cm/3in basal cuttings in spring and insert in a peat/sand mixture in a cold frame. Plant out when rooted. Divide established plants between autumn and spring.

POSSIBLE PROBLEMS Cold winds and frosts may damage young shoots.

▪ PLANTING TIP

The light green flowers and leaves of this plant provide a striking contrast to other, more colourful flowers in a border. Try combining them with orange or golden-coloured lilies for an eye-catching display. This plant is popular with flower arrangers on account of its unusual colouring and can also be used dried.

▪ CUT FLOWER TIP

This tall attractive plant is a good choice for flower arranging, as the dark leaves and lime-green flowers contrast effectively with bright flowers.

DICENTRA

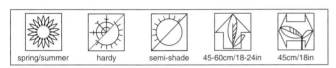

spring/summer	hardy	semi-shade	45-60cm/18-24in	45cm/18in

Dicentras make excellent plants for the border, and by growing two or three different species you can be assured of flowers from spring to late summer. All have fern-like foliage and slender stems bearing nodding flowers of white, pale pink or rose red.

GROWING Set out young plants from autumn to early spring, taking great care not to damage the fragile roots. Soil should be moisture-retentive but well-drained and, for best results, rich in humus. Apply a mulch of well-rotted organic matter each spring.

PROPAGATION Divide established plants between autumn and spring, or take root cuttings 7.5cm/3in long in early spring. Insert in a peat/sand mixture in a cold frame. When the young leaves are well formed, transfer to a nursery bed and grow on until transplanting to the permanent site in autumn.

SPECIES *D. formosa*, large clusters of pink, white or red flowers, early summer; *D. spectabilis* (bleeding heart), arching stems of rose flowers in summer – 'Alba' (*above*) is a white form; *D. eximia*, only 30cm/12in high, rose pink or white flowers right through summer.

POSSIBLE PROBLEMS Generally trouble-free.

ACHILLEA

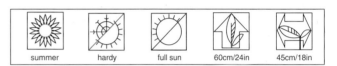

summer	hardy	full sun	60cm/24in	45cm/18in

The garden relatives of the common yarrow bear yellow or white flowers in flattened clusters. With fern-like, grey-green leaves, they are handsome additions to the summer border.

GROWING Set out young plants from autumn to spring in well-drained soil. Cut the stems back to ground level in late autumn each year.

PROPAGATION Divide established plants in spring into portions each bearing 4-5 young shoots and replant immediately.

VARIETIES *A. filipendula* 'Gold Plate', yellow flowers bloom all summer, good for dried flowers; A. × 'King Edward', forms low (10cm/4in high) hummocks of long-lasting primrose yellow flowers, suitable for rock gardens; A. × 'Moonshine' (*above*), feathery leaves, sharp yellow densely packed flowerheads; A. × *taygetea*, 45cm/18in high, pale yellow flowers 5-10cm/2-4in across, the best variety for cutting.

POSSIBLE PROBLEMS Generally trouble-free.

▧ SPECIAL CARE TIP

Does best in a semi-shaded spot with shelter from any cold winds. Enjoys wooded clearings where the young foliage will be protected from late frosts.

▧ DRIED FLOWER TIP

This is an easy and attractive plant to dry, with its flat flower-heads, which are generally white or yellow. Cut and tie in bunches and dry either from the roof of a shed, or in an indoor drying cupboard. The variety A. filipendulina holds its colour well, with masses of vivid yellow flowers.

OENOTHERA

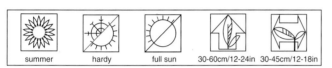

| summer | hardy | full sun | 30-60cm/12-24in | 30-45cm/12-18in |

The oenothera family of North America includes the evening primrose, *O. biennis*. Most species bear yellow flowers, though some are white. Lightly scented, they are funnel-shaped at first but open almost flat. They bring prolonged and brilliant colour to the border, and because they self-seed freely are also good for wild gardens.

GROWING Set out small groups of young plants in the autumn, on light, free-draining soil. Oenotheras like an open, sunny site but will tolerate light shade. Water well in dry weather and dead-head regularly unless you want plants to self-seed. Cut down the stems after flowering.

PROPAGATION Divide established plants between autumn and spring. These perennials are short-lived but self-seed freely and successfully.

SPECIES *O. perennis*, syn. *O. pumila*, small, yellow flowers, pale green leaves, mid-summer; *O. missouriensis*, suitable for rock gardens or the front of the border at 15cm/6in high, abundant yellow flowers all summer; *O. fruticosa*, the variety 'Yellow River' bears a profusion of deep golden yellow flowers, mid-summer; *O. tetragona* 'Fireworks' (*above*) bears yellow flowers throughout the summer.

POSSIBLE PROBLEMS Heavy, waterlogged soil encourages root rot.

MECONOPSIS

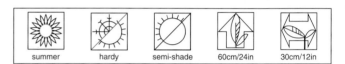

| summer | hardy | semi-shade | 60cm/24in | 30cm/12in |

Meconopsis bear showy, poppy-like flowers in spring and summer on slender stems above neat rosettes of attractive leaves. They are beautiful plants for a mixed border.

GROWING A free-draining but moisture-retentive soil is essential, preferably non-alkaline. Meconopsis like a position in semi-shade and sheltered from wind. Water well in summer and support with pea sticks. Clear away old seedheads and foliage in late summer.

PROPAGATION Collect ripe seed from the plants in late summer and sow in a cold frame. Transfer the seedlings to boxes and keep over winter in a cold frame. Transplant to nursery rows until planting in the permanent site in the autumn.

SPECIES *M. cambrica* (Welsh poppy, *above*), vivid golden flowers in summer, self-seeds very freely, does not withstand hot summers; *M. betonicifolia* (Tibetan poppy), up to 90cm/3ft high, large, deep blue flowers in early summer, best choice for higher temperatures; *M. napaulensis*, up to 2m/6½ft high, with beautiful leaves and large blue, purple, red or pink flowers in early summer.

POSSIBLE PROBLEMS Downy mildew, black bean aphid.

■ ORGANIC TIP

Ideal for the organic garden as its night-scented flowers will attract moths from dusk onwards. Other insects will be attracted in daytime to the nectar.

■ SPECIAL CARE TIP

The Himalayan poppy was only recently brought to this country. It is a tall plant, with striking, blue flowers, and like other Asiatic species it should have a cool, partly shaded position, for example in a clearing among trees, in a lime-free soil kept moist with plenty of humus or well-rotted compost.

COREOPSIS

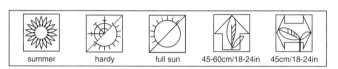

summer	hardy	full sun	45-60cm/18-24in	45cm/18-24in

Native to North America, the coreopsis is an accommodating plant, producing cheerful yellow star-shaped flowers throughout the summer even in polluted atmospheres.

GROWING Set out young plants between autumn and spring in well-drained, fertile soil. Chalky soils are tolerated. A position in full sun in an open border is preferred. Cut back some stems in late summer to encourage perennial growth.

PROPAGATION Divide established plants in early autumn or very early spring, making sure that each portion has 4-5 new shoots. Replant immediately. *C. grandiflora* can be increased by 7.5cm/3in basal cuttings taken in summer and rooted in a cold frame.

SPECIES *C. verticillata* (*above*), very fine leaves, a succession of star-shaped flowers 2.5cm/1in wide from mid to late summer; *C. grandiflora*, a short-lived perennial, up to 90cm/3ft high, bearing large daisy-like flowers all summer. This is the best species for cutting; named varieties include 'Mayfield Giant', 'Sunray', double flowers, and 'Goldfink', dwarf at 23cm/9in.

POSSIBLE PROBLEMS Froghoppers damage young shoots.

DORONICUM

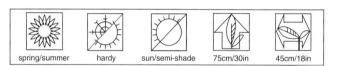

spring/summer	hardy	sun/semi-shade	75cm/30in	45cm/18in

Commonly known as leopard's bane, doronicums bring the first glow of colour to the mixed border in spring, and if regularly dead-headed may produce a second flush of flowers in the autumn. The yellow, daisy-like flowers are excellent for cutting.

GROWING Set out young plants in the autumn, in fertile, moist soil in sun or dappled shade. Remove faded flowerheads regularly. Cut the stems back in autumn.

PROPAGATION Divide established plants in the autumn, using only the healthy outer portions. Replant immediately.

SPECIES *D. plantagineum* (*above*): vigorous plant, heart-shaped leaves, flowers 6.5cm/2½in across; good named varieties include 'Miss Mason' and 'Harpur Crewe'; *D. pardalianches* (great leopard's bane), up to 90cm/3ft high, requires staking; *D. cordatum*, only 20cm/8in but with golden yellow flowers 5cm/2in across.

POSSIBLE PROBLEMS Powdery mildew may appear on leaves.

▓ CUT FLOWER TIP

The large, yellow, daisy-like flowers of C. grandiflora are ideal for cutting. It flowers profusely, providing a good supply of blooms all summer.

▓ PLANTING TIP

Doronicum is the ideal plant if you have a shaded, cool border which rarely sees the sun. This plant thrives in cold, draughty places and is thus an excellent candidate for gloomy borders which it will cheer up in spring with its golden daisy-like flowers.

PAPAVER

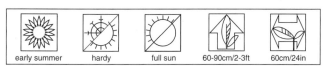

early summer	hardy	full sun	60-90cm/2-3ft	60cm/24in

The oriental poppy, *Papaver orientale (above)*, is an eye-catching border plant bearing vivid but short-lived scarlet flowers up to 10cm/4 in across. Cultivated varieties extend the colour range to pink, crimson and white.

GROWING Set out young plants in small groups in autumn or early spring in free-draining soil in a sunny, open site sheltered from wind. Provide supporting canes for the growing plants. Cut back to ground level after flowering.

PROPAGATION Divide established plants in early spring and replant immediately. Alternatively, take root cuttings in winter and insert in a cold frame. Transfer to 7.5cm/3in pots of compost when 3 or 4 pairs of leaves have appeared. Stand outdoors in summer and set out in the autumn in the permanent site. Plants may also be raised from seed sown in spring in the greenhouse.

VARIETIES 'Black and White', white flowers, black centre; 'Perry's White'; 'King George', scarlet, frilled petals; 'Mrs Perry', soft coral; 'Enchantress', carmine.

POSSIBLE PROBLEMS Downy mildew on leaves.

VERBENA

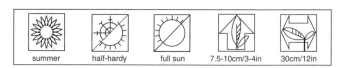

summer	half-hardy	full sun	7.5-10cm/3-4in	30cm/12in

Verbena peruviana (above), a native of South America, is a low-growing perennial that looks best where its tiny though startlingly bright red flowers can spill over a sunny wall. It does well in a sheltered rock garden or a stone trough in a favoured corner. There are no named varieties of the species.

GROWING Light, free-draining, reasonably fertile soil is best. Give verbenas a sunny open site protected from wind. Pinch out growing tips of young plants to encourage sturdy, branching growth. Remove faded flowerheads regularly. Protect with cloches over winter.

PROPAGATION Raise plants from seed sown in winter/early spring in a greenhouse or propagator at 20-25°C/68-77°F. Prick the seedlings off into boxes when they are large enough to handle. Harden off before planting out in late spring/early summer.

POSSIBLE PROBLEMS Aphids may damage young shoots.

■ DRIED FLOWER TIP

The seed heads of poppies are widely used in dried flower arrangements. In a good year the seed heads can be allowed to dry out on the plant, or you can pick them and hang them up to dry in a loose bunch – no need to avoid sunlight in this case. Avoid picking flowers when they are wet or covered with dew.

■ ORGANIC TIP

Another plant that is a must in the organic garden, as its flowers are a good source of nectar, thus attracting bees and other nectar-feeding insects. Its sweet-smelling flowers are ideal if you want to create a scented border. Remember to dead-head regularly to keep it flowering.

TROPAEOLUM

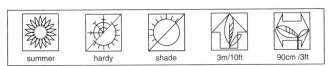

| summer | hardy | shade | 3m/10ft | 90cm /3ft |

Tropaeolums include the familiar garden nasturtium, *T. majus*, and the canary creeper, *T. peregrinum*, both annuals, which climb by twisting their leaf stalks around any available support. *T. speciosum* (*above*), or flame nasturtium, is a rhizomatous perennial which bears bright red flowers on slender stems from mid to late summer. Attractive green leaves echo the radiating form of the petals. There are no named varieties of the species.

GROWING Despite its South American origin, the flame nasturtium does not like full sun – a shaded wall is ideal. Set out plants in spring in fertile, slightly acid soil, if necessary adding peat. Supports are essential, but a leafy shrub will serve this purpose as well as wires or canes.

PROPAGATION Divide the rhizomes in spring.

POSSIBLE PROBLEMS Aphids may infest the stems.

POTENTILLA

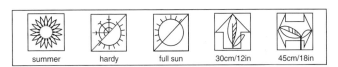

| summer | hardy | full sun | 30cm/12in | 45cm/18in |

Potentillas, commonly known as cinquefoil, were a favourite in sixteenth-century England and still claim a place in many modern gardeners' affections. *P. atrosanguinea* is a perennial species which is the parent to many garden hybrids. All are characterized by strawberry-like, grey-green leaves and sprays of five-petalled flowers like small wild roses. They are very long-lived plants and merit a prime spot in the border.

GROWING Set out young plants from autumn to spring in well-drained soil in full sun. Water generously in dry weather and apply an annual mulch of well-rotted manure in spring.

PROPAGATION Divide established plants in autumn or spring and replant immediately.

VARIETIES Choose from the hybrids 'Gibson's Scarlet' (*above*), semi-prostrate, useful for ground cover, single flowers; 'Yellow Queen', pure yellow, semi-double blooms, early flowering; 'Glory of Nancy', semi-double, crimson flowers; 'Wm Rollison', semi-double, bright orange flowers.

POSSIBLE PROBLEMS Generally trouble-free.

■ PLANTING TIP

To minimize attack by aphids, plant alongside tagetes. These will attract hoverflies which feed on the nectar and the larvae of which will eat aphids.

■ ORGANIC TIP

The marsh cinquefoil P. palustris *is ideal if you are creating a wetland area in your garden. It will also thrive in any damp shady corner under trees.*

POLYANTHUS

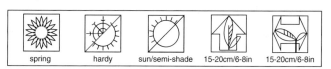

| spring | hardy | sun/semi-shade | 15-20cm/6-8in | 15-20cm/6-8in |

The primula family comprises a number of hardy perennials including *Primula veris*, the cowslip, and *P. vulgaris*, the primrose. The polyanthus is a hybrid of these two, with characteristic whorls of primrose flowers in a huge variety of colours, carried on strong stems above a rosette of oval leaves. They can be treated as indoor pot plants, but are ideal at the front of the border or in tubs and window boxes.

GROWING Set out plants in autumn or spring in heavy, moist soil into which plenty of organic matter has been incorporated. A site in full sun or partial shade will do.

PROPAGATION Divide the plants every 3 years immediately after flowering and replant straight away.

VARIETIES Pacific strain (*above*), large blooms, early flowering, bright colours including white, yellow, pink, red, purple and blue; 'Cowichan', mixed colours, no central eye.

POSSIBLE PROBLEMS Slugs on leaves in spring; grey mould; leaf spot on older plants.

LUPIN

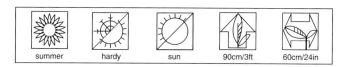

| summer | hardy | sun | 90cm/3ft | 60cm/24in |

Lupins are traditionally a feature of informal cottage gardens, but their tall spires in a range of soft colours make a striking contribution to the border in any garden design. The most reliable types are hybrids of the species *L. polyphyllus*.

GROWING Set out young plants in early spring or in the autumn, in light, slightly acid soil. Neutral soils will do, but lupins hate lime, and in heavy soils the stems become too soft to support the flowers. Stake with twiggy sticks when plants are 15cm/6in high. Wait until late winter before cutting back, to prevent water lodging in the hollow stems.

PROPAGATION Take 7.5cm/3in cuttings, with a little rootstock attached, in spring. Insert in sandy soil in a cold frame; pot on when rooted or set in nursery rows before planting out in the autumn. Named varieties do not come true from seed.

VARIETIES Choose forms of the Russell lupin strain. Many are bi-coloured. 'Blushing Bride', cream and white; 'Cherry Pie', crimson and yellow; 'Jane Eyre', violet and white; 'Lilac Time', rose-lilac and white; 'Limelight', butter yellow; 'Guardsman', vermilion.

POSSIBLE PROBLEMS Crown rot, root rot, honey fungus.

■ ORGANIC TIP

To protect plants from slugs, sink a yoghurt pot into the ground nearby and fill with beer. The slugs are attracted to the liquid then fall in and drown.

■ SPECIAL CARE TIP

Lupins seed themselves very easily, so if you don't want lupins all over the garden the seed heads should be removed in good time. Remove the tips of the flower spikes before the seeds have time to form – it will also ensure that the plant keeps on flowering.

IMPATIENS

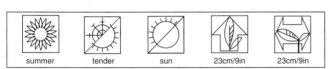

| summer | tender | sun | 23cm/9in | 23cm/9in |

Familiar even to non-gardeners, *Impatiens walleriana* or busy lizzie is a short-lived perennial native to Africa. Usually grown indoors or in a greenhouse, dwarf hybrids between *I. walleriana* and *I. sultanii* can be used in outdoor bedding schemes and are ideal for tubs and windowboxes. They are admired for their dense foliage and five-petalled flowers of red, pink or white which appear throughout the summer.

GROWING Set young plants out in early summer in well-drained soil in a sheltered position. Pinch out the growing tips to promote bushy growth. Dead-head regularly.

PROPAGATION Sow seed in pans in spring at 16-18°C/61-64°F. Prick the seedlings off into boxes when they are large enough to handle, then into individual 7.5cm/3in pots of compost. Harden off before planting out.

VARIETIES The Imp strain (*above*) includes varieties in white, shocking pink, carmine, scarlet and purple; 'Tangleglow', orange; 'Zig Zag', striped.

POSSIBLE PROBLEMS Aphids infest leaves and stems. Slugs may damage seedlings.

BELLIS

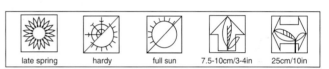

| late spring | hardy | full sun | 7.5-10cm/3-4in | 25cm/10in |

The perennial daisy, *Bellis perennis*, is a charming if short-lived plant for the front of the border or as attractive ground cover. Unlike the simple daisy of the meadows, flowers are large, the foliage glossy and almost evergreen, and the colour range includes pink, red and white as well as bi-coloured forms.

GROWING Treat as biennials. Set out young plants in autumn in any ordinary garden soil. Daisies prefer sun but do reasonably well in partial shade. Dead-head regularly – though daisies will self-seed, the resulting seedlings are poor. Discard or divide plants after flowering.

PROPAGATION Divide named varieties immediately after flowering. Sow seeds in boxes or in the open in late spring and grow on in a nursery bed before planting out in autumn for flowering the following spring.

VARIETIES Monstrosa forms include double-flowered varieties such as 'Giant Double', mixed or single colours. Double miniature varieties have tiny pompon flowers; try 'Pomponette' (*above*); 'Dresden China', pink; 'Quilled Mixed'; 'Rob Roy', red; 'Victoria', red and white.

POSSIBLE PROBLEMS Generally trouble-free.

■ PROPAGATION TIP

To propagate by taking cuttings: in spring, make a clean cut from new shoots of plants which have over-wintered indoors or in a heated greenhouse.

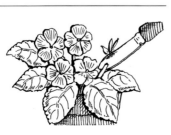

■ PLANTING TIP

One of the more traditional plants used in raised flowerbeds. To make a raised bed, cut a geometric shape in the turf. The soil is slightly heaped up, rising towards the centre so that the flowerbed is about 40cm/16in higher than the rest of the garden. Plant out in autumn for spring flowers.

HELLEBORUS

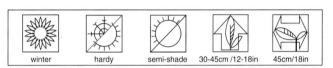

| winter | hardy | semi-shade | 30-45cm /12-18in | 45cm/18in |

No gardener who wants to enjoy flowers all the year round can afford to ignore the Christmas rose, *Helleborus niger*, which produces its exquisite white blooms in deepest winter. The Lenten rose, *H. orientalis*, is equally valuable, blooming from winter into early spring with dramatically coloured flowers of green, white, pink, red-purple or black-purple, often splashed inside with a contrasting colour. As cut flowers hellebores are very long-lasting.

GROWING Set out young plants in small groups in autumn in deep, moisture-retentive but well-drained soil into which plenty of well-rotted compost or leaf mould has been incorporated. Choose a site where they can be left for years: they dislike disturbance. Protect the flowers of the Christmas rose as they open with cloches. Cut stems right back after flowering; apply an annual mulch in the autumn.

PROPAGATION Divide well-established plants in spring and replant immediately. Alternatively sow seeds in sandy soil in a cold frame in summer. Prick off the seedlings into a nursery bed and grow on until planting out in the autumn of the following year. They will not flower for 2-3 years.

VARIETIES *H. niger* 'Potter's Wheel' (*above*), exceptional white form.

POSSIBLE PROBLEMS Leaf spot.

ALTHAEA

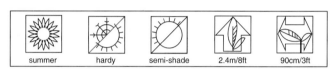

| summer | hardy | semi-shade | 2.4m/8ft | 90cm/3ft |

Althaea rosea (above), the familiar hollyhock, is well suited to cottage gardens and because of its great height looks impressive at the back of an informal border, particularly when a fine old wall provides protection. The showy, trumpet-shaped flowers of the species are in shades of pink, but named varieties are available in red, cream and white.

GROWING Hollyhocks do best if treated as biennials. Set out young plants in autumn in any ordinary soil, in a sheltered site. Strong stakes should be provided from early spring. On light soils, apply a moisture-retaining mulch in hot weather. For perennial growth, cut back plants after flowering to 15cm/6in; otherwise discard the plants.

PROPAGATION Sow seed in trays of compost in early spring. Prick the seedlings out into 7.5cm/3in pots when they are large enough to handle and plant out in late summer for flowering the following year.

VARIETIES 'Chater's Double', peony-like double flowers, all colours; 'Begonia Flowered Crested', mixed colours.

POSSIBLE PROBLEMS Caterpillars damage the stems and leaves. Rust is more likely on plants treated as perennials and can be severe.

■ PLANTING TIP

If using a container-grown plant, ensure that the root ball gets enough moisture when first planted. Dig a hole that is big enough for the roots, sprinkle a general fertilizer around the rim and firm in. 'Puddle in' the plant by giving enough water so that a puddle forms. Avoid moving hellebores once sited.

■ ORGANIC TIP

Rust occurs when growing conditions are poor. Instead of using chemical sprays, make sure the soil is fed properly with manure or compost before planting.

CONVALLARIA

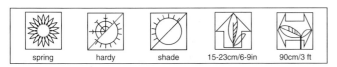

| spring | hardy | shade | 15-23cm/6-9in | 90cm/3 ft |

The lily-of-the-valley, *Convallaria majalis (above)*, is one of the prettiest spring flowers, its graceful stems clothed with pure white bell-shaped blooms. With handsome leaves, it makes excellent ground cover in shady spots, spreading by means of creeping rhizomes. The lightly fragrant flowers are popular with flower arrangers.

GROWING Start with 'pips' (root pieces with buds). Plant in autumn 5cm/2in deep in heavy, moisture-retentive soil that has previously been enriched with plenty of well-rotted organic matter. Mulch with leaf mould every autumn.

PROPAGATION Lift the rhizomes between autumn and spring and separate into crowns; replant, just covering with soil, and dress with leaf mould. Water well.

VARIETIES 'Fortin's Giant', white; 'Rosea', pink; 'Variegata', leaves striped with gold.

POSSIBLE PROBLEMS Caterpillars damage the rhizomes; grey mould on leaves in wet weather.

TIARELLA

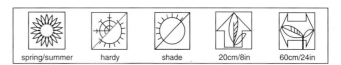

| spring/summer | hardy | shade | 20cm/8in | 60cm/24in |

The foam flower, *Tiarella cordifolia (above)*, like lily-of-the-valley *(left)* is a good subject for cool shady places, where it will spread out to smother weeds with its soft green pointed leaves. Foliage is retained throughout the winter. Spikes of tiny, very pale pink flowers appear in early summer. No named varieties of this species are available. *T. wherryi* is similar but slow-growing, with attractive autumn foliage.

GROWING Set out young plants in autumn or spring in moist, rich, well-drained soil. Water in dry weather to maintain growth and apply an annual mulch of leaf mould or peat in spring.

PROPAGATION Divide established plants of foam flower in autumn or spring and replant rooted pieces immediately. *T. wherryi* does not divide easily.

POSSIBLE PROBLEMS Generally trouble-free.

◼ PLANTING TIP

One of the essential plants when creating a scented border. Make sure you choose a shady spot near the house so the scent can waft in on summer nights.

◼ ORGANIC TIP

Nature's answer to the problem of weed control are the perennial ground-cover plants which in time will spread out to smother most troublesome weeds.

Tiarella is a perfect example – low-growing with nice leaves, it is the organic solution to the weed problem being dense enough to kill off all competitors.

49

Pelargonium

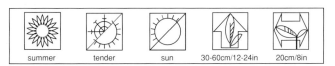

summer	tender	sun	30-60cm/12-24in	20cm/8in

Pelargoniums are often (wrongly) called geraniums, the name properly given to the hardy perennial cranesbill (*see page 56*). Native to Africa, these tender species with their showy blooms are an essential element in hanging baskets, window boxes and tubs as well as summer bedding schemes. Among the most popular types for this purpose are the hybrids known as Regal and Zonal pelargoniums, which are available in all shades of pink, red, maroon and white. Zonal hybrids have beautifully coloured leaves.

GROWING Set out young plants in early summer in moderately fertile soil in full sun. Remove faded flowerheads. Water freely, giving a high-potash feed occasionally. In autumn put plants under protection. Cut back older plants and put up in good compost.

PROPAGATION Take cuttings from overwintered plants in spring and insert in a peat/sand mixture. Pot on when rooted. Plants may also be raised successfully from seed sown under protection in early spring.

VARIETIES 'Princess of Wales', frilled, strawberry pink; 'Grand Slam' (*above*), abundant rose-red blooms; 'Nomad', white, blotched pink. Many other good varieties.

POSSIBLE PROBLEMS Low night temperatures cause reddening of leaves and stems. Leaves turn yellow if soil is too dry.

Malva

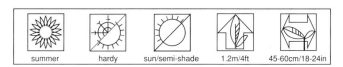

summer	hardy	sun/semi-shade	1.2m/4ft	45-60cm/18-24in

The mallow, *Malva alcea*, is a tall, bushy plant particularly useful on poor soils. It bears abundant mauve trumpet-shaped flowers all summer.

GROWING Plant from autumn to spring on light, well-drained soil in sun or partial shade. Provide twiggy sticks for support. Cut down dead stems in late autumn or winter.

PROPAGATION Take 7.5cm/3in basal cuttings in late spring. Insert in sandy soil in a cold frame and transfer to the flowering site in autumn. Plants may be raised from seed sown under protection with gentle warmth in spring. Prick the seedlings out into a nursery bed when they are large enough to handle and grow on until transferring to the flowering site in the autumn.

VARIETIES *M. alcea* 'Fastigiata' (*above*) is more upright than the species and reaches only 90cm/3ft.

POSSIBLE PROBLEMS Rust may affect the leaves and stems.

▓ PLANTING TIP

Pelargoniums are the perfect flowers – ideal for a host of situations and almost trouble-free. Whatever your needs, there are types to suit: regal pelargoniums for bedding or massed border display schemes, trailing ivy-leaved ones for hanging baskets and zonal foliage ones for window-boxes and tubs.

▓ ORGANIC TIP

Rust is often a symptom of poor soils. If it is a real problem, try mulching the soil with well-rotted compost or provide a feed of liquid seaweed.

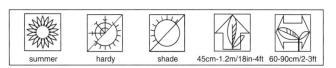

STOKESIA

summer	hardy	sun/semi-shade	30-45cm/12-18in	45cm/18in

Stokesia laevis is a wonderfully rewarding plant. It bears corn-flower-like blooms of blue, lavender or creamy-white that are 10cm/4in across and continue right through the summer. Its long-lasting foliage and spreading habit contribute useful ground cover.

GROWING Set out young plants in spring in sun or partial shade in light, well-drained soil. Shelter from cold winds is appreciated and the plants should be staked with light twigs in early summer.

PROPAGATION Divide established plants in spring and replant without delay.

VARIETIES 'Blue Star', light blue flowers, 7.5cm/3in across; 'Silver Moon', white with lilac centre; 'Cyanea' (*above*), lavender.

POSSIBLE PROBLEMS Generally trouble-free.

ASTILBE

summer	hardy	shade	45cm-1.2m/18in-4ft	60-90cm/2-3ft

Astilbe species come from China and Japan. From these the garden hybrid *A. × arendsii* (*above*) has been developed to display the best qualities of the family. They are bushy, erect plants, forming impressive clumps of fern-like leaves; the taller types are most effective for ground cover. Feathery plumes of pink or white flowers are carried on delicate stems. They make excellent waterside plants.

GROWING Plant from autumn to spring in moist soil in a cool, shady position (although a sunny site is acceptable if the soil is never allowed to dry out). Astilbes dislike chalky soil. Water well in dry weather and apply an annual moisture-retaining mulch such as leaf mould, well-rotted compost or manure in early spring. Do not cut the plants back until the end of winter, as the faded flowerheads and foliage are attractive in their own right.

PROPAGATION Divide woody clumps in spring, ensuring that each portion has 2-3 developing buds.

VARIETIES 'Fanal', 60cm/24in, red; 'Bressingham Beauty', 90cm/3ft, rose-pink; 'Deutschland', 60cm/24in, brilliant white.

POSSIBLE PROBLEMS Generally trouble-free.

■ SPECIAL CARE TIP

This attractive perennial is quite easy to grow, but it must have a well-drained soil – on heavy, wet or clay soils it will be very short-lived. If necessary, there-fore, improve drainage before planting by digging deep, and incorporating one or two bucketfuls of gravel and organic material into the soil.

■ PLANTING TIP

This tall, bushy plant is ideal for the centre or back of the border. As with most perennials, remember to give it enough 'elbow room' to allow for future growth.

PULMONARIA

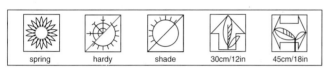

| spring | hardy | shade | 30cm/12in | 45cm/18in |

Pulmonarias are ideal plants for a shady part of the garden, where they will spread their handsome oval leaves to make dense ground cover. In early spring clusters of drooping bell-shaped flowers appear, held clear of the foliage on erect stems. The blooms are pink, often turning blue later.

GROWING Set out young plants in autumn or spring in reasonably moist fertile soil. Apply an annual mulch of peat in spring and water well during the growing period. Remove dead leaves in the autumn.

PROPAGATION Divide established clumps in autumn or spring.

SPECIES *P. angustifolia* (blue cowslip), height 23cm/9in, dark green leaves, spring-flowering; *P. officinalis* (Jerusalem cowslip), height 23-30cm/9-12in, light green leaves blotched silver, late spring-flowering; *P. saccharata* (*above*), 30cm/12in, pointed leaves beautifully marked cream, late spring-flowering; the variety 'White Wings' bears white flowers.

POSSIBLE PROBLEMS Slugs may eat young shoots.

ASTRANTIA

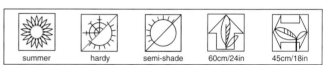

| summer | hardy | semi-shade | 60cm/24in | 45cm/18in |

Native to Europe and Western Asia, this group of herbaceous perennials includes three species which are well suited to summer borders or informal planting schemes. All have attractive divided leaves and bear tiny but numerous white or pale pink star-shaped flowers. They last well as cut flowers.

GROWING Set out young plants between autumn and spring in well-drained, fertile soil. Semi-shade is best but full sun is tolerated, as long as the soil does not dry out. Apply a moisture-conserving mulch in spring. Cut plants back to ground level in late autumn.

PROPAGATION Divide roots in autumn or spring

SPECIES *A. major* (*above*), fresh green leaves, pinkish-green flowers surrounded by silver bracts; *A. maxima*, similar to *A. major* but bolder in effect, with pink bracts; *A. carniolica*, mid-green, slender leaves, white flowers – the variety 'Rubra' is only 30cm/12in high with deep crimson flowers and bracts.

POSSIBLE PROBLEMS Generally trouble-free.

■ ORGANIC TIP

With attractively marked leaves and clusters of drooping bell-flowers, this is the perfect answer if you need weed control or ground cover for shady parts of the garden, such as under trees and shrubs, or in the shade of hedges. Brighten up dark corners with the 'Argentea' variety which has white flowers.

■ CUT FLOWER TIP

An old favourite, grown for hundreds of years, and very highly regarded as a cut flower because the unusual star-shaped blooms last well. Suitable for drying.

CATANANCHE

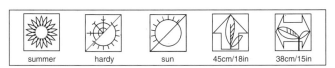

| summer | hardy | sun | 45cm/18in | 38cm/15in |

Catananche caerulea or cupid's dart bears blue cornflower-like flowers throughout the summer. It is a good plant for the border or for cut flowers, and can be dried very successfully for winter decoration.

GROWING Set out young plants from early autumn to late spring in light, well-drained soil. On exposed sites it may be advisable to support the plants with pea-sticks. Cut down the dead stems in autumn.

PROPAGATION Catananches are short-lived perennials. Take root cuttings in the spring of their third or fourth year to be sure of continuing stock. Insert 7.5cm/3in cuttings in seed compost in a cold frame and transplant to a nursery bed when the leaves are well formed. Transfer to the permanent position in the autumn or following spring.

VARIETIES 'Major' (*above*), large, lavender-blue flowers; 'Perry's White'; 'Bicolor', white with blue eyes.

POSSIBLE PROBLEMS Generally trouble-free.

BERGENIA

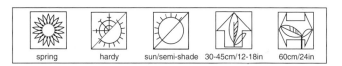

| spring | hardy | sun/semi-shade | 30-45cm/12-18in | 60cm/24in |

Bergenias are among the elite of evergreen ground cover plants, with large, glossy, handsome leaves and nodding clusters of bell-shaped flowers. Both foliage and flowers are prized by flower arrangers, too.

GROWING Almost any situation will do, as long as the soil is reasonably moist and fertile. The best winter leaf colour will be achieved on open sites. Plant in autumn or spring and leave undisturbed until the clump is overcrowded. Pick off damaged leaves and remove flower stems after flowering.

PROPAGATION Lift and divide established plants in the autumn. Select single-rooted portions and replant immediately.

VARIETIES Choose from hybrids such as 'Abendglut' (syn. 'Evening Glow', *above*), deep magenta flowers, leaves reddish-bronze in favourable conditions; 'Morgenrot' (syn. Morning Blush'), pink, often flowers twice, in spring and summer.

POSSIBLE PROBLEMS Leaf spot may discolour the leaves.

▥ DRIED FLOWER TIP

To dry the beautiful blooms of these plants, tie them in small bunches and hang upside down in a dark shed or attic (darkness prevents the colours fading).

▥ PLANTING TIP

This attractive plant will grow almost anywhere, in sun or shade, but you have to make a choice – grow in the open for best winter leaf colour, or in a sheltered spot, free from spring flowers for the best show of flowers.

BRUNNERA

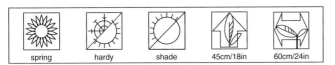

| spring | hardy | shade | 45cm/18in | 60cm/24in |

Brunnera macrophylla, sometimes listed as *Anchusa myosotid-iflora*, is related to the forget-me-not, as can easily be seen from its airy clusters of tiny blue flowers. It is a quick-growing plant with large, heart-shaped leaves that make attractive ground cover for shade and under trees. The leaves of variegated forms are splashed cream or silver.

GROWING Set out young plants between autumn and spring in any type of fertile soil, even chalk. Do not let the soil dry out. Variegated forms need a cool, sheltered position. Remove old stems after flowering and cut the plant down to ground level in late autumn.

PROPAGATION Divide and replant the roots in autumn or spring.

VARIETIES The species is vigorous and reliable. Interesting forms are 'Variegata', with leaves splashed creamy-white, and 'Langtrees', with silvery-grey markings on the leaves.

POSSIBLE PROBLEMS Generally trouble-free.

CAMPANULA

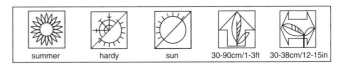

| summer | hardy | sun | 30-90cm/1-3ft | 30-38cm/12-15in |

The bellflower family includes a great number of attractive species including *Campanula medium*, the well-loved biennial Canterbury bell, and several exquisite alpine plants. For the border, *C. persicifolia*, the peach-leaved campanula, is an excellent choice with its impressive height, breathtaking flowers and evergreen foliage. *C. Lactiflora* (*above*) bears pale, lavender-blue, bell-shaped flowers in early and mid summer.

GROWING Set out young plants in autumn in well-drained fertile soil; chalky soils are tolerated. A sunny site is preferred but light shade will do no great harm. Stake the plants when they reach 15cm/6in high.

PROPAGATION Divide established clumps in autumn. *C. persicifolia* does not come true from seed.

VARIETIES *C. persicifolia* 'Telham Beauty', deep, rich blue; 'Planiflora' (syn. *C. nitida*), dwarf at 23-30cm/9-12in, blue flowers; 'Planiflora Alba' is a white form.

POSSIBLE PROBLEMS Slugs and snails may damage leaves and shoots. Leaf spot fungus and rust may damage leaves.

▍PLANTING TIP

Enrich the soil with manure or well-rotted leaf mould before planting. Mulch with manure or well-rotted compost in the spring to help conserve moisture.

▍PLANTING TIP

The best-known, and most popular, variety is probably the tall Canterbury bell, which needs lots of room. But even if space is a problem, it is still possible to enjoy this beautiful plant. C. Cochleavifolia is ideal for a wall or rock garden where it forms low mats of leaves with dainty bell-shaped flowers.

DELPHINIUM

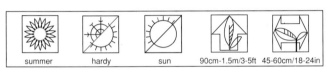

| summer | hardy | sun | 90cm-1.5m/3-5ft | 45-60cm/18-24in |

Delphiniums are unquestionably the most magnificent flowers in the herbaceous border. Quite apart from their great height, the profusion of blooms and intensity of colour – usually blue, but sometimes pink or cream – make an unforgettable impression. Most garden types are hybrids bred from *D. elatum* and other species, giving two strains known as Elatum or Large-flowered (up to 2.4m/8ft, and including the Pacific hybrids, *above*) and Belladonna (about 1.2m/4ft).

GROWING Set out young plants from autumn to spring in deep, rich soil on a sheltered site. Provide stout canes for support. Cut back to ground level after flowering.

PROPAGATION Divide established plants in spring or take 7.5cm/3in basal cuttings and insert in a peat/sand mixture in a cold frame. Transfer to a nursery bed when rooted and grow on until planting out in autumn.

VARIETIES The choice is wide. 'Blue Jade', Pacific, dwarf at 1.2m/4ft, sky-blue; 'Wendy', Belladonna, gentian blue; 'Butterball', Elatum, rich cream.

POSSIBLE PROBLEMS Slugs and snails damage young shoots.

ECHINOPS

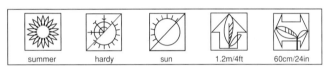

| summer | hardy | sun | 1.2m/4ft | 60cm/24in |

The globe thistle, *Echinops banaticus* (*above*) is a valuable addition to the border, with dramatic dark green foliage and round, steel-blue flowerheads held high. The flowers are prized for winter decoration when dried. No named varieties of the species are available.

GROWING Set out young plants from autumn to spring in deep, well-drained soil; echinops do well on chalk. A sunny, sheltered position is best. It may be necessary to provide stakes for support on exposed sites, but usually this is not required. Mulch lightly in spring, and cut the stems down in the autumn.

PROPAGATION Divide established plants between autumn and spring.

POSSIBLE PROBLEMS Generally trouble-free.

■ SPECIAL CARE TIP

Delphiniums are not difficult to grow, provided the young plants are well looked after. If necessary, make sure there is shelter from strong winds and provide staking early enough. Protect from slugs, otherwise the young plants can disappear overnight. Try 'slug pubs' (see page 46) or organic powders.

■ DRIED FLOWER TIP

The blue flowerheads are popular for arrangements. To dry the flowers, cut the heads before fully opened and hang upside down in a dark, airy place.

GERANIUM

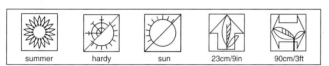

| summer | hardy | sun | 23cm/9in | 90cm/3ft |

Geraniums, popularly known as cranesbills, comprise a large family of flowering plants, including some alpine species. All summer and into the autumn, they bear open, five-petalled flowers about 25cm/1in or more across, in shades of pink, crimson, blue and white. The leaves are rounded, sometimes deeply cut; the plants form large round clumps that look attractive in the summer border or any informal planting scheme.

GROWING Set out young plants between autumn and spring in any type of well-drained soil. Do not let them dry out in hot weather.

PROPAGATION Divide and replant established clumps in autumn or spring.

SPECIES *G. endressii* reaches 40cm/16in in height and spreads to 60cm/24in or more. Named varieties include 'A.T. Johnson', silvery pink, and 'Rose Clair', white edged purple. The hybrid G. × 'Claridge Druce', with deep mauve blooms, makes excellent ground cover. *G. sanguineum* (*above*) is low-growing, mat-forming, with magenta flowers; *G. s. lancastrense* is a great favourite with pale pink flowers veined with red.

POSSIBLE PROBLEMS Slugs may eat young plants.

VIOLA

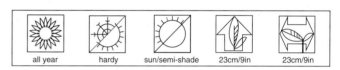

| all year | hardy | sun/semi-shade | 23cm/9in | 23cm/9in |

Garden pansies, *Viola × wittrockiana*, are short-lived perennial hybrids. They are among the most popular of all cultivated plants, with their large, colourful flowers, bushy foliage and easy-going nature. The colour range is huge and different varieties are in bloom almost all year.

GROWING Time of planting depends on variety. Set out in moisture-retentive but well-drained soil. Add peat and/or leaf mould to chalky soils. Snip off faded flowers to ensure a succession of blooms.

PROPAGATION Divide mature plants in early spring or take 5cm/2in cuttings of non-flowering basal shoots in summer and insert in a peat/sand mixture in a cold frame. Pot on when rooted and plant out in autumn or spring.

VARIETIES Countless varieties are available, in single colours – white, yellow, apricot, red, violet and blue – and numerous combinations, often with a black blotch.

POSSIBLE PROBLEMS Leaf spot; fungi of different kinds cause pansy sickness.

■ ORGANIC TIP

Geranium is also known as meadow cranesbill, and at one time was a common wild flower found in open meadows. It attracts bees and other insects, and the birds will feed on its seeds. It is an ideal flower to grow if you want to create a natural-looking flowery meadow at the end of your garden.

■ PLANTING TIP

A highly versatile plant which can be used to edge borders or paths, in rock gardens, in window-boxes and containers and as ground cover under trees.

AQUILEGIA

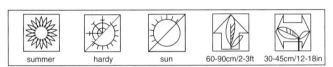

summer	hardy	sun	60-90cm/2-3ft	30-45cm/12-18in

A number of very beautiful hybrids have been raised from *Aquilegia vulgaris*, the columbine or, to give it its old country name, granny's bonnet. The plants are characterized by pretty fern-like leaves and graceful funnel-shaped flowers with a spur behind each petal. They are very effective in the border and in cottage garden schemes. Blooms may be single or bi-coloured in pink, blue, cream, green, yellow or red.

GROWING Set out young plants in autumn in fertile, well-drained soil. An open, sunny site is best but light shade is tolerated. Do not let them dry out. Mulch in early spring to conserve moisture. Unless seed is required, dead-head and cut the stems (not the leaves) to ground level after flowering.

PROPAGATION Divide established clumps into single-rooted pieces from autumn to spring. Columbines produce seed freely. Allow the plants to self-seed or collect the seed when ripe and sow in nursery beds in spring, transplanting to the permanent site in autumn.

VARIETIES 'McKana Hybrids', large flowers, many colours, 90cm/3ft high.

POSSIBLE PROBLEMS Aphids; leaf spot.

MONARDA

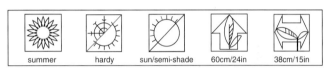

summer	hardy	sun/semi-shade	60cm/24in	38cm/15in

Bees and butterflies are irresistibly attracted to the vivid, shaggy flowers of *Monarda didyma*, a highly decorative relative of mint which is variously known as bee balm or Oswego tea. Native to North America, it was used by the Oswego Indians to make a soothing drink – the leaves have a minty fragrance. It is named after Nicolas Monardes, author of a sixteenth-century herbal first published in America. Quick-growing and perfect for cutting, Monarda is a good choice for the middle of the border.

GROWING Plant in groups of 4-6 in spring or autumn in moisture-retentive soil. Mulch annually in spring with well-rotted organic matter. A position in sun or partial shade will do. Cut down the stems in autumn.

PROPAGATION Monarda spreads from the roots. Divide established clumps every 3 years. Discard the centre and replant small outer tufts. Named varieties do not come true from seed.

VARIETIES 'Cambridge Scarlet', bright red; 'Croftway Pink', shell pink; 'Snow Maiden', white; 'Prairie Night', indigo-purple.

POSSIBLE PROBLEMS Generally trouble-free.

▮ ORGANIC TIP

Practise companion planting – plant tagetes and other insect-attracting flowers beside it in the border. The larvae of hoverflies eat aphids.

▮ ORGANIC TIP

One of the perfect plants for the organic garden as its scarlet, shaggy flowers attract butterflies and bees. To make the soothing drink of the Oswego Indians, steep 1 teaspoon of monarda leaves in a cup of hot water.

CALTHA

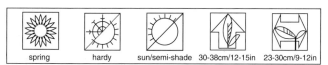

| spring | hardy | sun/semi-shade | 30-38cm/12-15in | 23-30cm/9-12in |

Caltha palustris, the kingcup or marsh marigold, will grow in water up to 15 cm/6in deep, but is happiest with the crown just submerged or at the water's edge. It produces a brilliant display of spring blooms up to 5 cm/2 in across. The glossy green leaves form rounded hummocks.

GROWING Plant in spring, in sun or partial shade. If in water, plants should be in containers or aquatic baskets. Use heavy soil, with a layer of shingle on top to prevent it muddying the water. In the garden, the best soil for calthas is heavy, moisture-retentive loam, preferably slightly acid. It must be kept constantly moist.

PROPAGATION Divide in early spring, when the young shoots appear.

VARIETIES 'Alba', white 'petals' (actually sepals), prominent yellow stamens; 'Plena' (*above*), low-growing, double flowers, green at first opening to rich golden yellow.

POSSIBLE PROBLEMS Rust on leaves caused by fungi.

PAEONIA

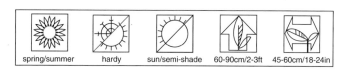

| spring/summer | hardy | sun/semi-shade | 60-90cm/2-3ft | 45-60cm/18-24in |

Peonies have an exotic air, with huge, bowl-shaped flowers that open in late spring or early summer. Large, handsome leaves set off to perfection the blooms of white, yellow, pink or red, some of which are double, some fragrant.

GROWING Peonies like moisture-retentive, well-drained soil, in sun or partial shade; choose a site that is sheltered from early morning sun. Before planting, dig the ground to a spade's depth, incorporating plenty of well-rotted organic matter. Set out young plants in suitable weather between autumn and spring, with the crowns just 2.5cm/1in below the soil surface. On light soil especially, mulch each spring with well-rotted compost. Peonies resent disturbance – choose a site where they can be left alone. Dead-head regularly. Cut back foliage in autumn.

PROPAGATION Divide and replant in early autumn, cutting the crowns with a sharp knife.

VARIETIES *Paeonia lactiflora* hybrids: 'Whitleyi Major', white, single flowers, golden stamens; 'The Moor', deep crimson, single; 'Felix Crousse', rose-red, double. *P. officinalis*: 'Alba Plena' (*above*): double, white; 'Rubra Plena', double, deep red.

POSSIBLE PROBLEMS Peony blight; leaf spot.

■ ORGANIC TIP

Ideal if you are creating a wildlife garden, or even a wetland area, as this plant enjoys wet or damp conditions on the edge of a pool, or any damp spot.

■ ORGANIC TIP

This is the ideal plant to benefit from your home-grown compost, well rotted down in a pit or container. Peonies don't like being moved, so prepare the site by digging plenty of compost before planting, to enrich the soil. Thereafter, mulch each spring with more compost or well-rotted manure.

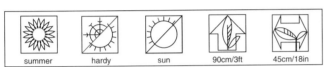

HEMEROCALLIS

summer	hardy	sun	90cm/3ft	45cm/18in

Three species of the hemerocallis are available, but much more popular are hybrids which can be found in dozens of different colours. The common name, day lily, refers to the fact that each flower lives for one day only, to be replaced by another the next morning. This process continues for 6-8 weeks; by choosing a mixture of varieties it is possible to have a display of these fabulous blooms for the entire summer.

GROWING Plant between autumn and spring in moist, rich soil. Full sun is preferred but a little shade is tolerated. Remove dead stems and leaves in late autumn.

PROPAGATION Divide established clumps in early autumn or spring just as young growth starts. Seeds do not come true to type.

VARIETIES 'Golden Chimes' (*above*); 'Chartreuse Magic', sharp yellow and green; 'Morocco Red', dusky red and yellow; 'Pink Damask', pink with yellow throat.

POSSIBLE PROBLEMS Generally trouble-free.

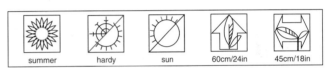

TROLLIUS

summer	hardy	sun	60cm/24in	45cm/18in

There are several species of trollius, the globe flower, in cultivation, all bearing impressive rounded blooms in various shades of yellow with prominent stamens. They are ideal for waterside planting or in the border, coming into flower in late spring and again in late summer if the stems are cut right back after flowering.

GROWING Plant out in autumn or spring in rather heavy, moisture-retentive soil. Keep well-watered, especially in hot-dry spells. Some shade is tolerated.

PROPAGATION Divide the fibrous rootstock in autumn and replant immediately.

SPECIES *Trollius ledebourii* (*above*), bright, orange-yellow, cup-shaped flowers; *T. × cultorum*, garden hybrid, only 30-45cm/12-18in high. Good varieties are 'Earliest of All', clear yellow; 'Salamander', reddish orange; 'Canary Bird', pale yellow.

POSSIBLE PROBLEMS Smut causes swellings on leaves and stems.

■ PLANTING TIP

If you are short of space, and need an attractive display for a container or a tub, this is the answer. Tall and striking, these exotic flowers will prove a real eye-catcher if planted to stand tall among the trailing foliage of variegated ivy, or another trailer or ground-cover plant.

■ PLANTING TIP

All parts of this plant are poisonous, so avoid planting it if you have young children who might be tempted to pick the attractive yellow flowers.

PERENNIALS

59

BULBS

Flowers grown from bulbs are inevitably associated with spring. The cheerful appearance of daffodils and crocuses announcing the start of a new year is a sight that raises everyone's spirits after the dull days of winter. There are, however, bulbs, corms and tubers for every season and indeed for every situation. It is this versatility that makes bulbs so valuable.

In botanical terms a bulb is a shoot, surrounded by tightly packed leaves arranged roughly in a sphere, with fine roots issuing from beneath. In some instances the leaves simply overlap each other; examples of these so-called scaly bulbs are lilies and fritillaries. In both cases these leaves are storage organs containing reserve food to nourish foliage and flowers. Corms, for example crocuses, gladiolus and colchicums, are storage organs composed of a thickened stem base; tubers, for example dahlias and begonias, are swollen underground branches with 'eyes' (buds) from which new plants are produced. Zantedeschias and some irises grow from rhi-

zomes, which are swollen underground stems from which a number of flowering stems arise. Bulbs are planted at different depths according to type. Most like sun or light shade and thrive in light, naturally rich soil. They should not be planted in contact with crude manure.

COLOUR THE YEAR ROUND Snowdrops (*Galanthus nivalis*) appear in the middle of winter, closely followed by the bright yellow flowers of the winter aconite (*Eranthis hyemalis*). Crocuses, scillas and chionodoxas enliven the cold bright days of very early spring, and then the glorious daffodil comes into its own. Daffodils – the genus *Narcissus* – have, like roses and chrysanthemums, attracted an enormous fan club, not only because of their individual beauty, but also their extraordinary variety. Most people are unaware of the range of narcissus (daffodils, strictly speaking, are narcissus whose central trumpet is as long as the surrounding petals). There are far too many individual species – about 60 – to describe here, but mention of three will demonstrate their diversity (and there are hundreds of hybrids as well). *N. bulbocodium*, at most 15cm/6in high, is unique, with leaves like chives. Very long, curved stamens protrude from 2.5cm/1in trumpets that open wide, almost concealing the tiny petals. The poet's narcissus, *N. poeticus*, reaches 45cm/18in with white petals but bright red, frilly cups. An old favourite is the hybrid *N. × odorus* (campernelle jonquil), 45cm/18in high, with 2-3 large, scented flowers to each stem. From this the richly scented, brightly coloured form 'Sweetness' has been developed.

Muscari, scilla, hyacinth and leucojum bring flourishes of blue, white, yellow and pink to the spring garden. For adding oranges and reds to the picture (as well as subtle hues of pink, yellow and cream), tulips cannot be bettered. Like daffodils, they have their devoted followers and display a dazzling variety of forms.

Blue, purple, yellow and white, irises bloom from late spring into summer. And in summer the colour range is stretched to the limit when gladioli and lilies come into

bloom. These beautiful flowers are much used for indoor decoration but because of their height and erect habit must be placed with care in the border. Lilies look splendid grouped together, rather than trying to integrate them, perhaps with a low-growing plant with decorative leaves at their feet. Clumps of the shorter gladiolus hybrids can be set in the middle of a mixed border, especially if offset with the interesting foliage of *Alchemilla mollis* or *Euphorbia robbiae*.

A garden with dahlias will never lack for autumn colour. These beautiful flowers come in a range of gorgeous colours and in a number of different forms, from neat pompons to the open anemone-flowered types. They bloom freely until the first frosts. Colchicums (autumn crocus) provide a subtler alternative for informal and cottage gardens. After they have faded, it is a matter of weeks before snowdrops reappear and the cycle begins again.

BULBS IN CONTAINERS Because of their varying sizes and flowering times, bulbs can be used in almost any part of the garden. They are also excellent for tubs, window-boxes and troughs. Miniature species are particularly well suited to containers which can be set at a level where tiny plants, which would be overlooked in the border, can be appreciated. An alpine garden in a trough could include the very early-

A display of zantedeschias provides the focal point of this cool green and white garden, the low box hedges providing a perfect foil for the tall, pointed leaves.

flowering *Iris histrioides* or *Narcissus juncifolius*. Some of the most brilliant effects are achieved by planting numbers of a single species in one container, so that they all flower at the same time. In fact, bulbs look best set in groups whatever the situation. Dwarf tulips with interesting foliage look marvellous in stone troughs or half-barrels. Try *T. clusiana*, the lady tulip, with narrow grey-green leaves and white flowers flushed red, or *T. greigii*, whose grey-green leaves are marbled purple and brown, the flowers vivid red.

LIFTING BULBS Some bulbs, such as gladiolus, are not hardy enough to withstand the winter in very cold areas, and must be lifted and stored. In formal bedding schemes bulbs are lifted when they are past their best in order to make way for the next feature, and when bulbs are congested they can be lifted, their offsets detached, and replanted at greater distances. Generally, however, bulbs can be left undisturbed for many years, another characteristic that endears them to modern gardeners with little time to spare for demanding planting schemes.

CROCUS

| spring | hardy | full sun | 7.5cm/3in | 7.5cm/3in |

The sight of budding crocuses is welcomed as a signal of spring. In fact these hardy plants, grown from corms, flower from late summer until spring, according to species. Colours include blue, purple, white, yellow and mauve. Some varieties are striped; many have vivid golden stamens. Very low-growing, with cup-shaped flowers rising directly from the ground, crocuses do well in rock gardens, troughs and at the edge of a border. Winter and early spring-flowering types can be used in lawns.

GROWING Plant in autumn in well-drained soil, preferably in groups, in a sunny position with protection from wind. Do not dead-head; leave the foliage until it is yellow and can be pulled off easily.

PROPAGATION Take offsets after flowering. Replant the larger cormlets for flowering the following year. The smaller ones can be grown on in drills until they reach flowering size.

SPECIES Try hybrids of *Crocus chrysanthus* such as 'E. P. Bowles', butter yellow, spring-flowering; *C. longiflorus* is scented, autumn-flowering, deep purple; spring-flowering Dutch crocuses deriving from *C. vernus* include 'Joan of Arc', white and 'Queen of the Blues', with large, lavender flowers. *C. imperati*, lilac streaked purple, blooms in mid-winter.

POSSIBLE PROBLEMS Mice and birds may damage the corms.

GALANTHUS

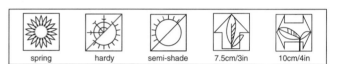

| spring | hardy | semi-shade | 7.5cm/3in | 10cm/4in |

No garden is complete without snowdrops, one of the first bulbs to flower outdoors. There are several varieties. *Galanthus nivalis* (*above*) is the common snowdrop, with nodding white flowers dotted green, the best for naturalizing in grass or beneath shrubs. Large-flowered varieties are a better choice for the open ground.

GROWING Plant the fresh bulbs as soon as they are available: snowdrops can be difficult to establish and the bulbs must not dry out. Set them in moisture-retentive loam in a position where they will receive good light in very early spring.

PROPAGATION Once established, snowdrops multiply freely. Lift and divide the clusters while in flower or just afterwards and replant immediately. Separate each bulb carefully so that its leaves and roots are undamaged. Plants may be raised from seed – in fact thriving plants may self-seed – and take 5 years to reach maturity.

SPECIES *G. nivalis reginae-olgae*, sub-species, flowers in autumn before the leaves appear; *G. n.* 'Flore-Plena', double, showy flowers; *G. n.* 'Viridapicis', large flowers, green spot on both outer and inner petals; *G. elwesii*, up to 25cm/10in high, spring-flowering, green inner petals.

POSSIBLE PROBLEMS Bulb eelworm; narcissus fly maggots; grey mould on leaves.

▓ PROPAGATION TIP

When bulbs are left to naturalize, do not cut the grass for at least 6 weeks after the flowers have faded so the bulbs can store food for next year's blooms.

▓ PLANTING TIP

Plant bulbs in clumps, rather than strung out in rows: they look much more effective when massed together (this applies to all bulbs). Bulbs are very good if you are short of space, as even one tub crammed with bulbs will brighten up a patio or balcony.

MUSCARI

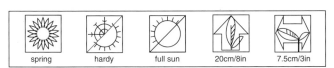

| spring | hardy | full sun | 20cm/8in | 7.5cm/3in |

The intense blue of the tightly packed little flower clusters of the grape hyacinth rivals gentians in richness. They look best in clumps at the edge of a border and last well as cut flowers.

GROWING Set out bulbs 7.5cm/3in deep from late summer to autumn, in well-drained, reasonably fertile soil. Plants grown in shade will produce excessive foliage at the expense of flowers.

PROPAGATION Clumps need dividing every 3 years or they become overcrowded. Just after flowering or when dormant, lift, divide and replant parent bulbs and offsets immediately.

SPECIES *Muscari armeniacum (above)*, 7.5cm/3in long spikes of violet-blue flowers; the variety 'Early Giant' bears electric blue blooms, while 'Cantab' is pale blue; *M. botryoides*: only 10cm/4in high, deep blue flowers, early spring; the variety 'Album' is pure white; *M. tubergenianum*, the Oxford and Cambridge grape hyacinth, is so called because the upper flowers are much paler than the lower, rich blue ones.

POSSIBLE PROBLEMS Generally trouble-free.

CHIONODOXA

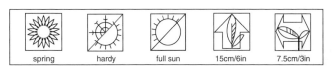

| spring | hardy | full sun | 15cm/6in | 7.5cm/3in |

The chionodoxa or glory-of-the-snow is a member of the lily family. It bears open, five-petalled flowers of pale blue or violet with white centres. Like the crocus, snowdrop and grape hyacinth, chionodoxa looks attractive in small groups and at the edge of a border. Indeed these four species do very well planted together in intermingling clumps.

GROWING Plant bulbs in autumn 7.5cm/3in deep in groups in moisture-retentive soil. No further attention is needed until the plants are overcrowded and need dividing.

PROPAGATION Lift, divide, and replant offsets as the foliage is dying down. Alternatively collect seed in spring when ripe (black) but before the seed box has split, and sow immediately in a frame or nursery bed. Transfer seedlings to the flowering site in the second summer.

SPECIES *C. luciliae (above)*, deep blue flowers with white eye, 2.5cm/1in across; varieties include 'Rosea', pink and 'Wanenburg', bright blue; *C. gigantea*, large, lilac flowers; the variety 'Alba' is pure white.

POSSIBLE PROBLEMS Slugs may eat flowers and leaves.

■ PLANTING TIP

An ideal spring bulb for early colour. Use in containers, beds, window-boxes, or plant as edging. If naturalizing in grass remember it spreads quickly.

■ PLANTING TIPS

Bulbs make a good showing in tubs and containers on the patio, as well as in borders. Chionodoxas are good spring-flowering bulbs which can be planted under or around permanent shrubs or flowers in a tub, providing early colour on your patio and garden.

TULIPA

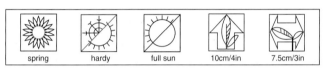

| spring | hardy | full sun | 10cm/4in | 7.5cm/3in |

Tulips were introduced to Europe from Turkey in the 16th century and have been firm favourites ever since. Most of the cultivated forms now seen are hybrids classified into 14 divisions according to their characteristics. Division 15 comprises the exquisite species tulips, many of which are ideal for rock gardens and containers. The colour range is extensive.

GROWING Plant bulbs 15cm/6in deep in late autumn in groups of 6-12 in well-drained soil in a site sheltered from wind. After flowering, remove the dead leaves and stems. Most species can be left in the ground to flower in subsequent years. Keep free of weeds. Bulbs that must be lifted should be stored in boxes in a dry shed.

PROPAGATION Lift the bulbs carefully when the leaves turn yellow. Remove the offsets, grade by size (discarding the very smallest) and store until planting time at 16-18°C/61-64°F. Replant small offsets 5cm/2in deep.

SPECIES *Tulipa urumiensis* (*above*); *T. tarda* (*above*) forms a rosette of leaves at the base of the stem, with several bright yellow blooms, tipped white, from each cluster; *T. greigii*, height 23cm/9in, vivid scarlet, pointed petals, leaves streaked dark red; *T. pulchella*, violet-red flowers, narrow leaves tinged red; must be lifted.

POSSIBLE PROBLEMS Mice may eat bulbs in store. See also other tulip entries.

▓ SPECIAL CARE TIP

Tulips are not difficult, but they should be planted slightly later than other bulbs – in late autumn/early winter. The bulbs can be left in the ground, but most will improve with being lifted every year and stored. Leave in the ground or container until the foliage has turned yellow, then store in a frost-free shed or cellar.

DARWIN TULIPS

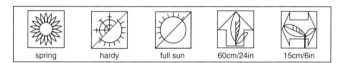

| spring | hardy | full sun | 60cm/24in | 15cm/6in |

Darwin tulips, classified division 6, are those most often used in formal bedding schemes. Their large, rounded flowers – 10-15cm/4-6in across – are available in a dazzling range of colours and are held erect on strong stems. They have been crossed with the species *T. fosteriana*, which has grey-green leaves and huge scarlet flowers, to produce Darwin hybrids (Division 5). Tulips in this group are vividly colourful with the largest blooms of all.

GROWING Plant the bulbs late in the autumn to avoid young growth being damaged by frost. Tulips like an alkaline environment; add ground limestone before planting on acid soils. Set the bulbs 15cm/6in deep, more on light soil. Planting distance can be varied for effect as when interplanting with wallflowers as shown. Lift and store when the foliage turns yellow.

PROPAGATION Remove offsets when lifting, grade by size (discarding the smallest) and store at 16-18°C/61-64°F until replanting.

VARIETIES Div. 5: 'Beauty of Appeldoorn' (*above*), yellow within, outside flushed red; 'General Eisenhower', vivid scarlet; 'Jewel of Spring', sharp yellow, spotted red, black base; Div. 6: 'Glacier', ivory; 'Margaux', wine red; 'Reliance', lilac shaded silver; 'Scarlett O'Hara', bright red.

POSSIBLE PROBLEMS Virus diseases such as cucumber mosaic virus. Damaged bulbs may develop mould in store.

▓ CUT FLOWER TIP

Cut thick-stemmed flowers like these under water, and cut at an angle, so that the stems do not sit on the bottom of the vase and fail to take up water.

PARROT TULIPS

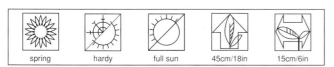

| spring | hardy | full sun | 45cm/18in | 15cm/6in |

Parrot tulips differ from the smooth-petalled, cup-shaped symmetry of most types, having petals that are often attractively fringed and twisted. Many varieties are bi-coloured: these colour 'breaks', originally caused by virus infections, were once greatly admired and became fashionable enough to constitute a single group, Division 10. Division 9, Rembrandt tulips, are Darwins with colour breaks. Both are great favourites with flower arrangers.

GROWING Plant bulbs 15cm/6in deep in late autumn, in alkaline soil. Lift and store when the foliage turns yellow.

PROPAGATION Remove offsets when lifting, grade by size (discarding the smallest) and store at 16-18°C/61-64°F until replanting.

VARIETIES Div 10: 'Black Parrot' (above), very dark purple; 'Gadelan', violet splashed green, white base; 'White Parrot', pure white; 'Texas Gold', deep yellow, narrow red edge; 'Orange Parrot', deep orange, mahogany within, richly scented. Div. 9: 'American Flag', deep red and white; 'Zomerschoon', coral pink and cream.

POSSIBLE PROBLEMS See left. Very dry soils may well cause 'blindness' – the flowers wither before opening. Grey bulb rot destroys bulbs.

DOUBLE TULIPS

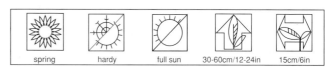

| spring | hardy | full sun | 30-60cm/12-24in | 15cm/6in |

The large, showy blooms of double-flowering tulips resemble peonies. Up to 10cm/4in across, they open wide and flat, looking spectacular on their stiff stems. Division 2, Early Doubles, are so-called because they can be forced to flower indoors for winter decoration. Double Lates, Division 11, earn their name because they stay in bloom for a long time unless damaged by bad weather.

GROWING Plant bulbs 15cm/6in deep in late autumn, in alkaline soil. Lift and store when the foliage turns yellow.

PROPAGATION Remove offsets when lifting, grade by size (discarding the smallest) and store at 16-18°C/61-64°F until replanting.

VARIETIES Early: 'Dante', blood red; 'Goya', deep coral, flushed yellow; 'Schoonord', pure white, very large; 'Peach Blossom' (above), rose pink on white. Late: 'Mount Tacoma', pure white, strong grower; 'Eros', rose pink, scented; 'Gold Medal', saffron yellow; 'Livingstone', red.

POSSIBLE PROBLEMS See left. Tulip fire is a serious fungus disease occurring in cold wet weather.

PLANTING TIP

These brilliantly coloured flowers look most effective planted in a block, rather than strung out in a thin row. This is especially true of the bi-coloured variety.

PLANTING TIP

To force tulips, bury the bulbs in their pots. Dig a trench in the garden 40cm/16in deep. Pot the bulbs with their necks just below the compost and place in the trench. Cover with soil and cover with straw in frosty weather. Check growth in mid-winter and remove from trench when necks are 7cm/2¾in.

ERANTHIS

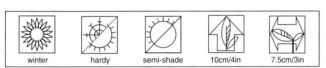

winter	hardy	semi-shade	10cm/4in	7.5cm/3in

The winter aconite, *Eranthis hyemalis (above)*, cheerfully bears its rounded, buttercup-like yellow flowers while snow is still on the ground. The stems are leafless, but each flower is surrounded by a neck-ruff of narrow leaves.

GROWING Plant the tubers in late summer, setting them 2.5cm/1in deep in small groups. They are happiest in soil enriched with peat or leaf-mould, preferably nestling beneath shrubs where they can naturalize undisturbed. Keep weed-free and well-watered, especially in spring.

PROPAGATION When the plants start to die down, lift the tubers and cut or break them into small sections. Replant immediately.

VARIETIES There are no named varieties of the species. The hybrid *E. × tubergenii* flowers a little later but bears slightly larger flowers. Named varieties such as 'Guinea Gold' have bronzed foliage.

POSSIBLE PROBLEMS Birds may damage the flowerbuds.

LEUCOJUM

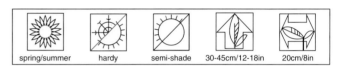

spring/summer	hardy	semi-shade	30-45cm/12-18in	20cm/8in

There are three species of leucojum in general cultivation. These bulbs bear delicate white flowers rather like a snowdrop but rounder in shape. Leucojums are taller and different species flower in spring, summer and the early autumn. They are not difficult to grow and require minimal attention.

GROWING Plant fresh bulbs in late summer/early autumn 7.5cm/3in deep. *Leucojum aestivum*, the summer snowflake, and *L. vernum*, the spring snowflake, require moisture-retentive soil. *L. autumnale*, the autumn snowflake, prefers free-draining soil and should be set only 5cm/2in deep. Leave the clumps undisturbed for several seasons and divide them when overcrowding reduces the production of flowers.

PROPAGATION Offsets will flower next to the parent bulb, but when they are overcrowded should be lifted, divided and replanted. Lift the bulbs when the foliage has died down.

SPECIES *L. aestivum (above)*, rich green strap-like leaves, white flowers tipped green, late spring; *L. autumnale*, grass-like foliage appears after the small, pure white blooms, late summer; *L. vernum*, only 15cm/6in high, single white flowers, tipped green, early spring.

POSSIBLE PROBLEMS Generally trouble-free.

▨ PLANTING TIP

All bulbs need moisture while growing, but because they are fleshy they will not tolerate waterlogged conditions. Plant where drainage is good.

▨ PLANTING TIP

L. aestivum, *the summer-flowering variety, likes a moisture-retaining soil, unlike most bulbs. It is ideal, therefore, for planting in a bog garden,* or for enlivening an otherwise dull, damp and shady corner of the garden.

CYCLAMEN

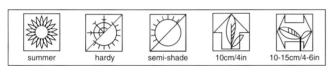

summer | hardy | semi-shade | 10cm/4in | 10-15cm/4-6in

Hardy cyclamens are cousins of the familiar flowering house-plant *Cyclamen persicum*. They are diminutive but charming plants and once established they flower for years. The beautifully marked foliage makes long-lasting ground cover in shady corners. *C. neapolitanum (above)* is the best species for this purpose, with flowers in various shades of pink appearing from late summer to late autumn. The deep green leaves are variable in shape – the alternative name, *C. hederifolium*, reflects their occasional resemblance to ivy – but are always streaked silver, and red on the underside.

GROWING Plant the tubers in late summer/early autumn in clusters barely covered with soil. Well-drained soil containing plenty of well-rotted organic matter is best. Choose a shady site sheltered from wind. Mulch annually with a 2.5cm/1in layer of leaf mould when the foliage has died down.

PROPAGATION As offsets are not produced, cyclamens must be increased from seed. Collect ripe seed in summer and sow in early autumn in pots of seed compost kept in a ventilated cold frame. Prick the seedlings out into small pots of potting compost. Overwinter in a cold frame and plant out in late spring.

VARIETIES *C. n.* 'Album' is a white form.

POSSIBLE PROBLEMS Generally trouble-free.

HYACINTHUS

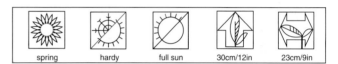

spring | hardy | full sun | 30cm/12in | 23cm/9in

The hyacinth bears spikes of fragrant flowers of white, blue, yellow, pink or red in early spring. Most of the generally available varieties belong to the group called Dutch hybrids, developed from the species *Hyacinthus orientalis*. They are commercially forced into flowering early for indoor plants, but are ideal for spring flowering outdoors in more formal schemes.

GROWING Plant the bulbs as soon as they are available in early autumn, in rich, well-drained soil. A sunny site is important if you want the bulbs to bloom for more than one year.

PROPAGATION Hyacinths are not prolific, but offsets can be taken from the parent bulb, which should be lifted after the foliage has died down. Replant the bulbils immediately.

VARIETIES Recommended for bedding: 'King of the Blues', deep blue; 'La Victoire', red; 'Pink Pearl' (*above*), deep pink; 'L'Innocence', white; 'City of Haarlem', primrose yellow.

POSSIBLE PROBLEMS Stem and bulb eelworm; narcissus fly maggots.

■ PLANTING TIP

This attractive bulb will last for years and is ideal for naturalizing. Choose a shady corner where it can stay undisturbed and it will provide excellent ground cover with its decorative leaves.

■ PLANTING TIP

To avoid bulbs rotting in heavy soils, improve drainage by planting bulbs in a 30cm/12in hole half filled with grit or fine gravel. Cover bulbs with soil.

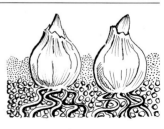

NARCISSUS HYBRIDS

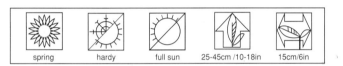

spring	hardy	full sun	25-45cm /10-18in	15cm/6in

Everyone can put a name to the cheerful daffodil, but few realize what an enormous number of species and hybrids are available. All bear six-petalled flowers with a trumpet-shaped central corona. Those with a corona as long as, or longer than, the petals are known as daffodils, the others as narcissi. The corona may be deeper in colour than the petals; both are usually a shade of yellow, but white, cream and pale pink varieties have been developed. Narcissi are divided into 11 groups, which include thousands of named varieties.

GROWING Plant bulbs in autumn in a hole three times the depth of the bulb, deeper if in a bed which will be cultivated through the year, where the hoe might damage the bulbs. Divide the clumps when overcrowded. Do not tie up the leaves after flowering.

PROPAGATION Lift the bulbs when the leaves are beginning to turn yellow. Remove and replant the offsets.

VARIETIES 'Suzy' (above), jonquil type, pale yellow and orange; 'Texas', double-flowered, yellow and deep orange; 'Thalia', triandrus type, with several white, nodding flowers per stem.

POSSIBLE PROBLEMS Narcissus fly; stem eelworm; slugs.

NARCISSUS SPECIES

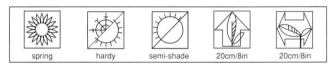

spring	hardy	semi-shade	20cm/8in	20cm/8in

Species of wild daffodils are generally smaller than the cultivated hybrids and the flower form is very varied. Most do well in the open, left alone to flower for many years. Some are good for rock gardens. Varieties suitable for naturalizing in grass, for which narcissi are perhaps the ideal subject, are described below.

GROWING Naturalized narcissi do best in rich soil, protected by the shade of larger plants such as trees and shrubs. Soil should not be waterlogged or too dry. Plant in late summer with random spacing; scatter the bulbs on the ground and plant them where they fall, in holes three times the depth of the bulb.

PROPAGATION If necessary, lift and divide the bulbs after flowering and replant immediately.

SPECIES Narcissus cyclamineus 'February Gold' (above), early-flowering species with rich yellow, swept-back flowers; in moist soil it will seed and increase freely; best in fine grass. N. pseudonarcissus, the wild daffodil or lent lily, up to 30cm/12in high, creamy petals with lemon trumpets; the better choice for tall grass.

POSSIBLE PROBLEMS Given suitable conditions, naturalized narcissi are relatively trouble-free.

▨ PROPAGATION TIP

If you want to lift bulbs after flowering to make room for other plants, carefully dig them up and heel in elsewhere until the foliage dies down.

▨ PLANTING TIP

Bulbs for naturalizing are best planted with a bulb planter. This tool removes a core of soil, and you then place the bulb in the hole and replace the soil 'plug'.

IRIS SPECIES

summer	hardy	full sun	45cm/18in	23cm/9in

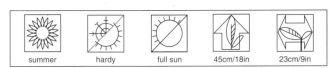

The iris family includes a great number of species and hybrids, with very beautiful flowers of blue or yellow in a distinctive arrangement of petals but varying greatly in size and use. Most irises grow from rhizomes, a few from true bulbs. Several are excellent rock garden plants; those described here are ideal for waterside planting or moist conditions.

GROWING Plant rhizomes in spring or late summer at the water's edge or in water up to 45cm/18in deep, depending on species. The clumps should be lifted every 3 years for division.

PROPAGATION Just after flowering, lift the rhizomes and divide by cutting off pieces from the outside of the clump, discarding the centre. Each piece should have one or two good fans of leaves. Replant immediately.

SPECIES *I. laevigata (above)*, deep blue flowers up to 15cm/6in across, water depth 15cm/6in; named varieties include 'Alba', pure white and 'Monstrosa', white blotched purple. *I. pseudocorus*, reaches up to 1.2m/4ft in 45cm/18in of water, half that height in a damp border; vivid yellow blooms; named varieties need only 15cm/6in water. *I. versicolor*, violet flowers, ideal lakeside plant in 7.5cm/3in water; 'Kermesina' is a wine-red variety.

POSSIBLE PROBLEMS Cucumber mosaic virus; leaf spot; iris sawfly.

IRIS BULBS

summer	hardy	full sun	60cm/24in	15cm/6in

Bulbous irises are a small group which include the dwarf reticulated types ideal for rockeries and pot culture. For general garden cultivation hybrids of the xiphium group are best. These fall into three categories: Dutch irises are first to flower in early summer; the Spanish irises bloom about 2 weeks later, and finally the English irises 2 weeks later still. All come in a range of delectable colours, but the English group, while it bears flowers 12.5cm/5in across, contains no yellows.

GROWING Plant the bulbs in autumn 10-15cm/4-6in deep, in light, fertile soil in the case of Dutch and Spanish hybrids. The English hybrids like rich, damp soil.

PROPAGATION Lift the bulbs after flowering. Detach the offsets and replant immediately, placing the smallest specimens in a nursery bed for a year.

VARIETIES Dutch: 'Golden Harvest', vivid yellow; 'National Velvet', deep purple, blotched orange. Spanish: 'Frederika', white blotched yellow; 'Blue River', aquamarine blotched orange. English: 'Prince Albert', silvery blue; 'Mirabeau', purple blotched white.

POSSIBLE PROBLEMS Narcissus fly larvae; grey bulb rot.

PLANTING TIP

There are almost too many irises to choose from, as there is a different type for every spot in the garden, from the herbaceous border to the edge of a pond. It is essential to know what type you want before buying and to buy with a definite spot in the garden in mind.

PLANTING TIP

Some varieties of the dwarf bulb iris will tolerate a dry soil, and so can be used for underplanting shrubs and trees, such as twisted hazel. The dwarf bulb iris is also ideal for brightening up tubs and containers in spring, as well as for rock gardens.

IPHEION

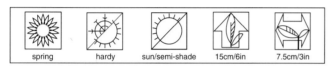

| spring | hardy | sun/semi-shade | 15cm/6in | 7.5cm/3in |

A member of the lily family, *Ipheion uniflorum* is native to South America. It is also known as *Brodiaea* or *Triteleia uniflora*. When closely grouped, the star-shaped flowers of white or shades of blue make an attractive addition to the front of the border. While the flowers have a pleasant scent, the leaves smell faintly of garlic.

GROWING Plant bulbs 2.5-5cm/1-2in deep in late autumn in well-drained soil. Choose a sheltered site. Ipheions prefer sun but tolerate partial shade. Remove dead flower stems and foliage in late summer. To prevent overcrowding lift and divide the clumps every 2-3 years.

PROPAGATION Ipheions produce offsets freely. Lift the bulbs as the leaves are fading, separate the offsets and replant immediately.

VARIETIES 'Violacea' (*above*), violet-blue; 'Caeruleum', pale blue.

POSSIBLE PROBLEMS Generally trouble-free.

FREESIA

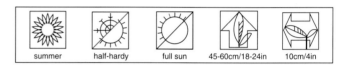

| summer | half-hardy | full sun | 45-60cm/18-24in | 10cm/4in |

Freesias are members of the iris family native to South Africa. The hybrid *Freesia × kewensis* is commercially cultivated in greenhouse conditions for its colourful, scented blooms on slender stems. Specially treated corms are available which will flower outdoors in mid-summer, but only for one season. In favoured areas ordinary, untreated corms can be used and will flower for several years.

GROWING Plant prepared corms in spring, 7.5cm/3in deep in well-drained, moderately fertile soil on a sheltered site. Even then, twiggy sticks will probably be necessary for support. Lift the corms when the foliage dies down. In warm areas, plant ordinary corms in late summer and leave in the ground after flowering.

PROPAGATION Offsets removed when lifting the corms can be brought to flower in cool greenhouse conditions in subsequent years.

VARIETIES 'Margret' (*above*), purplish-pink veined purple; 'Klondyke', yellow shading to gold; 'Snow Queen', cream with yellow throat; 'Stockholm', red with yellow throat.

POSSIBLE PROBLEMS Aphids and caterpillars damage leaves and young shoots.

■ PLANTING TIP

This attractive little plant looks very good in a rock garden, and it will appreciate an open, sunny position. Remember to divide clumps and detach offsets in autumn, to prevent overcrowding.

■ SPECIAL CARE TIP

A joy to grow because of their scent, outdoor freesias do need a warm, dry spot to flower well in late summer and autumn. They also need to be kept watered, but at the same time avoid planting in heavy, waterlogged soil. Like all bulbs, they will do best on well-drained fertile soil.

COLCHICUM

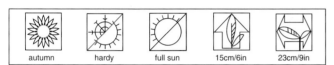

| autumn | hardy | full sun | 15cm/6in | 23cm/9in |

The autumn crocus is not in fact related to the crocus, though they look similar when in flower. Colchicums are members of the lily family (crocuses belong to the iris family), with oval (not flat) corms and long, rather untidy leaves. This feature should be borne in mind when choosing a planting site, as the leaves persist long after the flowers have died down. As they can be left undisturbed for years, it is a good idea to group them in rough grass.

GROWING Plant the corms in late summer in any type of well-drained soil. Set them 10cm/4in deep in small groups. Lift and divide when overcrowded.

PROPAGATION Lift the corms in summer, detach the offsets and replant immediately.

SPECIES *C. speciosum (above)*, flowers in shades of mauve. Beautiful hybrids developed from the species include 'The Giant', large mauve flowers, white centre; 'Album', pure white; 'Atrorubens', crimson-purple.

POSSIBLE PROBLEMS Slugs may eat the corms and leaves.

SCILLA

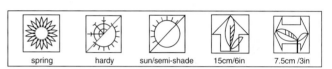

| spring | hardy | sun/semi-shade | 15cm/6in | 7.5cm /3in |

These hardy bulbs belong to the useful group of spring-flowering plants which are simplicity to grow yet produce brilliantly coloured blooms to brighten the border or create a splash of colour in grass. Most scillas, or squills to give them their common name, bear their star-shaped flowers in varying shades of blue. The shiny leaves are mid-green and precede the flower stems.

GROWING Plant the bulbs 5-7.5cm/2-3in deep in moist well-drained soil in late summer. A sunny or partially shaded position will do. Leave the bulbs undisturbed thereafter.

PROPAGATION Scillas produce their offsets slowly. Their presence is indicated by extra clusters of leaves. Lift the bulbs carefully after the foliage has died down, detach the offsets and replant immediately. They may not flower the first year.

SPECIES *S. sibirica*, 3-4 stems per bulb, brilliant blue flowers; *S. tubergeniana (above)*, very early-flowering, pale blue flowers, good in mixed spring planting; *S. peruviana*, flowers early summer, 23cm/9in high, profuse, intensely blue flowers.

POSSIBLE PROBLEMS Yellow spots on the leaves may be caused by rust.

▨ ORGANIC TIP

Bulbs left to naturalize in grass will enjoy a feed of liquid manure after flowering. If in a bed, mulch soil with well-rotted manure after foliage has died down.

▨ PLANTING TIP

Spring bulbs can be left to naturalize under trees and shrubs, but ideally the bulbs should flower before the shade from the leaves becomes too dense.

DAHLIA

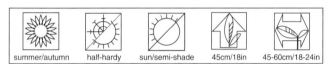

summer/autumn | half-hardy | sun/semi-shade | 45cm/18in | 45-60cm/18-24in

Long-lasting and excellent for cutting, dahlias are among the most popular summer flowers. The types grown from tubers are called border dahlias, which are divided into groups, namely: Single-flowered; Anemone-flowered; Collerette (with a collar of smaller florets); Peony-flowered; Decorative (large ray florets, reminiscent of chrysanthemums); Ball; Pompon; Cactus and Semi-cactus (pointed petals). Decorative, Ball and Cactus dahlias are further subdivided by size. The colour range is wide, excluding blue, but all shades have a characteristic clarity and brightness. Dahlias are in glorious bloom from high summer until the first frosts. The minimum height is given above – some varieties reach 1.5m/5ft.

GROWING Dahlias are best grown in a special bed on well-drained soil previously enriched with well-rotted organic matter. Just before planting, rake in bonemeal at 100g/m² (4oz/sq.yd). Place a stake in each planting hole to support the stem to within 30cm/12in of its ultimate height. Plant unsprouted tubers in spring, 12.5cm/5in deep. Plant sprouted tubers in late spring or wait until summer in cold wet seasons. As the plants grow, tie the stems loosely to the stakes. For additional growing advice, see next entry.

DAHLIA

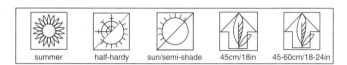

summer | half-hardy | sun/semi-shade | 45cm/18in | 45-60cm/18-24in

When dahlias are grown for exhibition purposes, a process of disbudding is carried out to produce fewer, larger flowers. This is not necessary in normal circumstances, but it is advisable to pinch out the leading shoots once, a month after planting. Lift and store the tubers annually. Raise them carefully, using a spade, a week after frost has turned the leaves black. Drain off water from the stems. Store healthy tubers only. Place them in boxes, just covered with peat, in a frostproof place. Inspect from time to time to make sure none is affected by mould.

PROPAGATION Set overwintered tubers in boxes of peat and sand in spring, with the crowns visible. Keep moist and frost-free. When the 'eyes' begin to swell, cut the tubers into pieces, each with an eye, and pot up or plant 10cm/4in deep in a cold frame. Plant out when danger of frost is passed.

VARIETIES Single: 'Sion', bronze; Anemone: 'Lucy', purple, yellow centre; Collerette: 'Can-Can', pink, yellow inner ring; Decorative: 'Little Tiger', red and cream, dwarf; Ball: 'Gloire de Lyon', white; Pompon: 'Nero', maroon; Cactus: 'Bach', yellow.

POSSIBLE PROBLEMS Aphids, caterpillars, earwigs; grey mould, petal blight.

■ PLANTING TIP

Dahlias are best planted in a bed on their own, to make an effective display. They are also useful for providing late colour in a border when most other flowers are fading or dying back. Taller varieties are available for the back of the border, while smaller ones, like 'Lilliput', will bloom in the front till the first frosts.

■ ORGANIC TIP

Dust tubers with sulphur before planting, to discourage any fungal attack. Set slug traps or use organic slug powder to avoid damage to new shoots.

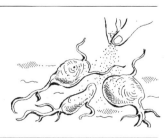

LILIUM SPECIES

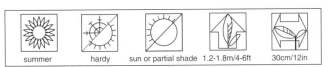

| summer | hardy | sun or partial shade | 1.2-1.8m/4-6ft | 30cm/12in |

In spite of its majestic, exotic appearance, the lily is generally not difficult to grow. The numerous species and hybrids are divided into 9 groups according to origin, with true species in Division 9. All lily bulbs, made up of tightly packed scales, produce roots from the base, but some also have roots from the stems; this type should be planted deeper than basal-rooting bulbs. Flowers may be trumpet-shaped, bowl-shaped or, in the form called Turk's-cap, with recurved petals. The colour range is very wide, excluding blue.

GROWING Plant fresh bulbs from autumn to spring (basal rooting bulbs always in autumn), about 15cm/6in deep depending on size. A south-facing site sheltered from wind is best; ordinary well-drained soil will do. While some species dislike lime, others prefer it. Enrich soil with well-rotted organic matter before planting.

PROPAGATION Some lilies produce numerous offsets which may be treated in the usual way. Scale propagation (see right) is suitable for all types.

SPECIES *Lilium regale* (*above*), China, fragrant, white, trumpet flowers 15cm/6in long, stem-rooting bulbs which increase quickly; *L. pardalinum* (panther lily), California, 5cm/2in orange-red Turk's-cap flowers, basal rooting bulb, needs lime-free soil.

POSSIBLE PROBLEMS Leatherjackets; lily beetle larvae.

■ PLANTING TIP

The blooms of these summer-flowering bulbs like sunshine, but the roots prefer shade. Ideally, plant the bulbs at the foot of a low-growing shrub.

LILIUM HYBRIDS

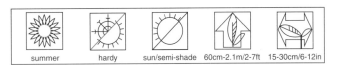

| summer | hardy | sun/semi-shade | 60cm-2.1m/2-7ft | 15-30cm/6-12in |

The many hybrid lilies raised from species are broadly grouped as Asiatic, European or American, and include countless stunning varieties.

GROWING Plant from autumn to spring about 15cm/6in deep depending on size. Lilies like well-drained soil enriched with well-rotted organic matter and a sheltered, sunny site.

PROPAGATION In spring or autumn, scrape away earth from the dormant bulbs and gently remove healthy scales. Replace the soil. Place scales at an angle in boxes of peat and sand to half their depth. Set in a cold frame at 10°C/50°F. New bulbs form at the base of the scales. When shoots form on these tiny bulbils, pot them up in compost and transfer to an open frame or sheltered bed. Transplant to permanent positions 2-3 years later.

HYBRIDS 'Orange Triumph' (*above*), from *L. × hollandicum* (formerly *L. × umbellatum*), upright cup-shaped flowers. The Mid-Century group, to 1.5m/5ft, includes 'Cinnabar', maroon; 'Joan Evans', bright yellow; 'Valencia', soft orange. The fine American Bellingham hybrids reach up to 2.1m/7ft and include 'Royal Favorite', Chinese yellow speckled deep red. 'Parkmanni' is an outstanding American lily with open, very fragrant flowers up to 30cm/12in in diameter, crimson inside, rose outside, tinged green and white.

POSSIBLE PROBLEMS Basal rot; lily disease.

■ PLANTING TIP

There is an enormous variety of these hybrids to choose from, in all kinds of colours and sizes. The bulbs must never be allowed to dry out, so plant immediately after purchase. Mid-autumn is best for planting lilium, when the soil is still free of frost.

BEGONIA

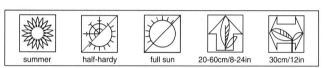

| summer | half-hardy | full sun | 20-60cm/8-24in | 30cm/12in |

The smooth, rounded leaves of tuberous begonia hybrids *(Begonia × tuberhybrida)* make a perfect foil for their large, rose-like flowers. The colour range includes white, yellow, pink, orange and red. Pendula hybrids, with slightly drooping stems, are seen to best advantage in hanging baskets or window-boxes.

GROWING Start tubers into growth in spring in boxes of moist peat at 18°C/64°F. Pot on into 12.5cm/5in pots of compost when leafy shoots appear, then into 20cm/8in pots. Plant outdoors in early summer in well-drained soil previously enriched with peat or leaf mould. Lift before the first frosts and overwinter at 7°C/45°F, just covered with dry peat.

PROPAGATION In spring, when potting up, divide the tubers into pieces bearing at least one healthy shoot each. Treat as above.

VARIETIES 'Single White' *(above)*; 'Buttermilk', cream; 'Festiva', rich yellow; 'Margaret Collins', true pink; 'Ninette', pale apricot, very large; 'T. B. Toop', orange; 'Olympia', deep scarlet, Pendula hybrid; 'Dawn', buff-yellow; 'Yellow Sweetie', lemon, lightly scented.

POSSIBLE PROBLEMS Weevils, eelworms, tarsonemid mites; grey mould.

GLADIOLUS

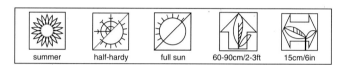

| summer | half-hardy | full sun | 60-90cm/2-3ft | 15cm/6in |

Gladioli bear their lily-like flowers on one side of an erect spike. Large-flowered hybrids are the best choice for the garden border; for cutting, choose Primulinus hybrids, 45-90cm/18in-3ft high, or Miniatures, the same height but with numerous smaller florets. The colour range is breathtaking, including both bright and subtle shades, but no blues.

GROWING Dig a layer of well-rotted manure into the site in early spring. Rake bonemeal into the surface at 75g/m² (3oz/sq. yd). Plant corms 10cm/4in deep, more in light soil, in spring. If the corms are not deep enough the mature plants may keel over. Space gladioli for cutting in rows 30cm/12in apart. Keep weed-free. Do not water for 8-10 weeks, then water generously. When the foliage yellows lift the corms and cut off the main stem to 1cm/½in. Dry off in warmth and store in a cool frost-free place.

PROPAGATION Detach cormlets from the base of the parent and treat in the same way, raising them in nursery beds and storing over winter until they reach flowering size in the second year.

VARIETIES Large-flowered: 'Peter Pears' *(above)*, salmon pink; Primulinus: 'Apex', warm red; Miniature: 'Greenbird', sulphur green.

POSSIBLE PROBLEMS Thrips, soil pests, gladiolus dry rot.

■ PLANTING TIP

The Pendula hybrid, with its drooping stems, is ideal for window-boxes or hanging baskets provided the soil is rich enough and kept watered during flowering.

■ SPECIAL CARE TIP

The one problem with gladiolus is that the flowers have such a short life, making them unsuitable for a mixed border. They are best grown in a special bed where they can be staked and cared for individually. Stagger the planting of the corms through spring to ensure a steady supply of blooms in the summer.

FRITILLARIA

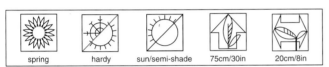

spring	hardy	sun/semi-shade	75cm/30in	20cm/8in

The small group of fritillaries in general cultivation range from the majestic *F. imperialis* (crown imperial), which may reach 90cm/3ft, to the 30cm/12in *F. meleagris* (snake's-head fritillary) with its distinctive checkerboard petals. The proud blooms of *F. imperialis*, coronets held high on straight stems clothed with glossy leaves, are best appreciated in a border. *F. meleagris*, by contrast, with its nodding, bell-like flowers, is suited to a semi-wild or at least informal setting.

GROWING Both species like fertile, well-drained soil. *F. imperialis* needs sun. *F. meleagris* does well in moist conditions, in short grass or at the border's edge. Set the bulbs on their sides to prevent water lodging in the depression on top. Plant them in autumn, 20cm/8in deep for *F. imperialis*, 10cm/4in for *F. meleagris*. Do not disturb for at least 4 years, apart from cutting down the stems after flowering.

PROPAGATION Take offsets from mature bulbs after the leaves have withered. Replant bulbils and parent bulbs immediately.

VARIETIES *F. imperialis*: 'Aurora', deep orange; 'Lutea Maxima' (*above*), golden yellow. *F. meleagris*: 'Alba', white, veined green; 'Artemis', purple-grey with purple checkers; 'Saturnus', violet-red.

POSSIBLE PROBLEMS Generally trouble-free.

▪ PLANTING TIP

F. imperialis, with its·tall stems and imposing flowerheads, is a real eye-catcher. For maximum effect, plant six or seven together, at the back of the border.

ZANTEDESCHIA

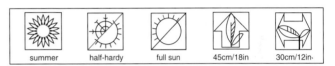

summer	half-hardy	full sun	45cm/18in	30cm/12in·

Native to South Africa, most species of zantedeschia are grown as greenhouse plants in temperate zones. The exception is *Zantedeschia aethiopica*, the calla lily or arum lily, which – if in pots – can be set outside in the summer, or – in a border or at the water's edge – left outside all year. These are exceptionally beautiful plants, with thick glossy leaves and large white flower spathes.

GROWING Pots: set rhizomes 7.5cm/3in deep in 25cm/10in pots of compost in early spring. Water in, and keep moist at 5°C/41°F minimum until growth appears. Increase watering gradually and feed with liquid fertilizer weekly in summer. Move pots outside in mid summer. Bring inside in autumn and repot in fresh soil. Outdoors: as a water plant *Z. aethiopica* needs 15-30cm/6-12in water. In the open ground, very rich soil is needed. In water or in the border, protect the plants from frost with a layer of bracken or straw.

PROPAGATION Divide the rhizomes when repotting or lift and divide outdoor plants in autumn. Replant immediately.

VARIETIES 'Crowborough', hardier than the species, recommended for outdoor cultivation.

POSSIBLE PROBLEMS Corm rot.

▪ PLANTING TIP

If you have only a patio or balcony to grow flowers in, a mixed selection of zantedeschia plants would make a stunning display and cheer up even the dullest spot. It is best raised indoors or in a greenhouse or conservatory and put outside in pots in summer.

Alpines

The strict definition of an alpine plant is one that is native to the alpine zone – the area between the end of the tree line and the beginning of the snow line. More loosely interpreted, the term is used to describe any small plant suitable for the rock garden.

What these plants have in common, as well as their jewel-like beauty and diminutive size, is the need for good drainage. Because they look best planted together, and have similar needs, alpine plants are not dotted around the garden – where their unique charms might well be overshadowed by larger varieties – but are given a special place of their own. This may take one of several forms, including that of the rock garden proper.

In order to succeed, a rock garden must look as natural as possible. This means positioning the rocks (and they must be rocks, not rubble) so that only two-thirds of each one can be seen protruding from the soil; often rocks are tilted at an angle, but if so each one should be set to the same degree. They must be distributed on a slope. If your garden does not have a sloping corner in the sun, you can build one, making sure that for every 30cm/12in of height the rock garden extends 1.2m/4ft wide.

Building a rock garden is hard work and achieving a successful design undoubtedly takes talent. A rather easier alternative is a raised bed, which can be of any size as long as it is 60cm/24in above the ground. Raised beds look best if irregular in shape, with the sides treated as a dry wall. They are, incidentally, well suited to elderly or disabled gardeners.

Whether you take up the challenge of a rockery or opt for a raised bed, you must provide at least 30cm/12in of drainage material. Dig out the soil an extra 30cm/12in deep and fill it up with clinker, gravel or rough stones. Construct the rockery or raised bed a layer at a time, filling each one with a compost made up of 3 parts (by volume) loam (or any good garden soil), 2 parts peat, compost or leaf-mould and 3 parts sharp sand or fine grit. Add 2.25kg/5lb bonemeal to every 0.75m³/1cu.yd of this mixture. When construction is complete, water well and leave the soil to settle. It will almost certainly need topping up as the level drops. Finally, strew an even, shallow layer of granite chippings over the soil (limestone chippings for lime-loving plants) and leave for 2-3 weeks before planting up so that any annual weeds that appear can be killed off.

You may be lucky enough to inherit a handsome rockery. If not, it takes time, energy and some cost to build one (rocks are not cheap). Fortunately, the lack of a rockery does not mean that you have to give up the pleasure of growing this exquisite group of plants. As long as you observe their paramount need for good drainage, you can also grow them in shallow troughs and pans or even in the cracks between paving stones on patios, paths and steps. Stone troughs look wonderful planted up with a selection of alpine plants. This particular version of container growing makes it possible to

include a wide number of different plants in a confined space, thanks to their small size. You can create a living patchwork of colour, choosing from the list of plants below, or confine yourself to a range of blues and pinks, perhaps – gentians and campanulas, dianthus and primula, beautifully set off by the weathered grey of old stone. Sedums and saxifrages are two of the easiest alpines to grow and make excellent companions in a trough garden.

Most alpines are sold as pot-grown plants which can, in theory, be planted at any time, but autumn and spring are best. Autumn planting allows the plants to establish themselves before winter comes. Spring planting means that the plants will start to grow away at once, but you will not see them at their best until the following year.

Alpines need watering until they are established, but not after that unless there is a long period of drought. In such conditions, water very thoroughly in the evening so that the water can soak through the soil all night.

Many alpine plants, and in particular alyssum, helianthe-

Here, a colourful selection of thymes are happily established over a set of stone steps. Cracks in walls and between paving stones make excellent homes for alpines.

mum, dianthus and veronicas, benefit from being cut back quite severely when flowering is over to encourage fresh growth and keep the plants compact.

Many experienced gardeners have highly prized collections of alpines, but this should not make the novice feel wary of growing them. Indeed, a trough of alpines is a good way to give children a suitable-sized garden of their own. In smaller modern gardens, too, or wherever there is a sunny corner, however tiny, alpines are the perfect choice.

ALPINES FOR CONTAINERS

Alyssum	*Gentiana*	*Saxifraga*
Arabis	*Helianthemum*	*Sedum*
Aubretia	*Juniperus*	*Sisyrinchium*
Campanula	*Primula*	*Veronica*
Dianthus	*Ramonda*	

SEDUM

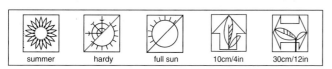

| summer | hardy | full sun | 10cm/4in | 30cm/12in |

Sedum spurium (above) belongs to the large family of succulent plants which includes biting stonecrop, *S. acre*, and that stalwart of the border *S. spectabile*, so attractive to bees. This diminutive perennial species bears deep pink star-shaped flowers on red stems. The rounded leaves cluster low and spread wide, giving ground cover that is both effective and attractive. Unlike *S. acre*, it is not invasive.

GROWING Plant in well-drained soil between autumn and spring. Full sun is essential. Like most sedums, *S. spurium* is drought-resistant. Do not remove the dead stems after flowering. Wait until spring when they can be picked off easily.

PROPAGATION Division is an easy and reliable method of increasing your stock. Divide and replant between autumn and spring.

VARIETIES 'Album', white; 'Schorbusser Blut', deep red, early-flowering.

POSSIBLE PROBLEMS Aphids on stems and leaves; slugs may eat foliage.

THYMUS

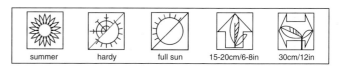

| summer | hardy | full sun | 15-20cm/6-8in | 30cm/12in |

There are several species of thyme suitable for the rock garden. The leaves of all of them are highly aromatic and two, *Thymus vulgaris* (common thyme, *above*) and *T. × citriodorus*, are used as culinary herbs (thyme is an essential ingredient in bouquets garnis). A perennial and very easy to grow, thyme spreads quickly and makes effective ground cover. The tiny flowers may be pink, red, lilac or white.

GROWING Plant from autumn to spring in well-drained garden soil. Full sun is important. After flowering snip off the faded flowerheads to encourage sturdy growth.

PROPAGATION Divide the plants in spring or late summer and replant at once directly in the flowering site.

SPECIES *T. vulgaris*, narrow, dark green, highly aromatic leaves, lilac flowers; *T. serpyllum* (correctly known as *T. drucei*), grey-green, very spreading leaves, purple flowers; 'Album' is a white form; 'Pink Chintz' bears salmon-pink flowers; *T. × citriodorus*, lemon-scented leaves, short-lived lilac flowers; the leaves of 'Aureus' are bright golden, those of 'Silver Posy' silver.

POSSIBLE PROBLEMS Generally trouble-free.

ORGANIC TIP

An ideal plant for the organic garden, as its bright flowers, full of nectar, will attract hoverflies (which will keep aphids at bay) and other insects.

ORGANIC TIP

Dried thyme is highly aromatic, and as such is an essential ingredient in bouquets garnis; the flowers provide a good source of nectar for insects.

DIANTHUS

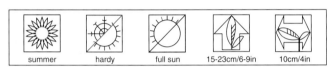

| summer | hardy | full sun | 15-23cm/6-9in | 10cm/4in |

The genus *Dianthus* includes garden pinks, border carnations and florists' perpetual-flowering carnations. Many of the so-called species pinks, exquisite perennials for the rock garden, are strongly scented. The narrow leaves are grey-green and the blooms white, red or shades of pink, sometimes with a central eye.

GROWING Set out young plants in spring or autumn, not too deep, in well-drained non-acid soil. Rake bonemeal into the surface just before planting. Water spring plantings in dry weather; keep autumn-planted stock free of fallen leaves. Pinch out the leading shoots in spring to encourage side-shoots. Remove old stems after flowering.

PROPAGATION Take 7.5cm/3in cuttings in summer and insert in a peat/loam/sand mixture in a cold frame until rooted. Pot up individually or transfer to the flowering site.

SPECIES *D. deltoides*, numerous tiny pink or white flowers until autumn, self-seeds freely, tolerates semi-shade; named varieties include 'Brilliancy' (*above*), bright pink, 'Albus', white; *D. caesius* (correct name *D. gratianopolitanus*, cheddar pink), long-lived, spreading, fringed fragrant pink flowers, early summer; 'Flore-pleno' is a double form.

POSSIBLE PROBLEMS Leaf rot in winter.

ZAUSCHNERIA

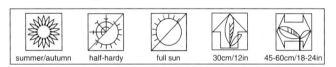

| summer/autumn | half-hardy | full sun | 30cm/12in | 45-60cm/18-24in |

Californian fuchsias, to give zauschnerias their common name, are sub-shrubby perennials from western North America and Mexico, suitable for hot, sunny positions such as the foot of a sunny wall. In the right conditions they are long-lived plants and produce their vivid red tubular flowers late in summer, persisting into the autumn.

GROWING Plant in late spring or high summer in light, well-drained soil. In cold areas, protect the plants with leaves or bracken over winter. Cut back in spring to just above ground level.

PROPAGATION Clumps may be divided in spring with difficulty. The better method is to take 7.5cm/3in cuttings of basal shoots in late spring. Insert in a peat/sand mixture in a propagator at 16-18°C/61-64°F until rooted. Pot up individually in compost and transfer to a cold frame. Plant out in late summer or the following spring.

SPECIES *Z. californica*, grey-green hairy leaves, sprays of red flowers 2.5cm/1in long; *Z. cana (above)*, distinguished by very narrow leaves.

POSSIBLE PROBLEMS Aphids on young shoots.

▪ SPECIAL CARE TIP

Alpine pinks are easy to grow, but there are a few points to remember for success. The plants need full sun, and do not thrive under a damp mulch. They only need watering after planting in dry weather, or in exceptionally hot summers. Most plants lose their vigour after a few years.

▪ SPECIAL CARE TIP

These heat-loving plants are obviously ideal for sunny gardens where the climate is mild all year round. In colder areas it might be better to grow this plant as a conservatory or greenhouse specimen.

AUBRIETA

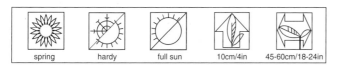

| spring | hardy | full sun | 10cm/4in | 45-60cm/18-24in |

It is easy to be dismissive of the ubiquitous *Aubrieta deltoidea* but it is in fact a very valuable plant, providing sweeps of dramatic colour on dry walls or in the rock garden in late spring, and lasting for weeks. The flowers are tiny but abundant, ranging in colour from lilac to deep purple. The plants form fast-spreading mats.

GROWING Plant between autumn and spring in well-drained soil containing some lime. Plants grown on the rock garden should be sheared right back after flowering to keep them neat; if trailing over a wall, just snip off the old stems.

PROPAGATION Divide rooted stems of established plants in autumn and replant immediately.

VARIETIES 'Gurgedyke', old favourite, deep purple; 'Dr Mules', reliable type, violet; 'Bressingham Pink', double, rosy-pink; 'Argenteo-Variegata', lavender flowers, leaves splashed silver.

POSSIBLE PROBLEMS White blister; downy mildew.

VERONICA

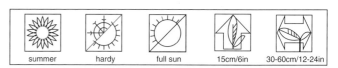

| summer | hardy | full sun | 15cm/6in | 30-60cm/12-24in |

The speedwell family includes six alpine species but two of these, *Veronica pectinata* and *V. filiformis*, are invasive. All bear pink or blue flowers in late spring or summer and are excellent on dry walls or as ground cover plants for rock gardens.

GROWING Plant in a sunny position in well-drained soil from autumn to spring.

PROPAGATION Divide all species, except those that are invasive, in spring, and replant immediately.

SPECIES *V. gentianoides (above)*, slender spikes of palest blue in spring; *V. prostrata* , dense spikes of pale blue flowers freely carried in early summer; named varieties include 'Pygmaea', only 5cm/2in high, 'Rosea', deep pink and 'Spode Blue', china blue; *V. cinerea*, mat-forming, with grey-green leaves and clear pink flowers, mid-summer; *V. teucrium*, variable species – choose named varieties such as 'Shirley Blue', deep blue, or 'Trehane', light blue with leaves variegated yellow.

POSSIBLE PROBLEMS Powdery mildew.

■ PLANTING TIP

Plant alpines in a rock garden in special 'pockets' for each plant among the rocks. Fill the holes with a mixture of soil, peat and grit before planting.

■ SPECIAL CARE TIP

To avoid mildew it is essential to provide a well-drained site, such as a rock or scree garden. If grown in containers, always place stones in the bottom.

CAMPANULA

summer	hardy	sun/semi-shade	23cm/9in	30cm/12in

Although the common name for campanulas is bell flower, not all the species bear flowers in this form. A number have star-shaped blooms, including two of the best species for rock gardens. *Campanula carpatica (above)* forms neat, bushy tufts of green, heart-shaped leaves and bears abundant blue, pink or white flowers 4cm/1½in across on erect, wiry stems. *C. garganica* is a rewarding choice – over the whole of the summer it bears so many blue flowers that the leaves are hardly visible. Both spread up to 30cm/12in.

GROWING Plant in well-drained soil in sun or partial shade between autumn and spring. Remove flowerheads when faded.

PROPAGATION Take 2.5cm/1in basal cuttings of non-flowering shoots in spring. Place in a peat/sand mixture in a cold frame until rooted. Pot up individually and grow on until planting out in the autumn.

VARIETIES The species are reliable, but good named varieties include: *G. garganica*: 'W. H. Paine', deep blue with a white eye; 'Hirsuta', grey, hairy leaves – protect from damp with an open cloche over winter. *C. carpatica*: 'Ditton Blue', only 15cm/6in high, indigo; 'White Star', 30cm/12in high, pure white; 'Turbinata', compact shape, blue flowers, hairy leaves need winter protection.

POSSIBLE PROBLEMS Rust.

RAMONDA

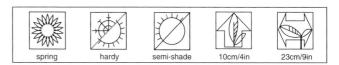

spring	hardy	semi-shade	10cm/4in	23cm/9in

Ramondas are native to southern and central Europe. Their predilection for shade and enriched soil distinguishes them from many alpine plants and enables gardeners to fill an awkward spot with an unusual and attractive subject. The dark leaves form a rosette on the ground rather like that of the primula, but are very deep green, crinkly and fringed with hairs. The straight stems bear pale mauve, saucer-shaped flowers with prominent yellow stamens.

GROWING Set out young plants in spring in a cool, shady crevice on soil previously enriched with peat or leaf-mould. Put them at a slight angle to prevent water collecting in the rosette of leaves. Do not let plants dry out in hot summer weather.

PROPAGATION Take leaf cuttings in summer, making sure each leaf has a dormant bud at the base. Insert at an angle 2cm/¾in deep in a peat/sand mixture in a cold frame until rooted (about 6 weeks). Pot up individually and grow on in the frame for two winters before planting out.

SPECIES *R. myconii (above)*, most popular species; named varieties are 'Alba', white and 'Rosea', rich pink; *R. serbica*, smaller rosette of leaves, stamens tipped with purple anthers.

POSSIBLE PROBLEMS Slugs may eat the leaves.

▦ PLANTING TIP

The massed display of flowers is most attractive, and makes this plant one of the prettiest choices when dense ground cover is required. C. carpatica is ideal for the rock garden, producing bushy leaves and abundant, bright blue bell-shaped flowers over a long period.

▦ SPECIAL CARE TIP

This species is the exception to the rule that rock gardens should be open and in full sun, since this prefers a shady spot. Like other plants which form rosettes, it should be planted at an angle to prevent water collecting in the centre of the rosettes, and should be protected with a mini-cloche in very wet winters.

LITHODORA

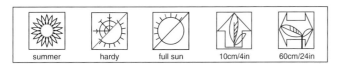

| summer | hardy | full sun | 10cm/4in | 60cm/24in |

Sometimes listed as *Lithospermum*, the genus *Lithodora* belongs to the same family as forget-me-nots, and, like them, bears bright blue star-shaped flowers. The flowers of *L. diffusa (above)* bloom all summer, emerging from a mat of dark green foliage that makes invaluable ground cover for the rock garden.

GROWING Plant in spring in light soil to which peat or leaf-mould has been added. This species will not tolerate lime.

PROPAGATION In the summer take soft green cuttings 4-6.5cm/1½-2½in long with a heel, and insert in a peat/sand mixture in a shaded frame until rooted. Water regularly. Pot up individually, overwinter in the frame and plant out the following spring.

VARIETIES 'Grace Ward', clear blue; 'Heavenly Blue' (rarely available), profuse, deep blue flowers.

POSSIBLE PROBLEMS Generally trouble-free.

OMPHALODES

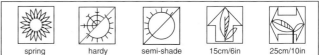

| spring | hardy | semi-shade | 15cm/6in | 25cm/10in |

Omphalodes verna (above), like lithodora, belongs to the for-get-me-not family. Fortunately it has a common name – blue-eyed mary – which is less of a tongue-twister than the Latin one. Suitable for the rock garden or the front of a border, this early-flowering perennial species forms tufts of long-stalked mid-green leaves with open sprays of bright blue flowers. The plant spreads by means of runners. Its slightly larger relative, *O. cappadocica*, is a clump-forming species that carries dense sprays of sky-blue flowers in early summer.

GROWING Plant in spring in peaty soil. Water generously in hot weather and dead-head regularly to prolong flowering.

PROPAGATION Divide and replant in spring or in summer when flowering is over.

VARIETIES The species are reliable. There is a white-flowered variety of *O. verna* named 'Alba'.

POSSIBLE PROBLEMS Generally trouble-free.

▨ PLANTING TIP

This plant definitely needs an acid soil. If your soil is alkaline, provide a special pocket in the rock garden or wall and fill with a peat mixture before planting.

▨ PLANTING TIP

Although this is described as an alpine, O. verna and O. cappadocica both do well in moist, shady woodland conditions, rather than in the dry, full sun conditions of a rock garden. O. luciliae is best kept in a conservatory or greenhouse as it is tender, and very prone to slug attacks.

PHACELIA

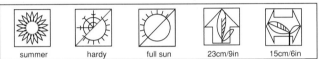

| summer | hardy | full sun | 23cm/9in | 15cm/6in |

Phacelia campanularia, or California bluebell, is an annual plant whose bright blue, bell-shaped flowers bloom all summer and are attractive to bees. The dark green, rounded leaves are fragrant when crushed. Annuals are useful in the rock garden for introducing a change of colour for one season, or for filling a gap if a perennial becomes exhausted. This species is also good at the front of a border. There are no named varieties.

GROWING Well-drained, well-cultivated sandy soil is best, in a sunny situation.

PROPAGATION Sow seeds in shallow soil in spring, directly in the flowering site. Autumn-sown seedlings need protection over winter but produce earlier-flowering plants.

POSSIBLE PROBLEMS Slugs may damage seedlings.

PLATYCODON

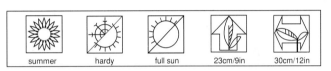

| summer | hardy | full sun | 23cm/9in | 30cm/12in |

Platycodon grandiflorum is a perennial member of the bell flower family. Because of the curious inflated form of its flowerbuds it is commonly called balloon flower. These 'balloons' open to become bells of blue or white. The compact species best for rock gardens is *P. g. mariesii,* with deep blue flowers 5cm/2in across. There are no named varieties.

GROWING Plant in late autumn or early spring in well-drained soil in a sunny position. Balloon flowers are slow to establish themselves and dislike disturbance. It is a good idea to mark the site so that the roots are not inadvertently damaged when top growth has died down.

PROPAGATION Divide mature (4-year-old) plants in spring and replant, handling the roots carefully. Raising from seed is more reliable. Sow seeds in spring in shallow drills in a nursery bed. Transplant to the flowering site when the seedlings are large enough to handle but before the fleshy roots have formed.

POSSIBLE PROBLEMS Generally trouble-free.

ORGANIC TIP

Alpines generally have little value in an organic garden, but the bell-shaped flowers of this plant will be sure to attract bees and other nectar-loving insects.

SPECIAL CARE TIP

Alpines rarely need any fertilizer or special feeding. Only feed plants if they look as if they have stopped growing completely, after a few years. The best *way to feed is to give a light dusting of blood, fish and bone, which can be lightly watered in.*

ARABIS

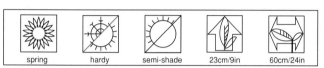

| spring | hardy | semi-shade | 23cm/9in | 60cm/24in |

Of the large number of species bearing the name, only one arabis, *A. albida* (syn. *A. caucasica*) is suitable for the rock garden. A perennial, it forms a cushion of grey-green, oval leaves covered in white flowers 1cm/½in wide from early spring to summer. The species is an invasive plant which cannot be allowed to range unchecked over the rock garden, but, in partnership with alyssum and aubrieta, can look wonderful scrambling over a dry wall or bank. Named varieties are recommended for the rock garden proper.

GROWING Plant in well-drained soil in autumn or spring. The stems can be pegged down for the sake of neatness; cut back hard after flowering to remove faded flower stems.

PROPAGATION Lift, divide and replant in autumn.

VARIETIES 'Flore-Pleno', double, white; 'Snowflake', large, single flowers, white; 'Corfe Castle', deep magenta.

POSSIBLE PROBLEMS Gall midge larvae on young growth; white blister, club root.

CERASTIUM

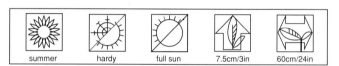

| summer | hardy | full sun | 7.5cm/3in | 60cm/24in |

Although the daisy-like white flowers are charming, cerastiums are chiefly valued for their dense, silvery foliage. The common name, snow-in-summer, is very apt, as these perennial plants form a thick white carpet over the ground. Some species are invasive, others nothing but weeds. Take care to obtain those recommended.

GROWING Plant in spring or early autumn in poor, well-drained soil in a sunny position. A south-facing bank is ideal. Protect the foliage from damp in winter with a pane of glass.

PROPAGATION Divide established plants in summer and replant immediately.

SPECIES *Cerastium tomentosum* (*above*) is pretty but invasive; the form *C. t. columnae* is neater and can be contained; *C. alpinum* can be recommended at 10cm/4in high, spreading only 23cm/9in and flowering all summer. A good late-flowering species is *C. pyrenaicum*, with tufted green leaves.

POSSIBLE PROBLEMS Generally trouble-free.

PLANTING TIP

Where there is no space for a rock garden proper, you can still grow trailing alpines such as arabis either by constructing a small two-level plot or by making a scree bed as an edging to a border or path. The bed is paved to form a box with sides about 25cm/10in high and a concrete base filled with peat and sand.

PLANTING TIP

This is the ideal carpeting, or ground cover plant, as it will smother any weeds around it. Although it is an alpine, avoid planting in the rock garden as even the less invasive variety will spread too much to keep under control.

LEONTOPODIUM

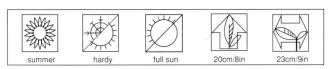

| summer | hardy | full sun | 20cm/8in | 23cm/9in |

Leontopodium alpinum, better known as edelweiss, is a perennial member of the daisy family which grows in alpine meadows
throughout Europe. It forms attractive clumps with woolly,
grey-green leaves and white 'flowers' (actually bracts) in
summer.

GROWING Plant in spring in well-drained, preferably sandy
soil, on an open sunny site.

PROPAGATION Edelweiss are easy to raise from seed. Sow in
early spring in boxes of a potting compost/grit mixture and
place in a cold frame. Prick off the seedlings into boxes when
they are large enough to handle and then into individual pots.
Keep in the cold frame until planting out the following spring.

VARIETIES The species is reliable. 'Mignon' is a good dwarf
form at 10cm/4in high.

POSSIBLE PROBLEMS Generally trouble-free.

NIEREMBERGIA

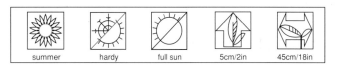

| summer | hardy | full sun | 5cm/2in | 45cm/18in |

Nierembergia repens is a member of the nightshade family, a
perennial from South America which forms a mat of rooting
stems. White flowers 2.5cm/1in wide with golden stamens are
borne in mid summer. Sometimes the petals have a rosy tinge.
There are no named varieties.

GROWING Plant in spring in moisture-retentive soil in a sunny
position.

PROPAGATION Divide in spring and replant immediately.

POSSIBLE PROBLEMS Generally trouble-free.

SPECIAL CARE TIP

*In the wild, alpines are pro-
tected by snow in winter. In
damper winter conditions,
protect plants with a small
plastic or glass housing to
keep off heavy rain.*

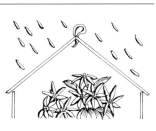

ORGANIC TIP

*Weeding alpines in a rock
garden can be a chore, as it
is so fiddly. Keep down
weeds by covering any soil
between plants with coarse
grit or ornamental stones.*

SANTOLINA

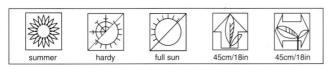

| summer | hardy | full sun | 45cm/18in | 45cm/18in |

Clumps of cotton lavender, studded with button-shaped yellow flowers, add height to the miniature landscape of the rock garden and look splendid in sunny borders. The fern-like silver foliage of this dwarf shrub is aromatic.

GROWING Plant container-grown plants at any time when the weather is favourable, but preferably in spring or autumn. Remove flower stems when they have faded. Cut back hard in spring to keep the plants compact.

PROPAGATION Take half-ripe cuttings 5-7.5cm/2-3in long in summer and insert in a peat/sand mixture in a cold frame. Pot up the following spring and harden off before planting out in autumn.

SPECIES *S. chamaecyparissus* (syn. *S. incana*) forms a compact mound, lemon-yellow flowers; *S. rosmarinifolia* (syn. *S. virens, above*), taller at 60cm/24in, spreads to 90cm/3ft, emerald green thread-like leaves, bright yellow flowers.

POSSIBLE PROBLEMS Generally trouble-free.

JUNIPERUS

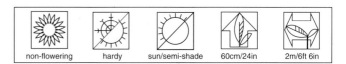

| non-flowering | hardy | sun/semi-shade | 60cm/24in | 2m/6ft 6in |

Juniper trees may be divided broadly into those that are columnar in form and those that are spreading, though there are variations. The leaves are usually needle-shaped when young, scale-like in maturity. They may be green, grey-green or blue; all are slow-growing. Some species bear fruits (berries or cones). Junipers make good focal points in a formal rock garden.

GROWING Plant seedlings in late spring, on well-drained soil in full sun or light shade.

PROPAGATION Take heeled cuttings 7.5cm/3in long in autumn and insert in a peat/sand mixture in a cold frame until rooted. Pot up individually and place outdoors or grow on in a nursery bed. Plant out after two years.

VARIETIES *Juniperus sabina* 'Tamariscifolia' (Spanish juniper); the bright green needle-like leaves release an aromatic oil if bruised; dense, prostrate habit, the stems building up in layers; prune to limit size. *J. communis* 'Compressa', dwarf form of the Irish juniper at 60cm/24in high, columnar, grey-blue foliage; best in groups of 3 or 5, no pruning. *J. virginiana* 'Globosa', dwarf rounded bush, 90cm × 90cm/3 × 3ft, pale green foliage, no pruning.

POSSIBLE PROBLEMS Scale insects; rust.

■ PLANTING TIP

A sunny, well-drained site is essential for this low-growing shrub. The rock garden is the ideal place for it, but if it is planted in a border, keep it to the front, and ensure that the soil is not heavy or waterlogged. If necessary, dig in some gravel and compost before planting, to improve drainage conditions.

■ PLANTING TIP

The compact size and columnar shape of this dwarf variety makes it ideal for patio or balcony containers, where it will provide all-year colour.

ALYSSUM

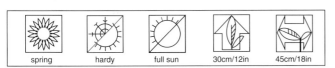

spring	hardy	full sun	30cm/12in	45cm/18in

Thanks to the brightness of its profuse yellow flowers, *Alyssum saxatile* (*above*) has an impact out of proportion to its diminutive size. This popular perennial, commonly known as gold-dust, is a shrubby plant with narrow, pointed, grey-green leaves. It carries its tiny blooms into the first weeks of summer. For a continuation of colour, plant with *A. argenteum*, which blooms all summer.

GROWING Plant between autumn and spring on light, free-draining soil. Over-rich soils are unsuitable. Cut back hard after flowering for sturdy growth and to keep the shape neat.

PROPAGATION Take 5cm/2in cuttings in early summer and insert in a peat/sand mixture in a cold frame until rooted. Pot up individually and grow on in the frame. Plant out the following spring.

VARIETIES 'Citrinum', sharp yellow; 'Compactum', neat, half the height of the species; 'Plenum' syn. 'Flore-Pleno', double golden-yellow flowers; 'Dudley Neville', dull gold.

POSSIBLE PROBLEMS Slugs may eat young plants; downy mildew on leaves.

CORYDALIS

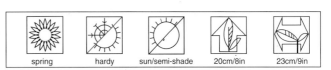

spring	hardy	sun/semi-shade	20cm/8in	23cm/9in

Corydalis lutea is the common yellow fumitory often found growing wild on old walls. More garden-worthy are *C. cheilanthifolia* (*above*) and *C. cashmeriana*. The former shares with its wild cousin a tendency to self-seed, which in the less formal settings which it suits may not be a problem. The fern-like foliage is slightly bronzed, arranged in tufts from which rise dense racemes of long-lasting yellow flowers. There are no named varieties. The species *C. cashmeriana* is a fussier plant, requiring cool, humid conditions, but its beautiful blue flowers make it well worth growing in areas where the climate is suitable.

GROWING Plant in spring on any good garden soil. *C. cashmeriana* must have cool, peat, totally lime-free soil.

PROPAGATION Self-sown seedlings of *C. cheilanthifolia* do well. Corydalis may be increased by careful division of the delicate tubers in early autumn. Replant immediately.

POSSIBLE PROBLEMS Generally trouble-free.

■ PLANTING TIP

With its tiny, bright flowers, this is the ideal plant where space is limited – plant in hanging baskets, tubs or containers. Some forms bloom all summer.

■ SPECIAL CARE TIP

The Himalayan version of this plant may prove difficult to grow as it likes a cool situation in a totally peat soil. Plant in a shady corner of the rockery, or on a shaded wall, in a specially made 'pocket' filled with peat.

PRIMULA

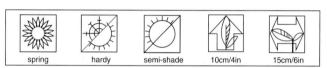

| spring | hardy | semi-shade | 10cm/4in | 15cm/6in |

For a cool, semi-shaded position, there are few alpine plants to better the diminutive species primulas. With primrose-like flowers in subtle shades of pink and lilac as well as white, these hardy perennials also look attractive in old stone troughs.

GROWING Plant between autumn and spring in well-drained, humus-rich, gritty soil. Species vary in their precise requirements.

PROPAGATION Divide after flowering and replant immediately. *Primula auricula* may be raised from 2.5cm/1in cuttings taken in summer.

SPECIES *P. frondosa* (*above*), rosette of grey-green leaves, each flower stem bearing up to 30 rose-pink flowers, needs a moist position; *P. clarkei*, only 5cm/2in high, bright pink flowers 1cm/⅜in across appear while the pale green leaves are unfolding; *P. reidii*, unusual bell-shaped flowers, white, fragrant, late spring; *P.r.* 'Williamsii' bears blue, more fragrant flowers; *P. auricula*, 15cm/6in high, umbels of long-lived yellow or purple flowers. Several fine varieties available including 'The Mikado', dark red, and 'Blue Fire'. *P. juliae*, low-growing, reddish-purple flowers; numerous excellent varieties including 'Snow Cushion', white, dwarf; 'Wanda', wine-red, flowers mid-winter; 'Our Pat', double dark crimson flowers.

POSSIBLE PROBLEMS Virus diseases, grey mould, rot.

ARMERIA

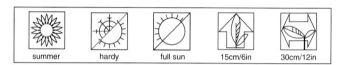

| summer | hardy | full sun | 15cm/6in | 30cm/12in |

Armeria maritima or sea thrift (*above*) is a familiar wild plant of coastal areas from which a number of attractive garden varieties have been developed. The perennial plants make neat hummocks and the long-lasting flower-heads – like pinks in form and usually pink in colour – are carried high on slender stems. The species *A. caespitosa*, by contrast, bears almost stemless flowers.

GROWING Plant between autumn and spring in well-drained soil in full sun. Snip off flower-heads as they fade.

PROPAGATION Lift, divide and replant in spring.

VARIETIES *A. maritima*: 'Alba', white; 'Vindictive', deep rose-red; 'Merlin', deep pink. *A. caespitosa*: 'Bevan's Variety', deep pink.

POSSIBLE PROBLEMS Rust.

■ SPECIAL CARE TIP

Alpine primulas are best given a layer of grit around their collars to prevent water collecting in the rosettes. As with other rosette-forming alpines, they should be protected from too much rain in winter by means of mini-cloches.

■ PLANTING TIP

An ideal sun-loving plant for the small rock garden. It will cope with a windy site even in seaside gardens. It can also be grown at the edge of tubs or between paving stones, where it will produce attractive hummocks of spiky, grass-like leaves.

ERINUS

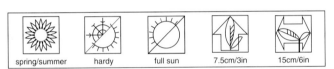

spring/summer	hardy	full sun	7.5cm/3in	15cm/6in

Erinus alpinus is one of those cheerful perennial plants that commends itself to the gardener by giving great rewards in return for almost no attention. Once established in a sunny position on the rock garden or a dry wall, it flowers for weeks, self-seeds freely to produce new plants after its short life is done, and as an evergreen gives year-round cover. The tiny, star-shaped flowers are bright pink.

GROWING Plant out seedlings in spring, in well-drained, poor soil in a sunny position. Trim lightly after flowering.

PROPAGATION Scatter the seed in spring where it is to grow. Most named forms come true.

VARIETIES 'Albus', white; 'Dr Hanaele', crimson; 'Mrs Charles Boyle', coral pink.

POSSIBLE PROBLEMS Generally trouble-free.

HELIANTHEMUM

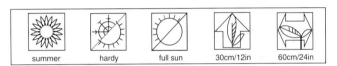

summer	hardy	full sun	30cm/12in	60cm/24in

There are several species of helianthemum available, but it is *H. nummularium* which has earned the name rock rose. This perennial forms dense mounds of small green or grey leaves and bears numerous yellow saucer-shaped flowers 2.5cm/1in across in early summer. The petals are papery, like those of poppies. *H. alpestre* is a more compact species, *H. apenninum* rather larger.

GROWING Plant in autumn or spring in light, well-drained soil. The rock rose should be cut right back after flowering to keep it neat; all species respond to trimming by flowering a second time in autumn.

PROPAGATION Take 2.5cm/1in cuttings of non-flowering side shoots in mid summer. Place in pots of a peat/sand mixture in a cold frame until rooted. Pot up individually in potting compost and overwinter in the frame. Pinch out the growing tips. Plant out in spring.

VARIETIES *H. nummularium*: 'Ben Heckla', copper; 'Ben Afflick', orange and buff; 'Wisley Pink' *(above)*, rose-pink; 'Cerise Queen', rose-red; 'The Bride', white; 'Beech Park Scarlet', red. *H. apenninum*: 'Roseum', rose red. *H. alpestre*: 'Serpyllifolium', very low growing at 5-7.5cm/2-3in.

POSSIBLE PROBLEMS In hot conditions powdery mildew may occur.

■ SPECIAL CARE TIP

Ideal for planting in a bare wall, where it will give all-year-round cover. Wrap the roots in a piece of old turf soaked in water, and push firmly into a prepared hole.

■ PLANTING TIP

Ideal for a site where you want quick growth and colour, this plant will provide a multitude of attractive yellow flowers. It is excellent for dry walls.

GENTIANA

autumn	hardy	semi-shade	15cm/6in	30cm/12in

A number of gentians are in cultivation, with widely varying requirements and flowering times. Broadly speaking, these perennials are divided into European species, which are spring-flowering, and the Asiatic species described here which flower in the autumn. The flowers are large, trumpet-shaped and of a uniquely intense blue. They are among the most distinguished alpine plants.

GROWING Plant out in spring, in deep soil previously enriched with leaf-mould or peat. Do not let the soil dry out. Always check the lime-tolerance of individual species.

PROPAGATION Lift, divide and replant in spring. All species may be raised from cuttings taken from the basal shoots in spring and treated as for helianthemums.

SPECIES *Gentiana sino-ornata (above)*, easy to grow in acid soil, abundant 5cm/2in long deep blue flowers striped purplish blue, a much admired species; *G. farreri*, lime-tolerant, clear light blue flowers with white throats from late summer; *G. ×* 'Stevenagensis', strong-growing prostrate hybrid, deep purple blue, late summer.

POSSIBLE PROBLEMS Root rot on poorly drained soil.

LEWISIA

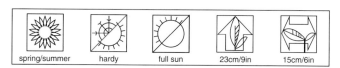

spring/summer	hardy	full sun	23cm/9in	15cm/6in

Lewisias are semi-succulent perennials. Those described here are reliably hardy, but there are other fine species which need the protection of an alpine house. Native to North America, the pink flowers rise on erect stems from rosette-forming fleshy mid-green leaves. *Lewisia cotyledon* is a variable species which has given rise to many named forms of varying colours, bearing masses of daisy-like flowers in late spring.

GROWING Plant in spring, placing the rosettes at an angle to prevent water collecting in the centre. Set in rich, gritty soil and place a collar of gravel around the neck of the plants to assist drainage. Water regularly, but give less in the winter.

PROPAGATION Remove offsets in summer and insert in boxes of a sand/peat mixture in a cold frame until rooted. Pot up individually in compost, overwinter in the frame and plant out in spring.

VARIETIES *L. c. heckneri (above)*, toothed leaves, deep pink striped flowers; *L. c. howelli*, narrow leaves, rose-pink flowers. Many good named hybrids include 'George Henley', terracotta; 'Sunset Strain', mixed colours, including orange and yellow.

POSSIBLE PROBLEMS Excessive moisture causes collar rot.

▮ PLANTING TIP

The ideal plant if you have a moist, peaty soil: if not, you will need to provide a special peat-filled pocket in the rock garden and ensure that it does not dry out.

▮ SPECIAL CARE TIP

Another alpine which needs winter protection from rain, as water collects in the rosettes and causes rot. A sheet of glass, supported on wire legs, will do the trick.

PULSATILLA

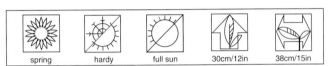

spring	hardy	full sun	30cm/12in	38cm/15in

Closely related to anemones, pulsatillas are perennials native to European mountain regions. Two species are suitable for rock gardens. *P. vulgaris* is known as the pasque flower. It is easy to grow and bears large purple flowers surrounded by a frill of fine, hairy leaves. The foliage is delicate and fern-like. *P. alpina* bears long-lasting white flowers flushed blue on the outside, followed by fluffy silver seedheads. Once established, both species are long-lived.

GROWING Plant in autumn in an open, sunny site on alkaline, free-draining soil. Do not disturb the plants thereafter.

PROPAGATION Sow fresh seed in summer in trays of seed compost in a cold frame. When the seedlings are large enough to handle, prick off into boxes and overwinter in the frame. Pot up individually when new leaves appear in spring. Water well as the plants develop and plant out in autumn.

VARIETIES *P. vulgaris*: 'Rubra' *(above)*, glowing red; 'Budapest', reddish-purple. *P. alpina*: 'Sulphurea', sharp yellow flowers last until mid summer.

POSSIBLE PROBLEMS Generally trouble-free.

SAXIFRAGA

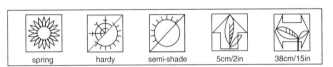

spring	hardy	semi-shade	5cm/2in	38cm/15in

The saxifrage family is large and complex, but all of its members are suitable for the rock garden. Certain types have rosettes of silvery or grey-green leaves that grow in hummocks or form mats; others are known as moss saxifrage because of the appearance of their densely packed leaves. The flowers may be star- or saucer-shaped, yellow, white, pink or red and are very freely borne. The species described here is the best-known mossy type, *S. moschata*.

GROWING Plant out in autumn or spring in any good garden soil in a shady site.

PROPAGATION After flowering, lift, divide and replant immediately. Alternatively, detach non-flowering rosettes in early summer, place in pans of a peat/sand mixture in a cold frame and water generously. Thereafter water sparingly until the following spring; water well over the summer, pot up individually in the autumn and plant out the following spring.

VARIETIES 'Dubarry' *(above)*, 15cm/6in high, deep red flowers; 'Peter Pan', hybrid, pink flowers on red stems, bright green leaves; 'Cloth of Gold', bright yellow leaves, white flowers.

POSSIBLE PROBLEMS Grubs and root aphids may attack the roots.

■ SPECIAL CARE TIP

This plant, with its beautiful violet flowers, thrives in full sun and in alkaline soil, but does not like to be disturbed after being established.

Its native habitat is mountainous, so its ideal position is in a rockery. Failing that, plant in an open position in a well-drained border.

■ PLANTING TIP

As with all rock plants, it is important to ensure that they have an open, sunny site well away from surface-rooting trees such as poplars or silver birch. If

the garden is small, or trees are established, it may be necessary to grow the plants in containers, raised above the ground and sited away from the trees.

ERODIUM

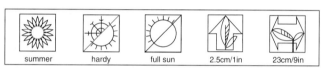

| summer | hardy | full sun | 2.5cm/1in | 23cm/9in |

Erodiums bear a close resemblance to their cousins the true geraniums or cranesbills. These are compact perennials, however, forming tufts or mats of small mid-green leaves studded with pink, white, or yellow flowers. They bloom throughout the summer.

GROWING Plant in spring in a sunny, sheltered position on well-drained, poor soil, preferably on the limy side.

PROPAGATION Take 5cm/2in basal cuttings in spring and insert in a peat/sand mixture in a cold frame. Plant out in the autumn or – after overwintering in the cold frame – the following spring. *E. chamaedryoides* must be increased by root cuttings taken in early spring. Treat as basal cuttings, potting them up when 3-4 leaves have formed, and plant out in the spring.

SPECIES *E. chrysanthum*, reaches 15cm/6in, silvery fern-like-leaves, sprays of acid yellow flowers; *E. chamaedryoides*, mat-forming, pink-veined white flowers; the variety 'Roseum' *(above)* bears clear pink flowers in late spring; *E. corsicum*, pink flowers in late spring, downy, soft leaves need protection from winter damp.

POSSIBLE PROBLEMS Generally trouble-free.

GERANIUM

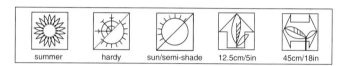

| summer | hardy | sun/semi-shade | 12.5cm/5in | 45cm/18in |

The large group of true geraniums or cranesbills includes several species indispensable to the rock garden. Flowers may be pink, lilac or white and the attractive leaves form dense ground cover.

GROWING Plant in autumn or spring in well-drained soil in sun or partial shade. After flowering, cut back stems to ground level to keep the shape neat and encourage a second flush of flowers.

PROPAGATION Lift, divide and replant between autumn and spring.

SPECIES *G. dalmaticum (above)* forms cushions of foliage flushed orange in the autumn, pale pink flowers; *G. ×* 'Ballerina', strong-growing hybrid, grey-green leaves, pink flowers veined red; *G. napuligerum*, slow-growing, suitable for a rocky bank, pink flowers – 'Album' is a white variety; *G. pylzowianum*, best ground cover plant for rock gardens, 7.5cm/3in high, relatively few pink flowers; *G. renardii*, clump-forming, with large lavender flowers veined purple; *G. subcaulescens*, bright crimson flowers in profusion from spring to autumn – the hybrid 'Russell Prichard' makes excellent ground cover with grey-green leaves and large, rich pink flowers.

POSSIBLE PROBLEMS Slugs eat young plants; rust on leaves.

▦ SPECIAL CARE TIP

This plant is native to the Mediterranean, so it is obviously a sun lover, well suited to a sunny, open position in the rock garden. Avoid too rich or acid soil – ideally the soil should be on the poor side – and make sure it is well drained.

▦ ORGANIC TIP

Deter slugs by mulching young plants with pine bark. You can also sink a small container into the ground and fill it with beer; the slugs fall in and drown.

SAPONARIA

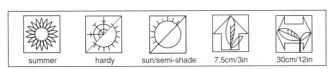

| summer | hardy | sun/semi-shade | 7.5cm/3in | 30cm/12in |

The common name of *Saponaria officinalis* – soapwort – gives the hint to its former use as a cleansing herb (the leaves produce a lather in water). This species is too large and invasive for the rock garden, however; *S. ocymoides (above)* is the one to choose, a vigorous perennial which forms trailing mats of small green leaves. Throughout the summer it bears a profusion of bright pink flowers.

GROWING Plant between autumn and spring in good garden soil in sun or partial shade. Cut back after flowering to encourage further blooms and cut back hard in late autumn.

PROPAGATION Divide and replant the roots or detach underground runners and replant between autumn and spring.

VARIETIES 'Compacta', slow-growing, neat habit; 'Rubra Compacta', rich pink flowers.

POSSIBLE PROBLEMS Generally trouble-free.

SILENE

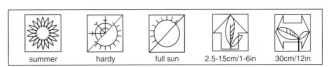

| summer | hardy | full sun | 2.5-15cm/1-6in | 30cm/12in |

Silenes, members of the carnation family, are commonly known as campions. Two perennial species are suitable for the rock garden; both are spreading plants bearing delicate pink flowers throughout the summer.

GROWING Plant in autumn or spring in well-drained soil on a sunny site.

PROPAGATION Take 4cm/1½in cuttings of healthy outer shoots in summer. Place in a peat/sand mixture in a cold frame until rooted. Pot up individually in compost, overwinter in the frame and plant out the following autumn. Silenes resent root disturbance.

SPECIES *S. acaulis* (moss campion or cushion pink, *above*), prostrate, tightly packed tiny leaves, may be slow to flower; *S. schafta*, easy to grow, reaches 15cm/6in high, deep pink flowers; tolerates some shade.

POSSIBLE PROBLEMS Generally trouble-free.

▪ PLANTING TIP

Rock gardens should always be open and in full sun, well away from any overhanging trees – dripping trees will soon destroy your plants.

However, saponaria will tolerate partial shade, or dappled sunlight. Plant in a container in a small garden or in the partial shade of a wall.

▪ PLANTING TIP

Prostrate alpines look charming planted in cracks in patios or in crazy paving, or between slabs of a path. Fill the gaps with a peat mixture before planting.

93

IBERIS

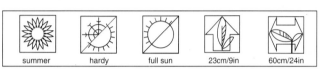

summer	hardy	full sun	23cm/9in	60cm/24in

There are three species of sub-shrubby perennial iberis, commonly called candytuft, suitable for the rock garden. All have dark green narrow leaves and bear numerous heads of densely packed flowers of white or lilac over a long period. As they are tolerant of polluted atmospheres iberis are a good choice for town gardens.

GROWING Plant between autumn and spring in any well-drained garden soil. They thrive on poor soils.

PROPAGATION Take 5cm/2in softwood cuttings of non-flowering shoots in summer. Place in a cold frame in a peat/sand mixture until rooted. Pot up individually and overwinter in the frame, setting out the young plants the following spring.

SPECIES *Iberis gibraltarica*, semi-evergreen, not fully hardy but self-seeds freely, lilac flowers in spring; *I. saxatilis*, only 7.5cm/3in high, spread 30cm/12in, neat form, white flowers spring to summer; *I. sempervirens*, variable in form. The variety 'Little Gem' *(above)*, with white flowers, is neat at 10cm/4in high, spread 23cm/9in; 'Snowflake' has pure white flowers and is more spreading in habit.

POSSIBLE PROBLEMS Flea beetles may puncture the leaves.

SISYRINCHIUM

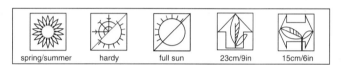

spring/summer	hardy	full sun	23cm/9in	15cm/6in

Sisyrinchiums are handsome members of the iris family. Their erect flower spikes, clothed with star-shaped flowers of violet, blue or yellow, are useful for bringing height to a rock garden design. The fresh green leaves are long and narrow. Different species are in flower from spring through to autumn.

GROWING Plant between spring and autumn on well-drained soil into which plenty of peat or leaf-mould has been incorporated. Choose a site where the plants will not be disturbed. In autumn remove the dead leaves and stems.

PROPAGATION Species come true from seeds, which will germinate where they fall if the ground is undisturbed. Alternatively lift, divide, and replant in autumn or spring.

SPECIES *S. striatum (above)*, reaches 45cm/18in, innumerable creamy-yellow flowers in mid summer; *S. angustifolium*, clumps of grassy leaves, violet flowers right through summer; *S. grandiflorum*, bell-shaped purple flowers in early spring; plant in close groups for best effect.

POSSIBLE PROBLEMS Generally trouble-free.

▉ PLANTING TIP

The perfect plant for poor soil or a problem site such as a hot, dry wall. This vigorous, trailing plant also thrives in a rock garden or on a dry, sunny bank.

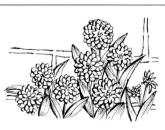

▉ SPECIAL CARE TIP

These flowers, members of the iris family, are native to Bermuda and Chile, so they need full sun and a sheltered position. In cooler areas of the world, they are better grown in containers. They can then be kept in a conservatory or greenhouse and brought out when the temperature is high enough.

SOLDANELLA

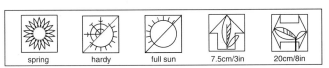

| spring | hardy | full sun | 7.5cm/3in | 20cm/8in |

Soldanellas are members of the primula family. They bear nodding, pale lilac flowers with fringed petals. Rounded mid-green leaves cluster at the foot of the erect stems. Native to European alpine meadows, these modest flowers suit informal planting schemes.

GROWING Plant in autumn or early summer in well-drained soil. A sunny position is preferred but some shade is tolerated. Place a collar of grit around each plant to assist drainage.

PROPAGATION Lift and divide the plants after flowering. Either replant in the permanent positions straight away or pot up in a compost/peat mixture and overwinter in a cold frame, planting out the following spring.

SPECIES *S. alpina (above)*, mat-forming foliage, lavender flowers; *S. montana*, larger, strong-growing species with bell-shaped flowers; *S. minima*, smallest at 5cm/2in high, best choice for ground cover, delicate lilac flowers; *S. villosa*, slightly hairy leaves, lavender flowers tinted deep blue.

POSSIBLE PROBLEMS Slugs may eat young plants.

AETHIONEMA

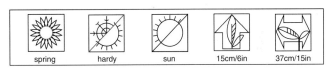

| spring | hardy | sun | 15cm/6in | 37cm/15in |

Aethionemas are evergreen perennials which will respond to a position in the sun with a long-lived display of beautiful pink or white flowers, the thick mat of leaves persisting through the winter.

GROWING Plant in spring in well-drained soil that is not too rich. Dead-head regularly and there may be a second flush of flowers.

PROPAGATION Plants may self-seed, but can be raised from non-flowering softwood cuttings taken in summer. Insert in a peat/sand mixture in a cold frame until rooted. Pot up individually, overwinter in the frame and plant out the following spring.

SPECIES *A.* × 'Warley Rose' *(above)*, the most popular hybrid, with small grey-green pointed leaves, rose-pink flowers; *A. grandiflorum*, height and spread 45cm/18in, deep pink flowerheads 7.5cm/3in long; *A. pulchellum*, 20cm/8in high, numerous rich pink flowers; *A. iberideum*, blue-green leaves, profuse white flowers.

POSSIBLE PROBLEMS Generally trouble-free.

▓ SPECIAL CARE TIP

Soldanellas are native to the Alps and Pyrenees, so conditions must be similar. The ideal situation is either in a coolish rock garden – possibly with some shade – or in a peat garden. You must protect plants against excessive moisture in winter with a mini-cloche or piece of glass.

▓ SPECIAL CARE TIP

This beautiful plant is no trouble given a well-drained site with lime-free soil. If necessary, provide a container and fill with a special peat mixture.

SHRUBS

Shrubs give the garden an established appearance, forming the main framework of most planting schemes around which perennials, annuals and bulbs are grouped.

As in all garden schemes, the principle behind choosing and siting shrubs is balance, for example between evergreen and deciduous species. Although all the shrubs in this chapter have been selected for their flowers, there is no denying the importance of foliage. An equally important factor is the season of interest. In a large garden with numerous shrubs you can include some specially for each season; in a smaller space with room for only two or three, it is a good idea to go for those that have something to offer all year, or at least at more than one time. *Mahonia aquifolium* 'Atropurpurea', for example, is an evergreen which flowers in mid winter, bears berries in spring and summer, and whose foliage turns a lovely red in autumn. Other worthwhile evergreens include camellia, *Ceanothus impressus*,

choisya, *Erica carnea*, pieris and many rhododendrons.

Spring-flowering shrubs are particularly useful at a time when most of the colour in the garden is at ground level, provided by swathes of bulbs. Try to limit the number of yellow-flowering spring shrubs, as there is likely to be a strong yellow element anyway at this time. For white, pink and red, try *Magnolia stellata*, rhododendrons and azaleas, enkianthus, choisya, pieris and chaenomeles.

It is a characteristic of the modern border that shrubs are included to add height and texture to the display. In summer, old roses, potentillas, fuchsias and spiraeas combine particularly well with other plants. Climbers at the back of the border complete the picture, whether against a fine old wall or a wooden fence. It is difficult to make a choice between such delectable species as clematis, climbing roses and honeysuckles (*Lonicera* species). Because many honeysuckles are fragrant they are often planted against the wall of the house, next to a window so that the scent will waft inside. Other scented shrubs are philadelphus, choisya, lavender and lilac.

Increasing emphasis on winter colour in the garden has put the focus on shrubs such as *Chimonanthus praecox* (winter sweet) and *Jasminum nudiflorum* (winter-flowering jasmine), two yellow-flowering species. The viburnums *V. tinus* and *V. farreri* both bear white flowers during the winter; consider too the little-known honeysuckle *Lonicera × purpusii*, which bears small, scented, cream flowers for many weeks in the middle of winter. For cold-weather glamour, nothing can outclass the camellia, with its huge red, pink or white flowers.

PLANTING SHRUBS Like trees, shrubs are sold bare-rooted, with a ball of soil around the roots, or in containers. Those in containers can be planted at any time of year as long as the soil is not allowed to dry out. Bare-rooted and balled-root shrubs should be planted between autumn and spring (see individual entries for variations). Cut off any damaged roots from bare-rooted specimens. Plants in

containers should be well-watered before planting.

1 Take out a planting hole to a depth such that the old soil mark on the stem, or, on a container-grown plant, the base of the stem, will be level with the soil. Fork over the soil at the bottom of the hole.

2 Mix the soil from the hole with half its volume of well-rotted compost, manure or peat.

3 Remove the plant from the container and place it in the hole. Do not remove sacking from a balled-root shrub until you have placed it in the hole. Holding the shrub by its stem, replace the soil in the hole, tread it down and top up with more soil. Tread the soil down again and water in generously.

4 When planting a bare-rooted shrub, spread the roots out and lift the shrub up and down a few times to make sure the soil settles around them.

PLANTING CLIMBERS Some climbers are self-clinging and need no supports; where supports are required, it is

The summer-flowering Deutzia × rosea is a rewarding shrub which, when pruned effectively, will produce an abundance of blossom.

essential to put them securely in place before planting. Wide-gauge plastic netting is suitable for a wide range of plants and soft enough not to damage delicate stems. A system of horizontal wires is efficient and inconspicuous. Whichever you use, mount the mesh or wires on battens to keep them at least 2.5cm/1in clear of the wall so that air can circulate. Start training the climber to the supports as soon as its tendrils become long enough to encourage it to grow in the desired direction.

When planting, follow the instructions for shrubs, but remember that because soil at the foot of a wall or fence is relatively dry, you need to give it a good soaking the day before planting and keep it moist afterwards. Do not set the plant too close to the wall or it will not benefit from rain – 30cm/12in is the correct distance.

FORSYTHIA

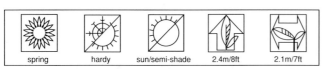

| spring | hardy | sun/semi-shade | 2.4m/8ft | 2.1m/7ft |

Forsythia is an easily grown shrub whose brilliant yellow flowers appear before the foliage. It is very successful in town gardens. *Forsythia suspensa* is suitable as a wall shrub for any aspect, while *F. × intermedia* is the best choice for hedging.

GROWING Plant from autumn to spring in any moderately fertile soil in sun or partial shade. *F. × intermedia* grown as a hedge should be planted in autumn. Set 45cm/18in high plants 45cm/18in apart. Cut back all shoots by one-third after planting. Pinch out the growing tips at 15cm/6in. Clip established hedges lightly in spring after flowering. Prune all species in spring to neaten and to clear damaged wood.

PROPAGATION Take 30cm/12in cuttings of the current season's growth in autumn and insert in a nursery bed outdoors for planting out one year later. The drooping branches of *F. suspensa* sometimes take root where they touch the ground. Separate the rooted layers in autumn and treat as cuttings.

SPECIES *F. × intermedia (above)*, hybrid form bearing abundant flowers on stiff branches. 'Spectabilis' is the most common variety, compact in shape with vivid flowers; *F. suspensa*, rambling habit, may exceed 3 x 3m/10 x 10ft on a wall. *F. s. sieboldii* has trailing stems.

POSSIBLE PROBLEMS Birds eat flowerbuds; honey fungus can kill plants.

CYTISUS

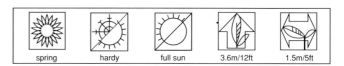

| spring | hardy | full sun | 3.6m/12ft | 1.5m/5ft |

Brooms are handsome shrubs, including both deciduous and evergreen species. All flower profusely in spring and early summer, with small cream, yellow, red or multi-coloured blooms of the pea-flower form. They are short-lived (particularly on limy soils) but easily propagated plants.

GROWING Set out young pot-grown plants in autumn or spring in well-drained, rather poor soil. Full sun is important. Prune species which flower on the previous season's shoots directly after flowering – remove two-thirds of all growth. Cut back those which flower on the current season's shoots just before flowering if necessary to maintain a compact shape.

PROPAGATION Raise species from seed sown in spring in pans in a cold frame. Pot on when the seedlings are large enough to handle and set outdoors. Plant out in the autumn. Raise named varieties from 10cm/4in cuttings taken in early autumn (see page 16).

SPECIES *Cytisus × praecox* (Warminster broom, *above*), hybrid, arching stems covered with pale yellow flowers; 'Allgold' has acid-yellow blooms. *C. scoparius* (common broom), early summer-flowering, upright habit. Good named varieties include 'Burkwoodii', crimson; 'Cornish Cream', cream and white, 'Goldfinch', purple, red and yellow.

POSSIBLE PROBLEMS Stems may be disfigured by gall mites.

▇ PLANTING TIP

Can be planted as informal hedging and clipped to keep in shape. Prune flowering shoots immediately after flowering to control the growth.

▇ PLANTING TIP

A good shrub for difficult positions: it will tolerate a hot, dry spot (such as against a sunny wall) that would kill off more tender shrubs.

CHIMONANTHUS

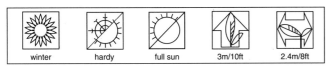

winter	hardy	full sun	3m/10ft	2.4m/8ft

Chimonanthus praecox, the winter sweet, bears its heavily scented cup-shaped flowers of yellow and purple in the middle of winter on bare twigs. When the leaves appear they are like those of the willow family.

GROWING Set out young plants from autumn to spring in reasonably fertile soil, preferably with the protection of a sunny wall. If trained against a wall, prune hard in spring, cutting flowered shoots right back almost to the base. Those grown as bushes should be pruned after flowering to remove old and overcrowded branches.

PROPAGATION Raise from seed sown in a cold frame in autumn. Pot on when the seedling are large enough to handle and set oudoors. Plant in nursery rows in the autumn and into the permanent site 3 years later. Plants take at least 5 years to reach flowering size. Alternatively, long shoots may be layered *(see page 17)* in the autumn.

VARIETIES The species is sturdy and reliable. Named varieties include 'Lutens', all-yellow flowers, slow to reach maturity; 'Grandiflorus', larger flowers but less fragrant.

POSSIBLE PROBLEMS Generally trouble-free.

JASMINUM

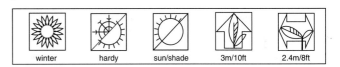

winter	hardy	sun/shade	3m/10ft	2.4m/8ft

The winter-flowering jasmine, *Jasminum nudiflorum*, is a rambler which will bear its bright yellow flowers in almost any situation except one where the buds might be nipped by cold winds. The flowers appear in the axils of the previous season's leaves and are excellent for cutting. There are no named varieties.

GROWING Plant from autumn to spring in any well-drained soil, against a wall or where the plant can clamber over a bank. Provide supports as the branches will need tying in regularly. Prune in early spring: cut out old, weak stems and cut back flowered side shoots to within 7.5cm/3in of the base.

PROPAGATION Layer in autumn *(see page 17)* or take 7.5cm/3in cuttings of semi-ripe wood in late summer. Cut just below a node and place in a peat/sand mixture. Overwinter at 7-10°C/45-50°F. Pot up when rooted and plant out in the autumn.

POSSIBLE PROBLEMS Mealy bugs on soft shoots.

▨ CUT FLOWER TIP

A must for the winter garden – its pretty yellow or lilac flowers will brighten up dark, winter days. The bare, flowering branches will also make very elegant indoor arrangements, and the delicate flowers will scent the whole house with their superb perfume.

▨ PLANTING TIP

Generously spangled with yellow blooms that are produced continuously, this climber will help soften the bare walls of a house, or a patio, when there is little else of colour in the garden. Give it a fence, trellis or netting to cling to, which will also provide protection from strong winds.

SENECIO

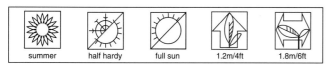

| summer | half hardy | full sun | 1.2m/4ft | 1.8m/6ft |

The best shrubby senecio for most gardens is *Senecio ×* 'Sunshine' *(above)*, sometimes inaccurately listed as *S. greyi* or *S. laxifolius*. Well-suited to coastal gardens, this evergreen has leaves of a beautiful silvery-grey. Though they turn green as the season progresses, the undersides remain silver. Clusters of daisy-like yellow flowers appear in early summer. It is not fully hardy in very severe winters.

GROWING Plant between autumn and spring in free-draining soil. Remove faded flowerheads as soon as you notice them. The minimum amount of pruning is required – simply remove dead or damaged wood in spring.

PROPAGATION Take 7.5cm/3in semi-ripe cuttings of side shoots in late summer. Place in a peat/sand mixture in a cold frame. Transfer the rooted cuttings to a nursery bed in spring or pot up individually and set outdoors. Plant out the following autumn.

POSSIBLE PROBLEMS Aphids.

THUNBERGIA

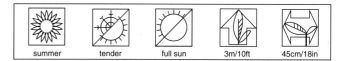

| summer | tender | full sun | 3m/10ft | 45cm/18in |

Native to South Africa, *Thunbergia alata* or black-eyed susan is a twining perennial grown as an annual in less favoured climates. It bears numerous funnel-shaped flowers of deep yellow with a black centre. Black-eyed susan can be grown on a sunny patio in a large pot, trained up a wigwam of canes which it will quickly obscure.

GROWING A position in full sun is essential, with fertile, moist soil. Plant against a wall, fence or post with the support of strings, wires or netting. Water in dry spells and discard after flowering.

PROPAGATION Sow seeds under glass in spring in small individual pots. Harden off and do not plant out until night temperatures exceed 10°C/50°F.

VARIETIES 'Susie', hardier than the species, profusion of yellow, orange and white flowers; 'Alba', white with black eye.

POSSIBLE PROBLEMS Generally trouble-free.

■ CUT FLOWER TIP

The beautiful yellow flowers are a marvellous source of cut flowers; they are also a good source of nectar for butterflies, so be sure to leave some.

■ PLANTING TIP

Remember to prepare the soil well when planting a climber against a wall, as this is likely to be a very dry spot. Make sure the soil is enriched with well-rotted manure or compost, and after planting, fork in some general fertilizer such as fish, blood and bone. Water well and mulch with compost to conserve moisture.

FREMONTIA

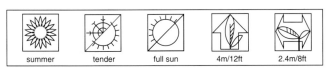

| summer | tender | full sun | 4m/12ft | 2.4m/8ft |

There are two species of fremontias but only one in general cultivation. *Fremontia californica*, as its name suggests, is a native of California (and Mexico). This deciduous shrub, though not a climber, is best grown against a warm sunny wall for protection as it is slightly tender. It should be trained against a trellis. Fabulous cup-shaped waxy yellow flowers, 5cm/2in across, are borne from late spring right through to early autumn.

GROWING Plant container-grown fremontias in autumn or spring in well-drained, sandy soil in full sun. Tie the trunk and main branches into the trellis. No pruning is necessary, but if any shoots are damaged by frost they should be removed in spring.

PROPAGATION Raise from seed sown in pots at 16°C/61°F in spring. Prick off the seedlings into individual pots of compost when they are large enough to handle. Pot on to larger pots (15cm/6in) and plant out the following spring.

VARIETIES *F.* × 'California Glory' *(above)* is a hybrid which is hardier than its parents.

POSSIBLE PROBLEMS Generally trouble-free.

POTENTILLA

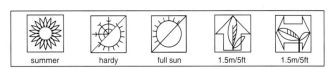

| summer | hardy | full sun | 1.5m/5ft | 1.5m/5ft |

The shrubby cinquefoil, *Potentilla fruticosa*, is a perfect subject for low-maintenance gardens. Totally hardy and requiring virtually no attention if given the correct conditions, it produces five-petalled flowers of yellow, white or orange for the whole summer. There are a number of low-growing varieties which are suitable for ground cover.

GROWING Plant between autumn and spring in light, well-drained soil in full sun. Fewer flowers will be produced in partial shade. To maintain bushy growth, remove old or weak stems at ground level. Cut off the tips of flowering shoots after the blooms have faded. No other pruning is necessary.

PROPAGATION Take 7.5cm/3in half-ripe cuttings with a heel in autumn and place in a peat/sand mixture in a cold frame. Place the rooted cuttings in a nursery bed in spring and transfer to the final positions in the autumn of the following year.

VARIETIES 'Farreri', very delicate foliage, bright yellow flowers; 'Tangerine' *(above)*, low-growing, scarlet in bud, opening to orange, or yellow if in full sun; 'Mandschurica', only 30 × 90cm/1 × 3ft, silver leaves, purple stems, white flowers.

POSSIBLE PROBLEMS Generally trouble-free.

■ SPECIAL CARE TIP

This tender plant, native to California and Mexico, is only suitable for warm, sunny, sheltered gardens where it can be grown against a wall.

In colder areas, it might be better off in a greenhouse or conservatory where it can be trained up a trellis.

■ PLANTING TIP

This shrub can be planted as an informal hedge. Simply remove flower shoots and old stems after flowers have faded. It flowers all summer.

PHILADELPHUS

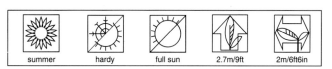

| summer | hardy | full sun | 2.7m/9ft | 2m/6ft6in |

White-flowered shrubs are an important element in gardens and the philadelphus or mock orange is a popular choice, not only for the attraction of its abundant blooms but also because of its delicious scent. The species and hybrids vary in size and habit, but all are summer-flowering and have mid-green oval leaves.

GROWING Plant between autumn and spring in fertile well-drained soil, preferably in full sun. The exception is the golden-leaved *Philadelphus coronarius* 'Aureus', which prefers semi-shade to retain foliage colour. Prune after flowering by cutting back flowered shoots to a developing shoot which will flower the following year. Cut weak growths right back.

PROPAGATION Take 10cm/4in half-ripe cuttings in summer and place in a peat/sand mixture in a cold frame. Transfer the rooted cuttings to a nursery bed the following spring and plant out in the autumn.

SPECIES *P. coronarius*, vigorous grower, good on dry soils; *P. microphyllus*, neat at 60 × 60cm/24 × 24in, suitable for rock gardens. Many good garden hybrids are available. Try 'Manteau d'Hermine' *(above)*, 90cm/3ft high, double, creamy flowers; 'Belle Etoile', 1.5m/5ft, intensely fragrant white flowers flushed red in the centre; 'Virginal', 2.4m/8ft, double, white flowers.

POSSIBLE PROBLEMS Leaf spot.

■ ORGANIC TIP

Ideal for a sunny border where its richly scented flowers will give much pleasure and will also attract bees, butterflies and other insects into your garden.

HYDRANGEA

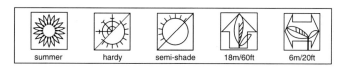

| summer | hardy | semi-shade | 18m/60ft | 6m/20ft |

The popular hybrids of the shrub *Hydrangea macrophylla* (1.8 × 1.8m/6 × 6ft) are known as Hortensias, with mop-heads of florets up to 20cm/8in wide, or Lacecaps, with smaller, open heads. Flowers are blue or pink. White-flowered species include *H. paniculata* and the climber *H. petiolaris*.

GROWING Plant in autumn or spring in a sheltered position in loamy, moisture-retentive soil previously enriched with well-rotted organic matter. *H. macrophylla* hybrids need top dressings of peat and an annual application of aluminium sulphate for blue flowers, or ground limestone for pink. Each spring, mulch with well-rotted organic matter and cut out damaged shoots. Remove faded flowerheads.

PROPAGATION Climbers: Take 7.5cm/3in cuttings in early summer and insert in a peat/sand mixture in a cold frame. Pot up individually when rooted, stand outdoors and set out in autumn. Shrubs: Take 15cm/6in cuttings in late summer *(see page 16)*.

SPECIES *H. petiolaris (above)*, self-supporting climber, 25cm/10in corymbs of cream flowers, early summer; *H. paniculata* 'Grandiflora', shrub with arching stems, maximum height 4.5m/15ft, 45cm/18in panicles of white flowers, late summer; *H. arborescens* 'Grandiflora', hardy American shrub, compact at 1.2 × 1.2m/4 × 4ft, pure white flowers all summer.

■ CUT FLOWER TIP

The spectacular flower heads are very popular with flower arrangers, but the faded heads can also be cut after flowering and dried for winter displays.

DEUTZIA

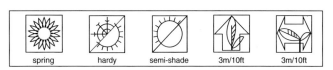

| summer | hardy | sun/semi-shade | 2m/6ft6in | 2m/6ft6in |

Most of the deutzias in cultivation are hybrids from parents of Asiatic origin. These rewarding shrubs are easy to grow and bear masses of pale pink, cerise or white star-shaped blooms in mid summer.

GROWING Plant in any type of fertile soil from autumn to spring, in full sun or in dappled shade. Avoid exposed sites. Prune after flowering, cutting back old flowering stems at ground level.

PROPAGATION Take 7.5cm/3in semi-ripe cuttings in late summer and place in a peat/sand mixture in a cold frame. Transfer the rooted cuttings to a nursery bed the following spring, grow on and plant out in the autumn.

SPECIES *Deutzia monbeigii*, arching stems, sheds bark to reveal orange-brown tints, abundant clusters of white flowers; *D. × hybrida*, strong-growing, of upright habit, older stems shed bark. The named variety 'Mont Rose' (*above*) bears large open flowers of rich rose ageing to white. *D. × rosea*, neat at 90cm/3ft high, pale pink bell-shaped flowers.

POSSIBLE PROBLEMS Severe cold may check vigour.

MAGNOLIA

| spring | hardy | semi-shade | 3m/10ft | 3m/10ft |

For many people, a magnolia blooming in early spring is the most beautiful sight of the gardening year. The shrubs of this much-admired genus bear magnificent white or pink flowers which are often fragrant.

GROWING Plant in spring in well-drained lime-free soil into which plenty of peat has been incorporated. Magnolias need a site giving protection from cold winds. Support with stakes for the first 3 or 4 years. Top-dress annually in spring with peat or leaf-mould. No pruning is needed.

PROPAGATION Magnolias may be raised from seed (germination takes up to 18 months), by cuttings taken in summer or by layering (*see page 17*) in spring.

SPECIES *Magnolia grandiflora*, evergreen with large, round creamy-white fragrant flowers. Excellent against a wall, where it can reach 10m/33ft. In this situation inward-growing shoots should be removed in spring. *M. stellata (above)*, the hardiest species with white, star-shaped, fragrant flowers; the variety 'Royal Star' bears larger, more showy blooms. *M. soulangeana*, maximum height 5m/15ft, cup-shaped white flowers tinged carmine at the base open before the leaves unfurl; *M. liliiflora*, 2.4m/8ft, cup-shaped purple flowers.

POSSIBLE PROBLEMS Frost damage leading to grey mould.

■ SPECIAL CARE TIP

This shrub needs a fertile soil, so prepare the ground before planting by digging in some bonemeal – fish, blood and bone - or other general fertilizer. After planting, mulch with well-rotted compost or manure, and thereafter mulch each spring, which will also help to protect new growth against frost.

■ SPECIAL CARE TIP

These shrubs are not so difficult to grow as you may think. However, it does need some care when planting, and in selecting a well-dug, sunny site. A moisture-retentive soil is essential, so dig in plenty of compost before planting, and lay more well-rotted compost around the roots. Mulch well after planting.

CEANOTHUS

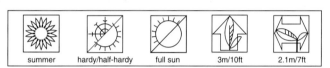

| summer | hardy/half-hardy | full sun | 3m/10ft | 2.1m/7ft |

This large genus of attractive evergreen and deciduous shrubs is often known as Californian lilac, revealing its origin. Most bear clusters of heavenly blue flowers; a few are pink or white.

GROWING Set out young plants in late spring in light, well-drained soil. Most types, especially the evergreen, need the protection of a warm, sunny wall, but will grow in the open if sheltered from wind. Tie shoots and branches of evergreens to wall supports and trim lightly when needed. Prune deciduous varieties in spring by cutting the preceding year's growth back to 7.5cm/3in. Remove faded flowerheads from all types.

PROPAGATION Take 7.5cm/3in soft cuttings in summer; root in sandy compost under cover; pot on when rooted and plant out the following year.

VARIETIES *Ceanothus* × 'Autumnal Blue', one of the hardier hybrids, evergreen, deep blue flowers; *C.* × 'Burkwoodii', evergreen, light blue, slightly scented flowers; *C.* × 'Gloire de Versailles', deciduous, panicles of powder blue flowers, a good choice for a sunny open site; *C. impressus* (*above*), half-hardy evergreen wall shrub, clusters of small deep blue flowers in spring; *C. thyrsiflorens repens*, evergreen, forms mounds 90cm/3ft high, light blue flowers in late spring.

POSSIBLE PROBLEMS Soils high in lime may sometimes cause chlorosis.

IPOMOEA

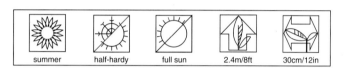

| summer | half-hardy | full sun | 2.4m/8ft | 30cm/12in |

Ipomoea tricolor is popularly known as morning glory, because its flowers open in the morning sunshine but fade by the end of the afternoon. A perennial grown as an annual, this climbing plant needs the support of netting or twiggy sticks for its twining stems. The funnel-shaped blooms are blue and white, up to 12.5cm/5in across.

GROWING Set out young plants in late spring or early summer after all danger of frost is past. Light but fertile soil is best, in a position sheltered from wind. Dead-head regularly and discard the plants after flowering is over.

PROPAGATION Sow seeds in spring under protection at 15°C/60°F, placing two seeds to a 9cm/3½in pot. Soak the seeds for 24 hours before planting to assist germination. Harden off the seedlings before transferring them to the permanent site. Alternatively, sow seeds where they are to grow in early summer.

VARIETIES 'Heavenly Blue' (*above*): large flowers of clear sky blue; 'Sapphire Cross', purple-blue; 'Flying Saucers', very large flowers, blue and white striped.

POSSIBLE PROBLEMS Aphids on young shoots; night frost distorts young leaves.

■ PLANTING TIP

This shrub can be hard hit by severe winters, and especially by a hard frost. Ideally, position in a sheltered spot, or against a hot, dry wall in the sun.

■ PLANTING TIP

Climbers such as morning glory can be used to hide unsightly items, such as an ugly chain-link fence. They can also be used to frame a window: grown in a container, this climber could be trained up lines of twine. It could also be trained up a narrow trellis on a patio to provide high-level interest.

MAHONIA

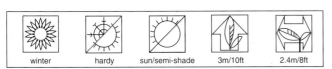

| winter | hardy | sun/semi-shade | 3m/10ft | 2.4m/8ft |

Mahonias are handsome shrubs, with dark green glossy leaves and racemes of fragrant, bright yellow flowers. The foliage is often used as winter decoration. All the species bear dark blue berries; those of *Mahonia aquifolium* are carried in clusters, earning it the common name Oregon grape. This species spreads by means of suckers and is an excellent ground cover plant.

GROWING Set out young plants in autumn or spring in sun or semi-shade in fertile, well-drained soil that is not markedly alkaline. Mulch annually in spring with leaf-mould or peat. No pruning is necessary except for *M. aquifolium* grown as ground cover, which should be pruned hard each spring.

SPECIES *M. aquifolium*, maximum height 1.5m/5ft unless regularly pruned, spread 1.8m/6ft, spring-flowering, dense clusters of flowers precede plump berries, wind-tolerant. Leaves of the variety 'Atropurpurea' turn red in winter; *M.* × 'Charity' *(above)*, hybrid, bearing 30cm/12in racemes of deep yellow flowers in mid winter.

POSSIBLE PROBLEMS Leaf spot; rust.

PASSIFLORA

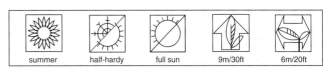

| summer | half-hardy | full sun | 9m/30ft | 6m/20ft |

Passiflora umbellicata and *P. caerulea*, the common passion flower, are the only members of their family – natives of Brazil – that can be grown outdoors and even then they must have a sheltered site. They bear exotic, star-shaped flowers with prominent stamens, which are occasionally followed by golden egg-shaped fruits.

GROWING Plant in late spring in well-drained soil, in a sheltered position against a warm, sunny wall with trelliswork or wire mesh for support. Tie in the young growths until the tendrils take over. Protect with cloches over winter. Plants may be cut down by frost but new shoots arise from the base. Prune in spring if necessary, removing overcrowded or frost-damaged stems.

PROPAGATION Take 7.5cm/3in stem cuttings in summer and place in a peat/sand mixture in a propagator at 16°C/61°F until rooted. Pot up individually and grow on. Harden off before planting out the following spring.

SPECIES *P. caerulea (above)*, vigorous plant with dense habit, white-petalled flowers 7.5cm/3in across have purple stamens. The variety 'Constance Elliot' is all white and hardier than the species; *P. umbellicata*, maximum height 6m/20ft, large purplish flowers.

POSSIBLE PROBLEMS Cucumber mosaic virus discolours the leaves.

■ PLANTING TIP

Good to plant as an informal hedge or as ground cover, especially in shaded conditions. For a small garden remember that the leaves are rather prickly.

■ PLANTING TIP

This beautiful climber will enhance any wall or fence when grown up trellis or netting for support. On a patio, it can easily be grown in a pot or other container against a wall, and this climber actually flowers better when it has some root restriction.

CLEMATIS HYBRIDS

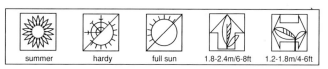

| summer | hardy | full sun | 1.8-2.4m/6-8ft | 1.2-1.8m/4-6ft |

Clematis are universally popular climbers, scrambling over a wall or fence, trellis or arbour, and covered with open star-shaped flowers of white, blue, pink or purple. There is a huge choice of beautiful hybrids. Some flower twice, in early and mid summer; others bloom from mid summer onwards.

GROWING Plant deeply between autumn and spring, preferably in alkaline soil, in a position where the base will be shaded from strong sun. Support for the twining stalks is essential. Prune those that flower twice by cutting back the shoots to 23cm/9in the second spring after planting. Remove all weak growth each spring and tie in replacement shoots. For summer-flowering clematis, train the shoots across wires at 30cm/12in from the ground and the flowering stems will grow upwards. Cut back flowered stems each spring to two good buds. Mulch each spring.

PROPAGATION Layer 18-month-old shoots in spring *(see page 17)*.

VARIETIES Early-flowering: 'Belle of Woking', double, silvery-mauve; 'Maureen', velvety purple; 'Lincoln Star', rich pink; 'Nellie Moser' *(above)*, pale mauve, crimson stripe. Summer-flowering: 'Huldine', pearly white; 'Etoile Violette', deep purple with cream stamens; 'Gravetye Beauty', cherry red.

POSSIBLE PROBLEMS Clematis wilt; powdery mildew.

CLEMATIS SPECIES

| spring | hardy | full sun | 9m/30ft | 15m/50ft |

Species clematis bear smaller flowers than the showy hybrids, but they are beautiful climbing plants that merit a place in any garden.

GROWING Treat as hybrids. Shade for the root-run can be provided by low shrubs. To prune, remove only weak growths and shorten the remainder by two thirds.

PROPAGATION Species can be raised from seed sown in autumn in pans of compost in a cold frame. After germination, in the following spring, pot up singly and set outdoors, transferring to the permanent site in autumn.

SPECIES *Clematis armandii*, vigorous evergreen, glossy foliage, white saucer-shaped flowers 6cm/2½in across; *C. orientalis*, fern-like leaves, abundant nodding scented yellow flowers in late summer followed by large silver seedheads; *C. tangutica*, grey-green leaves, lantern-shaped yellow flowers in late summer, attractive seed-heads; *C. flammula*, height 3m/10ft, bears a mass of tangled growth at the top with 30cm/12in panicles of fragrant white flowers in late summer/early autumn; *C. montana (above)*, 12 × 6m/40 × 20ft, easiest species to cultivate, profuse white flowers; the pink-flowered variety 'Rubens' is very popular.

POSSIBLE PROBLEMS Clematis wilt; powdery mildew.

▣ PLANTING TIP

To keep the roots moist and shaded after planting, cover the soil with flat stones and plant low shrubs and creepers to shield the base from the sun.

▣ PLANTING TIP

Clematis are rapid climbers that will quickly cover a wall, pergola, fence or even an unsightly building. They can also be used to scramble over an existing bush or tree, such as a dead apple tree. If you allow them to scramble through a flowering bush or tree, take colour into account to avoid clashes.

RHODODENDRON

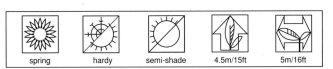

spring	hardy	semi-shade	4.5m/15ft	5m/16ft

Rhododendrons have much to offer gardeners who must work with acid soil. The magnificent flowers come in an unparalleled range of colours. In size the plants range from as low as 30cm/12in to an imposing 4.5m/15ft or more and spread wide. About 800 species are known and thousands of hybrids have been developed.

GROWING Plant in early autumn in well-drained but moisture-retentive acid soil. Most prefer light shade but hardy hybrids and small-leaved types tolerate full sun. Water well and mulch after planting. Remove dead flowerheads. Prune to restrict growth if necessary by cutting back lightly to a whorl of leaves in spring. Old, straggly hardy hybrids can be induced to make new compact growth if pruned heavily in late winter.

PROPAGATION Increase stock by layering (see page 17) or cuttings (see Azalea). Varieties do not come true from seed.

VARIETIES 'Bluebird', 90cm/3ft high, rich violet flowers; 'Praecox', 1.5m/5ft, rose-purple, very early flowering; 'Scarlet Wonder', 60cm/24in, compact shape. Hardy hybrids (all these up to 4.5m/15 ft, late spring-flowering): 'Cynthia', rose-crimson, vigorous grower; 'Mount Everest', white with red throat, fragrant; 'Purple Splendour', purple marked black.

POSSIBLE PROBLEMS Rhododendron leafhopper causes bud-blast disease; rhododendron bugs suck sap from the leaves.

■ ORGANIC TIP

If your soil is too alkaline, grow rhododendrons by constructing a raised bed with a wooden framework, or peat block walls, filled with a peaty mixture.

AZALEA

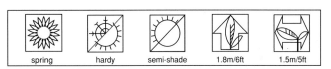

spring	hardy	semi-shade	1.8m/6ft	1.5m/5ft

Azaleas are types of rhododendrons, but generally smaller; the deciduous azaleas do not have scaly leaves, and the so-called evergreens actually drop some leaves in autumn. The showy flowers are bell-, funnel- or saucer-shaped.

GROWING See Rhododendron.

PROPAGATION Deciduous azaleas may be increased by layering (see page 17), rhododendrons (hardy hybrids), Kurume and other evergreen azaleas from cuttings. Take cuttings from young growths in summer and place in a mixture of sand and sifted peat at 2:1 in a cold frame. When firmly rooted pot up in a compost consisting of equal parts (by volume) of sifted peat, leaf-mould, lime-free loam and sand. Keep lightly moist, protect over winter and plant out in nursery beds in spring. The compact root system makes transplanting easy. In fact, if a plant outgrows its site, it is sometimes better to move it than prune it.

SPECIES Evergreens (give shelter from cold winds): 'Palestrina' (above), pure white; 'Orange Beauty', soft orange; 'Fedora', deep pink. Kurume hybrids (small glossy leaves, slightly tender): 'Kirin', rose-pink; 'Hinodegiri', carmine-red. Ghent azaleas (deciduous, hardy, fragrant): 'Corneille', double flowers, cream flushed pink; 'Narcissiflora', primrose yellow.

POSSIBLE PROBLEMS See Rhododendron; azalea whitefly infest the undersides of the leaves.

■ SPECIAL CARE TIP

Azaleas are like rhododendrons and thrive on acid, peaty soil. They also enjoy dappled shade and need shelter from frosts, which can blacken their blooms. If your soil has a trace of lime, water the foliage with sequestered-iron solution and mulch generously with peat.

FUCHSIA

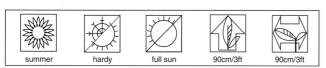

| summer | hardy | full sun | 90cm/3ft | 90cm/3ft |

So-called greenhouse fuchsias will not survive the winter out-doors. Fortunately there are a number of hardy fuchsias with the beautiful characteristic bell-like flowers which make decorative bushes or hedges. In cold districts they may die back above ground in winter, but shoot up afresh the next spring.

GROWING Plant in early summer when there is no longer any danger of night frost, in well-drained soil previously enriched with peat or leaf-mould. A sheltered spot is best. Water well in dry weather. In cold districts, cut the plants back to ground level in the autumn and sprinkle a shovelful of coarse grit around the crown before the first frosts. In warmer areas, simply cut out damaged wood in spring.

PROPAGATION Take 10cm/4in tip cuttings without flower buds in spring. Insert in individual pots of a peat/sand mixture at 16°C/61°F. Pot on when rooted and pinch out both leading and lateral shoots frequently to encourage bushy growth. Overwinter at 13°C/55°F and plant out in early summer.

SPECIES *Fuchsia magellanica*, hardiest species, about 1.5m/5ft, more as hedging in mild areas; crimson and purple flowers. Varieties include 'Gracilis', slender leaves and flowers; 'Gracilis Versicolor', beautifully variegated leaves; 'Pumila', only 15cm/6in; 'Alba', pale pink flowers; 'Mrs Popple' *(above)* profusion of large flowers.

POSSIBLE PROBLEMS Generally trouble-free.

■ SPECIAL CARE TIP

Hardy garden fuchsias will survive the winter, though they may die back completely. Mulch crowns heavily with compost when growth dies down, to protect from cold and frost. In the spring, prune back the previous year's growth to ground level. Clip fuchsia hedges in the spring.

CAMELLIA

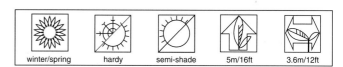

| winter/spring | hardy | semi-shade | 5m/16ft | 3.6m/12ft |

Camellias are beautiful, with large cup-shaped flowers of pink, red, purple or white and dark green glossy leaves.

GROWING Plant in autumn or spring in any good, lime-free soil, previously enriched with leaf-mould if light in texture. Give plants the protection of a sheltered wall which is shaded from the rising sun, since they are susceptible to damage from wind, frost and early morning sun after frost. Stake young plants until established. Mulch generously every spring with well- rotted organic matter or leaf-mould. Dead-head the species after flowering. If necessary, shorten wispy shoots in spring – no other pruning is required. Early-flowering species do well in small tubs containing a mixture of lime-free loam, peat and sand at 4:2:1, but should be moved indoors over winter.

PROPAGATION Layer specimens in autumn *(see page 17)*.

SPECIES *Camellia japonica (above)*, very early flowering, all shades of pink. Varieties include 'White Swan', single white flowers with prominent yellow stamens; 'Adolphe Audusson', semi-double crimson flowers 12.5cm/5in across; 'Anemonae-flora', deep red flowers; 'Elegans', large rose-pink peony-type flowers. *C. × williamsii*, outstanding hybrid, height up to 2.4m/8ft, free-flowering from late autumn to spring. Varieties include the exceptional 'Donation', pale pink.

POSSIBLE PROBLEMS Birds may damage the flowers.

■ ORGANIC TIP

If your soil is slightly chalky, you can grow this shrub by giving an annual dose of sequestered iron, seaweed fertilizer in the spring and a peat

SPIRAEA

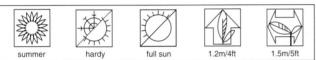

| summer | hardy | full sun | 1.2m/4ft | 1.5m/5ft |

Spiraeas bear tiny star-shaped flowers of white or shades of pink in flat or plume-shaped clusters. They are good subjects for a mixed border and are often grown as decorative hedging.

GROWING Plant between autumn and spring in deep, rich soil in an open sunny position. Prune *Spiraea* × *bumalda* and *S. japonica* in early spring, cutting back to 10cm/4in from ground level. Remove dead flowerheads. Thin out all species after flowering. Young plants for hedging should be set between 38 and 60cm/15 and 24in apart. Cut back the previous season's growth to within 15cm/6in of ground level after planting. Trim established hedges every year.

PROPAGATION Lift, divide and replant between autumn and spring. Or, take 10cm/4in cuttings of half-ripe side shoots in summer and insert in sandy soil in a cold frame. Transfer to a nursery bed the next spring and plant out in the autumn.

SPECIES *S.* × *arguta*, commonly known as bridal wreath, a beautiful hybrid bearing umbels of pure white flowers on arching stems in spring, max height 2.4m/8ft, excellent underplanted with crocuses or cyclamen; *S.* × *bumalda*, hybrid bearing 12.5cm/5in wide heads of bright pink flowers; 'Anthony Waterer' (*above*) is a popular variety with foliage variegated cream and pink when young; *S.* × *japonica*, maximum height 1.5m/5ft, large pink flowerheads on erect stems.

POSSIBLE PROBLEMS Leaves may be stripped by sawfly.

▦ ORGANIC TIP

Spiraeas like sandy or alkaline soils, but these may need enriching before planting. Dig in well-rotted compost to help retain moisture and nutrients.

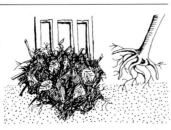

ENKIANTHUS

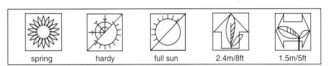

| spring | hardy | full sun | 2.4m/8ft | 1.5m/5ft |

Enkianthus campanulatus is a native of Japan and is prized for its foliage – dull green in spring and summer, vivid scarlet in autumn. Its abundant bell-shaped flowers are creamy-yellow, tipped and veined rose-pink. There are no named varieties.

GROWING Plant in autumn or spring in acid or neutral soil. Peat or leaf-mould should be added to ordinary lime-free soils. A sunny sheltered position, as in light woodland, is preferred. Pruning is generally unnecessary, but leggy overgrown species may be cut back hard in late winter.

PROPAGATION Take 7.5cm/3in heeled cuttings of lateral shoots in late summer and insert in a peat and sand mixture in a cold frame. Transfer the rooted cuttings to a nursery bed in spring to grow on for 2-3 years before planting them out in their permanent positions.

POSSIBLE PROBLEMS Generally trouble-free.

▦ PLANTING TIP

Otherwise known as the pagoda bush, because of its vivid colouring. If your garden is successful with rhododendrons and azaleas, you will succeed with this shrub. Lime-free soil is essential; dig peat into the soil when planting, and mulch with peat.

FLORIBUNDA ROSES

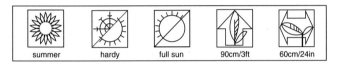

| summer | hardy | full sun | 90cm/3ft | 60cm/24in |

Floribunda roses are derived from the early hybrid teas, and have similar foliage. Whether matt or glossy, there are 7 oval leaflets, sometimes flushed red when young. These roses are very thorny. Flowering twice, in mid summer and early autumn, they bear their 7.5cm/3in wide blooms in large terminal clusters, and are good for borders and decorative hedges.

GROWING If conditions are favourable, roses may be planted at any time from late autumn to spring. Rich, loamy soil gives the best results. Prepare the site by digging it over well and mixing in plenty of well-rotted organic matter. Double-digging is recommended. Make a hole big enough to spread out the roots. Mix a bucketful of peat with a cupful of sterilized bonemeal and place 3 cupfuls of this mixture in each planting hole. Make sure the union of the rootstock and the rose is just below ground level. Give a mulch of partially rotted manure or well-rotted compost every other spring, and a mulch of leaves (rotted or unrotted) each autumn to conserve moisture. For pruning *see Hybrid Tea Roses.*

PROPAGATION Increase by budding (*see page 18*).

VARIETIES 'Iceberg' (*above*), 1.5m/5ft, large sprays of white, fragrant blooms, good for hedging; 'City of Birmingham', abundant scarlet blooms with wavy petals; 'Korresia', sweetly fragrant, golden yellow.

POSSIBLE PROBLEMS *See Hybrid Tea Roses.*

■ DRIED FLOWER TIP

Roses are lovely as cut flowers, but they can also be dried. The best roses for drying should have long, stiff stems and flowers that are well-formed but not so dense as to make drying difficult. Roses can be dried by hanging in the dark, in warm air, but it is best to use silica gel and follow manufacturer's instructions.

OLD ROSES

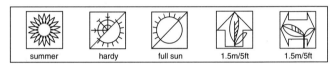

| summer | hardy | full sun | 1.5m/5ft | 1.5m/5ft |

Descended from true *Rosa* species such as *R. alba* (the White Rose of York) and *R. damascena* (damask rose), old roses were popular before hybrid teas were introduced, and are now enjoying a well-deserved revival. Intensely fragrant, the blooms of white, pink or red have a relatively brief flowering period.

GROWING *See Floribunda Roses.* Albas, Damasks and Gallicas do not need rich soil. Prune the spring after planting by removing weak and damaged wood. For established bushes just remove straggly stems and any laterals that bore flowers the previous year. Do not prune until flowering is over.

PROPAGATION Take cuttings in late summer (*see page 16*).

VARIETIES Moss Roses (from *R. centifolia*), stems and branches covered with bristles. Very fragrant flowers 7.5cm/3in across: 'Henri Martin' (*above*), semi-double, deep pink; 'Comtesse de Murinais', vigorous shrub, pure white flowers with green centre. Gallicas (from *R. gallica*, the French rose), stiff stems, double flowers 5-7.5cm/2-3in wide: 'Cardinal Richelieu', pale pink ageing to deep purple, good for hedging. Bourbon roses (from *R. × odorata* and *R. damascena*) Globular or cup-shaped flowers in bloom from early summer to first frost: 'Boule de Neige', white; 'La Reine Victoria', deep pink.

POSSIBLE PROBLEMS *See Hybrid Tea Roses.*

■ ORGANIC TIP

Roses appreciate a rich, well-fed soil, and well-rotted compost is the best medium for your old roses. If you provide a well-dug soil, enriched with well-rotted compost and manure before planting, and then mulch regularly with more, your roses will have no need of artificial fertilizer or rose feeds.

HYBRID TEA ROSES

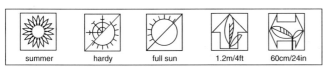

| summer | hardy | full sun | 1.2m/4ft | 60cm/24in |

Hybrid tea roses were first raised in the late nineteenth century and are distinguished by a high pointed centre surrounded by petals that curve back. Excellent for cutting, the colour range is extensive, and some varieties are scented.

GROWING *See Floribunda Roses.* This group is particularly susceptible to damage by wind and rain. Prune autumn-planted roses hard in the first spring to encourage strong shoots from the base. Remove all damaged wood then cut back to 3 buds (4 or 5 for floribundas). Spring-planted roses can be pruned immediately. Once established, remove dead and damaged wood early each spring and cut back all the previous season's growth by two-thirds (by one-third for floribundas)

PROPAGATION By budding only (*see page 18*).

VARIETIES 'Bonsoir' (*above*) or the following which are all fragrant: 'Alec's Red', deep red; 'Ingrid Bergman', dark red; 'Royal William', crimson velvet; 'Iced Ginger'; 'Just Joey', coppery-orange; 'Tynwald', cream; 'Pink Pearl'; 'Prima Ballerina', deep rose-pink; 'Lover's Meeting', soft tangerine; 'Fragrant Cloud', coral-scarlet; 'Peer Gynt', yellow shaded peach; 'St Hugh's', creamy-yellow; 'Valencia', orange-bronze (prize-winning scent).

POSSIBLE PROBLEMS Aphids; caterpillars; sawfly larvae. Black spot; die-back; grey mould; rust; powdery mildew.

▓ ORGANIC TIP

Help to avoid aphid attacks in your rose garden by using the companion planting method. Plant tagetes, calendula or nasturtiums nearby to attract hoverflies.

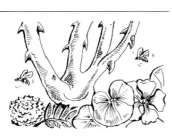

CLIMBING ROSES

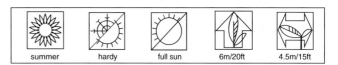

| summer | hardy | full sun | 6m/20ft | 4.5m/15ft |

All gardens, whatever their style, are enhanced by a climbing rose – or two. Climbers with species roses as parents are very vigorous (up to 9m/30ft), bearing 5cm/2in wide cream or yellow flowers in mid summer; climbers bred from hybrid teas are a better choice for more restricted areas such as pillars or fences, and bear flowers up to 12.5cm/5in wide.

GROWING *See Floribunda Roses.* Always plant climbing roses close to their supports. To prune, cut back strong growths after planting to 38cm/15in, weaker ones to within 10cm/4in of the base. Thereafter prune in early spring, leaving the basic framework but cutting back short laterals to 2-3 buds. Tie in new shoots in autumn.

VARIETIES The following are suitable for restricted areas: 'Caroline Testout', profusion of heavily fragrant, double pink flowers; 'Meg', pink and apricot; 'Danse du Feu', double, orange-scarlet; 'Golden Showers', pale gold; 'Parkdirektor Riggers', scarlet; 'Zephirine Drouhin', a bourbon rose, bright pink, fragrant, continuous flowering. Strong growers: 'Mme Gregoire Staechelin', clear pink, fragrant; 'Wedding Day', very vigorous, yellow in bud opening white; 'Mermaid', large, butter-yellow, fragrant, good on a cold wall. 'Fantin Latour' (*above*) double flowers over a short summer period.

POSSIBLE PROBLEMS *See Hybrid Tea Roses.* Climbers are particularly susceptible to powdery mildew.

▓ ORGANIC TIP

Powdery mildew is at its worst when the plant roots are dry. Avoid by mulching well in the spring with well-rotted manure or compost and renew if necessary.

SYRINGA

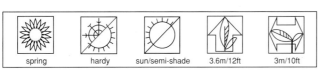

| spring | hardy | sun/semi-shade | 3.6m/12ft | 3m/10ft |

Syringa vulgaris, the common lilac, is one of the best-loved garden shrubs. There are a number of varieties, some double- flowered, all of them fragrant. Lilacs are deciduous, bearing panicles of white, lilac, pink or purple flowers up to 25cm/10in long in late spring.

GROWING Plant in autumn in sun or semi-shade on any type of fertile soil. Lilacs take 1-2 years to become established. Remove all the flowers in the first season to reserve the plant's energies. In later years dead-head after flowering. Remove lower buds and branches to form a single stem if desired. Pull off any suckers that appear. Prune old, straggly bushes in late autumn, cutting back to 90cm/3ft from ground level.

PROPAGATION Take 10cm/4in half-ripe cuttings with a heel in summer and insert in a peat/sand mixture in a propagator at 16°C/61°F. Pot up when rooted and grow on in a cold frame. Transfer to a nursery bed in the spring and grow on for 2 years before planting out.

VARIETIES 'Candeur', cream; 'Firmament', pale blue; 'Massena', deep purple; 'Maud Notcutt', the best white; 'Mrs Edward Harding', double, red; 'Marechal Foch', cerise; 'Primrose', pale yellow; 'Paul Thirion', double, rose-red, very fragrant; 'Souvenir de Louis Spaeth' (*above*).

POSSIBLE PROBLEMS Frost damage leading to grey mould; lilac blight.

■ ORGANIC TIP

The sweet-smelling flowers attract butterflies and other nectar-loving insects into the garden in early summer, when food may be in short supply.

ERICA

| winter | hardy | full sun | 25cm/10in | 60cm/24in |

The winter-flowering heath, *Erica carnea* syn. *E. herbacea*, is a low-growing shrub excellent for ground cover and, unlike other heaths, will tolerate chalky soils. The foliage is usually green, sometimes golden, the bell-shaped flowers white or pink. Easy to grow, heaths are invaluable in low-maintenance gardens and wherever winter colour is needed.

GROWING An open sunny position is essential. Prepare the site by digging it over well. Mix bonemeal into the top soil at 100g/m² (4oz/sq yd) and top dress with a 7.5cm/3in layer of peat. Plant in spring or late autumn, making sure the plants are well firmed in with the stem completely buried. Set the plants between 30 and 45cm/12 and 18in apart in groups of 6 or more. Water well – do not let plants dry out, particularly in the first year. Cut right back after flowering to keep the plants dense and bushy.

PROPAGATION Take 5cm/2in cuttings of side shoots in late summer and insert in pots of a moist mixture of sharp sand and peat at 2:1. Place in a mist propagator until rooted and transfer to a cold frame or nursery bed. Plant out when 10cm/4in high.

VARIETIES 'Cecilia M. Beale', white, and 'Eileen Porter', pink (*together above*); 'Aurea', golden leaves, pink blooms; 'Praecox Rubra', prostrate with pink flowers.

POSSIBLE PROBLEMS Generally trouble-free.

■ DRIED FLOWER TIP

All ericas are very easy to dry, including native wild heather, and preserve their vivid colouring. Simply hang up bunches in a draughty, warm place and allow to dry naturally. It is best to cut bunches of erica before the flowers are fully out.

LAVANDULA

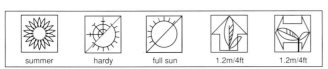

| summer | hardy | full sun | 1.2m/4ft | 1.2m/4ft |

Lavandula spica, the common lavender, richly deserves its popularity. Evergreen and intensely fragrant, it makes a charming low-growing hedge or edging to a pathway. The flowers may be dried and are often used in pot-pourri mixtures. Herbalists use a lavender infusion on a cold compress to treat headaches.

GROWING Plant between autumn and spring in any type of well-drained soil. Remove flowerheads when faded. Trim the plants with shears in late summer, and cut right back in spring to encourage bushy growth. For hedges, set young plants 23-30cm/9-12in apart. Trim established hedges in spring.

PROPAGATION Take 10cm/4in cuttings of non-flowering shoots in late summer and insert in a peat/sand mixture in a cold frame. Overwinter in the frame and plant out in the spring. Alternatively take 20cm/8in cuttings in early autumn and insert them where they are to grow.

VARIETIES 'Hidcote' syn. 'Nana Atropurpurea' *(above)*: compact at maximum height 60cm/24in, deep blue flowers; 'Alba': white; 'Twickle Purple': up to 90cm/3ft high, flowerspikes up to 12.5 cm/5in long.

POSSIBLE PROBLEMS Frost damage leading to grey mould; honey fungus.

HIBISCUS

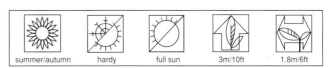

| summer/autumn | hardy | full sun | 3m/10ft | 1.8m/6ft |

The hibiscus belongs to the mallow family, and bears the beautiful characteristic funnel-shaped flowers in late summer and into the autumn. The blooms may be pink, white, blue or red and measure up to 7.5cm/3in across. Only one species, *H. syriacus*, is hardy enough for outdoor cultivation. This attractive shrub is suitable for the back of a mixed border.

GROWING Plant between autumn and spring in any type of well-drained soil in full sun. In cold districts it is necessary to give plants the protection of a wall. No regular pruning is necessary, but straggly shoots may be shortened after flowering.

PROPAGATION Take 10cm/4in cuttings of non-flowering lateral shoots in summer and insert in a peat/sand mixture at 16°C/61°F. When rooted, pot up individually and place in a cold frame over winter. Pot on in late spring, set outdoors and transfer to the flowering site in the autumn.

VARIETIES 'Blue Bird', blue with red centre; 'Coeleste', deep blue; 'Hamabo', white flowers flushed pink, crimson centres; 'Woodbridge' *(above)*, rosy pink, red centre. Double-flowered varieties include 'Violaceus Plenus', wine-red; 'Elegantissimus', white, red centre; 'Ardens', mauve-tinted rose.

POSSIBLE PROBLEMS Aphids; buds drop if soil dries out.

▓ DRIED FLOWER TIP

Lavender dries to a lovely faded blue. To dry, pick when in full flower on a dry sunny day (never after rain or dew). Hang upside down in a dry place.

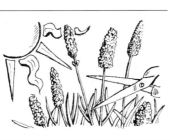

▓ SPECIAL CARE TIP

This shrub is not for every garden - it needs full sun, a well-drained soil, and protection from cold winds, eg against a wall. If these conditions are not possible, grow in a container or tub on a sheltered terrace or in a conservatory or greenhouse.

WISTARIA

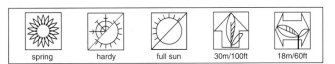

| spring | hardy | full sun | 30m/100ft | 18m/60ft |

Wistaria sinensis, or Chinese wistaria, is one of the loveliest climbing shrubs – and potentially one of the largest, though annual pruning will keep it within more reasonable bounds. Its twining habit can be supported by an arch or an old tree; against a wall, permanent supports are essential. The leaves consist of numerous delicate leaflets; before they are developed glorious lilac-blue or white flowers appear, in racemes up to 30cm/12in long.

GROWING Plant in autumn or spring on any good soil. The site should afford adequate room for root growth. A warm, sunny wall is ideal. Tie the young growths in to the supports. Pruning is advisable to encourage flowering; left alone, plants take up to 10 years to come into flower. Prune in winter, cutting back all growths to within 2-3 buds of the base of the previous year's growth. In summer, train the long leaders in the desired direction.

PROPAGATION By layering (*see page 17*).

VARIETIES The species with lilac-blue flowers is reliable and popular. 'Alba' (*above*) bears a mass of white flowers; 'Plena' has double mauve flowers.

POSSIBLE PROBLEMS Birds may damage buds and flowers; aphids; thrips. Bud-drop if soil dries out or night temperatures are very cold.

CHOISYA

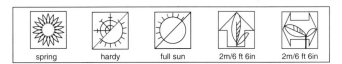

| spring | hardy | full sun | 2m/6 ft 6in | 2m/6 ft 6in |

The Mexican orange blossom, *Choisya ternata*, is one of the most accommodating of evergreens. An attractively rounded shrub, its three-part leaves are a dark glossy green and give off a pungent aromatic scent when crushed. A multitude of white, sweet-scented flowers appear in late spring. There are no named varieties.

GROWING Plant in spring in any type of well-drained soil. Full sun is best but semi-shade is tolerated. In cold districts it is best to site plants against a warm, sunny wall. No regular pruning is required, but any frost-damaged leaves or shoots should be cut out in early spring. As soon as flowering is over, cut out any straggly shoots.

PROPAGATION Take 7.5cm/3in cuttings of half-ripe lateral shoots in late summer and place in a peat/sand mixture at 16°C/61°F. When rooted, pot up the cuttings singly and over-winter in a cold frame. Pot on in the spring, set outdoors and plant out the following spring. In cold areas, transfer the pots to a cold frame over winter.

POSSIBLE PROBLEMS Frost damage; honey fungus.

▮ PLANTING TIP

The most vigorous variety is W. sinensis, but if grown against a wall, special attention is needed, as it can destroy guttering and get under the roof tiles.

If grown against a house wall, it is safer to grow the less vigorous Floribunda or macroborys - the latter has flowers 75cm/2 ½ feet long.

▮ PLANTING TIP

This is one of the neatest garden shrubs, forming a dome of glossy leaves, making it particularly suitable for a small town garden or patio.

LONICERA

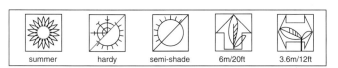

| summer | hardy | semi-shade | 6m/20ft | 3.6m/12ft |

The deciduous climber *Lonicera periclymenum*, better known as woodbine or honeysuckle, is a familiar sight in the wild, twining its stems in strong bands around anything in reach. The cultivated varieties will do the same in the garden, given wires, trellis or an old tree to scramble over. The beautiful tubular flowers have a delicious fragrance.

GROWING Plant from autumn to spring in any type of well-drained soil, previously enriched with humus. Honeysuckles like their roots in shade and the tops in sun. Give a light mulch of leaf-mould or well-rotted compost each spring. Prune after flowering if necessary to remove old wood.

PROPAGATION Take 10cm/4in stem cuttings in summer and place in a peat/sand mixture in a cold frame. When rooted, pot up individually and set outside. Transfer to the flowering site in the late autumn.

VARIETIES 'Serotina' (late Dutch honeysuckle), bushy habit, flowers red outside, cream within; 'Belgica' (early Dutch honeysuckle), red and yellow flowers appear in late spring. These two varieties planted together will provide flowers for a six-month period.

POSSIBLE PROBLEMS Leaf spot; powdery mildew.

VIBURNUM

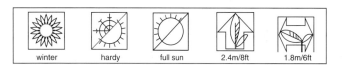

| winter | hardy | full sun | 2.4m/8ft | 1.8m/6ft |

There are some 200 species of viburnum, most of them hardy, some evergreen. One of the best evergreens is *V. tinus* or laurustinus, which bears its flat heads of white flowers from late autumn through to the end of spring.

GROWING Plant in the autumn or spring on fertile, moisture-retentive soil, in a position sheltered from cold winds. Do not site the plants where early morning sun after frosts could damage young growths. Prune in late spring, simply removing old and damaged branches.

PROPAGATION Take 7.5cm/3in cuttings of lateral shoots with a heel in early summer. Place in a peat/sand mixture in a propagator at 16°C/61°F. Pot up individually when rooted and set in a cold frame. Keep in the frame over winter. Transfer to nursery rows in the spring and grow on for 2-3 years before planting in the permanent site.

VARIETIES 'Variegatum': leaves splashed with gold; 'French White', pure white flowers; 'Eve Price', dense shrub with pink flowers.

POSSIBLE PROBLEMS White flies on underside of leaves; frost damage leading to grey mould.

■ ORGANIC TIP

An absolute must for the organic garden. Beautifully scented flowers attract bees and other insects into the garden. They also attract moths in the evening, when the scent is strongest. The red berries which follow flowering are enjoyed by the birds.

■ CUT FLOWER TIP

The wonderfully perfumed flowers of this shrub make it a delight in a border, and a few branches will scent a whole room in a winter arrangement.

PIERIS

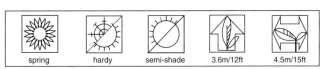

spring	hardy	semi-shade	3.6m/12ft	4.5m/15ft

Pieris formosa is a shapely evergreen shrub, the leaves of which are a warm red when young and turn green later. It bears drooping panicles of lily-of-the-valley-like flowers in late spring. Pieris are handsome slow-growing shrubs which may be planted as specimens or in a mixed border.

GROWING Lime-free soil is essential. Set out young plants in autumn or spring in a sheltered position. Do not allow the soil to dry out during the summer. Give an annual top-dressing of leaf-mould or peat in spring. Pruning is minimal – simply remove faded flowerheads and cut back straggling shoots at the same time.

PROPAGATION Take 10cm/4in cuttings of half-ripe shoots in late summer and place in sandy soil in a cold frame. Pot up individually the following spring, using a mixture of equal parts of peat, loam, leaf-mould and sand. Keep in the cold frame, transferring to a nursery bed in the autumn to grow on for 2-3 years before planting in their permanent positions.

VARIETIES 'Forrestii' (*above*), noted for the vivid red of the young foliage and quantity of flowers.

POSSIBLE PROBLEMS Generally trouble-free.

CHAENOMELES

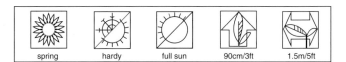

spring	hardy	full sun	90cm/3ft	1.5m/5ft

There are four species of chaenomeles in cultivation, collectively known as flowering quinces. They bear red, pink or white flowers like apple blossom, followed by small round yellow fruits. The plants, though attractive, have an untidy habit of growth and look best in an informal garden.

GROWING Plant from autumn to spring in any type of soil, even clay, in a sunny position or against a wall. In the open, the only pruning necessary is the thinning of overcrowded branches after flowering. If grown against a wall, cut back the previous season's growth to 2-3 buds after flowering.

PROPAGATION By layering (*see page 17*). Alternatively take 10cm/4in cuttings of lateral shoots with a heel in late summer. Insert in a peat/sand mixture in a propagator at 16°C/61°F. When rooted pot up the cuttings individually and overwinter in a cold frame. Plant out in the spring.

SPECIES *C. japonica* (Maule's quince, *above*), spreading shrub, coral-red flowers; named varieties include 'Brilliant', scarlet flowers. *C. speciosa* syn. *C. lagenaria* (Japanese quince), widely grown species, 1.8 × 1.8m/6 × 6ft in the open, higher on a wall, very early flowering. Named varieties include 'Apple Blossom', double pink flowers; 'Crown of Gold', deep red with showy yellow stamens; 'Fascination', orange; 'Nivalis', white.

POSSIBLE PROBLEMS Birds may damage flowers; chlorosis on very alkaline soils.

▇ PLANTING TIP

An acid soil is essential for this plant. Dig in plenty of peat and compost before planting, and mulch with more peat after planting. In following years, mulch with peat every spring to top up the acidity.

▇ PLANTING TIP

This early-flowering shrub is perfect for training against a fence or wall. It does well in partial shade, but is best in full sun. Trim back after flowering.

PYRACANTHA

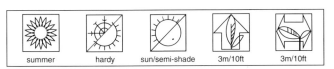

summer | hardy | sun/semi-shade | 3m/10ft | 3m/10ft

Firethorns are evergreen shrubs chiefly grown for their bright berries which stay from early autumn, after the flowers have faded, right through the winter. They look splendid against a wall, but as clipped hedges the berries will be relatively few.

GROWING Plant container-grown plants between autumn and spring in any fertile, well-drained soil. Wall-grown plants need trelliswork or a system of horizontal wires for support. During the summer tie in strong growths and trim the plant lightly. Plants for hedging should be set about 45cm/18in apart. Pinch out the growing points of young shoots when they are 20cm/8in long. Established hedges should be cut to shape in summer. Plants grown as bushes need no pruning.

PROPAGATION Take 10cm/4in cuttings of young shoots in summer and place in a peat/sand mixture in a propagator at 16°C/61°F. When rooted, pot up individually and transfer to a cold frame over winter. Pot on in the spring and set the pots outdoors in a bed of soil or peat. Plant out in the autumn.

VARIETIES *Pyracantha atalantioides* 'Aurea' (*above*), fast-growing, deep green leaves of variable shape, white flowers precede bright yellow berries; *P. crenulata* 'Rogersiana', abundant white flowers, orange-red berries; *P. × watereri* is a compact hybrid between these two producing masses of scarlet berries.

POSSIBLE PROBLEMS Woolly aphids; fireblight

ORGANIC TIP

This colourful shrub is ideal for attracting birds into your garden. The berries will provide food during the hard winter months when food is scarce.

FOTHERGILLA

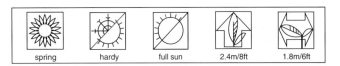

spring | hardy | full sun | 2.4m/8ft | 1.8m/6ft

Native to the United States, fothergillas are handsome shrubs highly valued for the brilliant tints of their autumn foliage. The flowers are composed not of petals but numerous white stamens arranged in bottle-brush-like spikes. Sweetly scented, they appear in spring before the leaves unfurl.

GROWING Plant in late autumn or spring in light, lime-free soil into which peat or humus has previously been incorporated. Fothergillas tolerate light shade. No pruning is necessary.

PROPAGATION By layering in autumn (*see page 17*). The layers generally take 2 years to take root, at which point they may be separated from the parent plant and transferred to their permanent sites.

SPECIES *Fothergilla major*, oval mid-green leaves, grey-blue underneath, take on orange, yellow or red colouring in autumn; *F. monticola*, leaves completely green when young, red or orange in autumn, of more spreading habit than *F. major*.

POSSIBLE PROBLEMS Generally trouble-free.

PROPAGATION TIP

This is another plant that must have a peaty, lime-free soil. When layering, it is essential to bury the stem in a hole filled with peat, for it to take root successfully. It will take 6-12 months to form roots. The rooted plantlet should then be planted out, again in a peaty soil.

TREES

Planting a tree is a sign of faith in the future. Most are planted at 3-4 years old and take about 30 years to reach their ultimate size (the sizes given in the entries in this chapter).

When you take over an established garden the chances are that you will inherit some trees, which, if you are lucky, will be mature, beautiful and in the right place. But even if they are not, cutting down a tree is a drastic measure from which many gardeners recoil. To be realistic, a garden cannot succeed if it is dominated by huge trees that literally put everything else in the shade and absorb all nutrients and moisture from the soil. One or more of the existing trees will have to go, with the choice dictated by practical factors such as direction of light and proximity to the house as well as the gardener's personal likes and dislikes. Tree-felling and the proper refurbishment and maintenance of old neglected trees is specialized work for which professional help is essential.

The small selection of trees described in this chapter have been chosen for their decorative qualities. Most of them make ideal specimen trees – that is, they merit being planted in a spot where they attract attention, for example in the middle of a lawn. When choosing where to plant a young tree, consider first its place in the overall design of your garden, taking into account its ultimate size. Even small trees are much bigger than the shrubs, perennials, bulbs and bedding plants that grow around it; simply by virtue of its size, a tree draws the eye. You can use this quality to emphasize a line of perspective or to distract from a less interesting or frankly ugly view, as long as a nice balance is struck between trees and other plants. The time at which a tree is at its best is important here. If there is a corner of the garden dependent for spring colour on bulbs, but comparatively dull in the autumn, incorporate a tree which blazes with autumn colour, such as a witch hazel (*Hamamelis mollis*). If you find the blossom of the flowering cherry irresistible, site the tree where it will have no rivals in spring, but where its fading blossom will be compensated for by a swathe of summer colour from the border.

An equally important consideration when deciding where to plant a tree is that in a competition for light and nourishment from the soil, mature trees will always win. Do not plant them too close to other plants which will suffer. Dappled shade from a nearby tree is ideal for some plants, and very pleasant for human beings on a hot summer's day; but a large tree too close to the house can make the rooms dark (and the roots may damage the foundations, necessitating costly repairs).

There are several factors influencing the choice of ornamental trees. Evergreens are prized for year-round interest and, if planted together, for the protection from wind they provide. Deciduous trees may have attractively shaped leaves which change colour in the autumn or pretty blossom and showy berries. The shape of the tree itself is important too. Where space is limited columnar or upright trees are useful, like eucryphias and spruces. In a formal garden a compact, neat outline looks best, as with a sorbus, while spreading trees like laburnums suit informal settings. The importance of a deciduous tree's skeleton – what it will look like in winter with bare branches – is related to some extent to the situation. If the tree is in a very prominent position it is as well to ensure that it bears scrutiny even without its leaves.

PLANTING A TREE Even though 3-4-year-old trees ready for planting are relatively small, they are large enough to merit two pairs of hands when planting. The best time to plant is between autumn and spring for deciduous trees, in autumn or spring for evergreens. Do not attempt to work on soil that is frozen hard or waterlogged. Young trees may have their roots covered in a ball of soil and wrapped in polythene; they may be bare-rooted or in a container. Container-grown trees can be planted at any time, even in summer as long as the soil is never allowed to dry out. Inspect bare-rooted trees before planting, cutting back any dead or diseased roots to healthy tissue.

1 Make a planting hole 45cm/18in deep and 90cm/3ft in diameter. If planting on grass, remove the turves from a neat circle and set them aside.

2 Fork up the soil at the bottom to aerate it and aid drainage.

3 Put a solid wooden stake, treated with preservative, in the middle of the hole, knocking it in with a mallet. Place it so that the top will be just below the point where the tree starts to branch.

4 If the soil is wet and heavy, place a layer of drainage material 15cm/6in deep evenly over the bottom of the hole.

5 Chop up the reserved turves, if any, into small pieces and place them in the hole grass side down.

6 Fork in a 15cm/6in layer of well-rotted manure or organic compost and replace the soil to the half-way point. Tread it down.

7 This is where you need a second pair of hands. Person

A holds the tree in place in the hole, gripping low on the stem, while Person B rests a flat piece of wood across the hole. Line up the tree so that the old planting mark on the stem is level with the wood. It may be necessary to add or remove soil beneath the tree to get it to the right depth.

8 With the tree held upright against the stake, gradually replace the remaining soil in the hole. Give the tree a shake from time to time to help the soil settle.

9 When the roots are covered, strew 2 cupfuls of sterilized bonemeal over the rooting area and cover with 3-4 shovelfuls of peat.

10 Continue filling up the hole with soil, treading it down occasionally, until the old planting mark is just visible and the soil level.

11 Attach the tree to the stake with a strap, placing a rubber buffer between stem and stake. As the tree grows, the strap will need to be loosened accordingly.

CARE OF TREES Give young trees a moisture-retentive mulch every autumn or spring. Suitable materials are well-rotted compost, leaf-mould or peat, applied over the rooting area to a depth of 10cm/4in. Young trees need generous watering, especially in dry spells and if the soil is light in texture. Feeding is not usually necessary because the mixture in the planting hole releases its nutrients over a long period of time.

Mature trees do not normally need watering. They may, however, need feeding. Signs of undernourishment are discoloured or undersized leaves, or premature leaf fall. Apply a general fertilizer in granular form to the roots. Bore 30cm/12in deep holes in the soil at 60cm/24in intervals. Pour the granules into the holes through a funnel to within 4cm/1½in of the surface and top up with soil.

PROPAGATION Although the method of propagation suitable for specific trees is described in the individual entries that follow, in many cases raising trees is a lengthy and skilled process beyond the scope of most amateurs. Grafting is a particularly demanding technique used for many species. A scion or shoot from the tree you wish to propagate is joined to a suitable rootstock by one of several methods. In approach grafting, for example, a shallow slice of wood is taken from both the scion and the rootstock and the two wounds are bound tightly together until they unite, which usually takes about 3 months. At this point the top of the rootstock and the bottom of the scion are cut away. Different methods are appropriate to different species.

MAGNOLIA

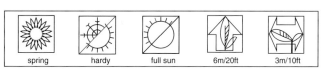

spring	hardy	full sun	6m/20ft	3m/10ft

Magnolias are among the most popular trees grown as specimens in a lawn or at the front of a town house. They bear huge, cup-shaped flowers of pink or white in early spring, often when it seems too cold for such beautiful blooms to survive – but they do, as long as they are sheltered from chilling winds.

GROWING Plant in spring in fertile, well-drained soil. Support with double stakes until well established. Top dress annually in spring with a 5cm/2in layer of well-rotted compost, peat or leafmould. No pruning is necessary.

PROPAGATION Take 10cm/4in cuttings of semi-hardwood shoots in summer and place in coarse sand in a propagating frame at 21°C/70°F. When rooted, pot on and overwinter in a cold frame. In spring, transfer to a nursery bed. Grow on for 3 years before transferring to permanent positions. Alternatively, layer suitable stems in spring (*see page 17*).

SPECIES *Magnolia salicifolia*, upright and fast-growing, star-shaped white flowers 10cm/4in wide open before the leaves unfurl. As the name indicates, the leaves are willow-like; *M. denudata*, up to 4.5m/15ft, slow-growing, abundance of fragrant white flowers 15cm/6in across.

POSSIBLE PROBLEMS Frost damage, grey mould, honey fungus.

▪ PLANTING TIP

When planting a new tree that needs staking, make sure the stake is placed in the hole with the roots before filling in to avoid damage to the root system.

LABURNUM

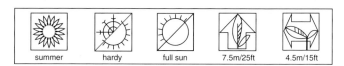

summer	hardy	full sun	7.5m/25ft	4.5m/15ft

Commonly known as golden rain, a laburnum tree in flower is a splendid sight. In late spring or early summer the branches are hung with long racemes of bright yellow flowers. All parts of the tree are highly poisonous, particularly the young green seedpods, which look like peas.

GROWING Plant between autumn and spring in any type of well-drained garden soil. A sunny site is best but semi-shade is tolerated. Provide stakes until the tree is established. No pruning is necessary.

PROPAGATION Species may be raised from seed sown in autumn in pots and set in a cold frame. Prick off the seedlings into boxes when they are large enough to handle. Transfer to nursery rows in spring and to the permanent site in the autumn. Hybrids and named varieties are propagated by grafting (*see page 119*).

SPECIES *L. alpinum* (Scotch laburnum), spreading habit, handsome bark in maturity, flowers in 25cm/10in racemes; 'Pyramidalis' is an erect form; *L. anagyroides* (common laburnum), 3m/10ft high, sometimes more, an early-flowering species with racemes 15-25cm/6-10in long. Named varieties include 'Pendulum', with a weeping habit, good for small gardens. *L. × watereri* (*above*), hybrid of moderate height. The variety 'Vossii' bears abundant, very long flower racemes.

POSSIBLE PROBLEMS Honey fungus, leaf miners.

▪ PLANTING TIP

Light and graceful, the laburnum is often chosen to be the focal point in a garden: it has the added advantage of casting dappled shade in which other plants can grow. The most spectacular variety is L. × watereri 'Vossii', which has very long tassels of flowers – up to 50cm/20in long.

SORBUS

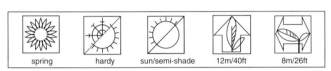

spring	hardy	sun/semi-shade	12m/40ft	8m/26ft

The genus *Sorbus* includes rowans, which are discussed here, and whitebeams. Rowans or mountain ashes are elegant trees admired for their pinnate leaves, which take on brilliant autumn tints. Flattened heads of tiny cream flowers appear in late spring, followed by attractive clusters of small round fruits.

GROWING Plant trees between autumn and spring in any type of well-drained soil in sun or semi-shade. Rowans tolerate the polluted atmosphere of towns well. No pruning is required.

PROPAGATION Pick the berries in autumn and take out the seeds. Sow immediately in seed compost in a cold frame. Prick the seedlings into boxes as soon as they are large enough to handle. Transfer to nursery rows in the following autumn to grow on for 5 years before planting in the final position.

SPECIES *S. hupehensis* (*above*), foliage blue-green, turning red in autumn, pale pink berries appear in late summer and last for weeks. *S. sargentiana*, height and spread 8m/26ft, leaves and fruit orange-red in autumn, best choice for colour; *S. vilmorinii*, height and spread up to 6m/20ft, dainty tree with fern-like leaves turning red in autumn, fruits red or white flushed pink.

POSSIBLE PROBLEMS Apple canker, fire blight, honey fungus.

PRUNUS

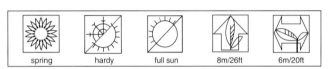

spring	hardy	full sun	8m/26ft	6m/20ft

The genus *Prunus* includes a huge number of trees that provide spectacular displays of spring flowers. Those described here are ornamental cherries; others are ornamental almonds, peaches, plums and cherry laurel. Easy to grow, all are popular in town gardens. Ornamental cherries have pointed, oval leaves and bear their blossom in heavy clusters.

GROWING Plant in autumn, not too deep in any well-drained soil, preferably with a little lime. Staking will be necessary until the tree is established, especially in exposed positions. Try not to disturb the soil around the trees too much, as they are shallow-rooting. No regular pruning is required. If necessary, damaged branches can be removed in late summer.

PROPAGATION By budding (*see page 18*) on to the rootstock *Prunus avium* (wild cherry).

SPECIES *P.* 'Amanogawa', upright habit, spread only 1.8-2.4m/6-8ft, good for small gardens, deep pink blossom; *P.* × 'Halle Jolivette', hybrid, height and spread 4.5m/15ft, suitable for small gardens, long-lasting double white flowers; *P.* 'Tai-Haku' (great white cherry, *above*), foliage red when young, bright white flowers 5cm/2in across, a vigorous grower.

POSSIBLE PROBLEMS Birds eat buds, caterpillars eat leaves; bacterial canker, chlorosis, honey fungus.

■ ORGANIC TIP

A good choice if you are hoping to attract wildlife. The bright red berries look attractive and are a good source of food for birds in the autumn.

■ ORGANIC TIP

This tree produces spectacular displays of flowers in spring, which are very attractive to insects and bees. Some varieties, such as the ornamental cherry, are sterile but others produce small fruits which will attract birds into the garden in search of food.

ROBINIA

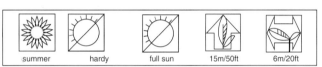

| summer | hardy | full sun | 15m/50ft | 6m/20ft |

The yellow-green, elegant foliage of *Robinia pseudoacacia* is best appreciated in larger gardens. Related to the laburnum (both are members of the pea family), robinias bear similar flowers in racemes up to 15cm/6in long in late spring or early summer. Short spines protrude along the stems.

GROWING Plant between autumn and spring in any type of well-drained soil in a sunny position sheltered from cold winds. Robinias tolerate atmospheric pollution and do well in areas of low rainfall; in waterlogged soils they are more vulnerable to wind damage. No pruning is required.

PROPAGATION Sow seed in pans of compost in early spring in a cold frame. Prick off into boxes when large enough to handle. Transfer to nursery beds and grow on for 3 years before planting in the permanent positions.

VARIETIES 'Frisia' (*above*), foliage opens bright yellow, turning light green in summer; 'Inermis' (mop-head acacia), compact, round habit, spineless branches, very few flowers.

POSSIBLE PROBLEMS Generally trouble-free.

SALIX

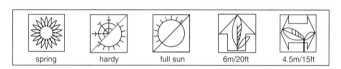

| spring | hardy | full sun | 6m/20ft | 4.5m/15ft |

Even if they cannot put a name to any other tree, most people can recognize a willow by its slender, pointed leaves and the woolly catkins which appear in spring. Some species also have colourful bark. All like moisture, and are often planted near water.

GROWING Plant between autumn and early spring in a sunny position. Light, sandy soils are unsuitable, especially for the larger species. To prune, remove dead wood during the winter and to encourage coloured shoots cut back to within 1-2 buds of old wood just before budbreak in spring.

PROPAGATION Take hardwood cuttings between autumn and spring and insert in moist soil. They should be ready for planting out in permanent positions after 1 year.

SPECIES *Salix daphnoides* (violet willow, fast-growing, with yellow catkins in early spring before the gleaming green leaves; in winter the stems are purple; *S. alba* (white willow), height up to 12m/40ft, greeny yellow catkins and grey-green leaves in late spring. *S. matsudana* 'Tortuosa' (*above*), slow-growing, erect willow. The variety 'Chermesina' has orange shoots in winter.

POSSIBLE PROBLEMS Caterpillars; anthracnose of willow.

PLANTING TIP

Always take into account final size and shape when choosing a tree. This one grows tall; the variety 'Pyramidalis' is slender, forming a neat column.

ORGANIC TIP

Ideal for the organic gardener, as the yellow woolly catkins not only look very attractive, but also provide food for early butterflies, moths and other insects.

SAMBUCUS

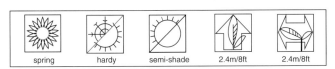

| spring | hardy | semi-shade | 2.4m/8ft | 2.4m/8ft |

The common elder, *Sambucus nigra*, which reaches 4.5m/15ft in height, is a familiar sight in the wild with its flattened heads of creamy flowers and the clusters of purplish black berries that follow. *S. racemosa*, the red-berried elder, is a slower growing cousin which makes a handsome addition to the garden.

GROWING Plant between autumn and spring in any type of fertile soil, in partial shade. Prune to encourage colourful foliage by cutting the stems right back in frost-free weather between autumn and spring: this will, however, reduce the quantity of flowers and berries.

PROPAGATION Take 25cm/10in hardwood cuttings in late autumn and treat as for salix (*see page 122*).

VARIETIES *S. nigra*: 'Aurea', yellow leaves; 'Aurea-variegata', green leaves edged yellow. *S. racemosa*: 'Plumosa Aurea' (*above*), finely cut yellow leaves.

POSSIBLE PROBLEMS Aphids; arabis mosaic virus.

RHUS

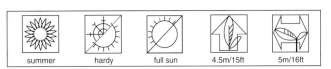

| summer | hardy | full sun | 4.5m/15ft | 5m/16ft |

The stag's horn sumach, *Rhus typhina*, is chiefly grown for its stunning autumn foliage, though it bears dense, 20cm/8in long panicles of minuscule flowers in summer. These are followed by clusters of red berries. Take care when pruning, as the sap contains a substance which irritates the skin.

GROWING Plant between autumn and spring in ordinary soil. This species thrives even in polluted urban atmospheres. To prune, cut stems right back to ground level in early spring. This will encourage foliage at the expense of flowers and fruit.

PROPAGATION This species produces numerous suckers, which may be pulled off in the autumn and planted where they are to grow. Alternatively, suitable shoots may be layered in spring (*see page 17*). They should be ready to sever from the parent plant in 1-2 years.

VARIETIES 'Laciniata' (*above*), fern-like green leaves turn orange and yellow in autumn.

POSSIBLE PROBLEMS Poor growing conditions may cause die-back.

ORGANIC TIP

The sweet-smelling flowers of the elder attract bees and other insects into the garden – and they also make excellent wine. They are followed by red berries which are highly attractive to birds as a good source. The black berries of the common elder are also good for winemaking.

PLANTING TIP

The stag's horn variety, the most popular, is extremely prolific: prune regularly or it will become too leggy and bare. It is unsuitable for planting in lawns because of the numerous suckers it produces, which can soon take over if not destroyed quickly.

EUCRYPHIA

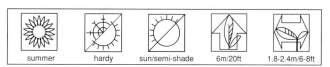

| summer | hardy | sun/semi-shade | 6m/20ft | 1.8-2.4m/6-8ft |

If you can offer a sheltered position, perhaps with the protection of a warm wall, *Eucryphia × nymansensis* would be a worthy candidate for the spot. Not fully hardy, in a favourable position it produces exquisite white, saucer-shaped flowers with a boss of red-tipped yellow stamens in late summer. These blooms are well set off by glossy oval leaves.

GROWING Plant in autumn on light soil, neutral or slightly acid. Eucryphias like sun or partial shade with a cool root run. In winter, protect young plants from frost with a covering of straw. Pruning is not necessary, but pinch out the leading shoots of young plants to encourage a bushy habit.

PROPAGATION Take 10cm/4in cuttings of non-flowering side shoots in late summer and insert in a peat/sand mixture at 16°C/61°F in a propagator. Pot up when rooted and overwinter in a cold frame. Harden off in the summer, keep sheltered over winter and plant out in the following spring.

VARIETIES 'Nymansay' (*above*), vigorous, upright habit, profusion of 7.5cm/3in wide white flowers in late summer.

POSSIBLE PROBLEMS Generally trouble-free.

PICEA

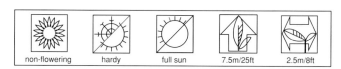

| non-flowering | hardy | full sun | 7.5m/25ft | 2.5m/8ft |

In natural conditions the Colorado spruce, *Picea pungens*, reaches 30cm/100ft, but numerous smaller forms of this beautiful tree have been raised for garden cultivation. Generally conical in shape, the trees bear stiff needles that are very pale blue-grey when young. After about 20 years cylindrical cones 7.5cm/3in long are produced.

GROWING Plant from autumn to spring on deep, moisture-retentive, slightly acid soil. Choose a sheltered position as young trees are vulnerable to damage by frost. Sprinkle a general-purpose fertilizer around the rooting area each spring. Pruning is not necessary.

PROPAGATION Sow seed in spring in boxes of compost in a cold frame. Place in nursery rows the following spring and grow on for 2-3 years before transferring to permanent positions.

VARIETIES 'Glauca', beautiful blue-green needles; 'Glauca Pendula', only 3 × 3m/10 × 10ft, a weeping form; 'Argentea', silver needles; 'Viridis', light green.

POSSIBLE PROBLEMS Green spruce aphids.

◾ PLANTING TIP

If the tree looks pot-bound when planting, the roots should be gently teased out and spread out flat around the new hole. Make sure the hole is big enough.

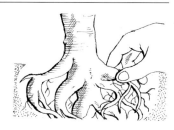

◾ PLANTING TIP

The silvery blue foliage of spruce is very attractive, so this tree is often used in gardens to provide a focal point. Remember always to keep in mind the final size of a tree when planting. After 10 years this tree will be approximately 2-3m/6-10ft tall but in time can reach 7.5m/25ft.

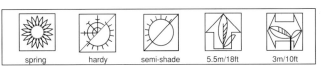

HAMAMELIS

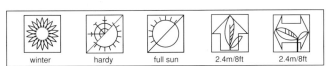

| winter | hardy | full sun | 2.4m/8ft | 2.4m/8ft |

Like the winter-flowering jasmine, witch hazels produce yellow flowers on bare stems before the leaves unfurl. They make good specimen trees or can be incorporated in a shrub border. The branches, with their spidery flowers, can be cut for decoration – they last well in water. In autumn the leaves take on beautiful coloured tints.

GROWING Plant between autumn and spring in slightly acid, moisture-retentive soil on a site sheltered from cold winds. Prune established specimens after flowering, cutting back unruly branches.

PROPAGATION Layer suitable shoots in early autumn (*see page 17*). Named varieties must be grafted on to rootstock of *Hamamelis virginiana* (common witch hazel) under glass.

SPECIES *H. × intermedia*, yellow flowers with crimped petals in very early spring, oval green leaves turn gold in autumn. Leaves of the named variety 'Hiltingbury' turn variously yellow, copper, scarlet and red in autumn – an outstanding choice. *H. mollis* (Chinese witch hazel, *above*), heavily fragrant yellow flowers flushed red appear in mid winter. Good, free-flowering forms are 'Brevipetala', with smaller blooms and 'Pallida', with paler petals.

POSSIBLE PROBLEMS Generally trouble-free.

ACER

| spring | hardy | semi-shade | 5.5m/18ft | 3m/10ft |

The maple family includes a large number of extremely handsome trees and shrubs, all bearing the characteristic palmate leaves which often take on vivid colours in autumn. The slow-growing *Acer palmatum* (Japanese maple) is a good choice for medium to small gardens. From this species a number of highly ornamental forms have been developed.

GROWING Plant from autumn to spring in well-drained, cool, moisture-retentive soil. Some lime is tolerated. Choose a site sheltered from sharp winds and early morning sun after frost. No pruning is required.

PROPAGATION The species may be raised from seed sown in the open in the autumn. Named varieties must be grafted on to species rootstock.

VARIETIES 'Atropurpureum' (*above*), bronze foliage; 'Dissectum', dwarf form with deeply cut leaves; 'Koreanum', striped bark, leaves brilliant red in autumn; 'Sessifolium Osakazuki' has the finest autumn colours – a combination of fiery orange, crimson and scarlet.

POSSIBLE PROBLEMS Aphids, red spider mites if conditions are too warm and dry; coral spot, honey fungus.

▌CUT FLOWER TIP

A few branches with their delicate yellow flowers will provide a welcome touch of indoor colour when not much else is available. They also provide a lovely scent.

▌PLANTING TIP

The beauty of this tree is that there are varieties available suitable for both small and large gardens. One particular variety, 'Atro-purpureum', is especially good for small gardens or patios, as it is only 60-90cm/2-3ft high and is highly ornamental, with purple leaves.

IN THE KITCHEN GARDEN

To grow fruit and vegetables successfully it is important to care for the soil and to raise healthy plants that can resist pests and diseases. Apart from the soil types described on pages 10-11, the vegetable gardener may also need to deal with *silt*. This is a very fine soil which packs down when wet in the same way as clay and so does not drain well either. Use the same methods as for clay (page 10) to improve the drainage. Dig over roughly in the autumn and add lots of organic matter plus coarse grit to open up the soil. A well cultivated silt soil will grow most vegetables and fruit well. Dig special deep beds if you intend to grow root vegetables, which will not otherwise do well on silt.

ANALYSING YOUR SOIL To find out what your soil is lacking and therefore enable you to improve it efficiently, send off a sample for professional analysis. Companies who offer this service advertise in gardening magazines. They will be able to tell you the chemical make-up of your soil and what type of fertilizer and how much you need to correct it. If you intend to garden organically, ask for information about organic fertilizers only.

Use one of the widely available testing kits to check the pH – the acidity level – of your soil (see page 10). Most vegetables grow best on soil with a pH value of 6-6.5. Be cautious when using lime, as over-liming can be very harmful, and only apply lime every three to four years.

IMPROVING KITCHEN GARDEN SOIL In cultivation, especially in the vegetable and fruit garden, nature's balanced soil re-generation cycle is broken because we harvest plants and tidy up the garden by removing dead material. We therefore need to replace naturally rotted organic matter each year by digging in manure or garden compost.

Animal manure (from herbivores) is excellent soil conditioner. Horse manure is better if based on straw bedding rather than wood shavings. Cow manure may be available from farmers with supplies to spare at the end of winter because they turn their cattle out in the summer. Sheep and pig manures are both high in nutrients and chicken manure is also very rich.

Do not use fresh animal manure on the garden. It needs to rot down completely first as in the fresh state it can burn plant leaves and stems, and the decomposing straw it contains will use up nitrogen in the soil.

Mustard is a quick-growing green manure, which is dug into the soil before flowering to provide nutrients and improve the soil's structure.

Three-part compost bin
Where space permits, it is best to have a compost heap with three compartments: one for filling with recent waste; one for the compost in the process of decomposing; and the last for the compost ready for using in the garden. Forking the compost from one bin to another has the advantage of aerating it. The heap can be built on either soil or concrete.

Leave it to decay for at least two to three months, longer if possible. If you can only get small quantities, add it to the compost heap where it will speed up decomposition. Larger quantities should be stacked and covered, especially through winter to protect the heap from bad weather. If you are worried about hormones fed to cattle or chickens, or pesticides that may remain in the straw, it is wiser to leave the manure for at least a year before using it.

Green manure Green manure is a quick growing crop that is dug back into the soil, while still young and green, to improve the soil's structure. If you have an empty bed, especially if your soil is light and free draining, it is better to sow a green manure like mustard, winter tare or red clover than leave the soil bare when rain can destroy the structure, nutrients drain away and weeds start to grow. Although the growing plants remove some nutrients, when dug back they provide more. As an alternative to digging the plants back into the soil they can be chopped off and left on the surface to be incorporated when they have decayed.

Garden compost A very good source of bulky organic material, free to us all, is household and garden vegetable waste. This again needs to decompose before it can be added to the soil. A compost container not only looks tidy but it speeds up decomposition by keeping the material warm. You can simply pile the material in a heap but it will take longer to rot down.

Waste material shrinks considerably when decomposing and the house and garden waste from one family results in a depressingly small heap, too small to provide all the bulk that a vegetable garden will need. You can increase the quantity by collecting waste from local vegetable shops or market stalls.

Tips on creating good compost Make the size of the container as large as you can: 1sq m/3sq ft is the minimum practical size. If your garden is very small, purpose-built compost bins are available.

Use good insulating materials for the container to help maintain the heat in the heap. Line the base of the container with a 15-cm/6-in layer of coarse material like straw or tough stalks or use wire mesh laid over widely spaced bricks to allow air to circulate.

Add about 20cm/8in of fresh mixed material to the container at any one time. The easiest way of doing this is to place waste materials first into a black dustbin liner, mix up, then add the contents when full. By adding a mixture of materials, the heap remains well aerated and doesn't pack down.

Include any fresh or cooked plant or vegetable waste from the house or garden, including lawn mowings. Slightly woody stems will need shredding or chopping.

Do not include animal waste which may attract vermin, woody material such as hedge clippings or rose prunings which will take a long time to break down, any diseased or infected plant material, weeds that have gone to seed or roots of perennial weeds like ground elder, couch grass or creeping buttercup.

The bacteria which act to decompose the material put on the heap need air, moisture and nitrogen. The water is mainly obtained from the leaves put on the heap but you should water dry materials like straw before adding them. Including animal manure in the heap will help to provide nitrogen, as will seaweed or seaweed extract or a proprietary compost activator. Adding lime helps to neutralize the natural acidity. The bacteria prefer a less acid environment so this will also help to speed up decomposition.

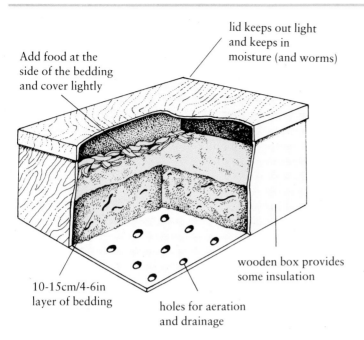

Add food at the side of the bedding and cover lightly

lid keeps out light and keeps in moisture (and worms)

10-15cm/4-6in layer of bedding

holes for aeration and drainage

wooden box provides some insulation

Worm box *Moist compost, shredded newspaper or leaves make up the bedding in the base. The worms are fed with vegetable and kitchen waste.*

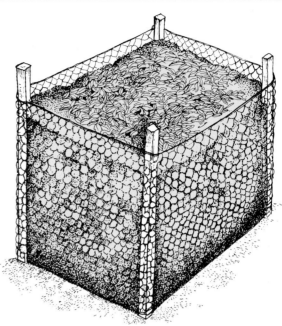

Leaf enclosure *Fill a simple, rectangular structure with leaves, watering them if dry. In 3 years, the resulting mould may be used for potting compost.*

Compost needs to be covered to keep the heat in and to prevent the material becoming too wet. An old piece of carpet or black plastic is suitable. In summer a heap should be ready for use in about three months, in winter it will take more like nine months.

MAKING A COMPOST BIN If you have the room make the compost bin with three separate compartments, one in which to put fresh waste material, one which has been filled up then left to rot down and one of compost ready for use. The sections can be made from timber planks or breeze blocks on three sides of the square with removable wooden boards on the fourth side so that the compost is easy to get at.

Worm compost Worm casts are very rich in nutrients in a form that is readily available to plants, so the compost produced in a worm box is closer to a fertilizer than a compost. The worms used are brandlings which are used by fishermen, and are available from fishing shops. In the base of the box (see illustration above), place a layer of moist compost, shredded newspaper or leaves. Feed the worms with a mixture of chopped-up vegetable and kitchen waste; include some protein which they also need. Animal manure is also suitable. Do not add huge quantities of material, no more than a 7.5-cm/3-in layer per week. Add some calcified seaweed because the worms do not like acid conditions. The worms will work best between 13-25C/55-77F and will die in freezing weather so cover the box with old carpet to insulate it. Some of the compost can be removed after 2 months.

Leaf mould Autumn leaves take a long time to rot down but are well worth collecting and making into leaf mould. In a dry, shady area make a simple frame from four posts pushed into the ground and with wire-netting stretched around them. Fill with leaves, pressing down each layer as you add it, and allow about two to three years for the leaves to decompose. Then use for potting compost or, sieved, for seed compost.

Seaweed A valuable source of organic material for the soil, seaweed can be added directly to the soil but leave it to stand for a few days for some of the salt to evaporate before using it.

Mushroom compost Mushroom compost is a dark, crumbly material. It is the growing medium for commercially cultivated mushrooms, which having been used once is discarded because mushrooms are extremely vulnerable to soil-borne diseases and each crop is grown on fresh, sterilized compost. It is good for improving the texture of the soil but as it contains lime it is more suitable for use on acid soils. Spent mushroom compost usually contains residues of chemicals as well as the fungus gnats they are used to destroy, so it is best to let it stand for 12 months before use.

CARING FOR PLANTS AND GARDEN

In most years it is only necessary to dig the soil, or fork it, to the depth of a spade blade. However, every three to four years it is a good idea to dig more deeply. This stops a compressed layer forming below the cultivated section which will impede drainage and it allows compost or manure to be included at a deeper level. The deeper cultivated soil encourages plant roots to go downwards, drawing nutrients from a greater depth, and this means that they are also more able to withstand drought. Plants can also be grown closer together.

DIGGING Double digging is done in a similar way to single digging (see illustrations below) except that the soil at the bottom of the trench is loosened to a further blade's depth with a fork. A good layer of manure or compost is put into the bottom of the trench, then the soil from the second trench is spread over the manure in the first and soil and compost are forked to mix them. The last trench is filled with the soil from the first.

Heavy soils are usually dug in autumn. The surface is left rough so that frost will help to break up the heavy clods. The surface is forked lightly in the spring, before sowing or planting. The soil in a narrow bed can be formed into a long ridge and covered in manure. This helps drainage and still allows the weather to break up the soil. With light soils it is better to cover the surface with compost or manure through the winter but leave any digging until the spring.

Once the soil has been dug it is important to keep off it. The structure of the soil is easily destroyed so it is wise to keep beds to a size that allows you to attend to growing plants without going on to the soil. Lay a plank on the surface if you have to walk on it.

WEEDING Perennial weeds with creeping root systems, like ground elder, or deep tap roots, like dandelions, need to be dug out and burned. Include even the smallest piece of root.

Annual weeds will gradually decrease over the years if you make sure that you never allow them to flower or seed and remove them as soon as you see them, or even better hoe to remove them before they reach the light. Mulching will help considerably by cutting off the light from emerging weeds but this cannot be done until vegetable seedlings are through.

WATERING In dry weather it is better to water less often but thoroughly than frequently and lightly. Light watering simply encourages roots to grow near to the surface and these will immediately suffer in dry weather whereas deeper roots have a reserve to draw on. It takes time for water to sink through the soil. Check by pushing a finger into the ground: it can look very wet on the top and feel bone dry only a short way below the surface. It is at a deeper level that roots need water.

The exception to the above rule is when watering seedlings which have just been planted out, as they can take up only a little water at a time and will need daily but light watering. Leafy vegetables need a lot of water throughout growth. Fruiting vegetables like tomatoes and cucumbers benefit most if they are watered well when flowering and when the fruits start to swell. Root vegetables should need little watering in the early stages unless it is very dry when, if they are not watered, subsequent heavy rain could result in the roots splitting.

MULCHING Mulching is adding a layer of material on top of the soil to stop the soil from drying out. It can also have a number of other benefits, including warming up the soil, but these depend on what material is

How to dig correctly
First, chop at right angles to the trench, marking out only a small bite at a time.

Holding the spade vertically, and placing one foot on the tread, cut down parallel to the trench.

Slipping one hand down to the base of the handle, turn the clod over into the previous trench.

used. Some materials, black polythene, biodegradable paper, or newspaper for example, will also act as a weed control because they cut out the light from growing weeds. The papers can be dug into the soil at the end of the season. Compost and manure mulches will eventually be drawn into the soil surface by worms and so continue to feed the soil and improve the structure but weeds, like the vegetables, will flourish. They are, however, more easily removed from a mulch. White plastic reflects on to plants and aids growing and ripening fruit, but does not suppress weeds.

Lay plastic mulches when planting out, either between rows of plants or cut crosses in the plastic and plant through them. The easiest way to water plants grown in this way is to lay a length of flat seep hose beneath the plastic and leave it there. Less water will be necessary as the plastic stops evaporation. Any sheet material and especially plastic needs to be held down securely or it can easily blow away. Place it on the soil and with a trowel make 10cm/4in slits in the soil along the edges. Feed the edges of the sheet into the slits and push the soil back over the top to hold the edges in place.

If you are using loose material, allow seedlings to come through before you spread it. Use enough material to make a layer at least 5cm/2in in depth. This can be put down in advance when planting out seedlings and simply be pushed to one side while planting, then moved back into place around the plants afterwards.

FEEDING PLANTS Fertilizers are used to supply extra nutrients to growing plants when needed. They are applied in two ways, either before planting or sowing as a base dressing, which is raked or forked into the soil, or as a top dressing, which is sprinkled around the growing plants, or, if in liquid form, applied with a watering can around the base of a plant.

Plants need the following nutrients plus some trace elements to grow.

NITROGEN – N This is important for leaf growth, so brassicas require large amounts of nitrogen.
PHOSPHATE – P This is necessary for root growth and for young plants and new shoots.
POTASH – K This aids the production of flowers and fruit and keeps plants healthy.

To provide supplies of one or all of these nutrients you can use a chemical or organic fertilizer.
Chemical fertilizers These can contain one major nutrient or are a compound, a balance of all three. They are easy to use, produce quick results and promote high yields but organic growers would argue that flavour suffers and plants are more prone to pests and diseases. Furthermore, artificial fertilizers do not put anything back into the soil itself for the next generation of plants.
Organic fertilizers These are usually gentler in action and so there is no danger of giving plants too much, which can occur with a chemical fertilizer.

CROP ROTATION The few perennial vegetables and a number of herbs require a permanent position but most vegetables are grown as annuals. Those of a similar type have similar requirements of the soil and therefore need to be grown together. They also attract the same pests and diseases, however, which, if the plants were continually grown in the same spot, would build up in the soil. Annually grown crops are therefore moved to a new spot and this is usually done – because of lack of space – on a 3-year rotation. This means that the same plants are only grown every third year in the same spot. In Victorian times a 7-year rotation was used.

Crop rotation also helps to care for the soil as one type of vegetable will remove more of certain nutrients, so the time lapse allows these to be replaced. Peas and beans add nitrogen to the soil which can then be utilized by the next crop and the rotation of shallow and deep rooting vegetables helps the soil structure. Unfortunately, moving the position of a crop does not guarantee that you will have no pests or diseases. Airborne pests will not be deterred and pests in the soil may attack any crop. However, rotation is a valuable

Organic fertilizers, ground minerals and liquid feeds

DRY ORGANIC FERTILIZERS

Dried blood A very quick-acting source of nitrogen.

Fishmeal A useful source of nitrogen and phosphorus, fairly quick acting.

Bonemeal Rich in phosphorus and also contains a little nitrogen. Fairly slow acting, depending partly on how finely it is ground.

Blood, fish and bone Supplies phosphorus and some nitrogen but scarcely any potassium – any brand listing a %K will almost certainly have it added in chemical form.

Hoof and horn Supplies mainly nitrogen; slow action, depending on how finely it is ground.

Seaweed meal One of the few organic fertilizers containing a significant amount of potassium; also supplies nitrogen and a small amount of phosphorus, so is near to being a complete fertilizer like the chemical Growmore.

Calcified seaweed Contains a very wide range of minerals, particularly calcium and magnesium, but none in large quantities, though it is said to help release phosphorus and potash locked up in the soil. It is valuable for poor soils needing trace elements and it can also be used instead of lime to increase alkalinity. It is claimed to work as a compost activator, not because it has a high nitrogen content but because its porous particles provide a good breeding ground for bacteria. This also helps its action in the soil.

Dried animal manures There are several brands of dried animal manure on the market, providing all the nutritional benefits of farmyard manure without the constraints of its bulk. The problem is that some come from intensive farms and contain contaminants. If in doubt about a particular product, contact an organization concerned with organic growing.

Worm casts A concentrated and balanced source of plant foods which you can produce at home (see page 128). The same reservations as for manures apply to products in the shops, as the worms may be fed on the output from intensive farms.

GROUND MINERALS

Rock potash From natural rock containing about 10 per cent potassium, ground to a fine dust; some is available fairly quickly, but it will last in the soil for up to five years.

Rock phosphate A natural ground rock providing a more lasting source of phosphorus than bonemeal.

Dolomite A ground rock similar to limestone, but containing magnesium as well as calcium. Use instead of lime for increasing the alkalinity of the soil, and for correcting magnesium shortage.

Gypsum A ground rock made up mostly of calcium sulphate, which supplies sulphur to the soil. However, it is most often mixed with dolomite and used as a 'soil conditioner' for clays, as it gradually helps the small clay particles to stick together and let water drain through.

LIQUID FERTILIZERS

Seaweed solutions Like calcified seaweed, liquid seaweed contains a wide range of minerals (the main plant foods and trace elements) but in small quantities. It is very useful as a foliar feed to correct deficiencies and to increase general plant health, especially of seedlings. It does not contain sufficient nutrients to feed plants in pots or high yielding greenhouse crops, though its effects are greater than a simple chemical analysis would indicate. Liquid seaweed also contains plant growth hormones; this supports claims that it helps rooting, gives plants some resistance to pests and diseases, improves fruit set, and extends the storage life of fruit and vegetables.

Liquid manures Proprietary liquid manures are available, or you can make your own by suspending a sack of well-rotted manure in a water butt. These liquids contain significant amounts of the main plant foods (although not as much as most chemical liquid feeds) and a range of trace elements.

Comfrey liquid This has a high concentration of potassium, and is therefore particularly useful for feeding fruiting crops such as tomatoes and courgettes. It is also the best feed for greenhouse plants in pots and houseplants. It contains concentrations of nutrients of the same order of magnitude as chemical tomato feeds.

VEGETABLE GROUPS FOR CROP ROTATION

Root crops	Brassicas	Legumes and salad vegetables	Permanent and specialist vegetables
Beetroot	Broccoli	Beans, broad, kidney and runner	Asparagus
Carrot	Brussels sprout	Celeriac	Aubergine
Chicory	Cabbage	Celery	Cucumber
Jerusalem artichoke	Calabrese	Endive	Florence fennel
Parsnip	Cauliflower	Land cress	Globe artichoke
Potato	Kale	Leek	Herbs
Swede	Kohl rabi	Lettuce	Marrow, courgette, pumpkin and squash
Turnip	Radish	Mustard and cress	Pepper
		Onion and shallot	Rhubarb
		Pea, asparagus and mangetout	Tomato
		Spinach, spinach beet and leaf beet	
		Sweet corn	

131

deterrent to those pests that are specific to one type of crop and move little – like the minute eelworms which affect potatoes and cabbages – or to the build-up of diseases caused by fungus such as club root. A good working plan is illustrated below.

It is not possible to be absolutely strict about rotation, because some crops require more space than others or have a specific requirement as regards position, or preferred harvesting time – but it helps to keep to it as closely as you can.

Crop rotation plan

Plot B
Legumes and salad vegetables need rich soil which has been recently manured.

Plot A
Root crops should not be given a plot which has been freshly manured. Grow them on a plot where manure has not been incorporated for two years.

Plot D
This can be reserved for permanent vegetables, speciality crops and your collection of herbs.

Plot C
Brassicas thrive in alkaline or neutral soil. The plot which has just been limed is best for them.

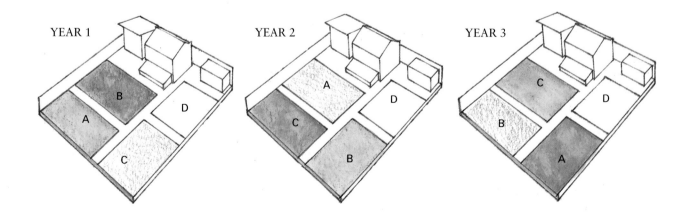

YEAR 1   YEAR 2   YEAR 3

GROWING FROM SEED

The most economic method of growing annual vegetables is to raise them from seed – you will also be able to try less usual varieties.

SOWING OUTDOORS The best seeds for sowing outdoors are those of hardy crops like peas and beans, those which germinate easily and those which dislike being transplanted, such as endive. Check under each specific vegetable for sowing time. Using cloches allows you to sow seeds up to a month earlier. Position the cloches two weeks before sowing so that the soil can warm up.

Preparing the bed A bed dug over in autumn, then left rough over winter, will need levelling with a rake before it is prepared. If it has been dug in spring leave it to settle before preparation. Don't work the soil if it is so damp it sticks to your boots. When it is dry, tread it firm, rake to a fine tilth and follow the steps illustrated on page 136.

Tips for successful germination Don't use old seed, especially if it has been stored at high temperatures or in damp conditions.

Sow at the time recommended, bearing in mind the weather conditions. Seed sown too early may not germinate unless given protection.

Place seeds at the recommended depth, no more (see symbols with each vegetable). If necessary water the drill before sowing, not afterwards, then cover with dry soil. If conditions are very wet, line and cover the drill with dry seed compost.

Thinly sown seeds, which do not have to compete for light, are less likely to be spindly. They are more resistant to diseases and will need less thinning.

Thinning and transplanting seedlings Before thinning or transplanting seedlings grown outdoors, water the plants well. To thin, pull up weak seedlings so that those left are spaced at the required distance. Discard spindly seedlings. If you have to pull up some healthy seedlings, to achieve the right spacings, and wish to transplant them, take them out with care (treat as for Pricking out seedlings – *see below*).

SOWING INDOORS Use fine lump-free seed compost for sowing in trays indoors and sieve if necessary. Fill seed trays almost to the top with compost, pushing it well into the corners. Firm with a flat piece of wood. Stand trays in water until the compost is thoroughly wetted. Sow the seeds thinly on top spacing them 1-2cm/$\frac{1}{2}$-1in apart. The easiest method is to pick them up individually on a wetted knife blade or place the seeds on a sheet of paper and push one off at a time. Lightly cover with a little dry compost, then gently press down the surface. Cover with a sheet of glass or put in a polythene bag. Remove the cover for a short time each day to prevent damping off and check to see if the seeds have germinated. As soon as the first true leaves have appeared, bring the tray into full light.

Tips for successful sowing indoors If you keep your trays on a windowsill, rather than in a greenhouse, place them in a box on its side lined with aluminium foil. This helps light to be reflected back on the seedlings ensuring more even growth.

Don't leave trays by a window at night when there is danger of frost nor in scorching sunlight.

Seed trays can be placed in the airing cupboard as long as the temperature is that required by the seeds for germination. Remove as soon as the first seedlings appear.

Pricking out seedlings
When young seedlings are large enough to handle, loosen their roots with a stick, and prick them out holding by the leaf, not stem.

Fill new trays with John Innes potting compost No. 1 and, making holes large enough to take the seedling roots, plant them up to their necks.

Place a fine rose on a watering can and gently water in the seedlings. Make sure that you keep them out of direct sunlight for a few days.

BEATING PESTS AND DISEASES

Healthy plants are much more resistant to pests and diseases than unhealthy ones which have been starved, forced or grown in overcrowded conditions; see the *Tips on maintaining a healthy garden* below on general prevention. Act as soon as a problem occurs.

ORGANIC CONTROL Attract predators into your garden so that they will do the work for you.

Birds eat grubs, caterpillars, slugs and aphids. Attract them with bird baths and nesting boxes.
Bats come out at dusk to feed on aphids, cutworm moths, craneflies and other insects.
Frogs and toads eat slugs, woodlice and other small insects. A garden pond will encourage them and will also appeal to another slug-eater, the slow worm.
Hedgehogs will remove slugs, cutworms, millipedes, wireworms and woodlice for you. Give them an undisturbed wild corner with a pile of rotting logs, leaves and a tree stump where they can hibernate.
Hoverflies, which look like slim wasps, lay their eggs in colonies of aphids on which the larvae feed. They are attracted to bright, open flowers like marigolds.
Ladybirds and their grey larvae devour aphids. Grow a wide selection of plants to attract them.
Lacewing larvae eat aphids in large quantities. They lay their eggs on the undersides of leaves.
Ground beetles hide under leaves during the day. At night they eat eelworms, cutworms, leather jackets, insect eggs and larvae. Ground cover plants, dense vegetation and organic mulch will all attract them.
Centipedes feed on small insects and slugs and, like ground beetles, need ground cover.

Organic control starts with physically removing any pests you find. When digging, look out for the fat, creamy coloured *leatherjacket* and squash it. Check plants for *grey mould or powdery mildew* and remove and burn any infected leaves or shoots. Remove *aphids* by hand or by spraying with a jet of water. Use an insecticidal soap to spray badly infected plants. Remove *caterpillars* by hand and drop into paraffin. Remove eggs laid by *moths* and *butterflies* on plants, especially cabbages.

Large *slugs* will not harm living plants – it is the small black and brown slugs that attack growing plants. Protect small plants with cut-off plastic bottles pushed into the ground. Surround larger plants with lime or soot, which slugs don't like. Collect slugs and snails at night, and drop into paraffin.

In late summer and autumn *millipedes* tunnel into potatoes and other root crops. A healthy soil with deep dug beds and plenty of manure will help to keep them at bay. During the day *cutworms* eat through the base of a plant and cut it off. Weed to reduce the risk of infestation and hoe around the plant searching for the grubs, as they live just below the soil. Drown in paraffin. *Wireworms* will be attracted by a potato, carrot or split cabbage stalk pushed into the ground. Fix on the end of a stick, then periodically remove the stick and bait and destroy the worms.

Sticky traps can be used to catch *flea beetles and whitefly.* Coat one side of a small piece of wood with heavy grease. Pass the board, grease side down, just over the top of infested plants. The flea beetles will jump up and stick to it. Hang up a grease-coated piece of yellow card to trap whitefly.

CHEMICAL CONTROL If you have a major pest or disease problem you may have to use chemicals. Choose the less toxic plant-based insecticides such as insecticidal soap, pyrethrum, derris, quassia and copper fungicide and follow the manufacturer's instructions closely. Spray on a windless evening when pollinating insects are no longer around.

Tips on maintaining a healthy garden

○ Improve your soil (see pages 11 and 126–7), and continue to dig and feed it well. A healthy soil will grow disease-resistant plants.

○ Crop rotation helps to prevent the build-up of some soil-based pests and diseases.

○ Remove rotting plants and weeds, which attract pests. Burn diseased vegetation.

○ Sow seeds thinly and thin early. Over-crowding encourages disease.

○ Harden plants off completely by placing outside for gradually longer periods before planting out.

○ Plants that grow steadily are much more healthy than those that have a setback. Water when necessary, feed regularly and mulch to retain moisture.

○ Damaged plants attract pests and disease so handle gently and hoe with care.

○ Protect fragile plants from wind with a shield of larger more robust varieties.

○ Act fast to remove aphids as these may be carrying virus diseases.

FRUIT PESTS, PROBLEMS AND DISEASES

Problem	Symptoms	Remedy
Aphids	Visible on shoots. Yellowing and distorted leaves. Sticky coating covered with sooty mould.	Wash off with soapy solution. Use tar oil to destroy over-wintering eggs. Spray with derris or malathion.
Big bud	Black currant buds become large and round and finally wither.	In winter, pick off enlarged buds to prevent spread of virus. Spray with lime sulphur.
Botrytis (grey mould)	Grey fluffy mould on stems, leaves, flowers and fruits.	Avoid overwatering. Remove affected parts. Spray with systemic fungicide.
Cane spot	Stems of raspberries and loganberries are covered with small purple spots in early summer. Spots enlarge to form white blisters.	Cut out affected canes. Spray with benomyl at 14-day intervals.
Canker	Bark of apple and pear trees shrinks in concentric rings.	Cut off damaged twigs. Cut out cankered bark. Coat wound with protective paint.
Capsid bug	Reddish spots and little holes in leaves. Fruits cracked and discoloured.	Keep garden free of debris. Spray apples and black currants in winter with malathion.
Codling moth	Grubs in apples, pears and plums in mid/late summer.	See spraying programme for apples. Trap larvae with corrugated cardboard bands round trunk in mid summer.
Damping off	Seedlings topple over as stems rot.	Sow thinly and do not overwater.
Die back	Branches of fruit trees die from the tips downwards, either from frost damage or fungal attack.	Cut off and burn affected part. Coat cuts with protective paint.
Flea beetle	Small yellow and black beetles puncture leaves with tiny holes.	Good garden hygiene will reduce the number of beetles hibernating in debris. A spray of derris may be used to protect young seedlings.
Leaf spot	Blotches on leaves of black currants and other plants.	Remove and burn affected leaves. Keep garden free of debris. Spray with fungicide.
Peach leaf curl	Rusty blisters on leaves of peaches, nectarines and apricots. Leaves fall prematurely.	Spray with lime sulphur or Bordeaux mixture in mid/late winter and again 14 days later.
Powdery mildew	Leaf surface and fruits covered with white powdery deposit.	Apply sulphur dust, benomyl or dinocap. Remove all diseased shoots in autumn.
Raspberry beetle	Small brown beetles damage flower buds of raspberry, blackberry and loganberry. Grubs eat berries.	Spray with derris as the flowers start to fall and again when berries begin to flush with colour.
Sawfly	Shows on apples as a ribbon scar on the surface with stickiness at entry hole. On gooseberries, leaves are reduced to skeletons.	Destroy fallen apples. Spray with malathion.
Scab	Affects leaves, twigs and fruits of apples and pears, discolouring and distorting.	See spraying programme for apples.
Slugs and snails	Eat stems, roots and leaves of a variety of plants.	Strew soot or sawdust around stems. Pick them up at night and drop into paraffin. Use metaldehyde bait.
Wasps	Attack soft-skinned or damaged fruits.	If damage is severe, catch wasps in jars of sweetened water.

SPRAYING PROGRAMME FOR APPLES

(Do not spray open blossoms with insecticides: remember the busy bees.)

Timing	Materials	Control
Blossom buds showing but still green	Benlate and Malathion (or Rogor)	Scab Mildew Aphids Caterpillars
Immediately after blossoming	Repeat spray 1	as above
14 days later	Benlate Karathane	Scab Mildew
Early summer	Benlate Karathane Malathion	Scab Mildew Codling moth

A KEY TO THE SYMBOLS USED IN THE INDIVIDUAL KITCHEN GARDEN PLANT ENTRIES APPEARS ON PAGE 7

PEAS AND BEANS

Following the crop rotation plan on page 132, peas and beans come under Plot B. They need plenty of organic matter dug in to keep their roots moist. Taller varieties of peas and beans are not suitable for deep dug beds as the soil is unlikely to hold stakes rigid enough. Because legumes make their own nitrogen they need little extra fertilizer. Taller pea and bean varieties can be used to shade summer grown lettuce, land cress or Chinese greens that would otherwise go to seed in hot weather.

STAKING CLIMBERS Most taller varieties of peas and beans need some support. Choosing the particular form of support, whether utilitarian or decorative, adds to the enjoyment of growing these vegetables.

Asparagus peas These do not grow very high, about 45cm/18in, but will still need some support. Use a short twiggy stick for each plant to cling to.

Broad beans Taller varieties of broad beans need supporting. Use stakes that when hammered into the ground stand 90-120cm/3-4ft above the soil and place on each corner of each short double row. You will need extra stakes in long rows. Tie twine from one stake to the next about 30cm/12in above the soil and across row ends. When the plants are about twice this height tie in a second row of twine higher up the posts and a third if necessary.

French beans Dwarf varieties will not need staking but climbing French beans which grow to about 2m/6-7ft need strings, canes or nets to climb up.

Runner beans The traditional support for runner beans is to use two 2.4m/8ft poles or canes, crossed and tied at the top, to form an inverted V. A row of these is placed with one pole at each point where a bean is planted and the row is held rigid by a horizontal cane at the cross points. Alternatively, a length of twine can be used pegged into the ground at each end of the row and attached where each pair of canes crosses. Another method is to use a T-shaped support with twine pegged into the ground at each plant point, then up and over the top of the T to form the inverted V.

If you want to grow the plants up a wall, fix two horizontal battens to the wall one just above the soil, one about 3m/10ft from the ground. Position nails at plant-spaced intervals along the battens and tie vertical lengths of twine between the two. Instead of using a soil height batten you can anchor one end of the string with the plant's root ball itself.

In the flower garden, beans are often grown up wigwam shapes constructed from canes but beans are ornamental enough to clothe a pergola, or surround an arch, particularly if you are waiting for a rose to climb around either.

Sowing seed outdoors
Rake ground previously dug over. Stretch a line down the rows and make straight, shallow drills, using a pointed stick.

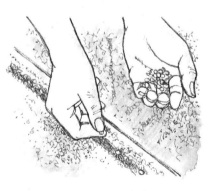

Water the drill lightly. Sow the seeds as evenly and thinly as possible to prevent wastage and reduce the need for thinning out later on.

Cover the seeds by shuffling along the rows, pushing the soil back over the drill. Write labels to indicate crop name and sowing date.

Dwarf varieties are also available or you can pinch out the growing tip of runner beans when they reach a height of about 30cm/12in to produce your own dwarf plants.

Peas Depending on variety, peas can grow from 45-120cm/18in-4ft. Although they can be grown without support, a system of posts with wires or netting stretched between them will keep the plants off the ground. Twiggy sticks about 120cm/4ft long are the traditional supports for peas, if you can find them. Place one beside each plant. Whatever supports are used, make certain they are sufficiently thin for the tendrils to grasp and as tall as the expected height of the variety grown.

In deep beds use a leafless variety and plant every 5cm/2in in rows 15cm/6in apart. Here the plants will support each other.

Mangetout and asparagus These can grow up to 2m/7ft tall depending on variety. Support tall varieties in the same way as runner beans. Dwarf varieties are also available.

AFTER HARVESTING In warmer areas, after harvesting early crops you can cut broad bean plants back to 5cm/2in above the ground and they will grow again to provide a second crop. Peas and beans and broad beans in particular have nitrogen-fixing bacteria in their roots which will improve soil fertility for future crops, so when beans are harvested cut off the stems just above soil level, cut them up and add to the compost heap. Dig in the stem bases and roots. If you have any seeds left after planting use these up in any spare plot of ground later in the season for a late harvest and to provide nitrogen for future crops.

PESTS, PROBLEMS AND DISEASES
Aphids Greenfly and blackfly group on plant stems, especially at new growth tips, and suck the sap. Broad beans are specially vulnerable to blackfly in early to mid summer. Remove the insects by hand or hose them off leaves and shoots. Use an insecticidal soap to spray badly infected plants. Attract ladybirds, lacewings and hoverflies, who eat quantities of these pests.

Chocolate spot Brown, chocolate-colour blotches on leaves and stems of broad beans are symptoms of chocolate spot fungus. Pull up and burn badly affected plants. This is a sign of overcrowding and lack of feeding. Prevent it in the future by following instructions for growing healthy plants and feed plants adequately.

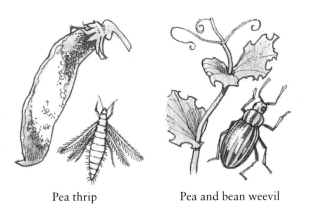

Pea thrip   Pea and bean weevil

Flowers don't set This usually occurs when the plant roots are dry. The flowers wilt and bees and other pollinating insects cannot reach the pollen. Water plants well in dry weather. Dig in plenty of organic matter before you plant beans so that moisture will be retained around the roots.

Halo blight A problem of French and runner beans, the leaves have dark spots surrounded with a lighter colour halo. Spray diseased plants with a copper fungicide. In future check seeds and reject those that are blistered as this is a seed-borne disease. Buy only from a reputable seed supplier and replace your own if they caused the problem.

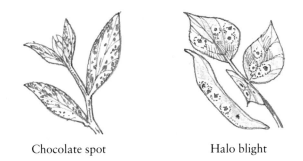

Chocolate spot   Halo blight

Pea and bean weevil This beetle eats pea and bean leaves, leaving serrated edges. If young plants are attacked dust with derris; older plants will be little harmed.

Pea moth Maggots inside the pods are the tiny caterpillars of the pea moth which lays its eggs on the flowers. In a severe attack use derris but as this is also harmful to beneficial insects it is not an ideal answer. Look out for pheromone traps which commercial growers use.

Pea thrips These live on pea foliage and leave a silvery trace behind.

Slugs Young plants are prone to attack by slugs. Protect with cut-off plastic bottles pushed into the ground around the plant.

CLIMBING FRENCH BEAN

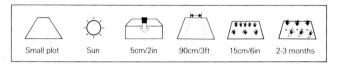

Small plot	Sun	5cm/2in	90cm/3ft	15cm/6in	2-3 months

Climbing French beans are half-hardy annuals which cannot be sown in the open until all danger of frost has passed. This type of bean is most popular in France – hence its common name.

GROWING Light, well-drained soils are required, while it helps if organic manure/compost has been worked in during the autumn preparations. Acid soils will not be tolerated. Incorporate a good general base fertilizer dressing during the final preparations before sowing: 25-50g/m²/1-2oz per sq yd of something like fish and bone meal will be suitable, provided that soft growth is not induced by too much nitrogen. Sow seeds 7.5cm/3in apart and 4-5cm/1½-2in deep from late spring onwards in single rows, spaced 90cm/3ft apart. Thin to 15cm/6in apart in the rows after the first leaves emerge. They are easily damaged by wind buffeting, so grow them in a sheltered spot. The beans can climb as high as 1.5m/5ft, so support with tall pea sticks.

HARVESTING Pick the beans when they are young and tender. Any delay will tend to cause stringiness, even though 'stringless' varieties are available. Regular picking will encourage more pods to develop. Small pods that snap easily and which have no sign of the beans showing through the skin are the tastiest.

POSSIBLE PROBLEMS Aphids may damage the pods.

DWARF FRENCH BEAN

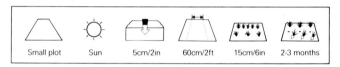

Small plot	Sun	5cm/2in	60cm/2ft	15cm/6in	2-3 months

Dwarf French beans are half-hardy annuals which cannot be sown in the open until all danger of frost has passed. They are grown for their edible pods, which are usually sliced before cooking. The traditional French bean varieties produce flat pods but cylindrical or 'pencil'-podded varieties are now available.

GROWING Light, well-drained soils are required, while it helps if organic manure/compost has been worked in during the autumn preparations. Acid soils will not be tolerated. Incorporate a good general base fertilizer dressing during the final preparations before sowing: 25-50g/m²/1-2oz per sq yd, of something like fish and bone meal will be suitable, provided that soft growth is not induced by too much nitrogen. Sow seeds 7.5cm/3in apart and 4-5cm/1½-2in deep from late spring onwards in single rows, spaced 45-60cm/1ft 6in-2ft apart. Thin after the first leaves emerge.

HARVESTING Pick the beans when they are young and tender. Regular picking will encourage more pods to develop. The beans are in prime condition for picking when the pods can be snapped cleanly. At the end of the crop, remove the visible parts of the plants and dig in the roots to provide valuable nitrogen.

POSSIBLE PROBLEMS Look out for slugs and aphids. Weeds may swamp young plants; hoe carefully, for they are very easily chopped off at ground level.

■ GARDENER'S TIP

Train climbing vegetables up a tepee of canes. Then while the plants are still small you can use the space beneath for a fast-growing crop like garden cress or lettuces.

■ COOK'S TIP

Use French beans when they are young, then you only need to top and tail them. Steam them for a short time so that they are still crunchy, then eat them on their own with butter and freshly ground black pepper or sprinkle with chopped, toasted almonds.

For a delicious salad, make a French dressing, mix with a tablespoon of Greek yoghurt and toss the beans in this. Chop up tomatoes, sprinkle with freshly chopped basil and add to the bean salad.

PURPLE-PODDED FRENCH BEAN

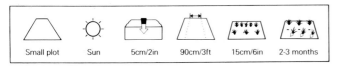

Small plot	Sun	5cm/2in	90cm/3ft	15cm/6in	2-3 months

Purple-podded French beans are half-hardy annuals which cannot be sown in the open until frosts are over. They lose the purple colour during cooking and compare well with other French beans for flavour.

GROWING Light, well-drained soils are required, while it helps if organic manure/compost has been worked in during the autumn preparations. Acid soils will not be tolerated. Incorporate a good general base fertilizer dressing during the final preparations before sowing: 25-50g/m²/1-2oz per sq yd of something like fish and bone meal will be suitable, provided that soft growth is not induced by too much nitrogen. Sow seeds 7.5cm/3in apart and 4-5cm/1½-2in deep from late spring onwards in single rows, spaced 90cm/3ft apart. Thin after the first leaves emerge. They are easily damaged by wind buffeting, so grow them in a sheltered spot. The beans can climb as high as 1.5m/5ft, so support with tall pea sticks, bamboo canes or strings.

HARVESTING Pick the beans when they are young and tender. Purple-podded French beans are stringless and remain tender longer than other types. Regular picking will encourage more pods to develop.

POSSIBLE PROBLEMS Aphids may damage the pods.

SCARLET RUNNER BEAN

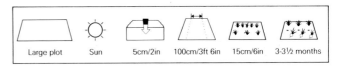

Large plot	Sun	5cm/2in	100cm/3ft 6in	15cm/6in	3-3½ months

A perennial, usually grown as an annual, the scarlet runner bean is a very tender plant and will be killed by very slight frosts either at the beginning or end of the season. By nature it is a climber and most crops reach a height of 1.5-1.8m/5-6ft when grown on supports. As well as producing quantities of beans both for fresh consumption and freezing, runner bean plants form very attractive living screens in summer.

GROWING The best results are obtained in fertile, well-drained land which has been deeply dug in the autumn and had liberal dressings of organic manure incorporated. This helps to improve soil structure as well as retaining moisture. Maincrop runner beans are sown outside from late spring onwards. Sow the seeds 5cm/2in deep and 15cm/6in apart in double rows, leaving 60cm/2ft between the two lines of plants and 100cm/3ft 6in between each double row. As soon as the young plants emerge, push 2.5m/9ft long poles or bamboo canes into the ground and when the plants are tall enough, train them on to the supports. Water regularly and very thoroughly in dry weather.

HARVESTING Pick before the seeds become obvious through the pod wall. Regular picking will ensure continuous flowering and fruiting.

POSSIBLE PROBLEMS Look out for aphids in summer.

■ DECORATIVE TIP

Grow the variety Purple Tepee up bamboo canes to form a wigwam shape. Pods are held above the foliage forming the shape of a North American Indian tepee. The pods have an excellent flavour. They are also suitable for late planting.

■ DECORATIVE TIP

While waiting for newly bought climbing roses or clematis to make their way around an arch or arbour, let runner beans clothe it with their decorative flowers and pods.

BROAD BEAN

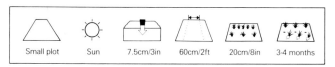

| Small plot | Sun | 7.5cm/3in | 60cm/2ft | 20cm/8in | 3-4 months |

Broad beans are the hardiest of the legumes that we grow. They are usually shelled from the pods when they are almost fully grown, although young pods may be cooked whole or sliced like French or runner beans.

GROWING The earliest of the successful sowings in the spring will need to be made into light, open-textured soils. In common with many other legumes, broad beans do not grow well in acid soils. On soils which are reasonably fertile and have had organic material worked into them, it should be possible to apply base fertilizers which just provide phosphate and potassium. You can grow broad beans in double rows, allowing 20cm/8in between the two lines and from 60-90cm/2-3ft, according to variety, between the double rows. Alternatively they can be grown in single rows spaced 60cm/2ft apart. Put each individual seed into a 5-7.5cm/2-3in deep hole made with a dibber.

HARVESTING Pick beans for slicing or cooking whole when they are 7.5cm/3in long. Those for shelling are ready when the seeds are about 2cm/³⁄₄in across.

POSSIBLE PROBLEMS Blackfly may attack from late spring onwards but the damage can be reduced by pinching out the tops of the plants when they are in full flower. Give support to large plants by knocking in stakes at each corner of the growing area and encircling the crop with string.

ASPARAGUS PEA

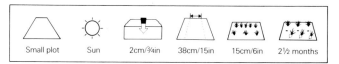

| Small plot | Sun | 2cm/³⁄₄in | 38cm/15in | 15cm/6in | 2½ months |

The asparagus pea is a half-hardy annual, grown for its curiously ribbed pods, which are eaten whole like a mangetout pea. The pods have a slight flavour of asparagus. This legume is not a true pea, but a type of vetch. Only the species *Tetragonolobus purpureus* is available.

GROWING Asparagus peas grow best in deep, rich soils which are moisture retentive. Sow in late spring, when the danger of frost is almost past. With its low-growing, bushy habit, the asparagus pea should be grown in a single, narrow drill with seeds sown 10-15cm/4-6in apart and 1-2cm/³⁄₄in deep. In dry weather, the bottom of the drill should be well watered and then allowed to drain before sowing. After sowing, rake the soil back over the seeds. Like ordinary garden peas, asparagus peas need pea sticks for support.

HARVESTING Pick as soon as the peas are 2.5cm/1in long or they will become stringy. Regular picking encourages the plants to go on cropping over a period of several weeks.

POSSIBLE PROBLEMS The asparagus pea tends to crop far less than peas but, by way of compensation, has fewer ailments.

▓ ORGANIC TIP

If you cut plants down to 5cm/2in after harvesting they should regrow to give you a second crop. The roots of bean plants take nitrogen from the air and fix it in the soil so plant any leftover seeds, then dig in the young plants as manure.

▓ DECORATIVE TIP

Asparagus peas, which grow to about 45cm/18in, make an ornamental addition to the flower garden with their clover-like foliage and unusual pods preceded by deep rusty-red flowers. They also make an attractive addition to the table and can be eaten raw in salads when very small, or steamed for about 5 minutes, seasoned and tossed in butter.

Mangetout

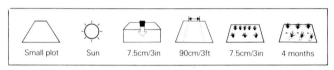

Small plot	Sun	7.5cm/3in	90cm/3ft	7.5cm/3in	4 months

Sugar pea is another name for the mangetout pea. The whole pod, complete with the young, immature seeds, is eaten, after topping and tailing and cooking.

GROWING Like all peas, mangetout grow best in deep, rich soils which are moisture retentive. Sow at intervals from early to mid spring in flat-bottomed drills which are 10-15cm/4-6in wide and 5-7.5cm/2-3in deep. Scatter the peas evenly in the bottom of the drill to leave the individual seeds 5-7.5cm/2-3in apart. Rake the soil back over the seeds. Distances between rows will vary from 60cm-1.2m/2-4ft and should be roughly equivalent to the expected height of the varieties being sown. When the seedlings are 5-7.5cm/2-3in high, provide support with well-branched and twiggy pea sticks.

HARVESTING Pick the pods while flat and immature – before you can see the seeds from the outside and when they are 7.5cm/3in long. Pick – regularly to encourage yield – from the bottom of the plant upwards.

POSSIBLE PROBLEMS Birds and mice may cause damage by eating or removing the germinating seeds. Two or three single strands of black cotton, not nylon thread, above the seed row will hinder birds. Shaking the seed in a little powdered seed dressing before sowing, or stretching a renardine-soaked string along the soil surface, will both deter mice.

Pea

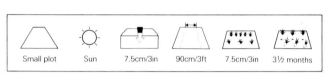

Small plot	Sun	7.5cm/3in	90cm/3ft	7.5cm/3in	3½ months

The early types of pea were round-seeded, but the less hardy, wrinkle-seeded or marrowfat peas have a much higher sugar content and, as a result, a better flavour. Round-seeded peas are now mainly used for winter and early spring sowings because of their greater hardiness.

GROWING Peas grow best in deep, rich soils which are moisture retentive. It is most important that the roots are always able to obtain enough water. Sow at intervals from early to mid spring in flat-bottomed drills which are 10-15cm/4-6in wide and 5-7.5cm/2-3in deep. Scatter the peas evenly in the bottom of the drill to leave the individual seeds 5-7.5cm/2-3in apart. Rake the soil back over the seeds. Distances between rows will vary from 60-1.2m/2-4ft and should be roughly equivalent to the expected height of the varieties being grown. When the seedlings are 5-7.5cm/2-3in high, provide support with twiggy pea sticks. Make certain that they are thin enough for the tendrils to grasp and as tall as the expected height of the variety being grown.

HARVESTING First early, second early and maincrop peas sown at intervals during early and mid spring will produce mature crops through early and mid summer. Your crop should be ready for picking to start about 3 weeks after flowering. Pick while young and tender, at 2 to 3 day intervals.

POSSIBLE PROBLEMS A serious pest is the pea moth.

◼ DECORATIVE TIP

Tall varieties, which grow to about 1.5m/5ft, can be grown in the smallest garden if you train the plants on wires or up climbers on the walls. Or use them in place of sweet peas as a decorative barrier between flower and vegetable garden.

◼ ORGANIC TIP

Planting can sometimes be planned to miss the worst period of attack by a particular pest. Peas that are sown early or late will miss most of the damage caused by pea moth larvae. Alternatively, see if you can procure pheromone traps.

Pheromone is a chemical secreted by the female moth to attract males and is available on a sticky tab. The attracted male sticks fast so is unable to mate with the female and reproduction is prevented.

SALAD VEGETABLES

Like many other vegetables the majority of salad plants require fertile soil, good drainage and some sun and shelter. Improvements can be made to your soil, whatever type it is (see pages 6-9), and the regular addition of organic matter will then ensure that plants receive their necessary supply of nutrients.

Waterlogging proves fatal to most salad plants, so check that the soil drains well and correct any problem before you start to prepare your salad garden.

WHERE TO GROW SALAD PLANTS Plants will grow far more sturdily if they are sheltered from wind. If your site is exposed then it pays to erect windbreaks. Vegetables such as runner beans or Jerusalem artichokes will provide shelter.

As the structure of the soil can be damaged if you walk on it, particularly in wet weather, it is a good idea to plan beds to a width that is comfortable for you to work on from a path on either side. The width is a personal choice but somewhere between 1-1.5m/3-5ft should allow you to do any work on the plants without treading on the bed. If you don't have the space for a separate vegetable or salad garden this need not stop you from growing a range of salad ingredients.

IN THE FLOWER GARDEN Some of the colourful varieties of loose-leaf lettuces, lemon-shaped cucumbers and purple-leaved beetroot are all decorative enough to earn a space in the flower garden.

However, vegetables require a more fertile soil than ornamental plants so if you want them to flourish, fork in compost where you are to plant them and mulch well afterwards. Allow small plants plenty of space in which to grow. Group them rather than dot individual plants around the space.

In containers Growing bags, boxes and pots can all be used to grow salad plants where space is very limited. The yield will not, however, be as great as from those planted directly into the ground.

Different plants require different soil depths. Lettuces need about 15cm/6in, larger plants like cucumbers, tomatoes and peppers need at least 23cm/9in. Tall plants that need staking must be sheltered from winds as they so easily become top heavy. Growing bags are probably the best containers to use. Because containers are exposed to all-round heat they dry out very fast in hot weather and need daily watering. Lining with plastic helps, but provide a few drainage holes first. Cutting out small crosses or slits in the tops of growing bags where plants are positioned, rather than cutting a larger opening, also helps moisture retention.

RESTRICTED SPACE Where space is restricted there are some useful techniques that can be put into operation to get the best possible value from the land. *Using the block system* Many more plants can be raised if plants are grown in blocks or staggered rows rather than in the traditional straight single or double rows. Each plant is provided with a circle of space which it will fill when fully grown. Plants protect each other equally on all sides, and, because each one is provided with exactly the right amount of space to grow well, there is little room available for weeds to flourish. *Deep digging* The block system can be used in conjunction with deep digging. The roots of plants grown in a deeply dug area will grow downwards, taking up less surrounding soil and thus allowing plants to be placed closer together. See page 129 for deep digging techniques.

Training plants vertically Trailing plants like cucumbers take up much less space, as well as looking decorative if they are grown up a wigwam or ridge tent shape of canes (see Tip on page 147). Where there are alternative forms and space is at a premium, choose varieties that will climb rather than bush out.

Grow trailing nasturtiums in hanging baskets or window boxes.

A CONTINUOUS SUPPLY There are a number of methods you can use to extend the growing season and to spread out the time when plants are in peak condition.

Mixing varieties By mixing varieties of one type of plant and by growing a wide range of salad plants suited to different weather conditions, the season when plants are available is greatly extended.

For instance, if you grow both globe and long beetroot, the round beetroot will provide a supply through the summer and the long varieties, which store well, will come into use through the winter. Young beetroot leaves can also be used in salads, either freshly chopped or cooked lightly.

Endive comes into its own when summer lettuce supplies die out. Curled-leaved endive can be used for salads from early to late autumn. Winter radishes, sown in late summer, are ready about 3 months later. Leave the crop in the ground during winter, lifting as needed.

The slow-growing corn salad, or lamb's lettuce, is a hardy plant that can survive low temperatures outside, although it will do better if protected. It therefore provides another useful winter or early spring crop.

Staggered sowing Salad plants which mature and then are quickly past their best, such as many lettuces and summer radish, need to be sown frequently in small quantities so that they mature over an extended period rather than arriving at peak condition all at the same time. It is difficult to plan staggered sowing accurately. Sowing seeds every 1-2 weeks is not exact enough, as the speed of plant growth can be erratic, affected by the weather. Rather than sowing at 10 or 14 day intervals, you may find it more reliable to start off a new batch when the last sown seedlings appear or reach a certain size.

Experiment to find out what works best for you, keeping a note of dates sown, and when the same plants are harvested. This will give you some idea of how often and how much you need to sow to provide the quantities you require.

To some extent, a staggered crop can also be obtained by planting out the larger size seedlings from one sowing first, then planting out another lot from the same group when these have reached the larger size and so on. Always keep a few seedlings ready to plant in a vacant space when it arises.

Seedling crops Use a vacant space, even a small one, early in the summer or in the autumn, to grow a seedling crop. Protected, many seedlings can even be

Successional sowing
Sow quick-growing crops, like lettuces, at frequent intervals to give you a steady supply of fresh produce.

grown into the winter. Plants are cut and eaten when they are still small, tasty and very nutritious and it is possible to get up to three cuttings from one sowing. Many lettuce seeds can be used in this way – experiment with any leftover seeds you have. Corn salad, or lamb's lettuce, and radish are other suitable salad plants for a seedling crop. Utilize growing bags left empty after tomatoes or peppers are harvested in this way, but bear in mind the soil will have few nutrients left in it by then and extra feeding will probably be necessary.

PROVIDING PROTECTION A greenhouse or walk-in polythene tunnel will not only allow you to bring on plants early and to grow more exotic salad plants successfully in summer, but also to grow a supply of leafy salad plants almost around the year. Where space is limited, use cloches and frames to provide valuable protection from cold and wind for low-growing plants allowing them to be harvested earlier in the year and grown further into the winter. The introduction to Fruiting Vegetables on page 152 gives more information on protecting plants. Cloches can also be used inside a greenhouse or walk-in tunnel to give extra winter protection.

PESTS, DISEASES AND DISORDERS
Aphids Greenfly may attack the plants. Remove by hand where possible or spray with insecticidal soap.
Bolting A check to growth, overcrowding or lack of water causes lettuces to flower, making them bitter and inedible. Transplant as soon as seedlings are large enough and keep well watered.
Damping off Seedlings collapse at ground level if affected by this disease. Always raise seeds in sterilized compost, do not sow too thickly and do not overwater.

GLOBE BEETROOT

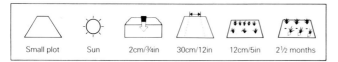

| Small plot | Sun | 2cm/¾in | 30cm/12in | 12cm/5in | 2½ months |

This type of beetroot has small, globular roots and is best for summer use and for pickling.

GROWING Light, sandy soils are best. Soil that is flinty or stony or which has been recently manured will produce mis-shapen roots. Deep digging should be done in the autumn, leaving the surface rough over winter. Prepare a fine tilth and work in a general purpose fertilizer just before sowing. Plants from sowings made too early may 'bolt', even if bolting-resistant varieties are used. Sow seed clusters from mid spring to early summer, soaking seed overnight to assist germination. Provide cloches to protect the earliest sowings and in colder districts. Keep weeds under control, but be careful not to damage the roots when hoeing. Water sparingly except in very dry summers, when beetroots tend to become woody.

HARVESTING Pick from early summer, lifting carefully to avoid damaging the roots, which will 'bleed' when pierced. Pick by hand if possible, or use a flat-tined fork and grasp the leaves like a handle. Twist off the tops carefully to keep the roots intact for cooking.

POSSIBLE PROBLEMS Keep aphids at bay on the young leaves. Plants sown too close together may attract carrot fly.

LONG BEETROOT

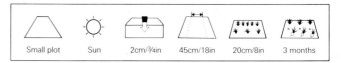

| Small plot | Sun | 2cm/¾in | 45cm/18in | 20cm/8in | 3 months |

Long varieties of beetroot can be stored over winter, making this an all-the-year-round vegetable. Beetroot make a delicious winter vegetable, served hot with creamy white sauce.

GROWING Soil requirements are as for globe beetroot, remembering that even heavy soils can be used, provided they have been lightened by the addition of peat or organic compost when digging in the autumn. Maincrop long beets should be sown in late spring, and the seedlings thinned 2-3 weeks after they emerge. Keep on top of weeds, always being careful not to damage the beets.

HARVESTING Long beetroot may either be left in the ground until required – in which case they should be strawed over to give protection against the severest frosts – or the roots can be lifted, cleaned and stored. Lift before late autumn as described for globe beets, discarding any that are damaged or diseased. If you cut the leaves off rather than twisting them, don't cut too close to the crown or 'bleeding' will occur.

STORAGE Place the trimmed beetroot on their sides in boxes of slightly damp sand. Keep the boxes in an airy frost-free place and inspect them at regular intervals.

POSSIBLE PROBLEMS Boron deficiency causes heart rot.

▦ COOK'S TIP

Young beetroot leaves can be used in salads raw or can be lightly cooked and eaten like spinach. Raw beetroot can be grated and used in salad in place of cooked beet. One of the most delicious soups, borsch, is made from beetroot cooked with other vegetables and stock. Tomato sauce, sugar and lemon juice are added towards the end of cooking. Finally it is topped with soured cream. Or try hot cooked beetroot coated in creamy white sauce.

▦ ORGANIC TIP

While seedlings are young hoe around them to keep weed free. Later the covering of beet leaves should keep weeds at bay. Layers of newspaper can be used as a mulch as they will eradicate the light from any growing weeds.

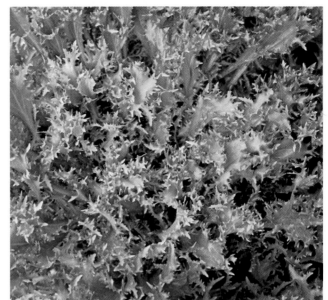

SUGARLOAF CHICORY

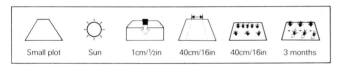

Small plot	Sun	1cm/½in	40cm/16in	40cm/16in	3 months

This variety of chicory, called *Pain de Sucre*, is the best if you want to use the leaves in salads, because they do not require blanching. It looks rather like a cos lettuce in shape.

GROWING A deep, fertile soil which has been well-manured for the previous crop is suitable. Sow seeds in the open from early to mid summer, and keep the rows well-hoed to eliminate weeds.

HARVESTING Sugarloaf chicory can be picked as soon as a heart has formed. Unlike lettuce, it can be left in the ground until it is needed without going to seed, a great advantage in dry seasons.

POSSIBLE PROBLEMS Watch for slugs and caterpillars.

CURLED-LEAVED ENDIVE

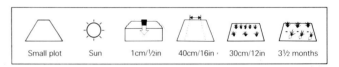

Small plot	Sun	1cm/½in	40cm/16in	30cm/12in	3½ months

Curled-leaved endive is the type most commonly eaten in salads. Its pale green, crisp leaves are deeply dissected and curled. As in the case of broad-leaved endive, for which see page 166, blanching is necessary to counteract its naturally bitter taste. Curled-leaved endive provides a summer and autumn crop.

GROWING As with most salad crops light, well-drained fertile soils are best, with a dressing of general, balanced fertilizer before sowing. Sow successively from early spring to late summer. Sow the seed in 1-cm/½-in deep drills spaced 40cm/16in apart. When the seedlings are 5-7.5cm/2-3in high, thin them out to 30cm/12in apart.

BLANCHING Endive plants are usually ready for blanching about 3 months after sowing and it may be done in one of two ways. The leaves can be gathered together when dry (damp plants may rot during blanching) and tied round with raffia string. This keeps the light away from all but the outer leaves. Alternatively, the plants can be completely covered with containers.

HARVESTING Blanching takes about 2 weeks in later summer. Only blanch the plants you require for immediate use, for they will soon rot once blanched.

POSSIBLE PROBLEMS Watch out for greenfly during the summer months, and avoid running to seed or bolting by correct watering during dry periods.

■ ORGANIC TIP

These chicories can be grown and harvested during autumn and winter when other salad materials are scarce. However, they will need protection in colder areas. Mix green-leaved chicories with the decorative red and variegated varieties which are expensive to buy and easy to grow. These start life green but their colour changes when the weather turns colder and, at the same time, they also form small, tight hearts.

■ ORGANIC TIP

Even dew can cause rot when blanching so dry leaves are very important. In summer, blanch plants in position using an upturned flower pot (cover any holes up first) or a bucket. You can also use a plate placed over each plant head.

LAND CRESS

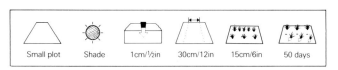

Small plot	Shade	1cm/½in	30cm/12in	15cm/6in	50 days

Otherwise known as American cress, land cress is a useful substitute for watercress (which is difficult to grow in the kitchen garden as it needs an uncontaminated stream of gently running water). Similar in flavour, land cress is easy to grow in a shady, damp corner.

GROWING Prepare the soil by forking in plenty of organic material and rake to a fine tilth. Sow seed thinly from early spring to late summer at 3 week intervals. Thin the young plants when they are large enough to handle. Late summer sowings should be protected by cloches to give useful supplies of winter cress.

HARVESTING Sowings made in spring and summer will be ready for cutting in 8-10 weeks. Cut the young tender shoots as soon as they are ready. If left to stand they may flower and become tough and bitter.

POSSIBLE PROBLEMS Flea beetle can be a problem in the early stages.

MUSTARD AND CRESS

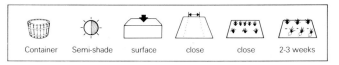

Container	Semi-shade	surface	close	close	2-3 weeks

This combination of slightly peppery leaves is easy to grow, and is delicious in salads and sandwiches or as a garnish.

GROWING To grow mustard and cress indoors during the winter, fill a small box with bulb fibre or a moist peat/soil mixture and strew cress seeds on top. Press the seeds into the growing medium with your fingers. Cover the box to exclude light. Mustard germinates faster than cress. After 4 days, strew mustard seeds over the cress, dampen slightly and cover again. When the seeds have germinated, bring the box into the light. During the spring and summer, mustard and cress can be grown in the open on light, moisture-retentive soils in the same way. Sow about every 2 weeks for a steady supply.

HARVESTING Snip off the fine stems and leaves when they are 4cm/1½in high.

POSSIBLE PROBLEMS Trouble-free.

▨ ORGANIC TIP

If you do not have a shady spot to grow land cress, position plants near to climbers like runner beans, or tall plants like sweet corn. These will provide the necessary shade and help to stop plants drying out. Water well on dry days.

▨ HEALTH TIP

Mustard and cress are high in vitamins and minerals, so they are a specially valuable addition to winter salads. Children will enjoy growing this quickly harvested crop. Use damp blotting paper, cotton wool or a flannel and spread the pre- *soaked seeds evenly over the base. Keep in the dark, rinsing daily. To do this, before the seeds have rooted, hold them in place with the back of a spoon. Bring out into the light to green up before harvesting.*

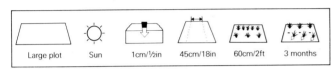

RIDGE CUCUMBER

Large plot	Sun	1cm/½in	45cm/18in	60cm/2ft	3 months

If you do not have a heated greenhouse and live in a cooler climate, you can still grow cucumbers if you choose the small variety that can be eaten in salads or pickled.

GROWING Dig the land deeply and thoroughly in the autumn and leave it rough for over-winter weathering. Before planting, take out a trench 30cm/12in deep and 45cm/18in wide. Half-fill it with manure and replace the soil to form a ridge. Plants must not be set out until all danger of frost is past. You can raise plants in the greenhouse and set them out in early summer, or sow seeds directly into the ridges at the end of spring covering them with cloches or jam jars. Sow seeds in pairs, and if both germinate, discard the weaker plant. Stop the plants after the sixth leaf and restrict side shoots to the space available. On ridge cucumbers both male and female flowers are needed to ensure fertilization. Water well and after the fruits have begun to set give the plants a high-nitrogen liquid feed.

HARVESTING Pick cucumbers when 15-20cm/6-8in long for salads, 5cm/2in long for gherkins.

POSSIBLE PROBLEMS Cucumber mosaic virus causes mottled leaves and fruits and stunted plants. Keep aphids under control.

■ GARDENER'S TIP

For the best use of space train cucumbers up canes. Create a wigwam shape by trying the canes together at the top. This also keeps the cucumbers out of the reach of slugs. Use soft string, to avoid damage, and tie the plants in as they grow.

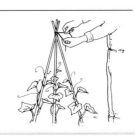

CUCUMBER

Greenhouse	Sun	1cm/½in	single row	90cm/3ft	4 months

Greenhouse cucumbers need careful attention but as few as two plants can be very productive.

GROWING Three weeks before planting, prepare a special cucumber bed on the greenhouse floor, using a mixture of 2 parts well-rotted organic manure to 1 part peat or loam. Build the beds 60cm/2ft wide, 45cm/18in deep with a domed top. Cover with a 15cm/6in layer of peat or loam. Water liberally and keep the temperature constant at 21-25C/70-75F. In late winter/early spring sow seeds singly in 9-cm/3½-in pots at the above temperature. After germination, give the seedlings maximum light and reduce the temperature slightly. At the three-leaf stage, pot on to 14cm/5½-in pots. Water and spray very thoroughly to maintain essential humidity. After 4 weeks, work a general purpose fertilizer into the prepared beds and plant the cucumbers out with a little of the rootball showing (this helps water drain away). The plants need the support of wires or strings as they grow upwards and outwards. Stop the main stem when it reaches the roof and allow the cucumbers to develop on side branches, which should be stopped after 2 leaves. Grow all-female plants in order to avoid fertilization, which causes bitterness. Maintain high temperatures and humidity.

HARVESTING Pick cucumbers when young and succulent, at about 30cm/12in.

POSSIBLE PROBLEMS Glasshouse whitefly; root rot fungi; grey mould.

■ COOK'S TIP

For a refreshing salad, slice up the cucumber and arrange in a bowl. Pour over a dressing made from strained yogurt, oil and lemon juice plus crushed garlic, chopped mint and seasoning. Add more yogurt to turn this into a dip for eating outdoors

with warmed pitta bread. Cucumber, onions, garlic and mushrooms sautéd, then simmered in chicken stock and garnished with soured cream and chives make a mouth-watering cold soup.

BUTTERHEAD LETTUCE

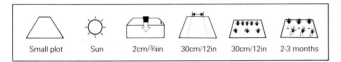

Small plot	Sun	2cm/¾in	30cm/12in	30cm/12in	2-3 months

COS LETTUCE

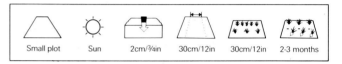

Small plot	Sun	2cm/¾in	30cm/12in	30cm/12in	2-3 months

Of all the varieties of lettuce available, this cabbage lettuce is the most popular. The name butterhead refers to the 'buttery' texture of the smooth, flattened leaves in named varieties such as Suzan and Fortune.

GROWING Butterhead lettuces can be raised in the open in the same way as crisphead types. The difficulty of watering lettuces under cloches makes the moisture-retentive quality of the soil even more important for over-wintering crops that can be picked in late spring. Sow seed of hardy varieties out in early autumn; alternatively, raise seedlings in trays and plant out in late autumn (in sheltered districts) or early spring (in more exposed areas). Apply fertilizer in the form of a top dressing just as growth recommences in the spring. Crops protected by unheated greenhouses, frames or cloches should be raised from transplanted seedlings. Sow in late summer and transplant a month later for mature plants in early winter; autumn plantings will be ready in early spring, while seeds sown in mid-winter and transplanted in late winter will be ready for cutting in mid to late spring.

HARVESTING Since lettuces contain a high percentage of water they wilt rapidly after cutting. Freshness will be improved by immersing the lettuce in ice-cold water for 15 minutes. Shake off the water and place the lettuce in the refrigerator until needed.

POSSIBLE PROBLEMS Aphids are the worst pest.

The leaves of cos lettuce are long and crisp, with a sweeter flavour than cabbage types. Since the plants take longer to reach maturity, they take up space in the vegetable garden for an extended period. In smaller gardens, a dwarf variety like Little Gem may be recommended for this reason.

GROWING For summer crops raised in the open, apply a base dressing of a general-purpose fertilizer before sowing and/or transplanting. Thin seedlings when large enough to handle, reducing the distances for Little Gem to 25cm/10in between the rows and 15cm/6in between the plants. Keep weeds in check. For over-wintering, see Butterhead lettuce, and choose a suitably hardy variety.

HARVESTING Cos lettuces are less likely to bolt than cabbage lettuces, but in hot, dry weather inspect the plants regularly and pick them as soon as they mature.

POSSIBLE PROBLEMS As well as aphids and slugs, lettuces are susceptible to damping-off diseases and mildew.

▓ ORGANIC TIP

Slugs are often a major problem when lettuces are small. One of the most effective methods of reducing numbers is to go out in the late evening with a plastic bag and pick up any that are feeding. Drop them in paraffin to kill them quickly. You can also use a mulch of pine bark or surround plants with soot or lime. On young lettuces use plastic bottles with the base removed and slip one, right way up, over each plant to protect it.

▓ GARDENER'S TIP

If some cos lettuces are grown close together they grow upright, produce good leaves more quickly and do not form hearts. Space 10cm/4in apart. Stumps of lettuces can also be left in the ground to regrow and provide a second crop.

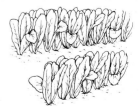

CRISPHEAD LETTUCE

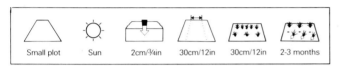

Small plot	Sun	2cm/¾in	30cm/12in	30cm/12in	2-3 months

The leaves of crisphead lettuce are large, curled and, as the name suggests, pleasantly crunchy. The old favourite, Webb's Wonderful, withstands heat and drought better than most.

GROWING Lettuces need light, moisture-retentive soil. For unprotected plants, sow seed in the open at fortnightly intervals from mid spring to late summer. Crisphead varieties of cabbage lettuce are not as well suited to over wintering as butterhead types. Thin out the seedlings as soon as they can be handled. Keep the beds free of weeds and water the plants well.

HARVESTING In warm weather, lettuces of all types run to seed ('bolt') quickly, so check regularly and pick mature plants as soon as they are ready. Pick in the cool morning if you can.

POSSIBLE PROBLEMS Aphids; slugs. Diseases include damping-off diseases and mildew if weather conditions are cold and damp.

LOOSE LEAF LETTUCE

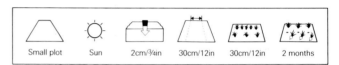

Small plot	Sun	2cm/¾in	30cm/12in	30cm/12in	2 months

Sometimes called chicken lettuce, these varieties are not harvested whole, nor do they form a heart like cabbage and cos lettuces, but individual leaves are picked as required. This cut-and-come again approach is useful as it allows space to be used for other crops. With the advent of frilly varieties like Lollo Rossa with red leaves, these lettuces are becoming very popular in gourmet salads. The long-established variety Salad Bowl is now also available with red leaves as well as the standard green.

GROWING Leaf lettuces should be grown as outdoor summer crops like crispheads, and need the same light, moisture retentive soil as other types.

HARVESTING Leaves are produced throughout the summer. Pick a few from each plant as needed. When all leaves have been used or died down, lift and discard the plant.

POSSIBLE PROBLEMS Aphids, which may carry virus diseases; slugs are a nuisance. Cold and wet weather encourages mildew and mould.

▪ GARDENER'S TIP

When growing hearting lettuces stagger the plants in adjacent rows for the best use of space. While these are young grow a seedling crop in the spaces, using up leftover seeds of loose leaf varieties and cutting off young leaves.

▪ COOK'S TIP

Grow an alternating border of differently coloured and shaped loose-leaf lettuces to provide a decorative edging to a vegetable, herb or flower bed. Choose from red and green oak-leaved, the frill-edged red and green Lollo or red-leaved Marvel of Four

Seasons. Picking a few leaves from each plant will give you an attractive salad that can be enhanced by adding borage or nasturtium leaves and flowers. These ingredients are costly to buy but easy to grow.

CORN SALAD

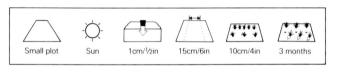

Small plot	Sun	1cm/½in	15cm/6in	10cm/4in	3 months

Also known as lamb's lettuce, this hardy annual has tender lettuce-like leaves ideal for a winter salad.

GROWING Corn salad grows over winter on well-drained soil in a sheltered site, preferably following a well-manured summer vegetable. It can also be grown in summer on deep rich soil. For winter crops, sow at 14-day intervals from late summer to early autumn; for summer, sow from late spring to early summer. Thin the seedlings as soon as possible. Cover the early autumn sowing with cloches in mid-autumn to give leaves in early winter; from unprotected sowings, you can pick leaves in spring.

HARVESTING In winter and early spring, gently pick a few leaves from each plant to make a good serving; in summer, lift the whole plant like lettuce.

POSSIBLE PROBLEMS Relatively trouble-free.

NASTURTIUM

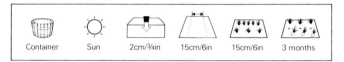

Container	Sun	2cm/¾in	15cm/6in	15cm/6in	3 months

This round-leaved trailing or climbing annual plant with brilliantly coloured flowers of red, yellow or orange makes a lively addition to salads. It has a strong peppery flavour similar to watercress, and is a valuable source of vitamin C and iron.

GROWING Nasturtiums grow well in light sandy soil. Sow seed in early summer in open ground where they are to flower. They are successful in window boxes and other containers. If space is at a premium, grow the variety Tom Thumb which reaches only 30cm/12in and does not trail.

HARVESTING The leaves and flowers should be eaten fresh and young, though the leaves can be dried successfully.

POSSIBLE PROBLEMS The worst pest is blackfly: do not grow nasturtiums near broad beans. Aphids such as these carry virus diseases.

■ ORGANIC TIP

Mix corn salad with stronger tasting chicory, or crisp cabbage for a winter salad and include citrus fruit, banana or apple. Crunchy roasted nuts or sesame seeds give extra flavour. Add yogurt to a vinaigrette dressing.

■ COOK'S TIP

Nasturtiums are specially valuable in the salad garden as flowers, leaves and seeds can all be eaten. Leaves and flowers have a peppery taste. The seeds can be pickled and used in the same way as capers. For a highly decorative effect in salads choose *the variety Alaska which has flowers in traditional colours, but the green leaves are marbled and striped with cream. Alaska grows to 30cm/12in in height.*

RADISH

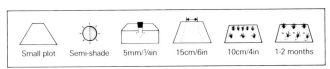

Small plot	Semi-shade	5mm/¼in	15cm/6in	10cm/4in	1-2 months

This popular vegetable can be grown for most of the year, adding colour, texture and taste to salads.

GROWING Rapid growth is essential to produce crisp, tender roots. Do not dig in fresh manure prior to sowing, but grow on rich soil which has sufficient organic matter to retain moisture. Always sow into a deep, fine bed. Because radishes are in the ground for a relatively short time, they are usually grown as a catch crop, between the rows of other vegetables that take longer to mature. Make the first sowing in mid-winter under frames or cloches, using varieties suitable for forcing such as Red Forcing. The first outdoor sowings of maincrop types like Cherry Belle can be made as soon as the ground is workable, in late winter/early spring, and thereafter fortnightly until late summer. Seed can be broadcast and lightly raked in or set at the recommended spacings. Water well, and give protected crops plenty of air on mild days.

HARVESTING Pick and eat as soon as they are ready. It takes up to 8 weeks for mid-winter sowings to mature but only 3-4 weeks for summer crops.

POSSIBLE PROBLEMS Damping off affects plants sown too thickly. Like brassicas, radishes are susceptible to club root, but if the soil is adequately limed this should not cause much damage as the plants are in the ground for such a short time.

WINTER RADISH

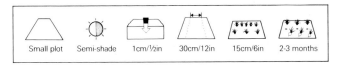

Small plot	Semi-shade	1cm/½in	30cm/12in	15cm/6in	2-3 months

Otherwise known as Chinese or Spanish radishes, depending on country of origin, winter radishes have solid roots, much larger than their summer cousins, which can be lifted and stored without becoming hollow. The skin can be red, white or black, the roots round or long. They can be peeled and grated to serve as a peppery garnish to roast meats or cooked like turnips.

GROWING Make sowings on fine, fertile soil in mid to late summer, thinning the plants when they are large enough to handle. Keep the seedbed moist and free of weeds.

HARVESTING Winter radishes will be ready to eat 2-3 months after sowing. Lift the plants and twist off the tops. Use fresh or store as described for long beetroot.

POSSIBLE PROBLEMS As for summer radishes.

▦ GARDENER'S TIP

Allow one or two of the early radish plants to go to seed and therefore supply you with a quantity of seeds for the next year for use as sprouted seed or as a seedling crop. As a catch crop sow with early carrots above potatoes or between rows of lettuce, beetroot or carrot. As radishes tend to bolt in hot weather sow mid-summer plants in a more shady position than earlier plants.

▦ COOK'S TIP

Seed pods of radishes that have run to seed are excellent in salads. Pick when they are crisp and young; the bigger the radish the better the seed pod. In spring when a winter radish crop is ready for digging up, leave some plants to seed.

FRUITING VEGETABLES

Although in a hot summer aubergines, peppers and tomatoes will produce fruit outdoors, the harvest is likely to be small in comparison with protected plants, and in poor summers all but non-existent. The ideal way of growing fruiting vegetables is in a greenhouse or walk-in polythene tunnel.

GREENHOUSE PROTECTION The glass of a greenhouse not only allows plants plenty of light but also helps to trap heat so that night temperatures do not drop as sharply as they can outside. It also provides protection from wind. Windows and roof vents allow ventilation. Good ventilation is vital as this is an important way of controlling the temperature inside the greenhouse.

The disadvantage of a greenhouse is that if plants like tomatoes and cucumbers are grown directly in the soil over a number of years soil pests and diseases can become a serious problem and the soil has to be replaced or sterilized.

Heating the greenhouse just enough to keep it frost free allows you to grow a far wider choice of vegetables through the winter and a greenhouse allows you to raise healthy vegetables from seed. Started off in the house, seedlings can never be as strong as those raised in a greenhouse because even on a window sill they will only receive light from one direction.

WALK-IN TUNNEL The less expensive alternative to a greenhouse is a walk-in polythene tunnel. This has the advantage of being comparatively easy to move to another site to avoid pest and disease build-up in the soil. However, the polythene will need replacing about every three years and ventilation is much more difficult. In winter, condensation can be a major problem, bringing the danger of disease with it. Providing a door at each end of the tunnel and incorporating ventilation panels will help. Added ventilation can be provided in summer by cutting out small, low level vents along the sides. These can be taped over with spare polythene in

winter. Alternatively, open mesh panels in doors and along the bottom of each side panel will provide extra ventilation. It is not feasible to heat a polythene tunnel.

COLD FRAME AND CLOCHE PROTECTION
It is important that outdoor varieties of tomatoes are not planted outside until early summer or they can suffer a severe setback in a late cold spell. Put them into cold frames in late spring to harden off first. Both bush and tall varieties can be started off under cloches or in a cold frame with the protection removed when plants outgrow it. Also, towards the end of the season, plants can be covered by cloches to help any green fruit to ripen. Upright varieties of tomatoes can be carefully removed from the stakes and lain on the ground on a bed of straw.

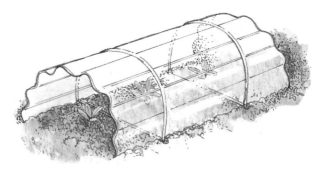

Cloches
A corrugated PVC cloche, held in position with wire hoops, is long-lasting and serves many uses. It is light and easy to move.

An improvised cloche, made by leaning some spare window panes against a wall.

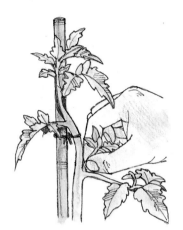

Training cordon tomatoes
Drive in a bamboo cane, before planting seedlings. They are ready when flowers on the first truss are opening.

As the tomato plant grows, loosely tie the main stem to the bamboo cane, using string.

Where a leaf stalk joins the main stem, side shoots will grow. Pinch these out, before they grow too large, sapping strength from the plant.

CULTIVATION In the greenhouse plants can be grown in pots, in growing bags or in the ground, but avoid growing plants in the same greenhouse soil for more than three years. As peppers grow best if their roots are restricted, they do well in pots.

In hot weather it is important to damp down the greenhouse. This means spraying plants and the greenhouse floor at least once a day to keep the temperature down and provide a humid atmosphere. Spraying is also important when fruit is setting.

Mature plants will need feeding every time they are watered; see specific plants for recommended fertilizers or use organic fertilizers. Liquid seaweed can be used on tomatoes and peppers, liquid animal manure fertilizer on tomatoes, peppers or aubergines. See the Organic Tip on page 160 for making liquid manure.

PESTS, DISEASES AND DISORDERS
Aphids Greenfly and blackfly, both aphids, are usually obvious as they group on plant stems, especially at new growth tips. They suck the sap but are unable to use the sugar in the sap and so excrete it as sticky honeydew. Where there is a large amount of honeydew, sooty mould will grow and virus can develop. Remove the insects by hand or hose them off. Use an insecticidal soap to spray badly infected plants. The organic solution is to attract ladybirds, lacewings and hoverflies, who eat quantities of these pests (see page 134).
Blotchy ripening in tomatoes Shading fruit in hot weather and watering frequently should help to prevent this. Another year, try growing a different variety.
Red spider mites Mottled leaves and fine webbing are signs that you have an infestation of this tiny green or red mite. It is too small to actually see. A problem in

greenhouses, red spider mites are a sign that the atmosphere is too dry. To avoid this pest, make sure you keep the atmosphere humid (see above). Spray small infestations with derris, following manufacturer's instructions. Alternatively, control by buying and introducing the predatory mite that feeds on red spider mites. Don't mix the two methods.
Tomato blight Black or brown spots appear on the leaves, tomatoes turn brown and rot. This is a problem that particularly occurs in warm, wet weather. Spray with Bordeaux mixture once a fortnight as soon as you discover the problem.
Tomato leaf mould This appears as yellow patches on the upper side of leaves, often with brown patches below. Spray with copper fungicide. Grow resistant varieties in the future.
Virus Yellowing and mottled leaves plus stunted plants is a sign of virus. Pull up and burn plants. This disease is carried by aphids.
Whitefly A common problem in greenhouses, these small white flies suck the plant's sap and can rise in clouds if you touch the plant.

Use a yellow grease-covered card to collect whitefly, as described on page 134. You can spray with derris. Do this three times at 5-day intervals, or alternatively use the parasitic wasp as a biological pest control. Don't use both methods as the derris will kill off the wasps.

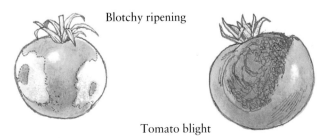

Blotchy ripening

Tomato blight

AUBERGINE

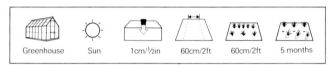

Greenhouse	Sun	1cm/½in	60cm/2ft	60cm/2ft	5 months

In cool districts aubergines can be raised only in a heated greenhouse, though if a sheltered, sunny site is available plants in pots can be moved outside in summer.

GROWING In late winter, or early spring for plants you plan to move outside, sow seeds thinly in trays of seed compost, cover lightly with compost and keep moist at a temperature of 21C/70F until germination occurs. When they are large enough to handle, prick the seedlings out into 9-cm/3½-in pots of proprietary compost. They can be planted out in late spring, either into the greenhouse bed or in 20-cm/8-in individual pots. A well-drained, moisture-retentive soil is necessary, and as with all greenhouse cultivation, it must be free of soil-borne diseases. Pinch out the leading shoot when the plant reaches 15cm/6in to encourage bushy growth. Aubergines like heat and humidity, so spray frequently with water and feed regularly with a nitrogenous fertilizer. Provide stakes for the plants to allow 3 or 4 shoots to develop on each.

HARVESTING The first fruits should be ready in mid summer. Cut them off with a sharp knife.

POSSIBLE PROBLEMS Aphids, glasshouse whitefly and red spider mite must be kept under strict control in the greenhouse. Control whitefly with the parasitic insect *Encarsia formosa*. Keep the atmosphere humid.

WHITE AUBERGINE

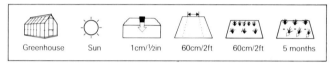

Greenhouse	Sun	1cm/½in	60cm/2ft	60cm/2ft	5 months

These fruiting vegetables are recently developed relatives of the familiar purple aubergine. They can be used in the same way and are particularly attractive pickled in vinegar in the Japanese style.

GROWING Sow seeds in late winter in trays of seed compost. Cover lightly with compost and keep moist at 21C/70F until germinated. When the seedlings are large enough to handle, prick them out into 9-cm/3½-in pots of proprietary compost. Maintain a constant temperature of 17C/65F. Set the plants into the greenhouse border or into 20-cm/8-in individual pots in late spring, using well drained, moisture retentive soil that is free of soil-borne diseases. Pinch out the leading shoot when the plants reach 15cm/6in. Keep the temperature steady, spray frequently to increase humidity and feed regularly with a nitrogenous fertilizer. Stake the plants so that 3 or 4 shoots develop in each: in good seasons it may be necessary to limit each plant to no more than 6 fruits. If you have a sun-trap patio, plants in pots can be moved outside in favourable weather.

HARVESTING The first fruits should be ready in mid-summer. Cut them off with a sharp knife.

POSSIBLE PROBLEMS Keep greenhouse pests under control, spraying against aphids, whitefly and red spider mite.

■ GARDENER'S TIP

Grow plants on a sunny balcony or in front of a south facing wall, which will reflect warmth and give protection. Buy sturdy plants from a nursery and plant out in organic soil grow-bags in early summer.

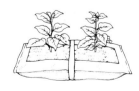

■ COOK'S TIP

Imam bayeldi is a famous Turkish dish made with aubergines. It is said that the sultan who first tasted it fainted from delight. Make it by frying 2 chopped onions and 2 garlic cloves; add a 400g/14oz can of tomatoes and cook until some *but not all of the liquid is reduced. Fry slices of 2 large aubergines, add to the mixture and garnish with chopped parsley and toasted pine nuts. Eat while still warm, but not hot, with fresh crusty bread.*

PEPPER

Greenhouse	Sun	1cm/½in	60cm/2ft	60cm/2ft	7 months

Peppers, the mature fruits of the capsicum plant are green, but if left on the plant will eventually turn red.

GROWING Peppers need very similar conditions to aubergines, and they make good companions in the greenhouse as well as the kitchen. Peppers are the less tender of the two, and can be grown outside in warm districts in good summers, in a sheltered site. All plants must be raised in a greenhouse. Sow seed thinly in trays of compost in late winter/early spring at 21C/70F. Pot the seedlings on into 9-cm/3½-in pots of proprietary compost when they are large enough to handle. Plant out in mid to late spring into the greenhouse bed or into 20-cm/8-in pots of soil into which plenty of well-rotted organic manure has been incorporated. Make sure the soil is warm when the plants are set out, and keep the temperature in the greenhouse at 18C/64F minimum. Keep the plants well watered and feed regularly with a high-nitrogen fertilizer. The developing plants need support, such as strings suspended from overhead wires, or canes if the plants are going outside. Pinch out the terminal flower in order to give continuous fruiting.

HARVESTING Begin picking green peppers in late summer, cutting them with a sharp knife. Pick regularly.

POSSIBLE PROBLEMS Watch out for aphids on young plants, red spider mite and whitefly in the greenhouse.

CHILLI PEPPER

Greenhouse	Sun	1cm/½in	45cm/18in	45cm/18in	5 months

There are numerous varieties of capsicum, the smallest of which are chilli peppers. These are very hot to the taste, providing the characteristic flavour of strong Oriental curries and chilli con carne. Always wash your hands after preparing chillies for cooking, and take care not to touch your eyes or lips.

GROWING Chilli peppers need heat, humidity and light. Sow seeds in spring in seed trays of compost kept at a constant 21C/70F, and prick out when large enough into 9-cm/3½-in pots of proprietary compost. Grow on at 17C/65F. Pot on in late spring to 20-cm/8-in pots. Spray daily with water and feed regularly with nitrogenous fertilizer. Give a stake to each plant and pinch out when they reach 20cm/8in to encourage bushy growth.

HARVESTING Pick the chillies when they are plump and glossy and use immediately. They will keep for up to 2 weeks wrapped in baking parchment in a box in the refrigerator.

POSSIBLE PROBLEMS Keep all greenhouse pests under control.

▪ ORGANIC TIP

To deter whitefly, surround pepper plants with French marigold plants. Grow outdoors against a sunny wall in home-made growing bags. Fill heavy duty plastic bags with garden compost and manure.

▪ PRESERVING TIP

Chilli peppers are best eaten fresh but they can also be dried to preserve them for use through the winter. Place the fruit on racks and put in the oven on a very low setting, leaving the door ajar. Chek regularly and remove when the fruits are crisp and dry.

Alternatively, place between sheets of absorbent kitchen roll and put in the microwave. Check every minute and turn the sandwich over. The chillies should be ready in 3-4 minutes.

GREENHOUSE TOMATO

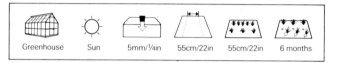

Greenhouse	Sun	5mm/¼in	55cm/22in	55cm/22in	6 months

A heated greenhouse gives a crop of early tomatoes. Choose a variety like Eurocross BB.

GROWING Bright light is essential. Sow in early winter to produce plants for setting out in late winter or in mid winter for an early spring planting. Sow seeds thinly in trays and cover lightly with compost. When 2 true leaves appear, pot the seedlings singly into 9-cm/3½-in pots using a proprietary potting compost. Plant out when the first flower on the first truss opens, earlier if they look pot-bound. The soil in the greenhouse border must be well-drained, moisture-retentive and completely free of soil-borne pests and diseases. Alternatively use 25-cm/10-in pots of a good proprietary compost. Water well after transplanting. Keep the temperature at a minimum of 17C/65F night and day. Support the growing plants with strings tied loosely around each stem and attached to an overhead horizontal wire. Remove the tiny side-shoots in the leaf axils. Feed the plants with a low-nitrogen, high potassium solution, gradually increasing the proportion of nitrogen. In mid summer wean the plants on to water only. Remove the growing point when the plants have 7-10 trusses. Spray regularly with water in hot weather.

HARVESTING Pick when the tomatoes are deep red.

POSSIBLE PROBLEMS The fungus cladosporum causes leaf mould: ventilate the greenhouse on hot days.

▪ GARDENER'S TIP

Use the plants themselves to hold the support strings in place at the base. Make a hole for a plant and fill with water. Take the tomato to be planted, loop the string end under the root ball, then firm the plant well in, anchoring the string.

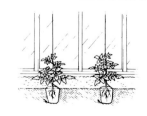

TOMATO

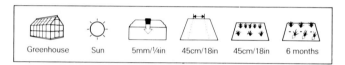

Greenhouse	Sun	5mm/¼in	45cm/18in	45cm/18in	6 months

Providing unheated protection is one of the most popular and successful methods of growing tomatoes.

GROWING Tomato plants raised from seed need the high temperatures and bright light described under greenhouse cultivation. Sow seed in mid/late winter. If you cannot raise plants in ideal conditions, it is better to buy sturdy plants from a nursery. Whether for an unheated greenhouse or outside under glass, prepare the soil by digging in generous quantities of well-rotted organic manure or compost the previous winter.
Harden off the young plants for 2-3 days before planting out in spring. Begin feeding with a medium-nitrogen feed and move on to a high-nitrogen solution when the plants are carrying fruit on the first 2 or 3 trusses. Water regularly. Support the plants as described for the heated greenhouse. Remove the side shoots from the leaf axils, and 'stop' the plants by pinching out the growing point when they have 7-10 trusses.

HARVESTING Pick the tomatoes with the calyx on, taking care not to damage the fruits. See outdoor tomato for ripening green tomatoes at the end of the season.

POSSIBLE PROBLEMS

To prevent the occurrence of soil-borne diseases, do not grow tomatoes on the same soil year after year.

VARIETIES Moneymaker, Tigerella (striped).

▪ GARDENER'S TIP

Tomatoes planted in an unheated greenhouse can be grown in the soil but, due to the fact that pests and diseases can build up in the soil over a number of years, it is best to grow the plants in large pots in garden compost on top of the soil. Some roots will find their way out of the pot into the soil but most will remain in the pot and this can be disposed of at the end of the season. Alternatively stand pots in trays containing a layer of damp pebbles.

OUTDOOR TOMATO

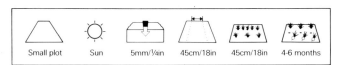

Small plot	Sun	5mm/¼in	45cm/18in	45cm/18in	4-6 months

Choose quick-maturing varieties like The Amateur for outdoor cultivation

GROWING To raise plants from seed, follow the instructions given under greenhouse cultivation, sowing up to early spring. If you cannot provide these ideal conditions, buy healthy plants from a nursery. Prepare the soil by digging in plenty of well-rotted organic manure or compost the previous winter. Set the plants out only after all risk of frost has passed and water well. Feed as for plants in an unheated greenhouse. Bush varieties do not need training, but long stemmed types should be staked. Water well every day. A useful protection technique is to plant 45cm/18in away from a wall and suspend a clear polythene sheet along the open side of the row. Remove weeds carefully or suppress them with a mulch of straw or grass cuttings. Bushy tomatoes grown outdoors do not need side-shooting, but as the fruits on the bottom truss begin to ripen, gradually remove the leaves below to allow light to enter and air to circulate.

HARVESTING Pick the ripe tomatoes with the calyx on. To ripen remaining green fruit, place in a single layer in a closed drawer with a ripening apple or pear.

POSSIBLE PROBLEMS Potato blight may strike in late summer if weather conditions are moist and warm.

VARIETIES The Amateur, French Cross.

CONTAINER TOMATO

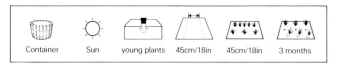

Container	Sun	young plants	45cm/18in	45cm/18in	3 months

Miniature tomatoes can be grown very successfully in window boxes or large pots on balconies and patios as well as in growing bags.

GROWING If space is limited, you are unlikely to be able to raise tomatoes from seed in the ideal conditions described under greenhouse cultivation (although you may have a gardening friend who will do so for you). In early summer, buy healthy plants from the nursery and set them in 25-cm/10-in pots containing a proprietary compost such as John Innes no. 3. Choose a sunny spot out of the wind. Water the pots every day or twice a day in very warm weather, adding liquid tomato feed to the water. Stop the plants at 7 trusses. Bush tomatoes do not need training, but it is a good idea to tie the stems to supporting canes.

HARVESTING Inspect the plants daily and pick the tomatoes as they ripen, with the calyx on.

POSSIBLE PROBLEMS Magnesium deficiency shows itself as yellowing of the leaves, starting at the bottom of the plant. Spray regularly with a solution of Epsom salts at 9g per litre/1½oz per gallon. Very high temperatures can cause blotchy ripening: light shade may be necessary at the day's height.

VARIETIES Tiny Tim, Pixie Hybrid and Gardener's Delight.

▪ GARDENER'S TIP

On all but bush tomatoes, remove the side shoots that appear in the angle between the leaf stems and main stem and remove lower leaves when they turn yellow. Use soft string to tie plants to canes to avoid damage.

▪ COOK'S TIP

The more tasteless, large-cropping tomatoes are cheap in the shops when home-grown tomatoes ripen. Instead choose to grow varieties with a wonderful flavour, like Gardener's Delight. If you are very short of space grow Pixie

F1, in a tub. It produces early tasty fruit. Cherry-sized Tiny Tim, expensive in the shops, do well in a window box or tub and look decorative, and taste good, whole in a salad.

LEAF VEGETABLES

Brassicas, which include broccoli, Brussels sprouts, cabbages, cauliflower, calabrese and kale, need a firm soil to help to give them anchorage, so do not dig the bed just before planting. They should always be moved to a new position each year to help to avoid the brassica disease, club root. In the rotation cycle on page 132, brassicas and leaf vegetables come under Plot C which follows peas and beans and salad vegetables. The plants in Group B will have been grown on very rich soil so fresh manuring may not be necessary and the peas and beans will have built up the supply of nitrogen in the soil from the bacteria in their root nodules.

SPECIAL SOIL REQUIREMENTS The soil pH is important and should be between 6.5 and 7.0 (see page 10). If your soil is too acid it is best to add lime in the autumn before growing brassicas. Do not lime and add manure or fertilizer at the same time as they do not mix. If you do not need to lime the plot, then it is a good idea to dig in well-rotted compost or manure in the autumn prior to planting as brassicas require a

deep and fertile soil. Before planting, add a general fertilizer like dried blood, fish and bone meal. If plant growth is sluggish half way through the year, feed plants with a seaweed-based fertilizer, watered in, or top dress with a nitrogenous fertilizer.

A CONTINUOUS SUPPLY By planting a range of leaf vegetables, it is quite possible to have a fresh supply available throughout the year, both for salads and as cooked vegetables. Varieties of cabbage are available to harvest in spring, summer, autumn and winter. Spring greens, winter purslane and annual sprouting broccoli will provide greens in the spring, and in summer New Zealand spinach, spinach beet, summer purslane and spinach are available. Starting in the early autumn, both Swiss and ruby chard can be harvested, then Brussels sprouts, broad-leaved endive and winter cabbage will take you through most of the winter while perennial sprouting broccoli is available all year round.

Planting Details of when to plant each variety are given under the specific vegetable. Plant brassicas very

Catch cropping
As broccoli and cauliflower are harvested, the ground they occupied is used for quick-growing crops.

Picking Brussels sprouts
As the plants grow, keep an eye on their progress and pick off any yellow leaves or loose-leaved sprouts from the bottom of the stem. This will create better air circulation.

When the sprouts are ready to harvest – they should be small and compact – pick them progressively from the base upwards a few sprouts at a time. There is an old saying that they taste better after a slight frost.

firmly when they have three to four proper leaves and are about 5-8cm/2-3in high. The block method of planting is especially suited to cabbages. If you want large heads, space 45cm/18in apart. For smaller heads space only 35cm/14in apart. If cabbages are more widely spaced they can be intercropped, as described below. When plants are harvested, use the spaces left for catch crops or seedling crops of salad lettuce (see below).

Larger brassicas like cauliflower and Brussels sprouts may need staking and earthing up to protect them in stormy winters.

Intercropping Where plants are in the ground for a long time and grow slowly, like cabbages or Brussels sprouts, it is a good idea to make use of surrounding space while the plants are still small. This space can be used for fast-growing salad crops, or for raising seedlings for transplanting later. In the same way, where plants are spaced widely apart, it is possible to start off the next crop just prior to the one already in the ground being harvested.

Catch cropping When large plants are harvested, or a crop fails, the space can be used for a catch crop. Any plants which are normally successively sown are suitable, such as beetroot, carrots, lettuces, spring onions or spinach.

Watering Leafy green plants need plenty of water while they are growing. In dry periods, water them thoroughly at least once a week or give one very heavy watering two to three weeks before you harvest. Seedlings and newly transplanted plants will need watering little and often, daily in dry weather until they have become established.

Harvesting Pick off any yellow leaves or loose-leaved Brussels sprouts from the bottom of the stem to create better air circulation. Pick the sprouts when they are small and compact, starting from the bottom of the stem.

Always remove roots and stems after harvesting brassicas to prevent club root.

PESTS AND DISEASES There are a number of diseases that can affect leaf vegetables but if you follow a crop rotation and the tips for growing healthy plants on page 134 these should be able to be kept to a minimum.

Caterpillars Appearing from early spring onwards they will eat holes in the leaves of most leaf vegetables. Remove them by hand and drop into paraffin. Look

Caterpillar

Cabbage whitefly

for eggs laid by moths and butterflies, on the plant, especially cabbages, and remove.

Cabbage root fly The larvae cause young plants to collapse. An adult female fly lays her eggs next to the stem in the soil and the larvae feed on the roots. Surround the stems of young plants with brassica collars at soil level so the fly cannot burrow down. These can be bought, or made from carpet underlay (see the Tip on page 162).

Cabbage whitefly Appearing from late spring to early autumn these tiny white flies can be found on the undersides of leaves of cabbages, Brussels sprouts and other brassicas. If the plant is touched a swarm will rise. Spray with insecticidal soap or derris. This fly can survive outside over winter so remove any old leaves and stems that it could feed on after harvesting.

Club root Young plants fail to develop and leaves yellow when this soil-borne fungus attacks the roots, making them swell and decay. There is no cure and the fungus can stay in the soil almost indefinitely. Pull up plants and burn them. Worst in acid soil and where there is poor drainage, so lime where necessary and improve drainage. By raising plants in pots in the greenhouse, then planting out later, you can produce crops after club root, except of cauliflower.

Mealy cabbage aphid A grey-green aphid that can appear in colonies on leaf undersides. Control as for cabbage whitefly above. Encourage ladybirds and hoverflies which are the predators of aphids, by growing a wide selection of plants.

Mosaic virus Also known as spinach blight, this virus causes yellowing of young leaves which then spreads to older leaves. There is no cure. Aphids spread the disease, so prevent it by controlling the aphids as soon as you discover them. Choose resistant varieties.

ANNUAL BROCCOLI

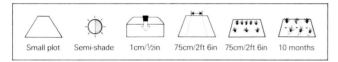

Small plot	Semi-shade	1cm/½in	75cm/2ft 6in	75cm/2ft 6in	10 months

Sprouting broccoli is similar to cauliflower, but produces a loose collection of flowerheads.

GROWING A well-drained, alkaline soil which has not recently grown a brassica crop is essential. It should be fertile, open and able to support a good root system. Broccoli plants thrive after well-manured crops such as early potatoes. Work in a top dressing of nitro-chalk in early spring. Sow seeds 2cm/³⁄₄in apart in an outdoor seedbed in mid spring, in drills 20-30cm/8-12in apart. In early summer, transplant the seedlings to the growing site, taking care not to damage the roots. Dip the roots in trichlorphon before planting to protect against cabbage root fly. Firm the plants in and water well. Mulch between the rows in summer to suppress weeds. Stake firmly against winter winds and earth up around the stems for extra support.

HARVESTING Sprouting may begin in mid winter, more likely late winter, and continues to late spring when the plants go to seed. Remove sprouting sideshoots when they are mature so that more will be produced further down. Snap off as close to the main stem as possible.

POSSIBLE PROBLEMS For club root, see Brussels Sprouts. Watch for aphids and whitefly.

VARIETIES Early Purple (or White) Sprouting; Late Purple (or White) Sprouting.

PERENNIAL BROCCOLI

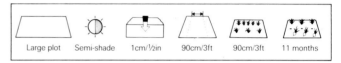

Large plot	Semi-shade	1cm/½in	90cm/3ft	90cm/3ft	11 months

This is a very useful winter-hardy vegetable, which matures in late spring and continues to be productive for several years. When the plants are exhausted, grub them up and do not use the plot for a brassica crop for at least 2 years.

GROWING Soil should be non-acid, fertile and well drained. Dig deep the winter before planting so that the soil texture will permit the formation of good strong roots. Raise plants by sowing seed in an outdoor seedbed in mid spring. Set the seeds 2cm/³⁄₄in apart in rows 20-30cm/8-12in apart. Choose only sturdy seedlings for transplanting in early summer to the permanent site, which should be given a worked-in top dressing of nitro-chalk in early spring. Dip the roots in trichlorphon to protect against cabbage root fly before firming the plants into place. Water well. To suppress weeds, put down a mulch in summer, and a layer of straw in winter. Stake firmly for support in winter winds.

HARVESTING In late spring perennial broccoli produces a large central head surrounded by about 6 smaller axillary heads. These must all be used to ensure continued productivity. Cut the central head first and remove all heads before the plant goes to seed.

POSSIBLE PROBLEMS See annual varieties.

VARIETIES Nine Star; Hen and Chickens.

▨ ORGANIC TIP

You can make an excellent liquid manure by suspending a sack of well-rotted animal manure in a water butt. Leave a couple of weeks before using and dilute it to the colour of weak tea before watering plants with it.

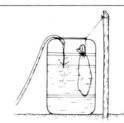

▨ HEALTH TIP

Broccoli is rich in vitamins A and B and has more vitamin C content even than oranges but it needs to be cooked in the right way to retain these important nutrients. Steam for only a few minutes or cook with a sprinkling of water in a microwave. After microwaving add yogurt to the cooking juices to create a sauce. Pour over the broccoli and sprinkle with toasted sesame seeds.

CALABRESE

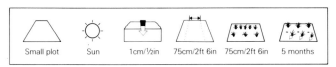

Small plot	Sun	1cm/½in	75cm/2ft 6in	75cm/2ft 6in	5 months

This delicious green relative of white and purple sprouting broccoli, hailing from Italy, is not winter hardy and must be harvested between late summer and mid autumn. It freezes beautifully.

GROWING To get the best results, calabrese must be grown rapidly. Soil must be non-acid, fertile and well drained but moisture retentive. Raise plants in an outdoor seedbed, sowing in mid spring. Place frames or cloches over the bed in advance to warm it up. Sow seeds 2cm/¾in apart in rows 20-30cm/8-12in apart and replace the frames/cloches. Water lightly. By early summer the plants are ready for transplanting, after a brief period of hardening off. Soak the seedbed before easing out the plants. Destroy any that are deformed or diseased. Dip the roots of sturdy specimens in trichlorphon and firm them in to the growing site. Dwarf types can be set closer together than the standards. Weed regularly. Constant supplies of water and nitrogenous fertilizer are needed if the necessary strong plant framework is to be produced.

HARVESTING Early-maturing varieties are ready for picking in late summer. Cut the terminal head first, using a sharp knife, to encourage formation of small axillary 'spears'.

POSSIBLE PROBLEMS See annual sprouting broccoli.

SUITABLE VARIETIES Mercedes (dwarf); Express Corona; Green Duke.

■ FREEZER TIP

Remove any outer leaves, trim the stalks and cut into sprigs, then wash well. Plunge into fast-boiling water for 3-5 minutes depending on stem thickness, then cool in ice-cold water for the same period. Pack head to tail in boxes.

BRUSSELS SPROUTS

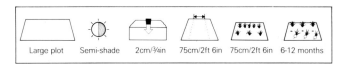

Large plot	Semi-shade	2cm/¾in	75cm/2ft 6in	75cm/2ft 6in	6-12 months

Brussels sprouts are hardy plants that stand over-winter, protected by the canopy of leaves.

GROWING Fertile soil is essential, worked deeply enough to sustain the deep root system necessary for a long growing season. Apply lime in the autumn/winter before planting. Raise plants outdoors in a seedbed in a sheltered part of the garden. Sow seed in early spring in drills spaced 25-30cm/10-12in apart. Transplant when the plants reach 15cm/6in, about 8 weeks later. Work a base dressing of a general purpose fertilizer into the soil of the growing site. Soak the seedbed before gently easing the young plants out with a fork. Discard any that are diseased, damaged or lack a growing point. Dip the roots into a bucket of trichlorphon to protect them against cabbage root fly. Firm them into place and give a good base watering. Weed well and water the base of the stems in dry seasons. Top-dress with a nitrogenous fertilizer in late summer. Tall varieties need staking.

HARVESTING Depending on variety, the first sprouts should be ready in early autumn. Pick from the bottom upwards, cutting with a sharp knife.

POSSIBLE PROBLEMS The most severe disease of all brassicas is the club root fungus. Do not grow on acid soils; rotate crops.

VARIETIES Peer Gynt; Roodnerf Early Button; Pegasus.

■ ORGANIC TIP

In winter birds are hungry too and may well take a liking to your Brussels sprouts. If you cover the leafy heads with a hood of wire or plastic netting, held aloft on long stakes, the birds will ignore the uncovered and easily-picked sprouts.

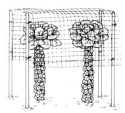

SPRING CABBAGE

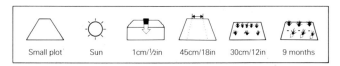

| Small plot | Sun | 1cm/½in | 45cm/18in | 30cm/12in | 9 months |

Very hardy varieties of cabbage stand over winter from summer sowings to mature at the beginning of the following year.

GROWING Go for rich, deep soil which is moisture retentive but well drained. Incorporate plenty of well-rotted organic manure the autumn before planting. Do not grow on soil that grew brassicas the previous year. Sow seed in an outdoor seedbed in mid-late summer in shallow drills 20-30cm/8-12in apart. In early autumn, before transplanting, work a base dressing of a general purpose fertilizer into the growing site. Water the seedlings well before lifting, being careful not to damage the roots. Retain healthy specimens only and dip the roots in trichlorphon before planting to deter cabbage root fly. Firm the young plants in well and give them a good watering. They overwinter as small plants; so that they will grow rapidly in the new year, hoe in top dressings of nitrogenous fertilizer from late winter onwards.

HARVESTING Spring cabbages are relatively small when mature. Pick as soon as they are ready and use fresh.

POSSIBLE PROBLEMS Cabbage root fly, aphids, club root fungus – see summer/autumn cabbage.

VARIETIES Harbinger (pointed, very early); Pixie (small, pointed); Durham Early (round).

▪ GARDENER'S TIP

Never let brassicas go short of water. Unless the weather is constantly wet, keep the soil deeply and evenly moist, especially for seedlings and new transplants.

EARLY SUMMER CABBAGE

| Small plot | Sun | 1cm/½in | 45cm/18in | 45cm/18in | 5-6 months |

The first cabbages of the year can be harvested in late spring or early summer. Both round and pointed varieties are available.

GROWING All cabbages prefer rich, deep soils which are moisture retentive but well drained. Incorporate plenty of well-rotted organic manure the autumn before planting. Do not grow on soil that grew brassicas the previous year. Sow seed in mid-late winter in cold or slightly heated greenhouses or frames (10C/50F), either in drills 20cm/8in apart directly into the soil or in seed trays. With the latter method the seedlings should be pricked out when large enough into other trays at 5 × 2.5cm/2 × 1in. Plant outside in mid spring, watering the seedlings well before lifting them carefully. Discard diseased or damaged specimens. Dip the roots of sturdy seedlings in trichlorphon to deter cabbage root fly. Firm in and water well. Continue to water the plants and give nitrogenous fertilizer regularly. Hoe weeds away.

HARVESTING Early cabbages are best picked as soon as they are mature, and used fresh and crisp. Cut heads with a sharp knife.

POSSIBLE PROBLEMS Cabbage root fly is prevalent in late spring. Spray with diazinon. Rotate crops to discourage club root disease.

VARIETIES Golden Acre; May Express & Primo (round); Greyhound, Hispi (pointed).

▪ ORGANIC TIP

To outwit the cabbage root fly take a 15-cm/6-in square of foam-rubber carpet underlay, cut a slit from the centre of one side into the middle. Add a small cross slit at the centre and slip this around the plant base.

SUMMER/AUTUMN CABBAGE

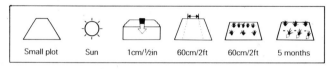

| Small plot | Sun | 1cm/½in | 60cm/2ft | 60cm/2ft | 4-8 months |

Cabbages sown outdoors in late spring are ready to pick from late summer to late autumn according to variety.

GROWING Cabbages prefer rich, deep soils which are moisture retentive but well drained. Incorporate plenty of well-rotted organic manure the autumn before planting. Do not grow on soil that grew brassicas the previous year. Sow seed in an outdoor seedbed during mid or late spring in drills 20-30cm/8-12in apart. Transplant to the growing site in early/mid summer, watering the seedlings well before lifting. Take care not to damage the roots. Retain healthy specimens only and dip the roots in trichlorphon before planting to deter cabbage root fly. Firm in well. Water generously and give top dressings of nitro-chalk to sustain growth. Hoe to control weeds until the leaves meet between the rows.

HARVESTING Most summer/autumn-maturing cabbages are best picked as soon as they are ready, but a few types stand well.

POSSIBLE PROBLEMS Spray against cabbage root fly in late spring. Spray young leaves against aphids. Rotate crops to discourage club root disease.

VARIETIES Autumn: Minicole (small, stands well); Holland Late Winter. Summer: Winnigstadt; Golden Acre.

SAVOY AND WINTER-MATURING CABBAGE

| Small plot | Sun | 1cm/½in | 60cm/2ft | 60cm/2ft | 5 months |

Savoy cabbage is distinguished from other winter-maturing cabbages, which are raised in the same way, by its beautiful crinkled leaves. All are frost-resistant, stand well and can be stored, unlike spring or summer/autumn types.

GROWING Soil should be rich and deep, moisture retentive but well drained. Incorporate plenty of well-rotted organic manure the autumn before planting. Do not grow on soil that grew brassicas the previous year. Sow seed in an outdoor seedbed during mid or late spring in drills 20-30cm/8-12in apart. Transplant to the growing site in early/mid summer, watering the seedlings well before lifting them. Take care not to damage the roots. Retain healthy specimens only and dip the roots in trichlorphon before planting to deter cabbage root fly. Firm in well. Water generously and give top dressings of nitro-chalk to sustain growth. Hoe to control weeds until the leaves meet between the rows.

HARVESTING Savoy cabbages mature from early autumn, while other winter cabbages stand throughout the winter. Cut the mature heads when required. To store white winter cabbages, cut in late autumn/early winter. Remove the outer leaves and stack the heads pyramid fashion in a cool, dry, frost-free shed.

◼ ORGANIC TIP

Keep aphids at bay by encouraging hoverflies to inhabit your cabbage patch. Entice them with their favourite flat, open flowers like yarrow, fennel and French marigolds which will add colour to the area too. The larvae of hoverflies flourish on aphids, *so are good friends to every organic gardener. Use a square of underlay to keep the cabbage root fly at bay (see early summer cabbage).*

◼ ORGANIC TIP

To keep weeds at bay, plant seedlings through cross slits made in a sheet of biodegradable brown paper. Push down the paper edges into a narrow channel made in the soil, then cover the exposed sides with more soil.

RED CABBAGE

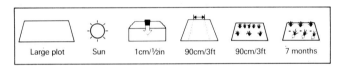

| Large plot | Sun | 1cm/½in | 90cm/3ft | 90cm/3ft | 7 months |

Red cabbages have large, firm spherical heads with deep purplish red leaves. Ready in late autumn, they stand well and have many uses in the kitchen, for pickling, grating in salads, or stewing with apple and onion to accompany roast meats.

GROWING Soil should be rich and deep, moisture retentive but well drained. Incorporate plenty of well-rotted organic manure the autumn before planting. Do not grow on soil that grew brassicas the previous year. Sow seed in an outdoor seedbed during mid or late spring in drills 20-30cm/8-12in apart. Transplant to the growing site in early/mid summer, watering the seedlings well before lifting them. Take care not to damage the roots. Retain healthy specimens only and dip the roots in trichlorphon before planting to deter cabbage root fly. Firm in well. Water generously and give top dressings of nitro-chalk to sustain growth. Hoe to control weeds until the leaves meet between the rows.

HARVESTING Cut from late autumn onwards. To store, trim off the outer leaves and stack the heads pyramid fashion in a cool, airy, frost-free place.

POSSIBLE PROBLEMS See summer/autumn cabbage.

VARIETIES Ruby Ball; Red Drumhead.

EARLY CAULIFLOWER

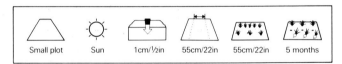

| Small plot | Sun | 1cm/½in | 55cm/22in | 55cm/22in | 5 months |

Tender early summer cauliflowers have the finest flavour.

GROWING An alkaline soil that has not recently grown another brassica is essential. It should be open, fertile and able to sustain rapid unchecked growth. If manured for a previous crop, moisture retention will be improved. Raise plants from seed sown in mid winter. Sow in seedtrays in the greenhouse at 13C/55F. When the seedlings are large enough to handle, prick them out into trays of potting compost, spacing them 5cm/2in apart. Before transplanting – in early or mid spring, depending on weather and location – dip the roots of the seedlings in trichlorphon to deter cabbage root fly and incorporate a general purpose fertilizer into the plot. If the soil is too cold, growth will be checked and a good head, or 'curd', will not form. Hoe to keep weeds down, and maintain growth with top dressings of nitrogen and regular waterings. Earth up the stems to prevent the plants shifting in the wind. To protect the developing curd from the sun and keep it white, break a leaf over it.

HARVESTING Cut cauliflowers as soon as they are ready throughout early summer, lifting them in the morning.

POSSIBLE PROBLEMS Watch out for aphids, whitefly, flea beetles and caterpillars as well as club root. Whiptail is a leaf distortion occurring on acid soils.

VARIETIES Snowball; Alpha.

■ DECORATIVE TIP

Add colour to autumn flower borders by planting decorative and colourful cabbages in groups. Apart from red cabbages use ornamental cabbage, Brassica oleracea, with pink, green and white variegated foliage.

■ ORGANIC TIP

Cauliflowers will immediately react to a soil deficient in nutrients. Check that you have included lime to ensure that the soil is not too acid, then use a liquid seaweed fertilizer. This contains potash and all the trace elements necessary to quickly correct any deficiencies. However, extra feeding should only be used when deficiencies are noticed. In an organic garden the well-fed soil should be able to supply all the nutrients that vegetables will need.

SUMMER/AUTUMN CAULIFLOWER

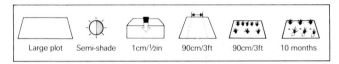

| Large plot | Sun | 1cm/½in | 60cm/2ft | 60cm/2ft | 5 months |

Summer- and autumn-maturing cauliflowers are the easiest to grow. While they are not frost-hardy, the flavour is more delicate than that of winter types.

GROWING Give cauliflowers a non-acid, open fertile soil, manured for a previous crop. Work in a base dressing of general purpose fertilizer before planting. Raise plants from seed sown in early spring in an outdoor seedbed that has not recently grown a brassica crop. Sow throughout spring in shallow drills 20-30cm/8-12in apart. Move the young plants to the growing site 8-10 weeks later, first dipping the roots in trichlorphon to deter cabbage root fly. Firm in well. Growth must be unchecked – give a top dressing of a nitrogenous fertilizer and water regularly. Keep weeds down and earth up the stems to keep the plants steady. If the variety you are growing has upright leaves, bend one over the maturing head to prevent it yellowing.

HARVESTING Cut cauliflowers as soon as they are mature, in the cool of the morning. Depending on variety the crop will be ready from late summer to late autumn.

POSSIBLE PROBLEMS See early cauliflower. Frost may damage late autumn crops.

VARIETIES All The Year Round; Wallaby.

WINTER CAULIFLOWER

| Large plot | Semi-shade | 1cm/½in | 90cm/3ft | 90cm/3ft | 10 months |

Winter-maturing cauliflower varieties, though relatively hardy, do better in mild coastal areas where frost damage is minimal. The leaves tend to be wrapped protectively around the white 'curd'.

GROWING Go for a non-acid, open, fertile soil that has been manured for a previous crop. Good drainage is important: a strong root system must develop to anchor the plants during windy winter months. Winter cauliflower plants are produced by sowing seed in an outdoor seedbed in mid/late spring as described for late summer/autumn crops. Thin the seedlings if necessary to 2cm/¾in to encourage short sturdy plants. Transplant to the growing site in mid summer, dipping the roots in trichlorphon to deter cabbage root fly. Keep weeds down during the winter and earth up the plants to keep them steady. When growth begins again in late winter apply a top-dressing of nitro-chalk, hoed in around the base of the plants.

HARVESTING Depending on variety, winter cauliflower are ready for picking from late winter to late spring. Cut at the base of the stem with a sharp knife.

POSSIBLE PROBLEMS See early cauliflower. Soil-borne fungi may cause damping off of seedlings.

VARIETIES Early White; Angers (south and west districts); Asmer Pinnacle (northern districts).

■ GARDENER'S TIP

Try growing mini-cauliflowers, which taste good and look very decorative. Choose a variety like Gorant or Predominant which will produce miniature curds, and space at 10cm/4in intervals in rows 22.5cm/9in apart. Then grow as for summer cauliflowers,
above. All will be ready about the same time but some can be frozen for use later. Raw cauliflower is delicious in a salad with nuts and raisins.

■ GARDENER'S TIP

Before transplanting a seedling, check that it has developed the tiny central bud from which the curd will come. If the seedling lacks this bud no head will form later on, so it is best to discard it at this point.

CHICORY

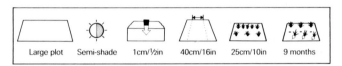

Large plot	Semi-shade	1cm/½in	40cm/16in	25cm/10in	9 months

The blanched chicon, or heart, which is forced from the roots of chicory plants is used in salads and braised as a vegetable.

GROWING Good chicons can only be produced from nicely shaped, healthy roots, which require soil that has been enriched for a previous crop, such as leeks. Recently manured soil will make the roots forked and misshapen. Sow in mid-late spring. Thin the seedlings when they reach the third leaf stage.

LIFTING When the most of the leaves have died down, in late autumn at the latest, carefully lift the long roots, discarding any that are damaged or forked, and trim the leaves to 2.5cm/1in of the crown. Store the roots on their sides on boxes in a cool frost-free place. Cover with sand or peat to prevent drying out.

FORCING AND BLANCHING Force a few roots at a time. Stand them upright about 6.5cm/2½in apart in deep boxes or pots in sand or light soil with 2.5cm/1in showing. Water lightly and then cover the containers completely to exclude all light.

HARVESTING Pick the chicons when 10-15cm/4-6in long. Discard the used roots and start again with a fresh batch from store.

POSSIBLE PROBLEMS Inspect for slugs when blanching.

BROAD-LEAVED ENDIVE

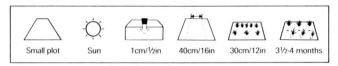

Small plot	Sun	1cm/½in	40cm/16in	30cm/12in	3½-4 months

A half-hardy annual and close relative of chicory, endive is blanched before picking to counteract its naturally bitter taste. Cook or eat raw in salads.

GROWING A well-drained, fertile soil is best, with a dressing of general, balanced fertilizer before sowing. Sow the seed into its final position from mid summer to early autumn for late autumn and winter picking. Transplanting the seedlings can damage the tap root and check growth. Sow the seed in 1-cm/½-in deep drills spaced 40cm/16in apart. When the seedlings are 5-7.5cm/2-3in high, thin them out to 30cm/12in apart in the rows.

BLANCHING Endive plants are usually ready for blanching about 3 months after sowing and it may be done in one of two ways. The leaves can be gathered together when dry (damp plants may rot during blanching) and tied round with raffia or string. This keeps the light away from all but the outer leaves. Alternatively, the plants can be completely covered with containers.

HARVESTING Blanching takes up to 3 weeks in the winter. Don't treat too many plants at a time because endive will not keep very long after blanching.

POSSIBLE PROBLEMS Watch out for greenfly during the summer months. Broad-leaved endive will need the protection of cloches in winter.

■ PRESERVING TIP

Once the chicons have been harvested they will need to be used fairly quickly or they will deteriorate, becoming green and bitter on exposure to light. Keep them chilled in the refrigerator and out of the light and wrap in foil.

■ COOK'S TIP

Endive goes well with other salad greens. Alternatively, toss with orange segments and watercress sprigs in a vinaigrette to which toasted almonds have been added. For a tasty hot bacon dressing to toss endive and dandelion leaves in, melt butter in a saucepan and add slices of bacon chopped up small, cook until the bacon starts to go crisp, then pour over the salad. Heat a little wine vinegar in the pan and pour this over the top. Serve at once.

KALE

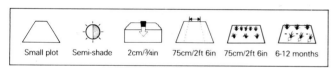

Small plot	Semi-shade	2cm/¾in	75cm/2ft 6in	75cm/2ft 6in	6-12 months

Kales are hardy winter greens that will stand very severe weather indeed. The type grown in vegetable gardens is curly kale – plain-leaved kale has a very strong flavour and is usually fed to livestock. Dwarf curly kales are useful for small gardens.

GROWING Kales do best if they follow well-manured crops such as early potatoes or peas. The soil should be non-acid and well drained. Raise plants in an outdoor seedbed, sowing seed thinly in mid/late spring, in drills 30cm/12in apart. Transplant the seedlings to the growing site in mid summer, setting dwarf varieties at the shorter distances of 45cm/18in each way. Fertilizer levels should be kept low to start with but increased by giving top dressings of nitrogenous fertilizer in mid winter.

HARVESTING Pick the young leaves off the plants from mid winter onwards. Regular picking will encourage sideshoots to develop which will produce more tender shoots in early and mid spring.

POSSIBLE PROBLEMS The usual brassica pests and diseases will need to be dealt with. See Brussels sprouts.

VARIETIES Dwarf Green Curled; Ragged Jack; Pentland Brig.

KOHLRABI

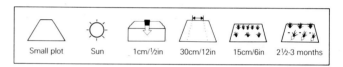

Small plot	Sun	1cm/½in	30cm/12in	15cm/6in	2½-3 months

This member of the cabbage family is grown for its swollen stem which is treated by cooks as a root – in fact its popular name is turnip-rooted cabbage. Gardeners like it because it can be grown quickly between rows of peas or carrots as a catch crop.

GROWING To sustain rapid growth, well-drained soil is important. Apply lime in late winter. Sow seed thinly from mid spring to mid summer, thinning the seedlings as soon as they are large enough to handle. Sow the white-skinned variety at the beginning, switching to the purple one for later sowings (both have creamy flesh). The plants withstand heat and drought but regular light watering assists development. Hoe carefully to control weeds, taking care not to damage the stems.

HARVESTING Do not let the globes exceed 7.5cm/3in in diameter before picking or the flavour will be coarse. Use immediately, as kohlrabi do not store well.

POSSIBLE PROBLEMS Relatively trouble-free.

VARIETIES Early White Vienna; Early Purple Vienna.

■ ORGANIC TIP

Club root cannot be cured and the fungus lives in and affects the soil for up to ten years. So it is important to grow plants that are as healthy as possible. Make sure the soil is not acid, is properly drained and rich in humus and dig up brassica stumps after harvesting. Some organic gardeners believe that a chunk of rhubarb or a moth-ball popped into the hole before planting a seedling helps mask the brassica smell from the fungus.

■ COOK'S TIP

Kohlrabi has a sweet, nutty flavour. To cook, scrub the bulb-shaped stems, then steam or boil for 15-25 minutes, depending on size. Peel just before serving and coat with a creamy sauce. Kohlrabi can also be sliced and stir-fried.

RUBY CHARD (SEAKALE BEET)

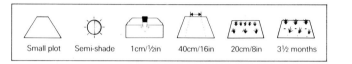

Small plot	Semi-shade	1cm/½in	40cm/16in	20cm/8in	3½ months

A showpiece in the vegetable garden, ruby chard's ornamental red stems can be eaten as a separate vegetable from the leaves, as in the case of Swiss chard. The leaves have a milder flavour than those of true spinach.

GROWING As is true of the other leaf beets – spinach beet and Swiss chard – any well-drained fertile garden soil is suitable for growing ruby chard. It should be given plenty of organic manure to encourage succulent leaf growth. The best results are obtained from spring-sown crops. Sow the seed thinly in 1-cm/½-in deep drills during mid spring. Leave 40cm/16in between rows and thin the seedlings to 20cm/8in apart when they are large enough.

HARVESTING A little ruby chard can be pulled in winter, but mainly in late summer and early autumn. Take only the young outer leaves while they are tender and pull them off complete with the base, being extra careful not to pull up the plant.

POSSIBLE PROBLEMS Weed control is particularly necessary during the early stages of this crop and extra watering in dry weather will help to prevent bolting.

SWISS CHARD (SEAKALE BEET)

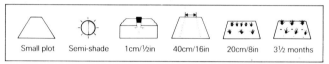

Small plot	Semi-shade	1cm/½in	40cm/16in	20cm/8in	3½ months

This distinctive-looking vegetable is grown for its wide white stalks as well as its leaves: the leaves are substituted for spinach and have a milder flavour than those of true spinach. The leaf stalks may be substituted for seakale itself. It is easier to grow than true spinach.

GROWING Any well-drained fertile garden soil is suitable. Swiss chard should be given plenty of organic manure to encourage succulent leaf growth. Sow the seed thinly in 1-cm/½-in deep drills during mid spring. Leave 40cm/16in between rows and thin the seedlings to 20cm/8in apart when they are large enough. Swiss chard can be sown in mid/late summer for an over-wintering crop, but the best results are obtained from spring-grown crops.

HARVESTING A little Swiss chard can be pulled in winter, but mainly in late summer and early autumn. Take only the young outer leaves while they are tender and pull them off complete with the base, being extra careful not to pull up the plant.

POSSIBLE PROBLEMS Weed control is particularly necessary during the early stages of this crop and extra watering in dry weather will help to prevent bolting. Feed with comfrey liquid if plants are not growing well.

▌DECORATIVE TIP

The red stems of ruby chard and the large spear-shaped leaves make it decorative enough to grow amongst flowering plants or as a border edging plant. The stems of rainbow chard can be red, yellow, orange, purple or white.

▌ORGANIC TIP

Grow comfrey as a plant food. The leaves of comfrey contain as much nitrogen and phosphorus as manure, plus far more potassium. Use a sunny position for a comfrey patch and cut down leaves to dig directly into the soil or use them as a mulch.

Make a concentrated feed by stuffing the freshly cut leaves into a plastic container with a hole in the bottom. The liquid that seeps out should be diluted with water 1:20 before use.

SPINACH BEET

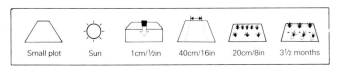

Small plot	Sun	1cm/½in	40cm/16in	20cm/8in	3½ months

Spinach beet belongs to the same family as garden beetroots. It is sometimes called perpetual spinach and is grown for the leaves and stalks, which are eaten whole for the spinach-like flavour. Its leaves have a milder flavour than those of true spinach.

GROWING Any well-drained, fertile garden soil is suitable. Spinach beet should be given plenty of organic manure to encourage succulent leaf growth. Spinach beet can either be sown in spring – for harvesting in the summer or autumn – or in late summer for harvesting in winter and early spring. The best results are obtained from spring-sown crops. Sow the seed thinly in 1-cm/½-in deep drills in mid spring. Leave 40cm/16in between rows and thin the seedlings to 20cm/8in apart when they are large enough.

HARVESTING Cut the entire leaves when young and tender. Regular harvesting encourages growth.

POSSIBLE PROBLEMS Weed control is particularly necessary during the early stages of this crop and regular watering is very useful in hot, dry summers. Aphids are a continual problem, especially on summer crops. Downy mildew produces the typical yellow blotches on the top of the leaves, accompanied by white fungal patches below. Protect winter spinach beet by lagging the plants with straw or bracken.

NEW ZEALAND SPINACH

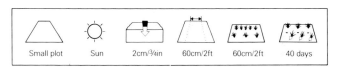

Small plot	Sun	2cm/¾in	60cm/2ft	60cm/2ft	40 days

New Zealand spinach is a useful vegetable for dry soils, and can be cropped regularly over a long period. It is a half-hardy sprawling plant.

GROWING New Zealand spinach must either be sown indoors in mid spring, hardened off and planted out in late spring after risk of frost has passed, or sown directly outdoors in early summer – or a little earlier under cloches. To assist germination, soak the seed in water overnight before sowing. Grow in stations 60cm/2ft apart. Sow 3 seeds per station, about 2cm/¾in deep, and pull out the two weakest seedlings as they grow. New Zealand spinach does best in hot summers, so choose a site in full sun with a light, well-drained soil.

HARVESTING New Zealand spinach should crop from early summer to early autumn, and must be picked regularly – otherwise it becomes tough, and knobbly seedheads are formed. Pick carefully, by nipping off the leaves without tearing. The plants are quite robust and up to half the leaves may be picked at a time.

POSSIBLE PROBLEMS Pick off any flowers to keep leaves growing. Hungry spinach of any kind will be bitter and possibly earthy flavoured. Give extra base dressing and liquid feed well throughout the summer.

▓ ORGANIC TIP

Mulch plants well, spreading around them garden compost, animal manure, seaweed, dried bracken, old straw, dried lawn mowings, or leaf mould. This will help to conserve moisture and keep the soil temperature stable.

▓ FREEZER TIP

Spinach and its substitutes, like New Zealand spinach, freeze well. Use young leaves and wash carefully to make sure no grit is left, then blanch, a little at a time, for two minutes, shaking the basket to separate the leaves. Cool fast by running very cold *water over the leaves for a further two minutes. Then press leaves to remove as much moisture as possible and freeze leaves whole in bags or chop up.*

SPINACH

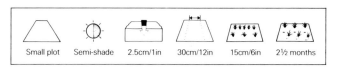

Small plot	Semi-shade	2.5cm/1in	30cm/12in	15cm/6in	2½ months

Spinach is very sensitive to day length, which is why it is apt to 'bolt' in the long days of summer. Steadier growth in autumn, winter and early spring allows several pickings.

GROWING A moist, rich, deeply dug soil is essential. For a summer supply, frequent small sowings are advisable, as in general only one cut can be made before spinach runs to seed. In warm parts of the country, the first sowing can be made under cloches in late winter, followed by outdoor sowings in early spring. Sow the seed thinly in 2.5cm/1-in deep drills spaced 30cm/12in apart. Water the bottom of the drill before sowing in dry weather. Thin the seedlings to 15cm/6in apart to allow reasonably sized plants to develop and to prevent excessive moisture loss and therefore bolting. Make further sowings at 2-3 week intervals until mid summer.

Winter spinach, which can be cropped between mid autumn and late spring, is sown in late summer and early autumn. In this case, however, growth rate and the danger of bolting will be less so the seedlings can be thinned, if necessary, to 7.5-15cm/3-6in apart. The plants will benefit from cloche protection from mid autumn.

HARVESTING Leaves can be eaten very small or allowed to grow larger. Pick them off the plant as required.

POSSIBLE PROBLEMS Copper spray will combat downy mildew. Pick off any flowers to keep leaves growing.

■ COOK'S TIP

Spinach has a distinctive taste and is delicious cooked or raw. Use young leaves in salads. Make a delicious appetizer with raw spinach leaves. Add to these hot streaky bacon bits, fried in butter until crisp, plus fried croutons. Toss the mixture in the hot butter *from the frying pan and add a little warmed wine vinegar. Spinach makes a tasty soup too. Add to it chicken stock, puréed tomatoes, a few carrots and potatoes plus freshly chopped dill leaves.*

SPRING GREENS

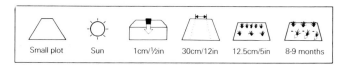

Small plot	Sun	1cm/½in	30cm/12in	12.5cm/5in	8-9 months

Spring greens are actually spring cabbages, cut before a heart forms, or the thinnings of a spring cabbage crop.

GROWING Spring greens are best sown in mid to late summer in their final positions with the shallow 1-cm/½-in drills spaced 30cm/12in apart. Once the seedlings have one or two true leaves, thin them to 7.5-12.5cm/3-5in apart in the rows. All members of the cabbage family prefer rich, deep soils which are moisture-retentive – but well drained – and have been given plenty of well-rotted organic manure. Spring greens over-winter as relatively small plants and must be encouraged to grow rapidly in the spring by hoeing in nitrogenous top dressings.

HARVESTING Harvest the first pickings of spring cabbages carefully so that the plants left have a 30cm/12in space between them. These can be left to heart up.

POSSIBLE PROBLEMS The soil will tend to become compacted during the winter, and this should be broken up when the fertilizer top dressing is hoed in during the spring. The fungus disease, club root, which causes the roots to become thick and swollen, is soil-borne, and most likely to occur in wet, acid soils which have grown continuous crops of brassicas without adequate rotational breaks. Mealy aphid can be treated with environmentally-sound soap sprays, with their combined insecticidal and wetting properties.

■ COOK'S TIP

Spring greens freeze well: wash, then blanch for two minutes in boiling, salted water, cool in icy cold water and press out any excess moisture before packing. Cook in a minimum of water for 5-10 minutes.

SUMMER PURSLANE

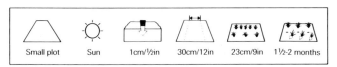

| Small plot | Sun | 1cm/½in | 30cm/12in | 23cm/9in | 1½-2 months |

Summer purslane is not a commonly grown leaf vegetable. It is worth trying if only because it grows very quickly. A low-growing plant, it can be cooked or eaten raw in salads.

GROWING Sandy soil suits summer purslane best, and a warm and sheltered position. Mixing the fine seed beforehand with moist sand will make sowing easier. Sow the seed broadcast from late spring until late summer. The plant usually grows well under the protection of glass or plastic cloches, but during wet, cold summers it often fails in the open.

HARVESTING Summer purslane is ready for picking in about 6 weeks – it may be ready in as little as 4 weeks, if the weather is warm or if it is grown under cloches. A length of stalk is usually picked with the leaves.

POSSIBLE PROBLEMS Over-close planting and over-watering can result in the fungus disease smoulder.

WINTER PURSLANE

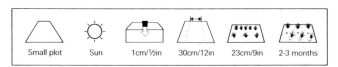

| Small plot | Sun | 1cm/½in | 30cm/12in | 23cm/9in | 2-3 months |

Late-sown crops of winter purslane survive mild winters and form a useful ingredient in the vegetable garden in early spring. Winter purslane is a low-growing, succulent salad plant.

GROWING Sow the seed from early spring to late summer in its final position. Most ordinary soils will be suitable and the plants tolerate light shade. Thin the seedlings to 10-13cm/4-5in apart each way.

HARVESTING The young leaves are ready for picking from 30 days.

POSSIBLE PROBLEMS Over-close planting and over-watering can result in the fungus disease smoulder. Protect winter purslane from frost by covering with cloches.

■ COOK'S TIP

When picking purslane leave a short length of stalk and a couple of leaves to encourage regrowth. Purslane has a crunchy texture and a rather bland taste that makes this salad plant best mixed with stronger tasting salad ingredients like rocket, sorrel, endive or chicory. The golden form adds an attractive yellow-green colour to a salad. Purslane can also be boiled briefly and eaten as a hot vegetable. It used to be pickled for winter use.

■ ORGANIC TIP

To reduce the slug and snail population encourage their predators: a pile of leaves in a dry and undisturbed corner could bring a hedgehog, an open-fronted nest box shaded and hidden by climbers may draw a pair of thrushes.

STALK AND SHOOT VEGETABLES

If you are following the crop rotation plan on page 132, stalk and shoot vegetables come into Plot B. Most need a well-drained soil that has been thoroughly dug to incorporate plenty of manure, but look under specific vegetables for more detail.

BLANCHING Blanching is done by excluding the light from stalks, shoots or leaves. This makes them more decorative, less bitter and crisp. Forced in the warm darkness new shoots of rhubarb can produce early supplies. Blanching can be done at any time of the year but colder weather produces the best results.

Plants can be blanched either while they are still in the ground or they can be lifted and transplanted for blanching in a dark position under cover in a frame, the greenhouse, garden shed or indoors where they will be protected from winter frosts.

Blanching in the ground There are a number of methods for doing this, suited to different plants.

Tying up plants The leaves are bunched up and then tied together with raffia or string either once about two-thirds up the plant or when necessary at two points. As light still reaches the outer leaves, they remain green but the inner leaves will be pale and crisp in 10-15 days. This method is used on endive.

Covering plants Light is totally excluded in this method where the plant is covered by a bucket, an inverted plant pot with the holes covered, black polythene-covered cloches or straw held in place with wire hoops or wire netting. Tie up the leaves to keep them off the ground.

Endive will take about 10 days; rhubarb protected and forced by this method in late winter will take about 5-6 weeks and seakale forced in mid winter takes longer, about 3 months.

Self blanching In this method, used for some varieties of celery, the plants are placed in squares, 30cm/12in apart, or 15cm/6in for larger quantities of smaller sticks. Because the plants exclude light from each other, they blanch without any additional work.

Covering stalks Cardoon stems are blanched by tying collars made of light-proof material, such as black polythene, around each stem. This method can also be used on Florence fennel and on celery instead of, or in conjunction with, earthing up where the collar is mainly used to stop the soil getting between the stalks.

Earthing up Here the plant stems are gradually covered with earth, increasing the height of the ridge in stages as the plants grow to keep out the light. This method is used on celery, asparagus, chard, leeks and Florence fennel.

If you leave a few salsify and scorzonera plants in the ground these can be completely covered in earth to provide blanched leaves for winter salads.

Lifted plants In winter plants can be lifted to be stored, then forced as required. Seakale can be blanched in this way. Blanching may be done in the dark in any frost-proof place; the greenhouse, a garden shed, a frame or in the house itself. A large flower pot, or a deep box filled with soil can be used to force and blanch the plants but the container needs to be covered with another of identical size and shape so that the light is completely excluded.

The plants are dug up in autumn, carefully to avoid damage, and the roots are stored until required for blanching. Those plants which are forced in warmth in the dark are not considered to have as much flavour as those which are blanched at low temperatures. Really early rhubarb can be produced by simulating forcing shed conditions used by commercial growers. Roots

Trench-grown celery
Dig a trench about 30cm/12in deep and 38cm/15in wide. Loosen the bottom to another spade's depth, add manure.

Tread down, return topsoil and firm to 10cm/4in of top. Ridge remaining soil and plant celery when it is 10cm/4in high. Tie polythene round plants when 30cm/12in high.

Earthing up is done in three stages, at three-weekly intervals. After the last earthing up only the leaves of the celery plants should be visible.

are lifted in the autumn and left on the soil surface until they have been frosted several times to break their dormancy. They are then taken into heated sheds where they are planted either in the soil or in boxes. After a thorough watering the crowns are then forced into growth – in absolute darkness – at temperatures around 13-18C/55-65F. Regular watering is necessary and the forced rhubarb is ready for pulling, at the higher temperature, in about 4 weeks. Home forcing should follow the same pattern but using smaller containers for the crowns. If tubs, pots or boxes are used then it should be possible to provide complete darkness by inverting a similar sized container over the top. After forcing in this way the crowns will be exhausted and should be thrown away.

Tips for successful blanching Make sure that plants are very dry before blanching. If damp they are likely to rot. In bad weather cover with cloches for a few days before excluding the light.

Remove any dead or rotting leaves before you blanch vegetables.

Handle plants with great care as damage to leaves or roots can lead to disease.

Once blanched a plant will quickly deteriorate so blanch only small quantities at a time for immediate use.

PESTS, DISEASES AND DISORDERS

Asparagus beetle This small orange beetle and its grubs may severely damage leaves, stripping the foliage, and encircle the stem, killing the plant. As soon as you see any sign of attack, dust with derris or use insecticidal soap.

Carrot fly Celery can be damaged by the larvae of the tunnelling carrot fly. To keep the carrot fly away from plants, surround the bed with a carrot fly barrier (see Tip on page 186). The insect has to fly up to go over the barrier and so misses the crop.

Celery fly The maggots appear in spring and leave brown blotches on leaves which then shrivel. They can kill the plant. Remove damaged leaves immediately and burn them.

Club root This disease of brassicas where roots distort and plants fail to develop can also affect seakale on acid soils. See page 159 for more information.

Damping off This is a fungus disease causing stems to blacken and decay on seedlings and plants to collapse. It should be prevented by sowing seed more thinly and watering less. Use sterilized compost.

Frit fly The growing points of sweetcorn will be stunted if larvae of the frit fly burrow in. Spray young plants with BHC.

Frost Asparagus shoots may be damaged by late frosts. In this likelihood, protect the tips with straw.

Leaf spot Dark, irregular spotting on celery leaves spreads and the leaves fall off. Remove and burn any affected leaves. Spray the plant with a copper fungicide.

Slugs Celery and young artichokes are attractive to slugs. Put a layer of soot or lime around the stems and weed regularly.

Violet root rot This fungus causes asparagus plants to wilt and die and the roots to turn purple and mouldy. This is rare but there is no cure. Make a bed in another part of the garden and do not use this area for asparagus again for at least three years.

GLOBE ARTICHOKE

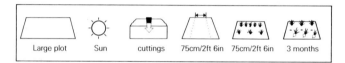

Large plot	Sun	cuttings	75cm/2ft 6in	75cm/2ft 6in	3 months

Although this vegetable needs a considerable amount of space, it is rewarding to grow. It is a handsome ornamental plant which produces edible flowerheads. The artichoke is an almost hardy perennial which will be productive for about 5 years.

GROWING Like all perennials, globe artichokes must be grown on well-prepared, manured and weed-free land. They prefer sheltered districts and light, well-drained soils. The best plants are raised from offsets detached from the parent plant in early spring or mid autumn. Early spring offsets are set into their permanent positions immediately; put autumn offsets into 9-cm/3½-in pots and keep in a cold frame until the following spring, when they can be planted out. Replace one quarter of the artichoke bed annually with offsets. Protect plants over winter with straw. Remove this covering in the spring, apply a top dressing of fertilizer and keep well-watered in dry seasons. Weed regularly or suppress weeds with a mulch.

HARVESTING Heads will be ready for cutting from midsummer onwards. Cut the terminal (king) head first: these are the largest, but the smaller lateral heads are very tender. To encourage continual cropping, harvest the heads as soon as they are mature.

POSSIBLE PROBLEMS None likely.

ASPARAGUS

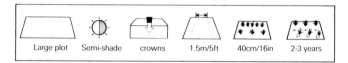

Large plot	Semi-shade	crowns	1.5m/5ft	40cm/16in	2-3 years

Start with 1-year-old crowns from a reputable supplier.

GROWING The ideal soil is a light, easily worked and well-drained loam. Dig deeply in the autumn before planting and work in well-rotted organic manure or compost. Remove all traces of perennial weeds. In late winter, rake in a general purpose fertilizer. In early spring/late spring, prepare double trenches 30cm/12in wide and 20cm/8in deep, 60cm/2ft apart. Replace a mound of soil 7.5cm/3in deep in the trench. Place the crowns on top, spreading out the roots. Quickly cover the roots with 5-7.5cm/2-3in of fine soil. Hoe the soil between the trenches regularly, each time drawing a little soil over the plants until the trench is filled. Continue earthing up as the shoots appear to make steep-sided beds.

HARVESTING Do not cut any spears in the first or second year. In the third year, cut for a 6-week period beginning in mid spring. Hold the tip of the spear and cut below the surface with a sharp knife, taking great care not to damage the crowns. At the end of the cutting period, leave the foliage to build up next year's crowns.
Cut down the foliage of mature plants when it changes colour and before the berries begin to drop.

POSSIBLE PROBLEMS Adult asparagus beetles and their larvae feed on shoots and foliage. Violet root rot fungus produces purple threads on the roots.

■ ORGANIC TIP

Save water and time by watering large, single plants efficiently. Sink a porous clay flower pot into the soil close to the plant and pour in water. It will seep down to the roots and a minimum will be lost by running away or evaporation.

■ ORGANIC TIP

Preparing the ground before planting is essential, since asparagus will crop for 40 years. When cutting back the foliage, cut as low as possible as the pupae of the asparagus fly overwinter in the stems. Slugs can be a problem with young asparagus. Distract them by growing a highly favoured crop nearby such as Chinese cabbage, hostas or sunflowers. Better still attract hedgehogs, thrushes, frogs and toads to do the work for you.

CARDOON

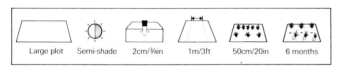

Large plot	Semi-shade	2cm/¾in	1m/3ft	50cm/20in	6 months

Cardoons are related to globe artichokes, but are cultivated for the leaf-stalks and ribs, although the thistle-like flowerhead is also edible. The stalks must be blanched in the same way as celery but the flavour is relatively bitter. Wear thick gloves when handling the prickly stems.

GROWING A fertile, free-draining but moisture-retentive soil is required. Prepare trenches 30cm/12in deep and 45cm/18in wide with well-rotted organic manure or compost dug into the bottom. Leave the soil from the trenches in ridges alongside. In mid spring, sow seeds at each station in the trench and later thin out all but the strongest seedlings. Alternatively, raise plants under glass at 15C/60F and harden off before planting out in late spring. Water lightly during the summer and keep weeds under control. Remove flowerheads and use as globe artichokes. On a dry day in early autumn, cut out any dead or yellow leaves before earthing up the plants. Tie up the tops and wrap the paper around the stems. Replace the soil from the ridges around the plants.

HARVESTING Blanching will be complete in four weeks. Remove the soil and use the stems – in salads, soups, and stews – as required, making sure all are harvested before the onset of severe winter frosts.

POSSIBLE PROBLEMS Relatively trouble-free.

TRENCH CELERY

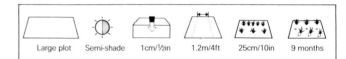

Large plot	Semi-shade	1cm/½in	1.2m/4ft	25cm/10in	9 months

Trench celery is winter-hardy and soil drawn up around the developing sticks blanches them.

GROWING Celery likes fertile, free-draining yet moisture retentive soil that is slightly acid. In early spring, dig trenches 30cm/12in deep and 40cm/16in wide, 90cm/3ft apart. Pile the soil you have removed in flat-topped ridges between the trenches. Fork over the trench bottom and work in well-rotted organic manure or compost. Earliest crops can be raised from seed in early spring. Sow thinly in trays, do not cover with compost and keep moist at 18C/65F to germinate. Prick out the seedlings after about 5 weeks into other seed trays, spacing them 9cm/3in apart each way. Do not let the temperature drop below 15C/60F. In late spring, transfer the plants to a cold frame for a few days to harden off before planting them in the trench. They are ready for planting when 10-12cm/4-5in tall. Plant firmly but carefully and water in well. Keep weeds down. When the plants reach 30-40cm/12-16in, begin to place earth from the ridges around the stems to the half-way point. Put a loose tie round the top to prevent soil getting into the heart. Repeat twice more at 3-weekly intervals, on dry days, making the soil slope away from the leaves.

HARVESTING Dig up bunches from mid autumn onwards.

POSSIBLE PROBLEMS As for Self-blanching Celery.

▣ COOK'S TIP

Remove the tough outer stalks, cut the remaining stems into 5-10cm/2-4in lengths, after discarding the leaves. Boil in water, to which a little lemon juice has been added, until tender, about 20-30 minutes.

▣ COOK'S TIP

Serve celery chopped up with apple and walnut with a creamy dressing by adding equal parts of cream cheese and Greek yogurt to vinaigrette. Celery is also good stir-fried. Chop small 1 onion, 1 clove garlic and 1cm/½in ginger and fry quickly, stirring all the time. Add chopped up lengths of 450g/1lb celery, lower the heat and cook for 2-3 minutes. Add a little sherry, and soy sauce, sprinkle with sesame seeds, cook for a further minute and serve.

SELF-BLANCHING CELERY

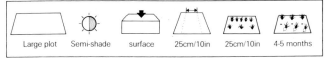

Large plot	Semi-shade	surface	25cm/10in	25cm/10in	4-5 months

All celery must be blanched for a good flavour. In contrast to trench celery, self-blanching types are grown on the flat. They are not frost hardy: their season of maturity stretches from mid summer until onset of frosts. Blanching is actually achieved by planting them close together in blocks and thus excluding the light.

GROWING Self-blanching celery needs the same soil type as trench varieties, and should also have well-rotted organic material dug in. Raise plants in the same way as for trench celery, but plant them out in a block, not in rows. Regular watering and a top dressing of nitro-chalk in mid summer are vital to encourage rapid growth.

HARVESTING Self-blanching celery will be available from mid summer. Lift the whole plant, and make sure harvesting is complete before the frosts begin.

POSSIBLE PROBLEMS Use seed treated against leaf spot fungus. Watch out for carrot and celery fly larvae. Seedlings can be affected by damping-off. Yellowing of the leaves and cracks in stems are caused by boron deficiency.

VARIETIES Golden Self-Blanching, Galaxy.

RHUBARB

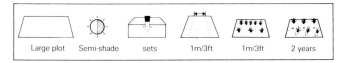

Large plot	Semi-shade	sets	1m/3ft	1m/3ft	2 years

Rhubarb is a perennial plant which can be forced to produce stems in late winter. The leaves are poisonous.

GROWING Because rhubarb occupies the ground for 5-10 years, the soil must be well prepared by incorporating plenty of organic compost or manure and digging deeply. Light soil is best. Start with healthy 'sets', obtained by dividing a mature crown in autumn, or buy in sets from a nursery. Remove all the roots and make sure each set has at least one bud. Plant with the crown just below the soil surface. Water lightly and do not let the new plant dry out. Clear away weeds and cut off flowering stems. Do not pull stalks for use in the first year. Remove them after they die down in winter, tidy the crowns and dig compost around the plants.

HARVESTING The first crop can be picked in the second season. Remove only half the stalks, twisting them off near the crown. Take more stalks in subsequent years.

FORCING Use an early variety. Cover the crowns with boxes or terracotta forcing pots if possible in early winter. Pack round with straw or fresh manure for warmth. After eight weeks, check that the growth has started. Pick stalks when 20-30cm/8-12in long. Let the plants crop naturally the following year.

POSSIBLE PROBLEMS Destroy any crowns affected by crown rot.

■ ORGANIC TIP

Feed with a seaweed-based fertilizer. Tuck straw around and between the plants to increase blanching. Also try growing leaf celery, a close relation of wild celery. It is hardy, usually continues to grow throughout the year and self seeds.

■ GARDENER'S TIP

Force rhubarb indoors to harvest in mid winter. Dig up clumps and leave exposed for 1-2 weeks. Place roots in a box, cover with a thin layer of soil and water, then another box and black polythene. Keep warm and moist for 4-5 weeks.

SEAKALE

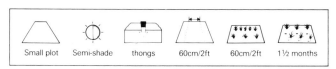

Small plot	Semi-shade	thongs	60cm/2ft	60cm/2ft	1½ months

The edible parts of this excellent spring vegetable are the shoots, which are blanched to eliminate bitterness.

GROWING A well-drained sandy loam is best. Seakale does not like acid soils. Shoots are forced from good healthy crowns. Cut the roots to 15-cm/6-in lengths (thongs) the size of your little finger. Trim the end which was nearest the crown horizontally, making an angled cut at the other end. Bundle the thongs together and heel them in under a cold frame over winter. In spring, remove all the buds except the strongest. Plant the thongs in early spring, angled ends downwards, so the tops are 1cm/½in below the soil's surface. In the growing season, control weeds, water regularly and remove flowering stems in order to build up the crown. Do not force the crowns in the first winter after planting.

FORCING Place pots or boxes over the crowns late in the second winter. To increase the temperature inside, fermenting organic manure can be packed outside.

HARVESTING Cut off the blanched, tender stems with a sharp knife. When all the shoots have been cut, clean up the crowns, apply a mulch and top-dress with fertilizer. Good crowns can be forced for at least 5 consecutive seasons, and from these new root cuttings can be taken.

POSSIBLE PROBLEMS Club root can occur on acid soils.

SWEET CORN

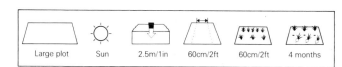

Large plot	Sun	2.5m/1in	60cm/2ft	60cm/2ft	4 months

Plant this half-hardy annual in square blocks rather than long rows to assist wind-pollination

GROWING Sow seeds in mid spring in seed trays at 10-13C/50-55F. Keep moist and when the seedlings are large enough to handle transfer them to 9-cm/3½-in pots. The plants need full light and good ventilation on warm days. Harden off before planting out in late spring. In warm districts, seeds can be sown in the open from late spring. Set 3 seeds at each station. in a well-drained and fertile soil on a sunny, sheltered site and retain the strongest seedling only. Incorporate plenty of well-rotted organic manure or compost the winter before sowing to assist fast vegetable growth, which is important to produce 2 cobs per plant (you may get only 1). Provide continual supplies of water and nitrogenous fertilizer during the growing season. Hoe the weeds out until the plants are tall enough – 60cm/2ft – to shade out further weed growth, being careful not to damage the stems. 'Tassels' and 'silks', the male and female parts of the plant, appear from mid-summer.

HARVESTING Pick about 4 weeks after the silk begins to wither. The ideal time is when a milky white fluid shoots out from the grains if pressed with your thumbnail.

POSSIBLE PROBLEMS Birds damage young plants. Fruit fly larvae tunnel into the stems.

▩ COOK'S TIP

Blanched seakale has a delicate, nutty flavour. It is best steamed for about 20-25 minutes. Don't overcook. Serve with a knob of melted butter or with a coating of bechamel sauce. Alternatively, use cheese sauce, top with nuts and breadcrumbs and put in a moderate oven for about half-an-hour until the topping becomes brown and crusty. A good flavour is produced, too, if the shoots are simmered in chicken stock. They can also be added raw, to salads.

▩ HEALTH TIP

Because the sugar starts to turn to starch as soon as a cob is picked, home-grown corns that are cooked immediately after picking are more nutritious and taste far better than those you buy in a shop.

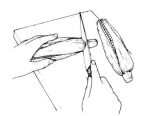

SQUASHES

Squashes do not need to be rotated to another plot yearly so they can be grown on a permanent site, Plot D on the crop rotation plan, page 132. They do, however, need well-drained soil and a sunny site. They also need a soil rich in organic matter.

PREPARING THE SOIL As roots do not reach down far into the soil each plant can be treated individually by providing it with its own supply of organic matter. Dig out a 30-cm/12-in cube where each plant is to be grown. Half fill the holes with well-rotted manure or garden compost then replace the soil on top and mix the two together to form a mound. Alternatively, if a row of plants is being grown you can dig a trench if you prefer.

When plants begin to fruit they will need feeding once a week with seaweed fertilizer or comfrey liquid (see page 168).

SEED GERMINATION Squash seed germination can be erratic. The best way to germinate the seeds is to place them on moist kitchen paper in a plastic container with a lid. Keep the container, covered, in a warm spot, such as the airing cupboard, and the seeds should start to germinate within 2-3 days. As squashes also dislike root disturbance, it is best to grow the seedlings individually in 7.5-cm/3-in pots or soil blocks. Sow in mid spring to plant out in early summer. Early courgettes to be grown under cloches may be sown in early spring and transplanted to the garden in late spring.

Alternatively, seeds can be sown outdoors, three to a mound, in late spring. Thin to leave one plant to each mound. A minimum of three plants of any squash variety is needed so that, in the early stages, there will be enough male and female flowers out at the same time for pollination to take place.

BUSH OR TRAILING There is a choice between growing bush or trailing varieties of most squashes. For small gardens, where space is at a premium, bush varieties are an obvious choice although trailing varieties can be grown up canes in a wigwam shape. In this case, pinch out the growing shoot when each plant reaches the top of its cane and support fruit other than courgettes in net bags.

Trailing varieties grown along the ground should have each branch stopped at 60cm/24in.

FROST TENDER Any squash planted out too early will suffer a severe setback that can be terminal if there is a late frost or even a cold spell, so don't be tempted to plant out before late spring or early summer, unless you are growing plants under cloches. It is also important to harden plants off gradually so that they adjust to the outdoor temperature before being planted out. A garden frame is ideal for this but a cloche can also be used. Place plants in the frame or under the cloche and during warm daytime hours gradually increase the

Growing squashes
Dig out a 30-cm/12-in cube where each plant is to be grown. Half fill the holes with well-rotted manure, replace the soil and mix with the compost.

When seven leaves have formed on each young plant, pinch out the growing tip. This encourages the side shoots – which will bear fruit – to develop. Select a support system of wire or canes.

Any side shoots which do not have flowers when their seventh leaf forms should have their tips pinched out. Water around the plants in dry weather and feed regularly with a liquid fertilizer.

time they are left uncovered. Protect at night until finally they are left uncovered altogether. They are then ready for transplanting.

EARLY COURGETTES By protecting courgette plants with cloches or a polythene tunnel you can bring forward the planting and fruiting dates by about a month. Prepare the soil as described on page 178, opposite, and place the cloches over the mounds about 4 weeks before planting out. If you dig out a trench instead of separate blocks of soil, you can cover the resulting soil and manure ridge with black plastic or biodegradable paper, then plant through this and finally replace the polythene tunnel. The plastic or paper will act as a mulch, conserving moisture and controlling weeds and will help to maintain soil temperature through the night.

MULCHING AND WATERING The fruit of squash plants contain a high proportion of water and plants need to be kept moist. Mulching the plants will help to conserve the moisture. It will also help to keep the fruit clean. It is also a good idea to place a piece of glass, a small square of timber or plywood or a brick under larger squash fruit to keep them away from slugs and help against fungal attack.

Large plants, like squashes, can be watered by sinking a clay plant pot into the soil close to the stem and filling this with water. The water will gradually sink through the soil providing a constant supply with a minimum of evaporation.

GARDEN COLD FRAME Really a miniature greenhouse, a cold frame is very useful for raising young plants and for hardening off seedlings prior to planting out. In winter a frame can be used for over-wintering seedlings, for growing lettuce or for forcing chicory. In spring it can protect the first crops of many plants including lettuce, carrot and radish. Tomato and pepper plants can be grown safely here until the weather is right for planting them out. A frame's use will be governed by its height. A low 23-cm/9-in frame can be used for seedlings and for salad plants like lettuces, but one of 45cm/18in high allows you to use it for a much wider range of plants.

Traditionally, garden frames are a permanent fixture, constructed of timber or bricks with glass, removable lights (top lid). These materials provide good insulation and the lights can be covered with an old piece of carpet for top protection in winter when forcing and blanching chicory.

Modern frames are lighter, with an aluminium frame and glass sides as well as glazed lights. They are also portable.

Like greenhouses, frames provide a restricted environment in which diseases can build up and pests multiply. Always clean the frame thoroughly at the end of the season.

PESTS AND DISEASES
Aphids Aphids are especially unpopular as the carriers of cucumber mosaic virus so need to be dealt with as soon as you see them. Remove small numbers by hand. Spray plants with insecticidal soap (direct on to the pests as this acts on impact) which is harmless to humans, animals, bees and other beneficial insects. Alternatively, spray with derris.

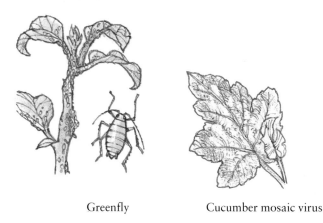

Greenfly   Cucumber mosaic virus

Cucumber mosaic virus This can affect all types of squashes. Leaves become mottled and yellow and the virus stunts growth. There is no cure. Pull up and burn an affected plant to stop it spreading. Take steps to remove aphids as soon as you see them as they carry the disease.
Foot rot Badly drained soil suffocates the roots and young plants rot at the stem. Keep the soil open and well-cultivated and observe recommended crop rotation patterns.
Leaf distortion A virus disease affecting marrows (and strawberries) causes the leaves to become crinkled and undersized. Burn diseased plants.
Slugs Slugs can be a problem when growing any squashes. Surround plants with a lime or soot circle which slugs hate going through or use a bark mulch which will also deter them. Attract the predators of slugs: toads and frogs, slow worms, birds and hedgehogs (see page 134).

COURGETTE

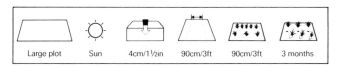

Large plot	Sun	4cm/1½in	90cm/3ft	90cm/3ft	3 months

Courgettes are marrows specially bred to be ready to pick and use at 15-20cm/6-8in long As well as the more common green types, yellow varieties are available as a colourful summer vegetable.

GROWING Fertile, well-drained soil is essential. Prepare ridges as for marrows or, alternatively, dig out planting holes 30cm/12in deep and 30cm/12in square and half fill with well-rotted organic manure before replacing the soil to make mounds. Like marrows, seeds need help germinating. Place on sheets of soaked kitchen paper and keep at 18C/65F until the roots appear. Plant immediately in pots if sowing in mid spring or directly into the growing site in late spring. The earlier sowings should be kept moist at 15-18C/60-65F and hardened off briefly before planting out in late spring. Feed and water liberally while growing. In cold weather pollination may need to be done by hand with a camel-hair brush or by removing the male flowers and inserting them into the open female blossoms. Leave the flowers in place.

HARVESTING As soon as they are large enough to use, pick regularly to encourage the formation of further fruits. Unlike marrows, courgettes cannot be restored.

POSSIBLE PROBLEMS Aphids attacking young shoots carry virus diseases. Spray with a suitable insecticide.

VARIETIES Zucchini; Green Bush; Eldorado (yellow).

■ ORGANIC TIP

For extra colour, mix varieties. Fruits can range from dark to light green, grey and yellow. Some are attractively striped. The flowers look effective in a saucer as a table decoration and can also be stuffed and cooked as a starter.

CUSTARD MARROW

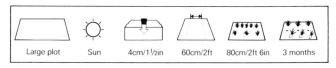

Large plot	Sun	4cm/1½in	60cm/2ft	80cm/2ft 6in	3 months

These members of the marrow and pumpkin tribe are very attractive fruiting vegetables which can be cooked like pumpkins.

GROWING Like long marrows, these plants need fertile, well-drained soil. Prepare a trench or planting holes as for courgettes, half filling with well-rotted organic compost before replacing the soil. Start the seeds into growth in mid spring by placing them on sheets of soaked kitchen paper kept moist at 18C/65F until the roots appear. Plant immediately, either into 9-cm/3½-in pots kept at 15-18C/60-65F until planting out in late spring or directly into the growing site, again in late spring. Feed and water generously during the growing period. Assist pollination if necessary, either using a camel-hair brush or by inserting the male flowers into the open female flowers (the females have a swelling behind the blossom).

HARVESTING Pick the circular fruits as soon as they reach 15cm/6in in diameter in order to encourage further fruiting. Not suitable for storage.

POSSIBLE PROBLEMS Slugs: lay down bait; aphids: spray with suitable insecticide. If virus diseases strike, destroy affected plants.

VARIETIES Custard Pie; Custard Yellow.

■ ORGANIC TIP

Make sleeves from plastic bottle sides to protect young plants from slugs; later surround them with lime or soot, both of which slugs hate crawling over. Use hoverfly larvae to control aphids (see summer and autumn cabbages) or, on a bad

infestation, spray with insecticidal soap directly on to the insect. Aphids also carry the cucumber mosaic virus and it pays to keep them at bay as there is no cure for this.

SQUASHES

MARROW

Large plot	Sun	4cm/1½in	60cm/2ft	80cm/2ft 6in	3 months

These half-hardy members of the cucumber family may be trailing or bushy in habit.

GROWING Marrows need fertile, well-drained soil. Prepare the growing site in late spring in a sheltered position, having dug the land deeply in the previous autumn. Dig out trenches 30cm/12in deep and 45cm/18in wide. Half fill with well-rotted manure and replace the soil to form a ridge. For early plantings, raise plants from seed sown in mid spring. To assist germination, place the seeds on sheets of soaked kitchen paper and keep at 18C/65F until the roots appear. Immediately transfer to individual 9-cm/3½-in pots of potting compost and keep moist at 15-18C/60-65F until planting out in late spring. Germinated seed may be sown directly into the ridges in late spring. Water very generously while growing and conserve moisture with a mulch of organic manure, peat or grass cuttings. Give regular feeds of liquid fertilizer.

HARVESTING Pick marrows as soon as they reach 30cm/12in for a tender texture. Those ripening in early autumn can be stored in an airy, frost-free place for winter use.

POSSIBLE PROBLEMS Spray with derris against aphids, which carry virus diseases. Watch for slugs.

VARIETIES Tender & True; White Bush (white).

ROUND MARROW

Large plot	Sun	4cm/1½in	60cm/2ft	80cm/2ft 6in	3 months

Very like melons in appearance, round marrows are good cooked with a savoury stuffing.

GROWING Prepare the site in the autumn for a spring sowing. Dig out trenches or planting holes 30cm/12in deep and half fill with well-rotted manure. Replace the soil to make a ridge or mound. In mid spring, prepare the seeds for sowing by placing them on sheets of kitchen paper soaked in water. Keep at 18C/65F until roots appear, then plant in individual 9-cm/3½-in pots. Keep moist at 15-18C/60-65F and transfer to the growing site in late spring. Water liberally, apply a moisture-retaining mulch and feed regularly with a liquid fertilizer. It may be necessary to hand-pollinate with a camel-hair brush if the weather is cold. Bush plants do not require staking.

HARVESTING Pick the marrows when they are about 30cm/12in in diameter. Late ripening specimens can be stored for winter use.

POSSIBLE PROBLEMS Aphids; slugs.

VARIETY Twickers.

■ COOK'S TIP

A whole marrow may be cooked remarkably easily in the microwave oven, provided it fits! Allow about 10 minutes for a stuffed 2kg/4½lb marrow, cooking it in a roasting bag on Full power.

■ GARDENER'S TIP

If you have only a small garden, you may well feel that you do not have the space to grow marrows. You can grow trailing varieties up tripods of canes but the fruit needs to be carefully supported. Alternatively, towards the end of the season, allow courgettes on a few plants to remain and grow large to provide you with a supply of marrows.

181

SPAGHETTI MARROW

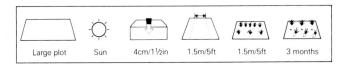

| Large plot | Sun | 4cm/1½in | 1.5m/5ft | 1.5m/5ft | 3 months |

Sometimes called vegetable spaghetti, these curious fruiting vegetables look like elongated melons. They are boiled whole, and when split in two reveal tender flesh in spaghetti-like strands, eaten simply with butter and seasoning.

GROWING Prepare planting holes as for courgettes but at the greater distances recommended. Raise plants from pre-germinated seed (see marrows). Sow seed in mid spring in individual pots of potting compost at 15-18C/60-65F and harden the seedlings off briefly before planting out in late spring, firming the plants in well. Alternatively, sow seed directly into the growing site, again in late spring. Feed and water well to encourage rapid growth. Because of its trailing habit, this plant needs training, on fences or tripods of 2-m/7-ft poles, if it is not to wander all over the garden. Support systems also help to keep the fruits out of slugs' way.

HARVESTING Pick spaghetti marrows at 20cm/8in long; do not leave them until the skin is so hard your fingernail cannot penetrate it. The plant will continue producing fruits for several weeks if they are harvested regularly.

POSSIBLE PROBLEMS Aphids carry serious virus diseases. Spray with a suitable insecticide.

MELON

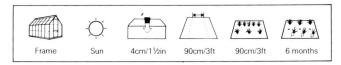

| Frame | Sun | 4cm/1½in | 90cm/3ft | 90cm/3ft | 6 months |

Some melon varieties must be greenhouse grown, but for others the protection of a frame is enough.

GROWING Sow seed in mid spring for planting in late spring/early summer. Strew seeds on a wad of wet kitchen paper. Keep moist at 18C/65F. Some of the seeds will root within 2 days. Plant them 4cm/1½in deep in individual 9-cm/3½-in pots of compost. Keep the temperature steady until the first true leaf appears, then gradually reduce it to 15C/60F. Harden off for 2-3 days before planting out, 1 plant per frame. To prepare the frame, see Tip below. Set the plants into the mounded beds with the rootball 4cm/1½in above the surface. Water in well. Spray regularly. Ventilate only on very hot days. Stop the plants after 3-4 leaves, again after another 4-5. Train 3-4 laterals into the corners, peg them down and stop them when they reach the edges. Open the frame on hot days to admit pollinating insects. After flowering, withhold water. Water the bed again when the fruits are egg-sized, keeping the atmosphere dry. Give liquid fertilizer every 10 days.

HARVESTING Fruits are ripe when they yield to gentle pressure and smell sweet. Cut off with a short stem.

POSSIBLE PROBLEMS Red spider mite; root rot fungi.

■ GARDENER'S TIP

Place ground-level developing fruit on sheets of glass or plywood. This helps to keep slugs away and discourages fungal attack.

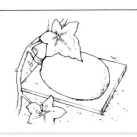

■ GARDENER'S TIP

To prepare the frame, in late spring take out a 30-cm/ 12-in cube at the back and fill with well-rotted manure. Replace the soil to make a mound. Water the bed and cover the frame to create warmth and humidity.

PUMPKIN

Large plot	Sun	4cm/1½in	60cm/2ft	80cm/2ft 6in	5 months

Although large pumpkins are impressive exhibition pieces and useful at hallowe'en, for cooking purposes smaller specimens are better. In fact it is difficult to grow giant pumpkins in the British climate. Full sun is essential. Both bush and trailing types are available.

GROWING In fertile, well-drained soil, prepare planting holes as for courgettes but at the greater distances recommended. To raise plants under glass, sow pre-germinated seed (see marrows) in mid spring and keep the seedlings moist at 10-13C/50-55F until planting out in early summer. Alternatively, sow directly into the growing site in late spring, covering the seeds with jars or cloches until they have sprouted two true leaves. Feed and water generously. Stop trailing types at 45cm/18in to encourage the flower-bearing sideshoots. For bigger pumpkins, leave only 1 or 2 fruits per plant.

HARVESTING Pumpkins are usually eaten as they mature in summer, but types that bear larger fruits should be left until autumn. Store in a cool, frost-free place.

POSSIBLE PROBLEMS Grey mould on the leaves: treat with benomyl. Use a systemic fungicide if powdery mildew appears on the leaves. See also courgettes.

SUMMER SQUASH

Large plot	Sun	4cm/1½in	60cm/2ft	80cm/2ft 6in	3 months

Summer squashes are popular vegetables in North America. Related to pumpkins and marrows, they cannot be stored but – like courgettes – should be used soon after picking.

GROWING Full sun and fertile soil is important. Prepare the site in autumn by digging out planting holes 30cm/12in deep, half-filling them with well-rotted manure and replacing the soil to form mounds. In late spring, prepare the seeds by placing them on sheets of soaked kitchen paper kept at 18C/65F until roots appear. Plant the seeds immediately after germination, one to each site, and cover with an upturned jar until the first true leaves appear. Feed and water generously. Stop trailing varieties at 45cm/18in to encourage the production of flower-bearing side shoots. Bush types are more compact and better for small gardens.

HARVESTING Pick squashes when they are young and tender for the best flavour. Harvest regularly to encourage the formation of more fruits.

POSSIBLE PROBLEMS Slugs; aphids.

VARIETIES Baby Crookneck.

■ COOK'S TIP

To make the traditional pumpkin pie in a 18-20-cm/7-8-in flan tin, you will need 1kg/2lb fresh pumpkin. Cut the flesh into cubes and steam in a bowl over simmering water for 15-20 minutes, then purée. When cool, add to this 3 eggs, 75g/3oz caster

sugar, ½ tsp ground cinnamon, ½ tsp ground ginger and a pinch of nutmeg. Mix well, then beat in 150ml/¼ pint single cream. Place in a pastry case and bake for about 55 minutes in a moderately hot oven (190C, 375F, gas 5).

■ GARDENER'S TIP

When the weather is cold early in the season, push a pollen-releasing male flower into an open female flower to pollinate.

ROOT VEGETABLES AND TUBERS

Following the crop rotation plan on page 132, roots are grown in Plot A. Because there is a danger of roots forking in freshly manured ground, in this plan they are grown on ground which was manured two years previously. However, if you use well-rotted manure or compost this should not occur.

PREPARING THE SOIL Land that has been deep dug, to the depth of two spades rather than one, is ideal for growing root crops as this improves the drainage and allows the roots to go downwards. For double digging see page 129. This greater depth of cultivated ground also allows you to grow plants much closer together which is a great advantage in a small plot. Plan beds to a width that allows you to work on them comfortably from both sides without moving on to the soil. This is important on all cultivated soil but specially so on deep dug beds. Somewhere between 1m/3ft and 1.25m/4ft depending on what is comfortable for you, is about the right size.

FLUID SOWING This is a method used by commercial growers to evenly sow small pre-germinated seeds and can be used on parsnips as well as many other vegetables.

First sow the seed on moist kitchen or tissue paper.

When the majority have produced a first root or shoot, wash them carefully in a sieve to remove the paper. Mix up a wallpaper paste – make sure you choose one that does not contain fungicide – and gently stir the seeds into it until they are evenly distributed throughout.

Pour into a polythene bag and tie up. When the seed drill is prepared cut off a corner of the bag and, like icing a cake, squeeze the mixture along the drill then cover in the usual way. Water regularly (very important or the wallpaper paste could harden) and tend the crop as usual.

TRANSPLANTING Most root crops cannot be transplanted as there is too much danger of damage to the single tap root causing distorted growth and double roots. They can however be planted individually in peat pots, then planted out pot and all. The roots produced by thinning can provide the wonderful tiny root vegetables that are so prized by nouvelle cuisine chefs.

INTERCROPPING Root vegetables, many of which are in the ground for some time, are ideal subjects for intercropping with fast growing crops like lettuces. Early carrots can be planted in spaces between slow-growing crops too, like cabbages.

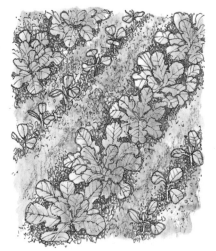

Intercropping
Left *While long-term crops are still young, use the ground in between for quick-growing crops.*

Earthing up potatoes
Right *Use a draw hoe to pull the earth between the rows up and around the top growth. If the tops are short, the soil can be drawn right over to cover the foliage, protecting it from frost.*

When intercropping, remember to choose plants to grow together which require the same conditions. Don't try to crush too many plants into the space. It is important to give both slow and quick growing plants plenty of space, light and moisture and enough room for you to cultivate and harvest them. Because the ground is being so heavily used it will need to be kept fertile with regular manuring and feeding.

Tips on keeping winter supplies Many roots such as parsnips, salsify, swedes and Jerusalem artichokes can be left in the ground to be lifted when required.

When harvesting roots and tubers, lift them carefully to avoid damage.

Pick only perfect vegetables for storage, eating any that are less than perfect first.

Potatoes should be lifted, cleaned of soil and left outdoors to dry for a few hours before sorting then storing in paper or hessian bags.

Most root crops are best lifted in late autumn. Store in layers in boxes in moist vermiculite or sand (see below). Small quantities can be stored in plastic bags.

Cool temperatures are best for storing vegetables: just above freezing is ideal.

Check stored supplies regularly and remove any roots or tubers that are starting to rot.

PESTS, DISEASES AND DISORDERS

Carrot fly larvae Both carrots and parsnips can be damaged by the carrot fly maggots which tunnel through the roots. Signs of attack are young seedlings that die or foliage of older plants that reddens. Avoid thinning as the smell attracts the fly. Surround beds with a plastic mesh barrier, described in Tip on page 186 to keep the fly away from plants.

Celery fly larvae The maggots leave brown blotches on the leaves of parsnips and celeriac which can then

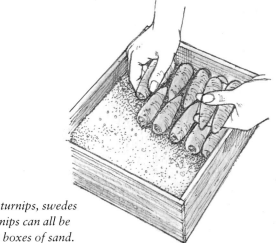

Carrots, turnips, swedes and parsnips can all be stored in boxes of sand.

wither and the plant may die. Remove affected leaves as soon as you see them and burn.

Flea beetle These jumping beetles make small holes in the leaves of turnips. As they act like fleas, leaping into the air when approached, they can be caught by running a small piece of wood over the crop which has been coated on the lower side with thick grease.

Forked roots Forked roots are caused by carrots or parsnips being grown on soil where fresh manure or compost has been used. Grow on ground manured for a previous crop or store manure and compost for a year, until it is well rotted.

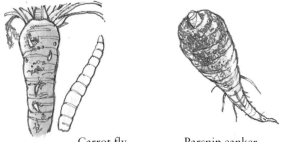

Carrot fly   Parsnip canker

Parsnip canker Reddish, orange brown or black cankers spread into the root and cause it to rot. In future dress the soil with lime and use good methods of cultivation plus resistant varieties.

Potato blight This is a fungus that causes black spotting on leaves and withered stems. Ultimately the tubers rot. Spray with Bordeaux mixture.

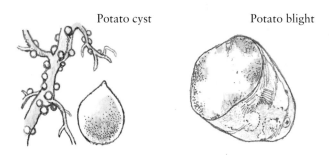

Potato cyst   Potato blight

Potato cyst eelworm
A minute pest that attacks potatoes between mid and late summer causing smaller tubers and plants to die. Rotate the crop to avoid this problem and grow resistant varieties.

Powdery mildew This powdery grey fungus thrives when days are hot and nights cool. It coats leaves and can eventually get into the plant and kill it if nothing is done about it. Spray with a copper fungicide.

Split roots Split roots can occur if plants suffer a very dry period followed by a very wet one. Do not allow the soil to get too dry before watering.

FORCING CARROT

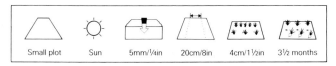

Small plot	Sun	5mm/¼in	20cm/8in	4cm/1½in	3½ months

The carrot varieties suitable for forcing or early cultivation are the stump-rooted types.

GROWING All carrot crops like a light, open-textured soil, and this is essential for early plantings. The soil must also be fertile and moisture retentive if good-sized roots are to develop. Dig over the plot in the autumn and leave it rough over winter for a tilth to form, but do not dig in organic manure, which will cause forking of the roots. Rake over the soil in mid winter to give a fine tilth, incorporating a general purpose fertilizer. Sow seed in shallow drills and lightly rake it in. Water evenly and regularly and cover with cloches or frames. Ventilate on warm, sunny days. Remove the cloches/frames in mid spring. Thinning the seedlings is unnecessary.

HARVESTING Pull the tender carrots for use as soon as they reach the required size. This crop will continue until late spring.

POSSIBLE PROBLEMS Early sowings escape the worst problems, but aphids may attack the leaves. Spray with a suitable insecticide.

VARIETIES Amsterdam Forcing; Nantes.

EARLY OUTDOOR CARROT

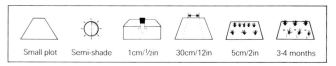

Small plot	Semi-shade	1cm/½in	30cm/12in	5cm/2in	3-4 months

If sown successively at fortnightly intervals, early outdoor sowings will produce carrots continuously throughout the summer. Like forced crops, stump-rooted types should be used.

GROWING The soil for early carrots should be light, open-textured and fertile with enough moisture to allow roots to develop to a good size. Prepare the plot by digging deeply in the previous autumn and leaving it rough to allow a tilth to develop. Apply a general purpose fertilizer, raking the soil to a fine tilth, as soon as the ground is workable, in early spring or a little later. Warm up the soil by covering it with cloches or polythene tunnels before the first sowing. Sow thinly in shallow drills. Water evenly and regularly and thin the seedlings as soon as they are large enough to handle. It is not usually necessary to water after this point. A further thinning may be necessary to produce really large roots. Thin in the evening, scattering soil over the holes from which carrots have been removed, to deter carrot fly. Keep weeds down, hoeing with care.

HARVESTING Lift the roots as soon as they have reached the required size and use immediately.

POSSIBLE PROBLEMS Carrot fly and aphids, which carry a virus which causes the leaves to be stunted and yellowed and the roots underdeveloped.

▨ FREEZER TIP

Small, young carrots are ideal for freezing whole. Scrub under running water then blanch by plunging into boiling water for 3 minutes then into ice-cold water. Pack in bags. They will keep well until the next year's crop. Steam the carrots or cook quickly in the microwave in a minimum of water and serve with butter, a squeeze of lemon juice and a pinch of sugar. Sprinkle with chopped fresh herbs, like parsley, marjoram, dill, chives or mint.

▨ ORGANIC TIP

Carrot flies are fairly easily foiled. As they fly low, simply erect a barrier around a carrot crop and they will move up to pass over it and miss your carrots too. Use plastic or fine mesh and put in place as soon as carrots have been thinned.

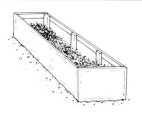

Maincrop Carrot

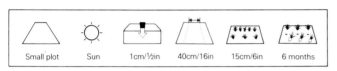

Small plot	Sun	1cm/½in	40cm/16in	15cm/6in	6 months

For maincrop carrots to be used in late summer both stump-rooted and long tapering varieties are available. Those picked in the autumn for winter storage must be long-rooted types.

GROWING While maincrop carrots prefer the light, open-textured soil essential for early crops, it is possible to grow them on heavier soils using stump-rooted types. If the soil needs manuring, this should be done for the previous crop. Dig the plot deeply in the autumn, leaving it rough over winter for a natural tilth to develop. Around mid spring, rake to a fine tilth, evenly incorporating a general purpose fertilizer. The first sowings can be made at this point, but seedlings will be vulnerable to carrot fly and it is better to wait until late spring or early summer if possible. Water regularly. Thin the seedlings when they are large enough to handle and withhold water unless conditions are very dry.

HARVESTING Maincrop carrots can either be left in the ground and dug up as needed – in which case they will need protection with straw during severe weather – or they can be lifted in mid autumn and stored. Place undamaged carrots only in boxes of sand in an airy frost-free place. They should keep until mid spring.

POSSIBLE PROBLEMS Carrot fly larvae feed on the roots and can kill young seedlings or damage older plants.

Celeriac

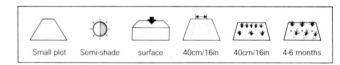

Small plot	Semi-shade	surface	40cm/16in	40cm/16in	4-6 months

This close relative of celery is not a true root crop since the edible part is the swollen stem base. The flavour is very like celery and the 'roots' can be cooked variously.

GROWING Deep, fertile, well-drained soil is essential. Dig in plenty of organic manure during the winter and incorporate a nitrogenous fertilizer when preparing the plot for planting. Raise plants in a heated greenhouse, sowing the seed thinly on the surface of compost in seed trays in early spring. Do not cover the seed with compost. Keep a steady temperature of 16C/61F and never let the trays dry out. After about a month, prick the seedlings out into small individual pots and grow on for another 4-5 weeks. Harden the plants off before setting them out in late spring/early summer. Water in well and continue to water generously through the season. If growth slows down give a light dressing of nitro-chalk and water it in. Keep weeds down.

HARVESTING Celeriac is ready for lifting from early autumn, but the roots will be bigger if left until late autumn. They can be left in the ground until required, covered with a protective layer of straw in severe weather.

POSSIBLE PROBLEMS Celeriac suffers from the same pests and diseases as celery. In poor growing seasons the flesh may be streaked brown.

VARIETIES Globus; Alabaster; Tellus.

▩ PRESERVING TIP

If you are short of space, use a plastic dustbin to store carrots in a garden shed. If they are left in the ground during a wet winter they may split. Twist off leaves and store in layers in sand, positioned so that they do not touch each other.

▩ COOK'S TIP

A classic French salad is made with raw grated celeriac coated with a mustard mayonnaise. Celeriac is also delicious cooked and served in a white sauce. Alternatively, layer celeriac and mushrooms in white sauce, cover with cheese and breadcrumbs and put in the oven to give a crusty topping. Yogurt or soured cream are also good partners for cooked or raw celeriac.

ROOT VEGETABLES AND TUBERS

187

Hamburg Parsley

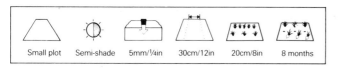

| Small plot | Semi-shade | 5mm/¼in | 30cm/12in | 20cm/8in | 8 months |

This hardy biennial, also known as turnip-rooted parsley, is grown for its roots, which taste rather like celeriac.

GROWING Sow seeds in early spring in well-drained soil manured for a previous crop. Thin the seedlings when they are large enough to handle. Keep weeds under control and water the plants regularly throughout the growing season.

HARVESTING Hamburg parsley needs a long growing season to develop the large roots which have the best flavour. Delay lifting the roots until late autumn. They can be left in the ground all winter, but are better lifted and stored, as beetroot, for winter use.

POSSIBLE PROBLEMS Root fly or fungus diseases can be problems.

Jerusalem Artichoke

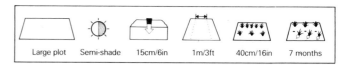

| Large plot | Semi-shade | 15cm/6in | 1m/3ft | 40cm/16in | 7 months |

This hardy perennial is a relative of the sunflower rather than the globe artichoke. It has underground tubers which are whitish in colour and club-like with knobbly protrusions. The delicate flavour is best appreciated if Jerusalem artichokes are served alone or as a creamy soup. The plants reach 2.5m/8ft and make excellent screens.

GROWING Jerusalem artichokes can be grown in even the poorest soils – in fact very fertile soils encourage too much foliage at the expense of the tubers. Save some tubers from a previous crop and plant them in early spring. The plants will need little attentiion but in exposed positions support the tall leafy stems with posts and wires.

HARVESTING The foliage dies down in the autumn. Pick some tubers in mid autumn if you wish, but the flavour improves if they are left in the ground to be lifted during the winter as needed. Make sure you lift all of them or they will come up again the following year.

POSSIBLE PROBLEMS A trouble-free crop.

▓ GARDENER'S TIP

Early sowing is necessary because of the long growing season but if the soil temperature is too low seeds may fail to germinate. Warm up the soil for a couple of weeks before sowing by protecting with cloches and keep them in place for a few weeks *after sowing.*

▓ ORGANIC TIP

These tall plants, when supported, can provide a useful windbreak to other delicate plants in the garden.

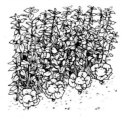

PARSNIP

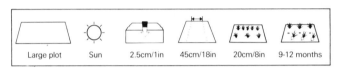

Large plot	Sun	2.5cm/1in	45cm/18in	20cm/8in	9-12 months

Because parsnips occupy the ground for such a long time – often a whole year – they are best in large gardens that can spare the space.

GROWING Parsnips need deep, rich, open-textured soils, free of stones and manured for a previous crop. Freshly manured soil produces misshapen roots. Work in a base dressing of a well-balanced fertilizer before sowing. Sow as early as possible to get the maximum length of growing season; late winter/early spring is ideal. As germination is erratic, sow seed liberally in the drills and thin seedlings later. Alternatively, sow 4-5 seeds at each station and discard all but the strongest seedling after emergence.

HARVESTING The leaves will go yellow and begin to die down from late autumn, and the roots can then be lifted as required. Tradition has it that the flavour is at its best when parsnips have been frosted. It is certainly better to leave them in the ground until you want them as they quickly go soft if stored. Regrowth begins in early spring so they must all be used by then.

POSSIBLE PROBLEMS Canker is a fungus which rots the roots and ruins the crop. Always grow resistant varieties.

VARIETIES Avonresister; White Gem.

LONG PARSNIP

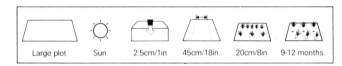

Large plot	Sun	2.5cm/1in	45cm/18in	20cm/8in	9-12 months

Because the sweet creamy flesh is high in sugar and starch, parsnips have always been valued as a winter vegetable.

GROWING Parsnips need deep, rich, open-textured soils, free of stones and manured for a previous crop. Freshly manured soil produces misshapen roots. Work in a base dressing of a well-balanced fertilizer before sowing. Sow as early as possible to get the maximum length of growing season; late winter/early spring is ideal. Sow 4-5 seeds at each station and discard all but the strongest seedling after emergence. Hoe regularly to keep weeds down.

HARVESTING The leaves will go yellow and begin to die down from late autumn, and the roots can then be lifted as required.

POSSIBLE PROBLEMS Aphids may infest young leaves. Spray with a suitable insecticide. Carrot fly larvae tunnel into the roots in summer. Spray with diazinon.

VARIETIES Lancer; Tender and True.

▨ ORGANIC TIP

Parsnips need a constant supply of water or roots can crack, so always water in dry periods. Use sub-surface irrigation; placed about 1m/3ft 3in apart the pipes are not difficult to install. Water leaks out through the pipes' surface and spreads out evenly in the ground. This method uses a tenth of the water a hose does to obtain the same result.

▨ GARDENER'S TIP

Forked roots in carrots and parsnips are caused by over-manuring. To avoid, use land which has been manured for a previous crop; do not add more.

FIRST EARLY POTATO

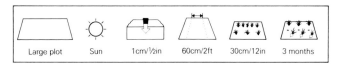

Large plot	Sun	1cm/½in	60cm/2ft	30cm/12in	3 months

For the first plantings, choose varieties like Arran Pilot.

GROWING Soil should be freely drained yet moisture retentive and preferably slightly acid. Double-dig the ground in the autumn, incorporating plenty of organic manure or well-rotted compost into the lower spit. Leave the top surface rough over winter to allow a natural tilth to develop. Before planting, evenly work in a general purpose fertilizer. Only use 'seed' potatoes that are certified virus-free. Order first earlies for mid winter so that they can be sprouted before planting. Growth begins from 'eyes', most of which appear at the rose end. Place the tubers close together, rose end upwards, in slatted-bottom trays. Leave in a light, frost-free but unheated place for shoots to develop. In mid or late spring, make 15-cm/6-in deep trenches with a hoe and plant the tubers, without damaging the shoots. Rake the soil back to cover and leave the surface slightly mounded over each row. Ridge up the plants as described for second earlies. Water when the tubers are 1cm/¹/₂in in diameter. Avoid watering late in the season.

HARVESTING Lift in early summer when the foliage is still green. Yield increases rapidly through mid until late summer.

POSSIBLE PROBLEMS Frost is a danger to young foliage. Aphids cause distortion of the foliage and may spread viruses from other plants.

SECOND EARLY POTATO

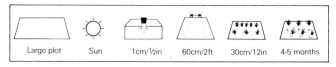

Large plot	Sun	1cm/½in	60cm/2ft	30cm/12in	4-5 months

To ensure a succession of new potatoes in late summer, and if space permits, plant varieties such as Craig's Royal or Pentland Dell.

GROWING The soil conditions for all types of potatoes are the same as for first earlies. Give them a site which provides maximum protection against frost. If spring frosts kill off young foliage there will be a 2-3 week setback to the crop. Second early varieties do not need to be sprouted before planting. Prepare a trench as for first earlies and set the tubers out in mid or late spring.

RIDGING When the potato shoots are 15cm/6in tall, loosen the soil between the rows with a fork and then draw it up around the plants with a hoe so that the sloping ridges meet near the top of the plants. Repeat at 3 week intervals until the foliage is touching.

HARVESTING Second earlies can be lifted in late summer and early autumn as needed. Neither first nor second earlies are suitable for storage, so do not lift the potatoes until you need them. Carefully dig up the potatoes using a flat-tined fork.

POSSIBLE PROBLEMS Keep aphids under control. Potato cyst eelworm is a pest living in the soil which attacks the roots, causing cysts to form. Long crop rotation is essential to eradicate it.

▓ GARDENER'S TIP

To avoid ridging up, lay a film of black polythene over the ground, make slits in the earth at the sides and push the polythene edges in this, holding in place with the soil as well. Make slits in the film and plant through these.

▓ ORGANIC TIP

Attract the predators of aphids, like ladybirds and hoverflies, by growing French marigolds as a companion plant to potatoes. These will also add a wonderful splash of colour. Aphids can be removed with a strong spray and insecticidal soap. If you grow
your own potatoes organically you have the added confidence that no persistent chemicals, including fungicides, have been used in their production.

MAINCROP POTATO

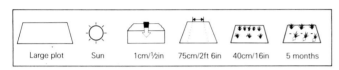

| Large plot | Sun | 1cm/½in | 75cm/2ft 6in | 40cm/16in | 5 months |

Maincrop potatoes like Desirée are the last to be harvested but can be stored through the winter.

GROWING Prepare the soil and make trenches as for early varieties. Maincrop varieties do not need to be sprouted before planting. Set the tubers out during mid spring. If frost threatens emerging shoots, scatter straw over them for protection. Ridge up the developing plants as described for second earlies.

HARVESTING Maincrop potatoes, harvested in early or mid autumn, will be easier to dig if the haulm (foliage) is removed about 3 weeks before. This also reduces the risk of disease spreading from the foliage to the tubers.

STORAGE Potatoes should be allowed to dry before storing. In warm, dry weather this can be done by leaving them in the open for 2-3 hours. Discard any damaged or diseased specimens. It is useful to grade the potatoes by size before placing them in boxes, trays or sacks. Keep in a dark, frost-free place. Dark is essential to prevent the tubers developing green areas containing poisonous substances which make them inedible. Inspect the tubers monthly. Remove rotting specimens and rub off developing 'sprouts'.

POSSIBLE PROBLEMS Potato blight affects foliage and tubers. Spray with fungicide from mid summer onwards whenever wet, humid conditions last for more than 2 days.

CONTAINER POTATO

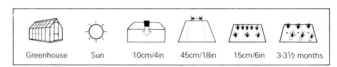

| Greenhouse | Sun | 10cm/4in | 45cm/18in | 15cm/6in | 3-3½ months |

If your garden is small, but you have a heated greenhouse, you can still grow some of your own delicious new potatoes. Choose a very early variety like Ulster Chieftain.

GROWING Sprout the tubers in mid winter as described for first earlies. In mid to late winter, plant the sprouted tubers 2 to a 25-30-cm/10-12-in pot containing a fairly rich potting compost. Water the pots well. Keep them at a temperature of 6-7C/43-45F at first and then at 10-13C/50-55F. Water regularly using a weak liquid fertilizer.

HARVESTING About 12 weeks after planting the tubers should be large enough to lift. Take the plants from the pot to remove the potatoes.

POSSIBLE PROBLEMS Usually trouble free.

■ GARDENER'S TIP

Most of the food value in a potato lies just beneath the skin and is lost when the potato is peeled. The skin itself also provides some important fibre, so cook potatoes in their skins whenever possible.

■ GARDENER'S TIP

Use a home-made automatic watering system to provide a constant supply of water to pot-grown plants. Fill a bucket with water and place on a higher level than the plants. Cut soft water-retentive material into 2-cm/¾-in wide strips to make wicks and *place one end of each in the bucket and the other end on the soil in the pot. The water is taken up by the wicks and seeps along them into the soil in each pot keeping it damp.*

SALSIFY

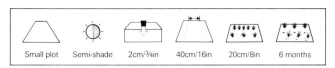

Small plot	Semi-shade	2cm/¾in	40cm/16in	20cm/8in	6 months

The common name of this long white root, vegetable oyster, gives a clue to its unusual flavour.

GROWING Deeply cultivated, moisture-retentive soils which have not been recently manured or limed are best. Sow seed thinly in mid spring, thinning the seedlings when they are large enough to handle. Keep weeds down, but do not damage the developing roots with the hoe – like beetroot, they 'bleed'. Keep plants well watered.

HARVESTING The best-flavoured roots are 5cm/2in wide at the crown and 25cm/10in long. Leave them in the ground and lift from mid autumn as required or store the whole crop in boxes of sand in an airy, frost-free place. The roots will keep until early spring. If roots are left in the ground until spring they will send up new shoots (chards) which can be cooked like asparagus.

POSSIBLE PROBLEMS None likely.

SCORZONERA

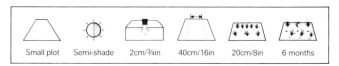

Small plot	Semi-shade	2cm/¾in	40cm/16in	20cm/8in	6 months

The delicate flavour of these black-skinned, white-fleshed roots is rather like Jerusalem artichoke, and is best simply boiled and served well seasoned with butter.

GROWING Fertile, well-drained soil is necessary, cultivated deeply to allow unchecked root growth. The roots will be mis-shapen if grown on recently manured soil. Sow seed in mid spring and thin the seedlings as soon as they are large enough to handle. Keep weeds under control and water well. A mulch of straw or grass cuttings will help to prevent the roots drying out.

HARVESTING Lift from mid autumn for immediate use or leave in the ground until required. Alternatively, lift the entire crop and store in boxes of sand in a frost-free place.

POSSIBLE PROBLEMS None likely.

▩ COOK'S TIP

This root has a taste similar to turnip. Cook gently for about 15 minutes until just tender then serve with a white sauce or a little butter. Otherwise salsify can be cooked in any way you might cook parsnips. The roots

discolour quickly when preparing, so scrub them and place in water to which lemon juice has been added.

▩ ORGANIC TIP

Mulches can be made from a wide range of decaying materials. Do not use fresh, but allow to rot down for two to three months first and use fairly coarse. Other mulches are a 5cm/2in layer of pine needles or softwood bark.

SWEDE

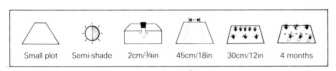

Small plot	Semi-shade	2cm/¾in	45cm/18in	30cm/12in	4 months

This hardy relative of the turnip is much larger and sweeter than its cousin. The skin may be white, purple or yellow but the flesh is usually yellow, sometimes white. Swedes store very successfully and are particularly popular in the north.

GROWING Any fertile, non-acid soil is suitable, manured for a previous crop as freshly manured ground will give forked roots. Work a little well-balanced fertilizer into the seed bed before sowing. Sow seed in drills in late spring/early summer in more exposed areas, and thin out when the seedlings are large enough to handle. Water well throughout the season.

HARVESTING Swedes are hardy enough to be left in the ground and lifted as required from early autumn through the winter. They store well in clamps, which is useful if the ground is likely to be frozen.

POSSIBLE PROBLEMS Flea beetle damage may occur on young seedlings. Spray with diazinon. Boron deficiency causes the flesh to discolour and harden. Water lightly with a solution of borax at 15g per 4.5 litres/½oz per 1 gallon.

SUITABLE VARIETIES Marian; Chignecto; Purple Top.

TURNIP

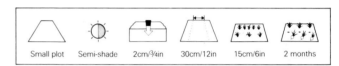

Small plot	Semi-shade	2cm/¾in	30cm/12in	15cm/6in	2 months

Turnips are best in spring and summer, young white globes flushed green and violet, but good varieties are also available for traditional winter use.

GROWING Fertile, well-drained yet moisture-retentive soil is best. Summer turnips must be grown rapidly, and can be treated as catch crops. Earliest sowings can be made outdoors in late winter. Sow 3 or 4 seeds to a station, soak the seedbed thoroughly and cover with frames or cloches. For summer crops, sow seed in drills in early spring. Winter turnips are grown from sowings made from mid summer to late summer and thinned so that the plants are spaced 40cm/16in apart each way.

HARVESTING Lift very early turnips when they are the size of a golf ball. Let summer turnips reach a maximum of 7.5cm/3in in diameter before lifting: this should be in late spring. Pick as soon as they are ready to be sure of a nice crisp texture. Winter varieties are ready in mid autumn for immediate use. They can also be stored: twist off the tops and place in boxes of sand in a cool, frost-free place. Roots which are left in the ground over winter will regrow in the spring, and the new tops can be used like spring greens.

POSSIBLE PROBLEMS Turnips share the problems of the cabbage family. Young seedlings may be attacked by flea beetle: dust the leaves with derris.

■ GARDENER'S TIP

Lift roots around mid winter, trim, pack in boxes in soil and put in part-darkness, such as the garden shed. The roots will sprout and the taste of the young, semi-blanched growth which results is delicious.

■ GARDENER'S TIP

Floating cloches made of woven polypropylene will float up with the crop as it grows beneath. Spread loosely over the ground and secure with bricks around the edge or hold in slits in the ground about 5cm/2in deep.

BULB VEGETABLES

If you are following the crop rotation plan on page 132, bulb vegetables are grown on Plot B. It is important to rotate onion crops to protect plants from soil-borne problems like white rot and stem eelworm. The soil pH should be above 6.5, so add lime if necessary. Bulbs require a sunny, sheltered position and a well-drained rich, fertile soil that has been previously dug and to which plenty of bulky organic matter, manure or compost has been added. As bulb plants have small leaves these are unable to smother weeds, so it is important to hoe around plants regularly to check weed growth.

BLANCHING LEEKS Plant stems can be blanched in one of two ways. In the first, the seedlings are placed in individual holes that are filled with water only. Gradually the holes fill up with soil and stems are blanched. They can be further blanched by drawing up

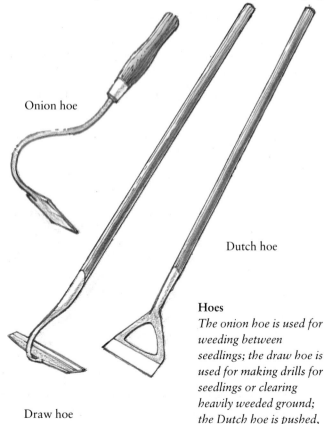

Onion hoe

Dutch hoe

Hoes
The onion hoe is used for weeding between seedlings; the draw hoe is used for making drills for seedlings or clearing heavily weeded ground; the Dutch hoe is pushed, leaving weeds on top of the soil to wilt and die.

Draw hoe

soil around the plants in late summer. Alternatively, seedlings can be positioned in a row down the centre of a trench. Soil is then gradually added to the trench as plants grow. In this way longer white stems are obtained. Tie paper collars around the stems to keep them clean.

HARVESTING AND STORAGE Onions are sown in autumn, winter and spring. Japanese onions, sown in autumn, provide the first harvest in mid summer. Onions store well, with the exception of Welsh onions which can be harvested fresh through winter in milder areas.

Spring onions are grown close together to keep the bulbs small and when sown in late winter under glass they are ready to lift in early summer. Sown in early summer, spring onions can be also harvested in the autumn.

Mild-tasting leeks, which can tolerate severe winter weather, are available to pull fresh when required from early autumn if sown in mid winter. Maincrop leeks sown in late winter are available for harvesting from late autumn to spring.

PROTECTION FROM COLD Early sown leeks and onions, like many other plants, need the protection of cloches if they are to survive the cold. Cloches are invaluable for extending the season when you can grow plants outdoors, both early and later in the year and for protecting tender vegetables.

A cloche should be at least twice as high and one and a half times as wide as the nearly fully grown crop to be covered. In fact it is wise to buy the largest size you can, one that covers your bed width is ideal. Larger cloches ensure that there is plenty of air circulation underneath and therefore less risk of pest or disease outbreaks. Some cloches have vents incorporated in the design to provide ventilation; on others a side or end can be raised or removed. Some designs include extra side pieces which can be added when plants grow tall.

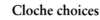

Cloche choices

○ **Glass cloches** provide the best protection from cold, but are heavier than plastic cloches to move around, expensive and not advisable where there are children.

○ **Rigid plastic** is lightweight, so make sure plastic cloches can be anchored to the ground.

○ **Corrugated plastic** diffuses the light which is excellent for use in summer or for winter protection of mature plants but not so satisfactory for use on seedlings.

○ **Transparent plastic bottles** make excellent cloches for small individual plants. Add a few small holes for ventilation.

○ **Polythene film** stretched over wire hoops is cheaper. Polythene tunnels are easy to move from crop to crop and the sides can be raised for ventilation. Since they are very light you will need to incorporate a secure method of holding the sheeting down. The film will deteriorate, usually lasting for two to three years at the most.

○ **Floating cloches** are sheets of perforated plastic or woven polypropylene which you weight down at the edges. As the crop beneath grows the cloche floats up with it. Water and air can penetrate the material and the polypropylene type will protect the plants from a few degrees of frost. This is the cheapest form of cloche to buy.

Tips on using cloches

Protection from draught Cloches need to include end pieces as a through draught can cause considerable damage to young or tender crops. You can make your own ends from panes of glass or rigid plastic.

Heating the soil Position a cloche or tunnel over the soil to be used a month before you intend to sow or plant there to warm it up.

Watering Don't forget that the cloche will keep rain off the plants inside so you will need to water regularly. If you place a length of seep hose inside then you will only need to fit the end of the hose to water.

Pollination Covered plants cannot be pollinated by insects so open or remove the cover during the daytime when the plants are flowering.

Ventilation As temperatures rise quickly under the protection, ventilation is important; where vents are not included in the design raise a side or remove one end only. Remove covers completely during the day in hot spells.

PESTS, DISEASES AND DISORDERS

Downy mildew In wet weather mildew may streak leaves with purple. Spray with zineb and rotate crops.

Onion eelworm Minute worms which get inside bulbs and cause distortion. Remove and burn plants. Move bed to another part of the garden and do not use this area for onions or potatoes for four to five years.

Onion fly Maggots, the larvae of the onion fly, can be a problem throughout the summer when they feed on the roots. First signs are yellowing leaves. Plants may die. The onion fly is attracted by the scent of the onions, specially strong when seedlings are thinned. If you grow onions from sets this avoids thinning. Hoe regularly around plants to expose grubs to birds.

Rot on stored onions A mouldy white growth can appear close to the neck of stored onions, which then become soft and rot. Others may become slimy due to fungal attack. Bending the tops of onions over to promote ripening can encourage the growth of mould later. Inspect stored onions regularly and remove any that are affected as soon as you find them. Only store ripe bulbs and store in nets or on strings to ensure air circulation.

White or neck rot This white fungus rots onions, leeks, shallots and garlic. Diseased plants turn yellow and die. Treat affected plants with Bordeaux mixture. Do not grow onions on the affected bed for at least three years as beds can be contaminated for up to eight years.

FLORENCE FENNEL

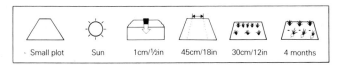

Small plot	Sun	1cm/½in	45cm/18in	30cm/12in	4 months

The bulbs for which this plant is chiefly cultivated are actually the swollen leaf bases. Florence fennel has a mild, sweet, aniseed flavour and has a range of culinary uses. The bulb can be sliced and used raw in salads or cooked in soups and stews, while the leaves make a useful flavouring.

GROWING Any reasonably fertile soil will do, but the best results are obtained on light, sandy soils. Because the leaf bases are blanched by earthing them up, an easily worked, stone-free soil is essential. Incorporate a base dressing of general fertilizer before sowing the seed thinly in mid spring. Thin the seedlings as soon as possible. Water well in dry weather and keep weeds under control. As soon as the bases start to swell, earth them up with soil to exclude the light. Alternatively, wrap them in paper collars secured with rubber bands.

HARVESTING Lift the plants as required during the late summer and autumn, once the bulbs have swollen. Cut the plants just below the swollen bases.

POSSIBLE PROBLEMS Florence fennel is a trouble-free crop.

EARLY LEEK

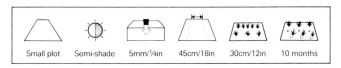

Small plot	Semi-shade	5mm/¼in	45cm/18in	30cm/12in	10 months

It is possible to bring the availability of leeks forward by raising plants of selected varieties under glass. This method is always used for growing leeks for exhibition purposes. Milder in flavour than onions, leeks are straight stems blanched at the base with green tops.

GROWING In mid winter sow seed thinly in trays in the greenhouse with the temperature at 10C/50F. When the seedlings are large enough to handle, prick them out into individual containers. They are slow-growing at first, but will be ready for planting out in late spring after a brief period of hardening off. Like maincrop leeks, early varieties can be grown on the flat or in trenches, as long as the soil is rich and deep and has been thoroughly cultivated in the previous autumn. Trench cultivation is necessary for exhibition leeks, which are fed regularly with a weak solution of nitrate of soda and superphosphate to increase size, staked to ensure straight stems and provided with cardboard collars packed with wood shavings to protect the foliage.

HARVESTING Early leeks are ready for lifting in early autumn but can be left in the ground until late autumn.

POSSIBLE PROBLEMS Relatively trouble-free.

VARIETIES Lyon Prizetaker; Early Market.

■ GARDENER'S TIP

This plant does not like being transplanted so if you want to start seeds off indoors or in a greenhouse use soil blocks, peat pots or cardboard rolls from toilet paper, kitchen roll or freezer bags cut into short lengths as containers. These decompose in the soil and all avoid disturbing the roots. This type of fennel can be frozen satisfactorily to provide a winter supply. Scrub young stalks and blanch for 3 minutes. Pack in boxes in blanching water, cool and freeze.

■ GARDENER'S TIP

An ingenious method of keeping leeks clean as they grow is to place a cardboard roll from toilet paper over each plant.

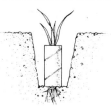

MAINCROP LEEK

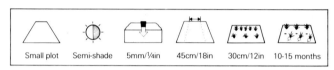

| Small plot | Semi-shade | 5mm/¼in | 45cm/18in | 30cm/12in | 10-15 months |

This hardy vegetable is particularly useful in the mid to late winter period, as it may well be available when the last of stored onion bulbs have been used.

GROWING Raise plants in a seedbed on light, well-drained soil. Sow in late late winter/early early spring in shallow drills 20-30cm/8-12in apart. Cover with cloches. When they are large enough to handle, thin the seedlings to 1-2cm/about ³/₄in apart. Hand-weed regularly or the emerging plants may be swamped. Water occasionally. Transplant to the growing site in early summer, watering the plants well before moving them. Here a rich, deep soil is best, well-cultivated in the previous autumn. Incorporate a base dressing of a well-balanced general fertilizer before planting. Make holes 15-25cm/6-10in deep with a dibber. Drop 1 plant in each and fill with water. During the season the holes gradually fill up and further blanching can be done by drawing up soil around the plants in early autumn. Hoe regularly to remove weeds.

HARVESTING Leeks are hardy enough to be left in the ground and lifted as needed from late autumn to mid spring, though late varieties will not be ready until mid winter. Do not leave them any later or they will start to regrow.

POSSIBLE PROBLEMS Relatively trouble-free.

VARIETIES Late autumn-mid winter: Musselburgh; mid winter-mid spring: Royal Favourite.

MAINCROP TRENCH LEEK

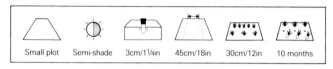

| Small plot | Semi-shade | 3cm/1¼in | 45cm/18in | 30cm/12in | 10 months |

Growing leeks in trenches produces a greater length of blanched stem and bigger specimens generally.

GROWING Raise plants from seed in exactly the same way as for cultivation on the flat. Before transplanting the seedlings, prepare the trenches well on rich-textured fertile soil. Make the trenches 30cm/12in deep and wide and heap the soil from the trenches in the pathways. Dig well-rotted manure or compost into the bottom. In early summer, set the leeks in a single row down the middle of the trench. Water in well. If birds pull out some of the seedlings, replant them immediately.

BLANCHING At monthly intervals, put soil from the pathways around the plants until the trenches are eventually filled in. To keep the plants clean and soil-free, wrap them in collars of corrugated cardboard before blanching begins. Weeding is important, but less of a problem as the regular movement of soil tends to discourage weed development.

POSSIBLE PROBLEMS Relatively trouble-free.

VARIETIES Late autumn-mid winter: Musselburgh; mid winter-mid spring: Royal Favourite.

■ COOK'S TIP

To clean home-grown leeks, cut off the green top leaves, and the root, plus coarse outer skin. Then slit down the length to the centre, open out and wash under cold running water.

■ GARDENER'S TIP

An alternative way of growing leeks is to place individual plants in 15-cm/6-in holes made with a dibber. Place holes at 15cm/6in intervals and in rows 30cm/12in apart. Drop a plant into each hole and fill with water but no earth. The water washes soil around and over the roots. When the seedlings have become established spread mulch around the plants. Harvest the plants as they are required.

197

ONION

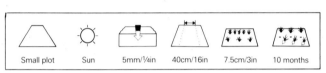

| Small plot | Sun | 5mm/¼in | 40cm/16in | 7.5cm/3in | 10 months |

Raise onions under glass for outdoor planting in spring.

GROWING Sow seed at the turn of the year (on Boxing Day, traditionally) in seed trays kept at 10C/50F. When the seedlings are large enough to handle prick them out into individual containers. Gradually harden them off from early spring before planting outside in mid spring. Fertile non-acid soil is essential. Dig in well-rotted manure or compost in the autumn and leave the ground rough to develop a natural tilth. Before planting, rake in a fertilizer with nitrogen and potassium in the ratio 1:2, as too much nitrogen encourages soft growth. Plant carefully: make a hole for each plant with a trowel or better still a dibber, deep enough for the roots to go their full depth but with the bottom of the bulblet not more than 1cm/½in below the surface. Firm each plant in well. Do not damage the leaves. Weed regularly with a short-handled onion hoe: don't damage the bulbs or cover them with earth. Water only in hot dry conditions. When the leaves wilt in late summer, fold them over neatly.

HARVESTING When the leaves are brittle, and on a warm sunny day, lift the bulbs. Lay them in the sun to dry, turning them frequently. When they are fully ripe, about 4 weeks later, store in wire-bottomed trays in a cool, frost-free place until the following spring.

POSSIBLE PROBLEMS Onion fly larvae tunnel into the bulbs: spray with diazinon.

SPRING-SOWN ONION

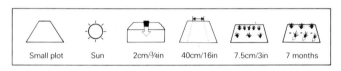

| Small plot | Sun | 2cm/¾in | 40cm/16in | 7.5cm/3in | 7 months |

Spring-sown onions are best in areas where cold, wet winters may damage an over-wintered crop.

GROWING A rich-textured, fertile soil is ideal. Onions do not tolerate acid soils, so it may be advisable to add lime. Prepare the ground in the autumn, digging in well-rotted manure or compost and leaving it rough over winter for a tilth to develop. In late winter, incorporate a fertilizer with nitrogen and potassium in the ratio 1:2, and rake the soil to a fine tilth. Firm the plot by treading up and down. Sow fairly thinly in the rows. While thinnings can be used for salads, the less disturbance to the plants the better. Watering is only necessary in dry seasons, but weeding must be carried out regularly. The bulbs begin to ripen in late summer, when the leaves fall over: if they don't, bend them over gently so that the ripening sun can get to the bulbs.

HARVESTING By the time the leaves are shrivelling the bulbs are ripe enough to lift. Choose a warm sunny day and pick the bulbs by hand or ease them out with a fork. Let them dry in the sun if possible, otherwise spread them out in the greenhouse. When the leaves are brittle, store the onions in wire-bottomed trays or make them into ropes. It is essential that they are in an airy, frost-free, dry place.

POSSIBLE PROBLEMS Many of the diseases afflicting onions can be avoided by observing crop rotations.

■ COOK'S TIP

To avoid crying when peeling onions, leave the root end of the onion in place until you have finished peeling and chopping each individual vegetable, then remove it. Alternatively, remove any necessary layers of skin under water.

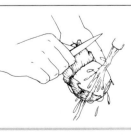

■ PRESERVING TIP

Onions can also be stored hanging up: place them, one above the other, in an old stocking, making a knot between each one to keep them apart. Cut off the required number from the bottom as you need them.

ONION SETS

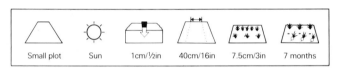

Small plot	Sun	1cm/½in	40cm/16in	7.5cm/3in	7 months

Onion sets are bulbs which have been partially grown in the previous season, then lifted and dried, and finally kept in temperature-controlled stores so that the small bulb continues to grow when it is replanted (rather than running to seed). Growing onions from sets means that less suitable soils can be used.

GROWING Prepare the soil as for onions grown from seed, digging and manuring in the previous autumn, and raking it to a fine tilth in early to mid spring. Firm the soil before inserting the bulbs so that only the necks protrude above the surface. If birds, worms or frost dislodge the bulbs, replant them immediately. Keep weeds down, while avoiding damage to the bulbs, and water only if prolonged dry conditions threaten to slow down growth. In late summer, when the leaves begin to topple, bend them over to speed up ripening.

HARVESTING In early autumn, when the leaves have shrivelled, the onions are ready for lifting. Pick on a warm sunny day and let the bulbs dry completely in the sun. A net supported on 4 low posts makes a good 'hammock' for drying the onions with warm air all round. Thick-necked onions must be used as soon as possible, but undamaged specimens can be stored in an airy, frost-free place until the following spring.

POSSIBLE PROBLEMS Rotate crops to avoid a build-up of diseases such as white rot and downy mildew.

JAPANESE ONION

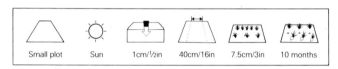

Small plot	Sun	1cm/½in	40cm/16in	7.5cm/3in	10 months

Japanese onions have been developed to mature from an autumn sowing, giving a midsummer crop before spring-sown onions are ready to use. Sowing onions in the autumn has a long tradition, but the crop was often spoiled by plants flowering in the spring warmth rather than producing a bulb. These can be relied upon to mature correctly, and can only be sown in the autumn.

GROWING A rich-textured, fertile, non-acid soil is essential. Incorporate well-rotted manure or compost in the previous winter and leave rough to allow a natural tilth to develop. Add fertilizer with nitrogen and potassium in the ratio 1:2 before planting and rake to a fine tilth. Firm the soil and sow seed in late summer. It is useful, but not essential, to protect the plot with cloches from mid autumn until frosts have passed. Not all the seeds will germinate, and some seedlings will not make it through the winter. Growth begins again in spring. Keep weeds down during the growing period.

HARVESTING The leaves begin to flag in early summer. Bend them over and let the bulbs ripen for 4-5 weeks before lifting. Pick on a warm sunny day and let the bulbs dry completely in the sun before use or before storing in a dry, airy place.

POSSIBLE PROBLEMS Rotate crops to avoid a build-up of soil-borne diseases. Grey mould sometimes appears after frost damage. Use a systemic fungicide.

▧ ORGANIC TIP

Growing onions from sets helps to keep the onion fly away. Onion scent attracts the female fly and this is specially strong when seedlings are thinned. Before planting, trim off old stems to deprive birds of a grip to pull on.

▧ COOK'S TIP

The simple Italian way to cook tomatoes with onions is to blanch and peel 397-g/14-oz tomatoes and sprinkle with salt, pepper and a pinch of sugar, then slice 2 large onions; arrange with 100g/4oz breadcrumbs, in alternate layers in an ovenproof dish, finishing with a layer of breadcrumbs and grated cheese. Bake in a moderate oven for 30 minutes. Lightly fried onions are also delicious with pine nuts, raisins and white wine added.

PICKLING ONION

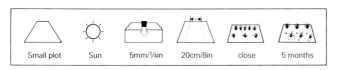

| Small plot | Sun | 5mm/¼in | 20cm/8in | close | 5 months |

Little yellow silverskin onions for pickling are very quick to mature and easy to grow. The flavour is milder than that of bulb onions.

GROWING While pickling onions prefer the fertile, rich-textured soil important for bulb onions, they can be grown on poorer soils as long as they are not acid. Rake the bed to a fine tilth in spring and tread it flat. Sow seed in mid spring in shallow drills, sowing very closely to make sure that the individual bulbs remain small. Water lightly but regularly to speed growth. Remove weeds by hand. The crop does not need thinning. In mid summer the leaves turn yellow and topple over – bend them over to speed up the ripening process.

HARVESTING Pick at the end of late summer. Fork up the onions and, if conditions are favourable, leave them on the ground for about a week to dry, turning them over from time to time.

POSSIBLE PROBLEMS See spring-sown onions. Onion fly is the most likely pest: spray with diazinon.

VARIETIES Paris Silverskin; Aviv.

SHALLOT

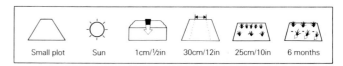

| Small plot | Sun | 1cm/½in | 30cm/12in | 25cm/10in | 6 months |

Shallots are small bulbs of the onion family about 2.5-5cm/ 1-2in in diameter, milder in flavour than large onions and commonly used for pickling or for flavouring casseroles and soups. They grow in clumps of 6-12.

GROWING Shallots are raised from the best bulbs saved from the previous year's crop and are planted like onion sets. They like the same soil as other onions: rich-textured, fertile and non-acid, manured in the autumn before planting. Rake the plot to a fine tilth and firm the soil before setting out the little bulbs. Plant as early in late winter as possible, firming them in well. Any bulbs dislodged by birds, worms or frost should be replanted immediately. Keep weeds down, taking care not to damage the bulbs. As they begin to dry off in early/mid summer, gently remove the soil from around the clumps.

HARVESTING The leaves will turn yellow and wither when growth has finished. Lift the shallots with care and spread them out individually in the sun to dry for a few days, or under protection if the weather is wet. Use immediately if required for pickling or store in an airy, frost-free place for future use. Select the best bulbs for planting next season.

POSSIBLE PROBLEMS There is a danger of soil-borne diseases building up if onions are grown on the same plot year after year, so rotate the crop.

■ COOK'S TIP

To pickle onions place them, unpeeled, in brine for a day. Drain and peel the onions, put in jars and cover with spiced vinegar. Seal. To make brine, dissolve 450g/1lb coarse salt in boiling water, allow to cool, strain and make up to 4.5 litres/8

pints. To make spiced vinegar add to 1 litre/1³/₄ pints white cider vinegar, 5-cm/2-in piece cinnamon, 1 tsp cloves, 2 tsp allspice, 1 tsp black peppercorns, 1 tsp mustard seed, 2-3 bay leaves, cover and bring to boil.

■ PRESERVING TIP

To dry shallots, lay them on chicken wire nailed to four short posts stuck in the ground to create a hammock. To store, hang up in string or mesh plastic bags, the sort that you get oranges in from the supermarket.

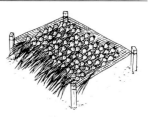

SPRING ONION

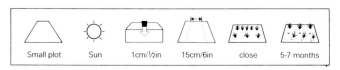

| Small plot | Sun | 1cm/½in | 15cm/6in | close | 5-7 months |

Otherwise known as salad onions, these small white bulbs with slender green stems are mild enough to be eaten raw but with enough pungency to enliven salads (the larger the bulb, the stronger the flavour).

GROWING Spring onions are grown close together to restrict the development of the bulb. The ideal soil is rich-textured, fertile and non-acid, and manured for a previous crop. Rake the plot to a fine tilth before sowing and tread it firm. For an early spring crop, sow seed of a hardy variety fairly thickly and protect with cloches. For lifting in early summer, sow in late winter under glass or early spring in the open. Seed sown in early summer will give onions for lifting in the autumn. All crops should be kept weed-free – hand weeding is best to avoid damaging the developing bulbs. No thinning is required.

HARVESTING Pull the onions as soon as they are big enough to use, with the leaves still green and tender. Unlike bulb onions, salad onions cannot be stored and should be used very fresh.

POSSIBLE PROBLEMS Rotate crops to avoid a build-up of soil-borne diseases. Onion fly larvae may be a problem on lighter soils: spray with diazinon.

VARIETIES For overwintering: White Lisbon Winter Hardy; spring and summer plantings: White Lisbon.

WELSH ONION

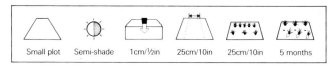

| Small plot | Semi-shade | 1cm/½in | 25cm/10in | 25cm/10in | 5 months |

Also known as the ever-ready onion, the so-called Welsh onion is in fact the most popular onion in Japanese and Chinese cooking. It is a perfectly hardy perennial and can be grown easily even in cooler zones. Plants grow in clumps in the same way as shallots or chives, reaching a height of 30cm/12in, but do not form large bulbs. Use the onions, stems and all, as a substitute for spring onions or for flavouring winter stews and soups.

GROWING Any fertile, well-drained soil will do in any handy part of the garden, perhaps as an edging to the vegetable or herb garden. The most satisfactory results are obtained by setting out new young plants rather than raising from seed. Set the bulblets out in mid spring, weed regularly and water lightly. The bulblets will multiply into thick clumps during the summer. Lift and divide the clumps every 3 years, replanting on new ground.

HARVESTING By early autumn you should be able to detach a few onions from each clump, continuing to pick throughout the winter. Use immediately – Welsh onions do not store. Always leave some onions in each clump to multiply the following year.

POSSIBLE PROBLEMS Trouble-free.

■ GARDENER'S TIP

You can have spring onions almost around the year if you make successive sowings every three weeks from late winter until early summer. Plants should be ready to eat in about eight weeks. Sow seeds in 8-cm/3-in bands, 1-2cm/½-¾in apart with 23cm/9in between bands. In all but the coldest areas you can also sow hardier varieties in late summer to harvest the next spring.

■ COOK'S TIP

Both the leaves and bulbs of Welsh onions can be used in salads. They can be used in place of leeks. Chop, then steam them until just tender. Use hot, coated in a sauce, or allow to cool, then toss them in vinaigrette.

201

HERBS

The value of herbs for food and medicine has probably been recognized almost as long as man has been around. Cultivating these wild plants became popular in Britain with the arrival of the Romans and in medieval England they were mainly grown in monastery gardens. Mixed with flowers and vegetables they became an important component of the cottage garden.

With their capacity to add delicious natural flavours to food and a renewed interest in curing illness with natural herbal remedies, herbs have come back into their own in the last decades. Many people have discovered the delights of including herbs in the garden. They are easy to grow, have a wide range of leaf shapes that are decorative in flower arrangements, and often have their own richly scented and colourful flowers. Add to this the benefit of some herbs in keeping away a range of plant pests and their attraction for pollinating insects, essential in the fruit and vegetable garden, and you will see that a garden without herbs is sadly lacking.

CREATING A HERB GARDEN Even if you have only a balcony or backyard, or no outdoor space at all, it is still possible to grow a range of herbs in pots. A small area of, preferably sunny, free space will give you the chance to plan a decoratively-shaped herb garden. Alternatively, the plants can be intermingled with flowers, or grown in a bed on their own close to the kitchen.

DESIGNING A DECORATIVE HERB GARDEN First, design the garden on paper. In a square plot you could copy the old cartwheel shape, using treated timber fence posts in place of spokes and a bird bath or sun dial as the centre point. Or use the same shape but divide off the sections with 'spokes' of shingle, grass or brick paths. Paths can also be used to divide up a rectangle and form beds of triangles, diamonds and hexagon shapes to break up the space. On a long, narrow plot use an old wooden ladder, or timber laid in a ladder shape, to act as a decorative plant divider.

Leave some of the paving slabs out when designing a patio and plant low-growing evergreen herbs in the spaces, such as thyme and winter savory. Group a number of decorative pots together and grow tall herbs, such as lovage, angelica and fennel, in the larger pots at the back. Place smaller plants in the front. A line of lavender, rue or rosemary plants can form a low dividing hedge between patio and grass.

Among the flowers Herbs mingle well with flowers and fruit, encouraging pollinating insects with their wonderful scents. Group different varieties of one herb together. Thyme, sage and mint all come in a range of leaf colours and patterns. Create a border for a herbaceous bed with parsley, thyme, chives, marjoram or salad burnet. Tall herbs like angelica, lovage, fennel, southernwood and evening primrose will add decorative leaf shapes towards the back of a bed and shelter smaller, more delicate flowers.

Kitchen herb bed If the area outside your kitchen door is sunny then this is an ideal spot for a culinary herb bed and some pots. It also means that you don't have to make a damp dash for a fistful of parsley in wet weather. A bed about 1 by 3 metres/3.3 by 10ft is ideal. If it is wider, you will need stepping stones to help you care for and harvest plants at the back without treading on the soil.

Limited space herb garden Hanging baskets can be used for herbs that will trail decoratively, like marjoram, thyme, nasturtiums, tarragon and chamomile. Boxes will take the more upright varieties, or plant a number of window boxes, each containing plants for specific uses, one of culinary herbs, one of herbs for making herbal teas, one for those herbs used in beauty preparations.

A box on a bedroom or living room window sill could be used for strongly scented herbs so that on sunny days herbal fragrances fill the room.

Rampant herbs like lemon balm and mint are more easily controlled if you grow them in a container, so plant them in pots, even if you intend growing them in a window box, then sink them into the soil with the

Herbs grow well in pots and hanging baskets. A good thick moss is required for lining the baskets to prevent loss of moisture.

rims about 2cm/³/₄in above soil level. Delicate herbs like basil and lemon verbena are best grown in pots so that they can be brought indoors in the autumn for protection from frost.

Indoor herb garden Herbs grown or brought indoors will be available for picking later into the winter than those grown outdoors. However, plants raised indoors cannot be expected to grow to the same extent as outdoor plants. Therefore, more plants are needed to provide a comparable harvest.

Indoor-grown herbs need ventilation, but not draughts, humidity, a moderate temperature of about 15C/60F, good light, and sunshine. The kitchen, unfortunately, is not the ideal spot to grow herbs as temperatures tend to fluctuate too much and unless the ventilation is good, the plants' leaf pores can become clogged with grease and dust. Consider growing them in hanging baskets, pots, or a window box in a sunny window. If you are short of space just grow the herbs

necessary for a bouquet garni in a decorative pot: parsley, thyme and bay.

Choosing the herbs to grow The herbs you decide to grow will depend on your own requirements. Some herbs provide a wide range of uses and are found in all categories. Given below are some of the most widely used herbs under each of four main headings.

For culinary purposes Start off with a limited number of the herbs you use most, then gradually extend the range, experimenting with species new to you. The ten most popular culinary herbs are: parsley, thyme, bay, rosemary, chives, tarragon, mint, sage, marjoram and fennel.

Medicinal herb garden Most herbs are in one way or another good for health. Ten starter herbs to treat some minor ailments are: peppermint for indigestion and as a pick-me-up, chamomile for indigestion, fennel for flatulence, lemon balm for insomnia and to relax, bergamot for insomnia, hyssop for coughs and colds, and parsley to stimulate digestion and as a diuretic herb – it gives gentle stimulation to the kidneys. Rosemary helps to stimulate circulation and when steeped in oil is a help for rheumatism, if gently rubbed into the affected part; sage is an expectorant while thyme stimulates appetite and aids digestion.

Cosmetic herb garden Many herbs can be included in shampoos, conditioners, moisturizers, cleansers and for bathtime relaxation. Some aid a healthy skin, others hair, eyes, hands, feet or nails. Elder cleanses, softens and whitens skin and is helpful for freckles and wrinkles. It also makes a soothing eyebath. Chamomile, *Matricaria chamomilla*, is good for skin, hair and eyes. Lavender can be used for skin and feet, rosemary for hair and skin, dill for eyes and nails, sage for skin and fennel for cleansing.

For scent Close to a window plant lemon thyme, lemon verbena, lemon geranium, pineapple mint and sweet marjoram. To attract butterflies and bees include borage, hyssop and thyme.

GROWING HERBS Most herbs are a delight to grow. They take little from the soil, while giving off scent, taste and colour. Most also have an in-built rejection of pests and disease.

In fact even if you are totally committed to fertilizers and pesticides, this is an area of the garden where it is important to use organic principles, a start to becoming a committed organic gardener perhaps. As many herbs are used uncooked, and taste to some extent is lost through washing, it has to be better to refrain from including chemicals in their cultivation.

Choosing a position Choose a sunny corner if possible as most herbs thrive in the sun. Those suitable for more shady areas are angelica, fennel, mint, tansy, sorrel and bergamot. Some protection from wind, such as walls or fences, is valuable.

Drainage A well-drained site is important for almost all herbs so that air can circulate around the plant roots. Soggy soil is airless and cold. The aim is to have a soil that does not dry out too quickly but has good drainage. If you are unsure if your drainage is adequate you can do a simple test. Dig a hole twice the depth of your spade blade and leave it open for a few days. If water collects in the hole over this time it shows that the drainage is poor. The surest way to improve poor drainage is to install pipes laid on gravel and leading to a soakaway point. In practice this is expensive and troublesome for the amateur gardener. An easier, but still laborious, alternative is to dig narrow trenches and partly fill them with large stones before replacing the soil. In most domestic gardens it is enough to dig the ground over to twice the spade's depth and incorporate as much bulky organic matter as you can get.

Soil and nutrients Most herbs grow best in a slightly alkaline soil. The soil should be well dug before planting and organic matter, animal manure, green manure, or garden compost included. For more information see pages 126-7. A healthy organic garden includes a good worm population to aerate the soil, improve drainage and convert materials into plant food. See page 126 for attracting and increasing worm population. When making your own compost, include any herb refuse as this is specially valuable to the compost heap. Add organic matter in autumn and mulch with a thin layer of compost in spring. This should be all the feeding necessary.

INCREASING HERBS Annual herbs can be sown in warm weather on the spot where they will grow or started indoors to give earlier crops (see page 133 for sowing). Recycle seeds for use in the next season but buy new every two to three years.

Perennials can be increased by layering: mint, marjoram, lemon balm, southernwood and sage are all suitable for this method of propagation, which is described and illustrated in the Gardener's Tip for sage on page 216. During the growing season stem cuttings can be taken from healthy plants (as described and illustrated step by step opposite). In autumn or early spring when plants are dormant many can be dug up and divided (see below).

HARVESTING Small quantities of most herbs can be cut for use fresh throughout the growing season. However, if you wish to preserve them then the best time to pick is when the volatile oil content is greatest. The time of day and the time in the plant's cycle are the two points to consider. Most herbs should be cut in the morning when the dew has dried naturally but before the sun is fully on the plant. In bright sun the volatile oils, which carry flavour and value, diminish.

If it is the leaves you require, the ideal time to pick is between the formation of flower buds and the opening of the flowers, when the oil content is highest. If you wish to harvest flowers these should be picked when fully open, and in prime condition. Seeds are gathered when the flowerheads begin to turn brown. To check if seeds are ripe, tap a head lightly; the seeds will fall when ready. Cut the heads, including a length of stem, and hang upside down in a dry airy shed. You can either encase the head in a paper bag so that the seeds fall into it or place a basket lined with paper or a cotton cloth below to catch the seeds. Place seeds in airtight containers in the dark to retain the full flavour.

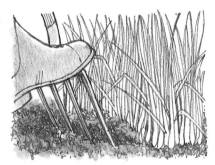

Lifting and dividing chives
Lift mature or over-crowded clumps out of the ground, using a garden fork.

Divide the chives into smaller clumps by prising the roots apart with your hands or a small fork.

Plant out the new divisions, without delay, in the desired position. Make sure that the chives are well watered.

Taking cuttings of shrubby herbs
Take a cutting of a semi-ripened shoot in summer. Neaten off the end by making a sharp diagonal cut with a knife.

Carefully strip the leaves off the lower end of the cutting to leave sufficient stem bare to insert into the compost. Do this gently with your hands.

Wet the bottom end of the cutting with water and dip it in a pot of hormone rooting powder, which will encourage roots to grow.

Fill trays or pots with seed compost or a half-sand, half-peat mixture. Using a matchstick, make holes in the compost and insert the cuttings.

Firm in the cuttings carefully with your fingertips, then gently water them; it is best to use a fine rose on a watering can to do this.

Cover the cuttings with a clear polythene bag, keeping the polythene off the leaves. Place on a warm windowsill but keep out of direct sunlight.

PRESERVING Herbs can be dried in three ways. The traditional method is to tie them in small bunches so that air can circulate freely around the herbage, then hang them upside down in a warm, airy spot for a few days.

The modern alternative is to dry them in the dark on racks. Stretch muslin over a frame (alternatively use metal drying racks) and place leaves, still on the stem, on these. Spread out well in a single layer. Place another layer of muslin on top to keep off any dust and place the trays in a warm, dark place – either an airing cupboard, or the plate warming drawer of an oven, with the door left ajar is ideal. Check if they are ready after 24 hours. When dry, the leaves will feel dry and be brittle to the touch. They should still be green; if they have turned brown the heat was too intense and the flavour will have been lost. Store immediately after cooling in glass jars, preferably dark in colour but otherwise in the dark, to retain strength. Flower-heads should be dried in the same way. Remove as much stalk as possible and handle very carefully as they disintegrate easily.

It is also possible to dry herbs in a microwave. Lay out on a double layer of kitchen paper, place a second double layer of paper over the top and using the lowest setting on the microwave check every minute, turning the sandwich each time. They should be ready in 2-4 minutes.

Some herbs, in particular basil, parsley, chives, chervil, dill and tarragon, are difficult to dry successfully and are better frozen. Chop parsley and chives and store in small bags or add a little water and freeze in ice cube containers. Chervil, fennel, dill and tarragon can be left as small sprays and packed in plastic bags. Basil leaves are best picked off the stem and stored in the freezer in small bags.

ANGELICA

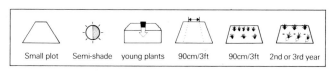

| Small plot | Semi-shade | young plants | 90cm/3ft | 90cm/3ft | 2nd or 3rd year |

Angelica is a lovely herb for the back of the garden, where it can act as a windbreak for more delicate herbs. Clusters of small greenish white flowers appear on the tops of the stems in the second year of growth.

GROWING It is easiest to buy your first angelica plant growing in a container and put it into a rich moist soil, in a partially shaded position, in spring. Once your plant is established, you can start to use the leaves, although for full flavour and scent you should wait until the second year. The seed which falls from the plant in the late summer of the second year will germinate early the following spring to provide a mass of seedlings growing round the old plant. Angelica can grow to 1.8m/6ft.

HARVESTING Gather leaves and flower stems in late spring and early summer. Cut off the flowerheads as they appear in summer, leaving one or two to set to seed.

POSSIBLE PROBLEMS Watch for leaf-mining caterpillars and remove affected leaves as soon as seen.

USES Candied angelica is well known as a cake decoration and can be easily made at home. Cut the young hollow stems into 5cm/2in lengths and boil them in a heavy sugar syrup until transparent and tender. Strain and allow the stems to dry completely before storing in screw-topped jars. They impart a delicious flavour when cooked with rhubarb or gooseberries.

BALM

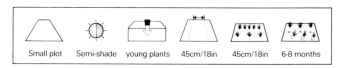

| Small plot | Semi-shade | young plants | 45cm/18in | 45cm/18in | 6-8 months |

Also known as Lemon Balm and Bee Balm, the leaves of this bushy plant carry a strong lemon fragrance; the flowers, insignificant in appearance, contain a lot of nectar and are very attractive to bees. A shorter form of balm, with yellow-variegated leaves, is more ornamental.

GROWING The scent of lemon balm will be strongest if it is grown in a fairly rich, moist soil. A sunny position is preferred. A plant bought from a herb nursery or garden centre and put in the garden in spring, can be increased in the autumn by root division.

HARVESTING Pick leaves as required after flowering throughout the summer.

POSSIBLE PROBLEMS Lemon balm spreads fairly rapidly so cut it back periodically to keep it a compact shape.

USES The chopped leaves, fresh or dried, can be used in recipes wherever a hint of lemon is called for. Try lemon balm in stuffings for lamb or pork, and cover a chicken with the leaves before roasting. Add to fruit drinks, wine cups, ice creams, fruit and vegetable salads, and to stewed fruit of all kinds. Melissa tea, made with the crushed leaves, is a refreshing drink sweetened with a little honey and taken hot or cold.

▦ PRESERVING TIP

Although angelica usually flowers in the second year it can take up to 4 or 5 years. After flowering the plant will die. If you want it to last for a further year remove the flower heads as soon as they appear. After harvesting large stalks for candied angelica remove the leaves and dry separately. Place on a rack in the dark in a warm, well-ventilated spot. They should then remain a bright green and retain their scent making them ideal for adding to pot pourri.

▦ GARDENER'S TIP

Lemon balm, like mint, can quickly take over a herb bed so contain the roots by growing this plant in a container. If you prefer to grow balm in a herb or flower bed, plant it in a pot or bucket and sink this into the soil.

BASIL

Container	Sun	1cm/½in	40cm/15in	20cm/8in	1½ months

There are two kinds of basil plants, sweet and bush. They are both treated as annuals in temperate climates. Sweet basil has largish, shiny, dark green leaves and bush basil has lots of small, pale green leaves and is good for growing in pots.

GROWING Basil has to be grown from seed or purchased as a pot plant. Sow seed in a rich, well-drained soil in a sunny, sheltered position out of doors after the danger of frost is over. Alternatively, sow in pots indoors. Plant out seedlings in summer and pinch out the flowerheads as they appear, allowing one plant or stem to flower and set seed for next year's plants. The compact habit of bush basil makes it ideal for container growing, where it will provide more leaves for use over a longer growing period.

HARVESTING The leaves are ready for picking about six weeks after the seedlings are planted out.

POSSIBLE PROBLEMS To avoid danger of damping-off disease, do not sow seed too thickly or over-water.

USES Basil is one of the best herbs to add to tomatoes and eggs, mushrooms and pasta dishes. It has a strong flavour, which tends to increase when the leaves are cooked. Fresh leaves are good in green salads and in oil and vinegar dressings. Add a tiny amount to butter sauces to accompany fish.

BAY

Container	Sun	young plants	not applicable	not applicable	4 months

Bay, or sweet bay, forms a shrub-like evergreen tree. The glossy dark green leaves have a leathery texture; small yellow flowers bloom in early summer and are followed by purplish black berries. Bay is a good plant for container cultivation, when it can be trained into a pyramid, or a round-headed standard.

GROWING Good soil or compost, drainage and sun are essential, also shelter from cold winds. Bay will die quickly in a wet soil. It is easiest to buy a small bay plant from a herb nursery. Do not disturb the rootball when taking it out of its pot. Dig a hole large enough to accommodate the roots. Put the plant in the hole and gently fill in with soil, firming it down as you go. Tread round the plant to secure against wind. If grown in a pot or tub, bay can be taken indoors in a severe winter.

HARVESTING Once bay is established, the fully matured leaves can be picked for use. Pick and dry some leaves during the growing season for winter use, rather than pick them from the bush all the year round.

POSSIBLE PROBLEMS Scrape off any brown scale insects appearing on the undersides of leaves or on stems.

USES Add a bay leaf to the water when poaching fish; use a leaf in marinades. Bay leaves add their spicy flavour to meat and vegetables, soups and stews. Store a leaf or two in a jar of rice for a delicious flavour.

■ COOK'S TIP

The famous Italian sauce Pesto is made from basil leaves and is delicious with fresh pasta. Use it, too, to enhance the flavour of minestrone. Place about 75g/3oz leaves, torn into small pieces, in a food processor with 3 garlic cloves and 100g/4oz Parmesan cheese. Slowly add to this 2 tablespoons olive oil until the mixture has a thick cream-like consistency. This sauce can be kept for a few days in the refrigerator or for some weeks in the freezer.

■ COOK'S TIP

A bay leaf is an essential part of the well-known culinary flavouring bouquet garni. This should also include 2 sprigs of parsley, 1 of thyme and 1 of marjoram. Tie together and use to flavour sauces, stews and casseroles.

207

BERGAMOT

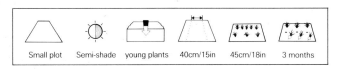

Small plot	Semi-shade	young plants	40cm/15in	45cm/18in	3 months

One of the many varieties of bergamot, the *Monarda didyma* is also called bee balm because bees are so attracted by its scent. A perennial plant, bergamot is highly ornamental, producing vivid red flowers in early summer.

GROWING Plant bergamot in spring or autumn in a sunny moist spot. Some shade will be accepted. Clumps are prettiest as the flowers of single plants get lost amongst others in the border. After planting, put peat or leaf mould round the plants to keep the roots moist. The plants grow to 45cm-1m/1-3ft high, but they die down in winter, so use a stake to mark their position. Bergamot is easily increased by dividing the clumps in spring. To obtain bigger and better flowers for display, cut off all the flowerheads in the first season. The following year there will be a lovely show of much larger flowers.

HARVESTING Pick flowers and leaves in summer.

POSSIBLE PROBLEMS In early spring, watch for caterpillars and snails, which attack the new leaves.

USES Bergamot leaves and flowers dry well, retaining their scent and flavour, and make a delicious tea. A few dried crushed leaves mixed in with Indian tea adds a delicate flavour. Chopped leaves and flowers add flavour and colour to green salads, fruit and wine cups. Add leaves and flowers to fresh fruit salads and jellies.

▥ COOK'S TIP

Tea made from bergamot is soothing and was very popular with America's Oswego Indians. North Americans, when refusing to use British tea at the time of the Boston Tea Party, also took to drinking it. To make a cup of tea, fill the cup to be used, with cold water and pour into a saucepan. Bring to the boil, then add a teaspoonful of dried leaves and flowers, reduce heat and simmer gently for 5-6 minutes. The resulting tea is a rich wine red.

BORAGE

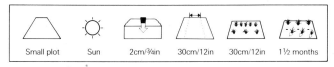

Small plot	Sun	2cm/¾in	30cm/12in	30cm/12in	1½ months

Borage is a tall, hairy-leaved annual with vivid blue star-shaped flowers. It is a strong-growing plant and continues to bloom for many months of the year. Both flowers and leaves have a fresh cucumber flavour.

GROWING Sow borage seeds in spring where they are to flower. Any soil and site will be suitable. Young plants should be thinned to leave at least 30cm/1ft between them. In a windy spot, it is best to stake the plants, because the many-branched fleshy stems become top heavy and after a downpour of rain or high winds will be found lying on the ground.

HARVESTING Seeds germinate quickly and the plants are fully grown in five to six weeks. Borage leaves are always used freshly picked.

POSSIBLE PROBLEMS Borage is not recommended for the small herb garden. It seeds itself freely, so keep it in check, or seedlings will come up all over the garden.

USES Pick only the young tender leaves, with a few fresh flowers and add them to green salads.

Candied borage flowers make a pretty decoration on cakes and ice creams and floating in a fruit salad. Dip the flowers first in beaten egg white, making sure they are completely covered, then into fine sugar. Leave the flowers to dry and harden on a nylon sieve. Candied in this way the flowers are for immediate use only.

▥ ORGANIC TIP

Borage is sometimes known as beebread because, like many other herbs, its scent and bright star-like blue flowers are very attractive to bees. Plant close to fruit or vegetables that require pollination.

CARAWAY

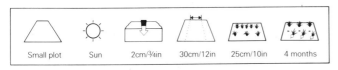

Small plot	Sun	2cm/¾in	30cm/12in	25cm/10in	4 months

Caraway is a feathery-leaved biennial plant grown mainly for the warm and spicy flavour of its fresh ripe seed, although the roots can be eaten too. Small white flowers are followed by the fruit in the second year.

GROWING Caraway can be sown in its flowering position in late spring or autumn. A well-drained soil and sunny place are important. Thin the seedlings to 25cm/10in apart. The plants reach their full height of 60cm/2ft in the second year. Once the seedheads have formed, keep a close watch to see when the seeds are ripe. To make sure no seeds are lost, cover the seedheads with fine muslin secured lightly round the stem.

HARVESTING When fully ripe, cut off the seedheads with long stems, tie the stems together and place the heads in a paper bag. Hang the bunches upside down so that when fully dried the seeds will fall into the bag. Dig up the roots for eating after harvesting the seeds.

POSSIBLE PROBLEMS As caraway takes over a year to flower and seed it is best to sow seeds as soon as they are ripe. Hoe around young plants to keep weeds at bay.

USES Caraway seeds can be used to flavour pork and liver, and vegetables such as cabbage, cauliflower and potatoes. The roots can be boiled and eaten like carrots with a parsley sauce. Use, too, in baking cakes, biscuits and buns, and sprinkle on Irish potato cakes.

CHAMOMILE

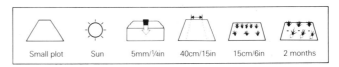

Small plot	Sun	5mm/¼in	40cm/15in	15cm/6in	2 months

There are two kinds of chamomile: *Matricaria chamomilla*, the true annual chamomile, and the Roman perennial chamomile, *Anthemis nobilis*, used for making lawns. Both are strongly aromatic. The true chamomile has white daisy-like flowers from late spring to mid autumn and fine needle-like leaves on a plant about 15cm/6in tall. Each plant produces many flowers, the only part of the herb which is used. Chamomile plants have for centuries been considered the physician of other plants and necessary for healthy life in the organic garden.

GROWING Very easy to grow from seed, chamomile prefers a dry, sunny position. Sow seed in early spring where it is to flower and keep seeds watered until the leaves appear. Thin the plants to 15cm/6in apart.

HARVESTING Flowers will appear eight weeks from sowing, and should be picked as soon as they open. The flowers can be used fresh or dried. Dry on nylon netting in an airing cupboard and store the flowers in glass screw-topped jars.

POSSIBLE PROBLEMS Mix sand with the tiny seeds to make sowing more even.

USES Chamomile makes a soothing tea for stomach upsets and indigestion, and with a spoonful of honey added, is a pleasant tonic or pick-me-up.

■ PRESERVING TIP

Caraway seeds add spicy fragrance to pot pourri and help to retain the scent of other herbs used in the mixture. Dry, then crush, the seeds before adding them to the other ingredients.

■ HEALTH TIP

A relaxing bath additive, chamomile will perfume the water and help to cleanse the skin. Use a square of muslin tied with ribbon to form a bag to hold the flowers and tie the bag by length of ribbon to the hot tap so it lies in the water as the bath

fills. If you have fair hair use chamomile to lighten and condition it. Add a small cup of flowers to 150ml/¼ pint purified water. Pour boiling water over the flowers for a facial steam bath.

CHERVIL

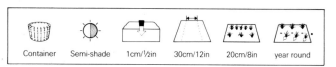

Container	Semi-shade	1cm/½in	30cm/12in	20cm/8in	year round

Chervil is an annual with lacy foliage and clusters of little white flowers, which appear from early to late summer. The flavour is sweet and aromatic, reminiscent of aniseed, and the leaves are best used fresh.

GROWING Chervil seeds germinate so quickly that with successive sowings it is possible to have a supply of fresh leaves almost all the year round. From early spring to late summer, sow seed where the plants are to grow, in well-drained garden soil in partial shade. When they are large enough, thin the seedlings to 20cm/8in apart. Remove flowers when they appear. The plants die down in winter but will come up very early in spring, long before many other herbs appear. Chervil can also be grown in window boxes and containers.

HARVESTING Chervil leaves can be used when the plant is about 10cm/4in high.

POSSIBLE PROBLEMS Leaves wilt quickly and the flavour is soon lost. Avoid sowing chervil where it will be in the summer sun a few weeks after germinating, or it will bolt and die quickly, especially if dry.

USES The chopped fresh leaves are at their most delicious in chervil soup. Add to butter sauces to go with delicate vegetables and to green salads. As a garnish, use chervil generously over pork or veal chops and beef steaks. Sprinkle over glazed carrots and peas.

▓ GARDENER'S TIP

Pick leaves, especially in the early stages, from the outside of the plant so the plant continues to grow from the centre. If chervil is not permitted to flower, but instead cut almost back to the ground, it will continue to produce leaves until heavy frost occur.

CHIVES

Container	Semi-shade	young plants	30cm/12in	20cm/8in	year round

A clump of chives is essential in the herb garden. The neat growing habit of chives makes them good edging plants in the herb bed, and if one or two clumps are left to bloom, their bright mauve pompom flowers provide a splash of colour.

GROWING Chives do best in a rich, damp soil and in sun or partial shade. They can be grown from seed sown in spring but germination is slow. It is quicker to divide clumps of established bulbs in spring or autumn. Grow several clumps of chives in order to have a succession of new growth and use the plants in rotation. Remove the flowers when they appear to keep the flavour in the leaves. Cover with cloches in autumn through winter, or dig up a small clump in autumn and transfer it to a pot to take indoors, where it will continue growing in the warmth. In spring throw out the exhausted plant.

HARVESTING Make sure new plants are well established before picking the leaves.

POSSIBLE PROBLEMS Do not allow the plants to dry out. At intervals during the growing season, feed them with a liquid fertilizer.

USES Chives chopped finely add a delicate onion flavour to soups, sauces and salad dressings. Blend chives with cream cheese or butter to use as a topping for baked potatoes and use to perk up fish and egg dishes.

▓ FREEZER TIP

Chives thrive when cut constantly. Use scissors to do this. This is not a suitable herb to dry, instead chop up leaves into short lengths of about 5mm/¼in and freeze with a little water in ice cube containers.

Dill

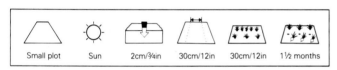

Small plot | Sun | 2cm/¾in | 30cm/12in | 30cm/12in | 1½ months

A decorative herb, dill looks at its best when a number of plants are clumped together in the herb bed. The needle-like leaves, and tiny yellow flowers from early to late summer, make it difficult to distinguish from fennel. Both the aromatic leaves and seeds are used.

GROWING Sow seed where it is to grow, in a well-drained soil and a sunny position. Cover the seed with a light sprinkling of soil. Make successive sowings from mid spring to early summer for a continuous supply of leaves. Stake the plant if the site is windy. Cut off the flowers of some of the plants as they appear so you can pick and use the leaves. Other plants can be left to go to seed. As soon as the flower-heads are brown, the seeds are ripe. The whole plant should then be cut down and the seed drying completed indoors.

HARVESTING Leaves can be used from six weeks after germination.

POSSIBLE PROBLEMS Watch for aphids.

USES Dill leaves make a particularly good sauce to go with fish. Add chopped leaves to green and raw vegetables, especially cucumber, and sprinkle over grilled lamb chops. Use whole or ground dill seed in lamb stews, herb butters, bean soups and in pickled baby cucumbers. Dill seed tea is good for the digestion and will also help you to sleep.

Fennel

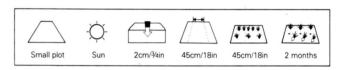

Small plot | Sun | 2cm/¾in | 45cm/18in | 45cm/18in | 2 months

Fennel is highly ornamental and grows up to 1.5m/5ft high. Tiny yellow flowers come in mid/late summer. The bluish-green needle-like leaves, the sweeter aniseed flavour, and the size of the plant help to distinguish it from dill. The seeds, which are dried for use, are oval in shape and have a much stronger flavour than the leaf.

GROWING Sow the seed in spring, in well-drained good garden soil and in a sunny position. If seed is not required, remove flower stems as they appear. Otherwise, leave some flowers on the plants to go to seed.

HARVESTING The seeds are ready to harvest when hard and a grey-green colour. Cut off the heads and complete the drying indoors.

POSSIBLE PROBLEMS Staking may be needed for this tall plant. Keep weeds under control; water fennel well in dry weather.

USES Seeds or leaves give an excellent flavour when added to the water for poached or boiled fish. Use the chopped leaves in fish sauces, or as a garnish to counteract the oiliness of rich fish. Add leaves to salads and raw or cooked vegetables, and try finely chopped leaves sprinkled over buttered new potatoes. Seeds can be used whole or ground to flavour bread, savoury biscuits, soups and sweet pickles. Fennel tea, made with leaves or seeds, is good for the digestion.

▦ PRESERVING TIP

Leave the seeds on the plant until they start to turn brown, usually in late summer, and then harvest. If left to ripen completely on the plant they can easily fall to the ground and be lost. Cut off the stems that hold the seedheads and tie a few together with elastic bands to form small bunches. Hang upside down in a dry, airy shed. Place a cotton cloth spread out in a bowl below to catch the falling seeds. Store seeds in a tightly sealed container.

▦ GARDENER'S TIP

If the seeds of fennel are required for culinary purposes it is important to sow seeds under cover in early or mid spring, then transplant them to the spot where they are to be grown. This early start allows time for the seeds to ripen.

HORSERADISH

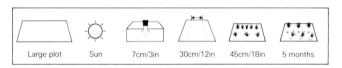

| Large plot | Sun | 7cm/3in | 30cm/12in | 45cm/18in | 5 months |

Horseradish is a hardy perennial with large floppy leaves growing from the base of the plant. The flowers are white on a single stem but they do not appear every season. The large thick roots are used sparingly, because of their hot flavour.

GROWING Plant 7-cm/3-in long root cuttings in a rich, moist soil in early spring, 30cm/1ft apart, just covered with soil. An open sunny place is best. These will establish to produce new plants. Lift all the plants in autumn, cut and store the larger roots in sand for winter use, and retain the smaller roots, also in sand, for planting the following spring. This ensures a constant supply of the best quality roots.

HARVESTING Established roots can be dug up as required, but the flavour is improved by cold weather.

POSSIBLE PROBLEMS The roots can become a great invader, so grow horseradish where it can be confined.

USES Horseradish is primarily used as a condiment, grated into cream, and makes a pleasant change from mustard. It is a superb accompaniment to roast or boiled beef. Add grated raw root to coleslaw and uncooked vegetable chutneys. Horseradish sauce helps in the digestion of rich smoked fish, such as eel, mackerel or herring. Horseradish paste made with cream cheese makes a tasty sandwich filling.

HYSSOP

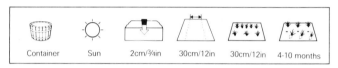

| Container | Sun | 2cm/¾in | 30cm/12in | 30cm/12in | 4-10 months |

A hardy evergreen perennial with a long flowering season, hyssop is a good herb to grow in garden or pot. It has woody stems and small pointed leaves which are pleasantly pungent. Hyssop flowers grow in long spikes of either blue or deep pink and have a heavy fragrant scent; they are loved by bees and butterflies. Hyssop leaves, the part used, have a slightly bitter taste, between rosemary and lavender.

GROWING Sow seed in spring in well-drained soil and a sunny position. You can increase the number of plants by taking stem cuttings 5cm/2in long in mid/late spring; they soon take root. Hyssop also reseeds itself and the seedlings come true to form. It grows to about 60cm/2ft. After three or four years, the plants become too woody and need replacing.

HARVESTING Remove the leaves for drying when the flower buds first appear and before flowering. Lay out in a warm and well-ventilated spot until brittle to the touch.

POSSIBLE PROBLEMS Cut hyssop back after the flowers have died to maintain a neat shape.

USES The faintly minty taste of hyssop leaves gives an unusual tang to green salads and vegetable soups. Hyssop is traditionally added to cranberries, stewed peaches or apricots, and to fruit drinks, tarts and pies. An infusion of hyssop makes a good cough syrup.

▋ GARDENER'S TIP

For replanting in early spring, use roots of pencil thickness and plant in holes made with a dibber at an angle of 45° with the thick end uppermost. Seed can also be sown in early spring and the plants thinned to 30cm/12in apart.

▋ ORGANIC TIP

To help relieve colds and coughs make hyssop tea. Place 2 to 3 tsp dried flowers in a tea pot and pour over boiling water. Leave to infuse for about 8 minutes. A cup of this liquid can be drunk hot or cold, three times a day. To dry the flowers remove from the plant before the sun shines on it and when the flowers first appear, as this is when the volatile oils are strongest. Spread out on foil and dry slowly at the lowest oven setting with the door ajar.

LOVAGE

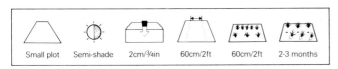

Small plot	Semi-shade	2cm/¾in	60cm/2ft	60cm/2ft	2-3 months

Lovage is a vigorous, handsome perennial. Greenish yellow flowers are followed by oblong deep brown seeds. All parts of the plant can be used for flavouring and have a pleasant yeasty taste, rather like celery.

GROWING Lovage grows well in a moist soil in either sun or partial shade. It can be raised from seed sown in early autumn in pots or seed boxes filled with compost. Cover the boxes with wire netting to stop the birds eating the seed, and leave the boxes in a sheltered place. In the spring, plant out the seedlings. In a good year, lovage will seed itself and in spring the seedlings appear near the parent plant. It can grow up to 2m/6ft tall. Towards the end of the season, leave one or two flowerheads to go to seed.

HARVESTING During the summer, when leaves are needed for cooking, freezing and drying, keep cutting off the flowerheads as they appear.

POSSIBLE PROBLEMS As lovage seeds only have germination power for a short period, harvest when they are just ripe on the plant, then immediately sow them.

USES Lovage soup is delicious and can be made from fresh or dried leaves. Chopped fresh leaves, young stalks or lovage seeds can be added to meat stews in place of celery. Use lovage leaves with boiled ham, in salads and with haricot beans.

MARIGOLD

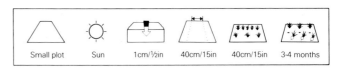

Small plot	Sun	1cm/½in	40cm/15in	40cm/15in	3-4 months

The cottage garden marigold, *Calendula officinalis*, or pot marigold, has long been popular as a flavouring.

GROWING Sow seed in early spring for summer flowering or in early autumn for late spring flowering the following year. A light, rich soil is best but marigolds do well even on poor soils. Water well and thin the plants when the seedlings are large enough to handle. Pinch out the growing points to encourage bushy growth. Keep weeds down until the plants are large enough to suppress them. Marigolds reach about 30cm/12in in height and can be grown in pots as well as in the border.,

HARVESTING Pick flowers for use when they are fully open. If you keep removing the flowerheads new blossoms will be produced for months.

POSSIBLE PROBLEMS Caterpillars eat the stems and leaves. Leaves may be spotted with smut in wet weather.

USES Use the petals, fresh or dried, to add a delicate colour and aroma to savoury rice, egg and cheese dishes. The fresh petals bring brightness and nutrition to a green salad.

▧ PRESERVING TIP

Use young leaves, still on their stalks, and dry at the oven's lowest temperature with the door ajar. Allow 1-2 hours for small quantities. When dry, the leaves will be brittle. Rub them off the stalks, keep in airtight containers in the dark. You can also dry herbs in the microwave. In this case sandwich small quantities between layers of kitchen paper. Use a low setting, check each minute and turn the sandwich over. Drying will usually take 2-4 minutes.

▧ PRESERVING TIP

Petals for drying should be gathered when the flowers are fully opened and perfect. They are as vivid when dry as when in full bloom. Add to a pot-pourri mixture or use in cooking in place of saffron.

MARJORAM

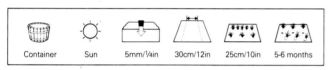

Container	Sun	5mm/¼in	30cm/12in	25cm/10in	5-6 months

Of the three forms of marjoram, the sweet, or knotted, annual marjoram has by far the best flavour for cooking. It is sweet and spicy but mild compared to the others. Wild marjoram is sometimes called oregano, from its Italian name; a perennial, it has the strongest spiciest taste of the three. The flavour of pot marjoram is not so pronounced as in the other marjorams. Combining the flavour of wild and sweet marjoram is a perennial named Daphne ffiske: the result is the best flavour with the growing habits of the perennial.

GROWING *Sweet* (knotted) *marjoram*: sow the fine seed mixed with sand under glass in early spring. Plant out seedlings in light, rich soil and a sunny, sheltered position. *Pot Marjoram*: propagate by seed sown in early spring or by rooted cuttings taken in autumn or spring. Ideal for growing in containers and indoors. *Wild marjoram*: easy to grow from seed sown in spring or by division of roots taken in spring or autumn. *Daphne ffiske*: grow in a pot either outside or indoors where it can be in the sun.

HARVESTING Marjoram leaves can be easily dried; gather sprigs just before the flowers appear.

USES The annual or the new perennial marjorams can be used sparingly in meat dishes and in salads. Marjoram adds good flavour to potatoes and pulses.

MINT

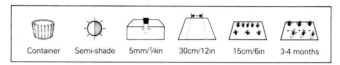

Container	Semi-shade	5mm/¼in	30cm/12in	15cm/6in	3-4 months

Common or garden mint (spearmint) is probably one of the oldest culinary herbs to be used in the Mediterranean region, and the best known of the mints. The long spikes of lilac flowers are a hit with bees. Peppermint and apple mint have the same growing requirements and are also enjoyed for their distinctive flavours.

GROWING In spring, sow mint seed in pots or boxes filled with compost and cover them with a piece of glass and newspaper until the seeds germinate. When the seedlings are large enough, set them out in the herb bed. Moisture and partial shade are the chief requirements. Spearmint grows to a height of about 30cm/12in, and is the best mint for window box and container growing, so long as the soil is kept moist.

HARVESTING Pick a few leaves from each plant as required. Cut right back in early summer to encourage a second crop in the autumn.

POSSIBLE PROBLEMS Mint is an invasive grower; in a small herb bed the plants can be restricted by surrounding them with old roofing slates sunk into the ground to a depth of 15-20cm/6-8in. The fungus disease rust can infect them, and such plants are best destroyed.

USES As well as using to make mint sauce and adding to the cooking water for peas and new potatoes, try mint with other young vegetables.

■ GARDENER'S TIP

To divide roots of pot or wild marjoram, lift the plant out of the soil and pull it into two separate sections at the centre. Break off young shoots from the outer sides, cut the leaves back to 2.5cm/1in from the roots and replant.

■ PRESERVING TIP

Mint can be stored in a box of compost to provide fresh winter supplies. Dig up a clump of mint and remove some of the sprigs with roots, then replant the rest. In a wooden box put a layer of moist compost, lay the sprigs on their sides in the compost and cover with more compost. Remove, cut and wash when required. Spearmint also dries well (see lovage for directions). In the Middle East dried mint is used in preference to fresh mint.

HERBS

PARSLEY

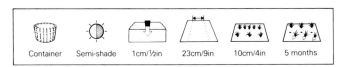

| Container | Semi-shade | 1cm/½in | 23cm/9in | 10cm/4in | 5 months |

The curly-leaved variety of parsley is the most widely used, perhaps because it makes an attractive garnish, but French, or flat-leaved parsley has more flavour. Parsley is a good plant for edging the herb garden, and ideal for container growing outside or indoors.

GROWING Though parsley is a hardy biennial, flowering in the second year of growth, it is usually treated as an annual and new seed is sown every year. Parsley does best in moist, slightly heavy soils and a shady position. Seed can be sown outdoors from early spring onwards, but if left until late spring, will germinate within ten days because of the increased warmth of the soil. Otherwise it can take three to five weeks. A second sowing in early mid summer will provide leaves through the winter. Thin the seedlings to 20cm/8in apart. Plants will sometimes grow on for two or three years. To ensure a long life for the plants, cut off all flowering heads in the second year.

HARVESTING Take only a few leaves at a time from curly-leaved parsley plants or you can affect growth.

POSSIBLE PROBLEMS Water well in dry weather to prevent bolting, and infestation by aphids.

USES Apart from its traditional use as a garnish, fresh chopped parsley is a good seasoning herb to add to meats, casseroles, soups, vegetables, stuffings, salads and eggs. Parsley is full of vitamins.

■ ORGANIC TIP

Allow one parsley plant to flower and go to seed. This will provide you with continuous plants as parsley self-seeds. Cut the flower stems off all other plants to extend the period when leaves will be produced. Parsley, especially the curly-leaved

variety, is not hardy in a severe winter so protect plants with cloches. This will also extend the season when you can cut fresh parsley.

ROSEMARY

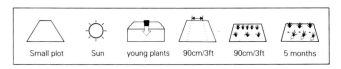

| Small plot | Sun | young plants | 90cm/3ft | 90cm/3ft | 5 months |

A strongly aromatic evergreen shrub, rosemary's small, narrow, grey-green leaves and blue flowers in late spring make it an ornamental addition to the herb garden. Eventually it grows up to 1.2m/4ft high. A dwarf variety is a neat alternative for a small garden or pot.

GROWING It is a slow process to produce rosemary from seed; it is best to start by buying a plant from a herb nursery or garden centre. In April, set the plant in a dry sunny spot towards the back of the herb garden. Increase the stock of plants by 5-7.5cm/2-3in cuttings of new shoot tips taken with or without a heel between mid spring and late summer. Place them in sandy compost and a warm, shaded place. In the autumn, cut back half the year's growth on a mature plant.

HARVESTING Although it is a slow-growing shrub, once the plant is established you can begin to use the leaves. Late summer is the best time to harvest for drying.

POSSIBLE PROBLEMS Protect young rosemary plants from frost in winter. Put a good layer of straw or leaves around the plant and surround it with wire netting.

USES Rosemary has a strong, spicy, sweet flavour which combines well in both sweet and savoury dishes. Add it, fresh or dried, to roast lamb and to beef or chicken casserole. Sprinkle it over potatoes when roasting and use it with other vegetables.

■ COOK'S TIP

Make a herbal oil to add to salad dressings and marinades. To 600ml/1 pint green olive oil add 2 branches rosemary, 2 sprigs thyme, a few black peppercorns and a peeled and cut garlic clove. Seal and leave for two weeks.

215

SAGE

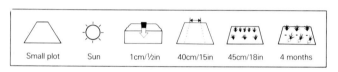

Small plot	Sun	1cm/½in	40cm/15in	45cm/18in	4 months

Garden sage is a strongly flavoured, small evergreen shrub. Varieties of sage, which have the same flavour, include Tricolor, with variegated leaves of white, green and purple-red, Icterina, with yellow-edged leaves, and purple-flushed Purpurascens.

GROWING Sage grows in any soil, provided it is well drained and in a sunny place. It can be grown successfully from seed sown in the early spring under glass and transplanted in late spring into the open ground. Alternatively, take cuttings from an established plant in late spring and put straight into the open ground. Plants should be 40-45cm/16-18in apart. When plants become leggy, pinch out the growing tips or cut the plants right back. Because sage plants become very woody over the seasons, renew every three or four years.

HARVESTING Garden sage produces leaves through the year which can be cut when needed. Decorative sages are not usually hardy so pot and bring indoors for the winter.

POSSIBLE PROBLEMS Stem cuttings or layering of side shoots are the only ways to increase the number of purple sage plants because its seed does not grow true to form but reverts to green-leaved sage.

USES Sage is most often used with roast pork but is also good with duck and sprinkled on to meat stews.

■ GARDENER'S TIP

To increase by layering make a slanting cut in the underside of a thick stem. Dab the cut into rooting powder and bend the stem at this point, pushing it into the ground. Hold in place with a peg until rooted , then cut off from the main plant.

SALAD BURNET

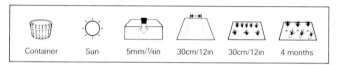

Container	Sun	5mm/¼in	30cm/12in	30cm/12in	4 months

Salad burnet forms a flat rosette of leaves on the ground, from which slender flowering stems grow up to 30cm/12in high. It is a hardy perennial and will stay green through a mild winter. The small, round red flowerheads bloom for three months in the summer.

GROWING You can buy the first plant from a herb nursery or grow salad burnet from seed. Set your plant in a sunny spot and renew the herb every year. In late winter or early spring, sow seed in boxes filled with a mixture of sand and compost. When the seedlings are large enough, prick them out into pots or seed boxes. Gradually harden off the plants and in late spring set them in their flowering positions, 30cm/12in apart. Salad burnet self-sows freely. To keep the flavour of the herb in the leaves, cut off the flowering heads as they appear.

HARVESTING Start to harvest leaves when the first flower shoots appear and cut when required. Cut the plant back periodically to 10-12.5cm/4-5in to ensure a continuing supply of young leaves.

POSSIBLE PROBLEMS This wild herb is easy to grow and should cause no problems. Do not try to transplant.

USES Mainly a salad herb as its name suggests, burnet leaves are at their best when used fresh. Add them to green and raw vegetable salads. Burnet vinegar has a delicious flavour, useful in making French dressing.

■ COOK'S TIP

To make salad burnet vinegar, heat 450ml/¾pint of vinegar to boiling point then pour this over ½ cup of salad burnet leaves which have previously been chopped, crushed and put in a heat-proof bowl (not metal). Pound the leaves in the vinegar then leave to cool. Pour the herbal vinegar mixture into a tall storage or jam jar, cork and shake every few days for two weeks. Strain and rebottle adding a few fresh leaves. Include basil and borage for extra flavour.

SORREL

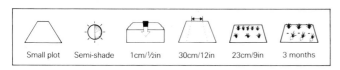

| Small plot | Semi-shade | 1cm/½in | 30cm/12in | 23cm/9in | 3 months |

Sorrel is a herbaceous perennial plant, dying down to ground level in autumn. The leaves are fleshy, light green and rather rounded; the tiny pink-red flowers that appear in early to mid summer should be removed.

GROWING A moist, fertile soil, such as a well-broken-down clay, gives good leaf size and succulence. Put in young plants in spring or autumn, 23cm/9in apart. Sun is preferred but sorrel will grow in shade.

HARVESTING Cut one or two leaves from each plant when individual plants have formed a group of more than five leaves, usually about three months after plants start to grow. Continue to harvest as required until the plants die back in autumn.

POSSIBLE PROBLEMS Soup recipes recommend 450g/1lb of leaves at a time, so a large harvest is needed. Whether you include this unusual herb in the kitchen garden depends upon how much space you want to devote to its cultivation.

USES Sorrel makes the famous and delicious sorrel soup, so popular in France, with a pleasantly sour flavour. It goes well with salads, and other vegetables, if used in moderation.

SUMMER SAVORY

| Container | Sun | 1cm/½in | 23cm/9in | 15cm/6in | 5 months |

An attractive herb, summer savory is a bushy, low-growing annual, with tiny lilac flowers continuing from mid summer to early autumn. The long, narrow leaves have a spicy flavour. Summer savory is an excellent plant to grow in a pot or window box. Another form of savory is the perennial winter savory. Although it is easy to grow, its flavour is not so delicate as that of summer savory.

GROWING Summer savory should be grown in a light, rich soil and a sunny position. Sow seeds in their flowering position in late spring and thin the plants to 15cm/6in apart.

HARVESTING Summer savory is best used when fresh, but it dries well and the plant should be harvested for drying when it is in full flower.

POSSIBLE PROBLEMS Problems in germination are probably due to too thick a covering on the seeds which germinate by light. Seeds also need damp conditions during sowing but fully grown plants are not normally sensitive to dry conditions.

USES As a seasoning herb, use summer savory with meats, fish and eggs. Add to all kinds of beans and sprinkle on to vegetable soup and meat broth. Put fresh sprigs into wine vinegar and leave to permeate. Use the vinegar to make a tasty French dressing.

FREEZING TIP

Build up a supply of sorrel leaves in the freezer until you have enough for soup-making. Wash, pat dry then place in plastic bags. If you want to preserve large quantities of sorrel it is best to blanch the leaves before freezing.

PRESERVING TIP

Well dried, summer savory will keep its flavour for a long time. Place cut sprigs on a frame and cover with net. Allow plenty of surrounding air flow. Place in a dark shed or cupboard where the temperature will not rise above 35C/95F. When leaves are dry they feel crisp but should retain their green colour. Reject any that turn brown. This happens when the drying temperature is too high. Rub leaves off the stalks and place these in an airtight container in the dark.

SWEET CICELY

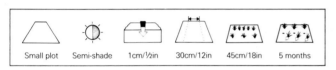

| Small plot | Semi-shade | 1cm/½in | 30cm/12in | 45cm/18in | 5 months |

Sweet Cicely is an ornamental perennial growing about 60cm/2ft high. Cut off the flowers that appear in late spring to retain the full aniseed flavour in the leaves. Let one or two remain to set seed. The seeds are long and jet black.

GROWING Easily grown, Sweet Cicely prefers a moist, deep soil and a little shade. Plant it in spring or autumn. Sweet Cicely self-seeds readily if the flowerheads are not cut off, so once you have purchased your first plant, you will have no problem in increasing the number. In the autumn, cut the large stems off at the base of the plant and leave the herb to die right down. Seed sown in autumn will produce seedlings the following spring.

HARVESTING Gather the leaves throughout the summer months and collect the seeds on any remaining flowerheads as they ripen.

POSSIBLE PROBLEMS Sweet Cicely's taproots go down very deeply, so be careful about where it is planted; the mature herb, once over a year old, cannot be moved to another part of the garden successfully.

USES Add finely chopped leaves when cooking gooseberries or rhubarb. Sweet Cicely reduces the acidity of tart fruits and less sugar is needed. It gives a delicious flavour when cooked with vegetables, too – particularly cabbage and swede.

TANSY

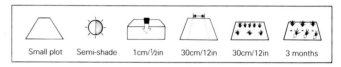

| Small plot | Semi-shade | 1cm/½in | 30cm/12in | 30cm/12in | 3 months |

A hardy perennial, 30-60cm/1-2ft tall with feathery leaves, tansy's yellow flowers appear in clusters from mid summer to early autumn. The common name comes from *Athanaton* – immortal – possibly because it lasts so long in flower, and its popular name, buttons, exactly describes the flower shape. Tansy has a curious, strong odour, not unpleasant and rather like camphor.

GROWING Tansy is easily grown from seed and is not fussy about either soil or situation. Alternatively, it can be grown by dividing the creeping roots. If cultivating by division, plant 30cm/1ft apart. The plant dies down in autumn.

HARVESTING Tansy has a bitter taste so use with care, cutting leaves as required. Dry for winter use.

POSSIBLE PROBLEMS This attractive herb can become invasive, so take care that it does not take up more of the herb garden than you would like it to.

USES Tansy can take the place of mint in sauce served with lamb and can be used in omelette and pancakes. Tansy cakes and tansy sauce were very popular in Elizabethan times and later.

▪ DECORATIVE TIP

To make a herb tuzzie muzzie start with a flowering herb in the centre, surround this with circles of herbs, mixing leaf shapes and colours. Tie each circle in place. Border with Sweet Cicely leaves and finally tie with a ribbon.

▪ ORGANIC TIP

Tansy leaves with their medicinal smell can be used to keep away ants, fleas and flies. Keep a few fresh leaves in a food cupboard to repel ants, or in a pet bed to put off fleas. Add these very decorative frilled leaves to a flower arrangement to keep away flies. Pennyroyal is also disliked by ants. Cut a few leaves and rub these over the point where the ants enter the house and they will not cross the area.

TARRAGON

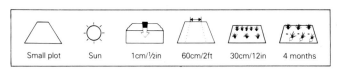

Small plot	Sun	1cm/½in	60cm/2ft	30cm/12in	4 months

French tarragon, *Artemisia dracunculus*, with its distinctive, slightly sweet-flavoured leaves, is one of the best culinary herbs for savoury cooking and no herb collection should be without it. It is a delicately bushy perennial plant, growing to 60-90cm/2-3ft. The Russian variety, *A. dracunculoides*, is inferior in flavour.

GROWING Tarragon needs a sunny, well-drained position in good garden soil. It will need feeding during the growing season to reach its full flavour. As tarragon does not set seed in temperate climates, propagate by taking cuttings of rooted shoots. Start by growing three or four plants set 30cm/12in apart in spring or autumn. Cut down plants in late autumn and protect from frost by covering them with leaves or straw.

HARVESTING Once the plant is established, leaves can be picked for use in the kitchen.

POSSIBLE PROBLEMS To keep it growing vigorously and prevent any risk of disease, tarragon should be divided every four years and replanted in fresh soil in the early spring.

USES Make tarragon vinegar by steeping the fresh herb in white wine vinegar. Use it when making French dressing. Add tarragon to roast meat, poultry dishes and fish. It is delicious in light buttery sauces to serve with mild-flavoured vegetables like marrow and artichokes.

▨ GARDENER'S TIP

To take a cutting, cut off the top 10cm/4in from a healthy stem with plenty of leaves. Remove the lower leaves, dip the cutting into water then rooting powder and place in moist cutting compost. Keep out of direct sunlight.

THYME

Container	Sun	1cm/½in	30cm/12in	30cm/12in	5 months

There are a large number of thymes that can be grown for their scent and as decorative plants, but for cooking the best flavours come from the common or garden thyme, *Thymus vulgaris*, and lemon thyme, *T. citriodorus*. Garden thyme is an evergreen shrubby perennial. Whorls of little mauve flowers bloom from early summer to late summer. Lemon thyme has a rather more trailing habit of growth. Thyme is a good container plant and can be used throughout the winter months.

GROWING Grow thyme in a dry sunny place in light, well-drained soil. Raise plants from seed sown in spring where they are to flower and thin the seedlings to 30cm/12in apart. Common thyme grows easily from seed. Lemon thyme is best bought as a plant. Thyme is easily increased from cuttings of shoot tips in summer.

HARVESTING Harvest thyme for drying when it is in full flower.

POSSIBLE PROBLEMS Cover the plants with leaves or straw in winter to protect from frost.

USES Use a little fresh chopped or dried thyme in stuffings and try finely chopped fresh leaves on potato purée, glazed carrots and other vegetables. Its fragrant leaves are an essential ingredient in bouquet garni, the seasoning posy used in all good cooking. Add sparingly to meats and fish, soups, stews and herb sauces.

▨ GARDENER'S TIP

To keep plants bushy and avoid woody stems, remove the growing tips regularly. To do this, pinch out the tiny new leaves between your thumb and index finger. Take cuttings in the same way as for tarragon.

SOFT FRUIT

Soft fruits have a long life, and because propagation is generally very easy, provide their own offspring so that you can continue to enjoy berries from new plants when the parents are exhausted. From raspberries and strawberries sweet enough to be served just as they are to refreshingly tart gooseberries, soft fruits offer a marvellous range of flavours. Strawberries alone among soft fruits do not freeze well – all can be made into delectable jams and jellies. The high vitamin, mineral and fibre content of these fruits makes a useful contribution to a healthy diet.

GROWING REQUIREMENTS   Because they occupy the ground for so long, as a general rule fruits need deep, well-drained but moisture-retentive, fertile soil. If your garden soil falls short of the ideal, it is well worth putting some effort into improving it by deep digging and incorporating as much bulky organic material as you can obtain.

During their life, fruit bushes need regular feeding and watering. This seems like stating the obvious, but it is easy to forget how important it is to nourish the permanent features of your garden in a busy summer making sure your lettuces don't bolt and earthing up your potatoes. A dressing of general purpose fertilizer worked in in spring is needed by many fruits.

The blueberry is an example of an unusual soft fruit that needs relatively little attention. If time is one of the commodities you are short of, it is worth growing a fruit like this.

If you have a large, sunny enclosed garden and plenty of time at your disposal, you can grow a whole range of fruits that thrive in a temperate climate.

Long hours of sunshine are crucial to ripening tender subjects like peaches, but not all fruits are so demanding. Only gardens in warm districts can support late-ripening apple varieties and dessert gooseberries, for example, but those in cooler zones will have successful results by choosing early-ripening varieties of all species. In between is the vast majority of varieties specially raised to do well almost anywhere.

PRUNING AND TRAINING   As with tree fruits, fruit bushes need pruning from time to time and for the same reasons. The main purpose of pruning is to keep the plant at an acceptable size and compact shape. This in turn encourages the formation of healthy fruits that are easy to harvest. A neglected bush with overcrowded and tangled stems will be prone to diseases and disorders, while what few fruits there are will be difficult to get at. For all pruning operations it is essential to have good equipment kept in perfect condition. A pair of secateurs is indispensable. Training systems make the most of every inch of space. In a tiny garden, grow gooseberries, apples and pears as cordons, with strawberries in a barrel.

Black currants   Black currants bear their fruit on two-year-old wood. To make sure the bushes have a healthy proportion of new (light) and old (dark) wood, prune established bushes every winter, taking out completely about one third of the old wood. Make a clean cut 2.5cm/1in from the nearest break. Leave behind and untouched as much of the new wood as you can; misplaced or diseased wood should of course be cut out.

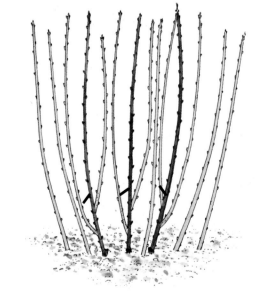

In winter, prune established black currant plants by removing one-third of the old wood.

If you inherit some neglected black currant bushes, revitalize them by pruning away all the old wood (which will be at the centre of the bush); and any broken or misplaced branches, old or new. Feed and water the bush carefully to help it back to productivity.

Red and white currants Unlike black currants, which shoot up from beneath the soil, red and white currant bushes sit on a short leg from which, ideally, 8 lateral branches radiate. If you are starting with cuttings, nick out with a sharp knife all but the top 4 buds before planting in late autumn. One year later 4 branches will have started to develop on a sturdy 10cm/4in stem. Transplant to the permanent growing site. Prune each branch by half, cutting to an outward pointing bud. By pruning the leaders in this way you will strengthen the plant, direct its habit of growth, furnish healthy new shoots and increase productivity. Repeat for the next 3 seasons, choosing suitably placed laterals to form further main branches up to 8. In the first growing season laterals will be produced from the main branches. Prune back any laterals not needed for new leaders to encourage the formation of fruiting spurs. In the winter, prune the leaders by about one third, and at the same time shorten the side shoots to 2.5cm/1in. Sub-laterals will be produced in subsequent years from the original cutback shoots, and these too should be cut back to 2.5cm/1in.

Although not essential, summer pruning of the laterals carried by the fruiting bush is an aid to fruitfulness. Cut back the side shoots as soon as the first fruits begin to colour, leaving about 10cm/4in. Cut back the same side shoots to 2.5cm/1in in the winter.

Gooseberries Gooseberry bushes are pruned in the same way as red and white currants, in order to achieve the same basic shape of strong branches radiating from a central stem. The difference is that bushes raised from cuttings are usually left in the nursery bed for 2 years, rather than one, to build up their strength. When pruning the bushes, cut back to an inward or upward rather than an outward pointing bud, in an attempt to prevent the branches from dropping. The summer pruning suggested for red currants is well worth doing for gooseberries.

Gooseberries can easily be grown as cordons, in which case pruning is rather different. For a single cordon, choose a single sturdy shoot on a newly planted 1-year-old and remove all the others flush with the stem. Tie the shoot to a cane for support. This cane should be firmly secured in the ground as the cordon will need it permanently. For a double cordon keep 2 shoots 23cm/9in above the ground and for a triple cordon keep 3 at the same height. Train the 2 shoots of a cordon horizontally on supporting wires until they are 15cm/6in long and then train them upwards. With a triple cordon, train the central shoot upwards and the 2 side shoots as for a double cordon. Every winter cut back the leaders of all cordons to two thirds of the new growth, and all side shoots to 3 buds.

Blackberries Most varieties of blackberry have biennial stems, which die after fruiting and are then replaced by the young canes, but the fruiting rods of some of the more vigorous varieties are perennial. It is useful to know this, because if there are not enough young canes produced in a particular year the old rods

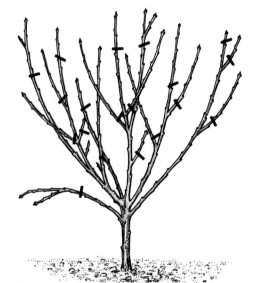

Cut back main branches of red currant to strengthen and cut back sideshoots near junction with main branches.

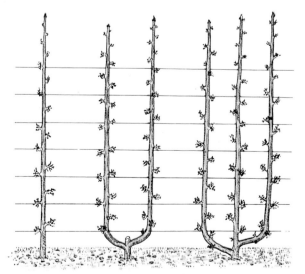

Single and multiple cordon systems of training, which are suitable for gooseberries and red currants.

Train blackberries to keep fruiting and young canes apart. Weaving is an efficient and decorative system: cut out old wood after fruiting. Weave in young replacement canes.

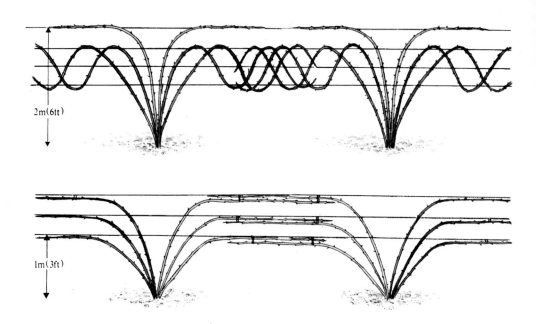

2m(6ft)

An alternative way of training blackberries is the one-way system. Train fruiting and young wood of adjacent bushes to left and right (the old wood in one direction and the new wood in the opposite direction).

1m(3ft)

can be retained for another season. All that is necessary, apart from any repositioning required, is to prune the laterals which carried the fruits back to 2.5cm/1in. An effective method of training blackberries to keep fruiting and young canes apart, is to weave the rods along the bottom of four wires – wearing thick gloves – then tie in the young cane as it develops during the summer and train it along the top wire. After fruiting, cut out the old wood and weave in the young replacement canes as illustrated at the top of this page. If this training method seems too tricky, train fruiting canes in one direction and young canes in the opposite direction, as illustrated beneath weaving.

Loganberries Pruning loganberries is simplicity itself, consisting of the complete removal of the fruited wood and the training in its place of the young cane. Gloves should be worn when handling loganberry canes. It is when pruning that the value of the thornless variety is particularly appreciated.

A fan system of training is ideal for loganberries: spread the fruiting canes on to the top wire, taking care to maintain a wide central area through which the young cane is trained initially, on to the top wire. After fruiting, prune by removing the fruited wood completely and tie in the young cane in its place. This training method is illustrated below.

As an alternative, the one-way system shown above for training blackberries, keeps the canes in their separate age groups, protecting the young canes from any risk of catching cane spot disease from the older wood, and avoids double handling but at the expense of unoccupied training space.

Raspberries For heavy and regular cropping, raspberries should be grown against posts and wires. Space each post about 3m/10ft apart, and standing 2m/6ft 6in out of the ground. Three wires should then be stapled to the posts, one at the top, the bottom one 60cm/2ft from the ground and the other mid-way

Using the fan system of training loganberries, tie young canes (light wood) on to the top wire, spreading the fruiting canes (dark wood) across the lower wires.

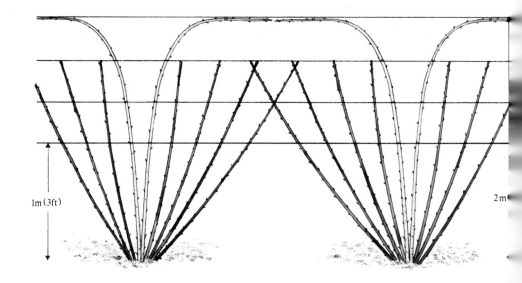

1m(3ft)

2m

Adopt a support system for raspberries: place wires at 2m/6ft, 1.2m/4ft, 60cm/2ft.

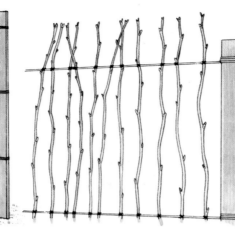

In the autumn tie in new canes at each level after cutting back old canes.

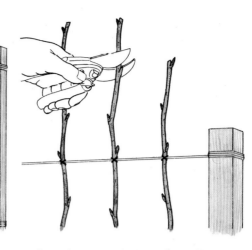

In spring, prune unripened tips. During the growing season pull out unwanted suckers.

between the two. In early spring, prune the tip of each cane. Pull out weak surplus suckers during the growing season. Once fruiting is over, cut out the old canes and tie the new canes to the supporting wires.

PROTECTING YOUR CROPS There are two kinds of protection available for fruit. One is protection from predators, which almost always means birds; and the other is protection from the elements – winds that rock the bushes and lash the berries and frosts that nip fruitfulness in the bud. Means of protection are also used to extend the season.

If you have a large garden and like to grow a lot of soft fruit, the ideal form of protection from predators, particularly birds, is a walk-in fruit cage. Most of us cannot accommodate such large structures and must resort to other means. Strong plastic netting can be draped over individual plants, though it should not be of so fine a mesh that pollinating insects cannot find their way through it. A number of scaring devices have been developed by exasperated gardeners, ranging from scarecrows, strips of fluttering plastic or glittering paper tied to the branches and tape-recorded frightening sounds.

The soft fruit crop which benefits most from protection from frost is strawberries, which because they are low-growing can be covered with cloches or a polythene tunnel and encouraged to fruit in early spring. Perpetual strawberries can be persuaded to fruit late into the autumn if placed under cover in early autumn.

PESTS AND DISEASES A pest is an animal – usually an insect – which is harmful to plants at some stage in its life cycle, for example as larva or caterpillar.

Generally speaking the substances used to combat pests are insecticides.

Diseases occur when plants are invaded by bacteria and fungi. Many troubles are caused by viruses, against which there are no chemical controls. As most diseases are caused by fungi the materials used to control them can be referred to as fungicides. Fungi are more difficult to control than insects.

Many of the things that go wrong with plants are the result of poor environment – not enough nutrition, for example. These disorders can usually be traced to neglect by the gardener. The first step in pest and disease control is to grow good plants that are living in fertile soil, correctly watered and kept free of competing weeds.

Always start with healthy plants bought from a reputable nursery, and in the case of such fruits as black currants, make sure you begin with plants certified free of virus diseases. While crop rotation is a discipline for the vegetable garden, the principle also applies to strawberries, which must not be grown on the same bed for two or three seasons after the original plants are exhausted. Never propagate from diseased stock, only from vigorous, healthy plants.

Prevention is better than cure. Spray in advance against inevitable troubles such as infestation by aphids. Prune at the correct time, making clean cuts that heal quickly without admitting disease. Whatever insecticides and fungicides you use, make sure you keep them in a safe place where they cannot be found by children. Always follow the manufacturer's instructions, and do not spray fruit immediately before picking it. Wash all fruits before use. A guide to control of pests and diseases is given on page 135.

BLACKBERRY

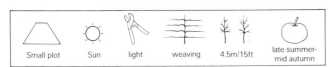

Small plot	Sun	light	weaving	4.5m/15ft	late summer-mid autumn

The blackberry is very accommodating and tolerant of adverse site and soil conditions.

GROWING Although the blackberry will grow and crop in poor soil and in shady positions, it does best in soil in which large quantities of farmyard manure or composted vegetation or other moisture-retaining bulky organic matter have been incorporated, and on an open site. Spread out the roots of the new plant so that they occupy as large a feeding zone as possible. Cut the plant back to about 30cm/1ft. Depending on variety, plants should be spaced from 3-4.5m/10-15ft apart.

PROPAGATION In the wild, young canes arch over, and the tips root eventually. To increase your stock, copy nature: bury the tip of a selected young cane shallowly in mid summer, securing the parent cane to ensure that the tip is properly anchored and keep moist. During the following winter or spring, the new rooted shoot can be detached, lifted and planted.

HARVESTING Blackberries should crop heavily each autumn, indefinitely. Leave fruit for eating fresh on the plant until ripe and sweet. Pick fruit for jams and pies just as the berries turn black.

POSSIBLE PROBLEMS Always plant healthy plants: never start with weak, scarred or cankered canes.

BLUEBERRY

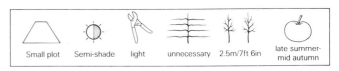

Small plot	Semi-shade	light	unnecessary	2.5m/7ft 6in	late summer-mid autumn

Blueberries are a favourite in the USA where they feature in a popular pie as well as being stewed with sugar. The flavour of the small, blue-black berries is pleasantly sharp.

GROWING An acid soil is essential for success, so if rhododendrons thrive in your garden, blueberries should do well. You can raise plants from cuttings like black currants – otherwise set out young plants from the nursery in mid autumn. The mature bushes can reach a height and spread of 2m/6ft 6in and are heavy croppers. The only pruning required is to remove overcrowded branches and cut the whole bush back occasionally to keep the shape neat. Do not let the soil dry out – mulch with peat once a year. Keep competing weeds under control while the bush is establishing itself.

HARVESTING Pick the strings of berries when fully ripe and use immediately or freeze.

POSSIBLE PROBLEMS Usually trouble-free.

VARIETIES Bluecrop.

▧ GARDENER'S TIP

An effective method of training blackberries to keep fruiting and young canes apart, is to weave the rods along the bottom of four wires – wearing thick gloves – then tie in the young cane as it develops during the summer and train it along the top wire. After fruiting, cut out the old wood and weave in the young replacement canes. If this seems too tricky, train fruiting and young canes to right and left.

▧ GARDENER'S TIP

You will need more than one plant as blueberries are not self-fertile and plants will take at least 3 years before they fruit but will then crop well for a number of years. High bush blueberries make an ornamental addition to the flower garden.

BOYSENBERRY

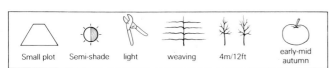

| Small plot | Semi-shade | light | weaving | 4m/12ft | early-mid autumn |

If you are interested in unusual fruits, the boysenberry is a rewarding subject. A hybrid of uncertain parentage, though certainly including members of the blackberry family, the fruits have a sweet-sharp flavour. The plants resist drought well.

GROWING Treat the boysenberry as a vigorous blackberry. Any soil will do as long as it is dug over before planting and a bucketful of well-rotted compost worked in. Set out young plants in the autumn and cut back to 30cm/12in. A system of horizontal wires makes it easy to control what would otherwise be a rampant bush. Tie fruiting canes in a fan shape on the lower wires. As new, light-wooded canes grow up, keep them out of the way on the top wires. After fruiting, cut the old wood right back and replace with the new canes. An alternative method which accommodates longer fruiting canes is to weave them in and out of the wires – wearing stout gloves to combat the thorns.

HARVESTING Pick the berries when they part easily from the bush. Use immediately in cooked desserts and conserves or freeze.

POSSIBLE PROBLEMS Cane spot fungus may damage the stems. Spray with bordeaux mixture just before and just after flowering.

SUITABLE VARIETIES No named varieties.

GOOSEBERRY

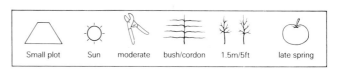

| Small plot | Sun | moderate | bush/cordon | 1.5m/5ft | late spring |

Most varieties of gooseberry are picked while green, for stewing; but some are so sweet when fully ripe they can be eaten straight from the bush.

GROWING Full sun is best, on a site sheltered from the wind. Deeply cultivated, fertile soil from which all perennial weeds have been cleared is best. Since gooseberries share red and white currants' need for potash, it makes sense to grow them together. A bush on a short stem makes it easier to weed and pick the fruit between the prickles. Plant healthy 2-year-old bushes between mid autumn and early spring, first incorporating a little sulphate of potash into the soil. Plant to the same depth as in the nursery. Pruning is important to achieve the desired shape. After planting, cut back new growth on 6-8 shoots by half, on the rest to 1 bud from the base. Thereafter, in summer cut back the side shoots to 10cm/4in and in winter cut them again, back to 2-3 buds. At the same time cut back the leading shoots by half and to an inward or upward pointing bud. Water well. Gooseberries can also be grown as cordons.

HARVESTING Fruits picked small and green can be stewed; use mid-season fruits for jam and preserves. Late ripening fruits can be eaten raw.

POSSIBLE PROBLEMS Aphids. Remove gooseberry sawfly larvae from the leaves by hand.

◼ COOK'S TIP

If you grow these and other fruiting canes organically there should be no reason to wash the fruit before serving or freezing. As they grow well above the ground they do not get mud spattered and washing will inevitably result in some loss of *flavour. Eat fresh with a little honey and yogurt or make into ice cream, put in a pie or turn into jam.*

◼ GARDENER'S TIP

Gooseberries flower early, so if there are few available bees pollinate the flowers by hand, using an artist's paint brush to transfer the pollen from one flower to another.

225

LOGANBERRY

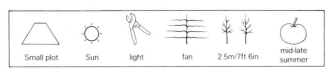

Small plot	Sun	light	fan	2.5m/7ft 6in	mid-late summer

Although the loganberry is not as easy to grow as its relatives, the raspberry and blackberry, it is a worthwhile addition to the fruit garden for its special flavour.

GROWING Loganberries do best in soil in which large quantities of farmyard manure or composted vegetation or other moisture-retaining bulky organic matter have been incorporated, and on an open site. Spread out the roots of the new plant so that they occupy as large a feeding zone as possible and if planting more than one, space the plants about 2.5m/7ft 6in apart. A fan system of training is ideal: spread the fruiting canes across three lower wires and tie the young canes on to the top wire, taking care to maintain a wide central area through which the young cane is trained initially. A thornless variety is available: if this is not chosen, gloves should be worn when handling loganberry canes. After fruiting, prune by removing the fruited wood completely and tie in the young cane in its place.

HARVESTING Pick when the full colour has formed. Ripe berries are easily crushed, so pick with care.

POSSIBLE PROBLEMS Because of proneness to cane spot, propagation is not recommended; training loganberries so that the young canes are either above or to one side of the fruiting canes avoids any fungus on the older wood being carried in raindrops on to new growth.

RASPBERRY

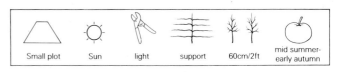

Small plot	Sun	light	support	60cm/2ft	mid summer-early autumn

One considerable advantage the raspberry has over all hardy fruits except the strawberry, is the ability to come into full bearing quickly, if the plants are well grown.

GROWING For best results, incorporate large quantities of farmyard manure or composted vegetation, or other moisture-retaining bulky organic matter before planting. Spread the roots out and plant the canes shallowly in a sheltered place when the soil is reasonably dry, spacing them 60cm/2ft apart. Late autumn is the best time. Pruning begins on planting, the aim being to prevent the formation of fruit (on summer fruiting varieties) in the first year: cut each cane back to about 25cm/10in above ground level. In early spring, prune the tip of each cane. Pull out weak surplus suckers during the growing season, wearing a protective glove. Once fruiting is over, cut out the old canes and tie the new canes to supporting wires.

HARVESTING Autumn-fruiting varieties fruit on the current year's canes, while summer-fruiting varieties produce their fruit on the previous year's canes.

POSSIBLE PROBLEMS Bad drainage can lead to the death of canes, so avoid waterlogging in the winter months. Weeds that appear should be pulled up or gently hoed away. The raspberry beetle gives rise to maggoty fruits. Dust the fruitlets with derris or spray with malathion as soon as the first pink fruits are seen.

▨ COOK'S TIP

One of the most delicious fruit vinegars is made with raspberries but loganberries are just as suitable to tint and add taste to white wine vinegar. One-third fill a glass jar with the fruit then top up with the vinegar. Use a glass or cork stopper. Place the jar on a sunny window sill and shake daily for two weeks. Leave a little longer in cooler weather. Strain the now pink vinegar into a clean bottle and seal with a cork stopper.

▨ GARDENER'S TIP

Raspberries are carried on side-shoots which are readily severed by a summer's gale, so plant them near a protective tree or shrub, as long as these produce only thin shade. Plant the canes in a relatively weed-free part of the garden.

ALPINE STRAWBERRY

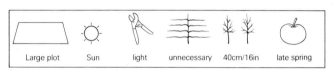

| Container | Sun | light | unnecessary | 23cm/9in | mid-late summer |

Alpine strawberries are small and grown on bushy plants that do not produce runners. While they are usually treated as summer strawberries, alpines are particularly suitable for growing in barrels. Large earthenware pots may also be used. These are the best strawberries for making jam as they are high in pectin.

GROWING Specially constructed strawberry towers are available, but old barrels are perfectly adequate and blend in nicely with the garden. They are sold with 5-cm/2-in holes bored in them 23cm/9in apart. Plant in late summer to fruit the following summer. Place drainage material such as broken pots in the base and lay turves grass side down on top. Make a central drainage column of wire netting filled with similar material. Use a rich potting compost, such as John Innes No. 3. As you fill the barrel, put the plants in place just inside the holes. Stop the drainage core 15cm/6in short of the top. Fill with compost and set more plants 23cm/9in apart on the surface. Do not let the compost dry out.

HARVESTING Start picking as soon as the fruits begin to ripen, removing the berries with the calyx and a little stalk. After fruiting, cut the leaves back to 7.5cm/3in. Replace stock and compost after the third year.

POSSIBLE PROBLEMS Birds, slugs and aphids.

VARIETIES Baron Solemacher.

▪ GARDENER'S TIP

To grow your own plants from seeds, sow the seeds in moist seed compost in autumn and overwinter in a cold frame. Alternatively, sow in trays in seed compost in early spring and keep at 17-21C/65-70F and covered until the seeds germinate. Prick out the seedlings when the first true leaves appear to 2.5cm/1in apart. Plant out at the end of spring. Spread bone meal on the soil shortly before planting, 2 handfuls per square metre/yard.

EARLY STRAWBERRY

| Large plot | Sun | light | unnecessary | 40cm/16in | late spring |

Certain summer-fruiting varieties of strawberry can produce fruit in late spring if grown under protection.

GROWING A light, fertile, well-cultivated soil is essential. Double dig before planting, working in plenty of well-rotted organic manure, compost and peat. Set new plants out in late summer, taking care that the crowns are level with the surface of the soil. Water lightly to encourage the formation of plump crowns for the following year. In late winter, cover the rows. The ideal protection is a tunnel of barn cloches. As an alternative, use lengths of polythene sheeting stretched over wire hoops and secured to a stake at either end. As the plants come into flower, ventilate the rows by day to let pollinating insects in and to prevent the interior becoming overheated: remove every fifth cloche or raise the sides of the polythene. Do not let the plants dry out.

HARVESTING Inspect the plants daily from the end of spring and pick the berries as soon as they ripen. After fruiting, remove the cloches/polythene, trim back the foliage, remove runners and weeds. Let the plants fruit in summer in the normal way the following year.

PROPAGATION It is not advisable to propagate from plants that have been forced into early fruiting.

POSSIBLE PROBLEMS Slugs, aphids, grey mould.

▪ GARDENER'S TIP

Give further protection and warmth to early strawberries grown under cloches by placing black polythene over a bed raised towards the centre. Tuck the edges in under the soil at the sides. Plant through slits in the plastic.

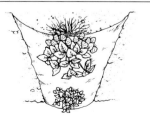

PERPETUAL STRAWBERRY

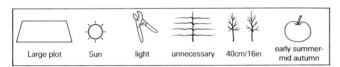

| Large plot | Sun | light | unnecessary | 40cm/16in | early summer-mid autumn |

Also called remontant strawberries, these varieties differ from standard summer-fruiting types in that they bear flushes of fruits from early summer-mid autumn instead of a single crop in mid-summer. The disadvantage is that certified virus-free stock is not yet available so perpetuals must not be grown near summer-fruiting strawberries.

GROWING Plant in spring in deeply dug soil in which well-rotted organic compost has been incorporated. Set the plants in the soil so that the crowns are level with the surface: make planting holes with a mound in the centre and spread the roots out and around before covering them with fine soil. Firm in and water well. In the first year, remove the flowers that appear up till the end of spring. A light, early crop follows in 6 weeks, but the later crop will be much heavier. Feed during the summer with a general purpose fertilizer and keep weeds down. Protect the ripening fruits with clean straw or strawberry mats.

HARVESTING Pick the fruits as soon as they are ripe, a few at a time from each plant. Remove all dead and decaying leaves after fruiting. The second year's crop will be lighter. Replace plants in the third year.

POSSIBLE PROBLEMS Birds, slugs, aphids, grey mould. See summer and alpine strawberries.

SUMMER STRAWBERRY

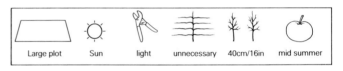

| Large plot | Sun | light | unnecessary | 40cm/16in | mid summer |

Using different varieties stretches the strawberry season throughout the summer and beyond. Because strawberries are prone to virus diseases, the bed should not be used for strawberries again for 2 seasons after the crop is exhausted, which may be 4-5 years.

GROWING The best soil is light-medium, well drained and quick to warm up in spring. Work in plenty of manure, compost and peat before planting. Choose a site that is sunny by day and retains warmth at night. Buy in certified virus-free runners to plant in late summer or late spring. Set the plants so that the crown is level with the surface of the soil (see perpetual strawberries). Cover with soil, firm well and water in. A well-prepared bed will retain moisture, but in dry springs it may be necessary to water to plump up the berries. Stop watering after the fruits take colour. Remove all weeds, preferably by hand. If night frost is forecast, cover the rows lightly with straw or strips of black polythene and remove it by day. Cut out all runners unless – in the first year – you want to raise new stock from a limited number of plants.

HARVESTING Pick the berries on dry days, with the calyx and a little stem as soon as they are ripe. Clean up the bed and cut the plants right back after fruiting.

POSSIBLE PROBLEMS Protect from birds with netting.

■ ORGANIC TIP

To stop birds harvesting the fruit before you do, upturn a series of glass bottles and push the necks in the soil. Light glinting on the glass appears to deter the birds from approaching.

■ ORGANIC TIP

To help to deter slugs, place the ripening fruits on a bed of straw, carefully placed right underneath them. Do this as the strawberries begin to swell, not before, because it also exposes them to any frost and insulates them from the soil's warmth. The straw will also help to keep the strawberries clean. To deter grey mould do not over-water or add more than 2 handfuls of fertilizer per sq m/sq yd. Cut off and burn infected shoots.

WINEBERRY

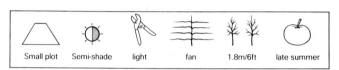

Small plot	Semi-shade	light	fan	1.8m/6ft	late summer

Related to the blackberry, and sometimes called the Chinese blackberry, the wineberry produces beautiful fruits which are at first yellow then turn through orange to red. The whole plant is very ornamental, its long stems covered with red bristles.

GROWING Choose a sheltered site and dig in plenty of well-rotted manure. Plant in late autumn, spreading the roots out well and covering them with fine soil. Firm in and water well. Cut new plants back to about 25cm/10in above ground level so that they will not fruit in the first year, but build up a strong root system. Cover the rooting area with a mulch to conserve moisture and suppress weeds. Wineberries, like raspberries, benefit from a support system, as they reach 2m/6ft 6in in height. After fruiting, cut down old canes and tie the new canes into the wires. Pull out all weak suckers during the growing season, wearing thick gloves for protection. In spring, lightly prune back the unripened tips of the new canes.

HARVESTING Pick the berries as soon as they are deep red, plump and ripe. They can be served with sugar and cream, cooked in a summer pudding or made into jam.

POSSIBLE PROBLEM Dust the immature fruits with derris to deter raspberry beetle.

BLACK CURRANT

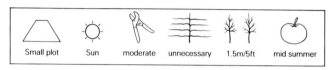

Small plot	Sun	moderate	unnecessary	1.5m/5ft	mid summer

The unique flavour of black currants is delicious in desserts, ice cream, jam and syrup.

GROWING In the autumn, start with 1-year-old plants certified free from disease. Buy half the number needed to fill the plot, which should be in full sun and sheltered from strong winds. Black currants need rich, deep moisture-retentive soil. Dig planting holes large enough to spread the roots right out. Set the plants 2.5cm/1in deeper than they were in the nursery. Cover the roots with fine soil or potting compost and tread it firm. With secateurs, cut each shoot down to leave not more than 5cm/2in. This is essential to encourage strong basal shoots for the future. Use the cutting to start new bushes (see below). No fruit is borne in the first summer, only strong young shoots which carry the first crop in the next year. The first winter after fruiting, and every following winter, prune out one third of the old, dark wood, leaving the young golden wood intact. The best fruit is borne on 1-year-old wood.

HARVESTING Currants turn black in mid summer and are ripe 2 weeks later. Pick a whole truss if ripe, otherwise take individual berries.

POSSIBLE PROBLEMS Reversion is a virus disease that makes the bushes barren and distorts the leaves. Destroy affected plants and begin again with new stock.

■ GARDENER'S TIP

The wineberry will grow best if fanned out against a wall or a fence. Its ornamental qualities will be highlighted too by this training system.

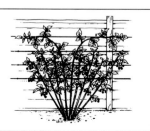

■ GARDENER'S TIP

To propagate black currants, discard the unripened tip of the cuttings and cut them into 25cm/10in lengths, cutting close to a bud at each end. Insert into the soil so that only 2 buds are showing, in groups of 3 set 20cm/8in apart in a triangle.

From these groups new composite bushes will form. In summer, give all the compost, lawn clippings and water you can spare as a weed-suppressing mulch.

RED CURRANT

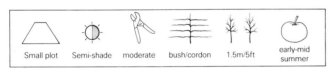

Small plot | Semi-shade | moderate | bush/cordon | 1.5m/5ft | early-mid summer

These gem-like fruits can be grown against a shaded wall if necessary.

GROWING Red currants like deeply dug, fertile, well-drained soil. Plant from late autumn-late winter, first incorporating a little sulphate of potash into the planting site. Buy 2-year-old bushes and plant to the same depth as in the nursery. While red currants can be trained as cordons to save space (see white currants), the ideal bush sits neatly on a short stem and carries 8 radiating branches. To achieve this, after planting cut the new growth on 6-8 strong shoots by half. Cut back other shoots to 1 bud from their base. Thereafter, prune twice a year. In early-mid summer, cut back all new side shoots to 5 leaves. Pull off suckers rising from the base of the bush. In winter, cut back the leading shoots by a half to an outward pointing bud. Cut the summer-pruned laterals back again to 2-3 buds. Water well in summer.

HARVESTING Pick red currants as soon as they are fully ripe and use straight away or freeze.

PROPAGATION Take hardwood cuttings in late autumn 30cm/12in long with a bud close to either end. Nick out all but the top 4 buds. Insert half-way in open ground. A small bush will be ready for transplanting in 12 months.

POSSIBLE PROBLEMS Tie strips of foil to the branches to scare off birds.

WHITE CURRANT

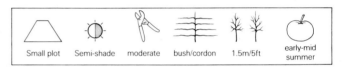

Small plot | Semi-shade | moderate | bush/cordon | 1.5m/5ft | early-mid summer

This unusual fruit is easy to grow and when fully ripe is very sweet. It is delicious in fruit salad.

GROWING Any well-drained, moisture-retentive soil is suitable, but like red currants, white currants need extra potash so work in a light dressing when digging over before planting between mid autumn and early spring. If space is at a premium, buy plants trained as cordons rather than bushes. Set 2-year-old plants in single rows 50cm/20in apart and support on wires between 5 × 5cm/2 × 2in stakes about 2m/6ft high. Prune in summer, cutting laterals back to 3-5 leaves. When the cordons reach 2m/6ft cut the new leader back to 4 leaves. In winter, cut the lateral shoots back to 1 bud. Before the leader reaches 2m/6ft, cut back new growth by up to 23cm/9in; after this point, remove new growth every winter.

PROPAGATION Take hardwood cuttings in late autumn, as for red currants.

HARVESTING Pick the fruits when fully ripe, either by the truss or individually. Use immediately or freeze.

POSSIBLE PROBLEMS White currants are relatively trouble-free. Scorching at the leaf edge is caused by a deficiency of potash. Aphids cause red blisters on the leaves. Spray with systemic insecticide just before flowering.

▨ COOK'S TIP

Red currants can be readily persuaded to part from their stems if the tines of a fork are used to isolate them. If the currants are to be frozen, leave them on the stalks. When solid, they will be very easy to remove.

▨ ORGANIC TIP

If leaves brown at the edges this is a sign of potassium deficiency. Currants need extra potassium. To remedy, spray plants with liquid seaweed and apply rock potash, one handful to the square metre. For the organic gardener, rock potash is an invaluable source of potassium so apply in quantities as above in the spring. To deal with bad aphid infestations, spray with insecticidal soap and attract predators of aphids, as described on page 134.

TOP FRUIT

From the gardener's point of view, the endearing thing about fruit is its longevity. Fruit trees such as apples, pears and plums may take a few seasons' nurturing to start with, but they repay the effort with many years of productivity. To the cook, too, fruits are a delight. Not only is there a range of flavours, but textures vary as well, whether in a crisp green apple or a juicy, tender peach. Apples and pears can be stored, while plums can be made into most delicious jams.

GROWING REQUIREMENTS Because they occupy the ground for so long, as a general rule fruits need deep, well-drained but moisture-retentive, fertile soil. The best site is sunny and open but protected from strong winds, which can easily uproot young trees and lay dangerously chilly fingers on older ones. Most town gardens enjoy some shelter from wind provided by the house to which they are attached, but you can do more to create an advantageous micro-climate with permanent windbreaks formed by hedges and fences.

Space is an important factor. Very few modern gardens can accommodate a mature sweet cherry tree, for example; but even standard or half standard apple trees are fairly majestic, and if two are necessary for successful pollination a substantial area will be used up. It is for this reason that dwarf bush apples have been developed, while trees like the plum – in nature a large specimen – are not raised on their own roots but grafted on to a suitable rootstock (St Julien A) that will keep growth within manageable bounds.

For apples the most popular rootstock is M9, which makes a dwarf bush reaching 2-3m/6-10ft. Where soil is poorer the large M26, reaching 2.5-3.7m/8-12ft, can be used. The very dwarf M27 needs extra care and feeding. Pears are grown on Quince A or C rootstock, cherries on F12/1, and while many a domestic peach has been raised from the kernel, the finest trees are grown on St Julien A, which is also used for nectarines and apricots. One of the purposes of pruning and training, discussed in detail below, is to keep fruit trees and bushes to shape and at an appropriate size. Some

pruning is necessary for all the most important fruit crops.

During their life, fruit trees need regular feeding and watering. A dressing of general purpose fertilizer worked in in spring is needed by many fruits. An annual mulch of well-rotted organic manure or compost spread liberally over the rooting zone feeds the plant, conserves moisture and suppresses weeds. While peat is a useful mulch, environmentally concerned gardeners are looking for alternatives to plundering a non-renewable natural resource. Grass cuttings and fallen leaves are obvious candidates, but other fibrous materials that can be made available in commercial quantities are being researched. Remember too that while a carpet of grass beneath your budding apple may look charming, it is probably starving the tree.

POLLINATION In the case of apples, pears, plums and some other top fruits, your choice will be affected by the need to have varieties that will cross-pollinate. It may be, of course, that a neighbouring garden contains a tree that will perform this duty for you. If not, you will have to plant two trees or choose a variety that is self-pollinating (self-fertile). Even with self-fertile trees, pollination needs your assistance in simple ways: the flowers of plants protected by sheets of hessian, for example, are inaccessible to pollinating insects unless you remove the obstruction to their flight path. Do not use insecticidal sprays when the blossoms are open and the bees are at work, but earlier in the season, at the bud stage.

PLANTING A TREE The best time to plant fruit trees is between late autumn and early spring, the earlier the better. Order your trees in advance from a reputable nursery to make sure you get exactly what you want. Whether you are starting with a 1-year-old – a maiden – which you will prune to shape from the start, or – in the case of a fan-shaped tree – an older tree whose branches have been trained into the basic fan framework by the nursery, the planting method is the same. (See Greengage for fan training). Prepare the soil very thoroughly by digging deeply, breaking up the subsoil with a fork. Work in as much rotted compost, farmyard manure or peat as you can get. Positioning the young tree and firming it into place is much easier with two pairs of hands. Drive a stout stake 1.2m/4ft long into the ground so that 75cm/2ft 6in is showing above the surface. If you are planting more than one tree, use a stake for each one, spaced according to type. Maiden apples on M9 rootstock should be placed 3m/10ft apart; dwarf pyramids on M27 can be half this distance and cordons as close as 75cm/2ft 6in. A half-standard tree needs the extra support of a double-stake and cross-bar, using two posts each 2m/6ft 6in long. The tree is tied to the cross-bar and padded to prevent chafing.

Take out a wide shallow hole, without loosening the stake, and spread the roots out so that they can make rapid use of the largest amount of ground. Take care to keep the union, the swollen piece on the stem which marks the junction between root stock and variety, at least 10cm/4in above the ground. If you bury the union, the inherently vigorous scion will root and the weak system of the rootstock will be overpowered, resulting in a large unfruitful tree rather than the neat productive one you hoped for. Firm the soil over the roots so that the two are in close contact. If you can lay hands on used potting soil, add a large bucketful to each planting hole to get the young tree off to a good start. Tie each tree to its stake, using a broad tie which will not bite into the stem. Allow room for the tree

trunk to expand rapidly without being choked. Place the tie as high on the stake as possible. If you are planting on a windy site, position the tree and stake so that the stake is on the side from which the strongest wind is likely, to avoid chafing. Prune immediately (see below). Over the winter cover the root area with composted material 5cm/2in deep to conserve moisture and suppress weeds.

PRUNING Left to themselves, fruit trees become overcrowded, diseased and pest-ridden, carrying small fruits on exhausted branches. On the other hand, excessive pruning can lead to too much growth and to light crops of poor quality. All pruning has a purpose. The main objectives are to: admit light and air; train the tree to an acceptable shape and size; increase the size of the fruit; encourage or control growth, whichever the tree demands; assist establishment after transplanting; remove diseased and broken parts; and finally, but importantly, to strengthen the branch structure.

The pruning of apple trees provides a good example of what is needed and is described and illustrated on this page and page 233. Other trees may vary slightly in their individual requirements.

The young tree The most common form is the open-centre bush tree. A one-year-old maiden tree without side shoots must be pruned as soon as possible after planting to compensate for the roots which are inevitably lost in transplanting. Cut the stem back to a height of 60cm/2ft, no more, making a clean cut just

Work plenty of well-rotted garden compost or manure into the bottom of the hole, and also into the earth that has been dug out. In addition, a light dressing of Growmore will be beneficial. Tread the soil well in as you fill in the hole.

Planting a tree
Dig out a hole large enough to accommodate the spread-out root system or the root ball. The depth should be sufficient to allow the soil mark on the stem to be level with the ground. Drive in the stake before planting to avoid damage to the roots.

The filling-in process is repeated until the hole is full and all the soil has been replaced. Use tree ties to steady the trunk against the stake. Lean this at a slight angle into the prevailing wind in an exposed site.

above a bud. The buds below the cut will grow outward in the first summer. You need 3 or 4 evenly spaced shoots, none of which grows towards the stake. Rub out unwanted or misplaced buds.

In the first winter after planting, cut back the branches which have formed from the chosen buds. If they are thick and strong, cut them back by half, but if they look weak and spindly, cut back by two-thirds. Prune to an outward pointing bud. This degree of pruning seems ruthless, but it is necessary in order to direct, strengthen and increase the numbers of the branches and their side shoots. During the second summer, water and manure the young tree, spraying at appropriate times to deter pests and prevent disease. Replace the tie that secures the tree to the stake if it has become too tight. The head will now have taken shape, with perhaps 6 to 8 strong and well-placed branches with a number of side shoots.

In the second winter, each of the main (primary) branches will have shoots at the end called leaders. They should be pruned only if it is necessary to strengthen the branch; to change its direction; to provide it with new side shoots or to remove diseased or overcrowded branches.

If it is necessary to do so for any of these purposes the leaders should be shortened again by about one third, two thirds if growth is weak, each to an outward pointing bud.

The side shoots are called laterals. Those growing to the outside may be left unpruned to form fruit buds. Those growing inwards should be pruned back to about 7.5cm/3in or removed entirely if there is overcrowding.

At the end of the third growing season look again at the leaders. Use your previous experience about the extent of cutting back, knowing that weak shoots should be pruned harder than strong shoots.

Follow a similar procedure with maiden laterals – leave alone those which are well placed and shorten or remove the others. You must also deal with last year's maidens, now burgeoning two-year-olds. Leave alone those which are well placed and not competing with the primary branches. Those for which there is no room for further extension should be cut back to the topmost fruit bud. Two-year-old budded laterals should fruit in the following summer.

The cut-back laterals of an earlier year may be pruned to any obvious fruit bud. If no fruit bud has appeared, the extension shoots should be pruned to 2.5cm/1in.

Although there are more complicated procedures undertaken by experts, amateur gardeners can be confident of success by following the rules given about leaders and laterals. These apply to apples, pears, plums and Morello cherries.

TRAINING The most convenient and successful form of tree is the open-centre bush described above or the open-centre half-standard or full standard, which are identical except for size.

An interesting variant on this form is the central leader tree, a development which makes it possible to train fruit trees into compact shapes such as the cordon, spindlebush and dwarf pyramid. Cordons are a very useful shape for small gardens as they can be planted as close together as 75cm/2ft 6in. The trees

Right *First winter: before pruning and after, selected leaders reduced by two-thirds.*

Far Right *Second winter: reduce leaders by two-thirds, cut laterals back to about 3 buds.*

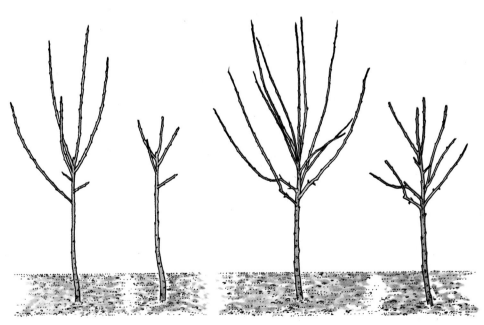

will be supported by a system of horizontal wires attached to posts firmly secured in the ground. The topmost wire should be 1.5m/5ft from the ground, with 3 further wires at 30cm/12in intervals below it. Plant in the same way as any 1-year-old tree. Attach a bamboo cane 2.4m/8ft long to the wires at an angle of 45 degrees. Tie the stem of the tree to the cane, using a soft twine so that the tree is not damaged. No pruning is needed until mid summer, and the same procedure is followed every year, cutting back the mature growth which is characterized by dark leaves and which is woody at the base. Prune back to 3 leaves from the cluster at the base. On the laterals there will be mature side shoots. These should be cut back to 1 leaf from the cluster at the base. Do not cut back the central leader.

When the leader reaches the top wire, remove the supporting cane. You can bend the stem to a more acute angle, gradually lowering it over a few seasons until it is 35 degrees from the ground. If you try to bend it lower than this the stem will break. When the tree cannot be lowered any further, prune the leader annually in late spring, cutting back new growth just above a bud to 1cm/½in.

The dwarf pyramid is a shape particularly useful for plums, and is described under dessert plums in the book. Shown in the illustrations below are the pruning cuts for the second year and for the mature tree.

For pruning fruit trees a heavy-bladed knife is very useful in addition to secateurs. A pruning saw is invaluable for dealing with older trees. Sharp blades help you make the clean cuts which are essential if the wound is to heal quickly.

PROTECTING YOUR CROPS Fruit trees grown in the open cannot be protected from wind and frost except when they are small enough to be draped with netting or have the bottom of the stem swathed in straw. Those grown against a wall, however, receive a good measure of protection from the wall, and can be covered with sheets of light netting or hessian, which should not touch the tree, on frosty nights.

Protection from birds is a perennial problem. Various scaring devices have been attempted. A resident cat is useful!

PESTS AND DISEASES Like soft fruits, tree fruits are subject to a number of pests and diseases, and to physiological disorders caused by adverse conditions or neglect. A brief guide to the control of common pests and diseases is given on page 135, with a spraying programme designed to protect apples.

Biological rather than chemical control is very useful in the greenhouse, where infesting white fly can be reduced by bringing in the parasitic insect *Encarsia formosa*, which eats them. A non-chemical way of attacking the codling moth larvae is to tie loose bands of sacking or corrugated cardboard around the trunks of susceptible trees in mid summer, before the larvae start their destructive journey up the trunk. Burn the sacking or cardboard in mid autumn. Similarly, trap the wingless females of the winter moth using greasebands placed on the trunks in autumn.

Preventing trouble in this, and other ways, is always better than cure: observe the rules of garden hygiene given in the general introduction, on page 134.

Far Left *Retain central axis, removing competing and unnecessary shoots on 2-year-old pyramid.* Centre *Remove upward growing shoots on mature pyramid.* Below *Greasebands trap the wingless female winter moths.*

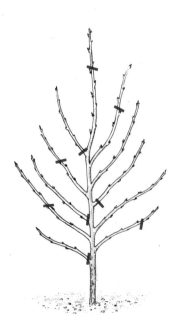

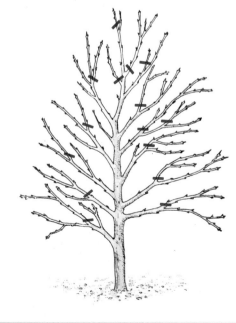

EARLY-SEASON APPLE

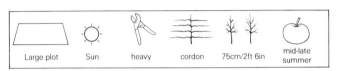

Large plot	Sun	heavy	cordon	75cm/2ft 6in	mid-late summer

The first apples to ripen are ready for picking in mid summer. Their skin is usually very pale yellow, sometimes with a reddish stripe, and the flesh soft, juicy and slightly acid. The flavour is not as good as that of varieties ripening in late summer. Early-ripening apples do not store well.

GROWING Irrespective of fruiting time, apple trees should be planted from late summer to early spring, the earlier the better. A slightly acid soil is best, well prepared by digging thoroughly. Break up the subsoil with a fork and work in ample quantities of well-rotted manure or compost. Choose self-pollinating or complementary varieties and plant as described on page 232. Dwarf bushes, pyramids or cordons are best for small gardens. Over winter, cover the rooting zone with a 5-cm/2-in layer of composted material to conserve moisture and suppress emergent weeds. For pruning see page 233. Apples need an annual mulch or manure and should never be allowed to dry out. Apply a general purpose fertilizer each spring.

HARVESTING Remove surplus fruits in early summer if pollination is over-successful, taking off the smallest fruits and any that are distorted or diseased. The fruits are ready to pick when they part readily from the tree when lifted to the horizontal. Pick gently to avoid bruising.

POSSIBLE PROBLEMS Aphids; codling moth caterpillar.

MID-SEASON APPLE

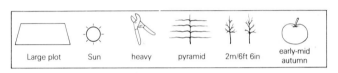

Large plot	Sun	heavy	pyramid	2m/6ft 6in	early-mid autumn

By choosing to grow apples that ripen in the period from early-mid autumn, you can include some of the most delicious varieties, among them James Grieve, Ellison's Orange, Devonshire Quarrenden and Discovery.

GROWING Start with 1-year-old trees – 'maidens' – if you are going for a dwarf bush or cordon. With a fan-trained tree it is best to buy one from the nursery with the basic framework of branches already formed. Plant from late autumn to early spring, as early as possible, in slightly acid soil. Prepare the site well by digging deeply and incorporating plenty of well-rotted organic compost. For planting, see page 232. Spread a thick moisture-retaining mulch over the rooting zone. For pruning, see page 233. Water well, give an annual mulch of manure and top dress with general purpose fertilizer each spring.

HARVESTING When the fruits begin to ripen, start by picking the outermost apples with the brightest colour, leaving the remainder to flush and put on more weight. Mid-season apples store well. Keep healthy specimens only in a cool, moist clean place. Place in polythene bags and inspect regularly for signs of rotting.

POSSIBLE PROBLEMS Aphids; codling moth caterpillar; scab; mildew.

▦ DECORATIVE TIP

In a small garden plant festooned trees in pots. These are grown on Pixy rootstock and the branches are trained to curve downwards by tying them, when they are young and supple, in summer to the stem or a lower branch.

▦ ORGANIC TIP

Use a pheromone trap to keep down the numbers of codling moth caterpillars, see page 238. Apple scab is a fungus which can flourish in wet weather. It appears as olive green blotches on leaves and small black or brown scabs on fruit and new shoots. Remove any infected leaves and shoots. Clear away fallen leaves that harbour spores. Apple aphids cause curled leaves and fruit distortion. Spray with insecticidal soap. Encourage bluetits in winter.

LATE-SEASON APPLE

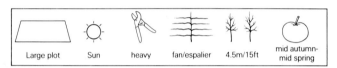

| Large plot | Sun | heavy | fan/espalier | 4.5m/15ft | mid autumn-mid spring |

The late season for apples is very long, extending from mid autumn right through to mid or even late spring, according to varieties. Those known as Reinettes, Pearmains and Pippins ripen in mid to late autumn, as well as the Russets. They are smaller than mid-season types, but the flavour is more aromatic and intense. All of these apples store very well. At the turn of the year, the choice of these varieties widens to include some with a long history, like Blenheim's Orange and the connoisseur's favourite, Ashmead's Kernel. The very late apples, those ripening late winter-early spring, need good soil and a long ripening season; these, like the old Cornish Gilliflower or the newcomer Golden Delicious, are best confined to warm districts.

GROWING Choose a prime site for late-season apples; if you want fan-trained apples on a sunny wall, these are the ones that merit such special treatment. Prepare the planting site with particular care, as the soil near a wall dries out more quickly. After planting (see page 232), apply a moisture-retentive mulch and keep the trees well watered and nourished throughout their life. Keep weeds under control.

HARVESTING Pick the outermost fruits first. Store undamaged fruits only in a cool, clean, moist place.

POSSIBLE PROBLEMS Mildew; scab; codling moth.

■ GARDENER'S TIP

When planting against a wall position trees at least 30cm/12in away from the wall so that roots can obtain sufficient water. Water each well initially. A little water merely encourages surface roots which suffer in dry weather.

COOKING APPLE

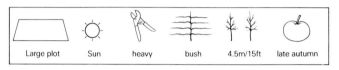

| Large plot | Sun | heavy | bush | 4.5m/15ft | late autumn |

While many dessert apples can also be cooked, there are a number of varieties with such a high acid content that they are always cooked before eating.

GROWING The best known cooking apple, Bramley's Seedling, is the finest flavoured cooker with the best texture. It makes a very large tree, however, and needs the company of others in order to pollinate successfully. Choose from two other cooking varieties, Emneth Early or Grenadier (late summer-early autumn) or the dessert apple Worcester Pearmain (late summer-early autumn). Plant in late autumn, first preparing the site by deep digging and incorporating plenty of well-rotted organic manure or compost. After planting (see page 232), apply a thick moisture-retentive mulch. Water well, give an annual mulch of manure and top dress with a general purpose fertilizer each spring. Keep weeds under control. For pruning see page 233.

HARVESTING The fruits are ready when they part easily from the tree when lifted to the horizontal. Pick carefully to avoid bruising. Store undamaged fruits only in a cool, moist, clean place.

POSSIBLE PROBLEMS As well as the usual pests and diseases affecting apples, Bramley's Seedling is susceptible to frost damage.

OTHER VARIETIES Woolbrook Russet; Crimson Bramley's Seedling.

■ PRESERVING TIP

When picking apples for storage select only those in perfect condition and place them in a cloth-lined container as you pick to avoid damage. Make a couple of small ventilation holes in each polythene bag you store them in.

CRAB APPLE

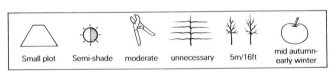

| Small plot | Semi-shade | moderate | unnecessary | 5m/16ft | mid autumn-early winter |

All apple trees are beautiful in blossom, but even lovelier is the crab apple, which carries a riot of flowers in spring. The wild crab, *Malus pumila*, is the parent of all cultivated apples. Crab apples are hybrids of this species and bear small fruits, round or conical in shape and golden, red or yellow flushed with pink in colour. They are used to make a delicious jelly.

GROWING Crab apples make compact trees if grown as standards on 1.2-2m/4-6ft stems, the exception being *M. baccata*, which may reach 15m/50ft in height. For best results plant 2 cross-pollinating varieties. They like fertile, well-cultivated slightly acid soils. Plant in autumn, giving the young trees the support of stakes. Cut the main stem back to 15cm/6in above the aimed-for height in early spring. A year later, cut back the resulting 3 or 4 shoots to 30cm/12in. Shoots appearing on the stem below these branches should be pinched back to 3 or 4 leaves. Remove them after 3 or 4 years when the trunk has thickened. Feed with annual mulches of well-rotted compost in mid spring until the tree is established.

HARVESTING Pick the fruits for use as soon as they part easily from the tree. They will stand on the tree for weeks if necessary.

POSSIBLE PROBLEMS Aphids are the most destructive pest. Any of the usual apple diseases may occur.

SWEET CHERRY

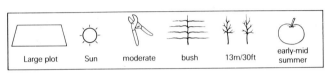

| Large plot | Sun | moderate | bush | 13m/30ft | early-mid summer |

Sweet cherries belong to the same family as the plum. The long-established type F 12/1 makes a very large tree, too big for most domestic gardens. Some gardeners have been successful growing it in a submerged pot to restrict the naturally vigorous growth. Because pollination is tricky it is essential to plant 2 compatible trees.

GROWING Give your cherries the choicest site and the best soil available in terms of depth, drainage and texture. Buy standards of certified virus-free stock with the head already formed and plant in autumn. Stake the young tree, firm in and water well. Apply a thick mulch over the rooting zone. Every spring, work in a top dressing of a general purpose fertilizer. Pruning is only necessary to assist the formation of a full head and to remove diseased or damaged branches in summer.

HARVESTING You will need a tall ladder to reach the whole tree. Ideally, wait until the fruits are completely ripe – in practice you may have to pick a little early to beat the birds. Use immediately. The crop potential from 2 trees is enormous.

POSSIBLE PROBLEMS Blackfly can quickly damage the foliage and the growing points of young shoots. Spray with malathion before the blossoms open. Birds are the worst pest. Fruits split after heavy rains.

■ COOK'S TIP

To make crab apple jelly, wash and quarter 2kg/4¼lb crab apples, put in a saucepan and cover with cold water. Add the rind of two lemons. Bring to the boil then simmer for about 1 hour until the apples are well cooked. Pour into a jelly bag and leave to strain overnight. Add 450g/1lb sugar for every 600ml/1pt juice and place back in a pan. Heat gently, stirring to dissolve the sugar. When the sugar has dissolved, boil fast until setting point is reached, then cool and pour into jars.

■ GARDENER'S TIP

In a small garden, grow sweet cherries against a south-facing wall. If you only want one sweet cherry, Stella is self-fertile, or grow a sweet and a Morello cherry that flower at the same time: so that the Morello can fertilize the sweet cherry.

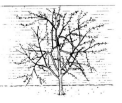

MORELLO CHERRY

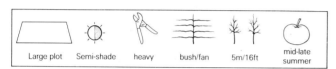

| Large plot | Semi-shade | heavy | bush/fan | 5m/16ft | mid-late summer |

The Morello cherry is a self-fertile tree quite distinct from the demanding sweet cherry – smaller, hardier and with sharper tasting fruits. Hybrids between the Morello and sweet cherries are called Dukes. The term Acid or Sour is used to describe the group as a whole. These cherries can be used to make delicious pies or jam.

GROWING Morellos are easy to grow and will even survive the rigours of a shady wall. Care is still needed when planting: dig over the planting site and incorporate plenty of well-rotted compost, manure or peat. Make a shallow planting hole, drive in a stake and arrange the young tree – a 1-year-old is best – with the roots carefully spread out. Cover with fine soil, firm well and water in. Attach the tree to the stake. Spread a thick layer of moisture-retaining mulch over the rooting area. Prune as for bush apples. Once the tree is established, simply remove crossing branches as well as cutting back to old wood on 3 selected branches annually in late spring to maintain a compact shape. Give copious top dressings of well-rotted manure and keep weeds well under control.

HARVESTING Remove fruits by the stalk when fully ripe.

POSSIBLE PROBLEMS Spray with malathion before blossom to deter blackfly. Birds are a pest. Cut out branches affected with silver leaf.

FIG

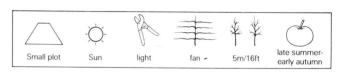

| Small plot | Sun | light | fan | 5m/16ft | late summer-early autumn |

These small, pear-shaped fruits, usually deep purple when ripe, are borne on handsome trees.

GROWING Figs are natives of warm countries. In cool climates they do best trained as fans against a sunny wall, as a bush if the site is sheltered, or in pots in a greenhouse. Well-drained but moisture-retentive soil is essential, and soil that is too rich will encourage the formation of soft shoots that are vulnerable to frost. Restricting the roots helps the tree to maintain its vigour; protected plants do very well in 23-25-cm/9-10-in pots. If grown outside, make a planting hole 1m/3ft deep and line it with bricks, placing drainage material in the base. Mix 250g/8oz sterilized bonemeal with the soil before replacing it. Plant in spring; if training a fan, have the supporting wires in place beforehand. Pruning consists of removing over-strong or misplaced shoots, either as they form or at the end of the summer. Where necessary, tie in young growths for next year's fruiting. Pull off any suckers that develop. Do not let the soil dry out in summer, especially near a wall. Spread a layer of moisture-retaining mulch over the rooting area in spring. Protect the shoots from frost with a wrapping of straw.

HARVESTING Wait until the fruits are fully ripe and soft before picking. The skin is delicate and splits easily.

POSSIBLE PROBLEMS Relatively trouble free.

▓ ORGANIC TIP

Use a codling moth trap hung among your fruit trees to lure male moths on to a sticky base from which they can't escape to breed. The trap lures the male with pheromone, used by the female to attract a mate. One kit protects up to five trees.

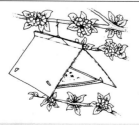

▓ GARDENER'S TIP

A fig tree will bear two crops a year but outdoors in this climate only one of these will ripen and this is the second set of fruits which are pea-sized at the beginning of winter. These overwinter, provided they are not caught by frost, to ripen in the following year. Remove the fruit which form earlier in the year in autumn. Our summer is not long enough for these to ripen. This allows all the plant's energy to go into the young fruit.

BLACK GRAPE

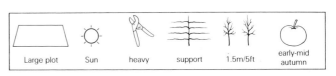

Large plot | Sun | heavy | support | 1.5m/5ft | early-mid autumn

Most of the black grapes which ripen well in cooler climates are best for wine, but Tereshkova is suitable as a table grape.

GROWING Choose a site open to the sun but sheltered from wind: a south-facing wall is ideal. Make windbreaks from netting or hedges if necessary. Any well-drained soil will do, though very heavy clays will need refining with compost or peat. Magnesium deficiency causes yellow veining on older leaves: correct this with agricultural Epsom salts. Put up the supporting posts and wires for the vines before planting. Set 2-m/6-ft posts into the ground 3m/10ft apart. Fix the lowest wire 45cm/18in from the ground. At 22cm/8½in above it set 2 wires 2.5cm/1in apart horizontally, then another double strand 30cm/12in above the second. These 2 wires are separated horizontally by spacer bars 30cm/12in long attached to the posts. Fix a final set of double wires exactly like the third 30cm/12in above it. On this system the branches are carried upwards and outwards, admitting light and air to foliage and fruit. Set out 1-year-old plants in spring, next to the posts, in holes filled with composted vegetation, peat or potting soil. Water well until the vines are rooting freely. Keep them supplied with a balanced fertilizer.

HARVESTING Fruit is borne the second year.

POSSIBLE PROBLEMS High humidity causes mildew.

WHITE GRAPE

Large plot | Sun | heavy | support | 1.5m/5ft | early-mid autumn

The choice of white grape varieties suitable for growing in cooler climates is wider than for black types. For growing, see black grapes.

PRUNING AND TRAINING After planting, cut back each new plant to 2-3 buds. When they start into growth, select the strongest, rubbing out the others, and tie it to the post to grow vertically. At the end of the season, cut back the single canes to 60cm/2ft from the ground. The next year, 3 shoots will emerge close behind the cut. Let them grow upwards, slipping them between the wires at the second level. At the end of the season, tie 2 canes to the bottom wire, one going left and the other right. Cut the middle cane right back to 3 buds from its origin. In year 3 the horizontal canes will bear flowers and fruit on upward growing laterals: secure these to the widely spaced double wires. When the flowers appear, remove weak laterals, leaving the remainder 20cm/8in apart. Stop the fruiting laterals at the top wire. Let the 3 new central growths grow upwards. After the harvest, remove the fruited canes from the bottom wire and replace them with 2 of the new canes. Cut the central cane right back to 3 new buds.

THINNING After fruit set remove some berries from the heart of the bunch with long-bladed scissors.

HARVESTING Remove ripe bunches with scissors.

■ PRESERVING TIP

Try making grape juice wine. After crushing the grapes check the amount of sugar they contain with a hydrometer and decide whether you wish to add extra sugar or not. If you intend adding sugar dissolve this in a little hot water then, cooled,
include with the crushed grapes. Add the yeast, cover and leave to ferment for ten days, stir each day. Squeeze out the pulp, strain the juice and make the wine following a home winemaking book.

■ ORGANIC TIP

Powdery mildew appears as grey powder on leaves and grapes. Downy mildew appears on leaf undersides. Mulching and watering help to prevent both. Spray with a copper fungicide like Bordeaux mixture.

COOKING PEAR

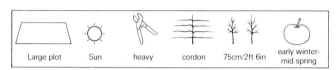

Large plot	Sun	heavy	cordon	75cm/2ft 6in	early winter-mid spring

While all dessert pears can be used for cooking if you wish, there are a few varieties which are used exclusively for this purpose. Stew them slowly in syrup. Ripening as they do in mid winter, cooking pears fill a gap in the gardener's calendar.

GROWING Cooking pears have the same requirements as dessert varieties: a slightly acid, deeply dug soil to which a fertilizer containing magnesium and potash is added before planting. Stake the young tree, taking care not to bury the union between rootstock and variety, and spread a thick layer of a moisture-retaining mulch over the rooting zone. Pears must not be allowed to dry out or to become waterlogged, and can take copious amounts of well-rotted organic manure both before planting and afterwards as mulches. Prune as for apples. In some years, following a frost-free spring, too many fruits may be set: the result will be small fruits and an exhausted tree, so thin in mid summer.

HARVESTING Check regularly to make sure you pick the pears just before they are completely ripe. Use immediately or store healthy fruits only in a cool, moist place until needed.

POSSIBLE PROBLEMS Birds, aphids and wasps are the worst pests. If pear scab is troublesome, spray with captan or benlate before the blossoms open.

DESSERT PEAR

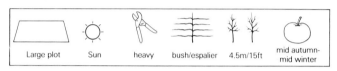

Large plot	Sun	heavy	bush/espalier	4.5m/15ft	mid autumn-mid winter

If pears are grown on Quince A or C rootstock they are compact enough for the average garden. Two open-centre bush trees that will cross-pollinate should be set 3m/10ft apart for best results.

GROWING Pears dislike lime, so shallow chalky soils are unsuitable. Choose the most sheltered site in the garden, while avoiding shade and competition from other trees. Before planting in the autumn, break up the sub-soil and work in large quantities of well-rotted manure or compost. Add a potash and magnesium fertilizer. Make a planting hole, drive in a stake as for an apple tree and arrange the tree with the roots spread out, taking care not to bury the union between rootstock and variety. Cover with fine soil, firm well and water in. Fix the tree to the stake and spread a thick mulch of rotted garden compost or other moisture-retaining material over the rooting zone. The initial pruning of a 3-year-old bush will have been done in the nursery. A 1-year-old will need pruning as for apples.

HARVESTING Pick pears just before they ripen: if the fruits part easily from the branch when lifted to the horizontal, they are ready. Keep in a cool, moist place.

POSSIBLE PROBLEMS Bullfinches eat the buds. Birds and aphids damage shoots. Pear scab is a fungus disease occurring in wet districts.

▨ ORGANIC TIP

Trap wasps before they attack the fruit by making a tasty concoction they can't resist. Half-fill a jar with jam and water or cider, cover the top with paper or polythene in which there is a smallish hole and tie a trap in each tree.

▨ GARDENER'S TIP

Choose the variety Conference if space is limited, as it will set its own pollen. Doyenne du Comice has the finest flavour of all pears. Pears can be trained as cordons, fans and espaliers on walls.

APRICOT

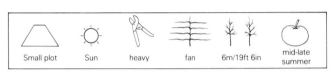

| Small plot | Sun | heavy | fan | 6m/19ft 6in | mid-late summer |

Apricots have been grown since the 16th century and can still be raised successfully even in cooler areas.

GROWING Apricots are best grown trained as fans on a south or west-facing wall. Prepare the ground thoroughly before planting in mid autumn by digging deeply and incorporating plenty of well-rotted organic manure or compost. Fix the supporting wires to the wall in advance, with brackets at the top from which to hang protective netting on frosty nights. Buy young trees on St Julien A rootstock with the framework of branches already formed in the nursery. Dig a shallow planting hole and spread the roots. Cover with fine soil, firm in and water well. Spread a thick mulch over the rooting zone. Fix the ribs on canes to the wires. Pruning is as for a fan-trained peach, except that apricots fruit on spurs as well as on young shoots. If there is space on an established tree you can encourage spurs to form by shortening sideshoots in mid summer. Water regularly in summer and put down a moisture-retaining mulch. Apricots are self-pollinating. If you put netting up at night, remove it by day to let insects in to do their work.

HARVESTING Twist off the fruits when ripe without bruising the flesh. They can be eaten raw or cooked.

POSSIBLE PROBLEMS Frost damage; cut out dead branches and paint the wound.

NECTARINE

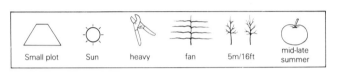

| Small plot | Sun | heavy | fan | 5m/16ft | mid-late summer |

The nectarine is a smooth-skinned peach. It has become very popular, but because it is not as hardy as the true peach should only be grown in warmer districts, preferably fan-trained on a sunny wall.

GROWING Soil should be well drained, deeply dug and moisture retentive. Plant in mid autumn, first working plenty of well-rotted organic material into the soil. Buy a young tree with the basic framework for fan-training already formed in the nursery. Fix the supporting horizontal wires to the wall before planting, and attach brackets at the top to hold a sheet of light hessian or plastic netting, which can be hung in front of – not touching – the tree on frosty nights. Remove the protective fabric by day to admit the light and warmth of the sun as well as pollinating insects. If these are few, use a tuft of cotton wool to speed things up. Nectarines are self-pollinating but flowering early as they do is a disadvantage. For pruning, see fan-trained peaches. Thin the fruits in mid summer to stand 20cm/8in apart. If the crop is too heavy the fruits will be all stone and no flesh, and the tree will be exhausted.

HARVESTING Pick the fruits when the flesh at the stalk yields to light pressure. Hold in the palm, twist off gently.

POSSIBLE PROBLEMS Frost damage; peach leaf curl; aphids; red spider mite.

▨ COOK'S TIP

Ripe fruit are deeper in colour and taste delicious picked from the tree and eaten raw, straight away. They also make a wonderful addition to a lamb or pork casserole. As a pudding poach them in honey syrup flavoured with lemon juice or vanilla. Glazed apricot tart is a favourite on the continent. Add slices of apricot to creamy Greek yogurt plus a little orange juice and some honey. Place in a glass bowl and decorate with chopped almonds.

▨ GARDENER'S TIP

Use a support system of wires and nails to tie branches in to protect them from wind damage. Make up a frame of horizontal wires, about 45cm/18in apart, held stretched taut away from the wall with vine eyes or wall ties.

PEACH

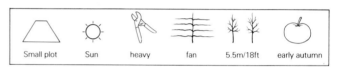

| Large plot | Sun | heavy | bush | 5m/16ft | late summer |

Peaches can be grown successfully in cooler climates in the open as long as you avoid obvious frost pockets or windswept sites. Early flowering exposes peach blossom to frosts; another disadvantage is that fewer insects are around and you may have to assist pollination with a tuft of cotton wool. All varieties, except Hale's Early, are self-pollinating.

GROWING Soil should be deep and well-drained but retentive of summer moisture. A pH level of 6.2 is about right. Buy a 1-year-old tree from a reputable nursery for planting in mid autumn. Incorporate plenty of well-rotted organic compost or manure into the soil. Take out a shallow planting hole, spread the roots out wide and attach the tree to a stake. Cover with fine soil, firm well and water in. Cut the tree back to 60cm/2ft and reduce the branches by two thirds. Apply a moisture-retaining mulch over the rooting zone. Subsequent pruning is as for bush apples, except that each spring it is necessary to prevent established trees from carrying all the fruit at the ends of the branches by cutting 3 chosen branches back to old wood. Water well and give an annual mulch. In heavy-cropping years thin out badly placed and damaged fruits to leave the remainder 20cm/8in apart.

HARVESTING Fruits ripen over a 6-week period.

POSSIBLE PROBLEMS Peach leaf curl; Aphids.

FAN-TRAINED PEACH

| Small plot | Sun | heavy | fan | 5.5m/18ft | early autumn |

The protection of a sunny wall allows you to fan-train late-ripening peaches like Bellegarde.

GROWING Soil should be deep, well drained and moisture retentive. It dries out much quicker near a wall, so water regularly. Buy the tree with the basic framework of branches formed in the nursery and fix the supporting horizontal wires to the wall before planting in mid autumn. Drape protective fabric from brackets in front of the tree on frosty nights and remove it by day. Pruning of an established fan is dictated by the fact that peaches fruit on the previous year's growth. Wood that has fruited does not fruit again and must be cut out at the end of the season, along with any damaged branches, so that a replacement shoot can be tied in. Spring-pruning encourages the production of these shoots. First, rub out any shoots pointing straight out or into the wall. From those remaining, leave healthy shoots at 15cm/6in apart on the ribs and one on the end. These will grow on as laterals. The next spring, growth buds will appear at the base of each lateral. Allow one to grow on as a replacement, and remove the others when they reach 5-7.5cm/2-3in. In the summer the laterals bear fruit – let the tips grow on but pinch out any sideshoots.

HARVESTING Lift off the ripe fruits in the palm of your hand.

POSSIBLE PROBLEMS Blackfly; peach leaf curl.

▌ ORGANIC TIP

A pH tester is an inexpensive and valuable piece of equipment with which to test how acid or alkaline your soil is. Once you know this you can adjust a too-acid soil by adding small amounts of lime in the spring before you sow or plant (not at the same time as manure though). A soil which is chalky and too high in lime needs to be deeply dug and to have lots of manure and compost added to increase the acidity.

▌ GARDENER'S TIP

Protect trees from frost by covering them with hessian. Place canes around the plant to stop the fabric touching the blossoms. Remove covers when temperatures rise to admit pollinating insects.

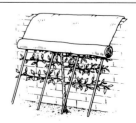

PEACHES UNDER GLASS

Greenhouse	Sun	heavy	fan	5.5m/18ft	late summer

Growing peaches in a glasshouse is a great luxury, since ideally the house should be devoted to the tree. Choose the variety Peregrine, which is dependably self-fertile.

GROWING Peaches grown under glass should be trained in a fan shape. The tree is best planted in a border 60cm/2ft wide and trained up the span on one side of the house. Make sure the roots have a minimum depth of 45cm/18in of well drained loam. The procedures for fan-training (see fan-trained peaches) must be assiduously carried out, and will be necessary at earlier stages of the year thanks to the protected environment. Keep the border well watered, especially in summer, and ventilate the house well during the day. The winter night temperature need not be more than 4C/40F, but not less than 10C/50F in summer. It is essential to hand-pollinate the flowers. As soon as the fruits set, spray the tree lightly every day with clear water to keep the foliage bright and the fruits swelling.

HARVESTING Pick the ripe fruits very gently, lifting them in the palm of the hand.

POSSIBLE PROBLEMS Dryness at the roots is the most important cause of failure. In these conditions glasshouse red spider mite can thrive and cause great damage.

QUINCE

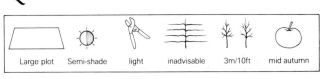

Large plot	Semi-shade	light	inadvisable	3m/10ft	mid autumn

The quince is a handsome tree, bearing flowers like apple blossom in spring. It has yellow pear-shaped fruits that are slightly acid and with a pungent aroma when ripe. They are used for making a delicious golden jelly.

GROWING Quinces need shelter and a certain degree of warmth. In cold districts it is possible to grow them as fans against a sunny wall, but in practice the trees dislike being trained. Unlike other tree fruits, quince – which is self-pollinating – is grown on its own roots, so you do not have to worry about choosing a suitable rootstock. In fact if there is a healthy tree growing in your area, a sturdy sucker can be detached in the winter and easily started into growth. Otherwise, start with a 2-year-old tree and plant in autumn in any fertile soil. Quinces may be planted near water. Give a generous mulch after planting and every subsequent spring until the tree is established. Keep down weeds. Pull off suckers and otherwise prune only to remove diseased, damaged or overcrowded branches.

HARVESTING Leave the fruits on the tree until late autumn. Store in a cool but frost-proof shed and pick over for use as they ripen. Apples and pears kept in store with quinces will inevitably pick up their stronger aroma so it is best to keep them separate.

POSSIBLE PROBLEMS Birds and aphids.

■ ORGANIC TIP

To prune, rub out any shoots pointing straight out. Leave healthy shoots at 15cm/6in apart on the ribs and one on the end to grow on as laterals. The next spring, growth buds will appear at the base of each lateral. Allow one to grow on.

■ ORGANIC TIP

Make delicious quince jelly. Simmer 1.75kg/4lb peeled, cored and chopped quinces in 600ml/1pt water until tender, then pour into a jelly bag. Leave overnight to drain through, add 1 tablespoon lemon juice, and 400g/14oz sugar to every

600ml/1pt liquid. Stir until the sugar dissolves, then boil briskly until setting point is reached.

243

DAMSON

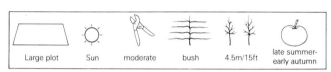

| Large plot | Sun | moderate | bush | 4.5m/15ft | late summer-early autumn |

Related to plums, but smaller and invariably deep purple in colour, damsons are usually used for jam or in preserves.

GROWING While damsons like the fertile, deep and slightly acid soil necessary for plums, they can cope better with heavy rainfall and high wind (particularly the variety Farleigh Damson). Start with a 2 to 3-year-old half-standard tree on St Julien A rootstock. Plant in autumn and double-stake as for cooking plums. Take care not to bury the union between rootstock and variety. Prune as for cooking plums, and remove any suckers that shoot from the base by scraping away the soil and pulling them away: if you cut suckers off they grow back even stronger. In heavy-cropping years, thin the fruits in early summer to take the weight off the branches, leaving the remaining fruits as evenly spaced as possible.

HARVESTING Pick the ripe fruits and make jam or bottle them immediately.

POSSIBLE PROBLEMS Birds, wasps and aphids are the major pests. Inspect for silver leaf: cut off and burn affected branches.

VARIETIES Farleigh Damson (pollinated by Czar or Golden Transparent Gage plums); Merryweather (self-fertile).

GREENGAGE

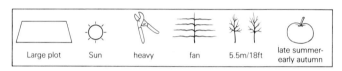

| Large plot | Sun | heavy | fan | 5.5m/18ft | late summer-early autumn |

As greengages are not completely hardy, most are trained as fans against a sunny wall.

GROWING A deeply cultivated, fertile and slightly acid soil is best. Incorporate plenty of well-rotted organic manure before planting in the autumn. If you are planting in the open, stake the young tree as described for cooking plums. For a fan-trained tree, choose St Julien A rootstock. Before planting, fix the supporting horizontal wires to the wall spaced 30cm/12in apart. Start with a 1-year-old tree and prune it back to 60cm/2ft. The 2 buds at the top will produce shoots which will make the first ribs of the fan, one left, one right. In the summer, when they have reached 23-30cm/9-12in, tie the shoots to canes and attach the canes to the wires at an angle of 45°. Follow a system of early spring pruning and summer training, selecting 3 evenly spaced shoots from each rib to start with until over the years you have built up 32 evenly spaced ribs. Always use canes to train the extension growth. They can be removed when the growth is woody. Do not allow any shoots to grow strongly upwards.

HARVESTING Let greengages ripen on the tree as long as possible, then pick them by the stalk to prevent bruising. Use immediately.

POSSIBLE PROBLEMS Bullfinches; aphids.

▥ GARDENER'S TIP

If necessary, thin the damsons when the stones have just formed by pulling off some of the fruit. Repeat if necessary when the fruits have expanded. Leave a final spacing of about 5cm/2in between the fruit.

▥ COOK'S TIP

Make tasty fruit crumble with greengages instead of apples. Stone 675g/1½lb ripe greengages and arrange in an ovenproof dish. Sprinkle with sugar to taste. Rub 75g/3oz butter into 175g/6oz flour until the mixture resembles fine breadcrumbs, then *add 75g/3oz sugar. Sprinkle over the fruit and bake at 200C/400F/gas 6 for 40 minutes. To freeze, leave unbaked and cover with clear film before putting in the freezer.*

COOKING PLUM

Large plot	Sun	moderate	bush/pyramid	4.5m/15ft	late summer-early autumn

Plum varieties, such as Czar and Marjorie's Seedling with a relatively low sugar content are suitable for preserving, jam-making or for use in cooked desserts. The popular Victoria can be used for cooking and for eating raw.

GROWING As long as the soil is fertile and slightly acid, most plums tolerate heavier, wetter (but not waterlogged) conditions than apples or pears. Dig in plenty of well-rotted organic manure, compost or peat before planting in the autumn. Buy a 2 or 3-year-old half standard tree of a self-fertile variety on St Julien A rootstock or on Pixie for a dwarf pyramid. Make a wide, shallow planting hole. Drive in a double stake using 2 posts 2m/6ft 6in long, connected by a 45-cm/18-in crossbar. Spread the roots out wide, cover with soil and firm well in. Do not bury the union between rootstock and variety. Attach the stem to the crossbar, padding it to prevent chafing. Cut back all branches to 60cm/2ft. Prune for the next 2 winters as for apples. Thereafter prune only in summer to remove diseased or crowded branches. Water well and apply a general purpose fertilizer in early spring. Mulch in summer to suppress weeds.

HARVESTING Pick the fruits as soon as ripe and use immediately or freeze. Plums cannot be stored.

POSSIBLE PROBLEMS Silver leaf (see tip). To avoid sharka disease, buy certified virus-free stock.

DESSERT PLUM

Large plot	Sun	heavy	pyramid	2m/6ft 6in	late summer-early autumn

Dessert plums are those which develop a high sugar content and are delicious to eat raw.

GROWING Dessert plums have the same requirements as cooking varieties: a well-cultivated, fertile, slightly acid soil on a site not too exposed. The trees are vulnerable to strong winds since they bear a lot of fruit. Dwarf pyramid trees on Pixie rootstock are useful for small gardens, but must be trained to shape. Give the leader of the newly planted tree a stout 3m/10ft cane for support. In the mid spring after planting, cut the tree back to 1.5m/5ft. Reduce any sideshoots by half, but remove completely any close to the ground, up to 50cm/20in to give a short leg. Toward the end of summer, shorten the ends of the branches, not the central leader, to 20cm/8in, cutting any sideshoots to 10cm/4in. In each case, cut back to a downward pointing bud. Next mid spring, reduce the central leader by two thirds. Repeat the end of summer pruning annually; cut the central leader well back every mid spring until it reaches 3m/10ft. After that, prune the leader every late spring to within 2.5cm/1in of the previous year's cut.

HARVESTING Pick and use as soon as ripe.

POSSIBLE PROBLEMS Silver leaf; aphids; birds.

VARIETIES Early Transparent Gage; Victoria; Severn Cross (all self-fertile).

▓ ORGANIC TIP

Silver leaf gives the leaves a silvery appearance and shoots and branches die back, with a purplish stain produced on the dead wood. The fungus enters through wounds from pruning, so treat large wounds with Trichoderma powder. All dead growth needs to be removed back to 15cm/6in of healthy wood. Inoculate infected trees with Trichoderma pellets. Insert them in 5cm/2in holes in the trunk. Spray aphid-infected trees with insecticidal soap.

▓ DECORATIVE TIP

Some plums do well in pots and can be trained decoratively in a pyramid shape or in a row as single cordons growing at 45 degrees against a wall or fence. Cover plants with netting in the spring to protect the blossoms against frost.

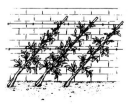

PLANTS FOR INDOORS

Such is the diversity of plants for indoor cultivation that no home need be without the enlivening effect of foliage and flowers. For those who have no space outdoors, growing plants indoors provides an opportunity for frustrated gardeners to practise their creative talents. The joy of indoor gardening is that because the warmer environment of the home makes it possible to nurture species too tender for life outside, even those lucky enough to have conventional flowerbeds will be attracted by the idea of raising more exotic species such as bromeliads, orchids and cacti in the house. There is a houseplant for every situation and to suit every taste: the design element is as important when choosing plants for indoor settings as it is outside, though the criteria may be different. Most important is choosing plants which will be happy and healthy in the environment you can provide.

No matter where they come from, all plants need light, warmth, water and nourishment to survive. In their natural habitat the plants which we cultivate indoors receive exactly what they need in order to thrive; indeed many of them reach very much greater dimensions in the South American jungle or the idyllic climate of South Africa than they do when confined to a pot. When grown indoors, however, it is the gardener's skill in imitating nature which determines how healthy any specimen will be. Every entry in this book includes a set of symbols which briefly summarize a plant's individual needs as far as light, humidity and minimum winter temperature is concerned, but it is

An interesting but restful effect is achieved by grouping together plants with different leaf shapes and habits.

246

useful to understand how these factors act and interact to maintain health. The first step to healthy indoor plants is choosing specimens which have been carefully grown and which are sold in peak condition. An obviously unhealthy plant will have yellowing leaves which may be drooping or suffering from drought; but some plants which look healthy enough may, once you get them home, go into a decline from which they never recover. This is most likely to happen in winter with foliage plants which are displayed outside the shop or on a market stall within a short time of leaving the automatically controlled atmosphere of a heated commercial greenhouse. If you want to buy houseplants in winter, buy them from shops which are kept warm and where they are stored away from draughts. Check that the compost is nicely moist. Choose tough plants like ivy, sansevieria or fatsia rather than the fussier kinds like codiaeum, maranta or tropical palms. Minimize their exposure to cold on the way home; keep them well wrapped and do not carry them around while you do more shopping. Put them in the car instead or take them home straight away. Repotting should not be necessary, but if you want to set a group of plants in a single container, wait for two or three weeks to let them become acclimatized to their new environment.

CHOOSING PLANTS

Plants admired for the beauty of their foliage look very tempting displayed in the shop or garden centre, but it can be disappointing to get your purchase home and discover too late that you cannot meet its particular needs. The chart on page 249 gives a guide to the plants which thrive in particular situations. Check before making your choice. Names in bold type need a humid atmosphere.

Hallways present particular problems for plants, especially if they are unheated, because of the inevitable draughts. Despite the unfavourable circumstances, fatshedera, fatsia, hedera and tolmeia will be happy enough as long as the light is good. Hedera and tolmeia can even cope with poor light (and if your hall is cold and dark, you will be glad of plants to cheer it up). Ideally, assess the kind of environment each room has to offer *before* going to the garden centre and choose plants to suit them.

CARE OF PLANTS

Looking at a garden through the seasons, it is easy to see that plants have a life cycle. The vast majority start into growth in spring, growing rapidly in the warmth and sunshine of summer, fading in autumn and resting and recuperating during the winter. Though the stages are not so clear, most indoor plants have a similar life cycle. The exceptions are those which are forced to flower in winter, or annuals which complete the cycle in one year and are then discarded. The resting period is important, allowing the plant time to build up its strength for the next season. Requirements for water and food diminish during dormancy. The amount and intensity of light is naturally less during the winter; this may suit the plant, or it may be necessary to reposition it to meet its needs.

Water More houseplants have met a premature end through an excess of water – or from drought – than any other causes. Plants like cyperus, which like to 'have their feet in water', are exceptional. Most will not survive if the compost is so waterlogged that air cannot get to the roots. If any water is left in the plant saucer 30 minutes after watering, tip it away. While giving to each plant according to its needs as described in the relevant entry, do not water without testing the compost first. Though it looks dry on the surface, it may be sufficiently moist beneath. Insert a small stick into the compost; if it comes out sticky, water is not needed. Clay pots make a dull sound when tapped if the compost is damp.

Different types of plants vary dramatically in their need for water, from cacti, fitted for life in the arid desert, to marsh plants like the acorus. The immediate environment also has an important effect. In hot, dry weather or in heated rooms, moisture evaporates from the potting mixture and much is lost through transpiration from the leaves. When it is cool, moisture is retained for much longer. Most important, plants need much more water during the period of active growth than when resting, when very little indeed may be enough – as always, depending on the individual.

To apply water, use a light watering can with a long, narrow spout so that you can aim the flow directly on to the potting mixture without wetting leaves or flowers. Some plants, such as cyclamen, must be watered

TOOLS AND EQUIPMENT

Pots, pot saucers and composts are obvious essentials. Keep two mist-sprays, one for water and one for insecticides/fungicides. A watering can is much the best way to apply water.

1. Clay pots (various sizes)
2. Clay half pots
3. Plastic pots (various sizes)
4. Plant saucers
5. Bags of soil-based, peat-based and seed composts.
6. Two mist-sprays
7. Watering can with thin spout
8. Liquid fertilizer
9. Small natural sponges
10. Mini-trowel and fork
11. Bamboo canes
12. Fine stakes
13. Trellis frame
14. Moss-covered stake (in pot)
15. Secateurs
16. Twine
17. Plant ties (metal rings)
18. Hygrometer
19. Maximum-minimum thermometer
20. Seed trays and pans.

from below as the tuber should never get wet. Others may be so bushy that the surface of the compost is inaccessible. In these cases place water in the saucer. The plant will take up what it needs within 30 minutes. After this period, empty the saucer.

Remember that a large pot will dry out more quickly than a small one as a greater surface area is exposed to the air; evaporation is faster from an unglazed clay pot than a glazed or plastic one, and growing mixtures containing sand, grit or perlite encourage fast drainage.

To revive a parched plant, first carefully break up the surface of the compost with a small fork, without damaging the roots. Plunge the pot in a bucket of water, holding it until bubbles stop rising. Spray the leaves with a fine mist at the same time. Let the excess water drain away and replace the plant in a suitable position. If the problem soon recurs, try repotting with fresh mixture.

Humidity Water vapour present in the air – the humidity level – is not related to how moist the potting mixture is. Nor is it easy to judge: the only time you can *see* water vapour is in mist or fog. Nevertheless, it can be measured by an instrument called a hygrometer, and many indoor gardeners use one (in conjunction with a thermometer) to ensure that humidity levels are correct. A reading of about 60 per cent suits most plants, but generally speaking those with thin, papery leaves like fittonias need more. All plants need increased humidity in higher temperatures. The simplest way to provide this is to stand the pot in a shallow tray holding a layer of pebbles at least 5cm/2in deep (up to 15cm/6in for very large pots). Pour in water without letting the water level rise higher than the pebbles (otherwise it may be absorbed by the potting mixture), and keep them moist. It is a good idea to group plants that need high humidity together, as they trap water vapour between the leaves and benefit each other. Hanging baskets often have built-in drip trays which can be used to hold water *below* the pot, so that water vapour rises around the leaves. It also helps to stand the pot containing the plant in another, larger pot containing peat kept constantly damp.

Feeding Regular feeding with a liquid fertilizer can make a tremendous difference to the health of houseplants. Most need feeding during the active period of growth (usually spring and summer), with little or none in the dormant period. Allowing unused nutrients to remain in the compost can lead to an accumulation of harmful salts. If you have been regularly feeding a plant which has not put on much growth, flush the pot out with water at the next two waterings and do not resume feeding until the plant shows signs of growth. After repotting, it is best not to feed for two or three months as the roots could be damaged.

Liquid fertilizers are useful as you can feed and water your plants at the same time. Top dressings are also available, which are sprinkled on to the surface of the compost. Sticks and tablets which are pushed into the compost last between four and eight weeks. As a plant can only make use of nutrients if they are dissolved in water, you must remember to water them regularly.

How much growth plants make depends directly on how much light they get. A pelargonium on a sunny windowsill might well appreciate a weekly feed, but if sited away from the window a feed every two weeks would be enough. Cacti, succulents, bromeliads, ferns and some palms need less feeding than the majority of plants. Having said that, plants in large pots need more feeding, and mature palms may well be in large pots.

Do not feed a plant just because it looks poorly; it may be in the wrong potting mixture, in the wrong situation, waterlogged or parched, so check these points first. And do not exceed the recommended dose: an overconcentration of fertilizers may well damage the roots. Foliar feeds made up to the correct strength and sprayed on to the leaves are useful as a quick pick-me-up when routine feeding has been neglected.

Temperature While it is true that all plants need a certain degree of warmth, the relationship between temperature and the amount of available light, water and humidity cannot be overemphasized. In higher temperatures, increased amounts of water and lighting levels are essential. The minimum temperature which individual plants tolerate is variable. In winter, poor light means slow or zero growth, for which low temperatures are needed (and, in nature, given). This is the important rest period in which many plants build up their strength for the summer. Tender plants which cannot tolerate temperatures lower than 16°C/61°F need correspondingly moderate, not poor, light at this time.

Constancy of temperature at all times of year is important: while a drop of several degrees at night is natural, dramatic fluctuations during the day are harmful. This is why plants should not be positioned in a draught, and why windowsills are not always the best place. Intense heat can be generated through glass, which quickly changes to relative chill when the window is opened.

Many houseplants are of tropical origin and thrive in hot summers, but those from temperate zones such as fatshedera will not be happy. They need a cool and airy position, as do many flowering plants.

Light Plants such as cacti can tolerate many hours of direct sunlight. Palms need bright but filtered light, with only a few hours of direct sunlight every day. In nature, ferns are sheltered from direct sunlight by the foliage of the trees under which they grow. Flower production depends on adequate bright light. Different plants obviously have varying needs, and the wise indoor gardener will identify them. Meeting them will be easier with some understanding of the effects of direct light. For example, an unobstructed sunny

TEMPERATURE CHECK CHART

	18–24°C/ 64–75°F	13–18°C/ 55–64°F	7–13°C/ 45–55°F
BRIGHT, INDIRECT LIGHT			
Adiantum	X		
Aphelandra	X		
Asplenium	X	X	
Begonia rex	X		
Caladium	X		
Calathea	X		
Chamaedorea		X	X
Chlorophytum		X	X
Cissus	X	X	
Cocos		X	X
Codiaeum	X		
Cyperus	X	X	X
Dracaena	X	X	
Dizygotheca	X		
Ficus benjamina			
Ficus elastica		X	X
Ficus pumila			
Hedera		X	X
Howea		X	
Hypoestes		X	
Maranta			
Nephrolepis	X	X	
Pellaea		X	
Peperomia		X	
Philodendron	X	X	
Pilea	X	X	
Pteris	X	X	
Sansevieria	X	X	X
Scindapsus	X	X	
Tolmeia			X
Tradescantia		X	X
Yucca		X	X
POOR LIGHT			
Adiantum	X		
Cissus	X	X	
Cyperus	X	X	X
Hedera		X	X
Maranta	X		
Nephrolepis	X	X	
Philodendron	X	X	
Scindapsus	X	X	
Tolmeia			X
SUNNY POSITION			
Cacti	X		
Cyperus	X	X	X
Hedera		X	X
Hypoestes		X	
Peperomia		X	
Pilea	X	X	
Sansevieria	X	X	X
Succulents			X
Tolmeia			X
Tradescantia		X	X
Yucca		X	X

This pretty bamboo plant gently brings some outdoor qualities indoors to great effect.

window will admit direct sunlight for most of the day. It can be filtered, if necessary, by a fine blind or curtain, or if there is a leafy tree outside. The light at a short distance from the window will still be bright. At a distance of about 2.4m/8ft the light could be called moderate. The areas to the side of even a brightly lit window receive much less light than you might think.

Poor light in dark corners or by obstructed windows is insufficient for most plants. One solution is artificial lighting. Ordinary light bulbs will not do, as they generate too much heat and scorch the leaves. They may be used at reasonable distances to emphasize an arrangement for decorative purposes, but have no practical value. Suitable artificial lighting systems include mercury blended lamps, which are rather expensive to run, but the best choice is fluorescent tubes, available in a wide range of shapes and sizes.

Versions of high pressure mercury lamps and metal halide lamps, widely used by commercial growers, are available from specialist outlets.

It is advisable to place plants against a white or light background, where a certain amount of available light will be reflected back on to them. Plants next to dark walls will grow towards a source of light much more markedly than those next to pale walls, giving a lop-sided appearance. To help even growth, give plants a quarter turn every two weeks or so. Do not turn a flowering plant that is already in bud as the sudden change in light levels may cause the buds to drop off. Stiff-leaved species and rosette-forming kinds do not turn to the light in this way.

Plant hygiene Plants not only look better when kept clean, but are likely to be healthier. Sponging with tepid water removes mites, insects and their eggs along with the dust which prevents light getting to the foliage. Palm fronds can be cleansed more easily by standing the plant outside in a gentle summer shower.

Support systems Climbing plants, which if left to themselves would become a messy, unhealthy jumble of stems, need to be trained up bamboo canes, trellis-work frames or a moss-covered stake. Whatever system is appropriate, it should be as inconspicuous as possible. If necessary, tie young growths in loosely using twine or fine metal rings. Put the stakes in position when repotting, taking care not to damage the roots. The moss on stakes for philodendrons and other plants with aerial roots must always be moist. Test with the fingertips and mist-spray when necessary.

Holiday care You cannot expect your houseplants to survive two or more weeks' neglect without suffering to some extent. Ask a friend or neighbour to take care of them while you are away, making the task easier if possible by grouping the plants together and leaving watering can and liquid feed ready to hand. If no such help is forthcoming, a few simple strategies will stave off disaster. Move plants out of direct sunlight. To conserve moisture, first remove all flowers and flower-buds, if any. Water the plants well and cover each one with a polythene bag. Blow it up first so that it will not touch the leaves and keep it in place with a rubber band. Alternatively, put all the pots in boxes, packed round with moist peat. Another simple watering system works by capillary action. Fill a bucket with water and position the potted plants around it. Tie a weight to one end of a 2.5cm/1in lamp wick (you will need one for each plant) and drop it in the water. Insert the other end of the wick into the compost of a pot. It is as well to try this system out for a week or so *before* going away to make sure water is getting to the plants and not on your furniture. For prize specimens it may be worth investing in self-watering pots. These contain a reservoir of water in the base which will usually keep the plants going for up to four weeks.

Pruning 'Pruning' conjures up images of wrestling with tangled rose bushes rather than any task associated with potted plants. But houseplants do need cutting to shape sometimes, or even cutting down to

WHAT CAN GO WRONG?

Pests and diseases afflict many plants but most problems that arise are caused by over- or underwatering, too low humidity, poor light and other cultural deficiencies, as described below. If the symptoms are not too far developed, plants generally recover when ideal conditions are restored.

SYMPTOMS	CAUSE
Lower leaves limp and yellowing. Flower drop. Soggy soil.	Overwatering
Leaves and stem wilting. Brown leaf tips. New leaves fail to develop.	Underwatering
Brown leaf edges, leaf drop.	Dry atmosphere
Lower leaves dry up, flowers fade quickly.	Overheating
Previously healthy plant drops leaves, which turn yellow.	Sudden change in environment
Long spindly stems reaching for light. New leaves too small. Variegated plants lose colouring.	Poor light
Leaves spotted brown, turning crisp.	Light too bright
Fast but feeble growth, white deposit on surface of compost.	Overfeeding
Failure to grow. Poor leaf colour. New leaves too small.	Underfeeding
Roots bulging through drainage holes and rising at surface of compost. Poor growth.	Needs repotting

size. The most frequently employed form of pruning is pinching out, that is removing the small growing point of a stem in order to produce bushy growth. It is important for tradescantias, coleus and beloperone, for example, which would otherwise become spindly. Pinching out can often be done with finger and thumb, but on tougher stems sharp scissors are more effective.

Cutting back is the term used when the main stem or a mature sideshoot (rather than the growing tip) has to be shortened to keep the plant size in reasonable bounds, as in reducing a ceiling-height *Ficus elastica* (rubber plant). Use pruning secateurs to make a clean cut, straight across the stem, as close to a growth bud as possible. Cutting back the main stem encourages sideshoots and vice versa.

Potting mixtures A number of reliable composts are commercially available, made up in different formulas to meet the needs of different plants at different stages of development. While exotic plants like orchids have very particular requirements, most are reasonably easy-going. This is not to say they would be happy in a potful of garden soil of questionable quality and probably carrying weed seeds, pests and diseases.

Soil-based mixtures are relatively heavy, an advantage for top-heavy plants, and they contain certain nutrients. Peat-based mixtures are light and easy to work with but are quite lacking in nutrients, so regular plant feeding is essential. When raising plants from seed, always start off with a good quality proprietary seed compost.

To top-dress a plant which is in the largest pot size you have room for, scrape away the top layer of old compost with a small trowel, taking care not to damage the roots or to expose too many of them. Fill up the pot with fresh compost to which some slow-release fertilizer has been added. Add enough compost to reach the previous level. Top-dressing should be done at the time when repotting would normally be carried out.

When potting on, prepare a pot or other container by placing crocks and moist compost on the base. Ensure that the compost of the plant to be moved is moist all the way through. Remove the plant from its existing pot by pulling the fingers of one hand across the compost surface, turning it upside down with the other hand and gently tapping the rim on a work surface. The plant will slide out. Cut back any long roots, place in the new container and fill compost around the sides firming with your fingers.

PROPAGATION

While some houseplants can only be successfully raised from seed in specialist nurseries, a number can easily be grown at home by various methods. Raising your own plants is one of the most creative aspects of gardening, indoors or out, and can save money too. The most common forms of propagation are described below.

SOWING SEED

Browallias, cinerarias, exacums, impatiens, pelargoniums and primulas can be raised from seed. Most are sown in early spring, but variations are given in individual entries.

Fill a seed tray with most seed compost and press it down evenly and firmly. Place the seeds on top, evenly spaced. Cover with 5mm/$\frac{1}{4}$in of sifted compost (unless the seeds are very fine) and water in gently until the compost is thoroughly wet (Fig 1a). Cover with a sheet of glass or polythene and place in a heated frame or propagator; or cover with a plastic bag and place in a warm place away from light, such as an airing cupboard (Fig 1b). Check daily for moisture on the inside of the bag, and flick it off. As soon as the seed leaves appear, remove the cover and move to a protected position in the light. When the true leaves appear the seedlings can be pricked off into trays or 7.5cm/3in pots of potting compost (Fig 1c). Prepare planting holes with a pencil, spacing them 4cm/$1\frac{1}{2}$ in apart. Carefully remove a small clump of seedlings with a plastic plant tag or similar tool, holding them by the leaves, never the roots. Separate them gently and lower them one by one into the planting holes. Use a pencil to firm the compost around each one. Water in using a fine rose watering can. Place the tray in a cold frame or on a windowsill away from direct sunlight for two or three days, then move into a sunlit position. Keep the compost moist. Gradually expose the seedlings to the environment they will occupy as mature plants. Transfer to pots of the standard growing mixture when well established.

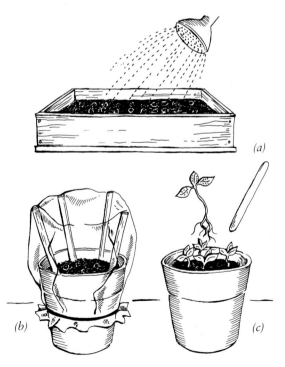

(a)

(b)   *(c)*

Fig 1 Sowing seed and pricking out.

Tip cuttings Many plants can be increased by tip cuttings, notably impatiens, tradescantia and zebrina, which have hollow stems, as well as all the ivies (hedera species).

Using a sharp blade, take 7.5cm/3in cuttings (or as given in individual entries) at the recommended time (Fig 2a). Remove the lower leaves and trim the stem just below a leaf node (Fig 2b). Stand the cutting in a small container of water (Fig 2c). When roots have appeared, about two weeks later, pot up the cutting in standard compost.

For plants without hollow stems, root the cuttings directly in small pots containing a mixture of peat and sand in equal quantities, or a proprietary potting compost. Make 4-6 holes around the edge of the pot with a small dibber or pencil. Insert each cutting so that the stem is supported by the edge of the pot (Fig 2d). Soak the compost with water and let the excess drain away (Fig 2e). Enclose the pot in a polythene bag, blown up so that it does not touch the leaves, and secure with a rubber band (Fig 2f). Leave in the shade at a steady 18°C/64°F. Keep the compost moist. The tips will show new growth when the cuttings have rooted, about four weeks later. Separate the cuttings carefully and pot them up individually in the standard compost. Gradually acclimatize them to the conditions recommended for mature plants.

Leaf cuttings To increase your stock of saintpaulias, sinningias and other fleshy-leaved plants, take leaf cuttings in summer.

Remove two or three healthy leaves, each with about 5cm/2in length of stalk, and trim the end with a sharp knife. Insert in evenly spaced holes made in small pots containing peat and sand in equal quantities or a proprietary potting compost. The stalks should fit neatly in the holes when gently firmed in, but the leaves must stand clear of the compost. Treat as tip cuttings, watching out for any excess condensation on the inside of the polythene bag. The appearance of tiny new leaves within four or five weeks indicates that rooting has occurred. Separate the cuttings carefully and pot them up individually in the standard compost. Keep warm and shaded for a further four weeks before treating as mature plants.

Numerous new *Begonia rex* plants can be raised from a single leaf by a fascinating method. In summer, select a large healthy leaf and cut it cleanly from the parent plant (Fig 3a). Trim the stem to 1cm/½in. Make

Fig 2 Tip cuttings.

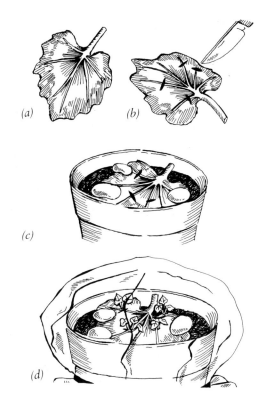

Fig 3 Leaf cuttings.

small cuts on the underside of the leaf where the main veins meet (Fig 3b). Place the whole leaf cut side down on a seed tray containing moistened potting compost, and anchor it with a few pieces of broken clay pot or clean pebbles (Fig 3c). Cover with polythene and keep at 21°C/70°F. Tiny plantlets will arise from the cuts within four to five weeks (Fig 3d). Remove the polythene and keep warm and shaded for a further two or three weeks before potting up in 7.5cm/3in pots.

It is also easy to increase sansevierias from leaf cuttings. Take a single leaf from a mature plant, cutting it away at the base with a sharp blade. Cut the leaf into horizontal sections, each about 2.5cm/1in deep. Place the sections four to a 12.5cm/5in pot of moist potting compost, making sure the lower end is set downwards. Give them a mist-spray and cover the pot with a polythene bag secured with a rubber band. Keep shaded at 21°C/70°F. New leaves will emerge from the base of each section within six to eight weeks. Remove the polythene and pot up in 7.5cm/3in pots.

Offsets Many different types of plants produce offsets or suckers at the base. Once these infants have achieved about half the height of the parent plant they can be detached and potted up individually. Summer is the best time to do this. Remove the whole plant from its pot, carefully shake off the soil from the root ball and separate out the rooted offset(s). If the parent plant is exhausted you may decide to discard it, or it may be well worth repotting. Fill small pots with compost to the three-quarter mark. Insert a thin bamboo stake if the offset is likely to need support. To pot up a single offset, hold it in the pot with the crown 1cm/2in below the rim, and with your other hand trickle compost around it until the pot is full; firm it down and water well, letting the excess drain away.

Division Splitting a mature plant into sections is an easy method of propagation used for chlorophytum, aspidistra, fittonia, sansevieria and adiantum, plants which all have numerous stems arising from beneath the surface of the compost. It can be done at any time during the period of active growth. Remove the plant from its pot and use your fingers to ease away the compost so that you can see the best places to divide the roots. It is usually possible to tear them apart, but occasionally a sharp knife is needed if the roots are

tough. Repot each section immediately in the standard compost, firming them in well. Water sparingly and keep warm and shaded until well established.

AIR LAYERING

This specialized method of propagation, appropriate to *Ficus benjamina* (weeping fig) and *F. elastica* (rubber plant) as well as dizygotheca, will appeal to the more experienced gardener. It should be done in spring. Make a length of stem bare of leaves by removing those within 23cm/9in of the topmost cluster (Fig 4a). Cut them off cleanly, flush with the stem. Make a slanting upward cut 5cm/2in long just below a leaf node (Fig 4b). Ease it open and brush with hormone rooting powder. Place a polythene tube around the cut, attaching it securely to the stem with tape. Fill the bag with moistened sphagnum moss (Fig 4c and d). Close the bag at the top with more tape. Roots should issue from the cut within ten weeks. Detach the rooted plant by cutting it from the parent just below the bag (the old plant will produce sideshoots and can be kept if it still looks good). Pot up in the standard compost and keep warm, shaded and just moist until well established (Fig 4e).

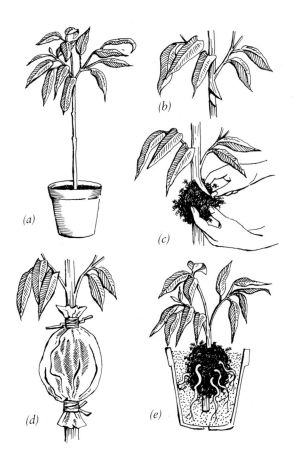

Fig 4 Air layering Ficus benjamina, F. elastica *and dizygotheca.*

A pair of healthy yuccas flanking a doorway add a mediterranean feel to an interior.

DESIGNING WITH HOUSEPLANTS

Every room in the house can be enhanced by plants, though some are better suited to certain situations. While the entrance hall is a place which should be welcoming it is often distinctly inhospitable for plants. A well-lit, airy hall offers scope for flowering plants that prefer cooler temperatures, such as cineraria and calceolaria. A bowl of spring bulbs would add colour – and scent too, if you include hyacinths. Space is likely to be limited, so avoid spreading or trailing foliage that may be damaged. A pedestal may provide the answer, supporting a decorative container with an arching fern or aspidistra. A stairwell lit from above by a skylight can be filled with hanging baskets or a shelf of trailing plants such as hedera, tradescantia or *Ficus pumila*. On the staircase itself, if space permits, the climber *Philodendron scandens* can be sited to great effect. As the amount and direction of light in most halls is problematic, it may well be worth installing an artificial lighting system to increase the range of possibilities.

In the kitchen Kitchens are popular spots for indoor plants; in a traditional, country-style room they fit per-

fectly with the warmth of wooden surfaces on which collections of favourite china sit beside bowls of fruit and piles of cookery books. In modern, clinical kitchens, plants are the perfect way to soften hard angles and straight lines, to offset the glint of chrome and glass with harmonious greens in arching forms. The problem with many kitchens is the likely fluctuation in temperature. In basically functional rooms, play safe with chlorophytum, tradescantia, chamaedorea and the tougher ferns. In rooms used by a family all day – and therefore kept steadily warm – add an asplenium, some pileas and peperomia. Gas fumes can only be tolerated by an aspidistra, and even that will need ventilation. Situate plants where they will not be disturbed. Hanging baskets are ideal, leaving surfaces clear, and shelves are suitable, as long as you can reach them easily enough to care for the plants. A small sunny window fitted with glass shelves is the ideal home for a group of succulents, their distinctive shapes outlined against the light.

In the bathroom Temperature and humidity levels fluctuate more dramatically in the bathroom than any other room. This limits the choice of plants that will do well – the warmth and humidity created by a steamy bath is great for exotics as long as it lasts, but for the rest of the time the room may be rather chilly, as windows are opened to release the steam. Ivies (hedera species) do well in colder rooms, but if a heated towel rail or small radiator keeps the temperature at a higher level, include philodendron and try a calathea. An all-white bathroom with mirrors and natural light will be good news for plants, and in aesthetic terms the perfect setting for fresh green ferns cascading over the sides of their containers. The leaves of all plants will need frequent cleaning if talcum powder and aerosol sprays are used. Plants may need an occasional break from the bathroom: move them to a steadier environment for a while.

In the bedroom People rarely choose to make a display of houseplants in the bedroom, but it is probably the room best suited to this purpose. The temperature is steady, and likely to be on the cool side, with correspondingly healthy levels of humidity. Perhaps setting out a fine display of foliage and flowering plants in the bedroom will encourage you to spend more time in it.

If the light is good, a yucca will do well, as will the reliable aspidistra. *Cissus antartica* needs a little more warmth, hederas will thrive, and many flowering plants do very well. Complement a blue colour scheme with streptocarpus, hydrangea or campanula. Add bright pink with cyclamen and azalea; if there is a sunny window, introduce pelargoniums. In winter, the bedroom is an excellent home for resting plants.

In the living room The design of the living room inevitably merits a good deal of attention as the busiest room in the house and the most likely to be seen by visitors. The contribution made by foliage and flowers can and should be much greater than the odd potted plant on a side table. Houseplants can completely change a room's ambience, becoming a permanent feature in the overall design in a way that bunches of cut flowers cannot do. Some might choose bold, eyecatching plants like *Ficus elastica* or a large-leaved philodendron, a yucca or magnificent palm. Exotic bromeliads are at home in modern settings, and are always a talking point. Ferns are the most versatile plants, their delicacy and grace inviting a sense of peace and blending with light, spare rooms as well as

cosy, homely interiors. They bring a note of calm to colourful, busy rooms, as do *Ficus benjamina*, cyperus, cissus and the elegant spathiphyllum. Low-growing plants such as fittonia, saintpaulia, *Ficus pumila*, tolmeia, schlumbergera and the pileas are beautiful viewed from above if set on a low table. Groups of plants playing on a variety of leaf shape and colour, some bushy, some upright and with different heights look stunning, and are the best way of adding interest to dull (not dark) corners. Plants with similar needs can be set in a single pot; another way to unify different species is to place all in similar containers – a row of identical pots, whether shining white or decorated in Mediterranean colours, looks disciplined but pleasing to the eye.

The constraints of light, temperature and humidity apply here as elsewhere in the house: advantages are that living rooms are generally kept reasonably and steadily warm and free of draughts. An atmosphere polluted by cigarette smoke is as unhealthy for plants as it is for humans – if this is a problem ensure adequate ventilation or move plants to a cleaner environment for a while.

In mid-winter bowlfuls of cyclamen add a cheering note of colour.

PESTS AND DISEASES

PEST	SYMPTOMS	REMEDY
Aphids (greenfly)	Suck the sap from leaves and stems, which become discoloured, distorted and stunted.	Remove by hand or spray with malathion if infestation is severe.
Tarsonemid mite	Outer leaves curl up, stems rot, flowers and buds wither.	Remove damaged foliage straight away in attempt to save plant. No effective chemicals available.
Red spider mite	Spin webs on the underside of leaves, but are difficult to see with the naked eye. Suck the sap from leaves, which become mottled and pale. Plants may die.	Maintain correct humidity and watering levels. Isolate infected plants and spray with malathion.
Scale insects	Live on underside of leaves, sucking the sap and weakening the plant. They excrete a sticky substance.	Scrape off insects, wash the plant with clear water and spray with malathion.
Whitefly	Pale green scales of young whitefly suck sap and produce sticky substance which weakens and distorts plants. Adult whitefly fly off when plant is touched.	Remove worst affected leaves, wash plant with clear water and spray with malathion.
Mealy bugs	Lives on underside of leaves. Young look like small flattened pale brown discs, adults are protected by a cottonwool-like fluff. Worst on necks of bulbs. Plants turn yellow and become deformed.	Scrape off with sharp blade. Wash plant with methylated spirits. Spray with malathion. **NB** malathion is not recommended for use on ferns or pileas. Use derris powder instead.

DISEASES	SYMPTOMS	REMEDY
Grey mould (botrytis)	Grey furry covering on leaves, stems and other parts. Infected parts rot and fall off, and the disease spreads rapidly if conditions are too cool and moist.	Improve cultural conditions, remove affected plants, and spray with a systemic fungicide.
Mildew	Patches of white powder, usually on leaves and stems, sometimes on flowers. Begonias are particularly susceptible if dry at the roots when the atmosphere is moist and warm.	Remove affected tissue and spray with benomyl.
Sooty mould	Black patches on leaves and stems which have been damaged by sticky excretions of pests.	Sponge leaves clean with tepid water. Deal with the insects.
Azalea gall	Fungus causing thickening of the leaves, which are covered with a whitish bloom.	Remove affected parts by hand as soon as seen.
Root rot	Waterlogged soil causes fungal decay. Leaves wilt and plant may quickly die.	Remove affected roots if possible.
Leaf spot	Damp conditions cause fungal decay. Small brown spots appear which soon cover all leaf surface.	Remove affected parts. Spray with benomyl.
Basal rot	Whole plant wilts, due to overwatering, poor ventilation, excessively high temperatures.	Remove affected part if possible, otherwise discard plant.

A KEY TO THE SYMBOLS USED IN THE INDIVIDUAL INDOOR PLANT ENTRIES APPEARS ON PAGE 7

FOLIAGE PLANTS

When early improvements in domestic heating made it possible to grow tender plants indoors, foliage plants (including palms and ferns) were the first to be used to decorate the garden rooms and conservatories of the privileged in the Victorian era. With characteristic zeal plant-gatherers sought as much variety and rarity as they could; by the end of the Edwardian age any conservatory worthy of the name was full to bursting. Social and economic changes may have swept all that away, but we still have the vast choice of plants at our disposal, beautifying and enlivening our homes and workplaces.

SHAPE AND FORM

Where once sheer quantity was the aim, now – for practical reasons as well as matters of taste – foliage plants are chosen for their individual qualities or for their effect in judiciously placed small groups. A pretty tiled fireplace made redundant by central heating, a broad landing lit by a skylight, a deep windowsill with a dull aspect: all are vacant spots which can be transformed by an arrangement of foliage plants.

A wide variety of leaf forms create a jungle effect in a conservatory.

When planning a foliage group, take into account how much individual species differ in shape, size and the texture of their leaves. They may be sword-shaped like chlorophytum; lobed like a fatshedera, oval like a maranta, circular like a saxifrage – there are many more variations. The leaves of a fatsia are huge and glossy; those of the fittonia tiny and soft.

COLOUR

A challenge comes with blending colours, too. Not all foliage plants are green, and those that are display a brilliant range of shades. Compare the fresh apple green of the plectranthus with the deep green of a healthy *Ficus elastica*. A group made up of peperomia species will offer greens of every hue, leaves of numerous shapes, some smooth and some deeply corrugated. Variegated leaves are those which are marked with a colour other than green, often white, cream, pink, silver or gold. It may be evident as a stripe, as in chlorophytum, for example; as an edging to the leaf, as in *Peperomia magnoliifolia* 'Variegata' or as irregular blotches, as in *Scindapsus aureus*. Hypoestes leaves are spotted pale pink; in fittonias the leaf veins take colour, either pink or cream. Beautiful colours and markings are seen on the leaves of the varieties of *Maranta leuconeura* and its relatives ctenanthe and calathea. In *Calathea picturata* 'Argentea' almost the whole leaf area is silver, with green just at the edges. Perhaps the most spectacular variegations are to be seen on the huge leaves of *Begonia rex* hybrids, splashed and banded variously red, purple, pink, silver and shades of green. They are rivalled by the caladium; its heart-shaped leaves, up to 37cm/15in long, may be entirely white, lightly veined green, or green splashed with vivid pink. There are a handful of plants which have completely abandoned all thought of green, such as *Iresine herbstii*, a startling red, and *Setcreasea purpurea,* rich purple. In a mixed group one of these two would make a good focal point. Some might find the colours too strong without a background of green, but if your taste is for the unusual, why not?

GROUPING PLANTS FOR INTEREST

A successful indoor planting scheme takes into account the same design principles applied to a herbaceous border: plants for height at the back, bushy medium-size specimens in the centre and miniatures or trailers at the front. A line of erect growers would look too formal, while trailers all together (unless in a hanging basket) might look doleful. For height choose climbers, such as *Cissus rhombifolia* or *Philodendron scandens.* The choice of middle height plants is huge and includes toleima, pilea, peperomia, hypoestes and maranta. *Ficus pumila* is one of the prettiest trailers. Others are *Peperomia scandens, Saxifraga stolonifera,* plectranthus and that popular pair, tradescantia and zebrina (as well as their colourful cousin, the aforementioned setcreasea). All of these are excellent for hanging baskets.

If you have space for several hanging baskets, do not feel they all have to be at the same level. Try varying the length of the strings to make a composite display of different plants. This idea works well with plants of different sizes – for example *Philodendron bipinnatifidum,* at 90cm/3ft high, and some of the larger ferns. Check that your ceiling joists will take the weight of several baskets before you organize your display.

An important consideration when grouping plants together is to use a selection which, as far as possible, have similar needs in terms of light, temperature and humidity. Set in a group, plants trap moisture under the leaves and help keep humidity high. It is also more convenient to water and feed all your plants at once, especially if you are short of time.

In terms of low maintenance, a bottle garden is hard to beat. Traditional bottle gardens with a stopper are ideal for moisture-loving plants which do not need full sun. Any type of attractive glass container will do as long as the neck is wide enough. Larger bottles like carboys are extremely effective. Small or slow-growing plants are essential. Some good subjects are pileas, fittonia, *Ficus pumila* and *Hedera helix.* The ferns *Adiantum capillus-veneris* and pteris also do well.

PLANTING UP A BOTTLE GARDEN

Work out the arrangement of your plants before you begin. Do not plant them too close together, as they will grow to cover any bare patches.

You will need three bamboo canes. Using twine or wire, fix to one a small spoon, to one a small fork, and wedge the third into an empty cotton reel. Also useful is a long-handled artist's paintbrush. Make up a potting mixture of equal quantities of loam or soil-based compost, sand and peat. Add a small quantity of crushed charcoal. A funnel or a piece of strong paper rolled into a cone is needed to pour the compost into the container. For watering, use a small watering can or a length of narrow plastic tubing.

The container must be clean and dry to start. Using the funnel, pour in enough mixture to come one-third of the way up the glass. Firm it down evenly with the cotton reel. Make holes for each of the plants using the spoon and fork. Working with one plant at a time, remove it from its pot and shake excess compost from the roots. Work from the outside towards the middle. You can drop the plants through the hole and then pick them up with the spoon and fork, or lower them in between two canes, chopstick fashion, or use a long piece of wire with a hook on the end. Set each plant upright in its hole. With the spoon, cover the roots with compost and firm it down with the cotton reel. When all the plants are in place, add water by pouring it down the sides of the container. This will clean the glass at the same time. The compost should be moist, not saturated. Any excess cannot drain away, so go carefully. Specks of compost on the leaves can be removed with the paintbrush.

Put the stopper in. If condensation appears all over the glass within the next few days, remove the stopper for a while. You may have to do this three or four times before the balance is right. A little condensation near the top is healthy and will come and go. No condensation at all means you should add water.

The bottle garden may need a light watering after some months, but otherwise can be left alone (apart from dusting the outside). The plants will probably have outgrown their space after three years and the garden can be re-made.

A CORUS

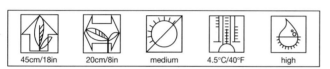

45cm/18in	20cm/8in	medium	4.5°C/40°F	high

The delicate, grassy leaves of *Acorus gramineus* rise in a close fan like those of an iris from a rhizome set just below the surface of the compost. They are best appreciated in a grouping of foliage plants where their grace and height contrast well with bushy or trailing specimens.

GENERAL CARE Acoruses are marsh plants, and the roots must never dry out. Grow in soil-based compost and stand the pots in saucers of pebbles kept constantly under water. In spring and summer, feed every 2 weeks with liquid fertilizer. Spray the leaves, using a fine spray, on hot days. The plants can tolerate direct sunlight if it is filtered through a fine curtain. Repot in spring if the fan of leaves touches the side of the pot. Once the plants have reached a 12.5cm/5in pot they should be divided into smaller sections.

PROPAGATION By division in spring or summer.

VARIETIES *A. g. variegatus*, leaves striped with white; *A. g. pusillus*, attractive dwarf form at 7.5cm/3in.

POSSIBLE PROBLEMS Generally trouble-free.

A SPIDISTRA

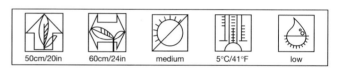

50cm/20in	60cm/24in	medium	5°C/41°F	low

Dubbed 'the cast-iron plant' by the Victorians because of its stoic constitution, *Aspidistra elatior* is indeed an extremely accommodating plant. Its leathery, glossy leaves are dark green, growing in a tightly formed cluster on short stems. A mature aspidistra in an old jardinière looks very dignified in a hallway or on a deep windowsill (out of direct sunlight, which will scorch the leaves).

GENERAL CARE Aspidistras need some attention, in spite of their reputation. Grow in soil-based compost and keep watered all year, so that the compost is just moist. Broken crocks at the bottom of the pot will assist good drainage. Feed every 2 weeks in spring and summer with liquid fertilizer. The plants are happy in cool or warm rooms. Repot in spring only when over-crowding demands it, upgrading to a pot one size larger. Once a mature plant reaches the largest pot you have room for, simply top-dress in spring (see page 252).

PROPAGATION Remove suckers bearing roots in spring and place one to a 10cm/4in pot.

VARIETIES *A. e. variegata*, leaves striped green and white.

POSSIBLE PROBLEMS Brown marks on leaves caused by overwatering.

■ GENERAL TIP

Acorus gramineus *has been naturalized and growing in East Anglia for 300 years or more, a region in which it is most at home in the wet area at the margins of ponds and similar water features. As indoor plants* *they are rather insignificant on their own unless clumps of growth are large. Plunged in moss in mixed plantings they offer pleasing contrast to other foliage.*

■ CARE TIP

The unusual flowers are produced at soil level and often go unnoticed as a result. Red spider mites can have very debilitating effect on aspidistras, turning leaves brown and crisp.

BEGONIA LUXURIANS

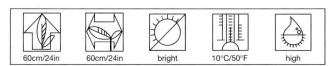

60cm/24in | 60cm/24in | bright | 10°C/50°F | high

Begonia luxurians is a fibrous-rooted plant with the slightly hairy leaves which characterize the 'hirsute' begonias. Its pale green leaves may be divided into as many as 17 pointed leaflets, giving them the appearance of palm leaves. The stems are tinged with red. No named varieties are available.

GENERAL CARE Treat fibrous-rooted begonias in the same way as rhizomatous types like *Begonia rex* hybrids. While both kinds need humidity, they need less water when resting during the winter. Let the top half of the compost dry out between waterings at this time.

PROPAGATION Take 10cm/4in tip cuttings in late spring and root in a compost of equal parts of peat and sand at a temperature of 18-21°C/64-70°F.

POSSIBLE PROBLEMS Powdery mildew; yellowing of leaves if too dry, overwatered or too cold.

BEGONIA REX

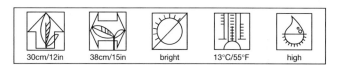

30cm/12in | 38cm/15in | bright | 13°C/55°F | high

The group of hybrids derived from *Begonia rex* are prized for their magnificent leaves. Roughly heart-shaped and slightly hairy, they reach as much as 30cm/12in in length and are almost as wide. The wrinkled texture and toothed edges emphasize the beautiful colours in shades of green, silver and pink or red, often with a metallic sheen. *Begonia rex* grows from a rhizome, which rests near the surface and sends down roots at several points.

GENERAL CARE Grow in a peat-based mixture with a layer of broken crocks at the bottom for good drainage. Set half-pots in trays of moist pebbles to maintain humidity and water the plants moderately during the growth period. At this time feed every 2 weeks with liquid fertilizer and keep at normal room temperatures. Bright light without direct sunlight is essential in order to maintain foliage colour. Repot overcrowded specimens in spring. Eventually old plants will need to be replaced.

PROPAGATION By leaf cuttings in late spring.

VARIETIES *B. r.* 'President', green and silver; 'Merry Christmas', red, pink, silver and green.

POSSIBLE PROBLEMS Powdery mildew; yellowing of leaves if too dry, overwatered or too cold.

■ DESIGN TIP

Something of a connoisseur's plant and one that will be difficult to obtain. Graceful, open plants on stout stems are fine as background subjects for setting off lesser plants in groups

■ PROPAGATION TIP

To be able to propagate new plants is something of an achievement among the enthusiastic growers of houseplants. Important needs are a heated propagating case and plants with firm and unblemished leaves. Take off a good leaf, reduce the petiole to one inch, cut through the veins in several places and rest the leaf on peat and sand mix with colour side up (see page 253, Fig 3).

261

CALADIUM

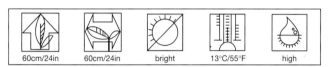

| 60cm/24in | 60cm/24in | bright | 13°C/55°F | high |

The extraordinary foliage of *Caladium bicolor*, native to tropical America, is not produced without some care. Given suitable conditions, this plant bears large, paper-thin leaves of silvery green, marked with white, magenta or dark green.

GENERAL CARE Grow in a peat-based mixture with a 2.5cm/1in layer of drainage material at the bottom of the pot. During the growing period maintain a temperature between 18 and 24°C/65 and 75°F. Mist-spray three times a day. Stand the pots in a tray of pebbles kept constantly moist. Feed with a liquid fertilizer at half-strength every 2 weeks. Avoid cold draughts at all costs. When the leaves die down in autumn, reduce the amount of water gradually. A dormant period of at least 5 months follows. Keep the tubers in their pots away from the light and do not let them dry out. Repot in the spring, placing them at about their own depth below the surface of the compost, and restore normal growing conditions.

PROPAGATION Detach and replant offsets when repotting.

VARIETIES *C. b. macrophyllum*, deep green, spotted white and rose-pink; *C. b. regale*, pointed bright green leaves edged purple, spotted white; *C. b. devosianum*, green edged crimson, spotted white and pink.

POSSIBLE PROBLEMS Leaves turn brown and wither if temperatures are too low.

■ CARE TIP

With leaves that are white with green venation the variety *C. candidum* is almost translucent – the movement of a hand being clearly seen on the opposite side of the plant. Purchased tubers should be firm and free of blemishes and when starting growth in late winter it is important that high temperature prevails, in excess of 20°C (68°F) if possible. Keep just moist to begin with.

CALATHEA PICTURATA

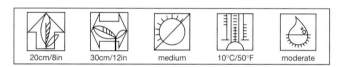

| 20cm/8in | 30cm/12in | medium | 10°C/50°F | moderate |

The leaves of *Calathea picturata* are similar in shape to those of its relative the zebra plant, but much smaller and predominantly silver in colour, with a bright green margin. They are deep red underneath, and this feature is easy to appreciate as the leaves are held almost upright on short stems.

GENERAL CARE Treat as *C. zebrina*. As an alternative to a peat-based mixture, you can use a mixture of soil-based compost and leaf-mould or peat in the ratio 2:1. In this case feeding during the active growth period can be reduced to once weekly.

PROPAGATION Divide and replant overcrowded plants in late spring.

POSSIBLE PROBLEMS Generally trouble-free.

■ CARE TIP

The leaves of *C. p. Argentea* have, as the name suggests, a glowing silver centre with a dark green margin – colouring seen in few other plants. As an ornament in the living room they are not likely to do well – needing warmth and humidity to succeed. A growing case, or a window extended outwards in the form of a large bay with sliding glass door to the room can be ideal.

CALATHEA ZEBRINA

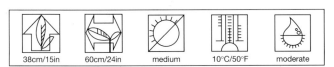

38cm/15in	60cm/24in	medium	10°C/50°F	moderate

Calatheas are closely related to marantas, and are sometimes difficult to tell apart. Most varieties have roughly oval leaves, prominently marked with stripes or with a broad margin of colour. *Calathea zebrina* (*above*) is commonly known as the zebra plant, because of the strong contrast between the leaves' pale green veins and midribs against soft-textured bright green. Each leaf rises from a stiff stalk on which it is held at a pronounced, almost horizontal, angle.

GENERAL CARE Grow in a peat-based potting mixture. When plants are actively growing keep the mixture constantly moist with cooled boiled water or rainwater. Feed with liquid fertilizer 3 times a week. The ideal temperature is 16-22°C/60-70°F. Stop feeding and reduce the amount of water during the winter resting period. Repot one size up annually in late spring.

PROPAGATION Divide and replant overcrowded plants in late spring. Enclose each small pot in a plastic bag until new roots have formed.

SPECIES *Calathea makoyana* (peacock plant); 30cm/12in leaves on long stems, marked green, silver and deep red depending on quality of light.

POSSIBLE PROBLEMS Generally trouble-free.

CHLOROPHYTUM

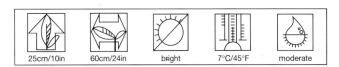

25cm/10in	60cm/24in	bright	7°C/45°F	moderate

Variously labelled *Chlorophytum capense*, *C. comosum* and *C. elatum*, the well-known spider plant is deservedly popular. Its long, grass-like leaves have a central white stripe. Each plant produces new plantlets at the end of narrow arching stems. They look their best in hanging baskets or on tall plant stands.

GENERAL CARE Chlorophytums are not difficult to cultivate. Grow in a soil-based compost and keep constantly just moist in spring and summer. During the winter resting period the compost should not be allowed to dry out completely. Feed mature plants all year round with liquid fertilizer every 2 weeks. Repot whenever the mass of fleshy roots has pushed up out of the compost.

PROPAGATION Peg young plants into small pots of potting compost and sever from the parent plant when rooted. Alternatively detach plantlets with little roots from the parent and place in water until the roots are 2.5cm/1in long. Pot up in soil-based compost.

VARIETIES *C. c. variegatum*, most common form, green leaves with central white band.

POSSIBLE PROBLEMS Generally trouble-free.

▓ GENERAL TIP

One of the testing plants that require skill and adequate temperature to maintain, but rewarding. Excellent subjects for growing in a heated plant growing case with moisture control.

▓ CARE TIP

The ubiquitous 'Spider Plant' is frequently neglected by being underfed and potted on too seldom, while attention to both of these aspects can produce superb plants for hanging containers.

CISSUS

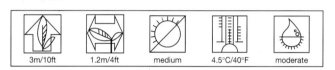

| 3m/10ft | 1.2m/4ft | medium | 4.5°C/40°F | moderate |

Cissus rhombifolia (formerly *Rhoicissus rhomboidea*) is commonly known as grape ivy. This beautiful plant is closely related to the true grape vine, and climbs by means of tendrils at about 60-90cm/2-3ft a year. Regular cutting back, however, will keep it bushy. The green, glossy leaves are composed of 3 diamond-shaped leaflets.

GENERAL CARE Grow in a soil-based compost and set in good light. Most types of cissus are tolerant of wide variations in light, but dislike direct sunlight. A tall stake is necessary on which to train the exuberant growth. Water well during active growth, allowing the top layer of compost to dry out between applications. Feed every 2 weeks from spring until late autumn. The ideal temperature while growing is around 16-18°C/60-65°F. Cut back the leading growths by one-third in spring to keep the shape attractive. Repot in early spring until a pot size of 25cm/10in has been reached. Thereafter top-dress annually in spring.

PROPAGATION Take 10cm/4in tip cuttings in spring and root in a compost of equal parts peat and sand at a temperature of 16-18°C/61-64°F.

VARIETIES *C. r.* 'Ellen Danica', a graceful plant with leaves more deeply cut and glossier than the species.

POSSIBLE PROBLEMS Red spider mite in dry atmospheres.

CODIAEUM

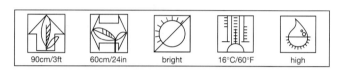

| 90cm/3ft | 60cm/24in | bright | 16°C/60°F | high |

There is a tremendous variation in leaf form and colour among the codiaeums, or crotons as they are commonly called. Red, yellow and green and varying combinations of these colours are flamboyantly displayed on leathery leaves that may be oval, lanceolate or deeply cut. In the variety 'Spirale' they are even twisted.

GENERAL CARE These handsome plants require at least 2 hours of direct sunshine every day to maintain leaf colour. Normal room temperatures are sufficient. Grow in a soil-based compost, water plentifully during the growth period and feed every 2 weeks. Set the pots on trays of pebbles kept just moist. Do not let the compost dry out completely in the dormant period. Repot each spring. When the largest convenient pot size has been reached, simply top-dress with fresh compost (see page 252).

PROPAGATION Take 15cm/6in tip cuttings in early spring. To stop the flow of milky sap from the stems, plunge the ends in water. Insert the cuttings singly in 6cm/2½in pots of equal parts peat and sand.

VARIETIES *Codiaeum variegatum pictum* 'Madame Mayne' (*above*), deeply cut leaves, golden yellow when young, green veined yellow in maturity; 'Reidii', oval, curved, wavy leaves, mid-green striped cream ageing to deep pink.

■ DESIGN TIP

Adaptable plants in that they may be used as either climbers or trailers. In the latter capacity they are seen to best effect when growing as a single subject in a hanging container of reasonable size. Alternatively, a trellis framework can be placed in the growing pot or attached to the wall adjacent to the growing container to allow the plant to cling naturally.

■ CARE TIP

In dry and hot conditions a major enemy of this plant is the minute red spider mite which is flesh-coloured rather than red, so difficult to detect. Use suitable systemic insecticide as a precaution.

COLEUS

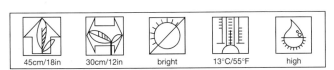

| 45cm/18in | 30cm/12in | bright | 13°C/55°F | high |

Popularly known as the flame nettle, *Coleus blumei* is a popular house plant valued for its beautifully coloured leaves and for its usefulness in plant groups. The delicate leaves are shaped like those of the nettle (to which it is not related) but are invariably very brightly marked. As these plants are easily raised from cuttings, they are usually discarded after one season.

GENERAL CARE Grow in a soil-based compost and keep it thoroughly moist at all times. Maximum bright light, including 2-3 hours of direct sunlight daily, is very important. Coleuses like warmth, but at temperatures above 18°C/65°F maintain humidity by standing the pots in trays of pebbles kept constantly damp. Feed every 2 weeks during the growing period and repot every 2 months so that the roots have room to spread. Pinch out the growing tips regularly to encourage bushy growth.

PROPAGATION Take 7.5cm/3in tip cuttings in the autumn and place directly in potting compost in a warm position.

VARIETIES There are innumerable good named varieties.

POSSIBLE PROBLEMS Leaves fall if the compost is allowed to dry out, and the colour will fade in inadequate light.

CTENANTHE

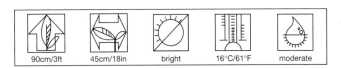

| 90cm/3ft | 45cm/18in | bright | 16°C/61°F | moderate |

Ctenanthes belong to the same family as marantas and calatheas. The matt leaves are rather more slender and pointed than those of its relatives. Splashed irregularly with cream, they are purple on the underside. Ctenanthes combine well with other plants in a mixed display.

GENERAL CARE Grow in a mixture of soil-based compost and leaf-mould. Set in bright light, not direct sunlight, at normal room temperatures. Stand pots on dampened pebbles and water regularly during active growth. Give a liquid feed every 2 weeks. Repot each spring. When the largest convenient pot size has been reached, simply top-dress annually (see page 252).

PROPAGATION Detach the basal offsets from the parent and replant immediately in the recommended growing medium.

VARIETIES *Ctenanthe oppenheimiana* 'Tricolor' and 'Burle Marx' (*above*), known as the never-never plant, with pointed leaves 25cm/10in long on slender stalks.

POSSIBLE PROBLEMS Leaves curl up if exposed to over-bright light.

▪ GENERAL TIP

Plants that are raised from seed will not be difficult to establish but these are not the best sort of coleus to acquire. There are also named kinds, such as C. 'Pineapple Queen' and 'Paisley Shawl' that are very much superior in respect of colour, growth and general appearance. Bought at the start of the season they need regular potting and feeding to prosper.

▪ DESIGN TIP

Ctenanthe oppenheimiana Tricolor is a fine plant if given modest warmth and shade from direct sun. Grown in pan type containers these are excellent among other plants when employed as ground cover.

CYPERUS

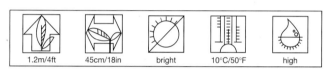

1.2m/4ft	45cm/18in	bright	10°C/50°F	high

Cyperus alternifolius (*above*) bears its leaves at the top of the stem, radiating outwards like the spokes of a wheel. Because of this formation it is commonly called umbrella plant, and the watery connotations are appropriate – this plant is aquatic, and needs to have its pot sitting in a shallow tray constantly filled with water.

GENERAL CARE Grow in pots of soil-based compost set in full or filtered sunlight. Normal room temperatures are suitable. Water frequently and spray mist the leaves daily in an upward direction. Feed every month with liquid fertilizer when actively growing. Cyperus grow quickly and will need repotting whenever the clumps become overcrowded.

PROPAGATION Divide the roots in early spring. Do not plant new sections too deep in their new pots. Alternatively detach a spray of bracts with a short length of stem and keep in water until roots appear. Pot up in the recommended mixture.

VARIETIES *C. a.* 'Gracilis', dwarf variety with darker green leaves; 'Variegatus', foliage striped white when young, ageing to green.

POSSIBLE PROBLEMS Generally trouble-free.

DIEFFENBACHIA

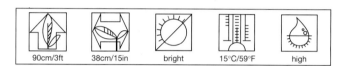

90cm/3ft	38cm/15in	bright	15°C/59°F	high

All dieffenbachias are poisonous, with very bitter sap. The common name, dumb cane, refers to the fact that loss of speech follows if any part of the plant is placed in the mouth. These negative qualities have not prevented dieffenbachias becoming popular houseplants. They are much admired for their large, handsome leaves, beautifully marked cream and green.

GENERAL CARE Grow in a soil-based compost. Set the plants where they can enjoy bright, filtered light during the growing period, with direct sunlight in the winter. Stand the pots in trays of pebbles kept moist and water so that the mixture is constantly damp. Feed every 2 weeks except when dormant. Repot annually in spring.

PROPAGATION Take 10cm/4in tip cuttings in early summer, insert in a compost of equal parts of peat and sand and keep the pots in plastic bags until the cuttings have rooted. Alternatively take cuttings from the main stem; the parent plant can be discarded but may well break into new growth from the base.

VARIETIES *Dieffenbachia picta* 'Exotica' (*above*), deep green leaves blotched white and yellow; 'Rudolph Roehrs' ('Roehrsii'), creamy leaves veined white; 'Bausii', leaves parti-coloured dark and light green, spotted silver.

POSSIBLE PROBLEMS Generally trouble-free.

■ CARE TIP

These are among the easiest indoor plants to manage and ideal for the person who is heavy handed with water. In fact, water is the name of the game in respect of cyperus and they do make excellent poolside features if one is fortunate enough to have a conservatory that can accommodate a small pool. In larger pools they are fine as island plants on a raised mound in the water.

■ PROPAGATION TIP

Success with propagation is always a bonus, and with this plant older stems can be cut into sections with an eye and laid horizontally, half buried in peaty mixture with the eye uppermost.

DIZYGOTHECA

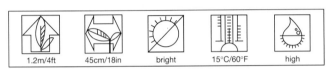

| 1.2m/4ft | 45cm/18in | bright | 15°C/60°F | high |

Dizygothecas, or false aralias, are elegant plants with narrow, serrated leaflets radiating from the tips of slender stalks. They are beautiful enough to stand alone – especially if planted 3 to a pot – but can also be used in a collection of tropical plants to add height and grace.

GENERAL CARE Grow in a soil-based compost and set the plants in bright light, not direct sunlight. Steadily maintained humidity is important. Stand the pots in saucers of pebbles kept moist, and do not let the compost become either waterlogged or dried out. Feed with liquid fertilizer every 2 weeks in the growing period. Pot on every other year in spring.

PROPAGATION New plants are normally raised from seed.

SPECIES *Dizygotheca elegantissima* (finger or false aralia, *above*), young leaves copper-coloured ageing to dark green, almost black; *D. veitchii*, wider leaflets of bright green, deep red beneath.

POSSIBLE PROBLEMS Plants become spindly in conditions that are less than ideal.

DRACAENA

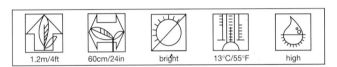

| 1.2m/4ft | 60cm/24in | bright | 13°C/55°F | high |

There are a number of dracaenas, all of them striking plants and well deserving of a place in a conservatory or sunny room. *Dracaena fragrans* has glossy, strap-like leaves radiating from the centre. As the plant matures the stem lengthens, bearing the rosette of leaves at the top.

GENERAL CARE Grow in soil-based compost and water well during the period of growth. Give a liquid feed every 2 weeks. Bright light, though not direct sunlight, is essential. The ideal temperature is in the range 18-23°C/65-75°F. Stand the pots in trays of damp pebbles and spray the foliage from time to time to maintain a high level of humidity. Repot annually in spring.

PROPAGATION Take tip or stem cuttings in spring or summer and root in a compost of equal parts of peat and sand at a temperature of 21-24°C/70-75°F.

VARIETIES *D. f.* 'Massangeana', dark green leaves with a golden central band; 'Lindenii', gold and green leaves edged gold.

POSSIBLE PROBLEMS Leaf drop in low temperatures; scale insects on leaves.

▪ GENERAL TIP

Dizygotheca elegantissima is never an easy plant to care for and one that will almost inevitably lose lower leaves as the main stem hardens with age. An interesting feature of this plant is the manner in which it changes character as the stem increases in height – the delicate filigreed leaves give way to much coarser leaves that are more typical of the araliaceae family to which it belongs.

▪ DESIGN TIP

Many fine plants here, almost all of erect growth – a feature that is very effective when groups of the same or mixed varieties are arranged in a large container or in decorative pots at floor level.

ELETTARIA

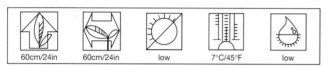

60cm/24in	60cm/24in	low	7°C/45°F	low

Native to India, *Elettaria cardamom* is the chief commercial source of cardamom seeds, one of the most expensive spices in the world. This rhizomatous plant bears numerous thick stems with pointed, slender mid-green leaves. It has a dense, bushy appearance and is useful for hallways and other poorly lit rooms. There are no named varieties.

GENERAL CARE Grow in a soil-based compost. Normal room temperatures and poor or moderate light are best; the leaves lose their colour in direct sunlight. Water moderately and give a liquid feed every 2 weeks when the plant is in active growth. The stems of elettarias soon fill the pot, necessitating repotting, which can be done at any time except when the plant is dormant. When they become too large for the largest suitable pot, the plants should be divided.

PROPAGATION Divide and repot plants in spring. Each clump of stems must be attached to a good piece of rhizome and roots.

VARIETIES *E. c.* 'Variegata' (*above*).

POSSIBLE PROBLEMS Leaves turn brown at temperatures below 13°C/55°F during the active growth period.

x FATSHEDERA

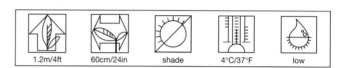

1.2m/4ft	60cm/24in	shade	4°C/37°F	low

The hybrid *Fatshedera lizei* (*above*) has characteristics of both its parents: the tough constitution of *Hedera helix hibernica* (Irish ivy) and the glossy, handsome leaves of *Fatsia japonica*. Fatshedera leaves may be up to 20cm/8in wide and are best appreciated when several plants are grown in one pot, giving a bushy appearance.

GENERAL CARE Grow in a soil-based compost. As the plants grow they need the support of thin stakes to prevent them toppling over. It is advisable to place these in the pot while plants are still young. Light shade is best, but the variegated type needs brighter light (not direct sunlight) to maintain its markings. Fatshederas are not fussy about room temperature, but the variegated type needs to be at a minimum of 15°C/59°F at all times. Water moderately and feed every 2 weeks when in active growth. Repot annually in spring, providing longer stakes if necessary.

PROPAGATION Take 10cm/4in tip cuttings in spring and root in a compost of equal parts of peat and sand.

VARIETIES *F. l.* 'Variegata', slower growing variety with white splashes on the leaves.

POSSIBLE PROBLEMS Red spider mite.

FATSIA

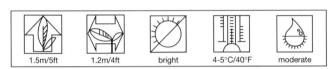

1.5m/5ft	1.2m/4ft	bright	4-5°C/40°F	moderate

Fatsia japonica, the false castor oil plant, is an imposing specimen with large, green, dark green, glossy leaves. Native to Japan, it is hardy to enough to grow outdoors, where it may exceed the dimensions given above. As a potted house plant, it usually reaches about 90cm/3ft. Small white flowers appear in autumn, but to preserve the handsome foliage it is best to remove the buds.

GENERAL CARE Grow in a soil-based compost kept thoroughly moist during the summer, and give a liquid feed every two weeks. Fatsias need good light, not direct sunlight, and prefer cooler temperatures, ideally about 15°C/59°F; over 18°C/64°F the leaves begin to flop. Pinch out the growing tips of young plants to encourage bushy growth. Clean the leaves by sponging them with tepid water. In the rest period, keep the compost just moist. Repotting may be necessary during the growing season as fatsias are fast growers. The final pot size will be 25cm/10in, after which simply topdress with fresh compost annually.

PROPAGATION Detach suckers, if any, in early spring, and pot up individually in potting compost.

VARIETIES *F. j. variegata (above)*: leaves tinged white; *F. j. Moseri*: leaves larger than the species, but the plant more compact.

POSSIBLE PROBLEMS Leaves shrivel in dry, hot atmosphere.

■ SPECIAL CARE TIP

The variegated form with cream blotches or edges to the leaves grows more slowly and is much less resistant to cold. If the temperature falls below freezing, it is likely to shed its leaves in winter. For this reason and because of its attractive light-coloured leaves it makes an ideal subject for a well-used room indoors.

FICUS BENJAMINA

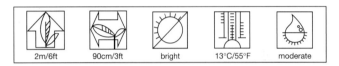

2m/6ft	90cm/3ft	bright	13°C/55°F	moderate

The ficus family includes an enormous variety of handsome foliage plants. *Ficus benjamina (above)*, the weeping fig, has some of the grace of *F. pumila* combined with the stature of *F. elastica*. It is ideal for the corner of a room, as it does not need to be rotated towards the light, but its glossy oval leaves on slightly drooping branches look good in any setting. There are no named varieties.

GENERAL CARE Grow in soil-based compost, using a pot that looks too small for the plant (ficus like their roots to be cramped). Water moderately, allowing the top half of the compost to dry out between waterings. Give a liquid feed every two weeks when in active growth. Good light, not direct sunlight, is essential. *F. benjamina* can thrive in cool or warm rooms, though sudden changes in temperature will be damaging. At high temperatures there is an increased risk of attack by red spider mite. Carefully sponge the leaves with tepid water from time to time to clean them. Repot in spring, but only when the roots are appearing through the drainage hole of the pot.

PROPAGATION Take 7.5cm/3in cuttings of side shoots in early summer. *F. benjamina* may also be increased by air layering.

POSSIBLE PROBLEMS Scale insects; red spider mite.

■ DESIGN TIP

Some rooms call for a single imposing plant and Ficus benjamina might very well be the answer particularly as it offers elegance and delicacy with significant height and a tree-like habit.

FICUS ELASTICA

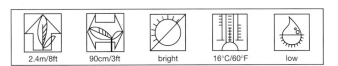

2.4m/8ft	90cm/3ft	bright	16°C/60°F	low

Ficus elastica, the rubber plant, is one of the most popular indoor plants. Though potentially very tall, it usually reaches about 1.2m/4ft – stately enough, and classically handsome with oval, shiny dark green leaves.

GENERAL CARE Grow in a soil-based compost, using a pot size that will cramp the roots slightly. Set in full light, out of direct sunlight. Water thoroughly, during the growing period, allowing the compost to dry out slightly between applications. Use cooled boiled water or rainwater if possible. Feed every 2 weeks. Wipe the leaves gently to remove dust. In winter, keep the compost just moist. Pot on in spring if necessary. To encourage a bushy habit, pinch out the growing point. Sap exuding from the wound can be stopped with powdered charcoal.

PROPAGATION Air-layering is the best method, but is difficult for the amateur.

VARIETIES *F. e.* 'Decora' (*above left*), best-known plain-leaved variety; 'Black Prince' (*above centre*), very dark green leaves; 'Variegata' (*above right*), slightly narrower leaves edged yellow and with yellow mottling.

POSSIBLE PROBLEMS Leaf drop in low temperatures; scale insects on leaves.

FICUS PUMILA

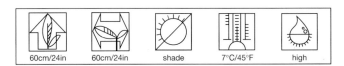

60cm/24in	60cm/24in	shade	7°C/45°F	high

In contrast to its relative the rubber plant, *Ficus pumila* – the creeping fig – climbs or trails on thin, wiry stems. Its diminutive leaves are bright green and attractively heart-shaped. It is best set in an arrangement with other plants where humidity is raised and where its low habit of growth can offset taller, bushier specimens.

GENERAL CARE Grow in a peat-based compost and keep evenly moist throughout the year – the leaves are too thin to retain much moisture. Pinch out the growing tips regularly to encourage a spreading habit. *F. pumila* likes shade and cool temperatures. In the growing period feed every 2 weeks with liquid fertilizer. Pot on when absolutely necessary in spring; all ficus like to have their roots rather cramped.

PROPAGATION Take 15cm/6in tip cuttings in spring and root in a compost of equal parts of peat and sand at a temperature of 16-18°C/61-64°F.

VARIETIES *F. p. variegata*, green leaves spotted cream; this variety needs slightly higher temperatures and better light than the species, or it will revert to plain green.

POSSIBLE PROBLEMS Red spider mite; mealy bug.

▪ PROPAGATION TIP

There have been many improvements in the rubber plant since the original F. elastica *came into favour, but they all seem to lose lower leaves with age. Top sections of such plants can be air-layered by removing a leaf,* cutting upwards through the node and putting a match into the wound to prevent it re-sealing – wet moss and plastic cover should ensure rooting.

▪ DESIGN TIP

The creeping fig is a fine plant for rapidly covering a damp wall in a heated conservatory – roots are self-clinging thus enabling the plant to travel long distances very effectively.

FITTONIA

7.5cm/3in	15cm/6in	shade	13°C/55°F	high

Fittonias, or snakeskin plants, are one of the prettiest low-growing indoor plants. Their pale green oval leaves, veined in a contrasting colour, completely cover the surface of the growing medium. Site the pots on a low table where this carpet of leaves can be viewed from above.

GENERAL CARE Grow in half-pots of peat-based compost and keep it just moist all the time. Spray the leaves frequently with a fine mist. Feed every 2 weeks with half-strength liquid fertilizer. A steadily maintained temperature of 18°C/65°F is the ideal; cold draughts are deadly. Fittonias like shade when in active growth, but should be moved into natural light during the winter months. It is not usually necessary to repot fittonias.

PROPAGATION Take tip cuttings with 4 pairs of leaves in spring. New plants may also be raised by layering.

VARIETIES *Fittonia verschaffeltii*, olive green leaves 5cm/2in long, veined pinkish-red; *F. argyroneura* 'Snakeskin' (*above*), smaller leaves veined cream; this variety cannot tolerate temperatures lower than 16°C/61°F. *F. a.* 'Nana' is a miniature form which is easier to grow.

POSSIBLE PROBLEMS Leaves shrivel up if conditions are too dry; stems rot if the compost is too wet.

GYNURA

90cm/3ft	45cm/18in	bright	13°C/55°F	high

Gynuras are prized for their colourful leaves, dark green but covered in purple hairs so soft they have given rise to the popular name 'velvet plant'. Flowers sometimes appear in spring but should be picked off before they open as the smell is unpleasant. As trailers, gynuras do well in hanging baskets, but they become straggly with age and should be replaced.

GENERAL CARE Grow in soil-based compost and keep it constantly just moist. To maintain humidity stand the pots in trays of moist pebbles, but do not spray the leaves: drops of moisture trapped in the hairs cause brown spots to develop. A few hours of direct sunlight every day helps keep the colours bright and encourages dense growth. Normal room temperatures are satisfactory. Feed every 4 weeks throughout the year. Repot in spring if the plant is still shapely.

PROPAGATION Take tip cuttings in early spring and root in equal parts peat and sand at a temperature of 18-21°C/64-70°F. Place 3 or 4 new plants in a pot for the best effect.

SPECIES *Gynura auriantica*, oval, bright green leaves up to 15cm/6in long, clothed with purple hairs; *G. sarmentosa* (purple passion vine, *above*), twining form with dark green pointed leaves, covered in deep purple hairs. Pinch out the growing tips of this variety regularly.

POSSIBLE PROBLEMS Aphids.

◼ CARE TIP

All of these attractively venated plants are very susceptible to low temperatures – the foliage being paper thin it simply shrivels and dies. A large plant propagator (perhaps with heating cables) can be utilized as a sort of miniature greenhouse to accommodate fittonias and other tender plants – particularly over the winter when plants are more vulnerable

◼ GENERAL TIP

Almost invariably untidy plants, but instantly attractive when seen growing on a windowsill where the sun can be seen shining onto and through their leaves and highlighting the purple effect.

HEDERA

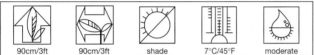

90cm/3ft	90cm/3ft	shade	7°C/45°F	moderate

There are numerous varieties of ivy, some of which are best set in mixed groupings while others can stand alone. *Hedera helix* (English ivy) has the characteristic ivy leaf and a branching habit of growth. Since most varieties do best in lightly shaded situations and are tolerant of cool temperatures, they have become very popular as house plants. Self-clinging, all will climb if provided with supports.

GENERAL CARE Grow in a soil-based mixture and water in moderation during the growing period. Variegated types need some sunlight every day. All are accommodating about temperature levels as long as there are no dramatic changes, and over 18°C/65°F humidity should be increased by mist-spraying the foliage. Feed with liquid fertilizer every 2 weeks during the growing period. Move plants to larger pots when roots can be seen protruding through the drainage holes.

PROPAGATION Take cuttings at any time and place in water until roots appear. Pot up in the recommended mixture.

VARIETIES *H. h.* 'Little Eva' (*above*), green leaves edged cream; 'Sagittaefolia', star-shaped, narrow leaves; 'Russell's Gold', golden leaves; 'Discolor', small neat leaves of green mottled with cream and pink.

POSSIBLE PROBLEMS Scale insects.

HYPOESTES

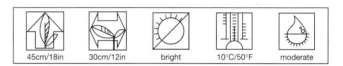

45cm/18in	30cm/12in	bright	10°C/50°F	moderate

Among a clutch of popular names, *Hypoestes phyllostachya* has acquired the label 'polka-dot plant', because of the pink and white spots that are liberally distributed over the oval, pointed leaves. If the growing tips are regularly pinched out the plants keep nicely bushy, but eventually become straggly and should be discarded (new plants are easy to raise from seed).

GENERAL CARE Grow in soil-based compost and keep constantly moist (not waterlogged) during the growing season, using cooled boiled water or rainwater if possible. Keep the compost barely moist during the resting period. To keep the attractive leaf markings the best light is bright sunlight filtered through a fine curtain. Normal room temperatures are suitable. Feed every 2 weeks with liquid fertilizer. Repot whenever the roots become overcrowded.

PROPAGATION Sow seed in seed compost in early spring or take 10cm/4in tip cuttings at any time and place in water until roots appear. Pot up in seed compost until large enough to transfer to 10cm/4in pot of soil-based compost.

VARIETIES *H. phyllostachya* 'Splash', similar to the species but with more pronounced pink markings.

POSSIBLE PROBLEMS Generally trouble-free.

■ DESIGN TIP

Lots of superb kinds to choose from and all natural climbers against a wall – Hedera (ivy) gold heart being an excellent choice for this purpose. Beside the small leaved forms there are those with larger leaves such as H. canariensis *which has beautifully marked cream and green variegated foliage. Larger leaved forms need some form of support to twine around.*

■ DESIGN TIP

When choosing plants, take some time to select those that are compact and of the brightest colouring. A group of small plants placed in a shallow container filled with wet moss can be a very attractive feature.

IRESINE

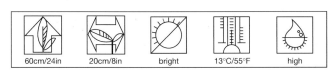

60cm/24in	20cm/8in	bright	13°C/55°F	high

The blood-red colour of its stems and heart-shaped foliage have earned *Iresine herbstii* the common name 'beefsteak plant'. Much used in outdoor bedding schemes, these shrubby plants have become increasingly popular for indoor decoration too.

GENERAL CARE Grow in a soil-based mixture. During the growing season water liberally and feed with liquid fertilizer every 2 weeks. To keep the leaves brightly coloured, several hours of direct sunlight every day are essential. Normal room temperatures are suitable throughout the year. Pinch out the growing tips to encourage a bushy shape. Repot whenever you can see the roots on the surface of the compost.

PROPAGATION Take 7.5cm/3in tip cuttings in spring and place in water until rooted. Pot up in the recommended compost, 3 cuttings to a 7.5cm/3in pot.

VARIETIES *I. h. aureo-reticulata*; red stems, leaves green splashed gold; *I. h. brilliantissima*, deep crimson leaves and stems; *I. h. wallisii*, dwarf variety with dark purple stems and leaves.

POSSIBLE PROBLEMS Aphids; red spider mite.

MARANTA

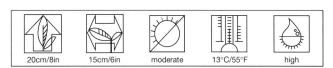

20cm/8in	15cm/6in	moderate	13°C/55°F	high

Maranta leuconeura is known as the prayer plant because it holds its leaves erect and close together at the end of the day, like praying hands. These are among the most beautiful foliage house plants, with broad oval leaves dramatically marked in regular patterns.

GENERAL CARE Grow in a soil-based compost, using half-pots as marantas are shallow rooting. Keep the compost constantly moist during the growing period, stand the pots in saucers of moist pebbles and spray the leaves regularly, preferably with rainwater. Feed every 2 weeks with liquid fertilizer. Light shade is best, for the leaves fade in direct sunlight, but a constant temperature in the range 18-21°C/65-70°F is required. Keep almost dry over winter and pot on in the spring, grading up one size.

PROPAGATION Divide and replant large clumps in spring.

VARIETIES *M. leuconeura*, slightly downy, pale green leaves marked white and darker green, purple beneath; *M. l.* 'Kerchoveana', larger leaves with red margins and sometimes also spotted red beneath; *M. l.* 'Massangeana' smaller leaves, marked almost black along the midribs, purple beneath.

POSSIBLE PROBLEMS Aphids; red spider mite.

▩ PLANTING TIP

Bright colouring of the blood red leaves of the 'Brilliantissima' variety are seen to best effect when plants are growing on a windowsill that catches the sun – both leaves and stems are red in colour. If used amongst bedding plants during the summer months this is the sort of plant that can be lifted prior to frosts and potted to use as a room plant.

▩ CARE TIP

Tolerant, shade-loving house plants that abhor bright sunlight. Often seen suffering in pots of inadequate size, they are seen to good advantage when growing in shallow pans as groups.

PEPEROMIA

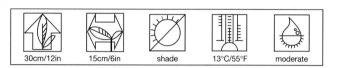

30cm/12in	15cm/6in	shade	13°C/55°F	moderate

There are numerous varieties of peperomia, with foliage of different shapes and colours. All types produce a long, thin flower spike, but it is the leaves which are of interest. A grouping of different varieties makes a beautiful display.

GENERAL CARE Grow in a peat-based compost using small containers or hanging baskets – peperomias do not have an extensive root system. Water very sparingly, and feed only once every 4 weeks with half-strength liquid fertilizer. Normal room temperatures are suitable. Pinch out the growing tips to maintain a bushy shape (this will, incidentally, discourage flower production). Repot if necessary in spring, placing a 2.5cm/1in layer of drainage material at the bottom of the pots.

PROPAGATION Take 7.5cm/3in tip cuttings in spring and root in pots of equal parts peat and sand at 18°C/64°F.

SPECIES *Peperomia argyreia* (*above*) shield-shaped leaves borne on long red stalks. *Peperomia magnoliifolia* (desert privet), 15cm/6in long dark green oval leaves. Leaves of the form 'Variegata' are almost completely cream when young, gradually acquiring more green as they age. *P. caperata*, small, heart-shaped dark green leaves tinged purple, with a ridged surface, a low-growing type; the variety 'Emerald Ripple' is particularly compact.

POSSIBLE PROBLEMS Leaf tips turn brown if the temperature drops suddenly.

■ GENERAL TIP

Many varieties of these are now available – quite enough for one to acquire an interesting collection. Methods of propagation attract considerable interest. The varieties P. caperata and P. hederifolia *are prepared* from single leaves dibbed into peat and sand, while P. sandersii can have its leaves cut into exact quarters to be stood upright in the mix. Bottom heat needed.

PHILODENDRON

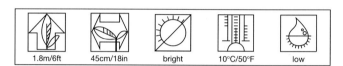

1.8m/6ft	45cm/18in	bright	10°C/50°F	low

There are a great number of philodendrons, many of them climbing plants, with beautiful, leathery leaves of differing forms. In the wild – they are native to central and South America – philodendrons clamber up mossy tree trunks, clinging by means of their aerial roots. Not difficult to grow, this rewarding group includes some of the finest foliage plants.

GENERAL CARE Grow in a peat-based compost, watering regularly during the growing period but allowing it to dry out slightly between applications. Give a liquid feed every two weeks. Philodendrons need good light, not direct sunlight, and are happy at normal room temperatures. In the rest period most species – with the exceptions of *P. scandens* – cannot tolerate temperatures lower than 13°C/55°F. At this time the compost should be kept barely moist. Climbing species need a moss-covered stake to support the aerial roots. Repot when the underground roots crowd the pot, at any time except when resting.

PROPAGATION Take 7.5cm/3in tip cuttings in late spring.

SPECIES *P. scandens* (sweetheart plant, *above*): heart-shaped leaves, evergreen, pinch out growing tips regularly; *P. erubescens* 'Burgundy': slow-growing, arrow-shaped leaves copper red when young; *P. selloum*: non-climber with a rosette of large, deeply incised leaves; *P. bipinnatifidum*: only 90cm/3ft tall, leaves heart-shaped when young.

POSSIBLE PROBLEMS Red spider mite.

■ DESIGN TIP

Philodendrons have two great features which may enable them to make a striking contribution to the look of a room. The first is their propensity for climbing which can be used to great effect for making a screen or for simply enhancing a tall piece of furniture; the second is their dark, glossy leaves which look good against light-coloured woods.

PILEA

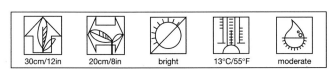

30cm/12in	20cm/8in	bright	13°C/55°F	moderate

Pileas are members of the nettle family, but their foliage is much more varied and attractive than that of the familiar weed. Roughly pointed-oval in shape, the leaves are in shades of green marked with silver or bronze and often of a quilted texture. The different types look striking set in groups together.

GENERAL CARE Grow in a peat-based compost kept continuously moist but not waterlogged during the growing period. Stand the pots in saucers or trays of moist pebbles. Give a liquid feed every 2 weeks in summer. Pileas like a warm atmosphere with good light, though not direct sunlight. Turn the pots round from time to time to ensure even growth, and pinch out the growing tips of any overlong shoots. Repotting is not recommended; replace tired plants with new ones grown from cuttings.

PROPAGATION Take 7.5cm/3in tip cuttings in spring.

SPECIES *Pilea cadierei* (aluminium plant), lightly corrugated green leaves splashed silver form a spreading mound; *P. involucrata*, deeply quilted green leaves; those of *Pilea mollis* 'Moon Valley' (*above*) are very light green veined bronze; *P. spruceana* 'Silver Tree', narrow pointed, dark green leaves with a silver central band.

POSSIBLE PROBLEMS Leaves fall in low temperatures.

PLECTRANTHUS

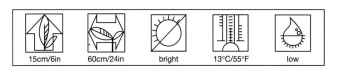

15cm/6in	60cm/24in	bright	13°C/55°F	low

There are around 120 species of Plectranthus many of which make suitable houseplants. Their foliage is similar to the coleus. *Plectranthus fruticosus* is scented and said to keep away moths.

GENERAL CARE Grow in soil-based compost and keep well-watered while in active growth, without actually letting the pots stand in water. Give a liquid feed every 2 weeks during the active growing period. Place the plants where they will receive several hours in direct sunlight every day. They like warmth, thriving in temperatures up to 21°C/70°F if humidity is correspondingly increased. Pinch out the growing tips to prevent the plants becoming straggly. Repotting is not recommended, as the plants are at their best when young and are easily increased by cuttings.

PROPAGATION Take 7.5cm/3in tip cuttings at any time and insert in small pots of the recommended growing medium.

SPECIES *P. oertendahlii*, trailing plant with almost circular leaves 5cm/2in across, bronze-green veined silver; *P. fruticosus* (*above*) bears lilac flowers in large branched racemes; *P. australis* (Swedish ivy), an erect, bushy species with bright green leaves; reaches up to 90cm/3ft in ideal conditions.

POSSIBLE PROBLEMS Generally trouble-free.

■ GENERAL TIP

Although P. cadierei *is the front runner in terms of popularity the Artillery Plant,* P. muscosa, *is a touch more fascinating. When the seed pods 'explode' they emit a puff of 'smoke'!*

■ GENERAL TIP

Not a popular plant with commercial suppliers of houseplants, but very adaptable plants that will tolerate much ill treatment and not seem much bothered. Their habit can only be described as sprawling as they are seldom tidy. But it can be an advantage, particularly when plants are seen growing in hanging containers in a location protected from the sun.

275

RHOEO

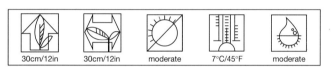

30cm/12in	30cm/12in	moderate	7°C/45°F	moderate

There is only one species of rhoeo, *Rhoeo spathacea* or boat lily, usually sold as *R. discolor*. The pointed, sword-shaped leaves first appear as a rosette, which in time grows to form a short, thick stem from which side shoots arise. These may be removed if preferred and, if they have developed their own roots, used to raise new plants. The leaves are very handsome, green above and rich purple on the undersides.

GENERAL CARE Grow in any good proprietary compost, watered constantly during the period of active growth but kept just moist when dormant. Bright light, not direct sunlight, and a minimum temperature of 16°C/61°F is essential when in growth. Stand the pots in trays of moist pebbles and feed every 2 weeks with liquid fertilizer. Repot annually in spring.

PROPAGATION Detach rooted basal shoots at any time and pot up singly in a mixture of peat and sand. Pot on using the recommended growing medium when firmly rooted.

VARIETIES *R. s.* 'Variegata' syn. 'Vittata', leaves striped golden.

POSSIBLE PROBLEMS Generally trouble-free.

RHOICISSUS

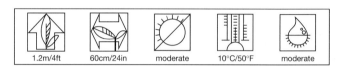

1.2m/4ft	60cm/24in	moderate	10°C/50°F	moderate

Commonly known as Cape grape, *Rhoicissus capensis* is a climbing plant which clings to supports such as bamboo canes with simple tendrils. The shiny, fresh green leaves are roughly heat-shaped and may be up to 20cm/8in across.

GENERAL CARE Grow in soil-based compost kept thoroughly moist during the growing period. Give overhead sprays with water and feed every 2 weeks. Rhoicissus tolerate light shade, but a reasonably bright situation out of direct sunlight is preferable. They are happy in cool or warm rooms as long as there are no sudden variations in temperature. Pinch out the growing tips to encourage a bushy shape. Keep the compost barely moist during the winter and repot in spring. When the largest practical pot size has been reached, top dress annually with fresh compost (see page 252). Plants that have become too big can be cut right back and will send out new growth. There are no named varieties.

PROPAGATION Take 10cm/4in tip cuttings in spring and root in equal parts peat and sand at 16-18°C/61-64°F.

POSSIBLE PROBLEMS Overwatering causes the leaves to turn yellow, shrivel and fall. Too little water makes the leaves turn brown.

■ **GENERAL TIP**

Common names make it easier for some to remember plants but they also lead to confusion – here we have the Boat Lily, but it is also Moses in the Cradle which alludes to the three white flowers in the boat.

■ **CARE TIP**

Not a plant for the faint-hearted, the Cape Grape is a prodigious grower that will be quick to fill its allotted space if conditions are in its favour. A framework of some kind for the vigorous growth is almost an essential

requirement, and it will be necessary to train the growth to fill gaps at lower level to provide a more attractive feature.

SANSEVIERIA

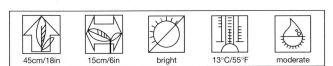

| 45cm/18in | 15cm/6in | bright | 13°C/55°F | moderate |

There are a number of sansevierias in common use, with some disagreement about distinction between species. Undoubtedly the most popular is *Sansevieria trifasciata*, generally known as mother-in-law's tongue, with dark green sword-like leaves.

GENERAL CARE Grow in a soil-based mixture to which one-third its volume of horticultural sand has been added to improve drainage. Use a heavy clay pot for upright varieties which may otherwise overbalance. Temperatures can be up to 26°C/80°F for these natives of West Africa, with plenty of light, preferably direct sunlight. Water moderately when in active growth and when resting allow the compost almost to dry out between waterings. Feeding should be stingy: apply half-strength liquid fertilizer every 4 weeks during the growth period only. Repotting is only necessary just before the overcrowded roots threaten to crack their pots. In other years, top-dress lightly with fresh compost (see page 252).

PROPAGATION Detach offsets from the parent rhizome and pot up, or take leaf cuttings and root in equal parts peat and sand at a temperature of 21°C/70°F.

VARIETIES *S. trifasciata* 'Laurentii', leaves edged golden yellow; *S. hahnii*, a rosette-forming species only 15cm/6in high, leaves edged gold or silver depending on variety.

POSSIBLE PROBLEMS Overwatering causes rot, especially if water is left to settle in the middle of the leaves.

▨ PROPAGATION TIP

Combination of cold and wet are the arch enemies of this plant. When propagating from 'toes' it is wise to remove the plant from its pot before cutting away the rhizome and its growth.

SAXIFRAGA

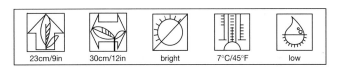

| 23cm/9in | 30cm/12in | bright | 7°C/45°F | low |

The saxifrages are a huge family of garden plants but only one, *Saxifraga stolonifera* (syn. *S. sarmentosa*) is grown as a house plant. It bears roughly circular, furry green leaves up to 10cm/4in across overlapping in an attractive rosette. Its distinction lies in the numerous little plantlets it bears at the end of long, delicate stolons (runners).

GENERAL CARE Grow in soil-based compost kept constantly moist during the growing period, though the pots should not stand in water. Tiny flowers appear in summer; after they have faded the amount of water should gradually be reduced until only enough is given during the rest period to prevent the compost from drying out. One or 2 hours of direct sunlight every day is recommended. As *S. stolonifera* prefers low temperatures – about 15°C/59°F – early morning sun is best. Repot in spring, putting plenty of drainage material in the pots, but do not expect to keep plants indefinitely.

PROPAGATION Detach plantlets from the parent plant and pot up in a 50:50 mixture of peat and sand. Pot on into the standard compost when rooted.

VARIETIES *S. stolonifera* 'Tricolor', small leaves edged cream, turning pink in good light; less vigorous than the species and needs more hours of sunlight.

POSSIBLE PROBLEMS Overwatering causes yellowing of the leaves.

▨ CARE TIP

Natural trailing plants are ever popular for hanging containers, and this is one of them. Many are sold in plastic containers with snap-on base saucers which is fine for preventing drips when watering. But it is important to tip away any water that has gathered in the saucer following watering – the alternative is soggy soil and sick plants.

SCINDAPSUS

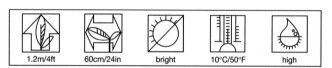

1.2m/4ft	60cm/24in	bright	10°C/50°F	high

The two types of scindapsus commonly available bear beautiful, glossy, heart-shaped leaves, sometimes marked silver or gold. They are climbers and need moss-covered supports to cling to.

GENERAL CARE Grow in a soil-based compost and water well during active growth. The plants like warmth but on very hot days will appreciate a misting over with water. Set in bright light, not direct sunlight, to maintain good leaf colour. Feed with liquid fertilizer every 2 weeks during the growth period. When the plant is resting, give it just enough water to prevent the compost from drying out. Repot annually in spring. When the plants have reached 20cm-8in pots, simply top-dress with fresh compost (see page 252).

PROPAGATION Take 10cm-4in tip cuttings in spring and root in equal parts peat and sand at 21-24°C/70-75°F. Plants raised from large-leaved cuttings will soon revert to producing small leaves.

VARIETIES *Scindapsus aureus* (*above left*), leaves a pointed oval when young, about 10cm/4in across, bright green marked yellow. Varieties include 'Golden Queen', almost completely yellow, and 'Marble Queen', white stems streaked green and cream leaves splashed with green and silver. *S. pictus argyraeus* (*above right*), matt green leaves spotted silver.

POSSIBLE PROBLEMS Overwatering causes leaves to yellow and fall.

■ CARE TIP

The Devil's Ivy may also be seen with its more recent name of S. epipremnum, but whatever the name it is one of the best indoor plants for poor light locations, but needs to be warm and moist.

SCIRPUS

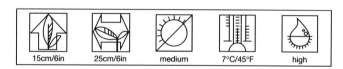

15cm/6in	25cm/6in	medium	7°C/45°F	high

Scirpus cernuus (*above*) is a member of the bulrush family, and, like its relative cyperus, likes to have its feet in water. The plant produces tufts of bright, slender green leaves from a creeping rootstock. So delicate are the leaves that they soon bend over the edge of the pot, making it almost impossible to place the plant anywhere else but in a hanging basket.

GENERAL CARE Grow in a soil-based compost kept constantly moist during the growing period. Water frequently – plants in hanging baskets dry out particularly quickly. Feeding is only necessary once every 4 weeks. Scirpus tolerate poor light well, for example at a north-facing window, but do not thrive in shade. During the resting period keep the compost just moist. Repot at any time if the surface of the compost becomes completely covered by the tufts of leaves. There are no named varieties.

PROPAGATION Divide overcrowded clumps in spring into 5cm/2in sections and replant immediately.

POSSIBLE PROBLEMS Generally trouble-free.

■ DESIGN TIP

Something of a fun plant with its weeping slender tubes of growth – the sort of growth that one is often at a loss to know what should be done with the plant to make it more effective. One suggestion is to seek out a ceramic head with a hole in the top rather than a mop of hair – the idea being that the scirpus placed in the hollow head becomes the flowing locks!

SETCREASEA

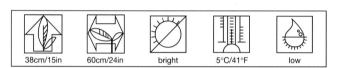

38cm/15in	60cm/24in	bright	5°C/41°F	low

Although setcreaseas bear tiny flowers in summer, it is for their extraordinary long pointed leaves that they are admired. In good light the foliage is a rich purple, contrasting well with the fresh green of the ubiquitous tradescantia, to which this plant is related. Setcreaseas are fast-growing and the trailing habit of growth can be rather untidy unless the shoots are regularly pinched out. There are no named varieties.

GENERAL CARE Grow in soil-based compost kept reasonably moist all year round, and feed with liquid fertilizer every 4 weeks. Good light is essential for leaf colour – several hours of direct sunlight every day is recommended. The ideal temperature is fairly warm, above 18°C/65°F. Repot whenever necessary; in practice setcreaseas are rarely kept beyond 2 years as they lose their good looks with age.

PROPAGATION Take 10cm/4in basal cuttings in summer.

POSSIBLE PROBLEMS Generally trouble-free.

SONERILA

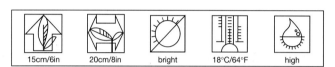

15cm/6in	20cm/8in	bright	18°C/64°F	high

Sonerila margaritacea is a low-growing, creeping plant with beautifully formed pointed leaves, green spotted silver, purple on the underside. The short stems are flushed with red. Tiny pink flowers appear in late summer. Because the plants grow continuously they are good subjects for closed containers or bottle gardens. For plants in room settings a short period of rest can be induced in the winter without doing any harm.

GENERAL CARE Grow in half-pots containing a peat-based compost to which a little leaf-mould, if available, has been added, with small pieces of crocks intermixed for improved drainage. Water moderately throughout the year. Sonerilas need good light, though not direct sunlight, and a warm atmosphere. Feed with liquid fertilizer every 2 weeks except for a brief period in winter if allowing the plants to rest. Repot annually in spring, and replace the plants when they become too leggy.

PROPAGATION Take 7.5cm/3in stem cuttings at any time except during a rest period. Set 3 cuttings to a 7.5cm/3in pot covered with a plastic bag until rooted, then gradually acclimatize them to normal conditions.

VARIETIES *S. m. hendersonii*, leaves more liberally spotted with white than the species; *S. m. argentea*, leaves almost completely silver; *S. m. marmorata*, leaves banded with silver.

POSSIBLE PROBLEMS Generally trouble-free.

◼ DESIGN TIP

Often seen as pathetic single stems in pots that are too large. Overcome this problem by putting lots of cuttings in the pot at the outset and pinching out the tips once into growth.

◼ CARE TIP

Not by any means the easiest of plants to manage, they are a bit like the fittonias that shrivel and die for little reason. As suggested for fittonias these would be much happier in the home if allowed the luxury of a large heated propagator in which to grow. A collection of these more tender plants with pots plunged in peat or moss can be a room feature.

TOLMIEA

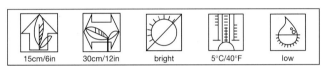

| 15cm/6in | 30cm/12in | bright | 5°C/40°F | low |

Tolmiea menziesii is a member of the saxifrage family, and like *S. stolonifera* is sometimes called mother-of-thousands because of the way it freely produces its young. In this instance, however, the plantlets arise on the upper surface of the leaves, which explains tolmiea's more common name of 'piggy-back plant'. The leaves are slightly downy, shaped like a maple leaf, and the plants are nicely compact. There are no named varieties.

GENERAL CARE Grow in a soil-based compost. When in active growth water moderately and feed with liquid fertilizer every 2 weeks. Set in good light, out of direct sunlight. Tolmieas are accommodating as to temperature and fast-growing. repot at any time of year, but be prepared to replace old plants after a year or 18 months.

PROPAGATION Detach a leaf bearing a healthy plantlet and with a short length of stem. Place in trays or small pots of potting compost until rooted. Pot up 3 to a pot for the best effect.

POSSIBLE PROBLEMS generally trouble-free.

TRADESCANTIA

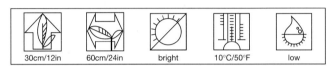

| 30cm/12in | 60cm/24in | bright | 10°C/50°F | low |

Tradescantias are the best-known trailing foliage plants, valued for their strong constitution and adaptabilty. The most popular varieties are those whose pointed oval leaves are variegated cream or white, but a green-leaved species is available. All look their best in hanging baskets or other situations where the trailing stems can fall freely.

GENERAL CARE Grow in soil-based compost kept reasonably moist during the active growing period. Feed with a liquid fertilizer every 2 weeks. Good light is important, though too much direct sunlight may scorch the leaves. Often these plants are kept at low temperatures, but they do best in warm rooms. Pinch out the growing tips to encourage bushy growth. Repot at any time of year, replacing old plants when they beome straggly.

PROPAGATION Take 10cm/4in tip cuttings at any time of year. Place in water, or place 6 cuttings in a 7.5cm/3in pot containing peat and sand until rooted and then pot up in the recommended compost.

SPECIES *Tradescantia fluminensis* 'Quicksilver' (*above*), strong-growing variety, prominent silver stripes; *T. blossfeldiana*, dark green leaves, purple beneath, in the variety 'Variegata' striped cream; *T. albiflora*, close growing species with many variegated forms, including 'Tricolor' with green leaves striped white and purple.

POSSIBLE PROBLEMS Overwatering reduces leaf colour.

▦ GENERAL TIP

Most useful plants that are not only attractive indoors but also hardy in the garden – if less attractive owing to the effects of wind and rain. Outdoors offer sheltered location.

▦ CARE TIP

Great favourites, these suffer from the old wives' advice of keeping them dry and unfed to preserve variegation in leaves. To maintain attractive colouring all poorly coloured foliage should be removed on sight and plants *should be fed and watered as one would any vigorous growing plant in a container. Five or six potfuls of cuttings in a hanging basket can be superb.*

YUCCA

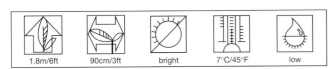

| 1.8m/6ft | 90cm/3ft | bright | 7°C/45°F | low |

The unusual yucca is a native of the south-east United States, and is commonly known as Spanish bayonet. At the top of a woody stem some 5cm/2in thick it bears a cluster of minutely toothed sword-shaped leaves. All forms of this eye-catching species are suited to a bright spacious entrance hall or porch.

GENERAL CARE Grow in a loam-based compost kept thoroughly moist during the growing period. Give a liquid feed every two weeks. Yuccas need bright light, including some direct sunlight, and are tolerant of a wide range of temperatures. They like a dry atmosphere. If possible, put them outside in a sunny spot for a few hours on summer days. Water sparingly in winter, and repot in spring if roots are overcrowded. Use heavy clay pots for stability.

PROPAGATION Professional growers cut the roots into 7.5cm/3in pieces and pot them up individually in sandy soil. This is difficult for amateurs, who do better to detach offsets, if they are produced, and treat them as cuttings.

SPECIES *P. aloifolia (above)*: blue-green leaves, stem normally unbranched except in the variety *P. a. draconis*: the leaves of *P. a. tricolor* have a central yellow stripe. *P. elephantipes*: several stems bearing glossy green leaves.

POSSIBLE PROBLEMS Leaf spot.

ZEBRINA

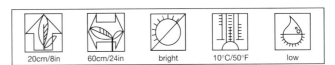

| 20cm/8in | 60cm/24in | bright | 10°C/50°F | low |

Zebrina pendula belongs to the same family as tradescantias and has much the same habit of growth. It is quick-growing and will do better in cooler temperatures than tradescantias. There are some interesting coloured forms available; a mixed planting of different varieties looks very attractive, especially if trained upwards on thin stakes rather than left to trail freely.

GENERAL CARE Grow in soil-based compost and set several plants to each pot for a bushy effect. Pinch out the growing tips regularly. Water moderately while in active growth and feed with liquid fertilizer every 2 weeks. Place in good light in order to maintain leaf colour. A warm atmosphere is preferred. Repot whenever the roots become overcrowded.

PROPAGATION Take 7.5cm/3in tip cuttings in summer and treat as tradescantias.

VARIETIES *Z. p.* 'Discolor', slender leaves striped silver and bronze; 'Purpusii', large green leaves flushed purple, carmine beneath; 'Quadricolor', striped white, green and purple, purple beneath.

POSSIBLE PROBLEMS Leaves turn brown and fall in poor light or if overwatered.

▌DESIGN TIP

Yuccas excel at the dramatic statement particularly in pairs flanking an archway or door. Especially effective when seen in silhouette, they look best against a plain, unpatterned background.

▌GENERAL TIP

Often passed over as being too ordinary, the sparkling silver colouring of this plant is almost without equal. Select best colours when purchasing and remove all inferior foliage.

FLOWERING PLANTS

In purely practical terms, the main attraction of flowering houseplants is that they last so much longer than cut flowers. Indeed, some will be in bloom for months. Many are easy to care for, while others are a little fussier and give you an opportunity to practise your gardening skills. A bushy shape is common – with the notable exceptions of jasmine, clivia and columnea – but apart from this common feature there is an enormous variety of flower colour, leaf shape and overall size.

There is a flowering plant for every season. In winter, while the garden is almost bare of ornament, the house can be full of exuberant colour, with the pinks, purple and blues of cheerful cinerarias, bright yellow chrysanthemums, shocking pink cyclamens and vivid red poinsettias (*Euphorbia pulcherrima*). Jasmines, ruellias and the impressive strelitzias (not forgetting primulas and the contribution made by bulbs – see page 316) bloom in spring. In summer the range of plants for indoor flowering is breathtaking. From the ever-popular fuchsia and fragrant Persian violet (*Exacum affine*) to the reliable buzy lizzie (impatiens) and exotic hoya, there is something to please all tastes and suit all situations.

SUCCESS WITH COLOUR

In terms of interior design foliage plants, including palms and ferns, have a certain versatility simply because they are, with some exceptions, uniformly green. While much of the charm of flowering plants naturally derives from the colour of their petals, to be displayed at their best some thought needs to be given to the overall colour scheme. In a room busy with patterns and prints, it is all too easy for plants to disappear against the background. In this situation, choose a plant whose flowers echo the brightest accent colour. The most effective is yellow, with vivid pink and red a close second and third. Draw attention to the plant with a careful choice of container; try a highly glazed pot in a plain colour complementing the flower, or a brass or copper pot with a burnished sheen. Display the pot against a plain wall which will act as a neutral background and, if painted in a pale shade, reflect some light back on the plant.

Modern room settings and offices tend to draw on a limited palette of subtle colours or simply stick to black and white. You can continue the understated feeling with a white cyclamen or hydrangea, especially in combination with sympathetic foliage plants; or use an unassertive colour scheme to set off plants that demand attention. Sinningias have it all: vivid, velvety trumpet-shaped flowers and huge dark green leaves. A collection of red or pink cinerarias looks stunning against white or cream. An orange clivia in full flower is like a piece of sculpture, perfect in light, spacious rooms.

PELARGONIUMS

Those fortunate enough to have sunny windows with deep sills have the ideal spot for a group of pelargoniums. The choice here is bewildering, and like roses and narcissi these are plants which have acquired a devoted following. As well as the zonal and regal types described on page 297, there are species such as *P. crispum*, with balm-scented leaves, edged with creamy white in the variety 'Variegatum', and *P. tomentosum*, a climber with velvety leaves strongly scented with peppermint. These two species bear modest blooms of pink and white respectively. The best lemon-scented variety is 'Citriodorum'; 'Attar of Roses' is rose-scented. Both have pale mauve flowers. Pelargonium leaves vary in shape, colour and texture. Ivy-leaved forms are bright green and glossy; these are varieties of *P. peltatum*, a trailing species. They include the aristocratic

'L'Elegante', whose white flowers are feathered purple, the green leaves edged cream and flushed with purple as autumn approaches. *P. quercifolium*, the oak-leaved pelargonium, is at 90cm/3ft a good choice for conservatories and bears pink flowers veined with purple.

Pelargoniums are easy to raise from seed and can be successfully propagated by cuttings taken in summer. This method is also suitable for fuchsias, but it is advisable to leave more leaves on the cuttings. New plants may also be raised from overwintered specimens by taking cuttings in spring. Healthy but smaller plants are produced in this way.

PRIMULAS

Some types of flowering plants have been developed by plant breeders to flower at virtually any time of year in the extra warmth afforded to plants grown indoors. The most successful of these is the chrysanthemum, which is raised commercially in particular conditions. You can have your own primulas in bloom most of the year too, by choosing different varieties and sowing seed at different times. *P. malacoides* and *P. obconica* will produce large plants from seed sown in very early spring, but perfectly healthy specimens will result from sowings as late as midsummer, flowering correspondingly later. Sow seed as described on page 252; for germination a temperature of 16°C/61°F is essential. Prick off the seedlings into boxes, then singly into 8cm/3¹/₂in pots. Spring-sown seedlings should be hardened off in an unheated frame during the summer. Transfer to the final pots in early autumn and bring indoors. They enjoy a cool spot indoors near a window to ensure constant light but without direct sunlight.

Primulas are available in a vast range of colours and can be grown from seed for winter and spring flowering.

ABUTILON

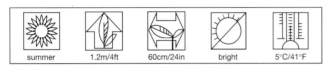

| summer | 1.2m/4ft | 60cm/24in | bright | 5°C/41°F |

Abutilons are members of the mallow family, though because of the shape of the leaves they are often called flowering maples. There are several species suitable for indoor cultivation, but most need the space of a greenhouse. *A. × hybridum*, at 60cm/24in high (it is unlikely to reach the maximum height given above), is the most suitable for the home. It bears nodding flowers of white, yellow, orange or red from late spring right through to the autumn.

GENERAL CARE Grow in a soil-based compost kept nicely moist throughout the growing period. Feed with liquid fertilizer every 2 weeks and position the plants in an airy room where they will receive several hours of direct sunlight every day. During the rest period water enough to prevent the compost from drying out. Repot in spring, upgrading by one size. Plants grow spindly after 3 years and should be discarded.

PROPAGATION Take 10cm/4in tip cuttings in summer and root in equal parts peat and sand at a temperature of 15-18°C/59-64°F.

VARIETIES 'Master Hugh' (*above*), rich rose-pink; 'Boule de Neige', snow-white with golden stamens; 'Canary Bird' yellow.

POSSIBLE PROBLEMS Scale insects; mealy bugs.

ACALYPHA

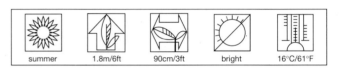

| summer | 1.8m/6ft | 90cm/3ft | bright | 16°C/61°F |

Known variously as the chenille plant or red hot cat's tail, *Acalypha hispida* is an exotic plant which can become very tall in a heated greenhouse. Even at 1.8m/6ft (the maximum height it will achieve in the home), it requires an unusual amount of space, which admirers of its spectacular flowers are happy to provide. These blooms are like catkins, up to 45cm/18in long and bright red. The vivid green leaves are pointed ovals up to 20cm/8in long.

GENERAL CARE Grow in a soil-based compost kept constantly moist during the growing season. Feed with liquid fertilizer every 2 weeks. Steady temperatures in the range 18-20°C/64-68°F or more are ideal, with humidity kept high with frequent mist-spraying. Stand the pots in trays of moist pebbles. Bright, filtered light is essential. Because acalyphas are naturally bushy, there is no need to pinch out the growing tips. Cutting back may, however, be necessary to restrict growth in confined areas. In winter, water just enough to keep the compost from drying out. Repot in spring, or at any other time if the roots are crowded. Discard after two seasons.

PROPAGATION Take 10cm/4in tip cuttings in early spring.

VARIETIES *A. h.* 'Alba', white-flowered type.

POSSIBLE PROBLEMS Red spider mite; mealy bug.

▮ PLANTING TIP

Only suitable if there is ample space for the amount of foliage that these plants are capable of producing. Over the summer months the problem can be sidestepped to some extent by planting plants as features in the garden. They can then be dug up, potted, trimmed back and re-introduced to a light and agreeable location indoors. Feed well when established.

▮ DESIGN TIP

In recent years often seen as a hanging plant in the Garden Centre, but it is far from happy in such elevated positions. Much better in large pots at ground level, by a pool perhaps.

ACHIMENES

summer	30cm/12in	20cm/8in	bright	2°C/35°F

Once their simple requirements are met, these bushy plants produce their beautiful tubular flowers of crimson, red, lavender or purple right through the summer. The small, pointed leaves are dark green, sometimes flushed red.

GENERAL CARE Achimenes grow from small rhizomes. Plant in a peat-based compost to which a little ground limestone has been added to reduce acidity. Set 6 to a 12.5cm/5in pot or 8 to 15cm/6in pot and position where they will enjoy good light, but not direct sunlight. When growth starts in early spring, water copiously using cooled boiled water and never let the compost dry out. Start feeding with liquid fertilizer every 2 weeks when flowerbuds appear and continue until the flowers have faded. Spray plants with a fine mist on hot days. Support the stems with thin canes. After flowering, gradually reduce the amount of water until, in the dormant period, the pots are quite dry. Keep in a cool, frost-free place over winter. Repot in spring.

PROPAGATION When repotting, separate out the brittle rhizomes and pot up in the fresh compost. Place them horizontally just 1cm/¹/₂in below the surface of the compost.

SPECIES *Achimenes heterophylla*, orange flowers 4cm/¹/₂in wide; 'Little Beauty' (*above*) is a bushy variety with bright pink flowers; *A. grandiflora*, up to 60cm/24in high, erect plant with magenta flowers; *A. longiflora*, suitable for hanging baskets; set 10-12 rhizomes to a pot and stems will trail over the edge.

■ CARE TIP

Bright and cheerful plants that are easy to manage on a light windowsill, but it is important to maintain good and steady temperature during the early weeks of development. The obscure common name of Hot Water Plant is difficult to reason with, but may allude to watering with warm water following winter rest.

ANTHURIUM

spring	23cm/9in	23cm/9in	medium	10°C/50°F

Anthuriums are natives of South America, where they grow to massive proportions. As house plants, however, they are compact but bushy. The best flowering species is *A. scherzerianum*, the flamingo flower, which is spectacularly colourful from spring right through to mid autumn. Its inflorescences consist of a large scarlet spathe from which a narrow, curly orange spadix emerges. They may need the support of thin canes. The pointed dark green leaves, up to 15cm/6in long, are equally handsome. There are no named varieties.

GENERAL CARE Grow in a fibrous open mixture consisting of fibrous peat, sphagnum moss, crushed charcoal and a little soil-based compost, with a generous layer of drainage material at the bottom of the pot. Plants should not be set too deep. Keep the compost thoroughly moist but not waterlogged during the growing period and feed with liquid fertilizer every 2 weeks. Success depends on steadily maintained temperatures between 18 and 21°C/64 and 70°F – draughts spell disaster – and high humidity. Stand the pots on trays of moist pebbles and spray the foliage with a fine mist daily. It helps to position anthuriums in groups of other plants, where humidity is usually higher. Place in slight shade. In winter, keep the compost just moist. Repot in spring, upgrading by one size.

PROPAGATION Divide the roots in early spring.

POSSIBLE PROBLEMS Aphids; leaf spot.

■ GENERAL TIP

Besides A. schertzerianum there is the more exotic and more demanding A. andreanum which has bold arrow-shaped leaves and spathe inflorescences in various colours on metre-long stems. Blooms are much in demand by the keen flower arranger and they have long-lasting qualities when cut that make them doubly useful. Generous warmth and moist surroundings are essential.

APHELANDRA

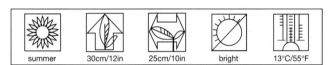

| summer | 30cm/12in | 25cm/10in | bright | 13°C/55°F |

Only one species of aphelandra, *A. squarrosa*, is grown as a house plant and while its vivid yellow flowers are showy enough, the foliage is equally eye-catching. The broad green leaves are up to 30cm/12in long, veined in a sharply contrasting cream, hence the popular name of zebra plant.

GENERAL CARE Grow in a peat-based compost kept constantly moist during the growing season. Feed with liquid fertilizer once a week and keep at a steady temperature of about 18°C/64°F. High humidity is important – stand the pots in saucers of moist pebbles and mist over with a very fine spray every few days. The plants need good but indirect light. In the brief winter rest period, water just enough to prevent the stems from drooping. After flowering, cut back the main stem to a healthy pair of leaves. This will encourage the production of side shoots for propagation. Repot in spring, upgrading to a final pot size of 15cm/6in.

PROPAGATION Detach side shoots when 10cm/4in long and use as cuttings. Root in equal parts of peat and sand at 21°C/70°F.

VARIETIES *A. s.* 'Louisae' (*above*), orange-yellow bracts, red stems; 'Leopoldii', red bracts, pure white leaf markings; 'Citrina', sharp yellow bracts.

POSSIBLE PROBLEMS Aphids, scale insects and mealy bugs on young growths.

■ PROPAGATION TIP

Keeping these from year to year is seldom successful indoors – much better to have a propagator and to raise cuttings made from shoots that form in the leaf axils of older plants.

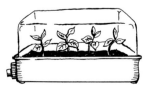

AZALEA

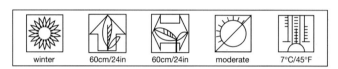

| winter | 60cm/24in | 60cm/24in | moderate | 7°C/45°F |

The pot plants sold in winter by florists as Indian azaleas are varieties of *Rhododendron simsii*, a Chinese species. Sometimes they are (wrongly) labelled *R. indicum*, which confusingly enough comes from Japan and is an evergreen that may reach 1.8m/6ft. *R. simsii* can reach 1.5m/6ft in a sheltered garden but is more compact grown in pots. Its gorgeous winter display of exotic blooms in a wide range of colours (except blue) has made the azalea very popular.

GENERAL CARE Choose a specimen just coming into bud. Place in a cool situation protected from draughts and keep moist by immersing the pot in water 2-3 times a week for 5 minutes. Always use rainwater or cooled boiled water. Do not feed. After flowering keep very cool and just moist. Place outside in a shaded position after all danger of frost has passed. Keep shaded and moist, spraying frequently, until bringing indoors again as winter begins. Repot in autumn using an acid compost.

PROPAGATION Take 7.5cm/3in cuttings in summer and root them in a mixture of 2 parts fine sand and 1 part peat. When rooted pot in compost of peat, leaf-mould, lime-free loam and coarse sand in equal proportions.

VARIETIES Florists' azaleas are unlikely to be named.

POSSIBLE PROBLEMS Lime in the water or growing medium will invariably result in yellow foliage, poor growth and ultimate collapse.

■ CARE TIP

The period following flowering is a critical time for these plants – often the time for most neglect. Remove dead flowers carefully so that new growth buds below the flowers are not damaged, and keep the plant moist and protected from frost until it is safe to put it outside in a lightly shaded, sheltered location. Keep watered and fed while outside – bring in before frosts occur.

BEGONIA SEMPERFLORENS

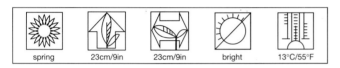

| spring | 23cm/9in | 23cm/9in | bright | 13°C/55°F |

Wax begonias, *Begonia semperflorens-cultorum*, bear their small but brilliantly coloured flowers all summer if grown outdoors. If you select F_1 hybrids, however, and grow them on a sunny windowsill indoors, they are almost perpetual flowering. Blooms are white and shades of pink or red; the foliage may be dark red or brown or green.

GENERAL CARE Grow in a peat-based compost kept moist but not waterlogged. Feed with liquid fertilizer every 2 weeks. Set the pots in good light, preferably where the plants can enjoy a few hours of direct sunlight every day. Normal room temperatures are suitable. Discard the plants after flowering.

PROPAGATION *B. semperflorens* are fibrous-rooted begonias, raised from seed. Sow seed in very early spring at 16°C/61°F. Plants should be ready for final potting up in about 10 weeks.

VARIETIES Red/brown leaves: 'Carmen', pink; 'Comet' (F_1), all colours; 'Coffee and Cream', white. Green leaves: 'Bella', rich pink; 'Scarletta', deep red; 'Organdy Mixture' (F_1), all colours.

POSSIBLE PROBLEMS Generally trouble-free.

BEGONIA TUBERHYBRIDA

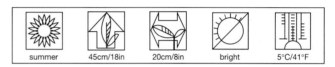

| summer | 45cm/18in | 20cm/8in | bright | 5°C/41°F |

The flowers of tuberous begonias, *Begonia tuberhybrida*, are among the most flamboyant of all house plants. Double-flowered varieties are available, as well as types with pendulous blooms, ideal for hanging baskets.

GENERAL CARE Buy tubers in spring and place concave side up in trays of damp seed compost. Set them 5cm/2in apart and press down to half their depth. Position on a warm windowsill and when 2-3 leaves have opened up, pot up in a peat-based mixture so that the tuber is just visible. Place in light shade, gradually pot on and bring into bright but filtered light. Water moderately during the flowering period and give a high-potassium liquid feed every 2 weeks. To allow the showy male flowers to develop, remove the small female flowers when they appear. In winter, let the compost dry out place in a frost-free place or remove the tubers and store them in clean dry sand over winter.

PROPAGATION In spring, cut large tubers into sections, each with a growing point, and treat as above.

VARIETIES Double: 'Buttermilk', cream; 'Crown Prince', crimson; 'Everest', white, frilled petals; 'Midas' golden yellow; 'Ninette', pale apricot, very large; 'Rebecca', light pink, blooms like rosebuds. *B. t. pendula* (trailing stems): 'Yellow Sweetie', scented; 'Roberta', scarlet.

POSSIBLE PROBLEMS Weevils, eelworms; grey mould.

▪ PLANTING TIP

Before frosts arrive dig up some of these from the garden and pot into containers for the summer display to continue on the windowsill indoors until the following spring – perhaps longer!

▪ GENERAL TIP

To see these at their best visit the British Begonia Championships – you may well not believe what your eyes are feasting on. But it must be said that such plants are grown from expensive named varieties. To do well all tuberous begonias should be started in late winter in almost dry peat and thereafter given little water until growth is evident.

BELOPERONE

spring	60cm/24in	45cm/18in	medium	7°C/45°F

Only one species of beloperone, a native of Mexico, is in general cultivation. *B. guttata* is commonly known as the shrimp plant because of the appearance of its inflorescences, pinkish bracts surrounding insignificant flowers. These hang on arching stems and are borne profusely from spring until the middle of winter. With its light green pointed leaves and bushy habit, the shrimp plant is very decorative. Provide thin stakes to support mature plants. There are no named varieties.

GENERAL CARE Grow in a rich, soil-based compost and keep well watered throughout the growing period. Strong sunlight will scorch the flowers, but reasonably bright light is best as long as the plants are in a well-ventilated room (as opposed to a draughty corner) and are not allowed to dry out. Temperatures of about 15°C/59°F will encourage long-lasting flowers. Feed with a liquid fertilizer once a week from the time flowering starts until autumn. Reduce watering during the winter, giving just enough to prevent the compost drying out. In early spring, cut back the plant to keep it bushy, and repot if necessary, adding a little peat to the compost.

PROPAGATION Take 7.5cm/3in stem cuttings in spring and root in a mixture of peat and sand at 18°C/64°F.

POSSIBLE PROBLEMS Generally trouble-free.

BROWALLIA

summer	45cm/18in	25cm/10in	bright	10°C/50°F

Browallias are annual plants grown for their display of vivid purplish-blue five-petalled flowers. Two species are available, bearing blooms in summer or winter depending on the time of sowing. The slender stems may need the support of thin stakes, or can be left to trail over the edge of the pot if displayed in hanging baskets.

GENERAL CARE Grow in 12.5cm/5in pots containing a soil-based mixture. Water moderately, allowing the compost to dry out a little between applications. Feed established plants with liquid fertilizer every 2 weeks. Browallias thrive in good light, including several hours of direct sunlight every day, but keep temperatures below 18°C/64°F to encourage long-lasting flowers. The ideal temperature is given above. Pinch out the growing tips regularly to encourage a bushy shape. Discard the plants after flowering.

PROPAGATION Sow seed in spring for late summer flowering, in late summer for a winter display.

SPECIES *B. speciosa* (*above*), 5cm/2in wide flowers in bloom for 4 months; *B. s. major* is the best variety for winter-flowering; 'Silver Bells' is a white-flowered form. *B. viscosa* is more compact at 30cm/12in, with smaller flowers.

POSSIBLE PROBLEMS Generally trouble-free.

■ CARE TIP

Much underrated plants on account of their need for frequent feeding and regular potting on. Both these actions will produce much more lush plants with infinitely more flowering bracts.

■ PROPAGATION TIP

Many of the seed-raised house plants are the prerogative of the commercial grower with ideal conditions at his disposal, but there are numerous kinds that can be raised on the windowsill indoors and this is one of them.

Sow lightly in shallow seed trays filled with peat and sand mixture and cover with a sheet of glass until seed has germinated. Protect with paper from sun.

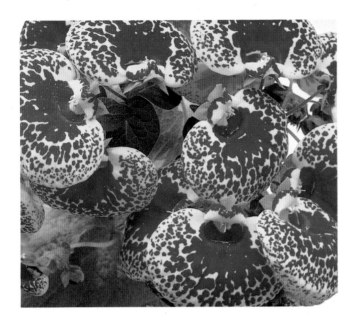

CALCEOLARIA

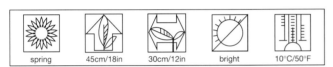

| spring | 45cm/18in | 30cm/12in | bright | 10°C/50°F |

The calceolaria family includes hundreds of species, including some alpines, but only one is in general use as a flowering house plant. This is the hybrid *Calceolaria herbeohybrida*, and although its flowering period is brief it is dazzlingly colourful. The slipper-shaped flowers, clustering above large, oval, slightly hairy leaves, are orange, yellow or red and often blotched with a contrasting colour. A dwarf strain with particularly attractive blooms is also available.

GENERAL CARE Grow in a mixture of soil-based compost and peat – calceoloarias like a slightly acid soil. Keep the compost constantly and evenly moist. It is a good idea to stand the pots in trays of moist peat to keep the humidity level high. While the flowering period (at best about a month) can be extended by keeping the plants cool, it is equally important to give them bright light, though not direct sunlight. Feeding is not necessary and the plants should be discarded after flowering.

PROPAGATION Calceolarias are raised commercially in great numbers and are widely available. If you wish to raise your own, sow the tiny seeds in summer. Overwinter the seedlings at 7-10°C/45-50°F before final potting up.

VARIETIES *C. h.* 'Monarch', a reliable strain which includes mixed colours; 'Multiflora Nana', up to 20cm/8in high, with abundant flowers.

POSSIBLE PROBLEMS Aphids.

▨ CARE TIP

These should be watered with care avoiding getting water onto the foliage of the plants. Ideally, the leaves should be lifted while water is carefully poured onto the soil surface.

CAMPANULA

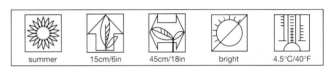

| summer | 15cm/6in | 45cm/18in | bright | 4.5°C/40°F |

The bell-flower family includes a huge variety of plants, one of which has become popular for indoor decoration. This is *Campanula isophylla*, native to northern Italy, a perennial which can successfully be grown outdoors in favoured districts. Low-growing, its long stems may be trained up thin stakes or left to trail gracefully over the side of the pot, especially if displayed in a hanging basket. Star-shaped pale lilac flowers appear in mid summer and persist for up to 12 weeks, becoming so numerous that the tangled, heart-shaped leaves are almost completely concealed.

GENERAL CARE Grow in soil-based compost kept well-watered though never waterlogged. Even in the rest period campanulas like their roots nicely damp. Feed with liquid fertilizer every 2 weeks until flowering is over. Keep cool during flowering, while ensuring bright light at all times. Spray with a fine mist to maintain humidity, especially if the temperature rises above 18°C/64°F. Deadhead regularly, and before the rest period cut all stems right back. Repot in early spring if necessary.

PROPAGATION Take 5cm/2in tip cuttings in early spring, ensuring that each has 4 pairs of leaves.

VARIETIES *C. a.* 'Alba' (above), white-flowered form; 'Mayi', blue flowers, variegated leaves.

POSSIBLE PROBLEMS Generally trouble-free.

▨ FLOWERING TIP

There are blue and white flowered forms and, though seen less often, the white form makes a much bolder and more attractive plant. In hanging containers in a cool room or conservatory they will flower for months on end during the spring and summer. But it is vital that dead flowers be removed almost continuously to prevent formation of seed and an end of flowers.

CAPSICUM

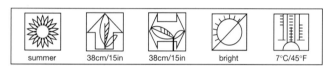

| summer | 38cm/15in | 38cm/15in | bright | 7°C/45°F |

The ornamental pepper, *Capsicum annum*, belongs to the same family as edible peppers; in theory the fruits of this species are edible too, but bearing in mind the fact that the smallest peppers are the hottest, these are likely to be unbearably fiery. Decorative they certainly are, in a range of colours including red, orange, yellow and purple, all of which are green, then creamy-yellow, when young. They last for weeks. The leaves are pointed and the whole plant attractively bushy.

GENERAL CARE Most capsicums are bought with the fruit already formed. Choose a compact, bushy plant with green (young) fruits. Keep at normal room temperatures – cooler if possible – and make sure that the compost is always thoroughly moist. Feed with liquid fertilizer every 2 weeks. Bright light is essential, including several hours of direct sunlight every day. The fruits stay colourful and plump for up to 12 weeks, but eventually shrivel and fall, at which point the plant should be discarded.

PROPAGATION Raising capsicums from seed is beyond the scope of most amateurs.

VARIETIES There are several named varieties, but the great majority on sale will be anonymous, even if of excellent quality.

POSSIBLE PROBLEMS Aphids, red spider mites.

CHRYSANTHEMUM

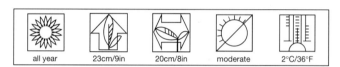

| all year | 23cm/9in | 20cm/8in | moderate | 2°C/36°F |

There are an enormous number of garden chrysanthemums of different kinds and sizes. A few of these have been selected for special treatment to keep the growth compact (in the garden chrysanthemums can reach 1.2m/4ft in height) and to permit flowering at any time of year. The colour range of these attractively bushy specimens includes white, yellow, red, pink and bronze.

GENERAL CARE Buy chrysanthemums with a few flowers opening, the rest still in green buds just flushed with colour. Keep well watered, in reasonable light and as cool as possible to encourage a long flowering period. In favourable conditions plants can be expected to last up to 8 weeks. Remove flowers as they fade. Neither feeding nor repotting is necessary and after flowering these plants should be discarded.

PROPAGATION It is not possible for amateurs to raise chrysanthemums under the artificial conditions necessary to produce these compact plants.

VARIETIES Chrysanthemums sold as pot plants do not usually bear a particular name.

POSSIBLE PROBLEMS Generally trouble-free.

■ CARE TIP

Hot, dry atmosphere will increase incidence of pests – aphids and red spider mites. To counteract both it is wise to treat plants with a systemic insecticide before pests appear.

■ CARE TIP

For their 6/8 week flowering life indoors these are foolproof plants if offered cool, light and reasonably moist conditions. Growers treat with growth retardants to control height.

CINERARIA

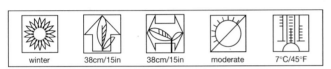

| winter | 38cm/15in | 38cm/15in | moderate | 7°C/45°F |

Although correctly named *Senecio cruentus*, these colourful, winter- and spring-flowering pot plants are always known as cinerarias. They produce masses of daisy-like flowers of pink, purple, red or blue, sometimes zoned with white. The compact mound of blooms is framed by large, dark green palmate leaves. Different strains have been developed, including dwarf varieties.

GENERAL CARE Cinerarias are available as pot plants from the late autumn. Buy specimens whose buds are just beginnning to show colour. Kept cool, moist and shaded, the plants will last up to 7 weeks. Water regularly as cinerarias lose moisture quickly through their large leaves. Feeding is not necessary. Discard the plants after flowering.

PROPAGATION Sow seeds in early summer for a mid-winter flowering, 4 weeks later for a spring flowering. Feed the young plants once a week in the autumn (before they come into flower) with half-strength liquid fertilizer.

VARIETIES Hybrida Grandiflora strain; 'Brilliant', up to 53cm/21in high with large flowers; Double-flowered strain: 'Gubler's Double Mixed', about 38cm/15in high with double or semi-double flowers; Multiflora Nana strain: 'Gem Mixed', about 30cm/12in high, broad-petalled flowers.

POSSIBLE PROBLEMS Aphids; leaf miners.

■ CARE TIP

To prolong flowering period indoors it is essential to offer these plants cool, airy and light conditions – in warm rooms, added to the shorter flowering life, there will also be a much greater incidence of pests. And these plants when in weak condition through improper care will attract all the pests in the book. Frequent inspection of undersides of leaves is needed.

CLIVIA

| spring | 60cm/24in | 30cm/12in | bright | 10°C/50°F |

The kaffir lily, *Clivia miniata*, is a spectacular flowering plant from South Africa. It produces several straight flower-bearing stalks from a bulbous base of overlapping leaves. The trumpet-shaped blooms of orange or yellow appear in abundant clusters. There are no named varieties.

GENERAL CARE Plant crowns when they become available in early spring, setting them in 12.5cm/5in pots of soil-based compost. Put in a position where they will enjoy good direct light, but out of the midday sun. Clivias thrive in average room temperature. Keep well watered during the spring and summer and start to feed with liquid fertilizer when the flower stalks are about 20cm/8in high. As autumn approaches, cease feeding and gradually decrease the amount of water leading up to a revitalizing rest period in early winter. During this time the compost should be almost dry and the temperature cool. Protect from frost. Repot after 2-3 years, after flowering, when the roots – which grow quickly – have filled the pot. Once plants have reached a 25cm/10in pot, simply top-dress annually (see page 252).

PROPAGATION Separate old plants into crowns, taking care not to damage the roots, and pot up singly. Clivias produce off-sets which can happily be left on the plant, but if wished can be detached with a sharp knife and potted up. Do this after flowering, selecting offsets with at least 3 good leaves.

POSSIBLE PROBLEMS Mealy bugs.

■ FLOWERING TIP

Extremely resilient plants in reasonable conditions, but not easy to bring into flower. Like many native South African plants they need a dry resting period to encourage flowering. Alternatively, if a heated conservatory is available they can be planted in a bed of good soil where they will produce an abundance of their rich, orange-coloured flowers.

COLUMNEA

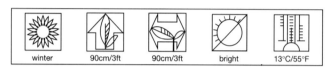

winter	90cm/3ft	90cm/3ft	bright	13°C/55°F

There are several species of columneas used as house plants; they are pendulous plants best seen in hanging baskets. Yellow or red flowers appear over many weeks in winter or spring.

GENERAL CARE Grow in a mixture of 2 parts peat-crushed compost and 1 part sphagnum moss, adding a little crushed charcoal to improve aeration. Keep the compost constantly moist, and mist the plants over with a spray of rainwater as often as possible. In summer, give a liquid feed at half-strength every week. Hang the baskets in full light, out of direct sun, and maintain a steady temperature of around 16°C/61°F in winter if possible. Pinch the stems back to encourage a bushy shape and cut them right back after flowering. Repot every other year.

PROPAGATION Take 7.5 cm/3in cuttings of non-flowering stems in spring and root in a mixture of equal parts peat and sand at 18-21°C/64-70°F. Pot up when established, setting 3 plants to a 25cm/10in basket.

VARIETIES *Columnea × banksii*, flowering winter into spring, orange-red blooms, glossy leaves; *C. gloriosa*, abundant scarlet flowers, splashed yellow, in winter, pale green leaves; *C. microphylla*, winter flowering, orange flowers, trailing stems up to 1.8m/6ft; *C.* 'Alpha' (*above*), hybrid bearing clear yellow flowers all year; *C.* 'Mary Ann', deep pink flowers all year.

POSSIBLE PROBLEMS Generally trouble-free if high levels of humidity are maintained.

▨ FLOWERING TIP

Some easy, some difficult, but all will flower more freely if they have a slightly drier and a cooler period prior to their normal flowering time, which may be winter or summer.

CYCLAMEN

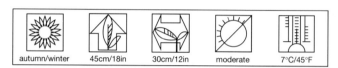

autumn/winter	45cm/18in	30cm/12in	moderate	7°C/45°F

Cyclamens developed from *Cyclamen persicum* are one of the most popular flowering house plants, bearing butterfly-shaped flowers of white, pink or red on straight stems rising from a cluster of heart-shaped mid-green leaves, often beautifully marked with silver. They require particular conditions to do well, and are rarely worth keeping for a second year.

GENERAL CARE Cyclamens are available from the autumn, potted up in a peat-based compost with half the corm visible above the surface. Choose a plant in bud; well-cared-for, it will be in flower for up to 3 months. Do not subject cyclamens to drastic changes in temperature. They like to be cool, ideally at 13°C/55°F; up to 18°C/64°F is acceptable with increased humidity, but any warmer and the plant will certainly suffer. Water daily by placing the pot in a plant saucer filled with water and leave to stand for 10 minutes. The plant will take up enough water for its needs. Water from above only if you have a steady hand and can be sure of not wetting the corm, which is subject to rot. Give a liquid feed every 2 weeks. Stand in good light, not direct sunlight. Remove faded flowers and discoloured leaves.

PROPAGATION Cyclamens can only be raised from seed.

VARIETIES 'Perfection Mixed', red, pink, magenta, white; 'Rex', all colours, leaves splashed silver; 'Ruffled Hybrids', all colours, fringed petals.

POSSIBLE PROBLEMS Grey mould.

▨ CARE TIP

The modern, quickly-grown, F_1 (first selection seed) cyclamen are brought from seed sowing to flowering in some eight months, but they seem much softer than the older style plant – perhaps the price of progress. Plants with large and firm corms can be kept from one year to the next by drying them off and storing in a cool, dry place until growth appears in new season.

EUPHORBIA

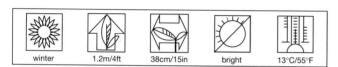

| winter | 1.2m/4ft | 38cm/15in | bright | 13°C/55°F |

Euphorbias are a huge family of plants, one of which is extremely popular as a decorative house plant. This is *Euphorbia pulcherrima*, the species universally known as poinsettia. The Latin suffix means 'most beautiful'. The true flowers are insignificant, all the colour deriving from showy bracts which are usually scarlet but may be pink or cream. These plants are commercially produced under special conditions which delay their development and inhibit their natural growth to make them compact enough for use in the home. The milky sap is poisonous.

GENERAL CARE Keep newly purchased plants at a moderate, steady temperature, preferably with other plants so that humidity is reasonably high. Place the plant in good light, such as sunlight filtered through a fine curtain. Water when the foliage begins to droop, and then give the plant plenty to drink, without allowing it to become waterlogged. No feeding is required. Discard the plant after flowering.

PROPAGATION Raising poinsettias is not recommended for the amateur.

VARIETIES Most commercially raised poinsettias do not bear names.

POSSIBLE PROBLEMS Generally trouble-free.

▓ GENERAL TIP

These can easily attain 2m (6ft) height when grown in pots, but to ensure short plants of compact appearance the grower treats his plants with a growth retarding chemical – a professional task.

EXACUM

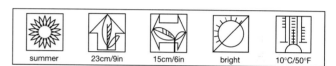

| summer | 23cm/9in | 15cm/6in | bright | 10°C/50°F |

Known as the Persian violet, *Exacum affine* (*above*) is in fact a member of the gentian family. Neat and bushy, its purple flowers, with prominent yellow centres, appear throughout the summer, cushioned by a mass of shiny, oval leaves. Some recently developed strains are fragrant, as is the species.

GENERAL CARE Buy plants that are just coming into flower, and keep them in a reasonably warm room protected from sudden changes in temperature. Keep the compost constantly and thoroughly moist and set the pots in saucers of moist pebbles to keep the level of humidity high. It also helps to keep several pots together (and they look particularly attractive in groups). While the plants are in flower, feed every 2 weeks with liquid fertilizer and remove faded flowers to prolong the flowering period. Set the pots in good light but not in direct sunlight. Discard plants after flowering.

PROPAGATION Exacums can be raised from seed sown in spring. Set the seedlings 5 to a 10cm/4in pot for the best effect. use a compost of equal parts peat and loam, with a little fine sand to assist drainage.

VARIETIES *E. a.* 'Starlight Fragrance', a reliable strain with spicy scent.

POSSIBLE PROBLEMS Generally trouble-free.

▓ GENERAL TIP

Neat and attractive windowsill plants that are reasonably easy to raise from seed. Alas, the average householders often feel that this is beyond them, but it is perfectly possible to sow and bring on young plants on a bright bedroom windowsill indoors – it is not necessary to have a greenhouse and attendant facilities for simple plants of this kind.

FUCHSIA

summer	60cm/24in	60cm/24in	bright	4.5°C/40°F

Fuchsias include literally hundreds of garden varieties, some hardy, some tender, and numerous perennial species which are suitable for the cool greenhouse – and, therefore, certain indoor situations. Their blooms are unique: pendulous, consisting of a bell-shaped flower (often purple) surrounded by 4 sepals (often bright pink).

GENERAL CARE Grow in a soil-based compost kept nicely moist during the flowering period. Feed with liquid fertilizer once a week as the buds are forming. Pinch out the growing tip to encourage bushy growth. Set in good light, not direct sunlight. Choose a cool, well-ventilated (not draughty) place where the temperature is steady. After flowering, reduce the amount of water and cut back to strong stems. Overwinter in a frost-free place, keeping the compost just moist. In spring, when new shoots appear, cut back to form a strong stem system.

PROPAGATION Take 10cm/4in tip cuttings in autumn or spring and insert singly in 5cm/2in pots containing equal parts of sand and peat at a temperature of 16°C/61°F.

VARIETIES 'Cascade', white sepals streaked pink, crimson petals; 'Falling Stars', red sepals, deep red petals; 'Golden Marinka', red flowers, golden yellow leaves; 'Swingtime', red sepals, white double petals; 'Thalia' (*above*), long, red flowers.

POSSIBLE PROBLEMS Aphids; whitefly.

■ CARE TIP

These often shed flowers alarmingly when brought indoors – to counteract, choose plants in bud, not in flower, and offer them the lightest and coolest window location in the room.

HIBISCUS

summer	38cm/15in	38cm/15in	bright	7°C/45°F

The rose of China, *Hibiscus rosa-sinensis* (*above*), can reach 1.8m/6ft in the wild. It is much more compact when grown in pots, and produces a succession of beautiful 12.5cm/5in wide flowers of white, red, orange, pink or yellow throughout the summer. The broad, pointed leaves are dark green and glossy.

GENERAL CARE Grow in a rich, soil-based compost kept evenly moist throughout the flowering period and give a liquid feed every 2 weeks. Bright light is important, including a few hours of direct sunlight every day. Normal room temperatures are suitable until flowering is over; during the rest period keep the plants cool and barely moist, and cease feeding. In spring the following year, cut back all growth to 15cm/6in after repotting into a pot one size larger.

PROPAGATION Take 10cm/4in tip cuttings in spring and root in a potting mixture of equal parts peat and sand at 18°C/64°F.

VARIETIES Hibiscus plants sold as house plants are generally unnamed, though they are reliable if bought from a reliable source. Look out for the variety *H. r.* 'Cooperi', with leaves variegated cream flushed red.

POSSIBLE PROBLEMS Aphids; mealy bugs.

■ CARE TIP

These are plants that can attain considerable age even when roots are confined to pots. Given time and care a main stem can be tied to a support so that it attains a height of 1m (3ft) or more, at which point the tip can be removed to encourage the plant to branch. The effect will be similar to that of a standard fuchsia with trumpet flowers set off to considerable advantage.

HOYA

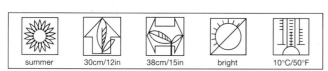

summer	30cm/12in	38cm/15in	bright	10°C/50°F

There are two species of hoya in general use. *Hoya carnosa*, the wax plant, is a climber reaching 5m/16ft and needs the space of a conservatory. More suitable for the average room is the diminutive *H. bella* (*above*), from India, which bears trusses of sweetly scented white or pink flowers all the summer.

GENERAL CARE Grow in peat-based compost kept nicely moist throughout the growing period. Set the plants in good light; an hour or two of direct sunlight every day will do no harm. Feed occasionally with liquid fertilizer – if the plant is becoming leafy with few flowers, dilute the feed and lengthen the intervals between applications. *H. bella* likes a warm room and high humidity; spray the leaves daily with rainwater or cooled boiled water before the flowers have opened. After flowering the faded blooms should be removed with extreme care, as the new flower is forming on the spur behind it. These buds can easily fall off if disturbed – so do not move the pot once you can see them. Keep the compost barely moist during the winter, but continue to give the plants full light. Repot every other spring, upgrading one size.

PROPAGATION Take 7.5cm/3in cuttings in early summer and root in equal parts sand and peat at a temperature of 16-18°C/61-64°F.

POSSIBLE PROBLEMS Overwatering, or the use of hard water, will turn the leaves brown.

▦ FLOWERING TIP

Getting these to flower can be a problem – to encourage keep dry in cool window over the winter and, when into growth for the new season, feed with a tomato fertilizer.

HYDRANGEA

spring	60cm/24in	60cm/24in	bright	13°C/55°F

Potted hydrangeas, varieties of the garden species *Hydrangea macrophylla*, are available in spring and bloom indoors for several weeks before being discarded (or planted outside). They are beautiful specimens for a table display. Flower colour is blue, white or pink.

GENERAL CARE Blue-flowered hydrangeas must be grown in an acid medium to retain their colour; the pink-flowered kinds need an alkaline medium. In the wrong potting mixture blues will turn purplish-pink and pinks turn blue-purple. Keep the plants cool to prolong flowering and in bright light, not direct sunlight. Do not allow the compost to dry out at any time. Submerging the pot in water for a few minutes each day is a good way to ensure constant moisture. Give a feed of liquid fertilizer every 2 weeks during flowering. Repotting is not necessary. After flowering either discard the plants or set them outside in a sheltered spot (remembering the effects of acid/alkaline soil on flower colour).

PROPAGATION Raising hydrangeas for pot culture is not recommended for amateurs.

VARIETIES Most varieties on offer are forms of *H. m.* 'Hortensia' (*above*) although lacecap types are sometimes available.

POSSIBLE PROBLEMS Aphids.

▦ DESIGN TIP

Naturally pink coloured, hydrangeas can be changed to blue (albeit, often a washed-out colour) by adding alum or a proprietary colourant to the soil. Following flowering indoors plants can be potted into tubs or large pots to become attractive features on the patio in subsequent years.

IMPATIENS

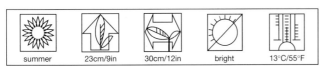

| summer | 23cm/9in | 30cm/12in | bright | 13°C/55°F |

A healthy specimen of impatiens, though spreading, is neat and compact. The leaves should be bright green and the whole plant covered in vivid flowers of red, pink or white from spring to autumn.

GENERAL CARE Grow in 12.5cm/5in pots of good soil-based compost kept moderately watered throughout the flowering season. Feed occasionally with a solution of Epsom salts (1 teaspoon to 600 ml/1 pint of water) to maintain good leaf colour. Mist over the plants regularly with a fine spray. Set them in good light, avoiding direct sunlight, in normal room temperatures. Pinch out the growing tips regularly or the plants become straggly. Overwinter at the recommended temperature, keeping the compost just moist.

PROPAGATION Raise hybrids from seed, named varieties of species from 10cm/4in cuttings taken at any time between spring and autumn and root in equal parts sand and peat at a temperature of 16°C/61°F.

VARIETIES *Impatiens holstii* (syn. *I. walleriana*), bushy, short-lived perennial, bright scarlet flowers; *I. petersiana*, up to 90cm/3ft high and needing support, bronze-red foliage, deep pink flowers. Hybrids include the Imp strain (*above*); flowers white, orange, scarlet, pink, red and purple; 'Fantastic Rose' (*above*), 'Orange Baby'; 'Scarlet Baby'.

POSSIBLE PROBLEMS Aphids; red spider mite.

■ CARE TIP

The New Guinea hybrid impatiens make an interesting change and have colourful foliage to add to their list of features. These must be kept wet, regularly fed and potted into rich compost.

JASMINUM

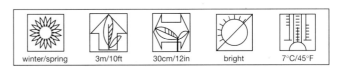

| winter/spring | 3m/10ft | 30cm/12in | bright | 7°C/45°F |

Delightful as they are, jasmines do not have a long life as house plants because they are such rampant growers that eventually a home has to be found for them elsewhere, in a conservatory or garden room. The most popular indoor species, *Jasminum polyanthum*, is a native of China, and bears abundant, heavily scented white tubular flowers in winter and spring. There are no named varieties.

GENERAL CARE Jasmines are often sold trained around a hoop, but they will soon need further support from canes or thin stakes. keep the plants cool, in the best light available, and water frequently, using tepid water, without allowing the compost to become waterlogged. Feed every 2 weeks with liquid fertilizer while in active growth. Pot on in the summer, upgrading one size and using a soil-based compost. The larger the pot, the greater the possible height of the plant; be aware that it may eventually outgrow the space you have available. Cut back hard after flowering. During the rest period keep the compost just moist.

PROPAGATION Take 10cm/4in tip cuttings in summer or early autumn and root in equal parts sand and peat at a temperature of 16°C/61°F.

POSSIBLE PROBLEMS Red spider mite.

■ CARE TIP

The skills of the commercial grower of these plants has made it possible for him to produce neat plants of about 1m (6ft) tall and full of flowers during the winter months when plants are normally purchased. Following flowering, the plant tends to grow apace needing a frame for its growth. Subsequent flowering is often difficult, but dry autumn conditions will help.

KOHLERIA

| summer | 60cm/24in | 30cm/12in | bright | 12°C/54°F |

Kohlerias come from South America, and need some of the warmth and humidity of their native habitat to succeed. Given congenial conditions, they produce beautiful bell-shaped flowers of pink or red throughout the summer; indeed, by taking cuttings at intervals you can have them in flower all year round.

GENERAL CARE Kohlerias grow from rhizomes. In very early spring, place rhizomes just below the surface in shallow trays of peat at 21°C/70°F. Pot them up when growth has reached 5cm/2in, placing 3 to a 12.5cm/5in pot containing a peat-based compost. Keep moderately moist until the plants are well established, then reduce the temperature to 18°C/64°F and increase the amount of water. Kohlerias like bright light, including direct sunlight; give protection from fierce midday sun. Give a liquid feed at half strength every 2 weeks. Spray frequently with a fine mist. Reduce the amount of water gradually as leaf colour fades. Remove dead top growth and overwinter the pots in a dry place.

PROPAGATION Divide the rhizomes in early spring, making sure each section has a growing point, or take 7.5cm/3in stem cuttings in summer, or in early autumn for winter flowering.

SPECIES *Kohleria erianthum* (*above*), scarlet flowers spotted red and yellow, dark green leaves clothed with purplish hairs; *K. amabile*, smaller with deep pink flowers spotted purple.

POSSIBLE PROBLEMS Generally trouble-free.

▦ GENERAL TIP

Specializing in one particular family of plants can have absorbing interest and the Gesneraceae (Kohleria and Saintpaulia for example) offer fascinating species for warm locations.

PELARGONIUM

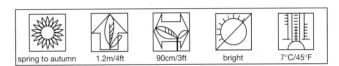

| spring to autumn | 1.2m/4ft | 90cm/3ft | bright | 7°C/45°F |

Pelargoniums are often called geranium (which is in fact the garden cranesbill). There are a number of species, and many varieties, with an astonishing choice of flower types in shades of white, pink, coral, red and purple.

GENERAL CARE Grow in 10-15cm/4-6in pots of good soil-based compost kept constantly moist while the plants are in active growth. Feed with a high-potash liquid fertilizer every 2 weeks. Place in good light where several hours of direct sunlight (preferably not fierce midday sun) are available every day. Good ventilation is important, especially at high temperatures – pelargoniums positively dislike humidity. Pinch out growing tips to encourage bushy growth. After flowering, cut right back and keep the compost just moist over winter. Repot in spring.

PROPAGATION Sow seed in early spring or take cuttings in the autumn (see pages 252-3).

VARIETIES Zonal (*above*), potentially very tall, best for conservatories, rounded leaves zoned bronze or wine-red, flowers in umbels: 'Delight', vermilion; 'Maxim Kovaleski', true orange; 'Lady Warwick', white edged red, distinctive blooms; 'Henry Cox', leaves zoned wine-red, red, green and cream. Regal, height up to 60cm/24in, long flowering period, large flowers; 'Black Knight', deep purple edged white; 'Lavender Grand Slam' (*above*); 'Princess of Wales', strawberry pink, frilled petals.

POSSIBLE PROBLEMS Generally trouble-free.

▦ CARE TIP

The winter months can be the most difficult for these plants, and not only because room temperatures are inadequate. More often there is a tendency for the custodian to cut back plants following flowering so that they occupy less storage space in the spare room, or wherever. The result of exposing cut areas late in the year is that rot sets in and ruins the plant.

PRIMULA

spring | 38cm/15in | 30cm/12in | moderate | 10°C/50°F

With their primrose-like flowers of yellow, mauve, pink, red, salmon or white, primulas are greatly valued as springtime indoor plants. Plants are usually discarded after flowering, but *Primula obconica* (*above*) can be kept for a second season.

GENERAL CARE Grow in a soil-based compost, using 12.5/5in pots. Stand in moderate light. Room temperature should not exceed 15°C/59°F, preferably less. Keep the compost always moist, not waterlogged, and give a feed of liquid fertilizer every 2 weeks from the time the first flower stalks appear. Pick off faded flowers regularly to ensure a succession of blooms. Repotting is not necessary. To save *P. obconica*, keep cool, just moist and shaded. In the autumn, tidy up the plants and top-dress with fresh compost (see page 248).

PROPAGATION Sow fresh seed in early spring. A mid-winter sowing of *P. obconica* will be in full flower a year later and bloom for 6 months in the right conditions.

VARIETIES *P. obconica*, pale green hairy leaves (to which some people are painfully allergic), flowers in clusters; giant-flowered strains are often named for colour, e.g. 'Delicate Pink', 'Red Chief', 'White'; *P.* × *kewensis*, light green powdered leaves, fragrant yellow flowers; *P. malacoides*, fragrant star-shaped flowers; 'Snowstorm', double white; 'Lilac Queen'.

POSSIBLE PROBLEMS Magnesium deficiency causes yellowing leaves.

▓ CARE TIP

Given reasonable care P. obconica *will often flower throughout the year. But plants can be a strong irritant to sensitive skin – not only when handling, sometimes being in the same room will induce irritation.*

ROSA

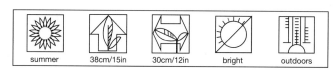

summer | 38cm/15in | 30cm/12in | bright | outdoors

Miniature roses are descended from *Rosa chinensis* 'Minima', a semi-double China rose still available under the name 'Rouletti'. This variety and others related to it generally reach between 23 and 30cm/9 and 12in. A group of slightly larger miniatures such as 'Starina' (*above*) has been developed, as well as tiny ones like 'Red Elf' (reaches 15cm/6in).

GENERAL CARE Grow in 12.5cm/5in pots of soil-based compost kept nicely moist during the flowering period. At this time, roses need good light and fresh air and are frankly happiest outdoors, being brought in to normal room conditions for short periods. Dead-head regularly and feed with a high-potash fertilizer every 2 weeks. After flowering put the pots outside or in the coldest day-lit spot you have available. Cut all old and damaged stems right back in autumn and top-dress with a 5cm/2in layer of peat to keep the root system from drying out.

PROPAGATION Take cuttings in summer and root in a mixture of equal parts peat and sand. When rooted, pot singly in 7.5cm/3in pots in potting compost.

VARIETIES Tallest: 'Josephine Wheatcroft', semi-double, sunflower yellow; 'Perla de Monserrat', double rose pink; 'Baby Gold Star', semi-double, yellow. Medium: 'Bo-peep', tiny deep pink flowers; 'Granate', velvety deep red, double; Tiny: 'Humpty Dumpty', soft pink; 'Peon', crimson/white eye.

POSSIBLE PROBLEMS Aphids.

▓ CARE TIP

Not the easiest of plants for indoors, as they need the lightest possible window in a cool room. As with most flowering plants they need high potash feed which can be found in tomato fertilizer.

RUELLIA

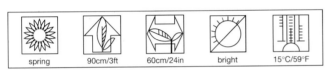

| spring | 90cm/3ft | 60cm/24in | bright | 15°C/59°F |

Ruellias are wonderful plants for winter/spring decoration. With their vivid pink trumpet-shaped flowers and long, pointed green leaves, they have an air of the exotic that enlivens the winter scene. Though tall, they are nicely bushy in shape if the growing tips of young plants are pinched out.

GENERAL CARE Grow in 15cm/6in pots of peat-based compost with the addition of charcoal granules for improved aeraton. Set in a warm room with good light, filtered in high summer. Keep the plants moist at all times, winter included. Repot established specimens in the autumn, but raise new plants annually, as young ones are more productive of flowers. Ruellias that have been repotted should be given a liquid feed at half strength every 2 weeks when in active growth. Immediately after flowering, cut back flowered shoots to within 7.5cm/3in of the surface of the compost.

PROPAGATION When pruning in late spring, take 7.5cm/3in basal cuttings and root them 4 to a 10cm/4in pot of equal parts peat and sand at 21°C/70°F. Pot up singly when growing well.

SPECIES *Ruellia macrantha* (*above*), clusters of rose-pink flowers 8cm/3$\frac{1}{2}$in long from mid winter to spring; *R. portellae*, small pink flowers from late autumn, beautiful green leaves tinted bronze, veined silver.

POSSIBLE PROBLEMS Plants deteriorate in cold, dry atmospheres.

■ PROPAGATION TIP

Where space permits it is always wise to have back-up plants of favourite species just in case something goes wrong with the pet plant, or it may be that older ones become ungainly and in need of replacement. Take cuttings of these in spring or early summer, but provide a heated propagator to encourage rooting. One with an electric cable offering bottom heat is ideal.

SAINTPAULIA

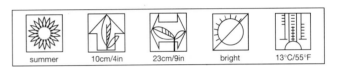

| summer | 10cm/4in | 23cm/9in | bright | 13°C/55°F |

African violets, properly called *Saintpaulia ionantha*, belong to the same family as sinningias, achimenes, streptocarpus and kohlerias, all plants noted for their beautiful flowers. They produce blue, purple or pink flowers all year, but mostly in summer. Violet-like, the blooms cluster above a dense rosette of dark green, oval, slightly hairy leaves.

GENERAL CARE Grow in 12.5/5in pots of a peat-based compost kept moist but never waterlogged. Place the pots on saucers of moist pebbles or immersed in larger pots of moist peat. Warmth as well as humidity is essential; the ideal temperature is in the range 18-24°C/64-75°F. Stand in good light, not direct sunlight, and feed with liquid fertilizer at half strength from late spring until flowering stops. Repot at any time, preferably spring, when the plants are pot-bound.

PROPAGATION In summer, take leaf cuttings with a 5cm/2in length of stalk and root in a mixture of equal parts sand and peat at 18-21°C/64-70°F.

VARIETIES 'Diana Blue', velvety royal purple; 'Blue Fairy Tale', rich blue; 'Grandiflora Pink', large-flowered pink.

POSSIBLE PROBLEMS Tarsonemid mites; water on leaves discolours the surface.

■ FLOWERING TIP

Producing flowers can be a problem – to induce the plant should be in a good light on a windowsill and under a table lamp in the evening. Good light is an important need for flower development.

SINNINGIA

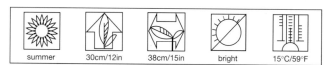

| summer | 30cm/12in | 38cm/15in | bright | 15°C/59°F |

The showy, trumpet-shaped blooms known commercially as gloxinias are in fact hybrids developed from *Sinningia speciosa*. A wide range is available in a stunning range of colours. The foliage is an added attraction, for the large oval leaves are a fine velvety green.

GENERAL CARE The simplest method of raising gloxinias is to obtain tubers in spring and place them in a bowl of moist peat at 21°C/70°F. Pot them up separately when 5cm/2in high in 15cm/6in pots of peat-based compost; each tuber should be just covered. Grow on in bright light, not direct sunlight, at no less than 18°C/64°F and keep constantly moist. Feed with liquid fertilizer every 2 weeks until flowering is over. Gradually reduce the amount of water as the leaves lose colour. Remove dead top growth, remove tubers from their pots and store over winter in a dry place.

PROPAGATION Divide tubers in spring, making sure each section has at least 2 shoots. Cut them up with a sharp knife, sealing the cut with powdered charcoal. Sinningias may also be raised from seed sown in early spring.

VARIETIES *S. s.* 'Emperor Frederick', scarlet edged white; 'Emperor William', purple edged white; 'Mont Blanc', white.

POSSIBLE PROBLEMS Tubers may rot if overwatered.

▇ GENERAL TIP

When purchasing it is wise to call on the grower of the plant as gloxinia are ill disposed to both packing materials and travelling. Reason for this is the very brittle leaves, and good reason for inspecting the foliage of plants that one intends purchasing to ensure that there are not too many damaged leaves present. Handle with care at all times.

SPATHIPHYLLUM

| summer | 60cm/24in | 60cm/24in | bright | 13°C/55°F |

Spathiphyllums are related to anthuriums, which they somewhat resemble, but are fortunately rather easier to grow. Known as peace lilies, their white spathes look exquisite against glossy dark green leaves. These blooms may appear at any time in congenial conditions, but most freely in late spring-early summer.

GENERAL CARE Grow in a peat-based loam-free compost kept moist at all times. Warmth and humidity are essential – spray the leaves frequently. Stand the pots in containers of moist peat and position in good light. Feed with liquid fertilizer all year round: every 2 weeks from spring until late summer, monthly at half strength at other times. Reduce the amount of water in winter. Repot every year in spring.

PROPAGATION Divide and replant established specimens in spring.

VARIETIES *Spathiphyllum wallisii* (*above*), only 30cm/12in high, bright green leaves, summer-flowering, will tolerate temperatures down to 10°C/50°F and needs shade in summer; S. × 'Mauna Loa', hybrid of more majestic proportions, large white spathes; needs as much warmth as can be given during spring/summer.

POSSIBLE PROBLEMS Sudden changes in temperature will damage the plant.

▇ CARE TIP

Superb plants with naturally glossy leaves and surprisingly tolerant of room conditions. To maintain appearance the leaves should be periodically cleaned with a soft, moist cloth.

STRELITZIA

spring	1.2m/4ft	90cm/3ft	bright	10°C/50°F

The extraordinary shape and colour formation of strelitzia blooms have given this species the popular name bird of paradise. Native to South Africa, *Strelitzia reginae*, *above* (a relative of the banana) bears its flowers in spring: 15cm/6in long, they are orange and blue, rising in a crest from a green bract, and last for several weeks. The mid-green leaves which surround the flowerheads are oval and may be 45cm/18in long. There are no named varieties.

GENERAL CARE Grow in a soil-based compost kept nicely moist throughout the active growing period, and feed with liquid fertilizer every 2 weeks. Situate the plant in bright light where it will receive several hours of direct sunlight every day. The leaves should, however, be protected from very fierce sun. Normal room temperatures are suitable. During the cool of the rest period, let the compost become nearly dry.

PROPAGATION Divide old plants in spring, or detach shoots bearing roots when repotting or just after flowering.

POSSIBLE PROBLEMS Scale insects.

STREPTOCARPUS

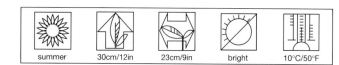

summer	30cm/12in	23cm/9in	bright	10°C/50°F

In spite of its popular name of Cape primrose, the flowers of *Streptocarpus* × *hybridus* do not resemble primroses at all; they are usually pink, purple, white or blue rather than yellow, and trumpet-shaped. The leaves, however bear some comparison; though those of streptocarpus are relatively large, they are similarly mid-green and corrugated.

GENERAL CARE Streptocarpus do best where they can enjoy high humidity. A well-ventilated greenhouse is the ideal place. Water freely in spring and summer, giving a liquid feed every 2 weeks. A moderately bright position out of direct sunlight will keep plants happy and prevent scorching of the leaves. Remove faded flowerheads. In winter, water sparingly and keep cool. Repot each spring, upgrading by one size until a 20cm/8in pot is reached; simply top-dress with fresh compost annually thereafter (see page 252).

PROPAGATION Take leaf cuttings and root in a mixture of equal parts peat and sand at 18°C/64°F or divide established plants in spring or late summer.

VARIETIES *S.* × *h.* 'Constant Nymph', purple-blue flowers; 'Purple Nymph' (*above*), reddish-purple; 'Merton Blue', purplish-blue with white throat.

POSSIBLE PROBLEMS Aphids.

◾ GENERAL TIP

Exotic flowers but unattractive foliage, particularly in older plants. Can be grown from seed but it takes at least four years for flowers to appear, and it may well be ten years!

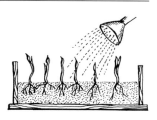

◾ PROPAGATION TIP

Old-fashioned they may be, but the white and blue varieties of 'Constant Nymph' are still plants worthy of acquiring. If plants are not available acquire a leaf and cut it into sections and stand them upright in peat and sand mix. Alternatively, cut through the middle of the central vein for its entire length and insert cut edge in same mixture.

FERNS

If you are sometimes bewildered by the complicated Latin labels given to plants, you should be warned that ferns have the most unpronounceable names. Even a fern-fancier has to be known by the jawbreaking title 'pteropodist'. It sounds prehistoric, but perhaps that is appropriate to families of plants which first appeared hundreds of millions of years ago. They had to wait until the late nineteenth century to be 'discovered' by Victorian plant explorers, who plundered the tropics to fill the ferneries of grand English houses. Some of these fern rooms still exist, havens of green tranquillity; but ferns do not in fact need a special room of their own to thrive – they have not survived the millennia by being over-fussy about their environment.

IDEAL CONDITIONS

Many ferns are hardy in temperate zones and make wonderful garden plants, but those grown as indoor plants are usually of tropical origin. In the wild they grow at the base of trees, terrestrial kinds with their roots in the earth, epiphytic types on the trees themselves with their roots in the rotting vegetation that accumulates in the trees' crevices. They are naturally

The foliage of ferns is seen at its best against a well-lit window.

shielded from the bright light of the sun by foliage above, and enjoy warmth and high humidity. Grown as houseplants they should therefore be protected from scorching sunlight; do not expect them to thrive, however, if permanently placed in deep shade. A certain amount of light is essential for growth. Because the fronds will turn towards the source of light it is a good idea to give the pot a quarter turn every week to prevent uneven development.

The ideal temperature range is between 18 and 21°C/64°F and 70°F (but see individual entries) with humidity correspondingly high and steady. Putting the fern's pot in another, larger one filled with peat kept constantly moist is an excellent solution. Before doing this, however, check that the pot of a newly purchased fern is large enough. Sometimes they need repotting, upgrading by one size. See page 248 for other methods of keeping the humidity level up. Since a great deal of moisture is lost through the delicate fronds, frequent mist-spraying is essential, and the best way to nourish ferns is with a foliar feed, that is, a liquid sprayed on to the foliage.

TRADITIONAL FERNERIES

The Victorians constructed their ferneries as cool, quiet retreats – and bearing in mind some of the gaudier herbaceous borders fashionable at the time, it is easy to see why. The same relaxing atmosphere created by ferns is what endears them to indoor gardeners today. Growing steadily all year (only adiantums positively benefit from a rest), they epitomize calm. Never flowering but always restfully green, ferns look wonderful grouped together, yet each is shapely enough to stand alone. They seem to look equally at home in every room in the house, and to suit cosy room settings as well as more formal designs. Ever-accommodating, ferns make a wonderful background to more colourful plants like tender summer-flowering bulbs, particularly vallotas, or in an arrangement with cyclamens, campanulas and hydrangeas. Those with arching fronds – particularly adiantum, blechnum, davallia, nephrolepis and pellaea – are ideal subjects for hanging baskets.

HANGING BASKET DISPLAYS

Some hanging baskets have a built-in drip tray which stops water getting on to the floor, but you can easily make a drip tray for a traditional wire basket from a large plastic plant saucer. Pierce a number of holes at regular intervals around the rim. Thread wire supports of equal length through the holes and fix them to the basket so that the saucer is about 5cm/2in below it. When filled with water, the dish will provide extra humidity for the plant.

To plant up a wire basket, rest it in a bucket for stability and line with sphagnum moss before filling it with the recommended growing mixture (see individual entries). When holding damp compost and a large plant, the basket will be very heavy and should be attached to fixtures screwed into the ceiling joists.

Hanging baskets are practical as well as decorative, in that they make use of otherwise vacant space and keep plants out of harm's way in busy domestic thoroughfares. The danger is that you will forget to water them, and ferns must be kept constantly moist.

PROPAGATION

Since they never flower, it follows that ferns do not produce seeds. Their method of reproduction is as fascinating as it is complicated, and few amateurs will want to attempt it. Spores, not seeds, contain the germ of a new fern. They are carried in spore cases called sori on the underside of some fronds (visible as dark-coloured dots). When the spores are ripe, the sorus bursts and millions of microscopic spores are scattered. In warmth, moisture and light, a spore will produce an organism called a prothallus, which has both male and female parts. If fertilization occurs, an embryo fern, called a sporophyte, begins to grow. This process takes months, and it is many more before the plantlet achieves a respectable size. Fortunately a number of ferns can be increased relatively easily by dividing the mature plants, and the trusty pteris spreads its spores so freely that you may be given offspring without doing anything at all. For the rest, reproduction from spores is probably best left to the experts.

ADIANTUM

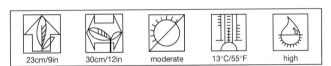

23cm/9in	30cm/12in	moderate	13°C/55°F	high

Adiantums are among the most delicate and decorative ferns. Two types are similar in appearance, with wiry black stems and light green, fan-shaped pinnae; a third species is distinguished by palmate fronds which are reddish-brown when young.

GENERAL CARE Grow in a peat-based compost to which one quarter its volume of sand has been added to improve drainage. Make sure there is a good layer of broken crocks at the bottom of the pot. Keep the compost moist but not water-logged all year round and give a liquid feed every 2 weeks in spring and summer. Withhold fertilizer and reduce the amount of water during the resting period. Adiantum lose their colour if the light is too bright, but should not be placed in full shade. Mist the fronds over daily with tepid boiled water or rainwater if possible. Repot in early spring only if roots can be seen.

PROPAGATION Divide the rhizome into small pieces, each bearing a few fronds, and repot immediately in a compost of equal parts of leaf-mould or peat, loam and coarse sand. Small sections can be broken off when repotting if wished.

VARIETIES *Adiantum capillus veneris* (maidenhair fern, *above*), fragile, fan-shaped pinnae on thin, arching stems; *A. cuneatum* (syn. *A. raddianum*), similar in appearance but slightly larger and coarser; *A. c.* 'Fragrantissima', scented fronds; *A. hispidulum* (rosy maidenhair), fronds reddish when young.

POSSIBLE PROBLEMS Root mealy bugs.

▨ CARE TIP

Perhaps the most popular of all the ferns for indoors – its delicate fronds having great appeal when seen on the retailers' plant benches. Dry air conditions are anathema to their paper-thin foliage, so offer moist surroundings where possible. With age, older fronds lose their appearance and may need to be cut completely away in the autumn to encourage new growth from base.

ASPLENIUM

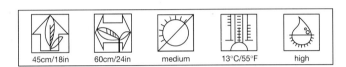

45cm/18in	60cm/24in	medium	13°C/55°F	high

Asplenium nidus (*above*), popularly known as bird's nest fern, is a native of tropical Asia. Its broad, strap-like fronds of fresh green grow in the form of a rosette, from the centre of which new fronds unfurl. In optimum conditions a frond can reach 1.2m/4ft in length but the dimensions given above are more likely in the home. Even large fronds are relatively fragile, and should be handled as little as possible. There are no named varieties.

GENERAL CARE *Asplenium nidus* is by nature epiphytic (see page 364). Grow in a mixture of 2 parts fibrous peat, 1 part loam and 1 part sand. Keep well watered when in active growth and feed with liquid fertilizer at half strength every 2 weeks. Stop feeding during the rest period and keep the compost just moist, but stand the plant in medium light all year round, turning the pot regularly to ensure even growth. Repot, preferably in spring, only when the roots have expanded to fill the pot. Because the roots cling to the side of the pot, it may be necessary to break it to release the root ball.

PROPAGATION This fern can only be raised from spores (see page 303).

POSSIBLE PROBLEMS Aphids; scale insects.

▨ CARE TIP

The shuttlecock arrangement of pale green leaves is particularly effective, but leaves should be kept clean by wiping occasionally with a damp cloth. Scale insects (on both sides of leaves) favour aspleniums and should be cleaned off with a firm sponge that has been soaked in insecticide solution. Wear rubber gloves and follow directions for the product.

BLECHNUM

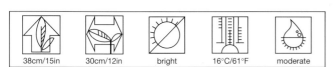

38cm/15in	30cm/12in	bright	16°C/61°F	moderate

Blechnums are a large group of arching ferns of different sizes suitable for a number of decorative purposes. The fronds are of the classic fern shape, rather like a nephrolepis.

GENERAL CARE Any good proprietary compost will do, but the best mixture is 2 parts peat (or leaf-mould if available), 1 part loam and 1 part sand, with a good layer of drainage material at the bottom of the pot. The compost should not be packed too tightly around the roots. Do not let the roots dry out at any time. To maintain humidity during the period of active growth, set the pots on saucers of moist pebbles, but do not spray the fronds as this will discolour them. Feed once or twice in summer with liquid fertilizer at half-strength. Give the plants good light, but not direct sunlight. Repot when the roots are visible on the surface of the compost.

PROPAGATION Most species are raised from spores, but sometimes *Blechnum gibbum* produces offsets which can be detached from the parent and potted up. Divide the rhizome of *B. occidentale* and repot each section individually.

SPECIES *B. gibbum*, most common species, shiny green slightly drooping fronds arising from a central rosette; *B. g. tinctum* has young fronds tinged pink. *B. occidentale*, robust species of neat habit.

POSSIBLE PROBLEMS At room temperatures above 21°C/70°F plants suffer serious damage and attack by thrips.

▥ CARE TIP

Many ferns suffer indoors because of the dry atmosphere that prevails – to counter such conditions it is wise to plunge the pots in larger pots with damp peat packed around them.

CYRTOMIUM

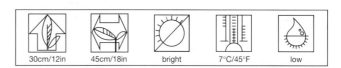

30cm/12in	45cm/18in	bright	7°C/45°F	low

Only one species of cyrtomium is generally available, and one variety in particular is preferred. Known as the holly fern because of the shape of its glossy, leathery pinnae, *Cyrtomium falcatum* 'Rochfordianum' (*above*) is an extremely sturdy rhizomatous plant, which can tolerate low temperatures and humidity. Quick-growing, these handsome plants will continue to thrive even when occasionally subjected to draughts and smoky atmospheres.

GENERAL CARE For all their toughness, holly ferns are not indestructible. They certainly appreciate good light, though not direct sunlight. Grow in a mixture of equal parts of peat, loam and sand, not packed down too tightly in the pot. If steady, normal room temperatures are maintained, no rest period is needed and the compost should be kept nicely moist all year; but if the temperature drops below 13°C/55°F for more than a few days, reduce the amount of water. Give a feed of liquid fertilizer every 2 weeks when in active growth. Repot only when the roots crowd the pot. Plants that have achieved a 15cm/6in pot should simply be top-dressed with fresh compost in early spring (see page 252).

PROPAGATION In spring, divide the rhizome into small sections, each bearing healthy roots and a few fronds. Pot up in 7.5cm/3in pots of the recommended mixture kept barely moist until well rooted. Thereafter treat as mature plants.

POSSIBLE PROBLEMS Generally trouble-free.

▥ DESIGN TIP

The Holly Fern is very distinctive among this type of plant, having foliage with a naturally high gloss. The latter is ever an advantage with plants that are used for indoor decoration. When arranged in groups with other house plants that have more colourful variegated foliage the contrast improves the appearance of all the plants in the arrangement.

DAVALLIA

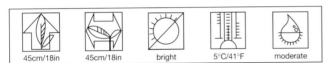

| 45cm/18in | 45cm/18in | bright | 5°C/41°F | moderate |

There are three species of davallia in common use, fine ferns with densely clustered, delicate triangular fronds of pale or medium green. All grow from rhizomes.

GENERAL CARE Grow in a mixture of 3 parts peat, 1 part leaf-mould and 1 part sand, with plenty of drainage material at the bottom of the pot. Keep the compost consistently moist, not waterlogged, during the period of active growth and feed with liquid fertilizer every 2 weeks. Do not spray the foliage. Keep the compost just moist during the winter. Place the plants where they will receive bright light, but not direct sunlight. They are happiest at normal room temperatures but will tolerate cooler conditions and low humidity. Repot small davallias in spring, trimming the roots and detaching a few sections of rhizome.

PROPAGATION Cut off tip sections of rhizome to which 2 fronds are attached. Place in 7.5cm/3in pots containing a mixture of equal parts peat and sand, pinning them to the surface with wire. Enclose in plastic bags until rooted. Gradually acclimatize to normal conditions and pot up after 3 months.

SPECIES *D. canariensis* (hare's foot fern, *above*), creeping scaly rhizomes covered with soft grey fur explain the common name, medium green fronds; *D. fijiensis*, very light green elegant fronds; *D. f. plumosa* is a feathery type; *D. mariesii*, pretty, dwarf, fully hardy species 15cm//6in high, light green fronds.

POSSIBLE PROBLEMS Generally trouble-free.

■ PROPAGATION TIP

The custom of placing propagating material in polythene bags when propagating is to reduce transpiration and so stop the potting material from drying out. It is suitable for most plants.

NEPHROLEPIS

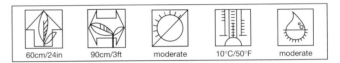

| 60cm/24in | 90cm/3ft | moderate | 10°C/50°F | moderate |

Of all the ferns used for indoor decoration, the nephrolepis in its various forms is the most important, and one of the most beautiful when in good health. Popularly known as the ladder fern, *Nephrolepis exaltata* (*above*) produces graceful, arching fronds of bright green, best appreciated when the plant is placed on a pedestal, or, if it is not too large, in a hanging basket.

GENERAL CARE Grow in a mixture of 3 parts fibrous peat, 2 parts loam and 1 part sand and keep well watered. Give a liquid feed every 4 weeks. Nephrolepis like normal room temperatures, but above 21°C/70°F the fronds will appreciate mist-spraying with tepid boiled water or rainwater. These plants are in active growth all year and like a position enjoying good light, though not direct sunlight. Repot in spring when the roots have filled the pot, upgrading by one size. When plants have reached the largest convenient pot size, trim the roots lightly and replace in the cleaned pot with fresh compost.

PROPAGATION Plantlets are formed from runners. Detach the young plants and pot up in peat and sand at 13°C/55°F until rooted.

VARIETIES *N. a.* 'Bostoniensis' (Boston fern), quick-growing, with broad fronds; 'Whitmanii', feathery fronds; 'Hillii', crinkled, pale fronds.

POSSIBLE PROBLEMS In high temperatures where the atmosphere is dry, fronds will turn yellow and shrivel up.

■ PROPAGATION TIP

To propagate plants from the naturally developing runners the growing pot should be plunged in a roomy box of peat so that runners can be pegged down in the peat to root and establish.

PELLAEA

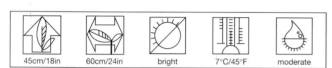

45cm/18in	60cm/24in	bright	7°C/45°F	moderate

There are many species of pellaea, small- to medium-sized ferns best suited to hanging baskets. The stalks are wiry, rising from rhizomes set just below the surface of the mixture.

GENERAL CARE Grow in a light, porous mixture composed of 2 parts peat, 1 part loam and 1 part sand. Do not let the roots dry out at any time: since pellaeas do not need a rest period, water moderately all year and give a liquid feed every 4 weeks. Do not spray the fronds. Give the plants a position in good light, out of direct sunlight. Repot in spring when the roots fill the pot.

PROPAGATION When the plants have reached pots of 20cm/8in, divide the rhizome into small sections, each bearing healthy roots and a few fronds, and pot up in the recommended mixture.

SPECIES *Pellaea rotundifolia* (button fern, *above*), almost round, tiny pinnae on long arching fronds. Good for ground cover in mixed plantings as it likes the humidity created by other plants; fronds trail over the side of the pot. Shallow-rooting, grow in half-pots. *P. viridis* (green cliffbrake), sometimes listed as a species of pteris, a bushy plant with upright, vivid green triangular fronds each up to 75cm/30in long and deeply divided.

POSSIBLE PROBLEMS Generally trouble-free.

PHYLLITIS

60cm/24in	20cm/8in	medium	7°C/45°F	moderate

One species of phyllitis, *Phyllitis scolopendrium* (the hart's tongue fern), is in general cultivation. A hardy, rhizomatous plant which can be grown in the garden, it will tolerate cool rooms as long as there is sufficient light. The strap-like, bright green fronds unfurl from a central rosette. A number of different blade forms are displayed in the varieties.

GENERAL CARE Grow in a mixture of 2 parts leaf-mould or peat, 1 part loam and 1 part sand. Keep the mixture just moist, reducing the amount of water if the temperature drops below 13°C/55°F for more than a few days. Give a liquid feed at half-strength every 2 weeks all year round. Repot only when the roots fill the pot, placing the rhizomes vertically. When the largest suitable pot size has been reached, trim away up to one-third of the rootball and replace in the cleaned pot with fresh mixture.

PROPAGATION In spring, cut off small sections of rhizome bearing a few fronds and insert in 7.5cm/3in pots of the standard mixture. Keep just moist until new fronds develop, then treat as mature plants. Sometimes bulbils form on the fronds or at the base of the fronds; these can be detached and grown on.

VARIETIES *P. s.* 'Crispum', blades bright green with wavy or ruffled edges; *P. s.* 'Cristatum', frilly blades with crested tips.

POSSIBLE PROBLEMS Generally trouble-free.

▧ CARE TIP

Many of the ferns are sensitive to the use of chemicals on their foliage, and to overdoses of fertilizer when feeding. One way of overcoming these difficulties is to use a slow release fertilizer in tablet form pressed into the pot soil for feeding and to employ impregnated fertilizer pins pressed into the soil to control many of the pests. Both treatments are clean and effective.

▧ PLANTING TIP

Tougher ferns such as the scolopendrium will benefit from a holiday in the garden during the summer. Choose a lightly shaded location and plunge plant pots in moist peat.

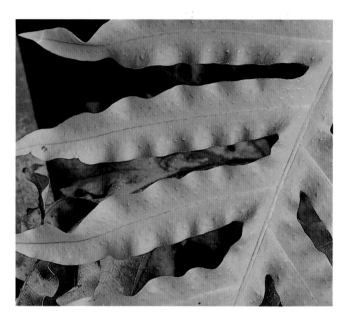

PLATYCERIUM

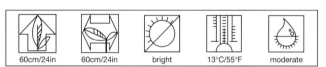

| 60cm/24in | 60cm/24in | bright | 13°C/55°F | moderate |

Platycerium bifurcatum (*above*) is an epiphytic fern (see page 302) which in its native Australia grows in the upper branches of trees, clinging to the bark by means of a single, sterile frond. From this, fertile fronds of mid-green overlaid with silver hairs arise, which divide at the end to look like antlers – hence the common name, stag's horn fern.

GENERAL CARE The best way to display these extraordinary plants is to wire them to a piece of bark wrapped in sphagnum moss and hang them up where they will receive bright light (not direct sunlight) in an airy room. A temperature of about 21°C/70°F is best in summer; higher than that, humidity must be correspondingly increased. To water, submerge the bark and sterile frond in a bucket of water for 15 minutes once a week, allowing it to drain before rehanging. Follow the same procedure during the rest period, but only leave the plant in water for 2-3 minutes. Do not wipe the fronds – in fact, try not to touch them at all. To clean them, spray very occasionally with a fine mist of cooled boiled water or rainwater.

PROPAGATION Detach young plants from the stems and attach them to fresh pieces of bark.

VARIETIES *P. b.* 'Majus', leathery fronds with fewer incisions than the species.

POSSIBLE PROBLEMS Generally trouble-free.

■ DESIGN TIP

Majestic plants when grown with care. Oddly, the anchor fronds that form at the base and secure it naturally to its anchorage will grow apace on natural materials, but not so on plastic pots!

POLYPODIUM

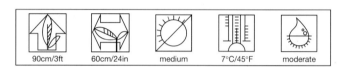

| 90cm/3ft | 60cm/24in | medium | 7°C/45°F | moderate |

There are numerous species of polypodium cultivated in gardens, though only one, *Polypodium aureum* (syn. *Phlebodium aureum*, *above*) is used for indoor decoration. It is commonly called hare's foot fern (like davallia, which has very different fronds), because of the creeping rhizomes with furry scales.

GENERAL CARE Grow in a mixture of equal parts of peat, loam and sand in a wide, shallow pot to accommodate the rhizomatous network. Water well, and give a liquid feed at half-strength every 2 weeks. Keep the plants out of direct sunlight, which will scorch the leaves, but in good light all year round. Normal room temperatures are best; if the temperature exceeds 21°C/70°F for several days increase the humidity by placing the pots in saucers of moist pebbles, and spray the fronds lightly with a very fine mist. Repot in spring.

PROPAGATION Cut off 7.5cm/3in sections from the tips of the rhizome and place on the surface of the standard mixture in small pots. Peg down each section, moisten the compost and place the pots in plastic bags in the warmth until rooting has taken place. Gradually acclimatize to normal conditions and then treat as mature plants.

VARIETIES *P. a. areolatum*, leathery, blue-green fronds; *P. a. mayi*, wavy fronds of silvery green, veins tinted purple.

POSSIBLE PROBLEMS Generally trouble-free.

■ DESIGN TIP

The greenhouse fernery is a very tranquil and soothing sort of environment – to emulate in some small degree indoors it is worth offering ferns a corner of their own in which to grow.

POLYSTICHUM

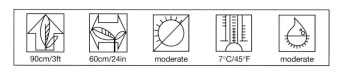

90cm/3ft	60cm/24in	moderate	7°C/45°F	moderate

There are a number of polystichums cultivated in gardens. The best for indoor use is *Polystichum setiferum* (above), the soft shield fern, which is an adaptable species tolerant of low temperatures. It is a handsome plant with abundant foliage and looks splendid alone or in a collection of ferns. The fronds are long, strap-like and deeply divided, soft in texture and not glossy.

GENERAL CARE Grow in a mixture of equal parts of leaf-mould or peat, loam and coarse sand, never allowing the mixture to dry out. At temperatures above 18°C/65°F, increase humidity by standing the pots in saucers of moist pebbles ad spraying the fronds with a very fine spray of cooled boiled water or rainwater. Feed with liquid fertilizer at half-strength every 4 weeks. Plants grow all year, and need good light (not direct sunlight) at all times; normal room temperatures are suitable. Repot in spring if the roots fill the pot.

PROPAGATION In spring, divide the rhizomes into smaller sections with a sharp knife and repot in the recommended mixture, setting each piece horizontally and only half-covered by the compost.

VARIETIES *P. s.* 'Plumoso-divisilobum', very finely divided, exquisitely delicate fronds up to 60cm/24in long, spreading up to 1.2m/4ft.

POSSIBLE PROBLEMS Generally trouble-free.

▤ CARE TIP

Ferns are seldom seen at their best when growing in tiny pots that restrict their development, however, continual potting-on means that they require ever more space in which to be housed. Where space is available plants can be potted on into a quite large container, but this is usually a two-handed task to reduce the likelihood of plants being damaged.

PTERIS

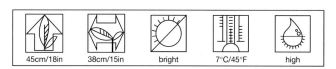

45cm/18in	38cm/15in	bright	7°C/45°F	high

Pteris species are collectively known as table ferns. All produce numerous clumps of fronds from rhizomes.

GENERAL CARE Grow in a mixture of equal parts of peat, loam and sand and keep well watered at all times. Pteris are in active growth all year, and like normal room temperatures. Give the fronds a misting over with tepid boiled water or rainwater if the temperature rises above 18°C/65°F for more than 2 days. Feed with half-strength liquid fertilizer every 4 weeks. Set the pots in good light (not direct sunlight) and give them a quarter-turn every day to ensure even growth. Repot when the roots fill the pot: in spring, transfer the plants to a pot one size larger, just burying the rhizome.

PROPAGATION In spring, cut the rhizome into 7.5cm/3in sections, each bearing both roots and a clump of fronds. Plant up in the recommended mixture and treat as mature plants. Pteris spread their spores freely, and you may well find tiny ferns which may be potted up in 5cm/2in pots and grown on.

VARIETIES *Pteris cretica* (ribbon fern), light to medium green fronds with wiry black stalks and strap-shaped pinnae which in the variety 'Albolineata' (*above*) are marked with a creamy central band; the fronds of 'Wilsonii' are crested at the tip. *P. ensiformis*, species with finer, deep green fronds.

POSSIBLE PROBLEMS Outer fronds of mature plants dry up. Cut them away at the base.

▤ CARE TIP

These are almost invariably purchased when growing in relatively small pots – often with a great deal of top growth. Such plants should have their roots examined on getting them home with a view to potting on the plant if, as is probable, there is a mass of congested brown roots in evidence. The new pot should offer at least 2cm (1in) of free space all the way round.

PALMS

Palms are the aristocrats of indoor plants. They have the dignified air of trees, and in their natural habitat, the tropics, most would of course grow into tall trees in time. Those available in plant centres are relatively young, but even so are the result of years of careful work by the nurseryman. Because it takes so much time and care to raise palms from seed, they are very expensive to buy, and only a small proportion of the large number growing in the wild are accorded this treatment. Despite their special status, however, palms are not fussy as houseplants. With attention to a few simple points, they will thrive for years, becoming a permanent feature of an interior design just as trees do in the outdoor garden.

KEEPING PALMS INDOORS

Many palms look different in their juvenile form from the way they do in maturity. Unlike an apple tree, which even at a year old is recognizably the precursor of a mature productive specimen, young palms are not miniature versions of their older selves. Most obviously, they do not have a long trunk, though some have a short stem; the leaves are naturally smaller, no flowers bloom (with the exception of chamaedorea, which may flower at about six years old) and therefore no fruit is produced. You will not be gathering your own dates and coconuts!

Unless kept in a special house in a botanical garden, palms are unlikely to achieve maturity for the many years of their life indoors, and this is to your advantage – no conventional room could accommodate them if they did. In the juvenile state, palms would naturally be protected from the sun's intense heat by the leaves of mature trees. It makes sense to imitate these conditions at home, placing palms in bright light that is filtered by a fine curtain. They can withstand a few hours of direct sunlight, however; and those which are usually

The sumptuous and exotic furnishings of this Eastern-inspired room need rather special plants. Palms have just the right combination of grace and flamboyance to work well with all the mirror, gilt and silk surfaces, without being too fussy.

positioned in poor light will certainly benefit from being moved outside on warm days – if they are not too heavy to lift. While palms can tolerate a degree of dryness in the air, the fronds look fresher in a slightly humid atmosphere and the possibility of infestation by red spider mite is reduced. The best way to achieve humidity is to stand the pots on trays of moist pebbles while the palms are in active growth. You can test humidity with a hygrometer.

TIPS FOR GOOD HEALTH

As important design features, if not for the sake of their health, palms should be kept clean. Sponge each frond by hand with tepid water, or place the whole plant in the bath and shower the leaves or move it outside if there is a warm summer shower of rain. Requirements for water vary (see individual entries) but generally the compost should be kept moist throughout the growing period. Always check the compost before watering, however; overwatering is the greatest single cause of damage to palms.

A winter rest period is essential; during this time palms can tolerate temperatures down to 13°C/55°F or 7°C/45°F depending on species, require very little water and no feeding. Do not automatically repot your palms in spring; the longer you can keep them in their present pot the better, to keep size within reasonable bounds. Repot – in spring – only when the pot is completely filled with roots.

Repotting is the time to detach suckers, if any, and take advantage of a natural method of propagation, since raising palms from seed cannot be achieved by the amateur. Suckers are produced by chamaerops, chrysalidocarpus and phoenix. After separating the sucker from its parent, pot it up in a moistened mixture of equal parts of peat and sand. Enclose the pot in a plastic bag secured with a rubber band. Stand in bright filtered light and keep warm – not less than 21°C/70°F. Rooting may take up to twelve weeks. Do not let the compost dry out during this time, and shake off any condensation that forms inside the bag. New top growth indicates that rooting has occurred. At this point, remove the bag, keep the plant lightly watered and feed with liquid fertilizer every four weeks. The following spring, pot up in the recommended growing mixture.

SITING PALMS

Even in youth, palms are impressive plants and some eventually reach the ceiling. This is the most important factor to be taken into account when deciding where to site them. In a small room with pale walls, good light and simple furniture, a single palm makes a striking feature. Only much larger rooms can accommodate a group of palms, for example a spacious porch, drawing room or conservatory. Keep the containers ultra-simple. As palms should not be situated where they are likely to be damaged, a busy kitchen or family sitting room is probably not a good choice. The beautiful shape of palm fronds is undoubtedly best appreciated against a pale, plain background. Having said that, they share with ferns the ability to combine gracefully with other plants. A stately palm could be the centre-piece of a group which included achimenes, cyclamen or sinningia, bushy in shape with foliage beautiful enough to hold its own. If you are lucky enough to have the space for it, such an arrangement would be the epitome of an indoor garden.

Palms add style and elegance to any interior. The most commonly grown indoor form is Howeia forsteriana. *When it reaches about this size, it makes a perfect floor-standing specimen. The wicker-basket container works well in this situation but any large, simple container would look good. In a period setting an elaborate cachepot would be particularly effective.*

CHAMAEDOREA

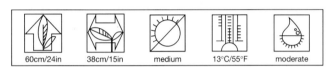

60cm/24in	38cm/15in	medium	13°C/55°F	moderate

The parlour palm, *Chamaedorea elegans* (syn. *Neanthe bella*, *above*), is one of the easiest palms to grow and much smaller than most others. The upright fronds are light and feathery. Young plants may produce small yellow-green flowers, which should be removed. No named varieties are available.

GENERAL CARE Grow in a mixture of 2 parts peat, 1 part loam and 1 part sand, and keep the compost thoroughly moist, not waterlogged, at all times. Chamaedoreas continue to grow all year, though more slowly in winter, when watering should be reduced slightly. Give a liquid feed at half-strength every 4 weeks. Temperatures in the range 18-24°C/65-75°F are best, with humidity provided by regularly spraying the leaves. Stand the pots in saucers of damp pebbles. Sponge the leaves with tepid water to clean them. In their natural habitat these small palms are shielded from the sun by taller trees: as house plants they need good light but not direct sunlight. Repot carefully when the roots fill the pot, upgrading by one size and adding peat or leaf-mould to the mixture.

PROPAGATION Chamaedoreas are best raised from seed, but this is a very lengthy process.

POSSIBLE PROBLEMS Red spider mite.

CHAMAEROPS

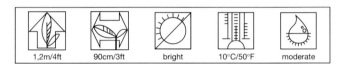

1,2m/4ft	90cm/3ft	bright	10°C/50°F	moderate

Chamaerops humilis, the European fan palm, *above*, is the only palm native to Europe. It is found in Mediterranean countries, varying greatly in size according to conditions. In the home it needs bright light, including 3-4 hours of direct sunlight every day. It needs space, too, in which to spread its arching fronds, and makes a statuesque contribution to a room setting.

GENERAL CARE Grow in a soil-based compost to which a little leaf-mould, if available, has been added. Keep well-watered, but do not let the pot stand in water. Feed with liquid fertilizer every 2 weeks when in active growth. Normal room temperatures are suitable. During the cooler rest period, water very sparingly. Repot every other spring until the palm is in a 30cm/12in pot. Simply top-dress with fresh compost in subsequent years (see page 248).

PROPAGATION Detach basal suckers from the stem whenever they appear, making sure healthy roots are attached to each. Set in small pots of the recommended compost kept just moist, warm and in good light until new growth appears. Thereafter treat as mature plants.

VARIETIES *C. h. argentea*; silvery green foliage; *C. h. elegans*; a slender, graceful form.

POSSIBLE PROBLEMS Red spider mite; leaf tips turn brown with sudden variations in temperature.

■ GENERAL TIP

The parlour palm is the best selection for smaller rooms. When purchasing, it is wise to seek plants that have numerous growing stems in the pot as opposed to single ones.

■ GENERAL TIP

Hardy in sheltered areas, the European Palm is only suitable where there is ample space. In its favour, however, it is very tough and able to tolerate low room or conservatory temperatures.

CHRYSALIDOCARPUS

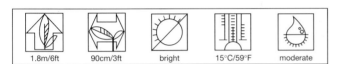

1.8m/6ft	90cm/3ft	bright	15°C/59°F	moderate

Variously known as the butterfly palm or areca palm, *Chrysalidocarpus lutescens* (*above*) is a native of India with slender, upright fronds. The description suffix *lutescens* means yellow, referring to the golden tinge of both stalks and foliage. This beautiful but rather slow-growing palm produces numerous small suckers at the base. There is only one species, and no named varieties.

GENERAL CARE Grow in a soil-based compost kept constantly moist. Feed with liquid fertilizer every two weeks. Normal room temperatures are suitable, and the plant should be positioned where it receives direct sunlight, filtered through a fine curtain. Clean the leaves with a spray mist or by standing the plant outside in a gentle summer shower. Repot every other year until the largest convenient pot size has been achieved, and simply topdress annually thereafter.

PROPAGATION In spring, detach basal suckers when 30cm/12in high and bearing some roots. Plant up individually in a 2:1 mixture of compost and sand, transferring to pots of the standard mixture after 1 year.

POSSIBLE PROBLEMS Scale insects; red spider mite.

COCOS

1.8m/6ft	1.2m/4ft	bright	16°C/61°F	high

The small, decorative plant known as the coconut palm is usually available at about 30cm/12in high, and it takes many years to reach the mature height given above. Its small size makes it useful as a house plant, but it needs particular conditions to do well.

GENERAL CARE Grow in a soil-based compost and water liberally from spring to autumn, gradually reducing the amount of water over a period of four weeks until during the winter rest period the compost is kept barely moist. When in active growth give a liquid feed at half-strength every three weeks. At this time the ideal temperature is 21°C/70°F; bright light and high humidity are essential. Spray the fronds frequently and stand the pots in saucers of moist pebbles. Repot as growth begins in spring; this should not be necessary more often than every three years.

PROPAGATION Coconut palms are raised from seed in high temperatures and in high humidity, conditions which the amateur is unlikely to be able to provide.

SPECIES There is only one species correctly known as *Syagrus weddeliana*, but always sold as *Cocos weddeliana* (*above*). The true coconut palm grown commercially for its fruit is *C. nucifera*.

POSSIBLE PROBLEMS Generally trouble-free.

▤ SPECIAL CARE TIP

Do not be deceived by the yellow leaves of this plant which could mistakenly give the impression that the specimen is suffering from an iron deficiency. Do not treat as for this.

▤ GENERAL TIP

Grown indoors, the coconut palm does not produce fruit and is in fact very short lived, lasting only one or two years. You can try propagating from a fresh coconut – it will sprout roots and leaves from the same eye – by

putting the fruit in damp sphagnum moss at a temperature of 20-25°C (68°-77°F).

CYCAS

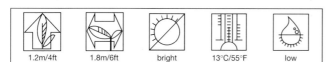

1.2m/4ft	1.8m/6ft	bright	13°C/55°F	low

Cycas revoluta is generally known as the sago palm. Cycas is the Greek word for palm, but in spite of its name and its palm-like appearance this plant is in fact a cycad, a very primitive plant type. Slow-growing, it produces arching fronds of many fine segments arising from a central base which looks rather like a pineapple. The graceful outline of the cycas belies its tough nature. As long as light is good, it is very tolerant of otherwise poor conditions. There are no named varieties.

GENERAL CARE Grow in a mixture of two parts soil-based compost to 1 part coarse sand, with the rounded base – actually a swollen stem – sitting on the surface. The base acts as a reservoir for water. Cycases are in active growth virtually all year, and need constant good light. Water moderately and give a liquid feed every four weeks; if poor winter light results in a period of rest, water sparingly and cease feeding. Slow growth means that repotting should not be necessary more often than every three years.

PROPAGATION Cycases are raised from seed, a lengthy process not recommended for amateurs.

POSSIBLE PROBLEMS Overwatering causes brown spots on the leaves; underwatering turns them yellow. Any disfigured leaves should be removed immediately.

HOWEA

3m/10ft	1.2m/4ft	medium	10°C/50°F	moderate

Howeas are slow-growing palms that eventually reach stately proportions, but even when young they have a dignified and formal beauty. The two species commonly available are tall with slender stems from which dark green, deeply cut fronds arise.

GENERAL CARE Grow in a soil-based compost and give moderate amounts of cooled boiled water or rainwater during the period of active growth, with a liquid feed every 2 weeks. To clean the leaves, sponge or spray them with water, or stand them outside in a summer shower. Do not use any of the proprietary leaf polishes. They thrive at a sunless window or in bright light; in direct sunlight or deep shade they will deteriorate. Normal room temperatures are suitable and low levels of humidity are tolerated. Repot every other spring, up-grading by one size, and firming the compost well around the roots. Provide a good layer of drainage material at the bottom of the pot.

PROPAGATION Howeas are raised from seed, a lengthy and demanding process.

SPECIES *Howea belmoreana*, the typical palm-court palm, imposing but graceful even when it reaches full size; *H. forsteriana*, a lower-growing species more suitable for the home, but because the leaflets are held horizontally the spread is considerable and it still needs plenty of space.

POSSIBLE PROBLEMS Red spider mite; tap water, or too much water of any kind, results in brown spots on the leaves.

■ SPECIAL CARE TIP

New leaves arrive curled like new fern leaves and gradually both the stem and new leaves uncurl from the base to the tip. Take extra care as these leaves are very delicate and easily damaged.

■ CARE TIP

The tall and stately kentia palm is often sold in pots of soil in which there is little root development. This can be an advantage as it obviates the need for potting on the plant for two, possibly three years. But there is a disadvantage with weakly rooted plants in that they are easily detached from the soil if lifted by the stems – lift by grasping the pot.

PHOENIX

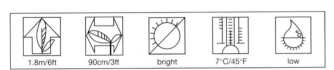

| 1.8m/6ft | 90cm/3ft | bright | 7°C/45°F | low |

The three date palms favoured for indoor decoration are hand-some species with arching pinnate fronds. They are slow-growing, and will take some years to reach their maximum size.

GENERAL CARE Grow in a soil-based compost kept constantly moist during the period of active growth. Feed with liquid fertilizer every 2 weeks. Phoenix species are happy in normally warm room temperatures in full light. When temperatures begin to fall and the plants enter the dormant period, gradually reduce the amount of water until the compost is kept just moist. Repot every 2 or 3 years, progressing to a pot 5cm/2in larger each time. When repotting, firm the compost down well and leave a good margin between the surface and the pot rim.

PROPAGATION Date palms are usually grown from seed, which is a very long process. It is sometimes possible to remove rooted suckers from *Phoenix roebelenii* and grow them on in 7.5cm/3in pots of the standard mixture.

SPECIES *P. canariensis* (Canary date palm), a robust and popular species, with stiff green pinnae arranged herringbone fashion on arching stems; *P. roebelinii* (pigmy date palm, *above*), max height 90cm/3ft with delicate, arching fronds. This species requires filtered light. *P. dactylifera* (true date palm), blue-green, prickly fronds; faster-growing and generally less fine than the other two.

POSSIBLE PROBLEMS Scale insects; mealy bugs.

■ CARE TIP

These develop into bold plants with rough stems that make it essential that they should be potted into heavier clay pots as they increase in size. The clay pot will give the plant much better anchorage while indoors, but more so if it is to spend some of the summer months on the patio outside. Larger plants require careful handling.

TRACHYCARPUS

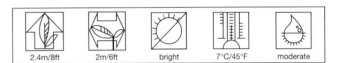

| 2.4m/8ft | 2m/6ft | bright | 7°C/45°F | moderate |

A native of China, *Trachycarpus fortunei (above)* is commonly known either as the chusan palm, or the windmill palm, from the shape of its fan-like fronds, which when fully developed are separated into distinct, narrow segments. In temperate zones it may be grown outside, where it may exceed the height given above. In the home, however, confined to a pot, growth is slow and plant size manageable. An average height of 1.2m/4ft is likely. There is a dwarf species, *T. f. surculosus*, which seldom exceeds 60cm/24in.

GENERAL CARE Grow in soil-based compost, kept constantly moist during the period of active growth. Chusan palm is one of the hardier kinds which can tolerate low winter temperatures, preferring normal room temperatures when actively growing. During this period give a liquid feed every four weeks. Good light is important, and some direct sunlight every day will be appreciated. As the leaves mature the colour fades to brown, and they can be pulled away or cut off. Repot when the roots have filled the pot – about every three years – placing a 5cm/2in layer of drainage material in the bottom of the new pot.

PROPAGATION *T. fortunei* is raised from seed, which is a lengthy affair. *T. f. surculosus* produces suckers which can be detached in spring and potted up.

POSSIBLE PROBLEMS Red spider mite.

■ ORGANIC TIP

The Trachycarpus has a useful advantage over other palms in that it will happily occupy a place on the patio during all but the coldest months making an attractive addition to the garden.

315

BULBS

At the mention of flowering bulbs, inevitably one thinks of spring, with daffodils and crocuses in bloom. But there are bulbs which bloom in all seasons; not only that, growing bulbs indoors means that tender species can be raised which will flower over several years. Species which are hardy enough to flower outside such as narcissi and iris usually spend only one flowering season indoors; these may be thought of as temporary indoor plants. Permanent, tender species include the fabulous crinum and vallota, both from South Africa, and ever-popular hippeastrums, from South America. Despite their exotic origins, none requires excessively high temperatures and are easy to grow indoors.

A bulb is constructed as a series of tightly overlapping leaves – as can be seen by slicing vertically into an onion – forming a storage organ for food and water and sending out fine roots from the base. Corms are modified stems which act in the same way. Buy fresh bulbs from a reputable supplier and plant them at the recommended time for the best results. They will have been raised at the correct pace and temperature to produce beautiful blooms.

GROWING HARDY BULBS INDOORS

Crocuses, narcissi, tulips, hyacinths and iris, which are all familiar spring-flowering garden bulbs, can be induced to flower in winter to provide indoor decorations. Specially prepared bulbs are recommended for this treatment. They will only flower once indoors, but will do so again if planted outside. Sometimes they skip a season while building up food supplies, then go on to bloom for several years. If you do not have a garden, pass the bulbs on to someone who does.

Bulbs for forcing are usually available in late summer/early autumn. Buy from a shop where they have been kept cool. Choose firm, clean specimens with no sign of root or shoot development. Potting compost is necessary if you plan to set the bulbs outdoors afterwards. If not, bulb fibre – which contains no nutrients – may be used, and the bowl need not have any drainage holes.

If you wish to keep bulbs for outdoor planting, remove faded flowerheads only, allowing the leaves and stems to die down naturally. Keep the bowls in a light place at about 4–7°C/39–45°F and water them regularly. In spring, remove the bulbs and their compost from the bowl and plant out the clump 15cm/6in deep.

Hyacinths and tazetta narcissi can be grown in water only in specially designed glass vases. This is an unusually attractive way of displaying bulbs which holds great charm for children. The bulb should fit snugly into the bowl of the vase with its base just touching the water – no deeper, or it will rot. Top up as necessary. Use specially prepared bulbs and start them off at any time from late summer to late autumn. Keep in a cool place – dark for hyacinths, well-lit for narcissi – until the roots are about 7.5cm/3in long and the leaves peeping through the neck of the bulb. Thereafter treat as bulbs grown in compost, with the difference that, having been deprived of food, these bulbs will not be any good for planting outdoors.

Because flowers last longer in cool rooms, forced bulbs are ideal to brighten a well-lit hall or landing, or set in the light of a shady, cool window. While you can plant bulbs singly, they invariably look best in groups, larger species such as hyacinths, some tulips and narcissi in sets of three or five. Increase the numbers for smaller narcissi such as 'Silver Chimes' and miniatures such as crocus and *Iris reticulata*. All can be planted close together, and this gives a more luxuriant effect when in bloom. If you have the space, it is well worth planting in succession so that you will have flowers in the house over many weeks.

The hippeastrum hybrids, popularly known as amaryllis, are striking by any standards and constantly gaining in popularity.

GROWING TENDER BULBS

The three tender bulbs described in this chapter are all members of the amaryllis family, with strap-like leaves and fabulous lily-like blooms borne on long straight stems. Hippeastrums are the first to bloom, the numerous hybrids in very early spring. The colour choice includes all shades of pink and red as well as white. Because specially prepared bulbs can be forced rather as hardy bulbs are, but without a necessary cold, dark period, you can pot up several at staggered intervals to ensure a succession of blooms. As well as the hybrids, try to obtain bulbs of the true species such as *H. aulicum*, which bears huge red flowers in winter or the exquisite *H. candidum*, which may reach 90cm/3ft and bears huge, drooping, scented white flowers tinted green – a stunning plant for a conservatory or sunny porch. It flowers in summer. *H. reticulatum*, about 45cm/18in high, will continue the display into the autumn, if given warmth, with pink flowers and leaves

striped white. Crinums, at 1.2m/4ft high when fully mature, are another good choice for a conservatory. Large, eye-catching plants need a spacious setting not only to look their best but to prevent damage to the petals and stems. Like vallotas, crinums bloom in summer, providing a colourful and exotic display for many weeks.

Tender bulbs flower year after year if properly treated, and then obligingly produce offsets to ensure a supply after the parent is exhausted. After flowering time, the aim is to build up a fresh store of nourishment in the bulb. Remove each flower as it fades, but let the foliage die down naturally – do not be tempted to tie it into a bunch for the sake of neatness – and cut off the flower stem cleanly when it is yellow and limp. Plants should be fed regularly during active growth and until all flowers have faded; then stop, and gradually reduce the amount of water until the compost is just moist (let it dry for hippeastrums). After the recuperative dormant period, the cycle begins again.

PROPAGATION

Detach offsets at repotting time. Knock the plant and all the compost clinging to the bulbs out of the pot. Ease off the compost and separate the offsets from the parent carefully, without damaging the roots. Pot up singly in suitably sized pots and grow on as mature plants. They will not reach full size for a year or two. Even so, raising plants in this way is very rewarding and an unmissable opportunity to increase your stock at minimal cost.

CRINUM

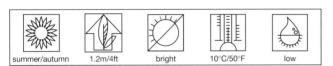

| summer/autumn | 1.2m/4ft | bright | 10°C/50°F | low |

Crinums or swamp lilies are natives of South Africa, and bear clusters of stunning lily-like flowers of pink, white or red at the top of strong straight stems, surrounded by strap-like leaves. Large, eye-catching plants, they need a spacious setting to be fully appreciated.

GENERAL CARE Plant large bulbs in a soil-based compost in pots no more than 5cm/2in greater in diameter than the bulbs themselves. Smaller bulbs may be set 3 to a 20cm/8in pot. Water well during active growth, but do not let the pots stand in water. Give a liquid feed every 3 weeks. Stand the plants where they will receive 2-3 hours of direct sunlight every day. Normal room temperatures are suitable. The plants rest at lower temperatures in mid winter. As the leaves become tired they fall or may be picked off, and new ones will appear. Repot as infrequently as possible; crinums do best when they are undisturbed. When necessary, repot in spring.

PROPAGATION Remove offsets when repotting over-crowded clumps and pot up firmly (individually or 3 to a suitable-sized pot). Water sparingly for 4-6 weeks then treat as mature bulbs.

SPECIES *Crinum × powellii (above)*, hybrid form, trumpet-shaped flowers of deep pink, green at the base; abundant foliage. *C. bulbispermum*, slender, narrow leaves, huge white flowers flushed pink.

POSSIBLE PROBLEMS Bulb mites.

▧ CARE TIP

Depending on variety these may be tender bulbs for the heated greenhouse or, in the case of C. powellii, they may be hardy and planted at the base of a sunny wall. During their rest period, bulbs should be stored in a heated greenhouse by laying their pots on their sides under the greenhouse staging – in this position water is prevented from getting into pots.

CROCUS

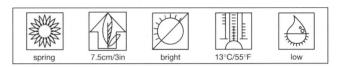

| spring | 7.5cm/3in | bright | 13°C/55°F | low |

There are a number of garden crocuses which bloom at different times of year, but the best forms for indoor cultivation are spring-flowering Dutch hybrids. These corms bear very large flowers which may be white, yellow or purple. Do not mix different colours in the same container as they come into flower at different times; a splash of a single colour lasting a few weeks is much more effective.

GENERAL CARE Plant the corms in a container of soil-based compost in the autumn, water very lightly and keep cool and dark, preferably burying them outside. Bring inside in late winter/early spring and place the container in good light, out of direct sunlight. Do not let the room temperature exceed 15°C/59°F and water moderately. If the bulbs are to be planted outside after flowering, cut off the dead flowerheads and let the foliage die down naturally. Remove the corms and store in a cool dark place until the following autumn.

PROPAGATION Remove offsets from bulbs after flowering and set outdoors in drills or pots of soil-based compost. They should reach flowering size in 2 years.

VARIETIES 'Pickwick', lilac, striped purple; 'Purpureus Grandiflorus', rich purple; 'Joan of Arc', white; 'Dutch Yellow', bright golden yellow.

POSSIBLE PROBLEMS Generally trouble-free, but corms in storage may rot or be attacked by aphids.

▧ CARE TIP

Following flowering in pots indoors, the foliage should be left on the plants to die back naturally, rather than be cut away. When purchasing bulbs for pots select only top quality.

HIPPEASTRUM

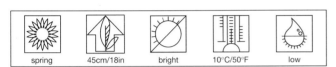

spring	45cm/18in	bright	10°C/50°F	low

Hippeastrums are sometimes incorrectly sold as amaryllis, another bulbous species to which they are related. While several species are known, the most popular types for indoor decoration are named hybrids which produce their spectacular lily-like flowers of red, pink or white in early spring.

GENERAL CARE Pot up newly obtained hippeastrums in a soil-based compost. Half of the bulb should stand clear of the mixture. Keep just moist until growth appears. When the flower bud appears, bring the pot into good light and gradually increase the amount of water until, when the plant is in full flower, the compost is constantly moist. Some direct sunlight every day is essential, but the temperature should not exceed 18°C/65°F. After flowering gradually decrease watering but start feeding with liquid fertilizer every 2 weeks. Good light is still important. By late summer the dried foliage can be removed and the dormant period begins. Keep the bulb in its pot, dry, and keep at 10°C/50°F until the cycle begins again. Do not repot, but replace the compost every 3 or 4 years in early spring.

PROPAGATION Remove offsets when renewing the compost and pot them up in 7.5cm/3in pots.

VARIETIES *Hippeastrum* 'Apple Blossom', white streaked pink; 'Candy Cane', cream; 'American Express', scarlet.

POSSIBLE PROBLEMS Generally trouble-free.

▮ CARE TIP

Following flowering, the flower stem should be left to die naturally and the plant should be fed to build up the bulb. During its dormant autumn period the bulb should be stored warm and dry and brought into normal growing conditions towards the end of winter. Flowers normally appear before the leaves, and may be encouraged if the bulb is kept very warm during this period.

HYACINTH

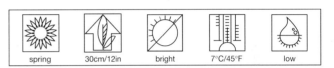

spring	30cm/12in	bright	7°C/45°F	low

Hyacinths are sold in the autumn for spring flowering, or as bulbs specially prepared to bloom in the middle of winter. The most common form is the so-called Dutch hyacinth, which bears fragrant flowerspikes of white, pink, blue or yellow.

GENERAL CARE Pot up bulbs singly or several to a container close together but not touching, with the nose of the bulbs exposed. Use bulb fibre if the container has no drainage holes, otherwise a good soil-based compost. The compost should be evenly moist. Put the container in a cold, dark place; preferably outdoors, covered with a 15cm/6in layer of peat and a sheet of polythene. Check after 3 weeks to make sure the compost has not dried out. As soon as 5cm/2in of leaf can be seen, the pots can be moved into the light at a temperature of 10°C/50°F. As growth progresses the temperature may be raised to 18°C/64°F, no more. The bulbs cannot be used for indoor decoration again, but will grow in the garden. To prepare them, remove faded flowerspikes but not the stems or foliage, which should die down slowly in a cool place. Plant out in late spring.

PROPAGATION Bulbs for indoor forcing are raised by special techniques not recommended for amateurs.

VARIETIES *Hyacinthus orientalis* 'Blue Jacket' (*above*), 'Queen of the Blues'; 'Pink Pearl'; 'City of Haarlem', primrose yellow; 'Madame Sophie', double white.

POSSIBLE PROBLEMS Eelworms; aphids.

▮ GENERAL TIP

Placing three bulbs in bulb fibre to flower in bulb bowls in mid-winter can be very appealing. But it is essential that one should specify prepared bulbs when purchasing.

IRIS

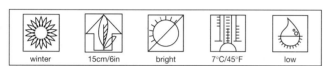

| winter | 15cm/6in | bright | 7°C/45°F | low |

Several dwarf irises are suitable for growing in pots to bloom in winter or early spring. One of the most successful is *Iris reticulata*, a fragrant miniature in shades of purple and blue with orange 'beards'. If planted in late summer they bloom in the middle of winter; autumn-planted bulbs flower in spring.

GENERAL CARE Plant the bulbs 6 to a 12.5cm/5in half-pot containing a light soil-based compost, with plenty of drainage material in the bottom. Keep cool, just moist and shaded for about 8 weeks. When the leaves show, bring the pots into full light and a room temperature about 13°C/55°F. Remove faded flowerheads but let the foliage die down naturally and feed with liquid fertilizer every 4 weeks. After a dormant period the bulbs should flower again and will almost certainly do so if planted outside.

PROPAGATION Divide the bulbs and offsets after the foliage has died down and pot up. Small bulbils may take 2 or 3 years to reach maturity.

VARIETIES *I. r.* 'Cantab', pale blue; 'Harmony' (*above*), royal blue; 'J. S. Dijt', reddish purple.

POSSIBLE PROBLEMS Aphids; mould on badly stored bulbs.

NARCISSUS

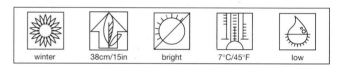

| winter | 38cm/15in | bright | 7°C/45°F | low |

Types used for forcing into early growth indoors are derived from the species *Narcissus tazetta* (bunch-flowered narcissus) and hybrids with *N. poeticus* called poetaz narcissi.

GENERAL CARE Bulbs specially treated to bloom early should be planted in the autumn. Use bulb fibre if the containers have no drainage holes, otherwise any good peat-or soil-based compost. Set the bulbs in groups, sitting half out of the growing medium, which should be thoroughly moistened before planting. Keep very cool and preferably in the dark, for example, wrapped in black polythene and left outside. Inspect the pots occasionally to make sure the compost is not drying out. When about 7.5cm/3in of growth is visible, move the container into a well-lit position, preferably in direct sunlight. Keep the room temperature below 16°C/61°F or the buds will shrivel before breaking into flower. Discard the bulbs after flowering.

PROPAGATION Bulbs for winter forcing are raised by special techniques not recommended for amateurs.

VARIETIES Tazatta: 'Paper White' (*above*), delicate very pale cream petals. Poetaz: 'Cragford', white petals, deep red cup, 4-6 flowers per stem; 'Geranium', cream petals, orange cup, 5-6 flowers per stem; 'Silver Chimes', small, 9-10 very pretty blooms per stem, white petals, lemon cup.

POSSIBLE PROBLEMS Blindness – buds failing to open – occurs if the compost is not kept moist.

▓ PLANTING TIP

There are numerous miniature flowering irises, such as I. reticulata, that are pleasing in pots. Simply plant several to shallow pans and stand in the garden to bring in as flower buds appear.

▓ PLANTING TIP

A single layer of these bulbs in a pot can sometimes be disappointing. For fuller effect it is possible to use deeper containers and to introduce a layer of bulb fibre or potting soil, followed by closely placed bulbs, *then more potting medium and a final layer of bulbs with finishing soil on top. The effect in the spring will be a double value display.*

TULIPA

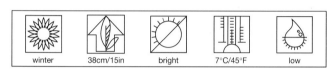

| winter | 38cm/15in | bright | 7°C/45°F | low |

Early-flowering tulips bring a splash of dramatic colour into winter displays. These species, which may bear single or double flowers, come in a breathtaking range of colours and combinations of colours (except blue). Both types have pointed, grey-green leaves. Like crocuses, only one variety should be placed in a pot, so that they will bloom together and achieve a pleasing uniformity of size.

GENERAL CARE Treat tulip bulbs exactly as narcissi. It is worth emphasizing that excessive room temperatures – over 16°C/61°F – will cause the flowers to fade quickly, while between 13 and 15°C/55 and 59°F they will bloom for up to 4 weeks. The bulbs cannot be used to flower indoors a second time, but if planted outside after the foliage has been allowed to die down naturally they may well flower for several seasons.

PROPAGATION Detach offsets, if any, from the bulbs after flowering and grow on in drills outside. They take 2-3 years to reach flowering size.

VARIETIES Single early, flowers pointed in bud, opening flat 7.5-12.5cm/3-5in across: 'Bellona', yellow; 'Pink Beauty', deep pink and white; 'Keizerskroon', yellow and red. Double early, peony-like flowers 10cm/4in across: 'Electra', pink-mauve; 'Wilhelm Kordes' orange and red; 'Peach Blossom', rose on white; 'Schoonord', white.

POSSIBLE PROBLEMS Mould on badly stored bulbs.

▪ GENERAL TIP

Always plant individual varieties. Taller growing tulips are often unwieldy indoors, which may be a good reason for choosing some of the species that are compact in growth and very colourful.

VALLOTA

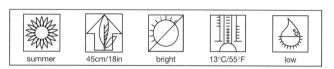

| summer | 45cm/18in | bright | 13°C/55°F | low |

Commonly known as Scarborough lilies, vallotas are related to hippeastrums. The two do look alike, but vallota flowers are only 10cm/4in across and the vallota blooms in summer. Up to 8 scarlet flowers are borne on a single erect stem.

GENERAL CARE Pot up in spring, one bulb to a 12.5cm/5in pot. Pack moist soil-based compost tightly around the bulb, so that half of it is visible above the surface. Place in good light at normal room temperatures. Water sparingly for 2 months then increase the amount of water to keep the compost just moist. At this point start giving a liquid feed every 2 weeks. When flowering is over substitute a high-potash fertilizer. Keep the plant in full light until the winter rest period, when indirect light will suffice. Water very sparingly and cease feeding during this time. Do not repot annually but top-dress (see page 252) with fresh mixture to which a little bonemeal has been added.

PROPAGATION When the pot becomes overcrowded with offsets and the original bulb has naturally divided into 3 or 4, separate them out gently and repot in the recommended mixture. This is best done in spring. Use 7.5cm/3in pots for small offsets and pot on the next year.

VARIETIES *Vallota speciosa* (*above*) is the only species available, with red flowers. Varieties include *V. s. alba*, white; *V. s. delicata*, salmon pink; *V. s. elata*, smaller with cherry-red flowers.

POSSIBLE PROBLEMS Mealy bugs on leaves.

▪ CARE TIP

Like almost all of the South African flowering bulbs these are plants that enjoy a bake in the sun during their dormant period, and good light at all times while in growth. Cool indoor conditions will suit them fine as they are hardy in sheltered areas if planted fairly deep at the base of a sunny wall. This is an old favourite that deserves to be more popular.

CACTI

These are plants that are indigenous to the American continent, where the vast majority grow in arid, desert regions. Many attain great age and a size that is totally out of keeping with the small plants that one may grow on the windowsill at home. However, it is the latter that we are concerned with here – the sort of plants that are grown for room decoration, or in the greenhouse if one has the facilities and sufficient interest in the subject. The greenhouse, offering modest winter warmth and maximum light, is the best location for the sun lovers, but that is not to say that the kitchen windowsill does not produce its quota of quality plants.

PURCHASING

There was a time when only a few specialist growers offered cacti for sale, but things have changed and they are now on offer at a wide assortment of retail establishments. The specialist growers still exist, many of them operating on a very large scale that allows them to offer plants of surprisingly good quality throughout the year. Cacti are available in tiny pots or as giant specimens that will give the chosen site an instant desert ambience if there is a little sand about to complete the scene. Even the smallest of the purchased plants will be in the region of 3 years old, so will be well rooted in their pots when acquired. In spite of the wide variety that is generally available it will be difficult to locate some of the less popular plants. If you cannot find the plant you want, contact specialist growers direct – they will usually be found at one of the many flower shows that are held in the spring and summer months.

LOCATION

The general rule in this respect, with but a few exceptions, is that cacti must have the lightest location available, and this will mean full sun in an arid atmosphere. In poor light the majority of plants become thin and etiolated with the result that they lose the tight, compact shape that is so important to their general appearance. Indoors, they should have a sunny window location. The tougher kinds can stand out of doors in good light during the summer, but care is needed to prevent their becoming too wet when it rains.

CONDITIONS

Dank and airless conditions can be fatal, so a light and airy atmosphere should be the aim. Although cacti are from desert regions the growing temperature should not necessarily be excessively high. In the desert the temperature can drop to a very low level at night, but cacti can tolerate these conditions as long as they are not wet at their roots; high temperatures will not be a problem, but if temperatures are to be below 5°C/41°F care is needed to ensure that the soil is dry.

WATERING AND FEEDING

Cactus plants that are permanently wet will have a very short life. Free-draining potting mixture is essential – a mixture that allows water to drain immediately through when it is poured on to the surface of the soil. During the spring and summer plants should be watered and allowed to dry before being watered again. During the winter months they should have no water whatsoever – this condition encourages flowering when water is given in the spring.

Fertilizers specially formulated for cactus can be bought, but a tomato fertilizer will usually do equally well. In general, one should feed established plants about once every 2-3 weeks during the spring and summer for the best possible results.

Cacti and other succulents can make a fascinating display. There are hundreds of species and varieties, many of which produce beautiful flowers.

POTTING AND POTTING MIXTURES

Mixtures formulated for cactus plants can be bought, and this is the best option for the beginner. When you have gained experience in the growing of these plants you can contemplate preparing your own concoctions, but it is not wise to experiment at the outset. All peat mixtures, or soil-less mixtures as they are termed, are unsuitable for cactus plants. It is much better to get a loam-based mixture – if it does not feel gritty when run through the fingers, additional grit or sharp sand should be added to improve the drainage. Never use potting soil that has been standing around unused for long periods of time. Plants should be repotted in the spring or early summer and should be well provided with roots; poorly rooted plants should be returned to the pot in which they are growing. When potting on 'spiteful' plants it may be necessary to put a paper collar around the plant to make handling easier.

PESTS AND DISEASES

Cactus plants are not too much troubled by either pests or diseases, but overwatering may well cause the fungal problem of botrytis which is seen as a blackish wet mould around the base of the plant. Treating with a fungicide might well save the plant, but it is doubtful. Affected plants should be isolated from others in the collection.

Mealy bug is the biggest problem, and these insects are normally detected as a waxy cotton-wool-like substance nestling between the leaves and stems of plants. The adult bugs look like powdery white woodlice which can be clearly seen as they move about, and will not be difficult to eradicate. The young of this pest are ensconced in the waxy wool and are much more difficult to make contact with. One way is to use an old toothbrush that has been soaked in methylated spirits to wipe them off the plant; this will also see off the adults.

Mealy root bug is often quite easy to see. The young are wrapped in a cottony coating resembling cotton wool and they leave a white deposit on the inside of the container – when detected immerse the pot to its rim in insecticide to eradicate. Always follow insecticide directions and wear rubber gloves.

Aporacactus Flagelliformis

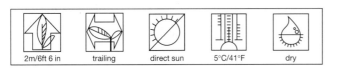

2m/6ft 6 in	trailing	direct sun	5°C/41°F	dry

Native to Mexico, *Aporocactus flagelliformis* (rat's tail cactus) can be grown as trailing plants in a basket, or as creeping plants in a large cactus garden.

GENERAL CARE When spring potting on is required use a peat or loam-based mixture and never allow the soil to dry out, keeping just moist over the winter months. While in active growth, spring and summer, feed fortnightly with a tomato fertilizer.

PROPAGATION Remove mature lengths of growth in early summer and allow to dry for a day or two before inserting in peat and sand mixture.

SPECIES *A. mallisonii*, pendulous spiny stems and large flowers, rarely found on sale.

POSSIBLE PROBLEMS Mealy bug and root mealy bug; treat the latter with a solution of Malathion insecticide by watering it into the soil, giving sufficient to see surplus draining through the holes in the bottom of the container. Mealy bug in the foliage should be treated with a systemic insecticide. Wear rubber gloves and apply out of doors.

Cephalocereus Senilis

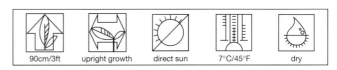

90cm/3ft	upright growth	direct sun	7°C/45°F	dry

Of Mexican origin, *Cephalocereus senilis* (old man cactus) will attain a height of some 12m/39ft in their native habitat, by which time they will be of considerable age. With roots confined to plant pots growth is very slow.

GENERAL CARE Provide the warmest possible position and very good light. Over the winter months the soil should be quite dry, but during the spring and summer it should be watered and allowed to dry out before repeating. When potting on, use a very open mixture containing a good proportion of grit.

PROPAGATION In late spring/early summer the top section of the stem may be removed and propagated in peat and sand mixture, but this does ruin the appearance of the plant. Allow the severed end to dry over a period of days before inserting.

SPECIES *C. sartorianus*, *C. chysacanthus*, both with upright columns of growth.

POSSIBLE PROBLEMS Mealy bugs and root mealy bug; treat with insecticide as soon as detected.

■ DESIGN TIP

These are excellent plants for suspending from a high ceiling near a window that offers good light, but it is important to check watering regularly during the summer months to ensure that the soil is not becoming too dry.

The cerise-coloured flowers, which each last for several days, are an added bonus and are produced in some quantity.

■ CARE TIP

The long grey hairs of old man cactus will become tarnished in time, and may be cleaned by giving the plant a shampoo with a mild solution of detergent.

CEREUS PERUVIANUS

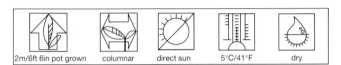

2m/6ft 6in pot grown	columnar	direct sun	5°C/41°F	dry

The erect habit of this easy-care plant, known as blue column, adds much to the cactus collection. The botanical name suggests that it is indigenous to Peru, but this is, in fact, a plant that is widely used in South America and there is doubt concerning its true origin.

GENERAL CARE Offer good light at all times and keep the soil dry over the winter. In spring and summer, water and allow to dry before repeating. Use clay pots and a free-draining mixture when potting on – avoid getting the plant pot-bound.

PROPAGATION Large sections of the stem of overgrown plants can be cut, allowed to dry and propagated in cactus mixture.

VARIETIES Numerous, but naming is confused unless plants are obtained from a reliable source.

POSSIBLE PROBLEMS Generally trouble-free, but there is always the possibility of root mealy bug – easily detected when the plant is removed from its container.

CHAMAECEREUS SILVESTRII

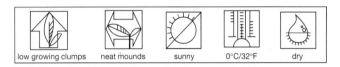

low growing clumps	neat mounds	sunny	0°C/32°F	dry

These accommodating little plants are colloquially known as peanut cactus. They must be almost everyone's introduction to the growing of cacti, as they are readily available, easy to grow and almost every little piece that breaks off will make excellent propagating material.

GENERAL CARE A high temperature is not needed, but if the temperature is unavoidably very low the soil must be kept dry. When potting use shallow pans as opposed to full-depth pots and employ a well-drained cactus mixture. Keep dry over the winter months.

PROPAGATION Growth resembles tiny green sausages and almost any piece that is detached will root readily in any reasonable mixture.

VARIETIES *Chamaecereus silvestrii*, bright scarlet flowers; *C. s.* 'Orange Hybrid', orange flowers.

POSSIBLE PROBLEMS The most likely cause of failure is that of having the soil in the pot much too wet when the prevailing temperature is very low.

■ CARE TIP

These are vigorous plants that will develop bold and spiteful columns of growth that are probably best suited to the greenhouse or large conservatory. They overbalance very easily so heavier clay pots are an important requirement when potting plants on – a task that should not be neglected. Moving larger plants is a two-handed task that needs care.

■ PROPAGATION TIP

Young children can be shown how to remove the little sausages of growth carefully with a pair of tweezers so that they can propagate their own plants.

CLEISTOCACTUS STRAUSII

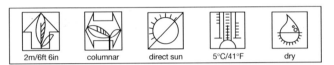

2m/6ft 6in	columnar	direct sun	5°C/41°F	dry

The common name 'silver torch' is very apt as the slender columns of growth are generously provided with white spines along their entire length, giving the plants a pleasing silvery appearance when seen in good light. Bolivia is generally credited with being the place of origin.

GENERAL CARE Because of their eventual height it is wise to use heavier clay containers when plants are being potted on. Use a loam-based, free-draining mixture and pot on in spring. Plants are reasonably vigorous in growth so potting on should not be neglected. In spring and summer feed with tomato fertilizer and keep moist, but keep dry in winter.

PROPAGATION Cut stems and allow them to dry before inserting in peat and sand mixture.

VARIETIES *Cleistocactus strausii juyjuyensis*, *C. baumannii* and *C. smaragdiflorus* may occasionally be available. A feature of these plants is erect, spiny stems.

POSSIBLE PROBLEMS Generally trouble-free, but watch for mealy bug.

ECHINOCACTUS GRUSONII

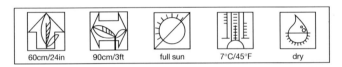

60cm/24in	90cm/3ft	full sun	7°C/45°F	dry

Native to Mexico and the aristocrat among cacti, *Echinocactus grusonii* (golden barrel) is seen at its best when very mature and developed into a huge globe of bristling yellow spines.

GENERAL CARE Best suited to shallow terracotta containers and a porous cactus mixture, golden barrel should be potted on in the spring, but only when it is necessary as a result of root development. Provide a dry atmosphere and sun and at all costs avoid dank and airless conditions. Water well and allow to dry before repeating. Keep dry over winter months.

PROPAGATION From seed collected from plants growing in the wild, but rarely available.

SPECIES *E. grandis* and *E. texensis* are available , but *E. grusonii* is the best choice.

POSSIBLE PROBLEMS Mealy bug and root mealy bug; cold and wet conditions present the greatest difficulty, hence the need for controlled temperatures in winter.

■ DESIGN TIP

Silver torch is one of the most attractive of cacti when seen in a group with other varieties, and it is generally better when forming part of a small collection rather than when used as a solitary specimen. Grouping of cacti is an exercise seen to best effect when plants are grown in the greenhouse or the conservatory where there is greater space available.

■ CARE TIP

Large specimens of E. grusonii will become the cactus grower's prize possession and must, consequently, be handled with great care. When potting or moving make it a two-handed task.

ECHINOCEREUS

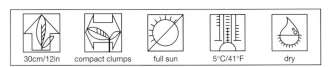

30cm/12in	compact clumps	full sun	5°C/41°F	dry

There are numerous varieties of these interesting plants, commonly known as lace and hedgehog cactus, mainly originating from the southern states of America and Mexico. A major benefit is that they produce flowers with little difficulty at an early age. Even without flowers the plants are attractive in appearance, some forming clumps of growth early on, whereas others take time for their true habit to establish.

GENERAL CARE To do well plants need the lightest possible location and the growing medium must be free-draining – add extra sand to the chosen potting mixture. It is important to allow the mixture to dry out between waterings.

PROPAGATION Cut mature pieces of stem and allow to dry before inserting.

SPECIES *Echinocereus viridiflorus, E. rigidissimus* and *E. fitchii*; large pink flowers are freely produced.

POSSIBLE PROBLEMS Mealy bug and root bug are the most likely pests to be found.

FEROCACTUS

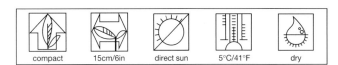

compact	15cm/6in	direct sun	5°C/41°F	dry

These become very large and very vicious plants in their natural habitat, but when pot-grown can be contained within acceptable dimensions. They do not produce flowers as pot plants until they have attained reasonable size. Their common name is 'fire barrel'.

GENERAL CARE These plants must have very good light in which to grow and at no time should the potting mixture become too wet – add extra sand or grit to the potting mixture when repotting in spring. Water and allow the soil to dry well before repeating.

PROPAGATION Ferocactus can be propagated from seed if available.

SPECIES *Ferocactus acanthodes* is the most popular, but *F. herrae* (*above*), *F. horridus* or *F. latispinus* may also be available.

POSSIBLE PROBLEMS Mealy bug or root mealy bug. Wet roots through poor culture will be fatal.

■ FLOWERING TIP

Although these are plants that will flower naturally at an early age it is important to offer the right conditions – a very long and very dry winter season, followed by spring watering to encourage flowering.

■ CARE TIP

This plant is also known as the fish-hook cactus and fish-hook barrel on account of its vicious hooked spines; handle it with the utmost care!

GYMNOCALYCIUM

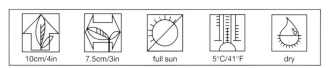

| 10cm/4in | 7.5cm/3in | full sun | 5°C/41°F | dry |

These are lovely plants that form neat clumps of growth in a reasonably short space of time, and they will also oblige with attractive flowers while still of tender age. There are numerous varieties available and all of them are delightful plants for the cactus enthusiast. The common name is 'spider cactus'.

GENERAL CARE Like most cactus gymnocalycium must have free drainage and any purchased potting mixture should have additional sand incorporated to improve its porosity. Watering can be fairly generous while the plants are in active growth, when they will also benefit from an application of tomato fertilizer every 2 weeks or so.

PROPAGATION Thin out congested clumps carefully, using a narrow-bladed knife, and insert the thinnings in a peat and sand mixture to produce new plants.

SPECIES *Gymnocalycium venturianum* (*above*), *G. bruchii*, *G. horridispinum*, *G. quehlianum* are among the many varieties. All are easy to care for.

POSSIBLE PROBLEMS Mealy bug, root mealy bug.

LOBIVIA

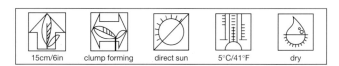

| 15cm/6in | clump forming | direct sun | 5°C/41°F | dry |

A pleasing characteristic of the lobivias (cob cactus) is their ability to flower at an early age, and the fact that flowers come in a range of colours.

GENERAL CARE Plants must be kept dry over the winter months, but it is important not to allow the soil to become excessively dry during the growing season. Pot on, if necessary, in spring – add sand to standard potting mixes to improve the drainage factor. Following potting on the soil should be well watered and thereafter kept on the dry side to encourage root development in the new mixture. Apply tomato fertilizer in the growing season to encourage flowering.

PROPAGATION From offsets allowed to dry before inserting in a peat and sand mixture in early summer. These should be kept in good light but out of bright sun until they have rooted.

SPECIES *Lobivia maximiliana, L. aurea, L. bruchii, L. famatimensis,* among others; most are indigenous to Argentina. Deeply ribbed growth – normally little trouble to flower.

POSSIBLE PROBLEMS Root mealy bug and mealy bug – careful inspection is needed to detect latter.

■ CARE TIP

Gymnocalycium '*Hibotan*' is much used for grafting on to stronger-growing stock, so a red, pink, yellow or even white gymnocalycium can be purchased perched on top of its host plant. It is important when overwintering such plants to maintain a minimum temperature of 10°C/50°F, as cold winter conditions can prove fatal.

■ PLANTING TIP

In shallow terracotta pans, lobivias make fine specimen plants when well matured. Preparation of these takes some time in the potting from one size of container to the next, so patience is needed!

MAMMILARIA

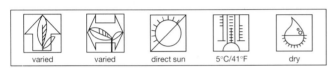

varied	varied	direct sun	5°C/41°F	dry

Almost all species of this greatly varied genus are indigenous to Mexico, and there are many excellent plants among them. The majority are easy-care plants that will not only grow well but will also flower well at an early stage in their development. Most form tight clumps of attractive colouring and can be encouraged to form into specimen plants in shallow containers in time.

GENERAL CARE Offer good light at all times and keep dry over winter to encourage flowering when water is again applied in early spring. Established plants will benefit from a weak solution of tomato fertilizer during the growing season.

PROPAGATION The majority are propagated from detached offsets. It is also possible to propagate from seed.

SPECIES *Mammilaria bocasans, M. backbergii, M. elongata, M. zeilmanniana* (*above*), plus many others that will enhance any cactus collection.

POSSIBLE PROBLEMS Root mealy bug and mealy bug – the latter may be difficult to detect among the clustered offsets.

NOTOCACTUS

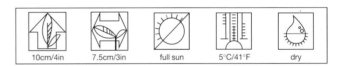

10cm/4in	7.5cm/3in	full sun	5°C/41°F	dry

Notocactus (ball cactus) are fine plants of attractive shape, mostly globular but some becoming columnar as they age. Spines and colouring are generally very attractive, and there is the added bonus that plants are not difficult to bring into flower. They are indigenous to tropical South America.

GENERAL CARE Provide good light for all notocactus and ensure that they are growing in a free-draining potting mixture by adding grit or sand to commercially prepared mixtures. Water with care during the growing season and feed occasionally. No winter watering is needed.

PROPAGATION From seed or offsets where available.

SPECIES *Notocactus horstii, N. herterii, N. ottonis; N. leninghausii* is particularly attractive, developing a stout column 25cm/10in tall with pale yellow spines.

POSSIBLE PROBLEMS The most common pests are mealy bug and root mealy bug. When detected both should be attended to without delay.

GENERAL TIP

An added interest for the keen cactus grower is to concentrate on one type of plant in particular (mammillarias, for example) and to become something of a specialist grower of these plants.

CARE TIP

Plants that form tight clusters of rosettes provide the perfect hiding place for mealy bug with the result that these pests often go unnoticed until they have become well established. Pick up the plants periodically and give them a closer inspection so that mealy bug can be controlled at an early stage of development.

OPUNTIA

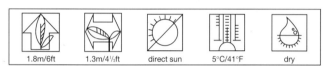

1.8m/6ft	1.3m/4½ft	direct sun	5°C/41°F	dry

'Bunnies' ears' is the perfect plant for children if they mind their fingers, and it is one of the most popular cacti of all. Some of the opuntias (prickly pear) have clusters of small bristle spines while others have vicious barbs, so all must be handled with some care. Most are easy to manage with the more robust, *O. robusta* for example, being very vigorous and needing to be reduced in size periodically – use trimmings for propagation. Opuntias are indigenous to the southern United States and tropical South America.

GENERAL CARE All need good light and dry winter conditions, but should be kept moist and fed during the growing season.

PROPAGATION From seed or from trimmings – allow to dry before inserting in peat and sand mixture.

SPECIES *Opuntia microdasys* (bunnies' ears, *above*), *O. leucotricha*, *O. tuna* plus many others.

POSSIBLE PROBLEMS Check frequently for mealy bug and root mealy bug.

PARODIA

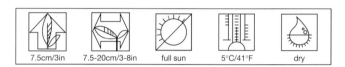

7.5cm/3in	7.5-20cm/3-8in	full sun	5°C/41°F	dry

Indigenous to Argentina, parodias (Tom Thumb) have become much more popular in recent years – much of the popularity being due to their willingness to flower as young plants. They are mostly of globular shape, with vicious hooked spines.

GENERAL CARE Over-wet conditions will cause rotting so water must be given with care. For the same reason plants must not be potted in containers that are too large – it is better to have smaller pots that allow the soil to dry more readily. Good light and free-draining soil mixture are important requirements. A sunny location will also help to alleviate damp conditions.

PROPAGATION From seed or offsets. Seed, when obtainable, should be sown in shallow seed pans filled with a proprietary seed sowing mixture to which grit or sand has been added.

SPECIES *Parodia chrysacthioa* (*above*), *P. aureispina*, *P. microsperma*, *P. sanguiniflora*, *P. mutablis*; all globular in shape and free-flowering.

POSSIBLE PROBLEMS Mealy bug and root mealy bug.

■ CARE TIP

Some of the opuntias will tolerate much lower temperatures than that indicated above if they are kept very dry. However, it is better to offer modest warmth.

■ FLOWERING TIP

Parodias have the considerable bonus as far as cactus are concerned in that they are able to produce their large red and yellow flowers at an early age. Given a reasonable collection of these plants one may have flowers over an extended period during the spring and summer months of the year.

PERESKIA

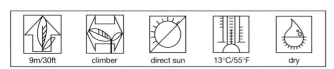

9m/30ft	climber	direct sun	13°C/55°F	dry

A cactus plant because of its barbs, but a most unlikely-looking candidate to be included in the family *Cactaceae* as the leaves are smooth and the plant is seen at its best when treated as a climbing subject. If grown in a pot indoors it can be trained on a light trellis placed in the pot, or if grown in the greenhouse it can be trained on a wall support. Its common name is 'Barbados gooseberry'.

GENERAL CARE Keep moist and feed occasionally during the spring and summer, but exercise care over winter as plants are susceptible to a combination of cold and wet.

PROPAGATION From cuttings in spring – place in small pots filled with a peat and sand mixture and root at a temperature of 21°C/70°F.

SPECIES *Pereskia grandiflora* (*above*), *P. rubescens*, *P. aculeata* 'Godseffiana'; the latter offers pale gold foliage and is the most widely available.

POSSIBLE PROBLEMS Mealy bug and root mealy bug.

REBUTIA

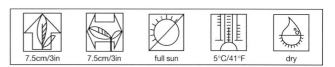

7.5cm/3in	7.5cm/3in	full sun	5°C/41°F	dry

The rebutias (crown cactus) have become very popular plants in recent years for the simple reason that they are small and easy to accommodate and that they flower very freely as young plants. There is a wide colour range of bright flowers. They are native to Argentina and neighbouring countries.

GENERAL CARE Plants must have a long winter rest from watering – from mid September to mid March. Begin watering again when flower buds are seen to be forming. Grow in small pots in good light and avoid overwatering. From the time of bud formation plants can be fed at fortnightly intervals with a tomato fertilizer.

PROPAGATION From seed or from offsets.

SPECIES *Rebutia pygmaea*, *R. senilis*, *R. deminuta* among others. Large numbers are grown from seed, so it might be difficult to obtain true named varieties.

POSSIBLE PROBLEMS Mealy bug and root mealy bug.

▨ FLOWERING TIP

Grow a single strong shoot attached to a cane and when strong enough use as a stock for grafting epiphyllum or zygocactus to the top to set them off more effectively when in flower.

▨ CARE TIP

These are ideal plants for the living-room windowsill as they occupy little space and, if offered good light, can almost be guaranteed to flower each year from an early age. When curtains are drawn in winter plants should be brought into the room rather than being left on a cold windowsill.

SUCCULENTS

These are different from the cacti in that they do not have areoles, a small cluster of spines that are found only on members of the family *Cactaceae*. Succulents belong to many different families of plants, but they do have one thing in common – their swollen stems or leaves are capable of holding moisture and nutrients to enable plants to survive long periods of drought in their natural habitats. In desert regions of the world these plants can withstand the most arid conditions with the capacity to burst into brilliantly coloured flower almost as soon as the first rains of the new season find their way to the roots of the plants.

This gives some indication of the watering requirements of these plants. In the UK, the winter represents the dry season and both cacti and succulents should have little or no water from about the end of September through to the early spring, when watering will induce many of the freer-flowering plants to produce their blooms.

LOCATION

Succulents are almost all sun-lovers, so the lightest possible location should be chosen for them, both indoors and in the greenhouse. In the home, plants ought to have a sunny windowsill, and where space is limited it may be possible to have narrow shelves at a higher level to accommodate smaller plants. High-level window shelves of this kind are frequently seen on the Continent, where the growing of all kinds of indoor plants seems to have reached almost the stage of obsession in some households! Such shelves need not be elaborate and can be supported on either side by appropriate fittings on the window frame.

CONDITIONS

The majority of succulents will tolerate temperatures around freezing point and will not be unduly harmed as long as the soil in the growing container is dry. However, it is generally better to offer plants a temperature of 10°C/50°F over the winter months, with higher temperatures tending to be beneficial rather than harmful. In most homes some rooms are warmer than others over the winter and if there are a number of plants they should be gathered together and placed in the warmest room so that they may benefit from the better conditions.

When these plants are grown as isolated decorative features in a room the tendency is to put the pots into decorative outer containers. A word of warning here – you must put a good thickness of pebbles in the bottom of the container before introducing the plant so that water draining from the growing pot will filter away into the gravel.

WATERING AND FEEDING

Dry winter conditions are essential – if plant roots are wet over winter and the temperature is low there is every chance that the plant will succumb. When it comes to caring for succulents (and cacti) there is a misguided belief that they need no attention other than the occasional drop of water. This is far from true, as will be seen from a visit to a succulent collection that is receiving proper care in respect of watering, feeding, potting on, suitable temperature and good light. Freshly potted plants should not be fed, but those that are established will benefit from feeding about every second week during the spring and summer months when growth is active. In terms of suitability and economy there is nothing better than a tomato fertilizer – it will not only benefit the plant generally, it will also encourage those that do flower to flower more freely.

POTTING AND POTTING MIXTURES

Established plants should be potted on in the spring to containers that are only slightly larger than the one in which the plant is growing. Specially prepared mixtures for cacti and succulents can be bought and this is probably the best option where only a few plants are concerned. In any event, it is most essential that the mixture should be free to drain, and that means that as you pour water on to the surface of the soil it should immediately soak away. To improve porosity of any mixture that is suspect you can add sharp sand, coarse grit or perlite.

CONTAINERS

There are all sorts of containers available and it does not seem to make a great deal of difference whether they are terracotta or plastic. However, to have a collection of plants in a hotch-potch of containers of different materials, sizes and colours tends to mar the overall appearance. Complete standardization is seldom possible but there should be a degree of uniformity, even if it means nothing more than having all plastic containers of similar colour.

PESTS AND DISEASES

Prevention is better than cure, which means that plants ought to be regularly inspected for the presence of pests such as mealy bug, which is the one most commonly found in succulents. These pests get into the most inaccessible places and their presence is only made known when a waxy substance rather like cotton wool is seen amongst the branches and leaves of plants.

A collection of succulents grown in a dish container look good with textured small rocks and stones.

AEONIUM

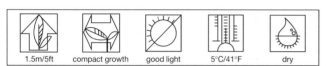

| 1.5m/5ft | compact growth | good light | 5°C/41°F | dry |

The most common of these is *Aeonium arboreum*, which is available with dark bronze or fresh green leaves. Both form strong stems from which rosettes develop. Indigenous to the Mediterranean region, aeonium require lots of sunshine and reasonably dry conditions in which to grow. As time goes on they will develop into quite substantial plants that look good growing in terracotta planters on a sunny patio. *A. domesticum Var.* has much softer rosettes of growth that do well on a sunny windowsill indoors.

GENERAL CARE Keep moist during the summer months and very much on the dry side at other times. Feed occasionally while in active growth.

PROPAGATION By mature offsets in free-draining mixture. Keep out of bright sunlight until they have rooted.

SPECIES *A. arboreum* (*above*), green form; *A. arboreum atropurpureum*, bronze form; *A. domesticum Var.*; pale green and cream rosettes; *A. urbicum*, large rosettes, yellow flowers.

POSSIBLE PROBLEMS Mealy bug, but not greatly troubled.

AGAVE AMERICANA

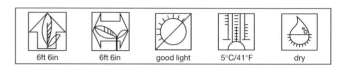

| 6ft 6in | 6ft 6in | good light | 5°C/41°F | dry |

Both height and spread will vary depending on location – in a container they will be much less, while planted out in a greenhouse the plant will be larger. The best location is probably a sunny patio in a terracotta container. The leaf tips are viciously pointed, so plants must be out of the way and care must be taken when inspecting them. In spite of these problems, *Agave americana* (century plant) is a magnificent plant when grown as a specimen. The large rosettes of leaves are an attractive grey and cream in colour.

GENERAL CARE Offer good light and never overwater. When container-grown, plants should be in a heavier loam-based potting mixture as opposed to a peaty concoction.

PROPAGATION From maturing offsets taken from around the base of the plant. Leave to dry for several days before potting in a potting compost.

VARIETIES There are many varieties available.

POSSIBLE PROBLEMS Generally trouble-free.

■ PLANTING TIP

A. domesticum var. is a splendid plant for growing indoors if it has a light location. Rosettes of softish growth develop on firm stems to provide a very attractive plant. Worth seeking out.

■ FLOWERING TIP

The century plant is seen growing in all tropical parts of the world where it develops into a plant of considerable size. Although it may take up to 10 years, plants do produce flowers and when they arrive they do so in style by attaining a height of up to 12m/40ft. Following flowering it is not unusual for plants to die.

ALOE

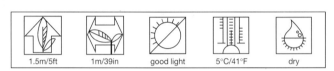

1.5m/5ft	1m/39in	good light	5°C/41°F	dry

Aloe variegata has a tight, spiralling rosette of leaves that are green with paler bands of colour, which gives the plant its common name of Partridge Breast Aloe. It is a very easy windowsill plant to manage. The Medicine Aloe, *A. Vera*, is much more rambling and untidy with appreciably larger rosettes of growth. The latter lives up to its common name in that the sap from a broken leaf has amazing curative qualities when rubbed on to burns or bruises – a plant that is worth having for this reason if for no other.

GENERAL CARE Aloe needs a light location. Keep plants moist during the spring and summer and on the dry side at other times. Feed occasionally with a tomato type fertilizer.

PROPAGATION Propagate from offsets; insert in sandy mixture to start them off.

VARIETIES There are numerous varieties, all rosette forming.

POSSIBLE PROBLEMS Occasionally mealy bug, but not greatly troubled.

CEROPEGIA

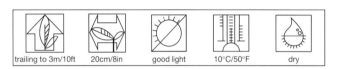

trailing to 3m/10ft	20cm/8in	good light	10°C/50°F	dry

Ceropegia is sometimes called rosary vine, but the heart-shaped leaves frequently get in a tangle, giving it the more commonly used name 'hearts entangled'. It is essentially a hanging container plant, be it in a conventional basket or decorative pot. The leaves are attached to very slender stems that will trail for yards if the container is suspended at reasonable height. The mauve-coloured tubular flowers are interesting, as are the peculiar round growths that appear on the stems of older plants. These can be used for propagating new plants.

GENERAL CARE These are very tolerant plants that put up with all sorts of varying conditions – their pet hate being a combination of wet soil and low temperatures.

PROPAGATION From cuttings or stem growths. Cuttings should go into peat and sand mixture, several cuttings to each small pot. A heated propagator will assist rooting.

SPECIES *Ceropegia woodii* (*above*), heart-shaped leaves, insignificant flowers.

◼ GENERAL TIP

While A. variegata is an excellent windowsill plant for the home, it is better to grow A. vera in the greenhouse to form clumps and to propagate single rosettes for a handy position on the windowsill.

◼ PROPAGATION TIP

When planting decorative hanging pots put at least 10 rooted cuttings into the soil and when these have reached manageable size peg them down in the soil to provide additional growth.

COTYLEDON

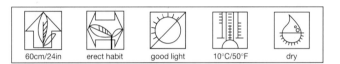

60cm/24in	erect habit	good light	10°C/50°F	dry

These South African succulents have particularly attractive foliage – not only do the leaves have a scallop-shell appearance, but they are also covered in an attractive mealy bloom. The stems of the plant also have similar covering which adds much to the general appearance.

GENERAL CARE Plants must have good light in which to grow and at no time should the soil be too wet – best practice is to water adequately and then to allow the soil to dry appreciably before repeating. A weak tomato fertilizer at fortnightly intervals in spring and summer will encourage growth. Sharp, well-drained potting mixture is important – the sort of mixture that allows water to drain through as soon as it is poured on to the surface of the soil.

PROPAGATION From seed or from cuttings.

SPECIES *Cotyledon elegans* (*above*), *C. undulata*, attractive grey foliage with undulating leaf margins.

POSSIBLE PROBLEMS Mealy bug and root mealy bug. Check for root mealy bug by removing the plant from its pot – white deposit on the pot confirms its presence. Eradicate by immersing the pot in malathion insecticide – wear rubber gloves and soak thoroughly.

CRASSULA

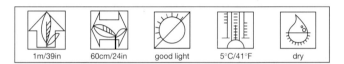

1m/39in	60cm/24in	good light	5°C/41°F	dry

In recent years the money plant (or jade plant) has become very popular. There is a green form and an excellent variegated form in *Crassula argentea* 'Hummels Variety', both of which have thick, strong stems on stout plants if not mollycoddled.

GENERAL CARE Keep in good light, avoid overwatering, restrict to modest-sized pots and feed every 10 days in spring and summer. Pinch out growing tips frequently early on so that compact and solid-looking plants develop. When potting on as plants of mature size use clay pots and a loam-based potting mixture.

PROPAGATION From cuttings – allow the severed end to dry before inserting in growing compost.

SPECIES *C. argentea*, *C. a.* 'Hummels Variety', *C. corymbulosa* (*above*).

POSSIBLE PROBLEMS Generally trouble-free.

▧ CARE TIP

The decorative mealy covering on the leaves can be very easily damaged through use of unsuitable insecticides. Check suitability first, or experiment with smaller plant first by treating it and leaving for a time before applying insecticide generally.

▧ CARE TIP

It is important to grow these in the manner that the professional would describe as 'hard', which means no high temperatures and little fussing. Plants can be outside all the time while the weather is not very cold.

ECHEVERIA

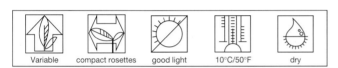

Variable	compact rosettes	good light	10°C/50°F	dry

These are among the most attractive of foliage plants, having many superb metallic shades of colour. By way of a bonus they will generally not be difficult to bring into flower. The majority form neat rosettes of growth that make it possible for a large collection to be fitted into a reasonably small space.

GENERAL CARE Care is needed to ensure that water does not lie in amongst the overlapping leaves of rosettes, and that watering in general is done with care, particularly during the winter months of the year. Use a free-draining mixture when plants are being potted on, and feed with a tomato fertilizer every 2-3 weeks during spring and summer.

PROPAGATION From offsets that form around the base of the parent rosette.

SPECIES *Echeveria derenbergii* (*above*), orange flowers; *E. hoveyii*, *E. setosa*, red flowers.

POSSIBLE PROBLEMS Mealy bug and root mealy bug.

EUPHORBIA

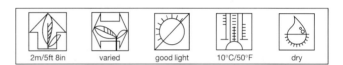

2m/5ft 8in	varied	good light	10°C/50°F	dry

There are many plants in this large family, all of them producing a milky sap when bruised or cut. Some resemble cacti and carry spines.

GENERAL CARE Plants should be dry from the end of the summer until the spring when watering for the new season can begin, but it must at no time be excessive. For this reason it is essential to employ a free-draining potting mixture when plants are being potted on. Avoid the use of shallow pans as plants are deep rooting.

PROPAGATION From seed, or cuttings where available.

SPECIES *Euphorbia obesa* (*above*), *E. melaformis*, *E. ingens* (giant form).

POSSIBLE PROBLEMS Generally trouble-free, but check for mealy bug.

■ CARE TIP

Allowing dead and dying leaves to remain on plants can cause the entire plant to rot and die. Check base of rosettes for discoloured leaves regularly and remove. Blemished leaves are nothing more than an eyesore, so should be removed during regular inspections. The most common reason for loss of leaves is wet and cold winter conditions.

■ PROPAGATION TIP

To propagate from seed you will need to have both male and female plants in your collection. The seed pods explode when ripe, scattering seeds widely, so place some muslin over the plant before the seeds ripen.

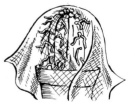

GASTERIA

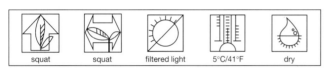

squat	squat	filtered light	5°C/41°F	dry

Gasteria are unusual in succulents in that these are plants preferring light shade as opposed to the sunny conditions that are normally needed. Grown from seed, gasterias will in time form attractive rosettes of growth but this takes some time to develop as plants will initially have a central stem from which leaves develop opposite to one another. Being shade tolerant, the gasterias make fine house plants that have the added advantage of being very compact so occupying little space.

GENERAL CARE A free-draining potting mixture is essential. Gasterias will need more frequent watering than the majority of succulent plants but it is necessary to allow the soil to dry out between each application. Reduce the watering over the winter months.

PROPAGATION From seed, or from offsets for true varieties.

SPECIES *Gasteria batesiana, G. maculata, G. verrucosa* (*above*).

POSSIBLE PROBLEMS Generally trouble-free.

KALANCHOE

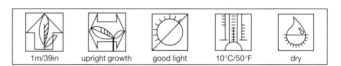

1m/39in	upright growth	good light	10°C/50°F	dry

There are numerous kalanchoes available that will add interest to a plant collection but none, perhaps, more pleasing than *Kalanchoe tomentosa* (*above*). The common name is Pussy Ears doubtless gained from the leaves, which are covered with fine silver hairs and edged with a rich brown colour.

GENERAL CARE Grow in full sun; water sparingly, especially in winter. Feed once every two weeks during the active growth period. Kalanchoes are no trouble to care for – they should be renewed when they become overgrown and ungainly.

SPECIES Other interesting species include *K. daigremontianum, K. tubiflorum.*

POSSIBLE PROBLEMS Generally trouble-free.

■ DESIGN TIP

One of the great pleasures of growing both succulents and cacti is to produce symmetrical plants of good dimension. The gasterias lend themselves well to this purpose, looking especially well in shallow pans. Pans planted with a single mature rosetting plant can be very effective if properly dressed with gravel on the soil surface to set off the plant.

■ FLOWERING TIP

The kalanchoe is a short-day plant, which means that it only develops flower buds when the day lasts for less than 12 hours. You can replicate these conditions at home by creating artificially dark conditions using a black plastic bag or bucket. Start the treatment in late summer and continue for between 12 and 15 weeks – removing the first few flower buds to promote flowering.

338

KALANCHOE BLOSSFELDIANA

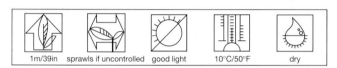

1m/39in	sprawls if uncontrolled	good light	10°C/50°F	dry

The most popular of all succulents, this plant is available in flower all year round as a result of growers manipulating the amount of light that is available to the plant. Long-lasting flowers in several colours are an attraction for many weeks. An excellent use for this fine kalanchoe is to group several in a shallow dish to provide a more impressive room feature. These are also good plants for edging decorative plant borders within the conservatory. They are commonly known as 'flaming Katie'.

GENERAL CARE Offer good light, modest warmth and pot on after flowering to produce bright and vigorous plants. Avoid overwatering, feed occasionally while in active growth and regularly remove dead flowers to keep plants in good fettle.

PROPAGATION Top sections of stem with a few leaves attached will root readily in peat and sand mixture.

VARIETIES Red, yellow, orange and pink-flowered varieties are available.

POSSIBLE PROBLEMS Generally trouble-free.

LITHOPS

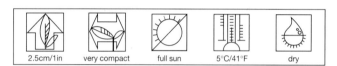

2.5cm/1in	very compact	full sun	5°C/41°F	dry

Fascinating succulent plants from South Africa, lithops (living stones) are almost guaranteed to capture the interest of younger members of the family.

GENERAL CARE A bright, sunny location is essential to their well-being, as is careful watering. Ensure that no water gets on to the plants and during the winter months do not water at all as dry soil conditions are essential during this time. There should be no hurry to apply water in the spring – allow plants to remain dry until the growth of the previous year has shrivelled away and fresh growth is evident. This will normally be in late spring. Water plants thoroughly but allow the soil to dry before repeating. Free-draining soil is needed when potting plants on.

PROPAGATION From seed, or by splitting older clumps during the summer months.

SPECIES There are many species, but plants are frequently sold as unnamed seedlings.

POSSIBLE PROBLEMS Generally trouble-free.

▓ FLOWERING TIP

This kalanchoe often fails through lack of attention following flowering. After flowering the dead flowers should all be removed and plants should be potted into larger containers to grow and prosper.

▓ PLANTING TIP

Because living stones take up little space they can be grouped together in a shallow terracotta pan along with a selection of pebbles – this will be something of a tease for anyone trying to identify the actual plants.

PACHYPHYTUM

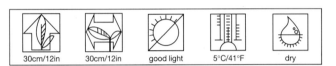

| 30cm/12in | 30cm/12in | good light | 5°C/41°F | dry |

With rounded, fleshy leaves, these are very much one's impression of what a succulent should be. Besides a pleasing shape, the leaves have the added benefits of being subtly coloured with an overall mealy covering. Rosettes of leaves form on long stalks that can be staked to remain erect or can be allowed to spread naturally to give a more pleasing appearance.

GENERAL CARE Water and feed occasionally during the spring and summer, giving no feed and only minimal watering over the winter months. Avoid getting water on to the foliage and be especially careful when using insecticides – malathion, for example, can be harmful. Use loam-based, free-draining potting mixture when potting on.

PROPAGATION From rosettes cut off and dried at severed ends before inserting in sandy potting mixture.

SPECIES *Pachyphytum bracteosum*, *P. longifolium*, *P. oviferum* (*above*), all having very colourful fleshy foliage.

POSSIBLE PROBLEMS Mealy bug and root mealy bug.

SEDUM MORGANIANUM

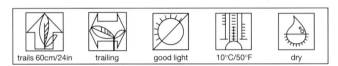

| trails 60cm/24in | trailing | good light | 10°C/50°F | dry |

Sedum morganianum (burrows tail) can only be grown as a trailing subject, having pendulous stems that are densely covered with overlapping succulent leaves that give the plant its very distinctive appearance. Older plants will in time produce clusters of pink flowers, but the foliage is the main attraction of this interesting plant.

GENERAL CARE Initially they should be grown in pots to establish; once well-developed a group of 5-6 plants should be planted into a hanging basket of good size (a large size is needed because it will be almost impossible to remove the plant to pot into a larger basket once it has become established as a trailer). Keep moist and in good light.

PROPAGATION Propagates very readily from leaves, which will break off and root of their own accord.

VARIETIES There are no varieties.

POSSIBLE PROBLEMS Generally trouble-free.

■ CARE TIP

The attractive mealy covering on the leaves is a principal attraction and it is necessary to grow these plants in full sun so that the mealiness and general colouring is enhanced. When handling plants with this sort of covering *it is important not to touch the leaves, and when watering one should do so with care, directing the water into the pot and not over the foliage.*

■ CARE TIP

One of the greatest difficulties with this plant is that it will shed leaves at almost the slightest touch. Since it has dense foliage a few leaves are not missed, but care in handling is important.

SENECIO ROWLEYANUS

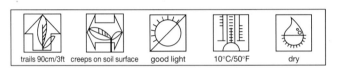

trails 90cm/3ft · creeps on soil surface · good light · 10°C/50°F · dry

With the fashion for trailing plants indoors this senecio has become very popular. The pendulous slender stems with green bobbles of leaves will, if grown in a greenhouse, eventually reach the staging or floor where they will root in and spread naturally in all directions. The common name is 'string of beads'.

GENERAL CARE Plants should be kept moist during the summer and only just moist over the winter. Feed occasionally in summer. When growing these plants indoors, as opposed to a greenhouse, they should be given the lightest possible location – hanging close by the kitchen window being ideal.

PROPAGATION Fresh plants can easily be made by severing rooted pieces from the main stem and potting them in a free-draining mixture.

VARIETIES there are no varieties.

POSSIBLE PROBLEMS Generally trouble-free.

STAPELIA

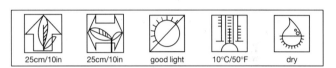

25cm/10in · 25cm/10in · good light · 10°C/50°F · dry

The stapelias (carrion flowers) have attractive succulent stems borne in clusters forming at soil level. They are quite easy to grow, but you may prefer to have them in the greenhouse rather than indoors – certainly while they are in flower, because the flowers have an abominable odour that has the very uncharming feature of attracting blowflies that help to pollinate the flowers. Nevertheless, the star-shaped flowers have fascinating patterns and colouring which might well outweigh the unpleasant smell that they produce.

GENERAL CARE Stapelias should be grown in a very sharp compost and should at no time be excessively watered. The latter is particularly important over the winter months.

PROPAGATION By removing mature stems and potting in small pots during the summer. If done with care it is possible to remove stems that already have roots attached.

SPECIES *Stapelia hirsuta*, *S. revoluta*, *S. variegata* (*above*), all have attractive flowers with an unpleasant odour.

POSSIBLE PROBLEMS Mealy bug and botrytis rot.

▪ DESIGN TIP

This senecio is seen to best advantage when growing in small hanging containers – the appearance of the hanging unit can be enhanced by placing it in a wicker hanging container. As with many such hanging plants the senecio will become rather sparse around soil level. To compensate for this, root a few cuttings and plant them in the soil.

▪ CARE TIP

Stapelias have a tendency to rot off at the base of their stems – a problem that is aggravated by wet conditions. Allow the soil to dry between waterings and cover the surface with a layer of gravel for added protection.

BROMELIADS

The bromeliads are a large family of plants from tropical America, a small number of which are popular for indoor decoration. They owe their name to a seventeenth-century Swedish botanist, O. Bromel. Bromeliads are distinguished in appearance by their stiff, spiky leaves, which are almost always stemless,

Stripes or prominent bands are features of the earth star. Good light gives best colouring.

and which form densely packed rosettes. The flowers may nestle in the cup of the rosette, emerge from closely packed bracts at the tip of a flowerstem, or droop from the end of it. The cup or 'vase' at the centre of the rosette in some genera collects a reservoir of water to supply the plant's needs. In most other plants, other than those that live in ponds, the constant presence of water at the heart would cause rot and ultimately death. In nature, most of the bromeliads grown as houseplants are epiphytic, that is they grow on another plant, often a tree, but take no nourishment from it (they are not parasites, in other words). They can do this because their roots are adapted to thrive without soil. While the roots can absorb moisture and nourishment from the air, very little moisture is lost through the strong leaves. Commonly called air plants, epiphytic bromeliads thrive where the atmosphere is humid and the temperature uniformly high. Terrestrial bromeliads grow in the ground.

With the exception of cryptanthus, bromeliads bear showy, colourful flowers, often surrounded by pink or red bracts. Some are borne on long flower spikes. Others have almost no stem at all and at flowering time the leaves or leaf bases surrounding the vase from which the bloom emerges change colour, taking on a gorgeous deep red hue. In nature this would attract pollinating insects and birds.

SPECIAL CARE

Despite their exotic appearance and unique characteristics, bromeliads are not difficult to grow indoors as long as a few basic requirements are met. Their adaptability is shown by the fact that bromeliads in the wild growing on the branches of a tree sometimes fall off and simply continue growing on the ground. For houseplants, the growing medium should be porous and completely free of lime. Suitable mixtures are (a) equal parts of peat and coarse leaf mould with half a part of coarse sand for improved drainage; or (b) equal parts of peat, sand and osmunda fibre or (c) equal parts of leaf mould, sphagnum moss and peat. Since the roots obtain relatively little nourishment from the mixture, pots as small as 12.5cm/5in are large enough; but because roots provide anchorage, the pots should be relatively heavy. Clay pots rather than plastic ones are recommended.

An intolerance of lime means that water used to fill the vases and spray the leaves should be either rain-water, the ideal choice, melted ice from a defrosting refrigerator (let it reach room temperature before use) or tap water, if unavoidable, which has been boiled and allowed to cool. The central vase, in plants which have one, should be full of water at all times. Replace it about every four weeks, turning the plant upside down to let the stale water drain away. Stand bromeliads outside in warm summer showers; the rain provides nourishment while washing the leaves. Indoors, maintain humidity at steady, reasonably high levels with the temperature between 16–18°C/61–64°F and in good light (see below). Many bromeliads do not have a natural rest period, but if it is not possible to maintain these conditions through the year they will survive the winter quite happily as long as the temperature does not drop below the minimum given in each entry – with a corresponding lessening of humidity. Requirements for light differ between those which have tough leathery leaves and can take a certain amount of direct sunlight, and those with softer, finer foliage which in nature would thrive in dappled light. For these, bright filtered light is best.

'Like a specimen tree on a manicured lawn, bromeliads invite individual attention. In a heated greenhouse or conservatory, they may be expected to co-operate in a larger display, but in a room setting they look best situated as one might a prize piece of china, enjoying pride of place on a table or pedestal. Having said that, the unique growing habits of bromeliads make it possible to combine a number of different species in a single setting, namely a bromeliad tree (see below).

PROPAGATION

Aechmea and billbergia, in particular, produce several offsets from each plant, and you can have four or five new plants from one parent. When bromeliads have flowered, the central rosette begins to die, but the offsets which have been produced around it will continue to grow. Treat them like the parent plant until they are at least 15cm/6in high and are ready to be detached. The best time to do this is in summer. Knock the whole plant from its pot and ease away the growing mixture. Pull away each offset, complete with its roots, taking care not to damage them. Pot up singly in 7.5cm/3in pots of moist compost. Sit the base of the plant on the surface, covering the roots. Do not bury the crown. Top up the vase with water, if there is one, and keep shaded until well-established. Young plants should have a resting period from late autumn to early spring. Although the leaves of the parent will remain handsome for several months, it will not flower again and should be discarded.

MAKING A BROMELIAD TREE

An artificial home for bromeliads can be formed from a seasoned branch cut from a hardwood tree, such as apple, although this will tend to rot in time. A very effective substitute can be made from pieces of cork bark fixed to a suitable support. This looks good and is long-lasting. Secure the trunk end of the 'tree' in a small tub or some other container, such as a stone trough, with a wide base and firm bottom. The size of the branch very much depends on the area in which the bromeliad tree will be positioned, but in proportion to the size of the plants a branch 1.2–1.8m/4–6ft is best.

One of the best ways of securing the branch is to place the end in the container, and to pour cement around it. Shingle or small stones can then be placed over the concrete.

Set the individual plants in the crevices of the branch; these can be found by pouring water down the branch and seeing where it naturally collects. Remove the plants from their pots and wrap the root-balls in sphagnum moss. Mould the moss around the roots so that it is firmly fixed to them. Put the plants in place and use green plastic-coated wire to hold each soil-ball together and also to attach it securely to the branch. Water the soil balls thoroughly and spray them regularly to prevent them drying out. Eventually the roots will bind themselves to the tree and the wires can be removed.

AECHMEA

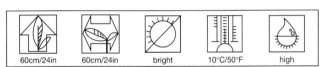

60cm/24in	60cm/24in	bright	10°C/50°F	high

Aechmeas produce long-lasting blooms that vary in appearance from species to species. All invariably have beautifully marked, curving strap-shaped leaves in rosette formation.

GENERAL CARE By nature epiphytic, in the home aechmeas may be grown in 15cm/6in pots of any of the recommended mixtures (see page 343). Keep the central vase filled with rain-water or cooled boiled water during the summer, replacing it with fresh water every 8-12 weeks. Keep the compost just moist throughout the year. Feed with liquid fertilizer every 4 weeks in summer, either by adding it to the vase or with a foliar spray. Maintain high levels of humidity by misting around the plant. Keep in full sun at a temperature in the range 16-18°C/61-64°F. A brief drop in temperature will do no lasting harm, especially if the compost is barely moist. If repotting is necessary, do so when new growth begins and use clay pots for stability.

PROPAGATION Detach rosettes when they are one-third to half the size of the parent plant and place in 5cm/2in pots of the standard compost. Keep in good light and just moist until well established.

SPECIES *Aechmea fasciata* (urn plant, *above*), green leaves banded silver, flowers blue in bud opening to rose pink, summer; *A. fulgens*, 38cm/15in high, broad green leaves, waxy blue flowers followed by scarlet berries.

POSSIBLE PROBLEMS Generally trouble-free.

▨ GENERAL TIP

The brush-like pink bract of this plant is colourful for many weeks. When no longer attractive it should be cut away, by which time one or more young growths will be evident at the base of the stem. Avoid damaging these as *they can be cut away when large enough and potted individually in an open, free-draining medium to flower in, perhaps, two to three years.*

ANANAS

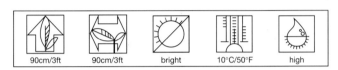

90cm/3ft	90cm/3ft	bright	10°C/50°F	high

The ananas family includes the edible pineapple as well as several highly decorative species suitable as house plants. They are slow-growing terrestrial bromeliads with arching spiny leaves in rosette formation. Mature plants produce 7.5cm/3in long blue flowers which are followed by distinctive pineapple-shaped fruits.

GENERAL CARE Grow in a mixture of 2 parts loam, 1 part leaf-mould or peat and 1 part sand. Ananas do not need a resting period, and should be sited in full sunlight all year. Temperatures in the range 16-18°C/61-64°F are ideal, though lower temperatures can be tolerated in winter. Give a feed of liquid fertilizer every 2 weeks throughout the year. Keep the compost constantly moist with rainwater or cooled boiled water and spray the foliage regularly with a fine mist. Repot young plants annually in spring until they reach 20cm/8in pots. Use clay pots for stability.

PROPAGATION Remove offsets with a sharp knife when about 15cm/6in long and pot up in a moistened peat and sand mixture.

SPECIES *Ananas comosus* (pineapple), edible fruits not produced in the home. *A. c.* 'Variegata' (*above*) has leaves edged yellow, tinged rose pink in good light; *A. nanus*, only 45cm/18in high with very graceful leaves, produces a fragrant green (inedible) fruit and numerous offsets.

POSSIBLE PROBLEMS Generally trouble-free.

▨ GENERAL TIP

Spectacular plants at any time when mature, but much enhanced in appearance as the pineapple fruit begins to develop and the plant colouring becomes suffused with reddish pink hues.

BILLBERGIA

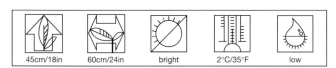

| 45cm/18in | 60cm/24in | bright | 2°C/35°F | low |

Billbergia nutans (*above*), popularly known as angel's tears or queen's tears, is one of the prettiest bromeliads and one of the easiest to grow. Its long, strap-like leaves arch over in an attractively random fashion, and the pendent flowers – which usually appear in late spring – are tinged blue, yellow, pink and green, encased in pink sheaths.

GENERAL CARE Grow this terrestrial plant in small clay pots (12.5cm/5in) containing any of the recommended mixtures (see page 343). As there is no need for a rest period, water the compost moderately all year using rainwater or cooled boiled water and give a liquid feed every 2 weeks, either into the pot or as a foliar spray. Normal room temperatures are suitable, but very low temperatures are well-tolerated for short periods. Stand the plants in good light, out of direct sunlight. Repot young specimens in spring.

PROPAGATION Detach offsets when they are half the size of the parent plant. Let the cut surface dry for 24 hours before potting up in one of the recommended mixtures.

HYBRIDS *B.* × 'Windii', a hybrid of *B. nutans* with stiff, grey-green leaves, blue-green flower petals reflexed to reveal long creamy stamens.

POSSIBLE PROBLEMS Generally trouble-free.

CRYPTANTHUS

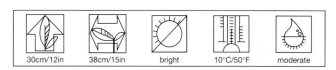

| 30cm/12in | 38cm/15in | bright | 10°C/50°F | moderate |

The many forms of cryptanthus or earth star have a tendency to hybridize easily, giving rise to an amazing variety of multi-coloured specimens. It is their unusual foliage for which they are prized, as the flowers are usually hidden by the abundant leaves, which grow in rosette form.

GENERAL CARE Cryptanthus are terrestrial bromeliads. Grow in small pots or half-pots of peat-based compost kept constantly moist during the growing season. When resting give just enough water to prevent the compost drying out completely. Very little feeding is required, perhaps 2 applications of a liquid fertilizer in summer. Bright light is important to maintain leaf colour. Normal room temperatures are suitable: above 18°C/64°F ensure humidity by placing the pots on trays of moist pebbles. Repot only when the pot is crowded with offsets.

PROPAGATION Detach offsets in spring and pot up in small pots of peat and sand.

SPECIES *Cryptanthus bromelioides tricolor* (rainbow star, *above*), wavy mid-green leaves striped white, tinged pink in good light, produces plantlets at the end of stolons rather than offsets; *C. zonatus*, spreading habit, wavy leaves striped olive and silvery green.

POSSIBLE PROBLEMS Generally trouble-free.

◾ DESIGN TIP

A much underrated easy-care plant that is seen to best effect when growing in a hanging container that will show off the pendulous bracts to full advantage. Whereas the majority of plants in elevated positions might suffer as a result of arid conditions the billbergias are much more tolerant. Small hanging pots can be plunged to give them a good soak.

◾ DESIGN TIP

The Earth Stars are composed, in the main, of tight clusters of rosettes that make these plants the perfect residents for bottle gardens and terrariums where compact growth is essential.

NEOREGELIA

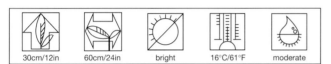

30cm/12in	60cm/24in	bright	16°C/61°F	moderate

The foliage is very beautiful, long, strap-like leaves arching outwards in a perfect rosette with a vase at the centre. Gorgeous reds and pinks tint the leaves for some months during the flowering period, though the flowers are insignificant.

GENERAL CARE By nature epiphytic, neoregelias have no clearly defined rest period. Grow in clay pots no larger than 12.5cm/5in containing a mixture of equal parts of sand, leafmould and loam, kept nicely moist all year. Use rainwater or cooled boiled water and keep the vase filled with water too, draining and replacing it every 4 weeks. Give a liquid feed at half-strength every 2 weeks to the compost, the vase and as a foliar spray. Stand in bright light, with some direct sunlight every day. Mist over with a fine spray to maintain humidity. Repot small plants in spring if necessary.

PROPAGATION Stolons are produced at the base of the plants. When they have formed roots of their own, carefully detach them from the parent, preferably in spring, and pot up in small pots of the recommended mixture.

SPECIES *Neoregelia carolinae*, bright green, long pointed leaves flushed red or purple at flowering time. 'Tricolor' (*above*) is a variety with leaves striped white. The whole plant turns rose red at flowering time; *N. spectabilis* (fingernail plant), leathery dark green leaves tipped bright red.

POSSIBLE PROBLEMS Generally trouble-free.

▦ CARE TIP

As with most bromeliads this is one of the toughest plants for growing indoors, so it is well suited for more difficult locations that offer reasonable warmth and light. Plants will be much better if the central urn is kept filled with water and only minimal watering is the aim in respect of the compost in the pot. The potting mix should be very open.

NIDULARIUM

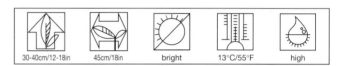

30-40cm/12-18in	45cm/18in	bright	13°C/55°F	high

Nidulariums resemble neoregelias in that they produce a rosette of glossy green leaves which acquire a pink tinge at the centre during the flowering period. The leaves are rather broader, however, and have spiny edges. Flowering only occurs in mature plants, after which they slowly decline, to be replaced by offsets produced in the leaf axils.

GENERAL CARE By nature epiphytic, nidulariums should be grown in clay pots no larger than 10cm/4in containing one of the recommended mixtures (see page 343). As there is no defined rest period, water moderately all year using rainwater or cooled boiled water. Feed with liquid fertilizer at half-strength every 2 weeks. Keep the vase filled with water, draining and replacing it every 6 weeks. Stand the pots in bright, filtered light at normal room temperatures. To keep the level of humidity high, stand the pots in saucers of moist pebbles. Repot in spring if necessary.

PROPAGATION Offsets are produced at the base of the plant, very close to the parent. When they have acquired the characteristic rosette shape, remove them carefully, leave to dry for 1-2 days and pot up in the standard mixture.

SPECIES *Nidularium fulgens* (*above*), shiny, arching, fresh green leaves spotted darker green, bright red central inflorescence; *N. innocentii*, green leaves tinged reddish-brown, white flowers surrounded by orange bracts.

POSSIBLE PROBLEMS Generally trouble-free.

▦ GENERAL TIP

Another of the cart-wheel type bromeliads with leaves radiating from a short central trunk. When significant flowers appear, the main rosette will begin to deteriorate before dying.

TILLANDSIA

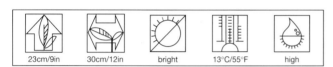

23cm/9in	30cm/12in	bright	13°C/55°F	high

Tillandsias are epiphytic bromeliads with a negligible root system. They can be grown on a bromeliad tree (see page 343) where they will absorb most of their food supply through their leaves, or they can be set in small pots. The grassy, arching leaves are attractive, but it is chiefly for their extraordinary inflorescence that tillandsias are grown. These blooms may appear at any time from late spring until late autumn. They consist of tightly overlapping pinkish bracts arranged in a flat, pointed oval, from which 1 or 2 small, bright purple flowers emerge.

GENERAL CARE Pot up in one of the recommended mixtures (see page 343). Keep the compost just moist but spray the leaves every other day. Set the pots in saucers of moist pebbles. Every 4 weeks, apply a little liquid fertilizer at half-strength. Tillandsias need bright, filtered light, and temperatures about 16°C/61°F. Repotting should not be necessary.

PROPAGATION Detach the small offsets and pot up in 7.5cm/3in pots in a peat/sand mixture.

SPECIES *Tillandsia cyanea* (*above*), narrow rosette of smooth green leaves striped brown, pink-purple inflorescence on short stem; *T. lindeniana*, 50cm/20in high, dark green leaves, purple beneath, 15cm/6in flower spike of pink bracts with blue flowers.

POSSIBLE PROBLEMS Generally trouble-free.

▇ GENERAL TIP

These have achieved tremendous popularity in recent years under their common name of Air Plants, which alludes to the fact that many of them virtually survive on what is blowing about or contained in the atmosphere.

You see them in all sorts of stores, often attached to anchorages with an adhesive. But it is better to buy plants with their roots growing in pots.

VRIESIA

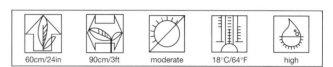

60cm/24in	90cm/3ft	moderate	18°C/64°F	high

Vriesias of various species are found all over Central and South America. They are impressive plants which require a stable environment to give of their best. All types produce handsome leaves in a perfect rosette with a central vase for retaining water. Mature plants produce erect, dramatic flower spikes.

GENERAL CARE Grow in 12.5cm/5in pots containing a mixture of sand and leaf-mould, loosely packed around the roots. In spring and summer water by filling the vase with rainwater or cooled boiled water, allowing it to spill over and moisten the compost. Every 4 weeks, feed with liquid fertilizer at half-strength. In winter, give enough water to keep the compost just moist. Normal temperatures are suitable, but bright filtered light is essential. To maintain high levels of humidity, place the pots in saucers of moist pebbles. Repot only if the roots fill the pots.

PROPAGATION Detach offsets bearing roots from the base of the plants when they are half the size of the parent. Allow to dry for 1-2 days then pot up in the recommended mixture.

SPECIES *Vriesia hieroglyphica* (king of bromeliads, *above*), wide, acid-green leaves irregularly banded purplish-brown, yellow flower in spring on erect, 75cm/2½ft stem; *V. splendens* (flaming sword), leaves banded green and brown, 60cm/24in flower stem bears a 30cm/12in scarlet inflorescence from which yellow flowers appear in late summer.

POSSIBLE PROBLEMS Generally trouble-free.

▇ GENERAL TIP

The larger species, such as V. fenestralis, are very difficult to acquire and would be much too large for the average room. Upright rosettes have spectacular flowers that last well.

ORCHIDS

Interest in these fascinating plants is clearly on the increase as more and more people find cut flowers in a local department store, or maybe even on a petrol station forecourt. Orchids in these places will almost certainly have been flown in from the Far East, where orchid farms cover vast acreages to provide cut flowers for virtually the entire world.

Some of the better garden centres stock a range of pot plants throughout the year, and this could well be the best initial source of supply. You may be able to purchase priced-down plants that have finished flowering but will be fine for the future if they are still in good condition. You can also order plants from such a garden centre, but as your interest increases you will want to acquire a list of orchid plant suppliers so that you can contact the grower direct.

LOCATION

The majority of orchids are epiphytic, meaning that they use other plants as hosts – often trees growing to considerable height. They do not take any nourishment from the tree, relying on what is available in the atmosphere for food and water. Consequently, you should provide a light and airy location. Indoors, this will mean having plants near a window as opposed to in a dark corner that is devoid of light, with little in the way of air circulation. If there is insufficient natural light in the room, you can grow many orchids very successfully under strip lights. Ordinary warm white fluorescent tubes will do, provided they are suspended at a reasonable distance from the plant material.

You may want to provide a plant window – a bit like a bay window, but with the extension going further out from the house to provide a comfortable area for plants. A sliding glass window can isolate this area from the rest of the room so that the plant window can be individually provided with heating, lighting and whatever else might be thought necessary.

CONDITIONS

Humidity is a key factor in the cultivation of most orchids and humid conditions can only be achieved by a combination of warmth and moisture. As far as temperature goes there are three distinct groups of orchids; cool growers (minimum temperature 10°C/50°F), intermediate growers (minimum temperature 13°C/55°F) and those needing a higher temperature of 18°C/65°F. When you buy plants you should make it clear to the supplier the sort of temperature you can maintain so that warm-loving plants are not acquired for conditions that are inadequate. It is also necessary to offer plants fresh air on warmer days of the year.

WATERING AND FEEDING

Plants should be kept moist at all times while they are actively growing, with a little less water needed while they are inactive. In the greenhouse it is necessary to perform the operation of damping down regularly in order to maintain humidity levels – much more important in summer than winter. Indoors, plants should be provided with trays containing a moisture-retaining material, such as gravel or Leca granules. In hot weather plants will benefit from misting of the foliage. Electrically-operated humidifiers are available.

Orchid fertilizers are available and these should be used as directed – plants normally require feeding during the spring and summer months.

POTTING AND POTTING MIXTURES

Because orchids are epiphytic, it is essential that any potting medium is as open and free-draining as possible. This means that almost all of the standard potting mixtures are unsuitable. Until you have had plenty of experience of growing orchids it is best to select an orchid potting mixture that has been specially prepared for these plants.

In general terms, the best time to pot orchids on into larger containers is the spring, with the summer months being the least suitable. Avoid the temptation to pot plants on for the sake of it – small plants in very large pots rarely do well, be they orchids or any other plant.

CONTAINERS

There is a wide range of containers you can use – not least the humble polypropylene pot that is available in many shapes and colours (although the majority of plants do better when grown in black pots). You can buy a special orchid pot made of polypropylene with open sides to provide maximum aeration. You may be fortunate enough to acquire clay orchid pots, even clay pots with pretty patterned holes in their sides, but you may have to visit a Far East orchid farm to obtain supplies! Many orchids will also grow happily on slatted wooden rafts or in square hanging containers that are made from slatted laths. Where there is high humidity and regular attention plants can be grown epiphytically by attaching them to sections of cork bark, or simply to well-soaked sections of timber. The inventive indoor gardener can devise all sorts of ways of displaying and growing his or her plants to full advantage.

PESTS AND DISEASES

Orchids have their problems in full measure with red spider mites, aphids, mealy bugs, scale insects, fungal diseases, viruses and, for full measure, petal blight.

A wonderful showy display of white orchid blossom enhances the neutral colour scheme of this interior.

ANGRAECUM

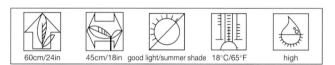

60cm/24in	45cm/18in	good light/summer shade	18°C/65°F	high

Angraecum are indigenous to tropical Africa. The flowers are greenish white in colour, some fragrant, with a distinctive spur that may be all of 30cm/12in long. Plants are seen at their best when growing on a raft or in lath basket that offers maximum aeration to the roots.

GENERAL CARE Angraecum are reasonably easy to care for if the minimum temperature can be maintained. Offer good light but shade from very strong sun and ensure a moist atmosphere at all times. Keep moist throughout the year and feed regularly while the plant is in active growth. Mist leaves frequently.

PROPAGATION Scandent species by severing stem below the aerial roots and allowing growth to show before removing and potting up.

SPECIES There are several species but only *Angraecum sesquipedale* (*above*) is likely to be available; it has creamy white fragrant flowers.

POSSIBLE PROBLEMS Generally trouble-free.

CATTLEYA

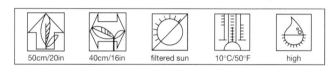

50cm/20in	40cm/16in	filtered sun	10°C/50°F	high

Cattleya (green orchid) are from tropical South America and are among the most desirable of orchid plants..

GENERAL CARE Watering can be a critical factor, and the best advice is never to be too generous. If the general area can be kept moist the plant will absorb moisture from the atmosphere, so needing less direct watering into its container. Feed with a weak fertilizer solution every 2 weeks, alternating with a foliar feed at every third feeding application. Offer good light but protect from sun. Potting on of established plants should be done in the spring. Put drainage material in the pot and use porous potting mixture.

PROPAGATION Divide mature clumps; the section for propagating should have at least four pseudobulbs to be successful.

SPECIES There are many species and varieties available. 'Pink Debutante' (*above*), *C. skinnerii*, *C. bowringiana* will give a good start, offering large exotic flowers..

POSSIBLE PROBLEMS Slugs on young shoots; thrips on opening flowers; scale insects and mealy bug.

■ CARE TIP

Indoors, only the miniature forms are suitable and these should be grown in an enclosed plant case. To economize in the greenhouse it is wise to section off a small area that can be kept warmer for the more demanding *plants. Given moisture and temperature the angraecums are not difficult to grow.*

■ CARE TIP

With pests, prevention is better than cure and immediate remedial action should be taken when pests are suspected as it is much easier to eradicate a few than an infestation.

COELOGYNE

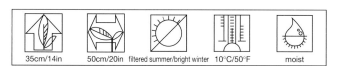

35cm/14in	50cm/20in	filtered summer/bright winter	10°C/50°F	moist

Coelogyne are indigenous to South-east Asia. They may produce upright or hanging flower spikes, and fragrance may be an added bonus. The smaller species may be grown successfully indoors but some species can become very large in time, needing ample growing space. Small plants should be grown in pans, larger plants in pots of suitable size and pendulous plants are best in hanging containers.

GENERAL CARE Plants require a dry winter rest with watering starting again when fresh growth is evident early in the year. Some species require higher growing temperature than that indicated above, so ascertain plant needs when purchasing.

PROPAGATION Divide plants when repotting in the spring.

SPECIES Coelogyne ochracea, C. cristata, 'Chadwort' (above), C. corymbosa; all reasonably easy to care for.

POSSIBLE PROBLEMS Slugs, aphids, mealy bug.

CYMBIDIUM

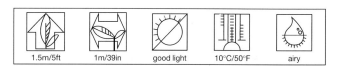

1.5m/5ft	1m/39in	good light	10°C/50°F	airy

Indigenous to South-east Asia, these are among the most spectacular of orchids. They are reasonably easy to manage indoors, bold groups being especially suited to a roomy conservatory. During the summer they can have a sheltered location out of doors.

GENERAL CARE Airy and cool conditions are essential during the summer months if plants are to bloom over the ensuing winter. Plants subjected to low temperature during the winter months will be very shy of flowering, so it is important to get the balance right. Cymbidium are evergreen and need no rest period.

PROPAGATION From seed (a specialized task) or by dividing mature plants.

SPECIES There is a very extensive range with highly coloured flowers.

POSSIBLE PROBLEMS Red spider mites, scale insect, mealy bug and others. Hygiene and regular inspection are essential.

■ PLANTING TIP

The coelogynes are epiphytic in their habit, meaning that they generally grow naturally in elevated locations, such as trees. The more pendulous types may be attached to trees in the greenhouse, but where space is limited a slatted hanging container will be more manageable. These should be lined with sphagnum moss before introducing potting mixture and the plant.

■ PROPAGATION TIP

Cymbidium are ideal beginners' plants as they flower freely and are reasonably easy to manage. They are also easily propagated. Healthy plants will quickly fill their containers with pseudobulbs; following flowering a sharp knife can be used to divide the bulbs for propagating. Select two bulbs, one with a shoot, and cut cleanly then pot into orchid potting mixture.

DENDROBIUM

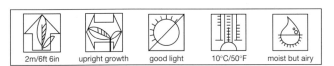

| 2m/6ft 6in | upright growth | good light | 10°C/50°F | moist but airy |

Dendrobium is one of the largest groups in the orchid family, some of the varieties being deciduous, some semi-evergreen and some evergreen. They are grown in South-east Asia, where humidity and conditions in general are ideal, for export in their thousands to destinations in the west.

GENERAL CARE Provide dry and light winter conditions, but ensure that the soil is not excessively dry as this will cause the canes to shrivel. When flower buds appear in spring give a thorough watering and keep moist throughout the summer. When repotting is necessary do it when new growth is evident, using orchid potting mixture. Never overpot these plants.

PROPAGATION Plants may form plantlets with roots on the main stem; remove and pot up.

VARIETIES *Dendrobium nobile* (*above*) and a vast selection of species and varieties available.

POSSIBLE PROBLEMS Red spider mites – treat and repeat is the best advice. Use a recognized insecticide to control.

ENCYCLIA

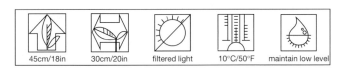

| 45cm/18in | 30cm/20in | filtered light | 10°C/50°F | maintain low level |

These plants from tropical South America prefer cool conditions in which to grow, which makes them reasonably suitable as indoor plants as well as good subjects for a cooler greenhouse than the norm. Different varieties will flower at different times of the year, with *Encyclia cochleata* seeming to flower the year round when established. Fragrance is an added bonus.

GENERAL CARE These are plants that prefer to grow on the dry side regardless of the season and for this reason they do well when attached to sections of bark or board rather than being grown more conventionally in pots.

PROPAGATION Propagation can be done quite simply by dividing bulbs and potting them singly.

SPECIES *E. cochleata, E. citrina, E. mariae, E. nemorale* (*above*) *E. radiata*; all compact and reasonably easy to grow.

POSSIBLE PROBLEMS Check regularly for the presence of slugs, aphids and mealy bug. The use of a systemic insecticide can be very helpful in controlling aphids and mealy bugs.

◼ CUT FLOWER TIP

A great benefit of the dendrobiums is their prolific flowering and their long-lasting qualities as cut flowers. If flowers have been removed from the plant for some time they should be immersed completely in water and left there to soak to extend their life when placed in the flower vase.

◼ PLANTING TIP

Sections of cork bark can be purchased for attaching orchid plants to. Soak the bark, knock in a few nails at the back for ties and wrap plant roots in moss before fixing. Water by immersing.

MILTONIA

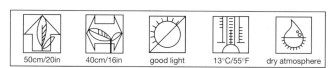

| 50cm/20in | 40cm/16in | good light | 13°C/55°F | dry atmosphere |

The miltonias (pansy orchids) produce flowers in numerous colours for many months of the year if one is fortunate enough to have a collection of plants. There are two distinct types – those originating in Brazil and those from Colombia. Many of the plants have pleasing fragrance and have the added bonus of flowering more often than the usual once in each year.

GENERAL CARE Miltonias need to be grown in warm conditions but not at excessive temperature. A winter rest is not needed so watering can continue throughout the year. Repot when the plants are showing signs of fresh growth. Use an open orchid mixture, but never repot unless it is necessary.

PROPAGATION By division of established clumps, or by removal of backbulbs.

SPECIES *Miltonia endressii*, 'Peach Blossom', *M. spectabilis*, offering an excellent colour range of attractive flowers.

POSSIBLE PROBLEMS Red spider mite.

OODONTOGLOSSUM

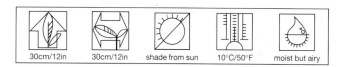

| 30cm/12in | 30cm/12in | shade from sun | 10°C/50°F | moist but airy |

Many Oodontoglossum (clown orchids) make excellent indoor plants that are not too difficult to care for, but check with the supplier that plants are suited to home conditions.

GENERAL CARE Moist atmosphere is important but it is also necessary to provide good air circulation, which may well mean having heaters in operation and ventilators open at the same time. Low-level vents are often better than those at higher level when plants are being grown in a greenhouse. Winter rest period should be checked with the supplier as winter care conditions vary with different plants.

SPECIES Numerous; *Oodontoglossum bictoniense* and *O. grande* (the attractive tiger orchid, *above*) are reasonably durable and easy to flower.

PROPAGATION By removal and potting of backbulbs from mature clumps. Large clumps provide the best flowers.

POSSIBLE PROBLEMS Aphids, mealy bug and red spider mite – control with malathion insecticide.

■ CARE TIP

Being plants that are in growth throughout the year these are orchids that will need constant attention to ensure that they remain in good health. As with most established orchids they will require regular feeding once established in their pots. For simple, easy-to-use stimulant use a tomato fertilizer which is high in potash and will encourage production of flowers.

■ PLANTING TIP

These are epiphytic plants so must have an open, free-draining potting mixture. Plants may be potted on at almost any time, but spring is favourable when new shoots are developing.

PAPHIOPEDILUM

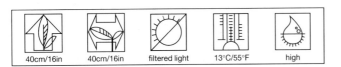

40cm/16in | 40cm/16in | filtered light | 13°C/55°F | high

Originating in South-east Asia and among the most popular of all orchids for indoor cultivation, the paphiopedilums (slipper orchids) are neat in habit, bearing erect flower stems with slipper flowers in many colours.

GENERAL CARE In a dry indoor atmosphere it is necessary to mist plants with water in warmer conditions. The controlled conditions of a plant-growing case are generally ideal for these easy-care plants. They should not be subjected to the bright light that may prevail on a sunny windowsill. Good air circulation is important in stuffy conditions – a fan may be necessary.

PROPAGATION By separating established clumps and potting severed smaller clumps individually in small pots.

VARIETIES There are many to choose from – when purchasing stipulate the easier kinds if you are a beginner.

POSSIBLE PROBLEMS Slugs and snails. Water in the centre of leaves can cause rotting.

PHALAENOPSIS

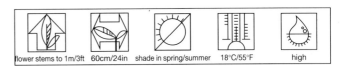

flower stems to 1m/3ft | 60cm/24in | shade in spring/summer | 18°C/55°F | high

Among the most rewarding of plants, all Phalaenopsis (moth orchids) need adequate temperature to succeed. Their individual arching stems produce a large number of spectacular long-lasting flowers, much used for floral displays. They originate from South-east Asia.

GENERAL CARE Shade from strong sunlight is essential during spring and summer, and at other times if very sunny. Offer high humidity and air circulation – electrically-powered fans are ideal for this purpose. Plants are evergreen and do not require winter rest so water, though reduced, must not be discontinued. Plants have no storage pseudobulbs so need regular feeding at intervals of 2-3 weeks.

PROPAGATION Difficult for the amateur grower – it is better to buy small plants for growing on.

SPECIES There are many species, among them *Phalaenopsis schilleriana, P. lueddemanniana, P. aphrodite*, with flowers said to resemble tropical moths flying in the night.

POSSIBLE PROBLEMS Check regularly for slugs and snails. Avoid getting water amongst the leaves.

■ PLANTING TIP

Quite small plants are occasionally available and these should be carefully potted into small pots using a fine grade of bark. Potting on of small plants should be more frequent than for older plants. For older plants *choose a coarser grade of bark mixture – preferably a mixture specially prepared for orchids. The best time for potting older plants is while in active growth.*

■ PLANTING TIP

Many of the phalaenopsis are propagated in culture flasks in laboratory conditions; pot these in very fine bark mixture. All potting should be done while growth is active.

PLEIONE FORMOSANA

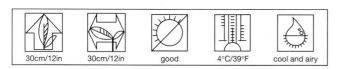

30cm/12in	30cm/12in	good	4°C/39°F	cool and airy

The alpine orchid, seen more frequently in a rock garden display rather than in an orchid house. These are attractive plants when well grown, producing healthy clumps of attractively coloured flowers on short stems. They are indigenous to the Far East, with some of the best forms growing close to the Himalayan snow line. Perhaps a good plant for the orchid beginner to take an interest in.

GENERAL CARE These may be grown in a greenhouse designed for alpine plants, or in the cool section of an orchid house should one be available. It is not impossible to grow pleiones in pots on an outside windowsill.

PROPAGATION From small pseudobulbs removed from the parent.

VARIETIES The species is most frequently offered for sale, but there are varieties including 'Oriental splendour' (*above*).

POSSIBLE PROBLEMS Slugs and snails.

VANDA

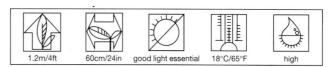

1.2m/4ft	60cm/24in	good light essential	18°C/65°F	high

Natives of South-east Asia and the Far East, vandas flower profusely over the winter months; they are capable of producing several flushes of flowers over one winter season. Flower colouring is very varied, with blue forms being especially choice.

GENERAL CARE Grow close to the window – if in a greenhouse suspend in a lath basket close to the glass and allow the roots to hang free. Water and allow to dry before repeating, but avoid long periods of drought. Feed fortnightly with balanced fertilizer. Provide a moisture-laden atmosphere, fresh air and bright light.

PROPAGATION From offsets removed from the parent plant when a few centimetres in length. Keep in moist, enclosed conditions until rooted.

SPECIES *Vanda coerulea*, *V. sanderana* and *V. rothschildiana*. Varieties include 'Rose Davis'.

POSSIBLE PROBLEMS Generally trouble-free.

▪ PLANTING TIP

To get the best from these plants they should be potted into fresh potting mixture in shallow pans each year prior to flowering. Plants are deciduous, the single pseudobulb lasting only one year. The bulb will produce 2 offsets and these can be removed for potting into fresh mixture, planted several to a pan of 12.5cm/5 in in diameter.

▪ CARE TIP

Vandas are plants that will often be seen growing in lath hanging baskets that seem absurdly small compared to the size of the plant; nevertheless, they will thrive like this if humidity, watering and feeding are attended to.

BONSAI

In the Far East the method of growing plants known as bonsai has been something of an art form for countless centuries, but 'indoor bonsai' seems to have crept into being with the advent of house plants. However, the many plants labelled 'temperate' or 'sub tropic' that are used for this purpose in the western world are run-of-the-mill materials in the tropics, suggesting that 'indoor bonsai' is not substantially different from the ancient art form. 'Indoor bonsai' has certainly raised the possibility of growing a very different range of plants within the home.

PURCHASING

The growing of indoor bonsai is one thing, but the first thought must be the acquisition of plant material that you can employ for bonsai purposes. Should you own some woodland, you can go out and dig up a few seedlings for the purpose of getting started with bonsai. Alernatively, there are specialist nurseries where more established plants may be acquired. However, for the average person seeking to experiment in a modest way with indoor bonsai the best source of material might well be your garden centre where, in the house plant department, you will find a wide range of plants that can be adopted for indoor bonsai culture.

LOCATION

Whether you intend to grow them as indoor bonsai or as conventional house plants, the location within the home for the assortment of plants you have chosen will

A bonsai grown juniper shows the pleasing tree shape characteristic of this art.

be relatively the same. House plants will generally have attached to them a care card with information concerning light, shade, temperature and such like, and a plant of, say, *Ficus benjamina* will require the same sort of location regardless of what your intentions in respect of culture may be. For the vast majority of plants for the home, the most important requirement is good light with some protection from strong sunlight. Generally speaking, plants with variegated or very colourful foliage require lighter locations than those with entirely green foliage.

CONDITIONS

Offering specific advice on this aspect of indoor bonsai culture is something of a problem as the chosen plants will be so varied in their temperature requirements. Temperate plants might well grow happily in the garden (to die in a severe winter!) or they may be of more delicate nature and need some cosseting to prosper. When buying you should get reliable advice concerning the needs of each particular purchase. Many of the less tender plants will normally do better if they can enjoy a sheltered and shaded spot out of doors for the summer months.

WATERING

Conventional plants in pots frequently become much too wet on account of the large volume of soil that is around their roots, and very wet conditions is one sure way of killing off container plants, regardless of the type of container. With indoor bonsai the containers are extremely shallow in many instances, with the result that there is very much less soil around the roots of the plant. A further advantage here is that the roots are very much better aerated, so providing ample oxygen for their well-being and, in turn, the well-being of the plant. But, with very little soil to retain moisture, it is important that indoor bonsai plants are checked very frequently for moisture requirements.

FEEDING

The need to keep indoor bonsai compact with frequent top and root pruning does not mean that nourishing

the plant should be neglected – failing to feed the plant during its active season of growth will simply result in the yellowing and eventual loss of leaves. As time goes by you will become more knowledgeable about your plants' feeding requirements by means of experiment. Initially, however, it is advisable to use a balanced fertilizer that has been prepared for potted plants. The fertilizer can be a foliar feed, and there is the choice of high potash or high nitrogen preparations. The beginner might well decide that a tomato fertilizer is the most convenient and the most satisfactory. Only feed plants that are in active growth, so little or no feed is needed in winter.

POTTING AND POTTING MIXTURES

For the first steps in potting indoor bonsai plants it is advisable to avoid attempts at preparing soil concoctions that might be some way off the mark in terms of suitability. The best advice is to buy a ready-made bonsai potting mixture, which will have all the ingredients that the plant is likely to need. The time for potting the majority of plants will be January, but this can vary a little either way. Potting on is not the correct term for this exercise, as the majority of plants will be removed from their pots/containers to be replanted in the same container following any root pruning that may be found necessary.

TOOLS

The growing popularirity of indoor bonsai means that there is a wide range of tools and general aids on sale that simplify the many tasks that will require attention. A good garden centre or a specialist supplier will be able to provide all that is needed.

PESTS AND DISEASES

Indoor bonsai will be affected by the same pests as any other indoor plants – vigilance is the answer, prevention being better than cure!

BOUGAINVILLEA

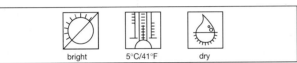

bright   5°C/41°F   dry

Bougainvillea (paper flower) is a true tropical exotic that will shed most, or all, of its leaves in winter. In nature plants will develop very strong trunks with age, and for bonsai purposes the aim should be to have a central stem of some substance. This may well be possible in the early stages by selecting a stout branch for propagating. Growth from such a branch can then be trained to shape by selecting only a few of the most promising growths. With normal cultivation plants will produce their bract flowers from early March.

GENERAL CARE Provide a cool, light and airy location and never overwater, particularly in winter.

PROPAGATION Taken in February and given bottom heat of around 25°C/76°F, a leafless stem section of some 15cm/6 in in length can be rooted without too much difficulty.

VARIETIES There are many to choose from in colours from white through orange to the deepest red.

POSSIBLE PROBLEMS Scale insects, aphids among others; excessive wet causes root failure.

BUXUS

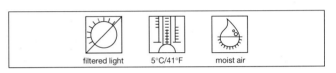

filtered light   5°C/41°F   moist air

The common box, *Buxus sempervirens*, could well be used for experimental purposes during the initial steps with indoor bonsai. However, there are more tender Asiatic species, such as *B. harlandii*, that will be a touch more exotic – the temperature above refers to this type of plant, which is not winter-hardy.

GENERAL CARE Plants should be watered by immersing the pot until all the air-bubbles have escaped – the exercise to be repeated only when the soil has dried out. Feed established plants at fortnightly intervals while in active growth. Offer a lightly shaded location in cool conditions.

PROPAGATION By top cuttings in late summer, by layering or by dividing older plants. Cuttings are slow to mature.

VARIETIES As mentioned above, but also any other varieties of interest that may be obtainable.

POSSIBLE PROBLEMS Red spider mites cause leaf discoloration and general debility; aphids on young growth.

▧ CARE TIP

In much of its native habitat bougainvillea is obliged to tolerate spartan conditions, which makes it a suitable subject for bonsai purposes. Bright conditions are important.

▧ CARE TIP

When establishing young plants it is important not to allow the development of too much clumpy growth as this leads to a very unattractive plant. It is much better to thin out the weaker shoots and to aim at providing *an attractive shape by selecting suitable stronger branches and training them into shape by using bonsai training wire. As with all bonsai, the establishment of a specimen tree is a long and slow process.*

CAMELLIA

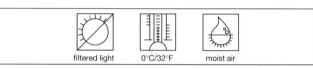

filtered light · 0°C/32°F · moist air

Native to the countries of the Far East, these are glossy-leaved, spring-flowering plants that must have frost protection for the blooms. For bonsai purposes a single stem that is trained to lean or is given a twist by careful wiring gives the plant a little more interest.

GENERAL CARE Ericaceous potting mixture, soft water and feeding with an ericaceous fertilizer are important needs of these decorative plants. Repotting is only needed every 2-3 years, and one should not be too severe when it comes to root pruning.

PROPAGATION From top cuttings taken in October and placed in fresh, moist peat with bottom heat in a greenhouse, or by layering.

VARIETIES Countless varieties, with the long-established C. 'Donation' still being one of the front runners.

POSSIBLE PROBLEMS Chlorotic conditions from using the wrong type of soil.

CITRUS

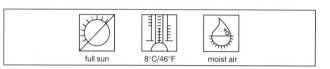

full sun · 8°C/46°F · moist air

The general name of citrus covers a number of exotic fruits,, many of which are too large to contemplate as bonsai for the average household. Choose one of the less robust varieties such as *Citrus mitis*, the calomondin orange, which can be had as a pleasing variegated form. The bonus here is that it also produces lots of small, edible oranges when growing well.

GENERAL CARE Root pruning at potting time must be done with care as these are not particularly strong-rooting plants. With judicious pruning of surplus shoots *C. mitis* will adopt a reasonably natural bonsai shape of its own accord.

PROPAGATION From firm top cuttings taken in the spring and rooted in bottom heat in a greenhouse. Results of seed propagation are unpredictable.

VARIETIES Numerous varieties are available from specialist growers, but one must stipulate compact or slow growth habit. Suitable plants are invariably in short supply.

POSSIBLE PROBLEMS Most troublesome are scale insects and red spider mites – take action as soon as detected.

▓ GENERAL TIP

It would be foolish to suggest that camellias would be at home if kept indoors throughout the year, as they really are outdoor plants. But they are also excellent plants for a window that is cool and light, or for decorating the conservatory while they are in flower. For most of the year they should enjoy a cool location out of doors.

▓ CARE TIP

The effects of scale insect attack on citrus plants can be especially displeasing as they leave an unattractive sooty deposit on the leaves – wipe clean with soapy water.

CRASSULA

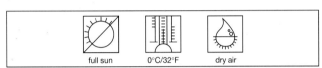

full sun   0°C/32°F   dry air

The best of these is *Crassula argentea* 'Sunset', with three-colour variegated leaves and a splendid pale brown stem. Mature container-grown plants have a distinctly bonsai look without need for bonsai treatment, but removal of the lower branches to expose the attractive stem and the stopping back of longer branches will much enhance the bonsai appearance.

GENERAL CARE To do well offer cool and light conditions and never overwater. Feed occasionally during the summer months. Plants that have spent the summer out of doors should be brought in as winter approaches, but never into very warm conditions. Plants will tolerate a touch of frost if the soil is very dry.

PROPAGATION Top cuttings allowed to dry before inserting in any reasonable soil in modest warmth will not prove difficult to root.

VARIETIES *C. argentea* 'Sunset', *C. argentea* (green foliage) and *C. arborescens* – a much bolder plant.

POSSIBLE PROBLEMS Generally trouble-free.

FICUS BENJAMINA

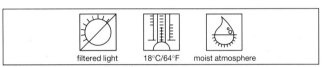

filtered light   18°C/64°F   moist atmosphere

Ficus benjamina (weeping fig) has naturally glossy leaves attached to elegant weeping branches; there are numerous close relatives. Bright green leaves against whitish stems set off this plant to perfection. It is an ideal subject for the beginner to indoor bonsai to experiment with, as it will not be difficult to train branches to provide interesting shapes. For a start young plants can be grown upright in their initial pots then potted on their sides to grow at an angle when introduced to their bonsai container.

GENERAL CARE Good light is essential for this plant, as are moist roots and regular feeding.

PROPAGATION From firm top or leaf cuttings taken at any time of the year provided bed temperature of 21°C/75°F can be maintained.

VARIETIES *F.b.* 'Golden Princess', *F.b.* 'Starlight', *F.b.* 'Hawaii' – all have variegated foliage.

POSSIBLE PROBLEMS Scale insects can be a problem; loss of leaves in poor light.

■ GENERAL TIP

The variegated form of this plant, C.a. 'Sunset', could be an interesting plant for the beginner with indoor bonsai as the cuttings root very readily, giving the opportunity of conducting a few experiments. Grow plants as single stems by removing side shoots as they appear until such time as a stem of reasonable size develops, then experimenf with shaping.

■ GENERAL TIP

The natural weeping of the plant stems could be further exaggerated by attaching light weights to the stems to induce them to hang more interestingly. Avoid heavy weights as these might break branches.

JACARANDA

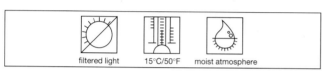

filtered light   15°C/50°F   moist atmosphere

With its full complement of amazing flowers this is a queen among tropical trees, but it is unlikely that flowers will be a feature when plants are being treated as indoor bonsai – for the later exercise the delicate foliage will be the main attraction. The best start will be to raise seed in a heated propagator and to plant a group of seedlings in a shallow dish filled with a loam-based free-draining potting mixture. When stems are still supple they can be wired into position to create a more pleasing effect.

GENERAL CARE These are plants that will do better in a light, sheltered location out of doors during the summer.

PROPAGATION From seed sown in moist conditions in a heated propagator.

SPECIES *Jacaranda mimosaefolia, J. obtusifolia.*

POSSIBLE PROBLEMS Aphids, scale insects and red spider mites.

MYRTUS

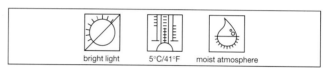

bright light   5°C/41°F   moist atmosphere

The flowers of myrtle are fragrant, as are the leaves when crushed, and the plant has a pleasing, fresh green appearance. These are fine plants for container growing, as bonsai or otherwise. Plants should be trained to shape in the spring by removing much of the inner growth to reduce the dense, clumpy appearance. At this time, too, the stouter branches that remain can be wired to the desired shape.

GENERAL CARE Provide cool, light and airy conditions for best results. Avoid late pruning of branches as this will result in many fewer flowers later in the season. During the spring and summer months plants will benefit from a sheltered outdoor location.

PROPAGATION From cuttings in early summer using a sandy mixture and a heated propagator.

SPECIES *Myrtus bullata* (common myrtle); *M.b.* 'Variegata', white variegation on leaves; *M. microphylla*, smaller leaves; *M. torentina*, more compact.

POSSIBLE PROBLEMS Aphids, red spider mites, among others.

■ DESIGN TIP

When preparing plants with feathery, delicate foliage for indoor bonsai it is advisable to plant them in groups rather than as individuals. This will mean obtaining a shallow dish of reasonably large dimension so that the plants can be arranged to maximum effect and the need for too much disturbance at an early date will be limited.

■ PLANTING TIP

When potting plants such as the myrtle that will spend long periods of time out of doors it is wise to cover the holes in the bottom of the container with perforated zinc to deter worms.

PODOCARPUS

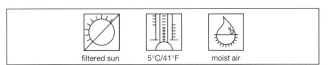

filtered sun   5°C/41°F   moist air

Podocarpus are tropical forest trees found from Africa to New Zealand. If there is a choice select those with narrow, yew-like foliage as they are more decorative as bonsai. With evergreen leaves it can become a substantial plant even when confined to a container. These are plants that can be wire-trained into interesting shapes with a true miniaturized forest look about them.

GENERAL CARE Protection from frost is necessary, but plants can remain outside for much of the year if desired. Keep moist and feed fortnightly while in active growth, giving less water and no feed over winter. Mist foliage during summer in a dry room atmosphere.

PROPAGATION From cuttings in a heated propagator or from seed.

VARIETIES *Podocarpus elongatus*, *P. macrophyllus* (Buddhist pine), and *P.m.* 'Maki', with larger, attractive glossy leaves.

POSSIBLE PROBLEMS Red spider mites, scale insects among others.

POLYSCIAS

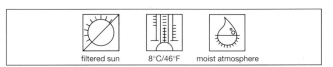

filtered sun   8°C/46°F   moist atmosphere

The polyscias (dinner-plate aralias) are tropical relatives of the ivy and when container-grown are painfully slow movers – an advantage in respect of indoor bonsai, as many of the numerous varieties have a bonsai appearance even when grown naturally. Grouping several plants in a flat dish is one way of setting plants off to advantage; the variety *Polyscias fruticosa* has finely segmented foliage that is well suited to this style of planting.

GENERAL CARE Keep moist and fed fortnightly when in active growth, with no feeding in winter and less generous watering. Although related to the ivy these are more temperamental plants, needing careful winter attention.

PROPAGATION From cuttings, or root cuttings taken in the spring and placed in a heated propagator.

SPECIES *P. balfouriana* and its several cultivars and *P. fruticosa* are the most readily available.

POSSIBLE PROBLEMS Red spider mites and scale insects; root loss from cold and wet winter conditions.

■ PLANTING TIP

The podocarpus belongs to the family Podocarpaceae, but has a pine-like appearance when grown as bonsai. Like the pine, it is a substantial plant when grown in a container. For this reason one should ensure that the *chosen container is reasonably substantial and that there are 2 holes in the bottom through which wires can be drawn to anchor the plant.*

■ DESIGN TIP

The stems of the polyscias will become bare lower down as they age – in many ways an attraction, but appearance will be improved if interesting stones can be incorporated in the design.

PUNICA GRANATUM

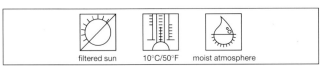

filtered sun   10°C/50°F   moist atmosphere

Of the numerous pomegranates, the plant most often offered for sale is *Punica granatum* 'Nana', the dwarf pomegranate. When container-grown, plants will produce their orange to red flowers but the fruits that develop are generally very small with a tendency to split. For indoor bonsai purposes these provide neat plants with a stout central stem once they have become established. The branches should be thinned out to provide a somewhat sparse effect, with wiring to shape done when the branches are firm but still pliable.

GENERAL CARE Keep soil moist and feed fortnightly during the growing season, with very much less water and no feeding at other times. The leaves are shed in winter; do necessary repotting prior to the appearance of new leaves.

PROPAGATION By seed, if obtainable, in the spring, or firm cuttings in mid summer – both done in peat and sand in a heated propagator.

VARIETIES *P.g.* 'Florepleno', 'Legrellei', and 'Nana'.

POSSIBLE PROBLEMS Aphids, red spider mites; chlorotic yellowing of leaves in poor growing conditions.

SAGERETIA THEEZANS

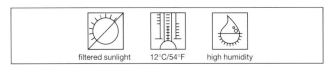

filtered sunlight   12°C/54°F   high humidity

This is a tender tree needing warm conditions to survive. The glossy evergreen leaves are an attraction in themselves, added to which the tree has attractive bark that is not unlike that of a mature plane tree.

GENERAL CARE Indoors, plants must be kept moist at all times with rather less water given in winter. A humid environment is also important and entails the need for periodic misting around the plant. Pruning can be undertaken at any time of the year; any repotting should be done in the spring every second or third year.

PROPAGATION Firm young cuttings should be taken in the spring and placed in a heated propagating case.

VARIETIES The above is the only plant that may be obtainable.

POSSIBLE PROBLEMS Aphids, red spider mites; chlorotic foliage from indifferent culture.

■ CARE TIP

In milder regions pomegranates can be planted out of doors against a sheltered wall, but it is preferable to grow them either indoors or in a greenhouse. A combination of spending part of the year in the greenhouse (winter), part indoors (spring) and part in a sheltered location outside (summer) is best of all.

■ CARE TIP

Root prune indoor bonsai when plants are pot-bound. Remove the plant from its container, disentangle the roots and, with sharp secateurs, trim off one-third of the roots. Repot in the same container with fresh soil.

GLOSSARY

Acid Used to describe soil with a pH reading below 7.0. Because acid soils contain little lime, lime-hating plants like azaleas and rhododendrons thrive; lime needs to be added to grow plants like brassicas.

Active growth The period during the annual cycle when a plant produces new leaves and flowers and increases in size.

Aeration Loosening of the soil to admit air.

Aerial roots Roots arising from stems above the growing medium, e.g. some orchids.

Alkaline Used to describe soil with a pH reading above 7.0. A slightly alkaline soil suits most plants.

Annual A plant that completes its life cycle in one growing season.

Aquatic A plant that lives in water, sometimes with leaves and flowers floating on the surface.

Axil The angle between the stem and a leaf, from which further growth arises.

Bedding plant A plant used for temporary garden display.

Biennial A plant that needs two growing seasons to complete its life cycle.

Blanching Excluding light from vegetables such as chicory and celery in order to whiten the stems or leaves and remove the bitter taste.

Bolt Running to seed prematurely. Lettaces and beetroot bolt if deprived of water in hot weather.

Bract A modified leaf, which may be brightly coloured and have the appearance of a petal, e.g. bromeliads, *Euphorbia pulcherrima*.

Broadcast To spread seed or fertilizer evenly over a wide area.

Bulb An underground storage organ made up of tightly wrapped fleshy leaves or leaf bases.

Bulbil A small bulb that forms at the base of mature bulbs which can be detached and grown on to achieve maturity.

Calyx The outer protective part of a flower which persists at the top of the fruit, e.g. tomato, strawberry.

Cane The woody stem of raspberries, blackberries and loganberries.

Catch crop A quick-maturing crop grown between rows of slower-growing species or sown and harvested in the brief time between one crop being picked and the next being sown.

Catkin A flower spike composed of bracts.

Chlorosis Deficiency of minerals in the soil or growing medium giving a pale appearance to foliage.

Clamp A store for root vegetables made of a mound of soil and straw.

Cloche Glass or plastic covering to protect plants in the open, usually in order to raise early crops.

Compost 1 a mixture of loam, sand, peat and leaf-mould used for growing plants in containers; 2 rotted remains of plant and other organic material.

Conifer Trees and shrubs with needle-like leaves which bear their seeds in cones.

Cordon A plant grown on a single main stem, achieved by strict pruning. Double and triple cordons have two and three stems respectively.

Corm An underground storage organ formed by a thickened leaf base. Unlike a bulb, a corm does not contain the young plant.

Corona From the Latin meaning a crown. Used to describe the trumpet of a narcissus.

Crown The bottom of a perennial or basal part of a plant from which roots and shoots arise.

Curd The heads of cauliflower and broccoli, made up of tightly packed flower-buds.

Cutting A portion of a plant removed and used to raise a new plant; usually from a stem or leaf.

Damping down Watering the greenhouse or frame in warm weather to increase humidity.

Dead-heading The practice of removing faded flowerheads in order to prevent seeding, encourage further flowering, or to keep the plant looking tidy.

Dormant Literally, sleeping. Used to describe the period when a plant makes no growth, usually in the winter.

Drill A straight furrow made in an outside bed to sow seeds.

Earthing up Drawing up soil around the stems to exclude light.

Epiphytic Used to describe plants which can live without having their roots in soil, e.g. many bromeliads and orchids.

Espalier A type of tree trained with the support of wires, often against a wall. The main stem is vertical with pairs of branches extending horizontally at regular intervals.

Evergreen A plant which bears foliage throughout the year.

Fertilization The fusion of the male and female elements of a plant (pollen and undeveloped seed) to form a mature seed.

Festoon A system by which tree branches are trained to curve downwards.

Forcing Bringing plants to fruit or flower before their natural time.

Frond The leaf of a palm or fern.

Fungicide A substance used to combat fungal diseases.

Germination The first stage in the development of a plant from a seed.

Ground cover Plants used to cover the soil, smothering weeds with attractive foliage.

Half-hardy Used to describe plants that require protection during the winter.

Hardening off Acclimatizing plants that have been grown under heated glass to outside conditions.

Hardy Description of plants that survive frost in the open.

Haulm The leafy stems of potato plants.

Heel The base of a piece of stem which has been torn away from a side shoot to be used as a cutting. Cuttings often root more readily if a heel is attached.

Heeling in Inserting shoots or roots of plants into the soil for a limited period to keep them moist until the time is right to put them in their permanent positions.

Hip Fruit of the rose.

Humus The substance remaining when dead vegetable matter has broken down.

Hybrid A plant that results from the crossing of two species or varieties, e.g. × *Fatshedera lizei*.

Inorganic A chemical substance, such as fertilizer, which does not contain carbon.

Insecticide A substance used for killing insects.

Larva The immature stage of some insects, such as caterpillars and grubs.

Lateral A stem or shoot that branches out from the leaf axil of a larger stem.

Leader The main stem of a plant or of a tree that extends the system of branches.

Lime Calcium, a chemical that may be used to neutralize acid soils. Too much lime makes it impossible for some nutrients in the soil to be absorbed by plants.

Loam Soil which is a compound of clay, silt, sand and humus. It is moisture-retentive and mineral-rich. It is an ingredient of soil-based composts and is always sterilized for commercial use to purify it of harmful organisms.

Maiden A one-year-old fruit tree.

Mulch A layer of organic matter spread on the soil surface in conditions that simulate nature.

Neutral Used to describe soil with a pH reading between 6.5 and 7.0, which is neither acid nor alkaline.

Node A joint in a plant's stem from which leaves, buds and side-shoots arise.

Offset A young plant naturally produced by mature (or 'parent') plants; can be detached and used for propagation.

Organic Used to describe substances that are the product of the decay of living organisms.

Pan A layer of hard soil that may form if soil is repeatedly worked to the same level.

Peat Partially decayed organic matter. Sedge peat is from the roots of sedges growing in bogs. It is an important ingredient of proprietary composts for indoor plants and is used in combination with sand to raise cuttings.

Pendent Literally, hanging. Used to describe flowers like those of the fuchsia.

Perennial A plant that lives for an indefinite period.

pH reading The pH scale is used to measure the acidity or alkalinity of soil. The neutral point is 7.0; a reading above this denotes alkalinity and one below it denotes acidity.

Pinching out Removing the growing point of a stem to encourage bushy growth.

Pollination Transferring pollen grains (the male cells of a plant) on to the stigma of a flower.

Potbound Used to describe a plant whose roots have completely filled the pot and can no longer efficiently support it; an indication that repotting is necessary.

Pricking out Planting out seedlings for the first time to larger trays, to a nursery bed, or to individual pots.

Propagation Increasing or raising new plants, either from seed or vegetatively, i.e. from cuttings, offsets or suckers.

Pruning Cutting back a plant to keep the shape neat, restrict the size and encourage the formation of flowers.

Pyramid A type of tree, trained to have an outline like a pyramid.

Repotting Transferring a plant which has outgrown its pot and exhausted the nutrients in its compost to a larger pot containing fresh compost.

Rhizome An underground storage organ composed of a creeping stem.

Rootball Used to describe a plant's roots and the growing medium supporting them.

Root run The soil area occupied by the roots of a plant.

Rootstock The name for the plant on to which another is grafted.

Rosette An arrangement of leaves radiating from a central point.

Runner An aerial stem which roots at the tip when it touches the soil, to make a new plant e.g. strawberry, blackberry.

Scion A shoot of a plant joined to the rootstock of another. Used to propagate trees.

Seedling A young plant.

Self-fertile Used to describe a fruit tree that does not need a pollinator to set fruits.

Self-sterile Used to describe a fruit tree that needs a pollinator to set fruits.

Spadix A flower spike containing numerous tiny flowers.

Spathe A large bract enclosing a spadix e.g. *Spathiphyllum* 'Mauna Loa'.

Spit A spade's depth – about 25-30cm/10-12in.

Spore A minute particle by which ferns reproduce themselves.

Spur A small lateral branch on a fruit tree which bears flowery buds.

Stake A support for plants, from a cane for delphiniums to a heavy wooden stake for young trees.

Stamen The male reproductive organ of a flower, arising from the centre of the petals.

Stolon A creeping stem which roots at the nodes where they make contact with the growing medium e.g. *Saxifraga stolonifera*.

Succulent A plant with fleshy leaves or stems which can store water and survive arid conditions.

Sucker A shoot that arises from below ground level. In some species of indoor plant the sucker can be used for propagation.

Tender Used to describe any plant susceptible to damage by frost.

Tendril A kind of leaf or stem that twines round supports permitting plants to climb.

Terrestrial Growing in the soil.

Tilth The surface layer of the soil, which is fine and crumbly.

Topdress Applying fresh compost to a plant after first removing 2.5-5cm/1-2in of the old compost. Useful for sustaining mature plants which have reached the largest convenient size pot.

Transplanting Moving young plants from one place to another to give them more room to develop.

Truss A cluster of fruits or flowers.

Tuber An underground storage organ, either a thickened root or stem.

Variegated Used to describe leaves which are marked with a contrasting colour.

Vegetative Propagation by a part of the plant, i.e. offsets, cuttings, division of roots, layering of a stem, rather than by sowing seeds.

Whorl An arrangement of leaves or flowers that project from a single point like rays.

INDEX

Including Common Names

Italic page numbers refer to illustrations.

***A**butilon* 284, *284*
Acalypha hispida 284, *284*
Acer 125, *125*
Achillea 41, *41*
Achimenes 285
A. grandiflora 285
A. heterophylla 285, *285*
A. longiflora 285
acid or alkaline soil 10
Acorus 247, 260, *260*
Adiantum 249, 254, 303, 304, *304*
A. capillus-veneris 259, 304
A. cuneatum 304
A. raddianum 304
Aechmea 343, 344, *344*
Aeonium 334
A. arboreum 334, *334*
A. atropurpureum 334
A. domesticum 334
A. urbicum 334
Aethionema 18, 95, *95*
A. grandiflorum 95
A. iberideum 95
A. pulchellum 95
African violet *see Saintpaulia ionantha*
Agave americana 334, *334*
Ageratum 36, *36*
air plants *see* bromeliads
Alchemilla 13, 39, 40
A. alpina 40
A. mollis 9, 39, 40, *40*, 61
almond, ornamental 121
Aloe 335, *335*
alpine orchid *see Pleione formosana*
alpines 9, 18, 76-95
Althaea rosea 38, 39, 48, *48*
aluminium plant *see Pilea cadierei*
Alyssum 25, 77, 84
A. argenteum 87
A. saxatile 87, *87*
amaryllis *see Hippeastrum*
Ananas 344, *344*
Anchusa myosotidiflora 54, *54*
angelica 202, 204, 206, *206*
angel's tears *see Billbergia nutans*
Angraecum 350, *350*
annuals 20-37
Anthemis nobilis see chamomile
Anthurium 285, *285*
A. andreanum 285
A. schertzerianum 285
Antirrhinum majus 32, *32*
ants 218
Aphelandra 249
A. squarrosa 286, *286*
aphid 23, 26, 29, 33, 45, 111, 134, 135, 137, 143, 153, 159, 163, 179, 190, 257, 349
Aporacactus 324, *324*
apple 135, 220, 231, 232-3, 235-7, *235*, *236*, *237*
apple mint 214
apple scab 235
apricot 135, 241, *241*
Aquilegia vulgaris 18, 28, 57, *57*
Arabis 77, 84
A. albida 84, *84*
A. caucasica 84, *84*
areca palm *see Chrysalidocarpus lutescens*
Armeria 88, *88*
Artemisia dracunculus see tarragon
artichoke 173
globe 131, 174, *174*
Jerusalem 131, 142, 185, 188, *188*
artillery plant *see Pilea muscosa*
arum lily *see Zantedeschia aethiopica*
asparagus 131, 172, 173, 174, *174*
asparagus beetle 173
asparagus fly 174
asparagus pea 131, 136, 137, 140, *140*
Asperula 18
A. odorata 30
A. orientalis 30, *30*
Aspidistra elatior 254, 255, 256, 260, *260*
Asplenium nidus 249, 255, 304, *304*
Astilbe x *arendsii* 39, 51, *51*
Astrantia 52, *52*
aubergine 131, *153*, 154, *154*
Aubretia deltoidea 77, 80, *80*, 84
autumn crocus *see Colchicum*
Azalea 11, 96, 107, *107*, 256, 286, *286*
azalea gall 257

Baby's breath *see Gypsophila*
ball cactus *see Notocactus*
balloon flower *see Platycodon grandiflorum*
balm 202, 203, 204, 206, *206*
bamboo *250*
Barbados gooseberry 331
Bartonia aurea 37, *37*
basal rot 257
basil 203, 205, 207, *207*
bats 134
bay 203, 207, *207*
beans 131, 133, 136-40, *138*, *139*, *140*
bee 25, 31, 32, 44, 56, 57, 83, 102, 121, 123, 203
bee balm *see* balm; bergamot
bee balm *see Monarda didyma*
beebread *see* borage
beefsteak plant *see Iresine herbstii*
beet 168-9, *168*, *169*
beetroot 131, 143, 143, 144, *144*, 159
Begonia
B. luxurians 261, *261*
B. rex 249, 253-4, 258, 261, *261*
B. semperflorens 287, *287*
B. tuberhybrida 60, 74, *74*, 287, *287*
bell flower *see Campanula*
Bellis perennis 39, 47, *47*
Beloperone guttata 251, 288, *288*
bergamot 203, 204, 208, *208*
Bergenia 13, 18, 39, 53, *53*
big bud 135
Billbergia nutans 343, 345, *345*
bird of paradise *see Strelitzia reginae*
birds 121, 123, 134
as predators 171, 174, 179
protecting crops from 161, 223, 228, 234
bird's nest fern *see Asplenium nidus*
black currant 135, 220-1, *220*, 223, 229, *229*
black-eyed susan *see Rudbeckia hirta; Thunbergia*
blackberry 135, 221-2, *222*, 224, *224*
blackfly 137
blanching 172-3, 194
Blechnum 303, 305, *305*
bleeding heart *see Dicentra*
blood, fish and bone 131
blue column *see Cereus peruvianus*
blue cowslip *see Pulmonaria angustifolia*
blue-eyed mary *see Omphalodes*
blueberry 220, 224, *224*
boat lily *see Rhoeo*
bonemeal 131
bonsai 356-63
borage 203, 208, *208*
Boston fern *see Nephrolepis*
botrytis 135, 257, 323
bottle gardens 259
Bougainvillea 358, *358*
box *see Buxus*
boysenberry 225, *225*
Brassica oleracea 164
brassicas 131, *132*, 158
broad bean 131, 136, 137, 140, *140*
broccoli 131, 158, 160, *160*
Brodiaea 70, *70*
bromeliads 248, 342-7
broom *see Cytisus*
Browallia 252, 288
B. speciosa 288, *288*
B. viscosa 288
Brunnera macrophylla 39, 54, *54*
Brussels sprout 131, 158, *158*, 159, 161, *161*
buddhist pine *see Podocarpus*
budding, propagation by 18
bulbs
bulb vegetables 194-201
flower gardens 60-75
houseplants 282, 316-21
bunnies' ears *see Opuntia*
burrows tail *see Sedum morganianum*
busy lizzie *see Impatiens*
butterflies 57, 102, 112, 122, 134, 203
butterfly palm *see Chrysalidocarpus lutescens*
button fern *see Pellaea rotundifolia*
buttons *see* tansy
Buxus 358, *358*

Cabbage 131, 134, 158, 162-3, *162*, *163*, *164*, 184
ornamental 164
cabbage root fly 159, 162
cabbage whitefly 159, *159*
cacti 247, 248, 249, 322-31, 332
calabrese 131, 158, 161, *161*
Caladium 249, 258
C. bicolor 262, *262*
C. candidum 262
Calathea 249, 255, 258
C. makoyana 263
C. picturata 258, 262, *262*
C. zebrina 263, *263*
Calceolaria herbeohybrida 289, *289*
Calendula officinalis 26, 111; *see also* marigold
California bluebell *see Phacelia campanularia*
Californian fuchsia *see Zauschneria*
Californian lilac *see Ceanothus*
Californian poppy *see Eschscholzia californica*
calla lily *see Zantedeschia aethiopica*
Callistephus chinensis 27, *27*
Caltha palustris 58, *58*
Camellia 9, 11, 13, 96, 108, 359, *359*
C. japonica 108, *108*
C. x *williamsii* 108
Campanula 39, 77, 81, 256, 303
C. carpatica 81, *81*
C. cochleavifolia 54
C. garganica 81
C. isophylla 289, *289*
C. lactiflora 54, *54*
C. medium 54
C. nitida 54
C. persicifolia 54
canary creeper *see Tropaeolum peregrinum*
candytuft *see Iberis*
cane spot 135
canker 135
Canterbury bell *see Campanula medium*
Cape grape *see Rhoicissus capensis*
Cape primrose *see Streptocarpus*
Capsicum
C. annum 290, *290*
see also chilli pepper; pepper
capsid bug 135
caraway 209, *209*
cardoon 172, 175, *175*
carnation *see Dianthus*
carrion flower *see Stapelia*
carrot 131, 159, 184, 185, *185*, 186-7, *186*, *187*
carrot fly 173, 185, 186
cast-iron plant *see Aspidistra*
Catananche 18, 39, 53, *53*
catch cropping *158*, 159
caterpillars 134, 159, *159*, 223
Cattleya 350, *350*
cauliflower 131, 158, 159, 164-5, *164*, *165*
Ceanothus 104
C. impressus 96, 104, *104*
C. thyrsiflorens repens 104
celeriac 131, 185, 187, *187*
celery 131, 172, 173, 175-6, *175*, *176*
celery fly 173, 185
Centaurea 18, 21, 31, *31*
C. cyanus 31
C. moschata 31
centipede 134
century plant *see Agave americana*
Cephalocereus 324, *324*
Cerastium 84, *84*
Cereus peruvianus 325, *325*
Ceropegia 335, *335*
Chaenomeles 96, 116
C. japonica 116, *116*
C. lagenaria 116
C. speciosa 116
chalk plant *see Gypsophila*
chalky soil 10, 11, *11*
Chamaecereus silvestrii 325, *325*
Chamaedorea 249, 255
C. elegans 310, 312, *312*
Chamaerops humilis 312, *312*
chamomile 202, 203, 209, *209*
chard 158, 168, *168*, 172
chenille plant *see Acalypha hispida*
cherry 231, 233, 237-8, *237*, *238*
ornamental *see Prunus*
cherry laurel 121
chervil 205, 210, *210*
chicory 131, 145, *145*, 166, *166*
chilli pepper 155, *155*
Chimonanthus praecox 96, 99, *99*
China aster *see Callistephus chinensis*
Chinese blackberry *see* wineberry
Chinese cabbage 174
Chionodoxa 60, 63, *63*
chives 202, 203, *204*, 205, 210, *210*
Chlorophytum 249, 254, 255, 258, 263, *263*
chocolate spot 137, *137*
Choisya ternata 96, 114, *114*
Christmas rose *see Helleborus niger*
Chrysalidocarpus lutescens 313, *313*
Chrysanthemum 21, 33, 282, 290, *290*
C. carinatum 33
C. coronarium 33
C. maximum 33, *33*
chusan palm *see Trachycarpus fortunei*
cineraria 252, 282, 291, *291*
cinquefoil *see Potentilla*
Cissus 249, 256
C. antarctica 256
C. rhombifolia 259, 264, *264*
Citrus 359, *359*
clarkia *see Godetia*
clary 35
clay soil 10, *10*
Cleistocactus 326, *326*
Clematis 9, 13, 18, 28, 96, 106, *106*
C. armandii 106
C. flammula 106
C. montana 13, 106
C. orientalis 106
C. tangutica 106
climate 9
climbing plants
flower gardens 97
houseplants 251
vegetables 142, 147
Clivia 282, 291, *291*
cloches 143, 152, *152*, 193, 195, *195*
clover as green manure 127
clown orchid *see Oodontoglossum*
club root 158, 159, 167, 173
cob cactus *see Lobivia*
coconut palm *see Cocos weddeliana*
Cocos weddeliana 249, 313, *313*
Codiaeum 247, 249, 264, *264*
codling moth 135, 234, 235, 238
Coelogyne 351, *351*
Colchicum 60, 61, 71, *71*
cold frames 143, 152, 179
Coleus blumei 251, 265, *265*
Colorado spruce *see Picea pungens*
colour 13, *15*
columbine *see Aquilegia vulgaris*
Columnea 282, 292, *292*
comfrey liquid 131
companion plants 23
compost 10, 11, 127-8, *127*, 204
coneflower *see Rudbeckia laciniata*
containers, growing plants in
automatic watering system 191
bulbs 61
flower garden 21, 76-7
herbs 202-3, *203*
strawberries 220
vegetables 142, 191
Convallaria majalis 13, 18, 49, *49*
Convolvulus tricolor 21, 29, *29*
cordon system of training 220, 221, *221*, 232, 233
Coreopsis 39, 43, *43*
corms 60, 316
corn salad 143, 150, *150*
cornflower *see Centaurea*
Corydalis
C. cashmeriana 87
C. cheilanthifolia 87, *87*
C. lutea 87
Cosmos 20, *21*, 22, *22*
C. bipinnatus 22
C. sulphureus 22
cotton lavender *see Santolina*
Cotyledon 336, *336*
courgette 131, 178-80, 180, *180*
cowslip *see Polyanthus veris; Pulmonaria*
cranesbill *see Geranium*
Crassula 336, 360, *360*
C. arborescens 360
C. argentea 336, 360
C. corymbulosa 336, *336*
creeping fig *see Ficus pumila*
Crinum 316, 317, 318
C. bulbispermum 318
C. x *powellii* 318, *318*
Crocus 13, 60, 62, *62*, 316, 318, *318*
C. chrysanthus 18, 62
C. imperati 62
C. longifloris 62
C. vernus 62
crocus, autumn *see Colchicum*
croton *see Codiaeum*
crown cactus *see Rebutia*
crown imperial *see Fritillaria imperialis*
Cryptanthus 342, *342*, 345
C. bromelioides tricolor 345, *345*
C. zonatus 345
Ctenanthe 258, 265, *265*
cucumber 131, 142, 147, *147*, 152
cucumber mosaic virus 179, *179*
cupid's dart *see Catananche*
cushion pink *see Silene*
cuttings 15-16, *205*, 253, *253*
leaf 253-4, *253*
cutworm 134
Cycas revoluta 314, *314*
Cyclamen 18, 247-8, 256, *256*, 282, 292, *292*, 303
C. hederifolium 67
C. neapolitanum 13, 67, *67*
C. persicum 67
Cymbidium 351, *351*
Cyperus 247, 249, 256, 266, *266*
Cyrtomium falcatum 305, *305*
Cytisus 18, 98
C. x *praecox* 98, *98*
C. scoparius 98

Daffodil *see Narcissus*
Dahlia 9, 60, 61, 72, *72*
damping off 135, 143, 173
damson 244, *244*
Daphne ffisk 214
date palm *see Phoenix*
Davallia 303, 306
D. canariensis 306, *306*
D. fijiensis 306
D. mariesii 306
day lily *see Hemerocallis*
Delphinium 13, 29, *29*, 38, 39, 55
D. ajacis 20, 29
D. consolida 29
D. elatum 55, *55*
Dendrobium 352, *352*
desert privet *see Peperomia magnoliifolia*
Deutzia 9, 18, 103
D. x *hybrida* 103
D. monbeigii 103, *103*
D. x *rosea* 97, 103
devil's ivy *see Scindapsus*
Dianthus 77, 79
D. barbatus 31, *31*
D. caesius 79
D. deltoides 79, *79*
D. gratianopolitanus 79
Dicentra 41, *41*
die back 135
Dieffenbachia 266, *266*
digging 15, 129, 135, 142
dill 203, 205, 211, *211*
dinner-plate aralia *see Polyscias*
diseases *see* pests and diseases
division, propagation by 16, 254
Dizygotheca 249, 254, 267
D. elegantissima 267, *267*
D. veitchii 267
dolomite 131
Doronicum 43, *43*
Dorotheanthus bellidiflorus 37, *37*
downy mildew 195, 239
Dracaena 249, 267, *267*
drainage 9
dried blood 131
drought 9, 18
dumb cane *see Dieffenbachia*

Earth star *see Cryptanthus*
earthing up 172
earwig 33
Echeveria 337, *337*
Echinocactus 326, *326*
Echinocereus 327, *327*
Echinops banaticus 39, 55, *55*
edelweiss *see Leontopodium alpinum*
elder 203; *see also Sambucus*
Elettaria cardamom 268, *268*
Encarsia formosa 154, 234
Encyclia 352, *352*
endive 131, 133, 172
broad-leaved 158, 166, *166*
curly-leaved 143, 145, *145*
Enkianthus campanulatus 13, 96, 109, *109*
Eranthis 18
E. hyemalis 60, 66, *66*
E. x *tubergenii* 66
Erica
E. carnea 96, 112, *112*
E. herbacea 112, *112*

Erinus alpinus 89, 89
Erodium 18, 92
　E. chamaedryoides 92, 92
　E. chrysanthum 92
　E. corsicum 92
Eschscholzia californica 35, 35
Eucryphia 118
　E. x nymansensis 124, 124
Euphorbia 13, 39, 40, 337
　E. ingens 337
　E. melaformis 337
　E. obesa 337, 337
　E. pulcherrima 282, 293, 293
　E. robbiae 39, 40, 40, 61
European fan palm see Chamaerops humilis
evening primrose 202; see also Oenothera biennis
Exacum affine 252, 282, 293, 293

False aralia see Dizygotheca
false castor oil plant see Fatsia japonica
fan training fruit trees 231-2, 244
Fatshedera 247, 249, 258, 268, 268
Fatsia japonica 247, 258, 269, 269
feeding plants and soil 15, 130, 134
　bonsai plants 357
　cacti 322
　houseplants 248-9
　orchids 348
　succulents 332-3
fennel 163, 202, 203, 204, 205, 211, 211
　Florence 131, 172, 196, 196
ferns 248, 255, 256, 258, 259, 302-9
Ferocactus 327, 327
fertilizer 130, 131, 248
Ficus
　F. benjamina 249, 254, 256, 269, 269, 360, 360
　F. elastica 249, 251, 254, 256, 258, 270, 270
　F. pumila 249, 255, 256, 259, 270, 270
fig 238, 238
fingernail plant see Neoregelia
fish-hook cactus (barrel) see Ferocactus
fishmeal 131
Fittonia 248, 254, 256, 258, 271
　F. argyroneura 271, 271
　F. vershaffeltii 271
flame nasturtium see Tropaeolum speciosum
flame nettle see Coleus blumei
flaming katie see Kalanchoe blossfeldiana
flaming sword see Vriesia
flamingo flower see Anthurium schertzerianum
flea beetle 134, 135, 185
Florence fennel 131, 172, 196, 196
foot rot 37, 179
forget-me-not see Myosotis
Forsythia 9, 18, 98
　F. x intermedia 98, 98
　F. suspensa 98
Fothergilla 13, 18, 117, 117
　F. major 117
　F. monticola 117
Freesia x kewensis 70, 70
Fremontia californica 101, 101
French bean 136, 137, 138-9, 138, 139
French marigold see Tagetes
frit fly 173
Fritillaria
　F. imperialis 75, 75
　F. meleagris 75
frogs and toads 134, 174
frost damage 173
fruit 220-45
Fuchsia 9, 18, 25, 26, 96, 108, 282, 283, 294, 294
　F. magellanica 108, 108
fumitory see Corydalis lutea
fungal diseases 349

Galanthus 18
　G. elwesii 62
　G. nivalis 13, 60, 62, 62
Gasteria 338, 338
Gazania 23, 23
Gentiana 77, 90
　G. farreri 90
　G. sino-ornata 90, 90
Geranium 39, 92
　G. dalmaticum 92, 92
　G. endressii 39, 56
　G. napuligerum 92
　G. prylzowianum 92
　G. renardii 92
　G. sanguineum 56, 56
　G. subcaulescens 92
Gladiolus 18, 60-1, 74, 74
globe artichoke 131, 174, 174
globe thistle see Echinops banaticus

glory-of-the-snow see Chionodoxa
gloxinia see Sinningia speciosa
Godetia 26, 26
gold-dust see Alyssum
golden barrel see Echinocactus
golden rain see Laburnum
gooseberry 135, 220, 221, 221, 225, 225
grafting 119
granny's bonnet see Aquilegia vulgaris
grape 239, 239
grape hyacinth see Muscari
grape ivy see Cissus rhombifolia
greengly 137, 179, 179, 257
green manure 10, 127, 140
green orchid see Cattleya
greenfly 137, 179, 179, 257
greengage 244, 244
greenhouses 152, 153, 234
grey mould 134, 135, 257
ground beetle 134
ground cover 13, 38-9, 84
growing bags 142, 153
Gymnocalycium 328, 328
Gynura 271, 271
Gypsophila elegans 21, 24, 24
gypsum 131

Half-hardy plants 9
halo blight 137, 137
Hamamelis 125
　H. x intermedia 125
　H. mollis 118, 125, 125
　H. virginiana 125
Hamburg parsley 188, 188
hanging baskets 21
　herbs grown in 202, 203
　houseplants 255, 259, 303
hare's foot fern see Davallia canariensis; Polypodium aureum
hart's tongue fern see Phyllitis scolopendrium
hearts entangled see Ceropegia
heath 11
heather 11
Hedera 247, 249, 255, 256
　H. canariensis 271
　H. helix 259, 272, 272
hedgehog 134, 171, 174, 179
hedgehog cactus see Echinocereus
hedges 9
Helianthemum 18, 77, 89
　H. apenninum 89
　H. nummularium 89, 89
Helichrysum 18
Helleborus 18
　H. niger 38, 48, 48
　H. orientalis 48
Hemerocallis 18, 59, 59
herb gardens 132
herbaceous border 21, 38
herbaceous perennials 38
herbs 131, 202-19
　harvesting and preserving 204-5
Hibiscus rosa-sinensis 18, 113, 113, 294, 294
Hippeastrum 316, 317, 317, 319, 319
　H. aulicum 317
　H. candidum 317
　H. reticulatum 317
hoes 194
holly fern see Cyrtomium falcatum
hollyhock see Althaea rosea
honesty see Lunaria
honeysuckle see Lonicera periclymenum
hoof and horn 131
horseradish 212, 212
hortensia see Hydrangea macrophylla
hosta 174
hot water plant see Achimenes
houseplants
　bonsai 356-63
　bromeliads 342-7
　bulbs 282, 316-21
　cacti 247, 248, 249, 322-31
　care of plants 247-52
　choosing 247
　ferns 303-9
　flowering 282-301
　foliage plants 258-81
　holiday care 251
　interior design 255-6, 258-9, 282
　orchids 348-55
　palms 310-15
　pests and diseases 257
　potting mixtures 252
　propagation 252-4, 252, 253, 254
　succulents 332-41
hoverfly 23, 29, 45, 111, 134, 137, 159, 163, 190
Howea 249, 314, 314

H. belmoreana 314
　H. forsteriana 311, 314
Hoya 282
　H. bella 295, 295
　H. carnosa 295
humidity, houseplants 248, 348
Hyacinthus 60, 67, 67, 255, 316, 319, 319
Hydrangea 102, 256, 282, 303
　H. arborescens 102
　H. macrophylla 102, 295, 295
　H. paniculata 102
　H. petiolaris 102, 102
hygrometer 248
Hypoestes 249, 258, 259
　H. phyllostachya 271, 271
hyssop 203, 212, 212

Iberis 18, 94
　I. gibraltarica 94
　I. saxatilis 94
　I. sempervirens 94, 94
Impatiens 21, 47, 47, 252, 253, 282, 296, 296
　I. holstii 296
　I. petersiana 296
　I. sultanii 47
　I. walleriana 47, 296
insecticides 135
intercropping 159, 184-5
Ipheion uniflorum 70, 70
Ipomoea tricolor 29, 104, 104
Iresine herbstii 258, 273, 273
Iris 60, 69, 316, 320
　bulbous 69, 69
　I. danfordiae 18
　I. histrioides 61
　I. laevigata 69, 69
　I. pseudocorus 69
　I. reticulata 316, 320, 320
　I. versicolor 69
ivy 247; see also Hedera

Jacaranda 361, 361
Japanese onion 194, 199, 199
Jasminum 9, 18, 99, 99, 282, 296
　J. nudiflorum 96, 99
　J. polyanthum 296, 296
Jerusalem artichoke 131, 142, 185, 188, 188
Jerusalem cowslip see Pulmonaria officinalis
jonquil see Narcissus
Juniperus 18, 77, 86, 86, 356

kaffir lily see Clivia
Kalanchoe 338
　K. blossfeldiana 339, 339
　K. daigremontianum 338
　K. tomentosa 338, 338
　K. tubiflorum 338
kale 131, 158, 167, 167
kentia palm see Howea
kidney bean 131
king of bromeliads see Vriesia
kingcup see Caltha palustris
Kohleria 297, 297
kohlrabi 131, 167, 167

Laburnum 118, 120
　L. alpinum 120
　L. anagyroides 120
　L. x watereri 120, 120
lace cactus see Echinocereus
lacewing 134, 137
ladder fern see Nephrolepis exaltata
ladybird 134, 137, 159, 190
lady's mantle see Alchemilla mollis
lamb's lettuce see corn salad
land cress 131, 138, 146, 146
larkspur see Delphinium
Lathyrus odoratus 9, 21, 32, 32
laurustinus see Viburnum tinus
Lavandula spica 9, 13, 18, 96, 113, 113, 202, 203
Lavatera trimestris 20, 36, 36
lavender 202, 203; see also Lavandula spica
layering, propagation by 17, 204, 254, 254
leaf beet 131
leaf mould 128, 128
leaf spot 135, 173, 257
leatherjacket 134
leek 131, 172, 194, 196-7, 196, 197
legumes 131, 132, 136-41, 138, 139, 140, 141
lemon balm see balm
lemon geranium 203
lemon thyme 203, 219
lemon verbena 203
Lenten rose see Helleborus orientalis
Leontopodium alpinum 85, 85
leopard's bane see Doronicum
lettuce 131, 138, 142, 143, 143, 148-9,

148, 149, 159
lamb's see corn salad
Leucojum 60
　L. aestivum 66, 66
　L. autumnale 66
　L. vernum 66
Lewisia cotyledon 90, 90
lilac see Syringa vulgaris
Lilium 73
　L. x hollandicum 73, 73
　L. pardalinum 73
　L. regale 73, 73
　L. x umbellatum 73
lily 13, 40, 60-1; see also Lilium
lily-of-the-valley see Convallaria majalis
lime-tolerant plants 18
Lithodora 82, 82
Lithops 339, 339
Lithospermum 82, 82
living stones see Lithops
Livingston daisy see Mesembryanthemum criniflorum
loamy soil 10
Lobelia erinus 21, 25, 26, 26, 27
Lobivia 328, 328
Lobularia maritima 21, 27, 27
loganberry 135, 222, 222, 226, 226
Lonicera 9, 13, 18, 96
　L. periclymenum 115, 115
　L. x purpusii 96
lovage 202, 213, 213
love-in-a-mist see Nigella damascena
Lunaria 30, 30
Lupin polyphyllus 13, 28, 39, 46, 46
Lychnis coronaria 21

Magnolia 103, 120, 120
　M. denudata 120
　M. grandiflora 103
　M. liliflora 103
　M. salicifolia 120
　M. soulangeana 103
　M. stellata 96, 103, 103
Mahonia aquifolium 13, 18, 96, 105, 105
maidenhair fern see Adiantum
Malus see apple
Malva alcea 36, 39, 50, 50
Mammilaria 329, 329
mangetout 131, 137, 141, 141
mangetout see pea
manure 11, 131, 160
maple see Acer
Maranta 247, 249, 258, 259
　M. leuconeura 258, 273, 273
marigold 13, 21
　French see Tagetes
　marsh see Caltha palustris
　pot 213, 213; see also Calendula officinalis
marjoram 202, 203, 204, 214, 214
marrow 131, 179, 181, 181
　custard 180, 180
　spaghetti 182, 182
marsh cinquefoil see Potentilla palustris
marsh marigold see Caltha palustris
Matricaria chamomilla see chamomile
mealy bug 257, 323, 349
mealy cabbage aphid 159
Meconopsis 42, 42
melon 182, 182
Mentzelia lindleyi 37, 37
Mesembryanthemum criniflorum 18, 37, 37
Mexican orange blossom see Choisya ternata
mildew 257
millipede 134
Miltonia 353, 353
mint 202, 203, 204, 214, 214
mixed border 38
mock orange see Philadelphus coronarius
Molucella laevis 25, 25
Monarda didyma 39, 57, 57; see also bergamot
morning glory see Ipomoea tricolor
mosaic virus 159, 179, 179
moses in the cradle see Rhoeo
moss campion see Silene
moth orchid see Phalaenopsis
mother-in-law's tongue see Sansevieria trifasciata
mother-of-thousands see Saxifraga stolonifera; Tolmiea menziesii
moths 42, 122, 134
mulching 9, 13, 129-30, 148, 179, 192
Muscari 60
　M. armeniacum 63, 63
　M. botryoides 63
　M. tubergenian 63
mushroom compost 128
mustard and cress 131, 146, 146
mustard as green manure 127
Myosotis 28, 28

myrtle see Myrtus
Myrtus 361, 361

Narcissus 13, 60, 68, 68, 316, 320, 320
　N. bulbocodium 60
　N. cyclamineus 13, 18, 68, 68
　N. juncifolius 61
　N. x odorus 60
　N. poeticus 60, 320
　N. pseudonarcissus 68
　N. tazetta 320
nasturtium 142, 150, 150, 202; see also Tropaeolum
Neanthe bella see Chamaedorea elegans
neck rot 195
nectarine 135, 241, 241
Nemesia 24, 24
Neoregelia 346, 346
Nephrolepis exaltata 249, 303, 306, 306
never-never plant see Ctenanthe
New Zealand spinach 158, 169, 169
Nidularium 346, 346
Nierembergia repens 85, 85
Nigella damascena 20, 28, 28
nitrogen 130
Notocactus 329, 329

Oenothera 18, 42
　O. biennis 42, 202
　O. fruticosa 42
　O. missouriensis 39, 42
　O. perennis 42
　O. pumila 42
　O. tetragona 42, 42
offsets, propagation from 17, 254
old man cactus see Cephalocereus
Omphalodes 82, 82
onion 131, 194, 198-201, 198, 199, 200, 201
onion eelworm 195
onion fly 195, 199
Oodontoglossum 353, 353
Opuntia 330, 330
orchids 252, 348-55
organic fertilizers 130, 131
oriental poppy see Papaver orientale
Oswego tea see Monarda didyma

Pachyphytum 340, 340
Paeonia 38, 39
　P. lactiflora 58
　P. officinalis 58, 58
pagoda bush see Enkianthus campanulatus
painted tongue see Salpiglossis sinuata
palms 247, 248, 249, 251, 256, 258, 310-15
pansy see Viola
pansy orchid see Miltonia
Papaver orientale 33, 44, 44
paper flower see Bougainvillea
Paphiopedilum 354, 354
parlour palm see Chamaedorea elegans
Parodia 330, 330
parsley 202, 203, 205, 215, 215
　Hamburg (turnip-rooted) 188, 188
parsnip 131, 185, 189, 189
parsnip canker 185
pasque flower see Pulsatilla
Passiflora 105, 105
pea 131, 133, 136-7, 140-1, 140, 141
pea and bean weevil 137, 137
pea moth 137, 137
pea thrip 137, 137
peace lily see Spathiphyllum
peach 135, 220, 231, 242-3, 242, 243
　ornamental 121
peach leaf curl 135
peacock plant see Calathea makoyana
peanut cactus see Chamaecereus silvestrii
pear 135, 220, 231, 233, 240, 240
peaty soil 10, 11, 11
Pelargonium 21, 25, 26, 50, 50, 248, 252, 256, 282-3, 297, 297
　P. crispum 282
　P. peltatum 282-3
　P. quercifolium 283
　P. tomentosum 282
Pellaea 249, 303, 307
　P. rotundifolia 307, 307
pennyroyal 218
peony see Paeonia
Peperomia 249, 255, 258, 259
　P. argyreia 274, 274
　P. caperata 274
　P. hederifolia 274

P. magnoliifolia 258, 274
P. sandersii 274
P. scandens 259
pepper 131, 153, 155, *155*
ornamental 290, *290*
peppermint 203, 214
perennial daisy *see Bellis perennis*
perennials 10, 38-59
Pereskia 331, *331*
Persian violet *see Exacum affine*
pests and diseases 134, 135, 143, 251, 257
bonsai plants 357
bulb vegetables 195
cacti 323
flower gardens 19
fruit plants and trees 135
fruiting vegetables 153, *153*
greenhouse 152
leaf vegetables 159, *159*
legumes 137
orchids 349
organic control 134
root vegetables and tubers 185
soft fruit 223
squash plants 179
stalk and shoot vegetables 173
succulents 333
top fruit 234
petal blight 349
Petunia 21, 25, *25*
pH scale 10, 242
Phacelia campanularia 83
Phalaenopsis 354, *354*
pheromone trap 235, 238
Philadelphus coronarius 18, 96, 102, *102*
Philodendron 249, 251, 255, 256
P. bipinnatifidum 259, 274
P. erubescens 274
P. scandens 255, 259, 274, *274*
P. selloum 274
Phleboodium aureum 308, *308*
Phoenix 315, *315*
phosphate 130, 131
Phyllitis scolopendrium 307, *307*
Picea pungens 124, *124*
Pieris formosa 13, 96, 116, *116*
piggy-back plant *see Tolmiea*
Pilea 249, 255, 256, 259, 275
P. cadierei 275
P. involucrata 275
P. mollis 275, *275*
P. muscosa 275
P. spruceana 275
pinapple mint 203
pineapple *see Ananas*
pink *see Dianthus*
pink, cushion *see Silene*
planning gardens
flower gardens 12-13, 38-9
herb gardens 202-3
Platycerium bifurcatum 308, *308*
Platycodon grandiflorum 83, *83*
Plectranthus 259, 275
P. australis 275
P. fruticosus 275, *275*
P. oertendahlii 275
Pleione formosana 355, *355*
plum 231, 233, 245, *245*
ornamental 121
Podocarpus 362, *362*
poinsettia *see Euphorbia pulcherrima*
polka-dot plant *see Hypoestes phyllostachya*
pollination 183, 195, 225, 231
Polyanthus 18, 39, 46, *46*
P. veris 46
P. vulgaris 46
Polypodium aureum 308, *308*
Polyscias 362, *362*
Polystichum setiferum 309, *309*
polythene tunnels 152
pomegranate *see Punica granatum*
poppy 13, 39; *see also Eschscholzia californica*; *Meconopsis*; *Papaver orientale*
potash 130, 131
potato 131, 134, 185, 190-1, *190*, *191*
potato blight 185
potato cyst eelworm 185
Potentilla 13, 39, 96
P. astrosanguinea 45, *45*
P. fructicosa 101, *101*
P. palustris 45
powdery mildew 111, 134, 135, 185, 239
prayer plant *see Maranta leuconeura*
pricking out seedlings 17, *133*
prickly pear *see Opuntia*
primrose *see Polyanthus vulgaris*
Primula 77, 88, 252, 282, 283, *283*
P. auricula 88
P. clarkei 88
P. frondosa 88, *88*
P. juliae 88
P. x *kewensis* 298
P. malacoides 283, 298
P. obconica 283, 298, *298*
P. reidii 88
propagation 15-18
bromeliads 343
bulbs 317
ferns 303
herbs 204
houseplants 252-4, *252*, *253*, *254*
pruning and training 18
houseplants 251
soft fruit 220-3, *220*, *221*, *222*, *223*
top fruit 232-4, *233*, *234*
Prunus 118, 121, *121*
Pteris 249, 259, 303, 309
P. cretica 309, *309*
P. ensiformis 309
Pulmonaria 13, 18, 39
P. angustifolia 52
P. officinalis 52
P. saccharata 52, *52*
Pulsatilla 91, *91*
pumpkin 131, 183, *183*
Punica granatum 363, *363*
purple passion vine *see Gynura*
purslane 158, 171, *171*
pussy ears *see Kalanchoe tomentosa*
Pyracantha 9, 18, 117
P. atalantioides 117, *117*
P. crenulata 117
P. x *watereri* 117

Queen's tears *see Billbergia nutans*
quince 243, *243*
flowering *see Chaenomeles*

Radish 131, 143, 151, *151*
rainbow star *see Cryptanthus*
rainfall 9
raised beds 76
Ramonda 77, 81
R. myconii 81, *81*
R. serbica 81
raspberry 135, 222-3, *223*, 226, *226*
raspberry beetle 135
rat's tail cactus *see Aporacactus*
Rebutia 331, *331*
red cabbage 164, *164*
red currant 221, *221*, 230, *230*
red hot cat's tail *see Acalypha hispida*
red spider mite 153, 257, 349
rhizomes 60
Rhododendron 11, 18, 96, 107, *107*
R. simsii 286, *286*
Rhoeo 276, *276*
Rhoicissus
R. capensis 276, *276*
R. rhomboidea see Cissus rhombifolia
rhubarb 131, 172-3, 176, *176*
Rhus typhina 123, *123*
ribbon fern *see Pteris cretica*
Robinia pseudoacacia 122, *122*
rock gardens 76
rock rose *see Helianthemum nummularium*
root crops 131
root rot 257
root vegetables *132*
Rosa
R. alba 110
R. centifolia 110, *110*
R. chinensis 298, *298*
R. damascena 111
R. gallica 110
R. x *odorata* 110
see also rose
rosary vine *see Ceropegia*
rose 9, 10, 13, 16, 18, 28, 96
climbing 111, *111*
floribunda 110, *110*
hybrid tea 111, *111*
old 110, *110*
see also Rosa
rose of China *see Hibiscus rosa-sinensis*
rosemary 202, 203, 215, *215*
rotation of crops 130, 132, *132*, 134, 158, 223
rowan *see Sorbus*
rubber plant *see Ficus elastica*
ruby chard 158, 168, *168*
Rudbeckia 21, 22, *22*
R. hirta 22
R laciniata 22
R. nitida 22
rue 202
Ruellia 282, 299
R. macrantha 299, *299*
R. portellae 299
runner bean 131, 136-7, 139, *139*, 142
rust 48, 50

Sage 35, 202, 203, 204, 216, *216*
Sageretia theezans 363, *363*
sago palm *see Cycas revoluta*
Saintpaulia 253, 256
S. ionantha 297, 299, *299*
salad burnet 202, 216, *216*
salad vegetables 131, *132*, 142-51
Salix 122, *122*
Salpiglossis sinuata 34, *34*
salsify 172, 185, 192, *192*
Salvia 18, 35, *35*
S. splendens 35
Sambucus 123, 203
S. niger 123
S. racemosa 123, *123*
sandy soil 10, *10*
Sansevieria 247, 249, 254, 277
S. hahnii 277
S. trifasciata 277, *277*
Santolina 9, 13, 18, 86
S. chamaecyparissus 86
S. incana 86
S. rosmarinifolia 86, *86*
S. virens 86, *86*
Saponaria 18
S. ocymoides 93, *93*
S. officinalis 93
sawfly 135
Saxifraga 258
S. moschata 77, 91, *91*
S. sarmentosa 277, *277*
S. stolonifera 259, 277, *277*
scab 135
scale insect 257, 349
Scarborough lily *see Vallota speciosa*
Schizanthus 33, *33*
Schlumbergera 256
Scilla 60, 71
S. peruviana 18, 71
S. sibirica 71
S. tubergeniana 71, *71*
Scindapsus 249, 278
S. aureus 258, 278, *278*
S. epipremnum 278
S. pictus argyraeus 278, *278*
Scirpus cernuus 278, *278*
scorzonera 172, 192, *192*
seakale 172, 173, 177, *177*
seakale beet 168, *168*
seaweed 128, 131
Sedum 18, 77, 78
S. acre 78
S. morganianum 340, *340*
S. spectabile *39*, 78
S. spurium 78, *78*
seed, propagation from 16-17, 133, 134, 184, 252-3, *252*
Senecio 100, *100*
S. cruentus see Cineraria
S. greyi 100
S. laxifolius 100
S. rowleyanus 341, *341*
Setcreasea 258-9, 279, *279*
shallot 131, 200, *200*
shield fern *see Polystichum setiferum*
shrimp plant *see Beloperone guttata*
shrubs, flowering 96-117
Silene 93, *93*
silver leaf 245
silver torch *see Cleistocactus*
Sinningia 253, 282
S. speciosa 300, *300*
Sisyrinchium 77, 94
S. angustifolium 94
S. grandiflorum 94
S. striatum 94, *94*
slipper orchid *see Paphiopedilum*
slow worm 179
slug 46, 92, 134, 135, 137, 148, 171, 173, 174, 179, 180, 182
snail 134, 135, 171
snakeskin plant *see Fittonia*
snapdragon *see Antirrhinum majus*
snow-in-summer *see Cerastium*
snowdrop *see Galanthus nivalis*
snowflake *see Leucojum*
soapwort *see Saponaria officinalis*
soil types 10-11, *10*, *11*
Soldanella 95, *95*
Sonerila margaritacea 279, *279*
sooty mould 257
Sorbus 121, *121*
sorrel 204, 217, *217*
southernwood 202, 204
Spanish bayonet *see Yucca*
Spathiphyllum 256, 300
S. wallisii 300, *300*
spearmint 214
speedwell *see Veronica*
spider cactus *see Gymnocalycium*
spider plant *see Chlorophytum*
spinach 131, 158, 159, 170, *170*
New Zealand 158, 169, *169*
spinach beet 131, 158, 169, *169*
spinach blight 159
Spiraea 18, 96, 109
S. x *arguta* 109
S. x *bumalda* 109, *109*
S. japonica 109
spring cabbage 162, *162*
spring greens 158, 170, *170*
spring onion 159, 194, 201, *201*
spruce 118
squash 131, 178-83, 183, *183*
squill *see Scilla*
stag's horn sumach *see Rhus typhina*
Stapelia 341, *341*
stem eelworm 194
Stokesia laevis 39, 51, *51*
stonecrop *see Sedum*
strawberry 179, 220, 223, 227-8, *227*, *228*
Strelitzia reginae 282, 301, *301*
Streptocarpus 256, 301, *301*
string of beads *see Senecio rowleyanus*
succulents 248, 249, 332-41
suckers, propagation from 254
sugarloaf chicory 145, *145*
summer savory 217, *217*
sun and shade 9
sunflower 174
swamp lily *see Crinum*
swede 131, 185, *185*, 193, *193*
Swedish ivy *see Plectranthus australis*
sweet basil *see* basil
sweet bay *see* bay
sweet cicely 218, *218*
sweet corn 131, 177, *177*
sweet marjoram 203
sweet pea *see Lathyrus odoratus*
sweet sultan *see Centaurea moschata*
sweet william *see Dianthus barbatus*
sweet woodruff *see Asperula odorata*
sweetheart plant *see Philodendron scandens*
Swiss chard 158, 168, *168*
Syagrus weddeliana 313, *313*
Syringa vulgaris 9, 18, 96, 112, *112*

Table fern *see Pteris*
Tagetes 23, 23, 26, 33, 111, 155, 163, 190
T. erecta 23
T. patula 23
tansy 204, 218, *218*
tarragon 202, 203, 205, 219, *219*
tarsonemid mite 257
thinning seedlings 16, 133
thrift *see Armeria*
Thunbergia alata 100, *100*
thyme *see Thymus*
Thymus 13, 18, *77*, 78, 202, 203, 219, *219*
T. x *citriodorus* 78
T. drucei 78
T. serpyllum 78
T. vulgaris 78, *78*
Tiarella 18
T. cordifolia 49, *49*
T. wherryi 49
Tibetan poppy *see Meconopsis*
tiger orchid *see Odontoglossum*
Tillandsia 347
T. cyanea 346, *347*
T. lindeniana 347
toads and frogs 179
Tolmiea 247, 249, 256, 259
T. menziesii 280, *280*
tom thumb *see Parodia*
tomato 131, 152, *153*, 156-7, *156*, *157*
tomato blight 153, *153*
tomato leaf mould 153
Trachycarpus fortunei 315, *315*
Tradescantia 249, 251, 253, 255, 259, 280
T. albiflora 280
T. blossfeldiana 280
T. fluminensis 280, *280*
transplanting seedlings 184
trees
bonsai 356-63
flowering 118-25
fruit 231-45
planting 119, 231-2, *232*
Triteleia uniflorum 70, *70*
Trollius 39
T. x *cultorum* 59
T. ledebourii 59, *59*
Tropaeolum 33, 45, 111
T. majus 45, 142, 150, *150*, 202
T. peregrinum 45
T. speciosum 45, *45*
tubers 60
tulip 13, 64-5
Darwin 64, *64*
double 65, *65*
parrot 65, *65*
Rembrandt 65 *see also Tulipa*
Tulipa 61, 316, 321, *321*
T. clusiana 61
T. fosteriana 64
T. greigii 61, 64
T. pulchella 64
T. tarda 64, *64*
T. urumiensis 64 *see also* tulip
turnip 131, 185, *185*, 193, *193*

Umbrella plant *see Cyperus*
urn plant *see Aechmea*

Vallota speciosa 303, 316, 317, 321, *321*
Vanda 355, *355*
vegetable oyster *see* salsify
vegetables 126-201
bolting 143
continuous crops 143, 148, 149, 158-9, 201
decorative 139, 142, 164, 168
velvet plant *see Gynura*
Verbena peruviana 44, *44*
Veronica 77, 80
V. cinerea 80
V. filiformis 80
V. gentianoides 80, *80*
V. pectinata 80
V. prostrata 80
V. teucrium 80
Viburnum 9, 18, 115, *115*
V. farreri 96
V. tinus 96, 115
Viola 18, 39
V. x *wittrockiana* 56, *56*
violet root rot 173
viral diseases 134, 153, 159, 349
Vriesia 347, *347*

Wasp 135, 240
watering 15, 129, 130, 174, 179
bonsai plants 357
bromeliads 343
cacti 322
cloches 195
houseplants 247-8
leaf vegetables 159
orchids 348
sub-surface irrigation 189
succulents 332-3
weeding 13, 129
weeping fig *see Ficus benjamina*
Welsh (ever-ready) onion 194, 201, *201*
Welsh poppy *see Meconopsis*
white currant 221, 230, *230*
white rot 194, 195
whitefly 134, 153, 234, 257
wild areas 13
willow *see Salix*
wind 9
windmill palm *see Trachycarpus fortunei*
wineberry 229, *229*
winter aconite *see Eranthis hyemalis*
winter savory 202
winter sweet *see Chimonanthus praecox*
winter tare as green manure 127
wireworm 134
Wisteria sinensis 18, 114, *114*
witch hazel *see Hamamelis*
woodbine *see Lonicera periclymenum*
worm casts 131
worm compost 128, *128*
worms 204

Yarrow 41, 163
Yucca 249, *255*, 256, 281, *281*

Zantedeschia 60, 61
Z. aethiopica 75, *75*
Zauschneria 79, *79*
zebra plant *see Aphelandra squarrosa*; *Calathea zebrina*
Zebrina 253, 259
Z. pendula 281, *281*
Zinnia 18
Z. elegans 34, *34*

osmos Rudbeckia Tagetes Gazania Gypsophila Nemesia Petunia Molucella
unaria Asperula Dianthus Centaurea Antirrhinum Lathyrus Schizanthus Chry
esembryanthemum Alchemilla Euphorbia Dicentra Achillea Oenothera Meco
upin Impatiens Bellis Helleborus Althaea Convallaria Tiarella Pelargoniun
ampanula Delphinium Echinops Geranium Viola Aquilegia Monarda Caltha Pa
ulips Parrot Tulips Double Tulips Eranthis Leucojum Cyclamen Hyacinthu
olchicum Scilla Dahlia Lilium Species Lilium Hybrids Begonia Gladiolus F
ampanula Ramonda Lithodora Omphalodes Phacelia Platycodon Arabis C
rimula Armeria Erinus Helianthemum Gentianum Lewesia Pulsatilla Saxifrag
orsythia Cytisus Chimonanthus Jasminum Senecio Thunbergia Fremontia F
assiflora Clematis Hybrids Clematis Species Rhododendron Azalea Fuchs
limbing Roses Syringa Erica Lavandula Hibiscus Wistaria Choisya Lonicera
runus Robinia Salix Sambucus Rhus Eucrypha Picea Amelanchier Pyrus H
ean Scarlet Runner Bean Broad Bean Asparagus Pea Mangetout Pea Glo
ustard and Cress Ridge Cucumber Cucumber Butterhead Lettuce Cos Lett
adish Aubergine White Aubergine Pepper Chilli Pepper Greenhouse Toma
alabrese Brussels Sprout Spring Cabbage Early Summer Cabbage Sumr
auliflower Summer/Autumn Cauliflower Winter Cauliflower Chicory Broad-lea
pinach Beet New Zealand Spinach Spinach Spring Greens Summer Purslane
g Celery Rhubarb Seakale Sweet Corn Courgette Custard Marrow Marrow P
arly Outdoor Carrot Maincrop Carrot Celeriac Hamburg Parsley Jerusalem
otato Container Potato Salsify Scorzonera Swede Turnip Florence Fennel E
ets Japanese Onion Pickling Onion Shallot Spring Onion Welsh Onion Ang
ennel Horseradish Hyssop Lovage Marigold Marjoram Mint Parsley Rosema
lackberry Blueberry Boysenberry Gooseberry Loganberry Raspberry Alpine
lackcurrant Redcurrant White Currant Early-season Apple Mid-season Appl
lack Grape White Grape Cooking Pear Dessert Pear Apricot Nectarine Pea
lum Dessert Plum Acorus Aspidistra Begonia luxurians Begonia rex Calad
tenanthe Cyperus Dieffenbachia Dizygotheca Dracaena Elettaria x Fatshec
ypoestes Iresine Maranta Peperomia Philodendron Pilea Plectranthus Rh
olmiea Tradescantia Yucca Zebrina Abutilon Acalypha Achimenes Anthuri
rowallia Calceolaria Campanula Capsicum Chrysanthemum Cineraria Cli
mpatiens Jasminum Kohleria Pelargonium Primula Rosa Ruellia Saintpaulia
yrtomium Davallia Nephrolepis Pellaea Phyllitis Platycerium Polypodium
owea Phoenix Trachycarpus Crinum Crocus Hippeastrum Hyacinth Iris Narc
ianus Chamaecereus silvestrii Cleistocactus strausii Echinocactus grusonii
arodia Pereskia Rebutia Aeonium Agave americana Aloe Ceropegia Cotyl
ithops Pachyphytum Sedum morganianum Senecio rowleyanus Stapelia A
ngraecum Cattleya Coelogyne Cymbidium Dendrobium Encyclia Milto
ougainvillea Buxus Camellia Citrus Crassula Ficus benjamina Jacaranda
udbeckia Tagetes Gazania Gypsophila Nemesia Petunia Molucella Godetia
sperula Dianthus Centaurea Antirrhinum Lathyrus Schizanthus Chrysan
esembryanthemum Alchemilla Euphorbia Dicentra Achillea Oenothera Meco
upin Impatiens Bellis Helleborus Althaea Convallaria Tiarella Pelargoniu
ampanula Delphinium Echinops Geranium Viola Aquilegia Monarda Caltha F
ulips Parrot Tulips Double Tulips Eranthis Leucojum Cyclamen Hyacinth
olchicum Scilla Dahlia Lilium Species Lilium Hybrids Begonia Gladiolus
ampanula Ramonda Lithodora Omphalodes Phacelia Platycodon Arabis
rimula Armeria Erinus Helianthemum Gentianum Lewesia Pulsatilla Saxifrac
orsythia Cytisus Chimonanthus Jasminum Senecio Thunbergia Fremontia
assiflora Clematis Hybrids Clematis Species Rhododendron Azalea Fuch
limbing Roses Syringa Erica Lavandula Hibiscus Wistaria Choisya Lonicera
runus Robinia Salix Sambucus Rhus Eucrypha Picea Amelanchier Pyrus